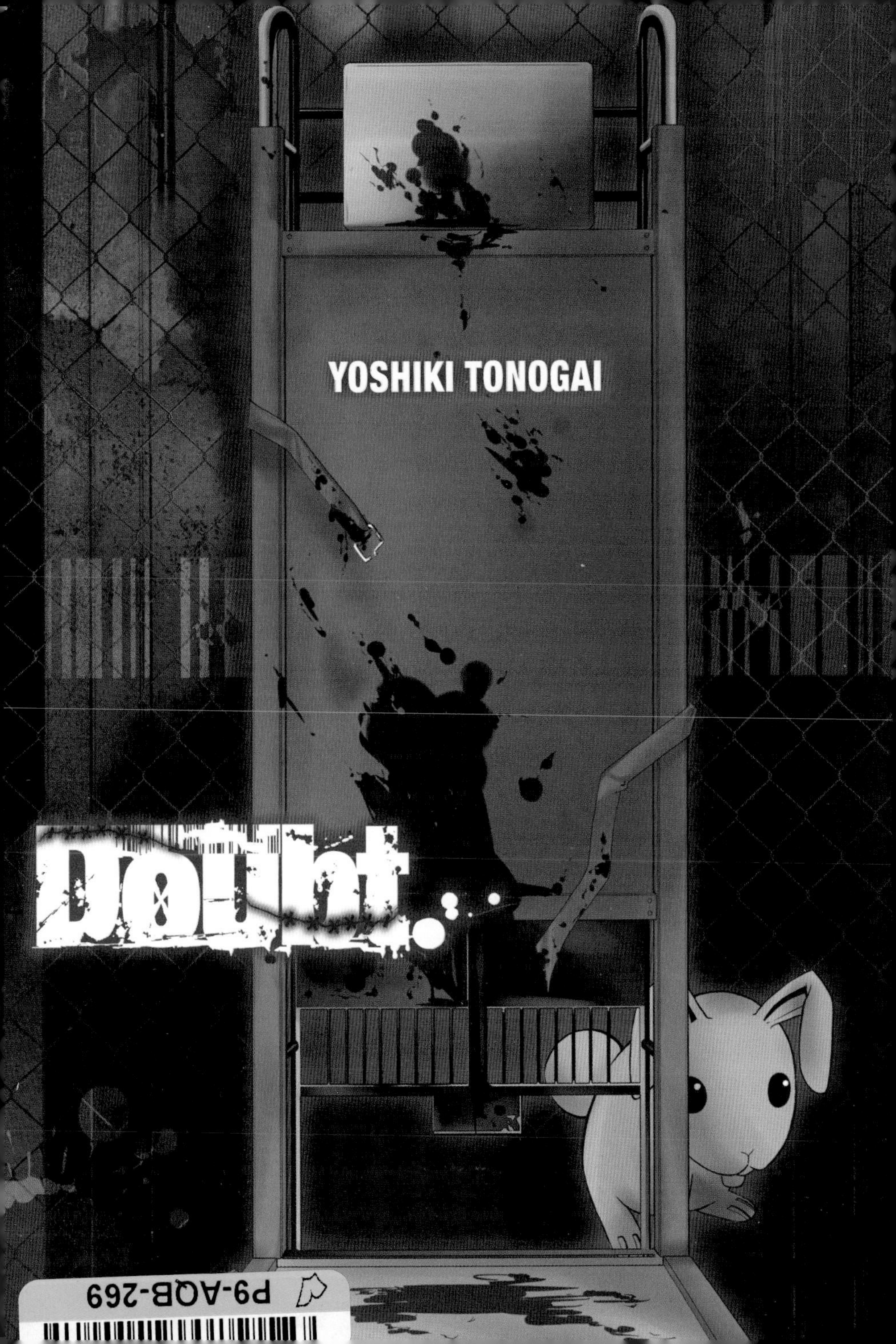
YOSHIKI TONOGAI
Doubt

CONTENTS

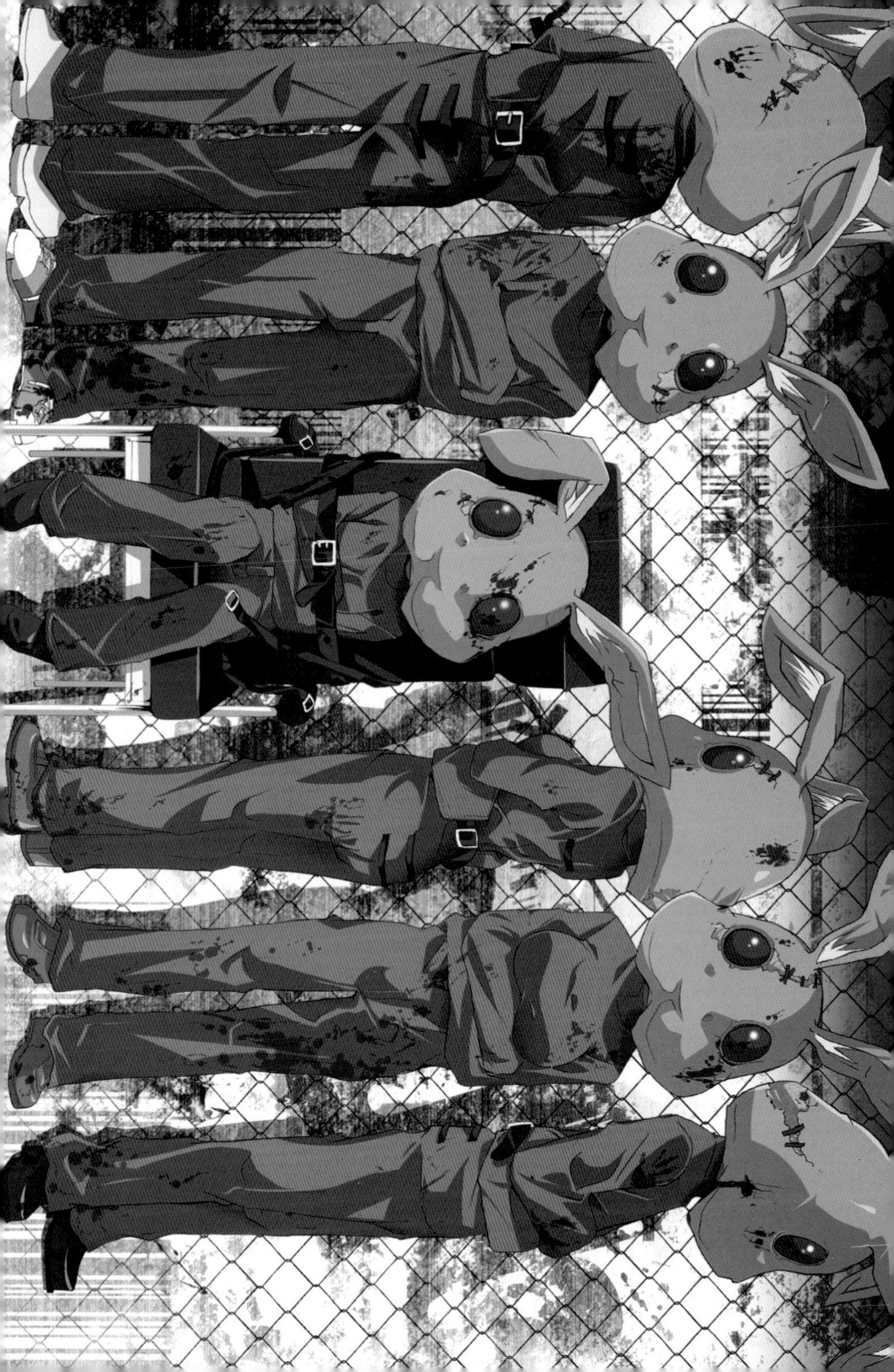

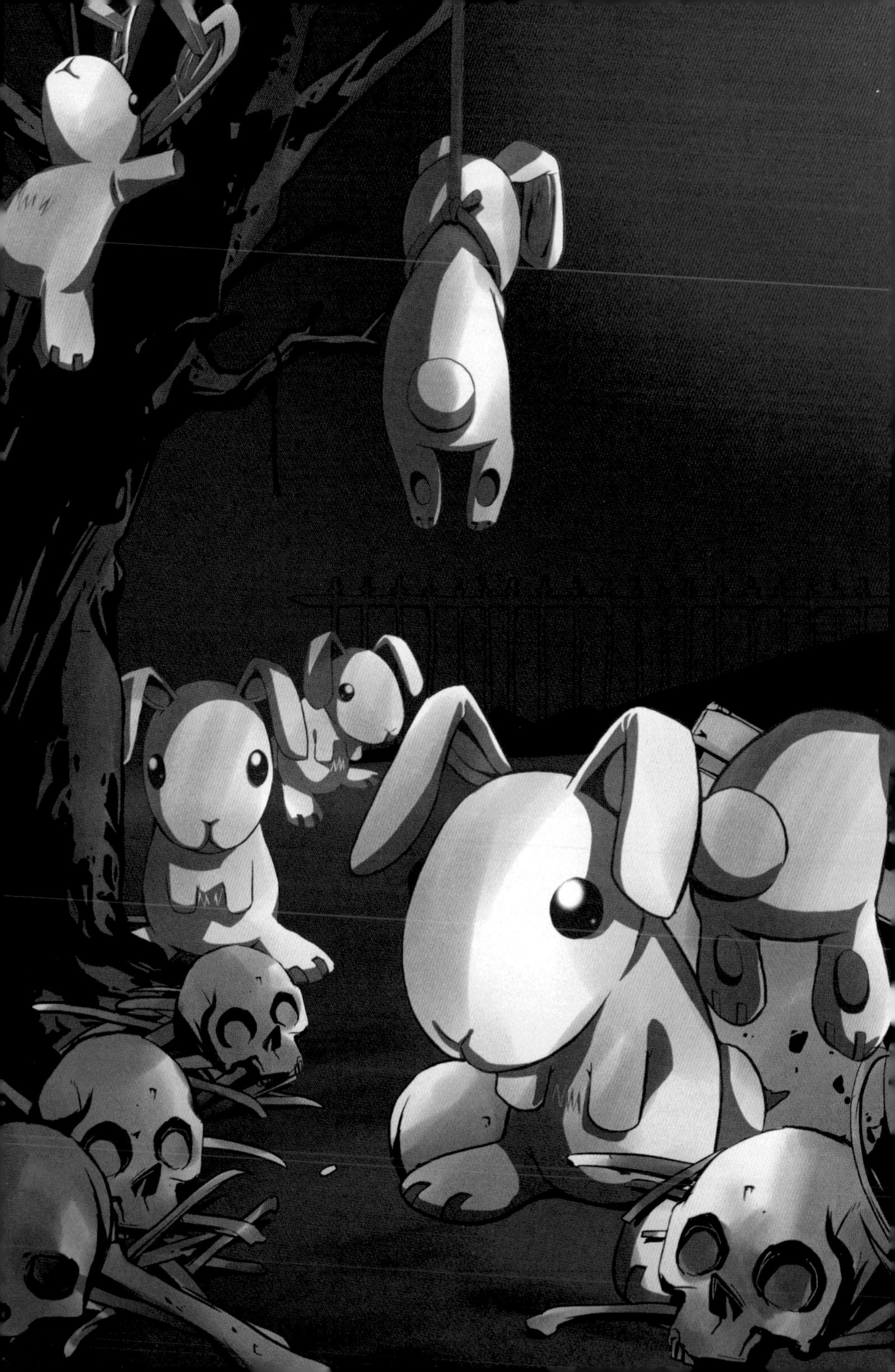

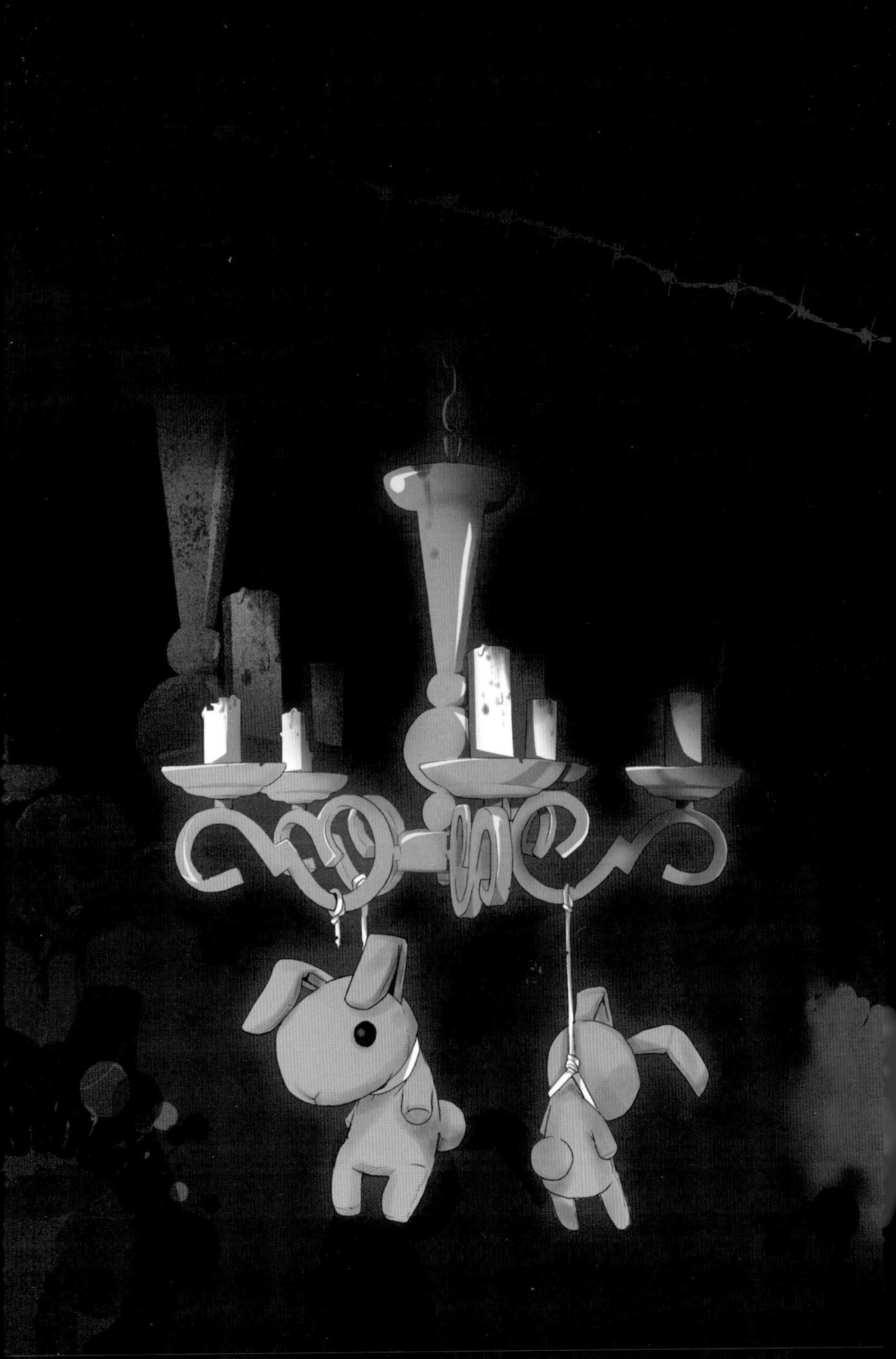

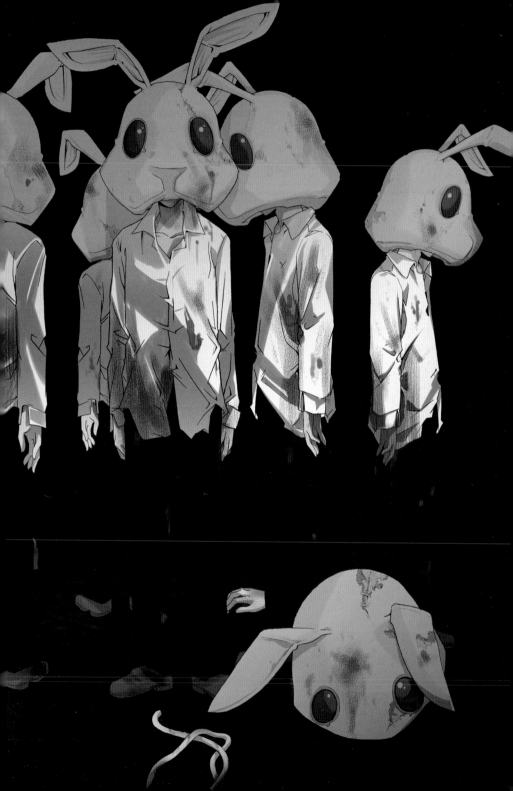

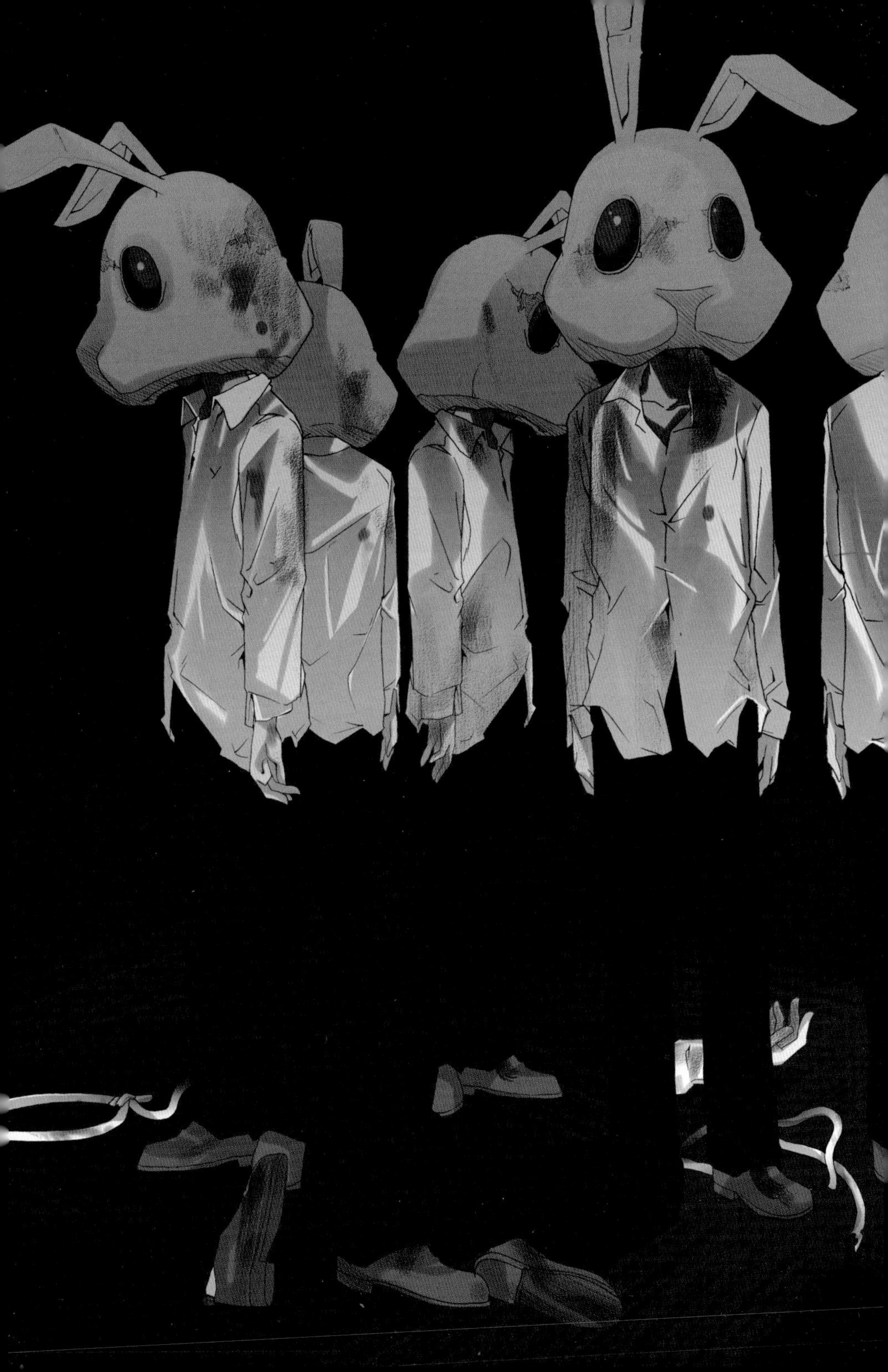

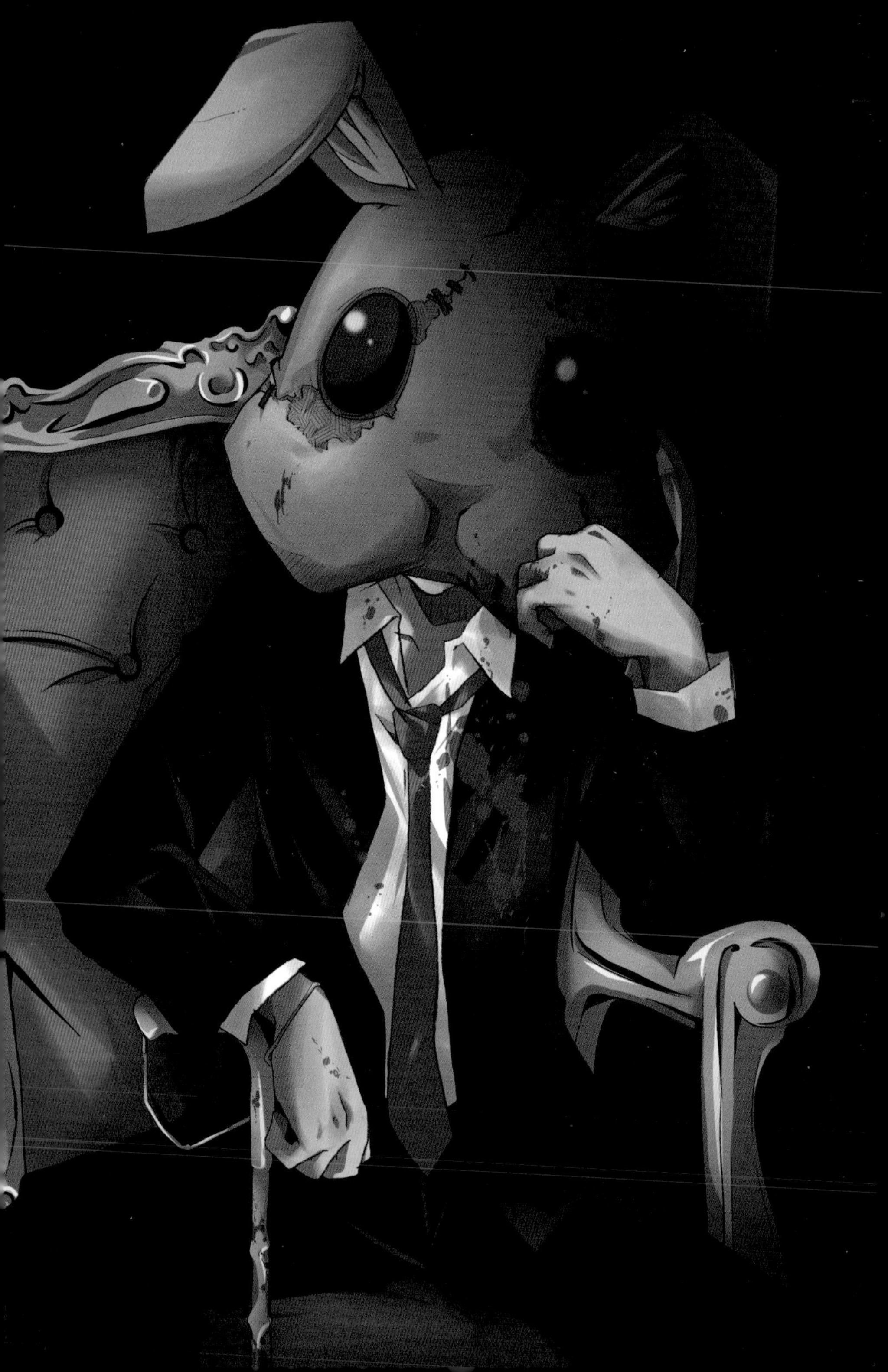

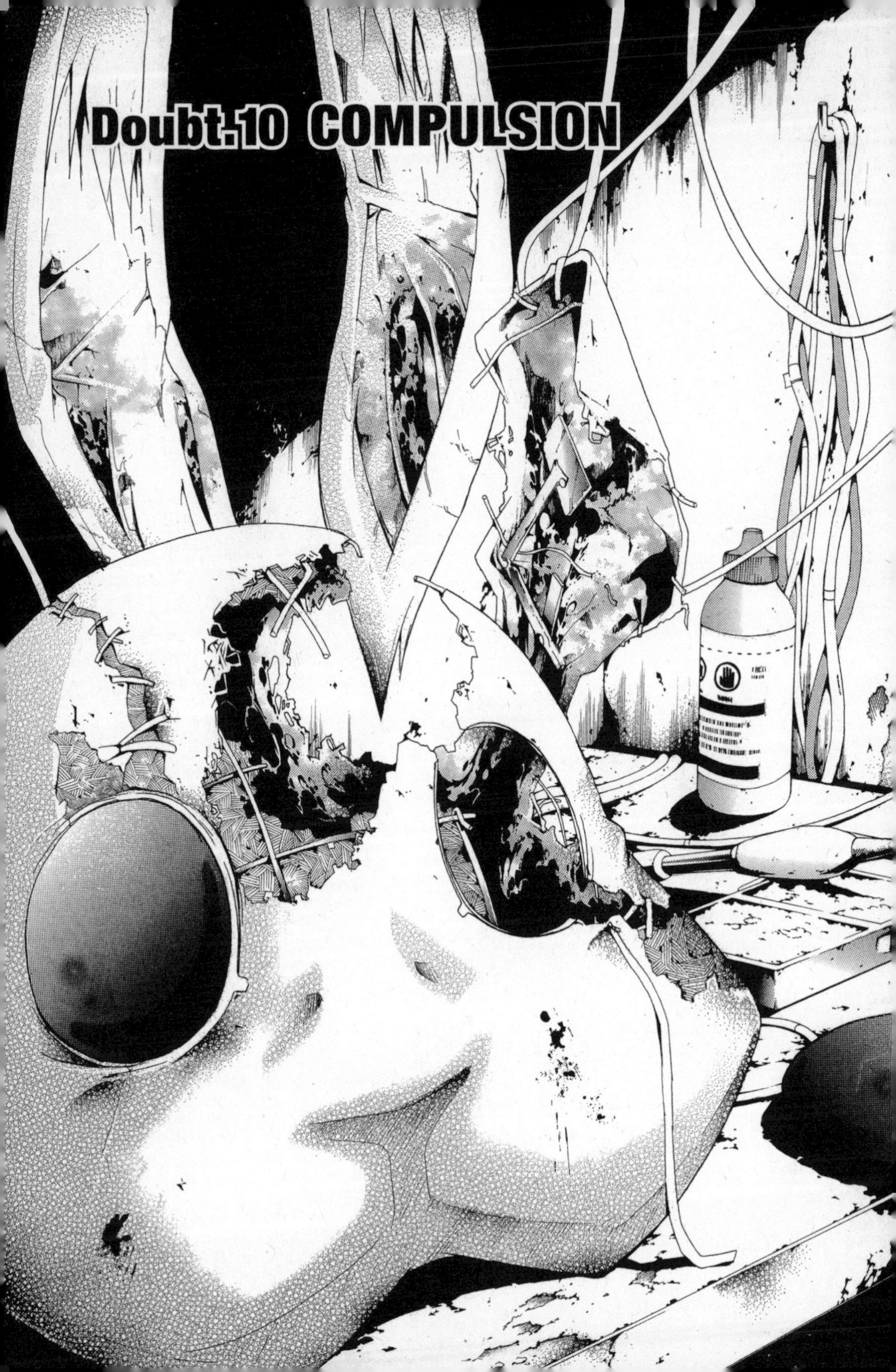
Doubt.10 COMPULSION

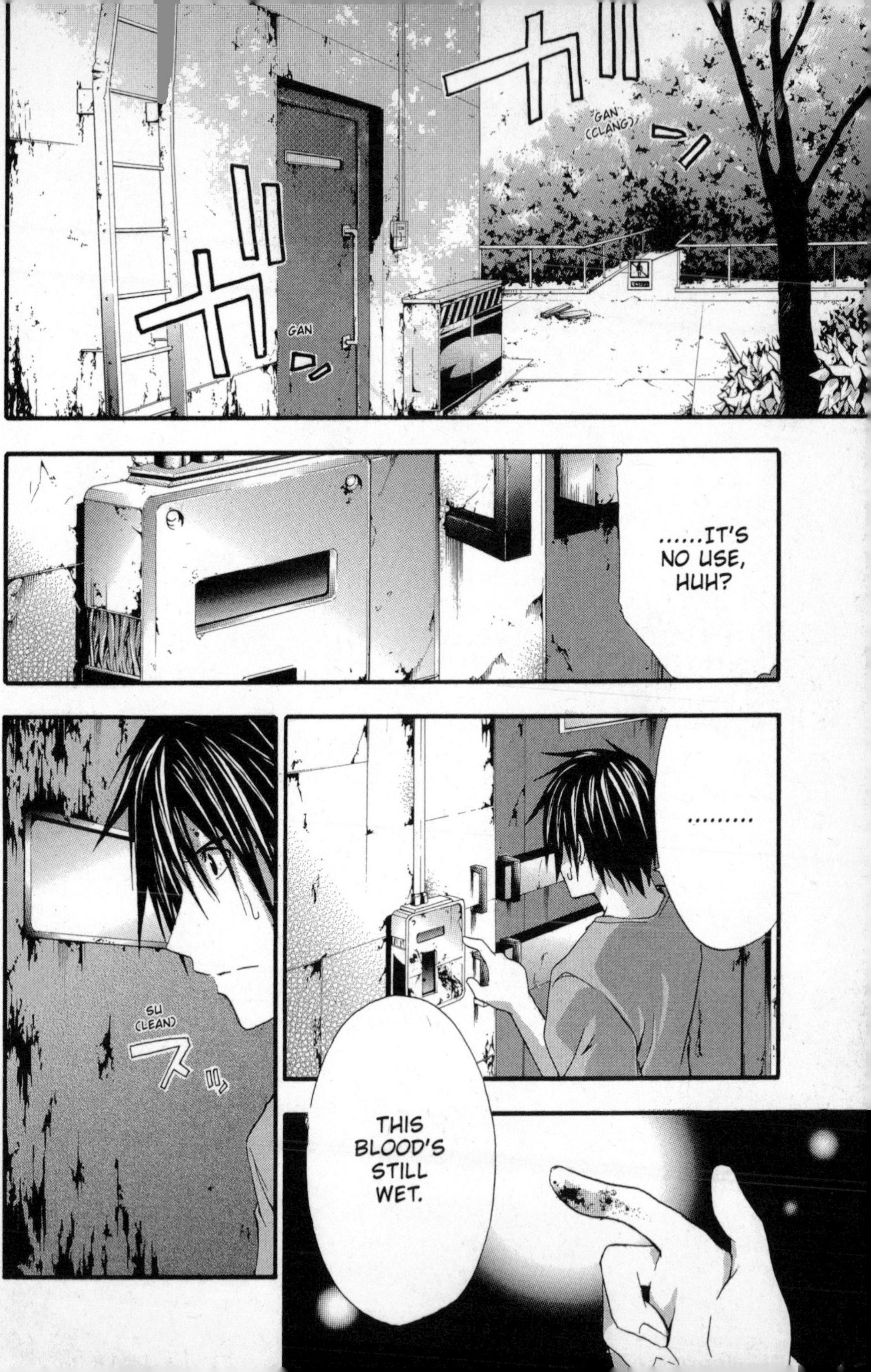
GAN (CLANG)
GAN
......IT'S NO USE, HUH?
....
THIS BLOOD'S STILL WET.
SU (LEAN)

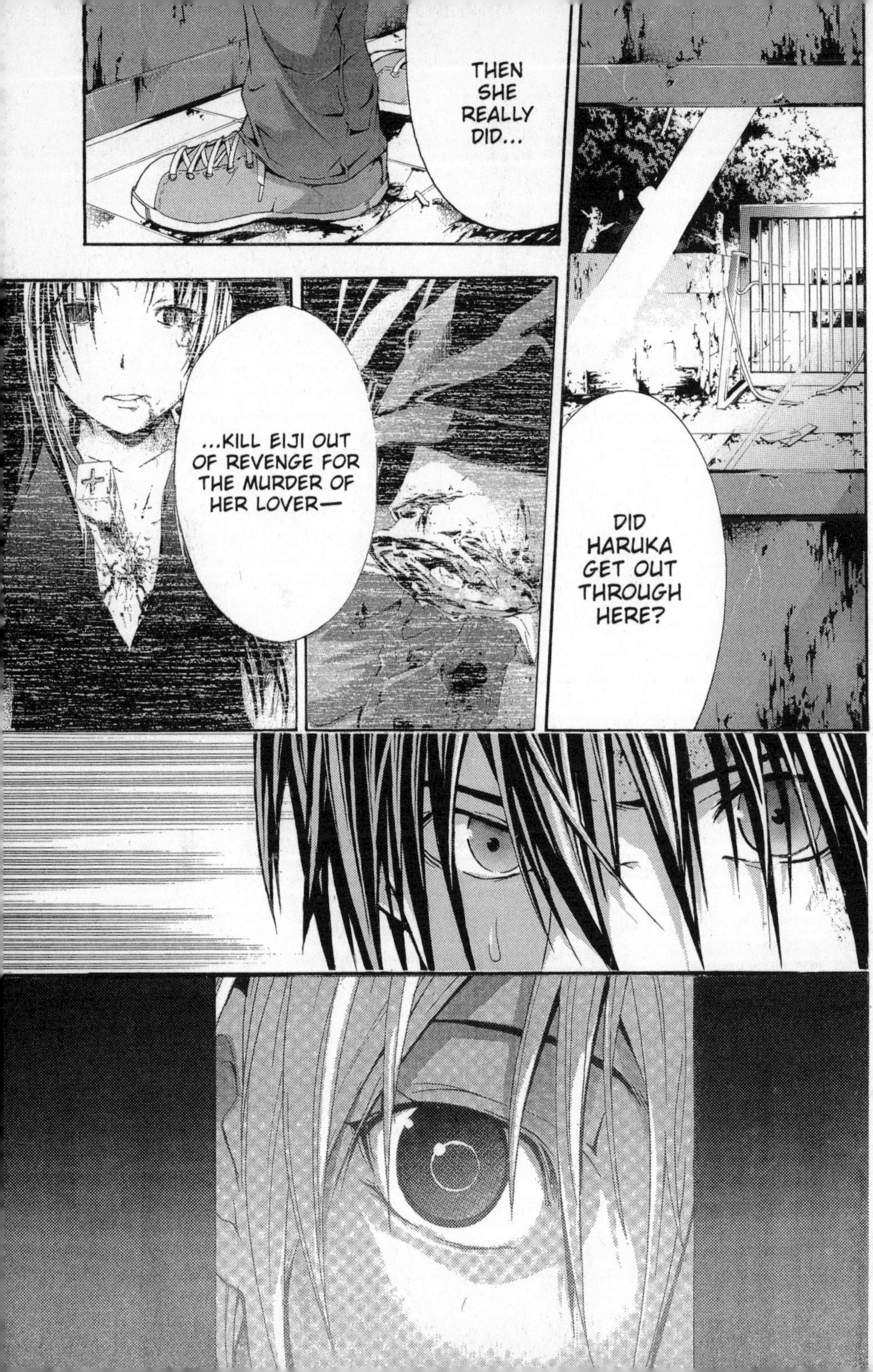
DID HARUKA GET OUT THROUGH HERE?
THEN SHE REALLY DID...
...KILL EIJI OUT OF REVENGE FOR THE MURDER OF HER LOVER—

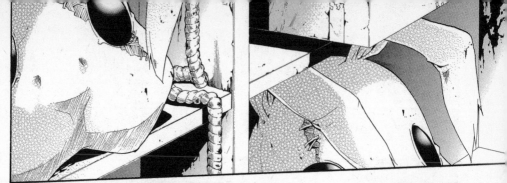

NO WAY
......

HAAH!

HAAH!

HAAH!

JIRI
(SCRAPE)

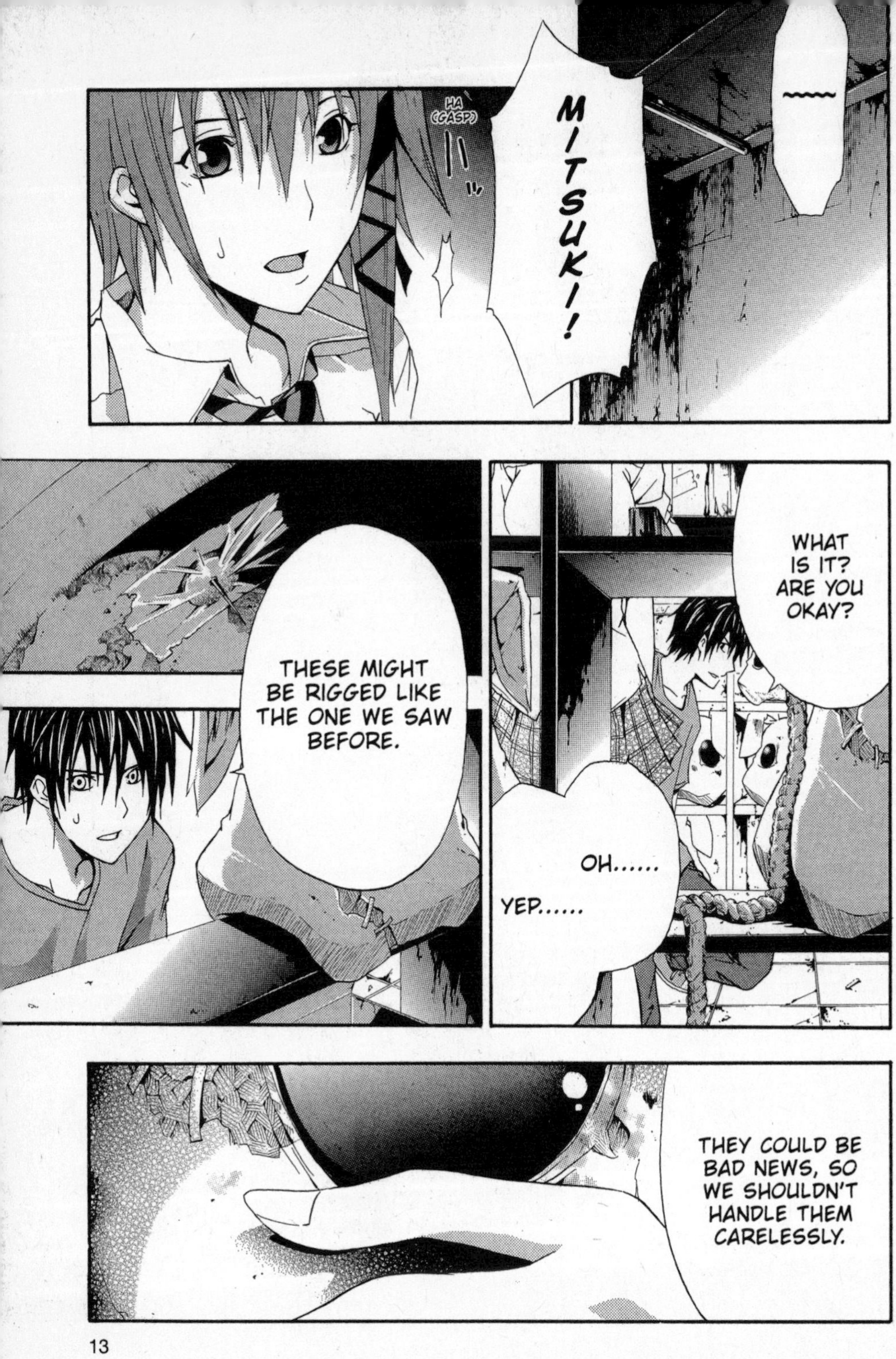

MITSUKI!!
HA (GASP)
WHAT IS IT? ARE YOU OKAY?
OH...... YEP......
THESE MIGHT BE RIGGED LIKE THE ONE WE SAW BEFORE.
THEY COULD BE BAD NEWS, SO WE SHOULDN'T HANDLE THEM CARELESSLY.

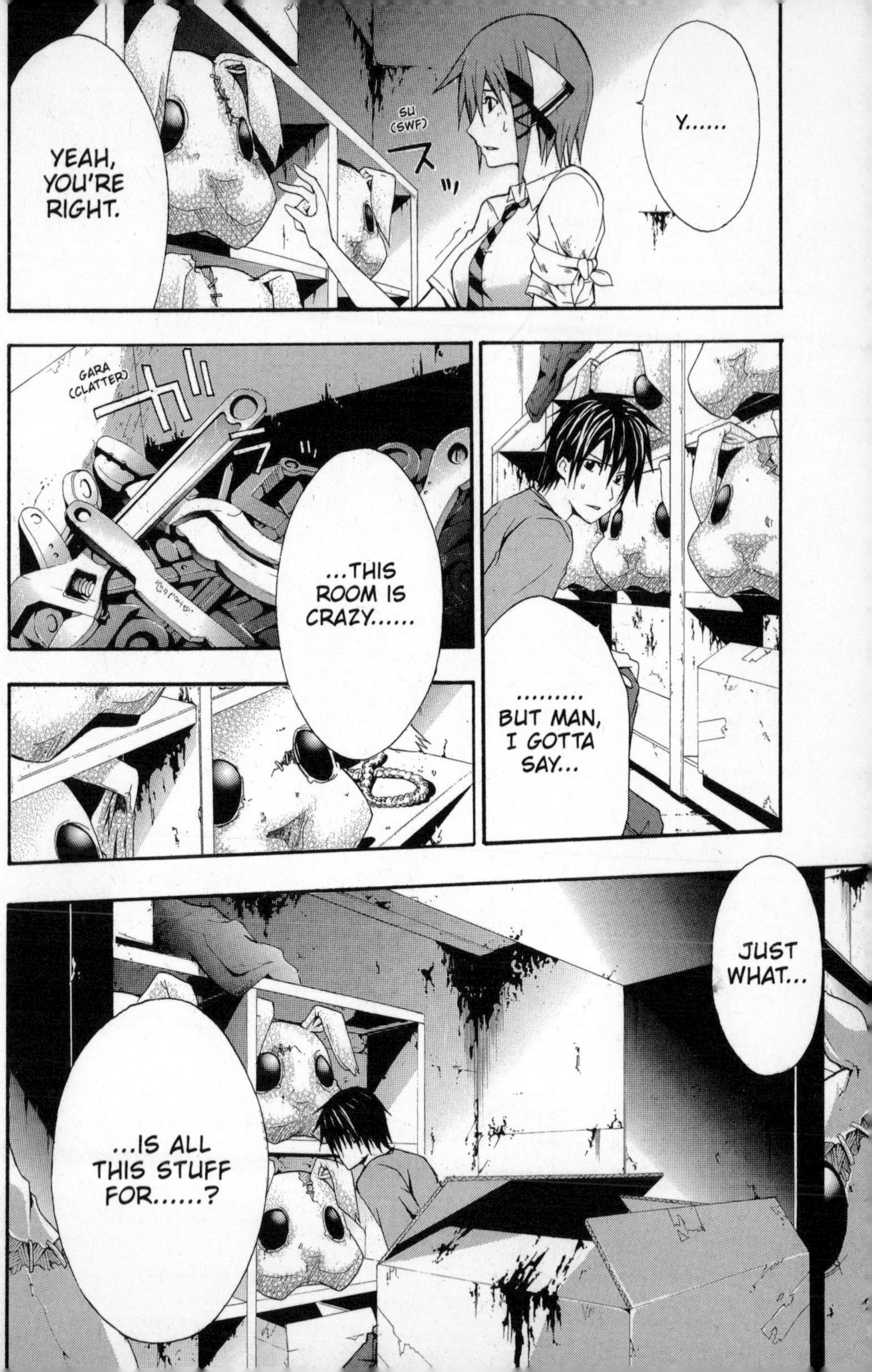

Y......
SU (SWF)
YEAH, YOU'RE RIGHT.
.... BUT MAN, I GOTTA SAY...
GARA (CLATTER)
...THIS ROOM IS CRAZY......
JUST WHAT...
...IS ALL THIS STUFF FOR......?

FILES LIKE THE ONES WE FOUND IN THE OTHER ROOM...

THERE'S SO MANY ......

!

.........?

PERA (FLIP)

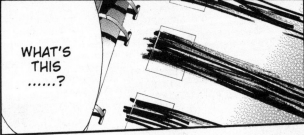

WHAT'S THIS ......?

IT'S ALL BLACKED OUT.

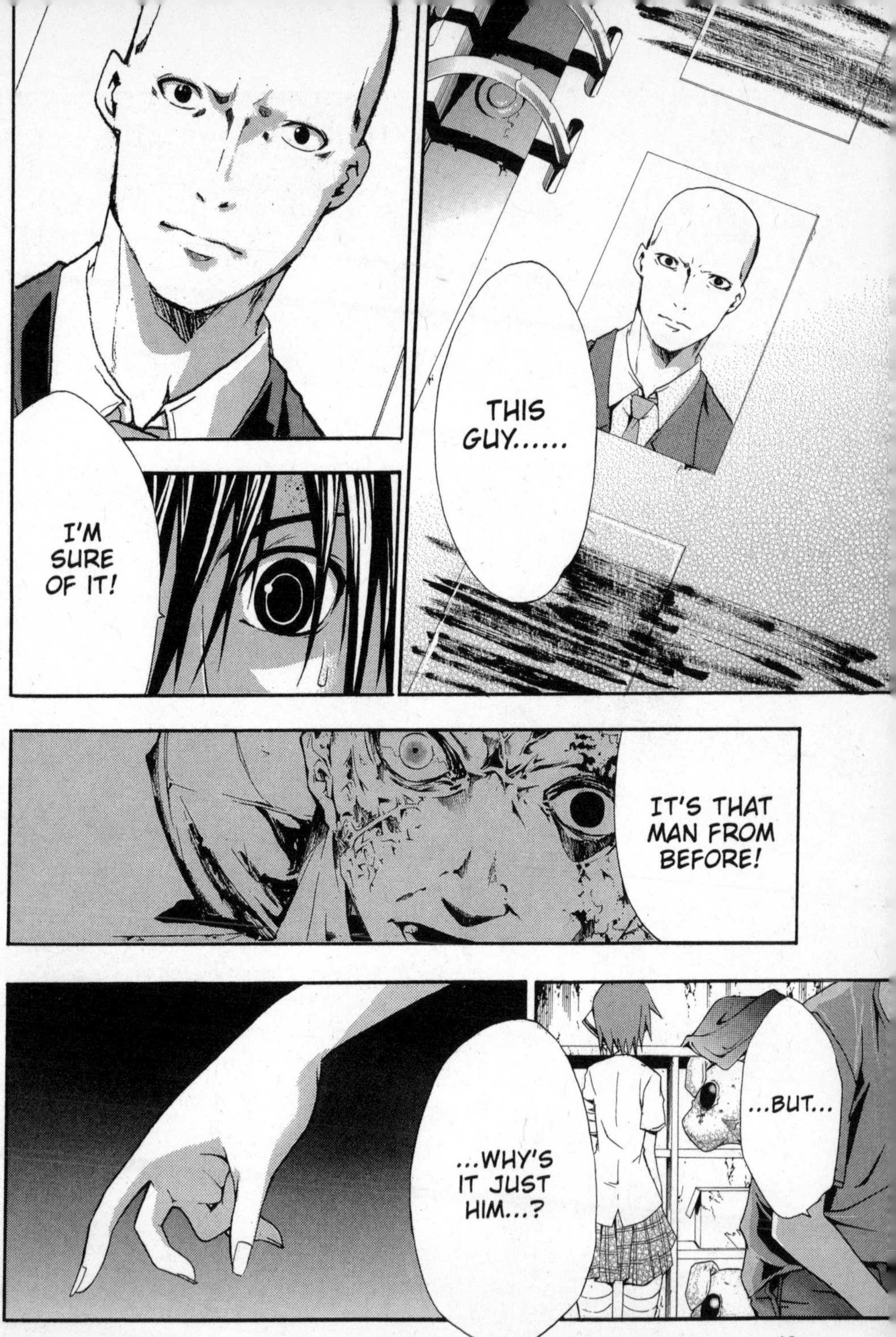
THIS GUY......
I'M SURE OF IT!
IT'S THAT MAN FROM BEFORE!
...BUT...
...WHY'S IT JUST HIM...?

RABBIT
DOUBT?

ALL THESE
OTHER PEOPLE
HAVE BEEN
BLACKED
OUT...

COULD
THIS
BE...

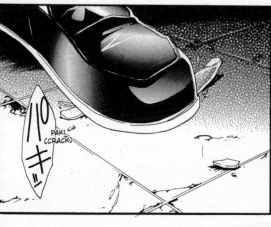

PAKI
(CRACK)

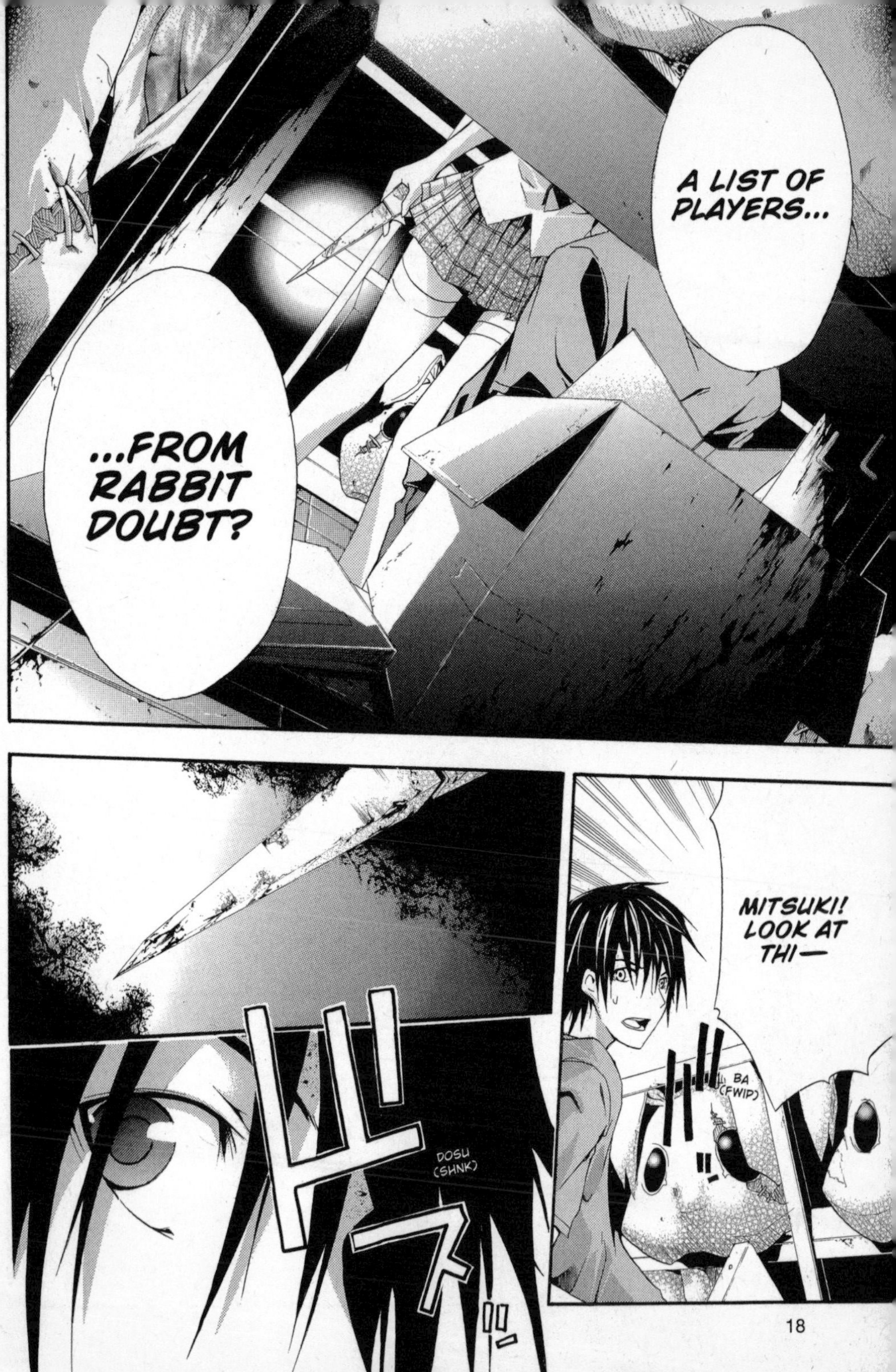
A LIST OF PLAYERS...
...FROM RABBIT DOUBT?
MITSUKI! LOOK AT THI—
BA (FWIP)
DOSU (SHNK)

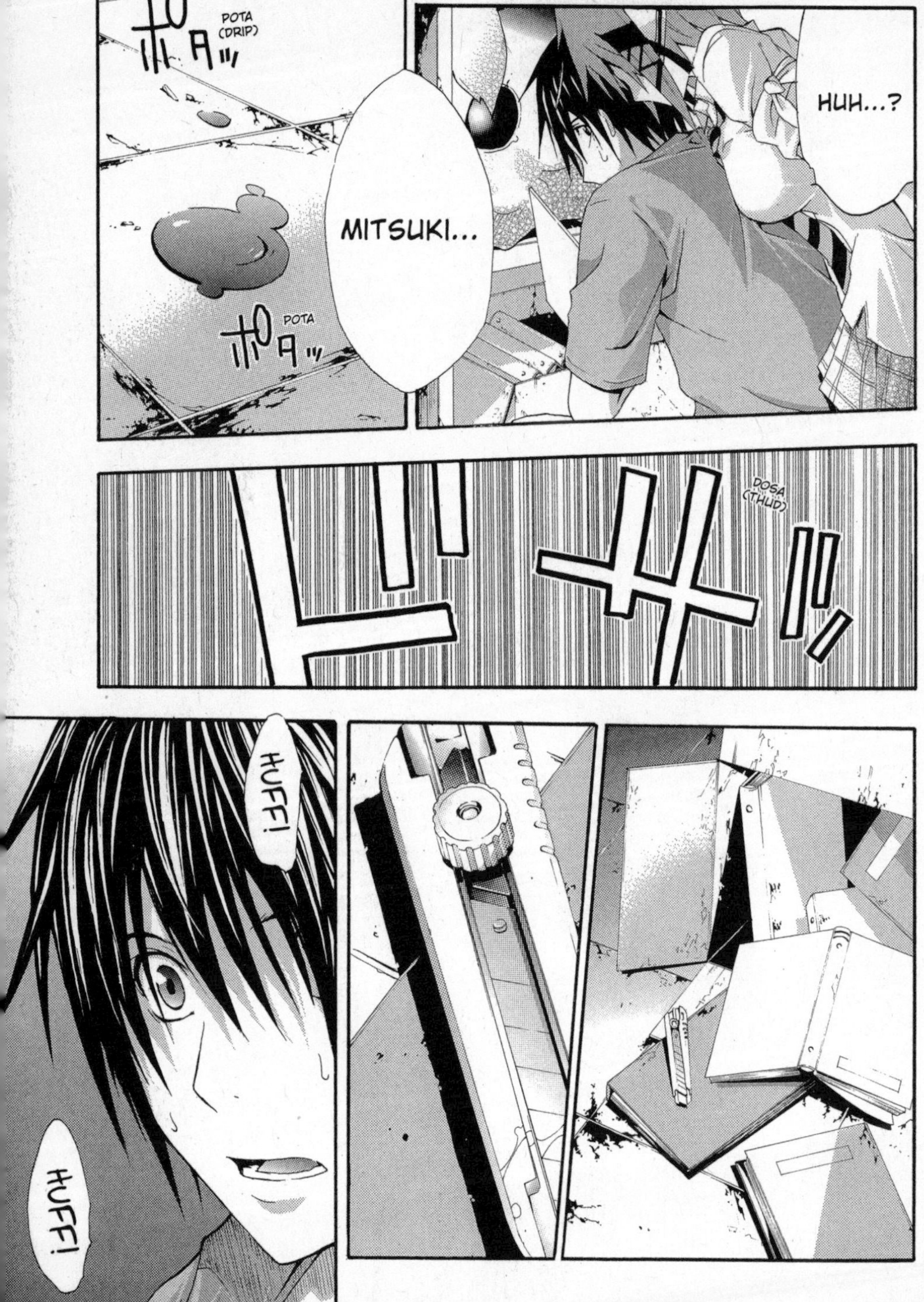
HUH...?
MITSUKI...
POTA (DRIP)
POTA
DOSA (THUD)
HUFF!
HUFF!

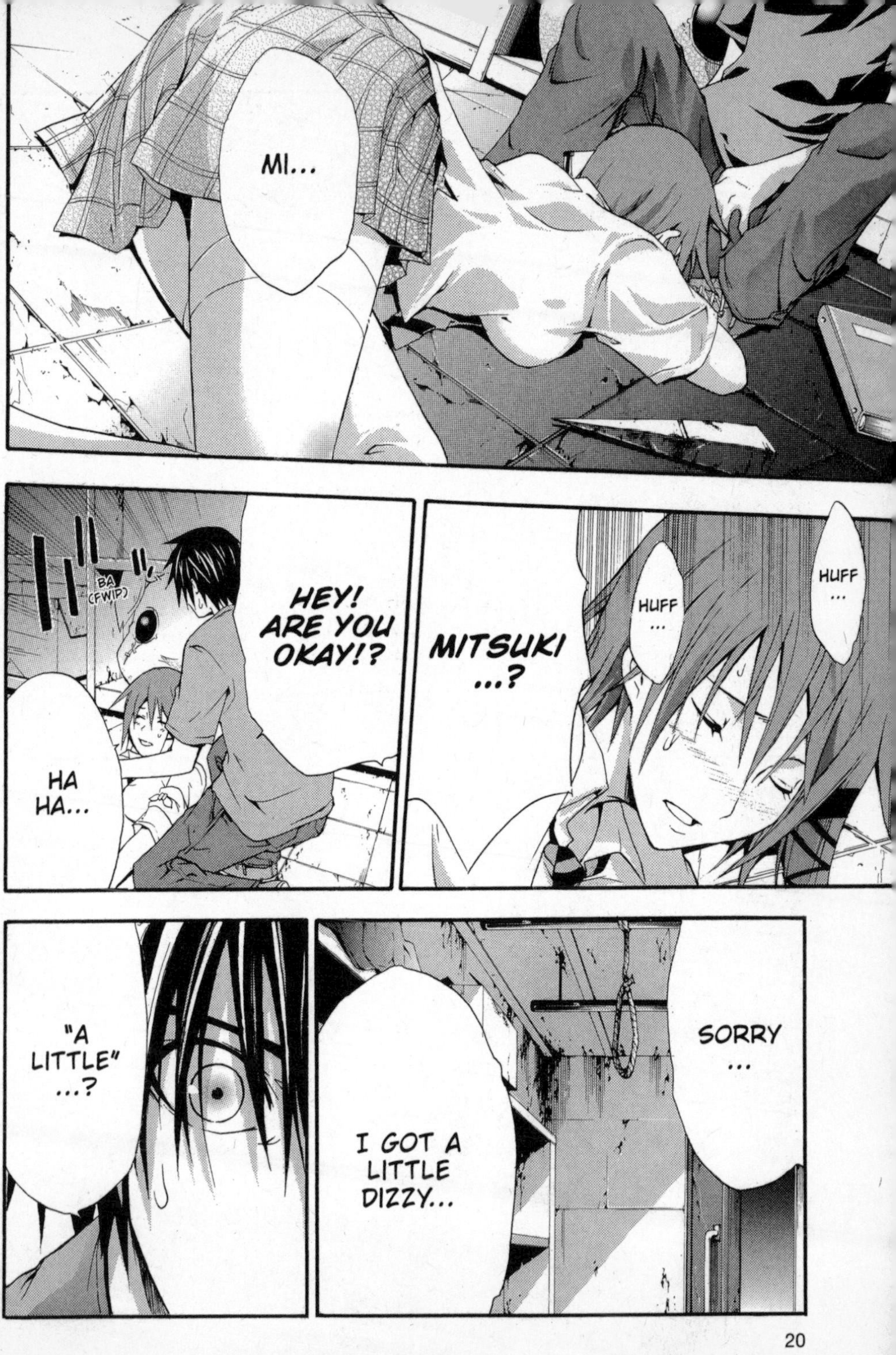
MI...
HUFF ...
HUFF ...
MITSUKI ...?
HEY! ARE YOU OKAY!?
BA (FWIP)
HA HA...
SORRY ...
I GOT A LITTLE DIZZY...
"A LITTLE" ...?

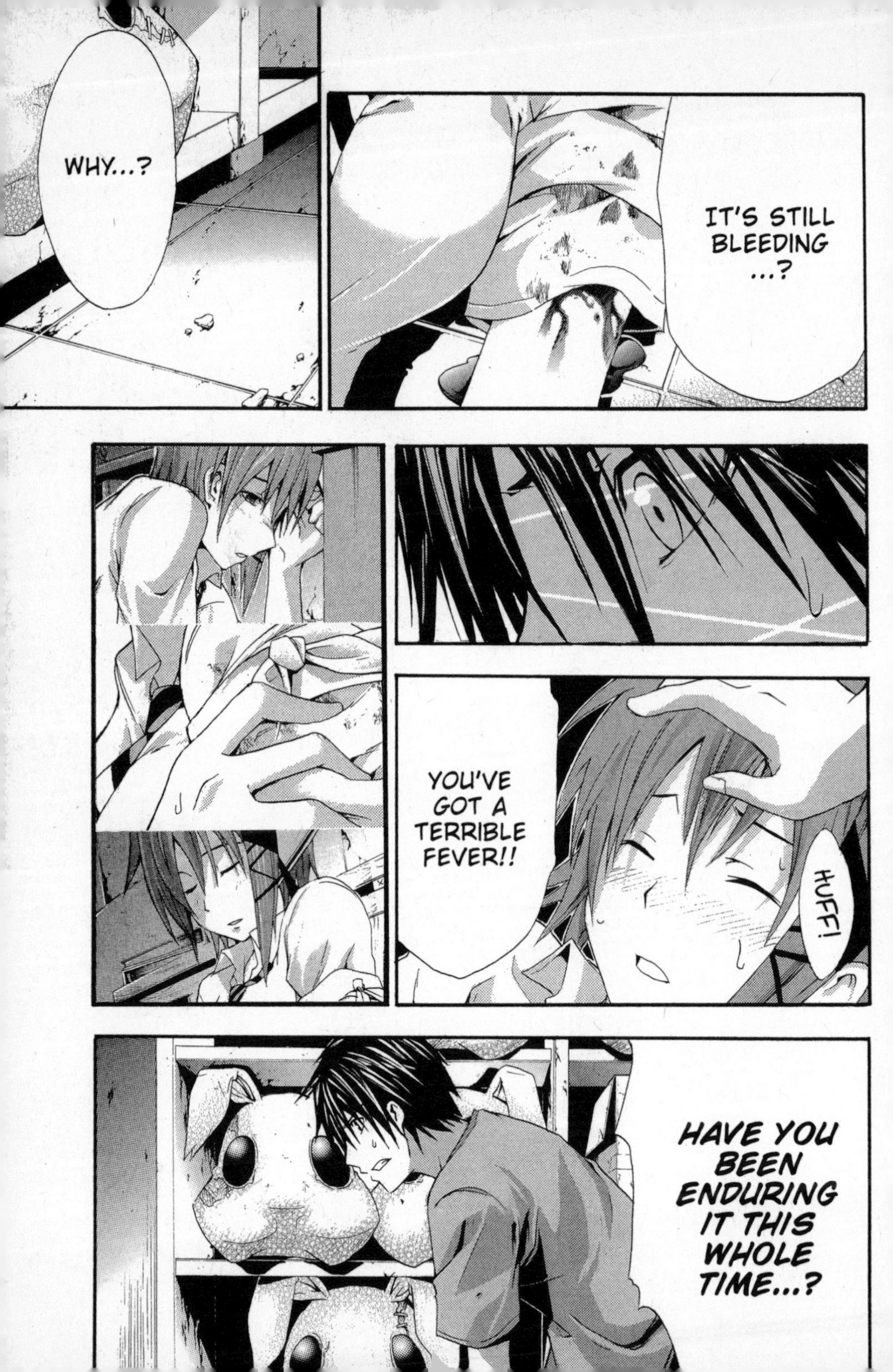
IT'S STILL BLEEDING ...?
WHY...?
YOU'VE GOT A TERRIBLE FEVER!!
HUFF!
HAVE YOU BEEN ENDURING IT THIS WHOLE TIME...?

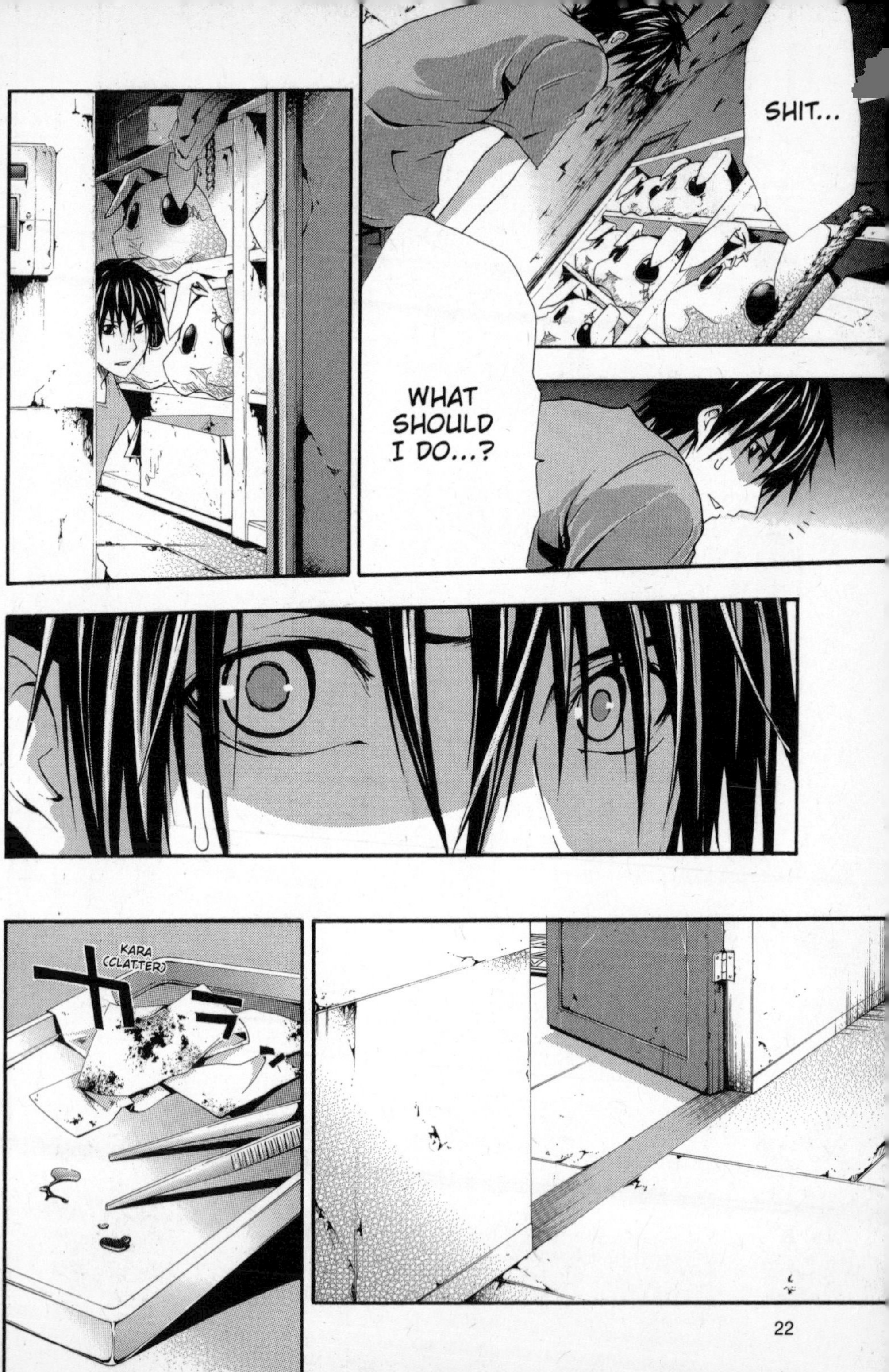
SHIT...
WHAT SHOULD I DO...?
KARA (CLATTER)

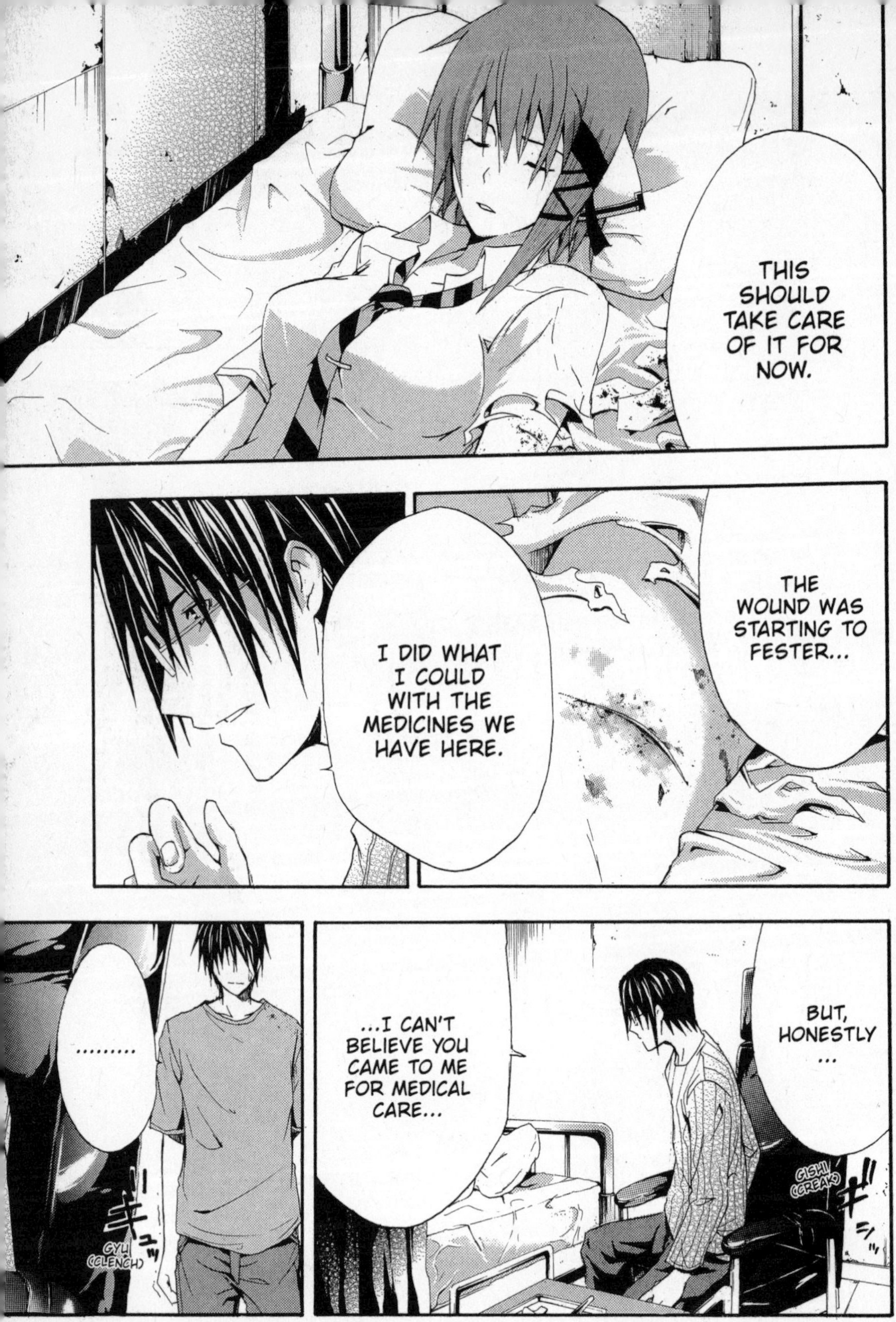
THIS SHOULD TAKE CARE OF IT FOR NOW.
THE WOUND WAS STARTING TO FESTER...
I DID WHAT I COULD WITH THE MEDICINES WE HAVE HERE.
BUT, HONESTLY ...
GISHI (CREAK)
...I CAN'T BELIEVE YOU CAME TO ME FOR MEDICAL CARE...
....
GYU (CLENCH)

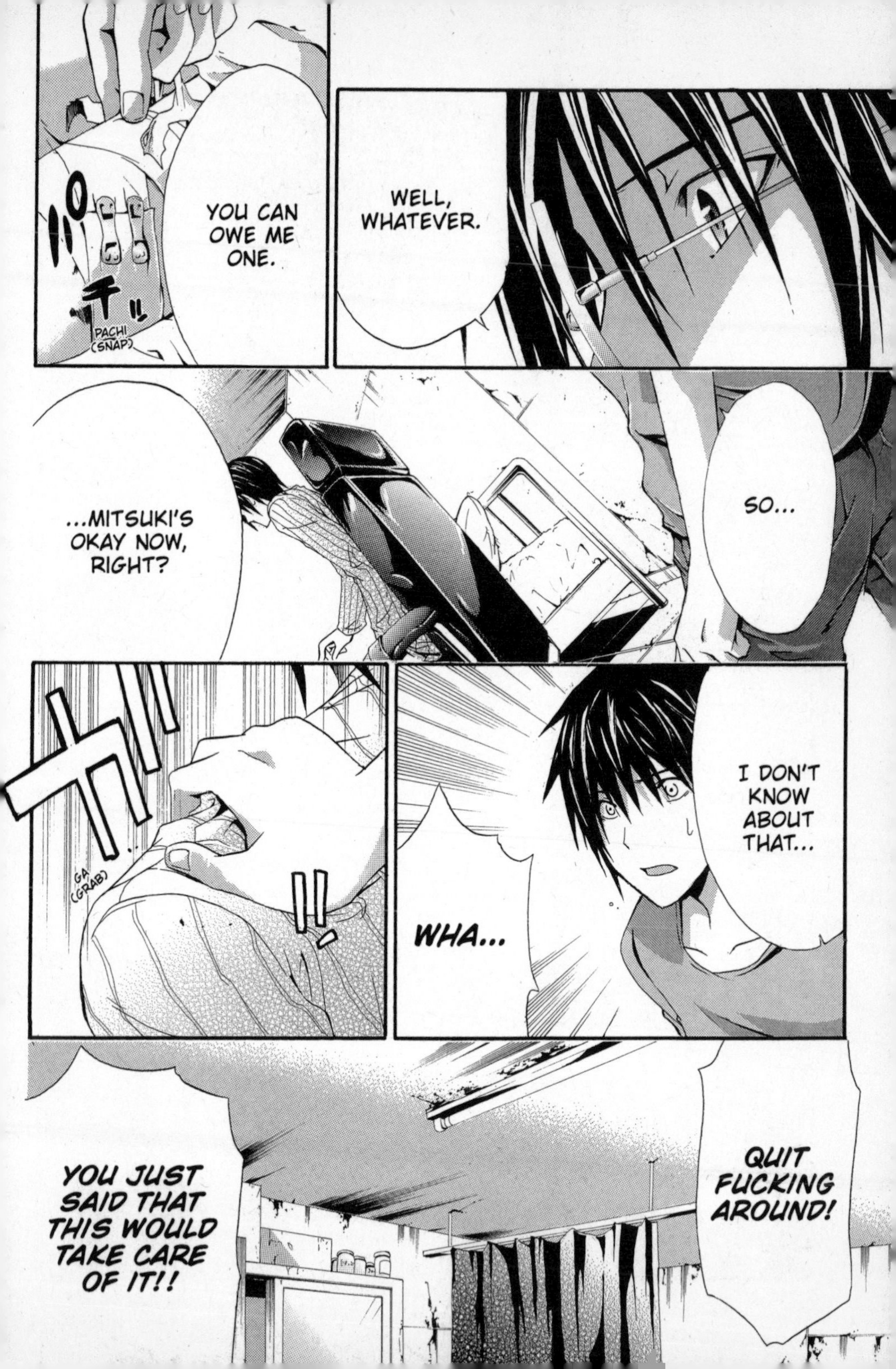
WELL, WHATEVER.
YOU CAN OWE ME ONE.
PACHI (SNAP)
SO...
...MITSUKI'S OKAY NOW, RIGHT?
I DON'T KNOW ABOUT THAT...
WHA...
GA (GRAB)
QUIT FUCKING AROUND!
YOU JUST SAID THAT THIS WOULD TAKE CARE OF IT!!

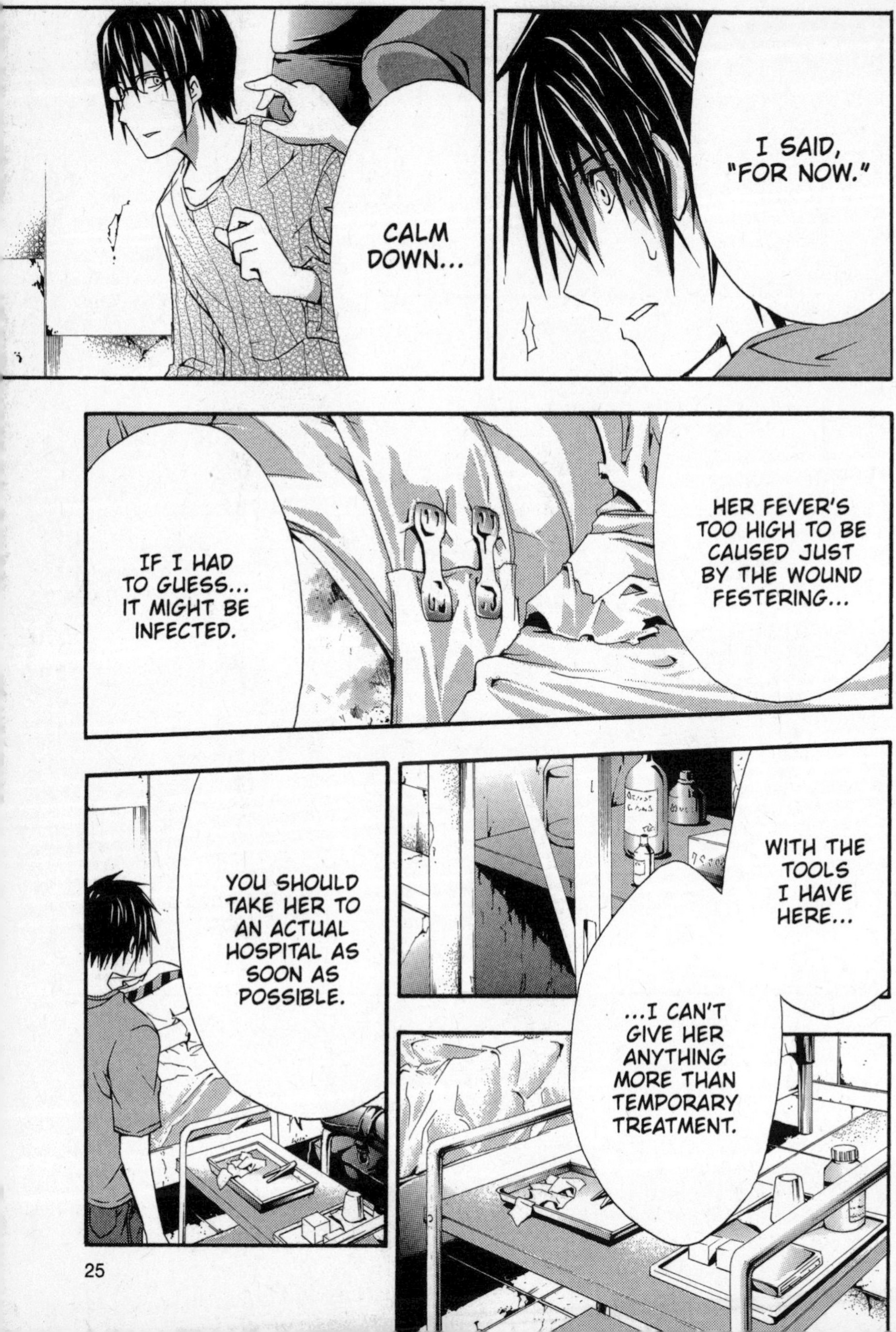
I SAID, "FOR NOW."
CALM DOWN...
HER FEVER'S TOO HIGH TO BE CAUSED JUST BY THE WOUND FESTERING...
IF I HAD TO GUESS... IT MIGHT BE INFECTED.
WITH THE TOOLS I HAVE HERE...
...I CAN'T GIVE HER ANYTHING MORE THAN TEMPORARY TREATMENT.
YOU SHOULD TAKE HER TO AN ACTUAL HOSPITAL AS SOON AS POSSIBLE.

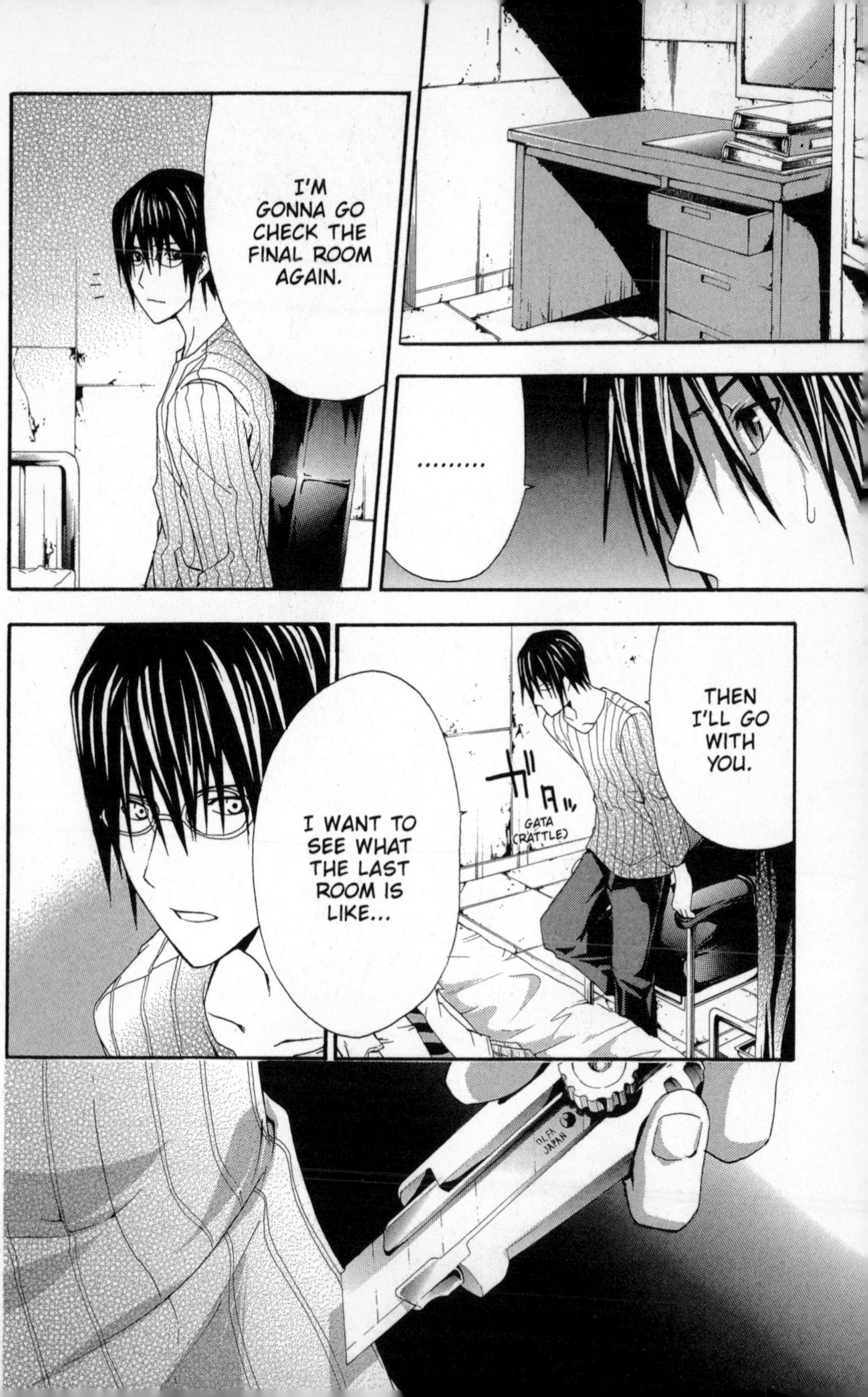
....
I'M GONNA GO CHECK THE FINAL ROOM AGAIN.
THEN I'LL GO WITH YOU.
ガタッ
GATA (RATTLE)
I WANT TO SEE WHAT THE LAST ROOM IS LIKE...
OLFA JAPAN

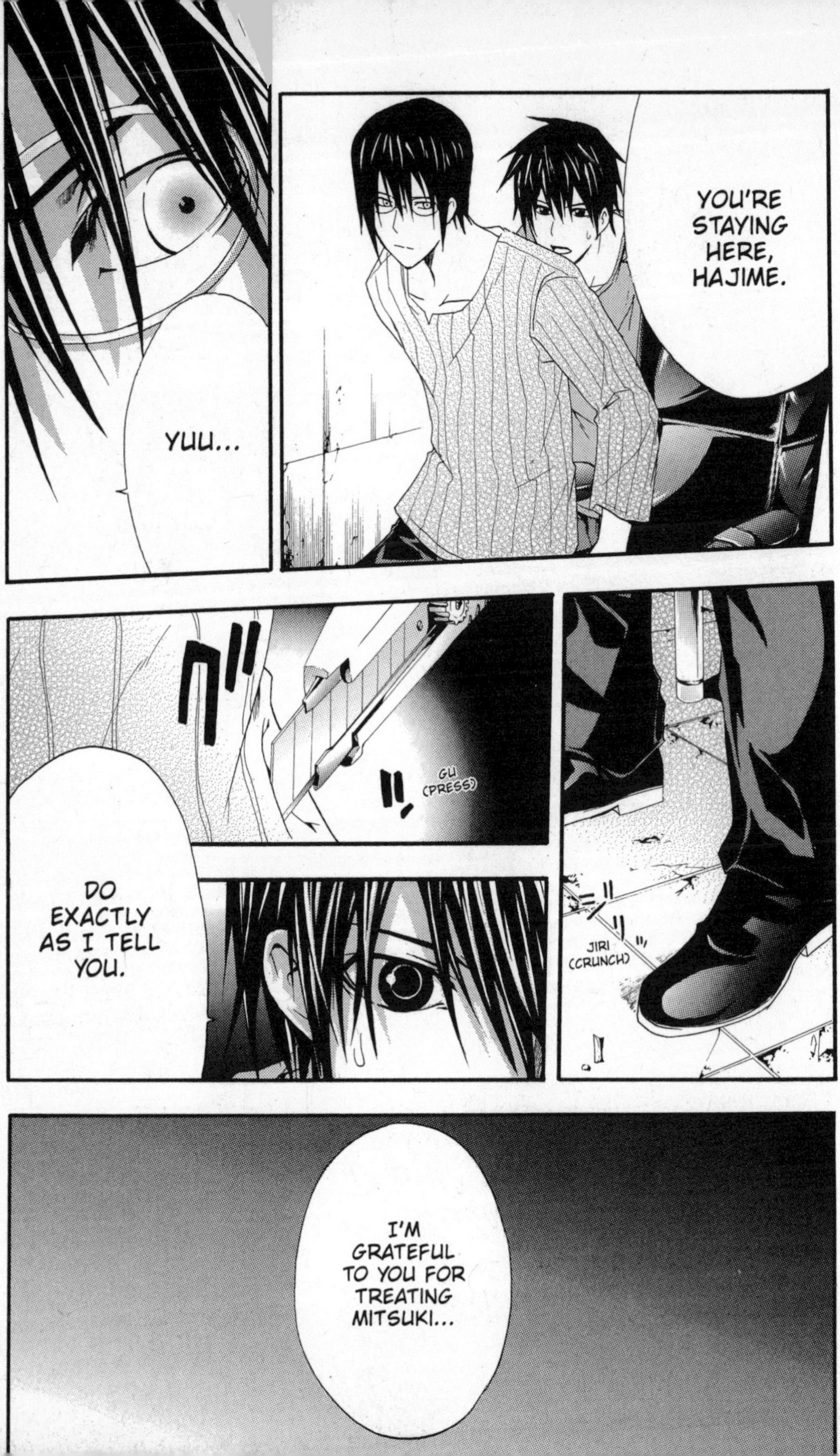
YOU'RE STAYING HERE, HAJIME.
YUU...
JIRI (CRUNCH)
GU (PRESS)
DO EXACTLY AS I TELL YOU.
I'M GRATEFUL TO YOU FOR TREATING MITSUKI...

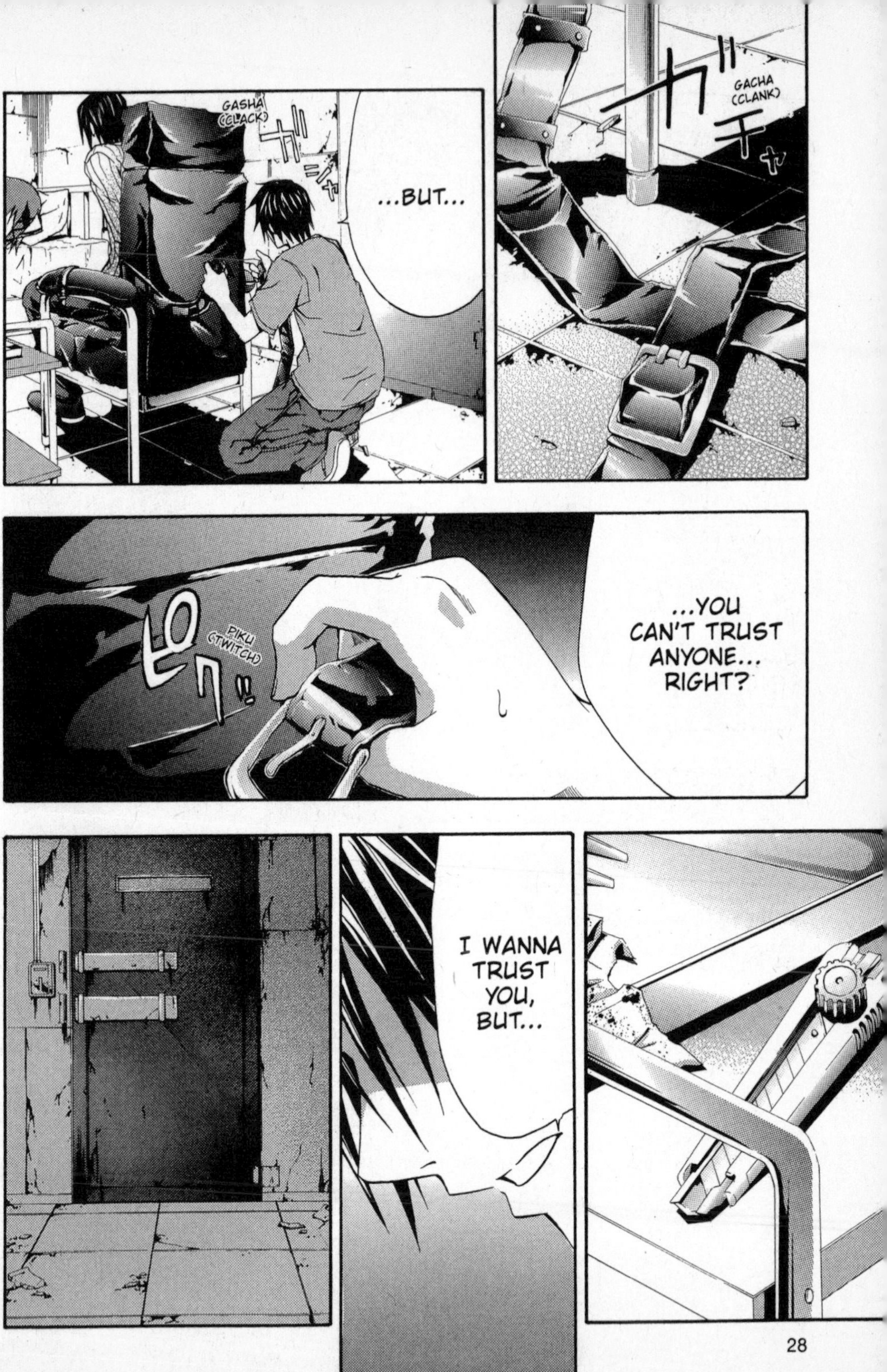
GACHA (CLANK)
GASHA (CLACK)
...BUT...
PIKU (TWITCH)
...YOU CAN'T TRUST ANYONE... RIGHT?
I WANNA TRUST YOU, BUT...

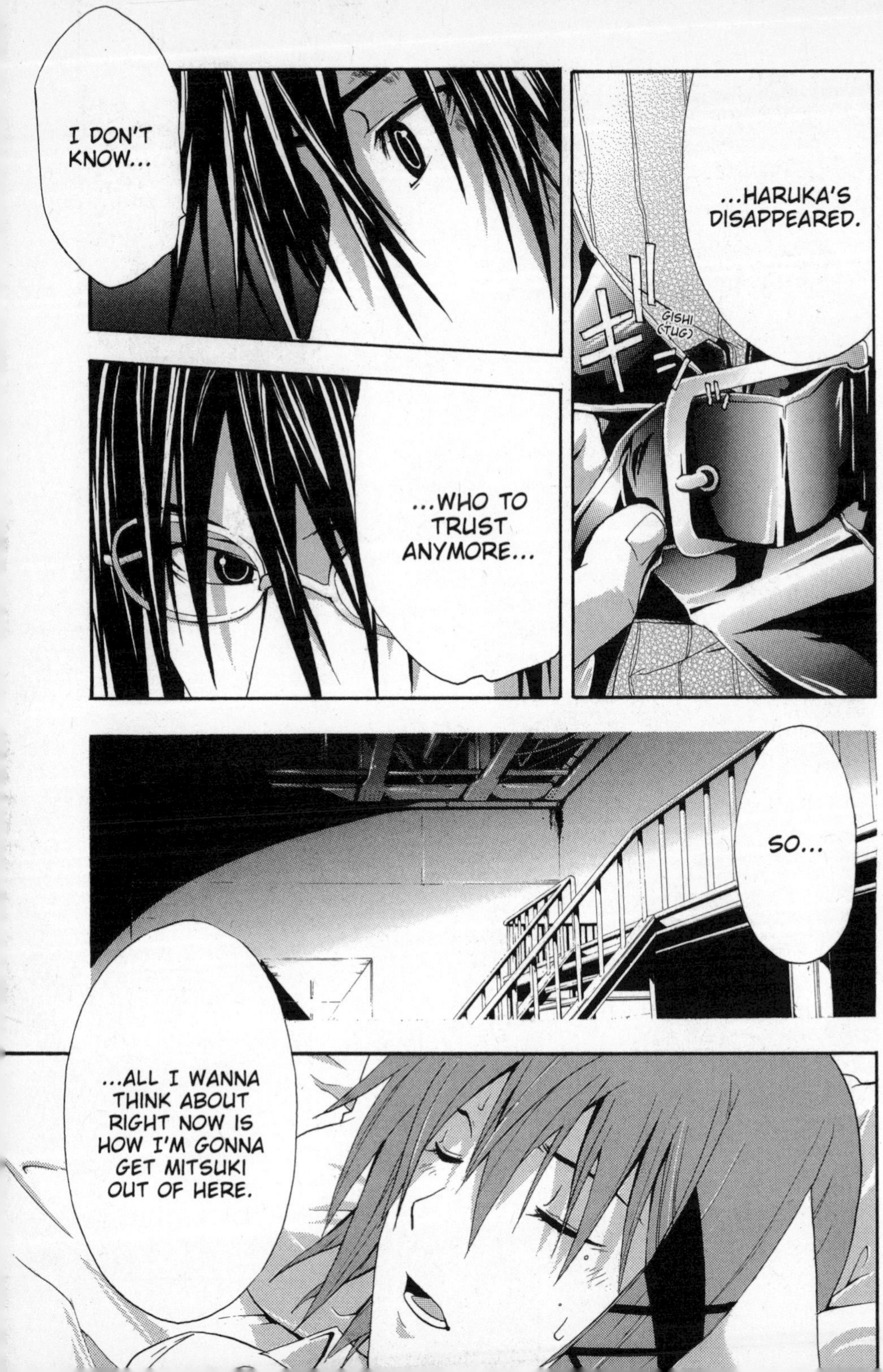
...HARUKA'S DISAPPEARED.
GISHI (TUG)
I DON'T KNOW...
...WHO TO TRUST ANYMORE...
SO...
...ALL I WANNA THINK ABOUT RIGHT NOW IS HOW I'M GONNA GET MITSUKI OUT OF HERE.

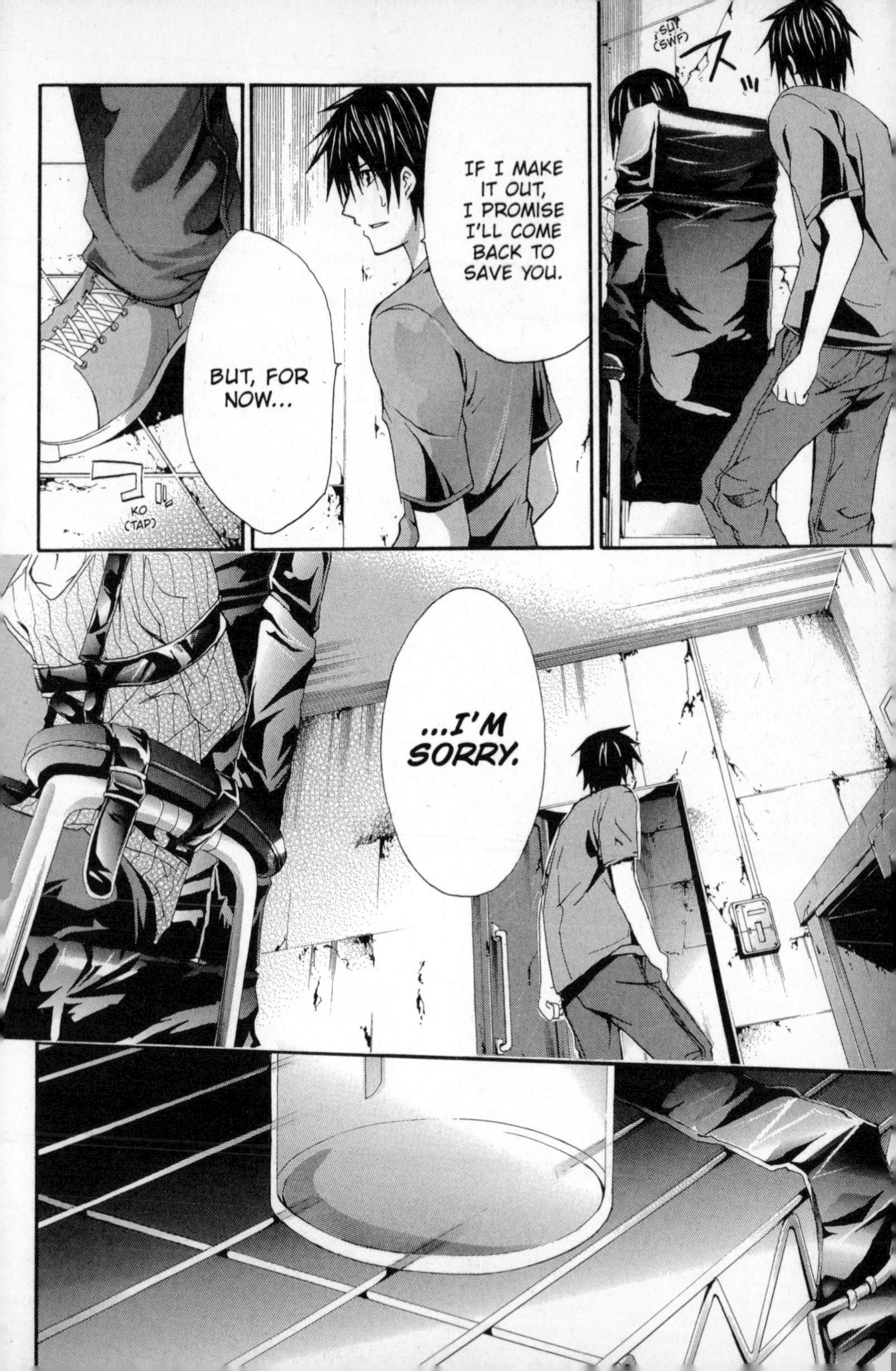
SU
(SWF)
IF I MAKE IT OUT, I PROMISE I'LL COME BACK TO SAVE YOU.
BUT, FOR NOW...
KO
(TAP)
...I'M SORRY.

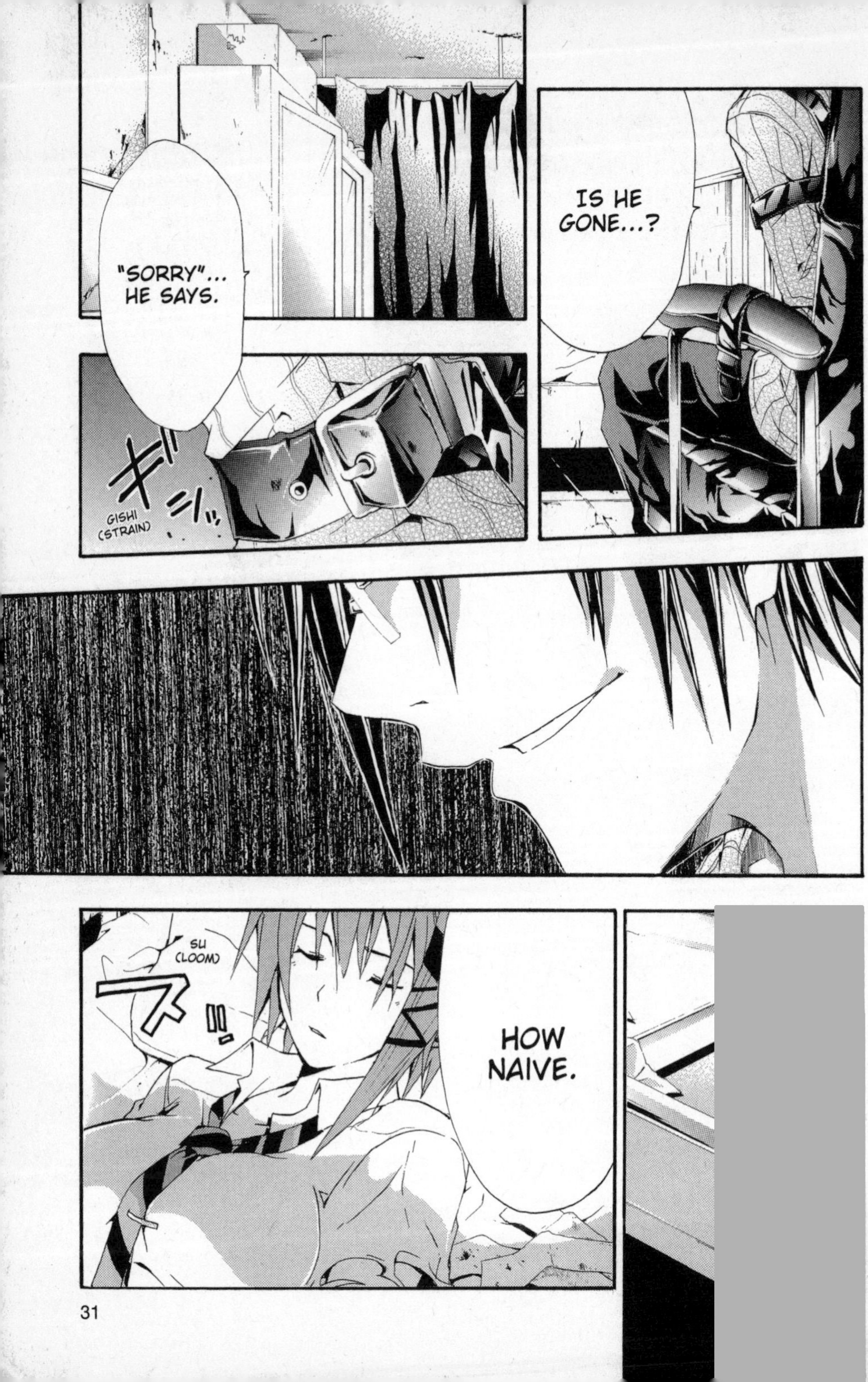

IS HE GONE...?
"SORRY"... HE SAYS.
GISHI (STRAIN)
HOW NAIVE.
SU (LOOM)

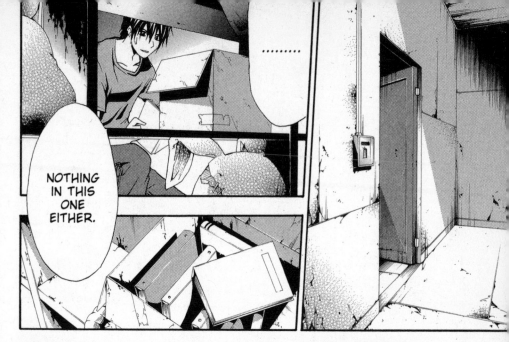

....
NOTHING IN THIS ONE EITHER.
I DON'T CARE WHAT IT IS...
...I NEED TO FIND SOMETHING TO OPEN THAT DOOR...
THAT'S...

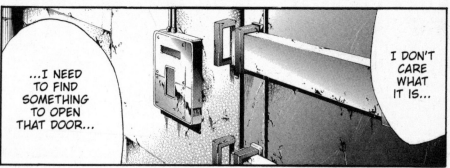

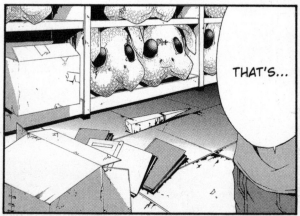

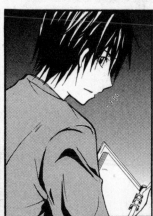

MITSUKI WAS HOLDING THAT EARLIER...

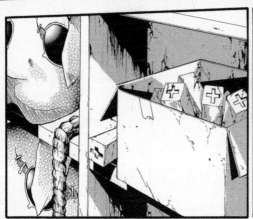

DON'T TELL ME...

ゴ||ク||
GOKU
(GULP)

33

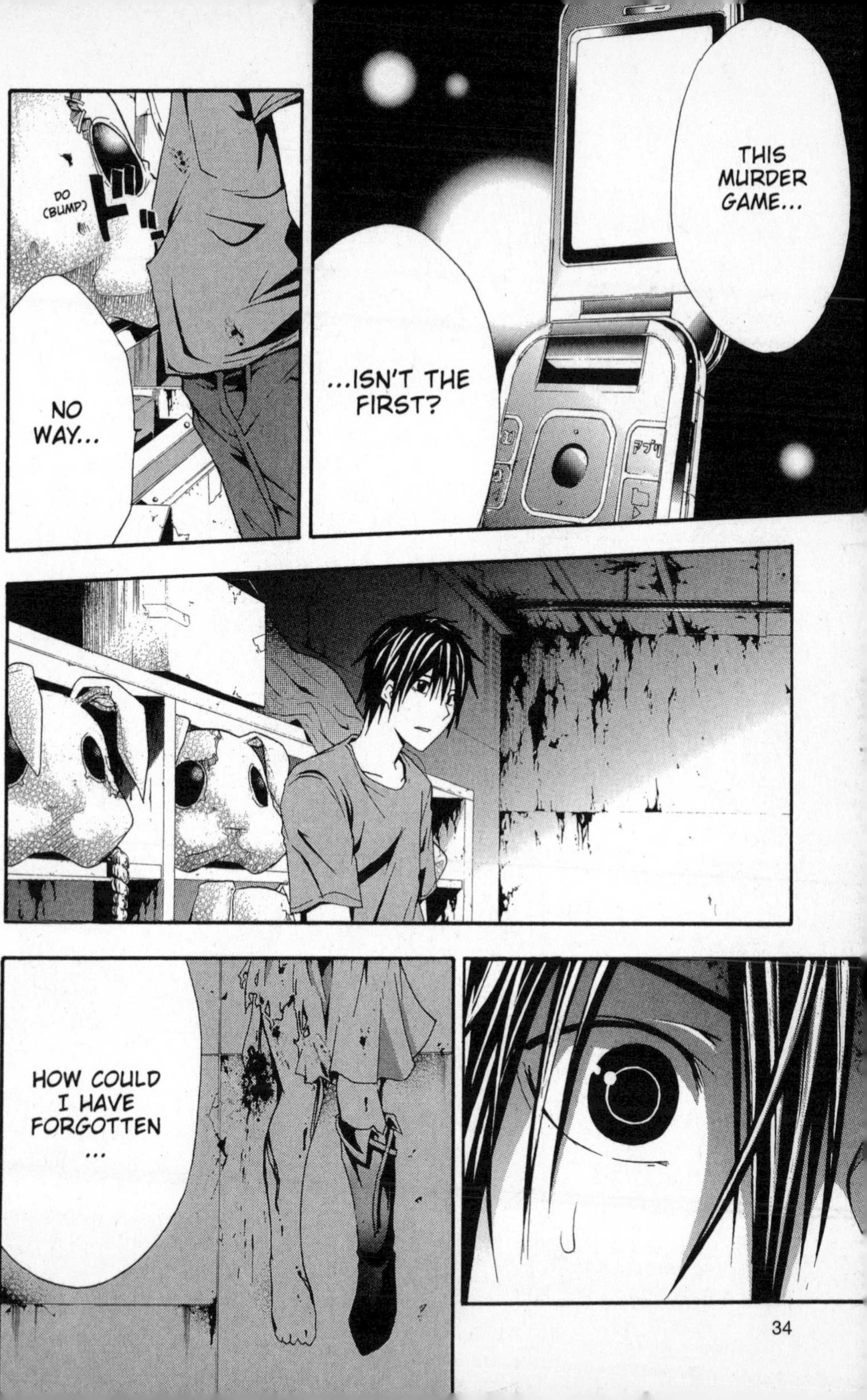
THIS MURDER GAME...
...ISN'T THE FIRST?
DO (BUMP)
NO WAY...
HOW COULD I HAVE FORGOTTEN ...

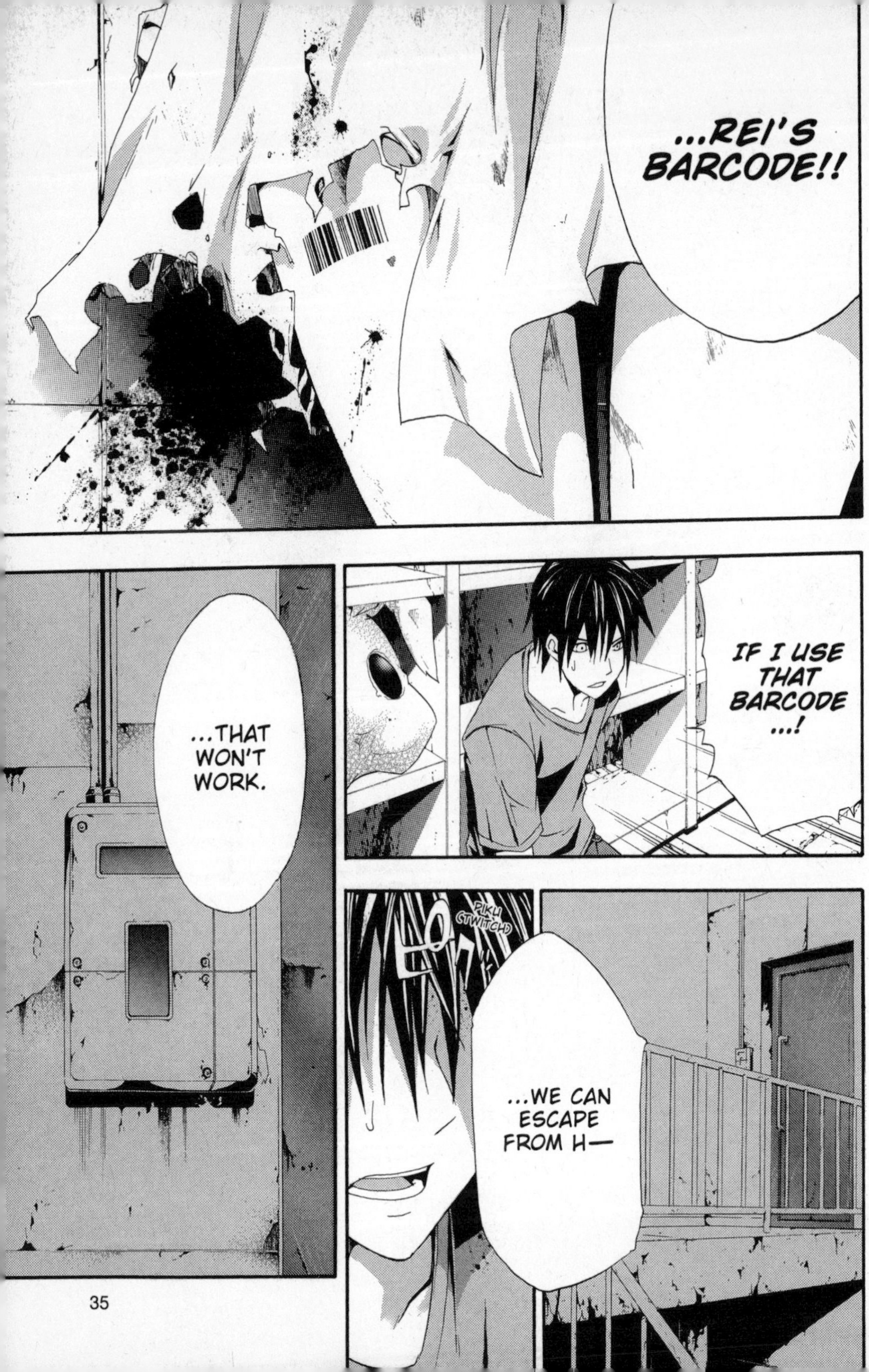
...REI'S BARCODE!!
IF I USE THAT BARCODE ...!
...WE CAN ESCAPE FROM H—
PIKU (TWITCH)
...THAT WON'T WORK.

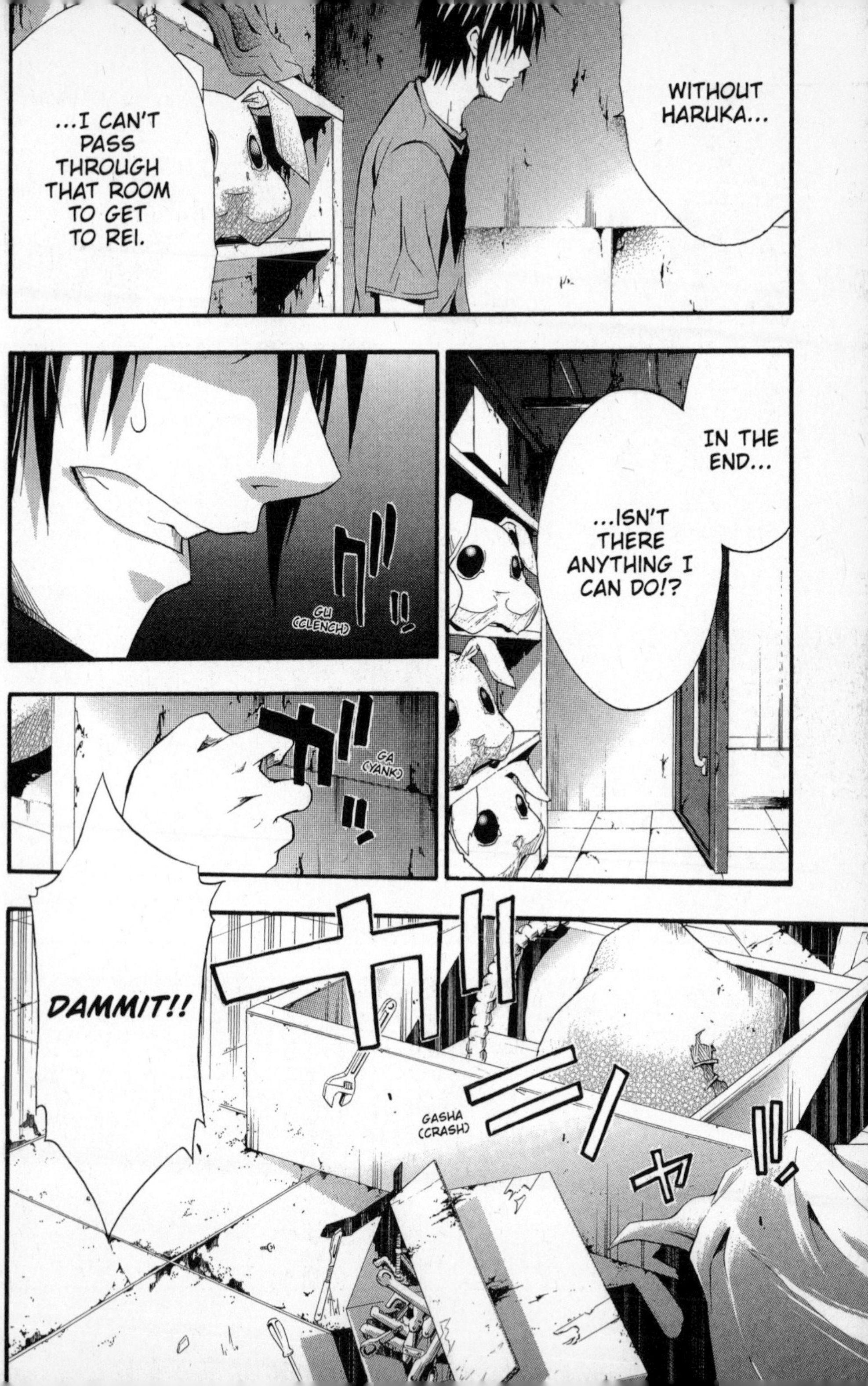

WITHOUT HARUKA...
...I CAN'T PASS THROUGH THAT ROOM TO GET TO REI.
IN THE END...
...ISN'T THERE ANYTHING I CAN DO!?
GU (CLENCH)
GA (YANK)
GASHA (CRASH)
DAMMIT!!

GORO (ROLL)
GORO
HUFF!
HUFF!
GORO

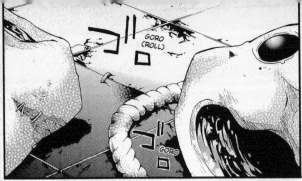

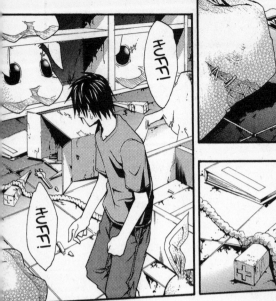

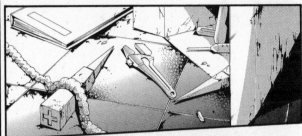

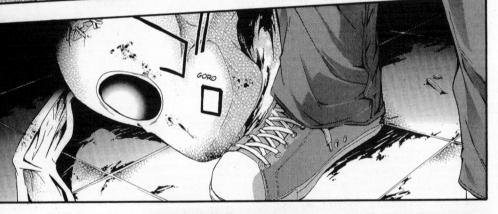

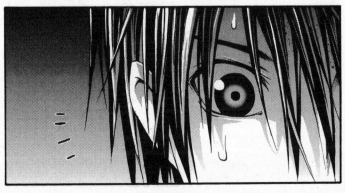

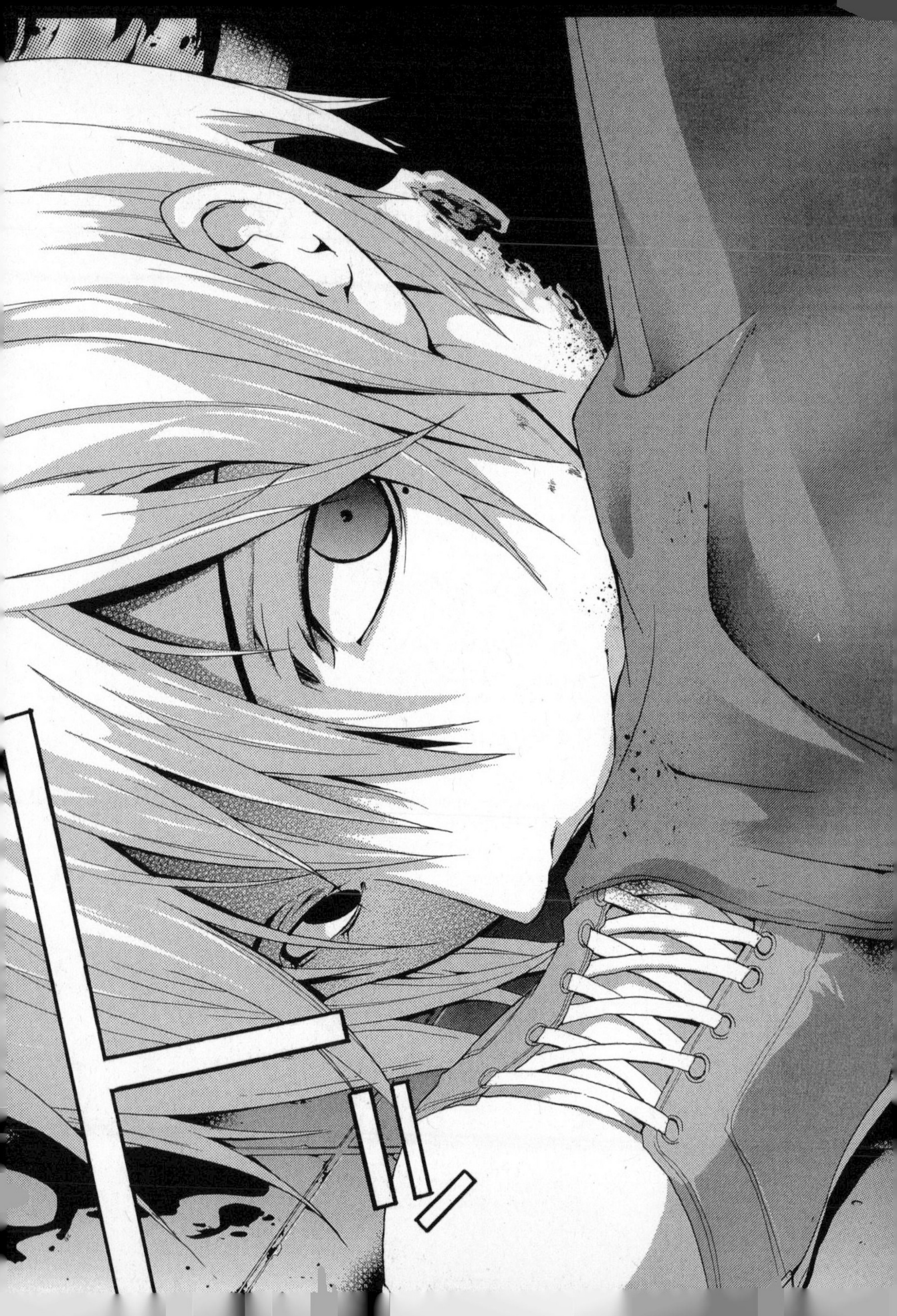

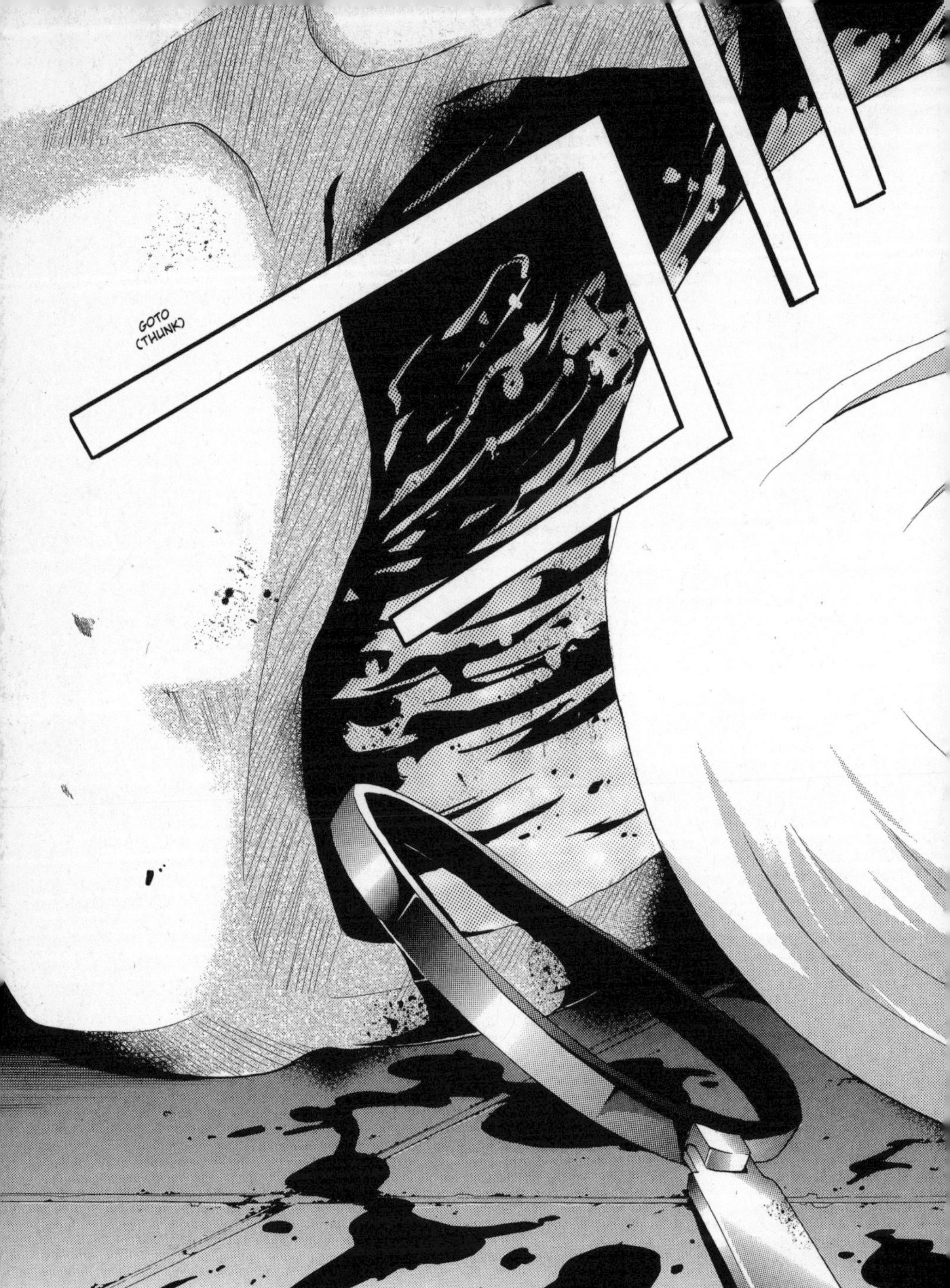
GOTO
(THUNK)

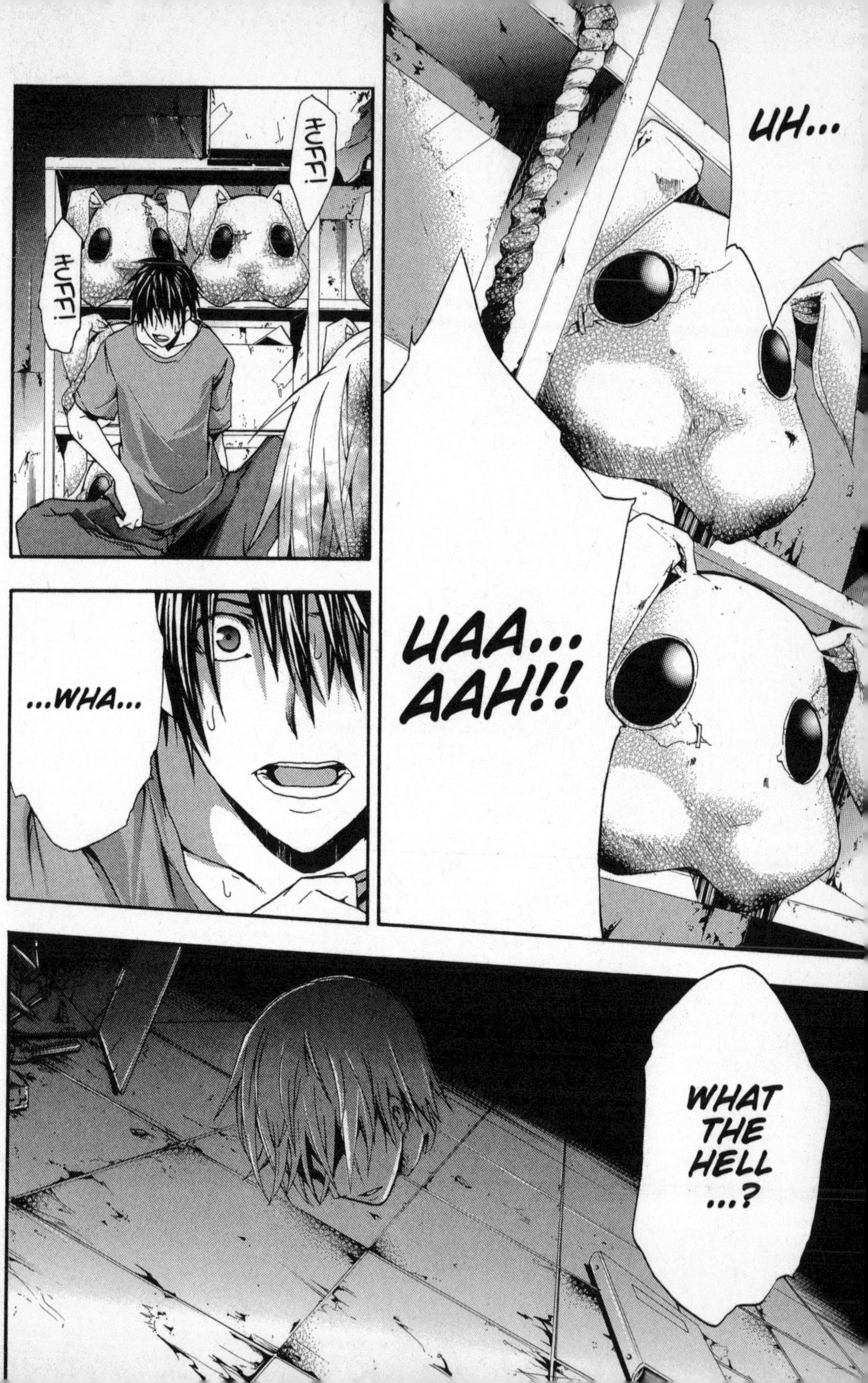
UH...
UAA... AAH!!
HUFF!
HUFF!
...WHA...
WHAT THE HELL ...?

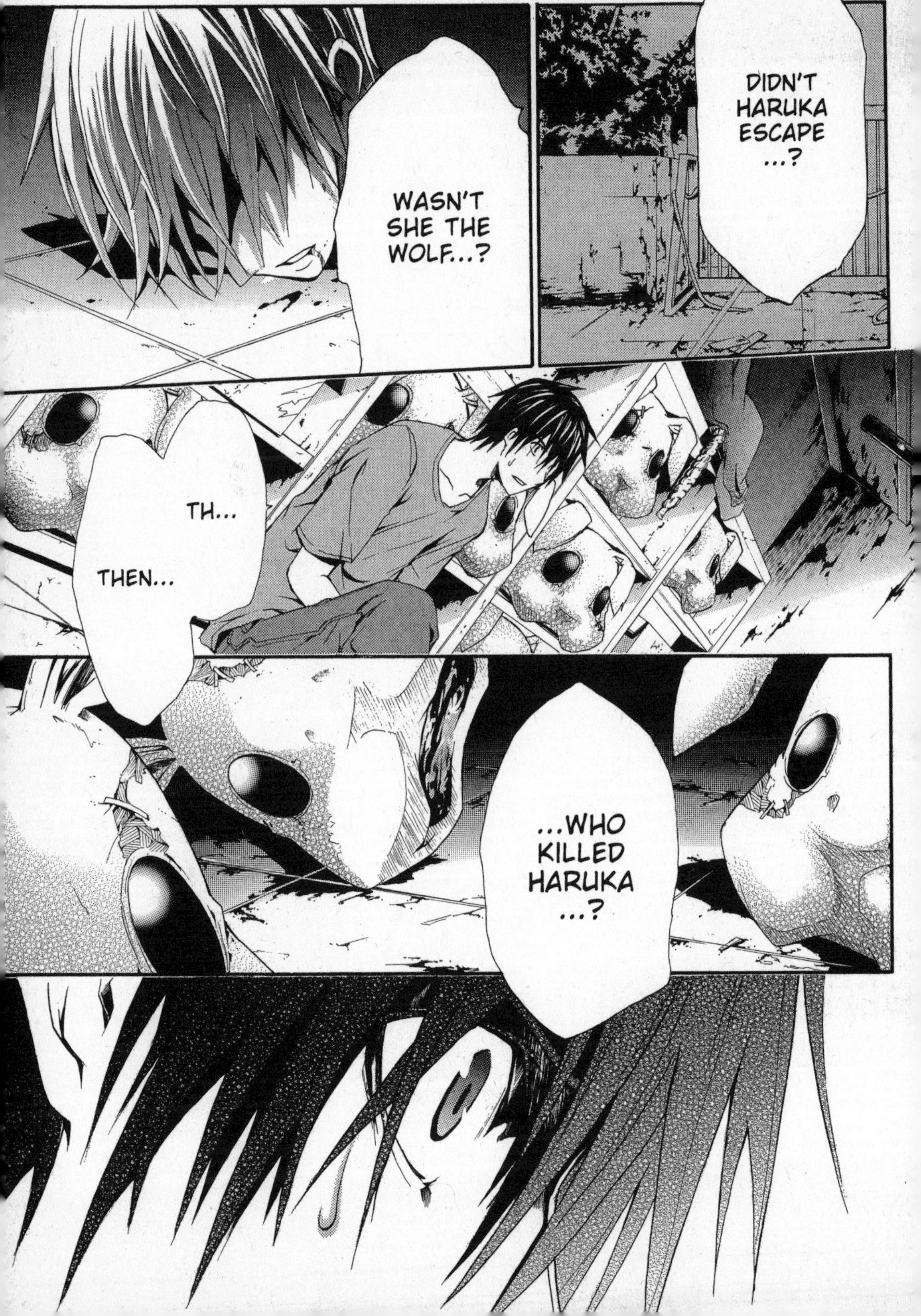
DIDN'T HARUKA ESCAPE ...?
WASN'T SHE THE WOLF...?
TH... THEN...
...WHO KILLED HARUKA ...?

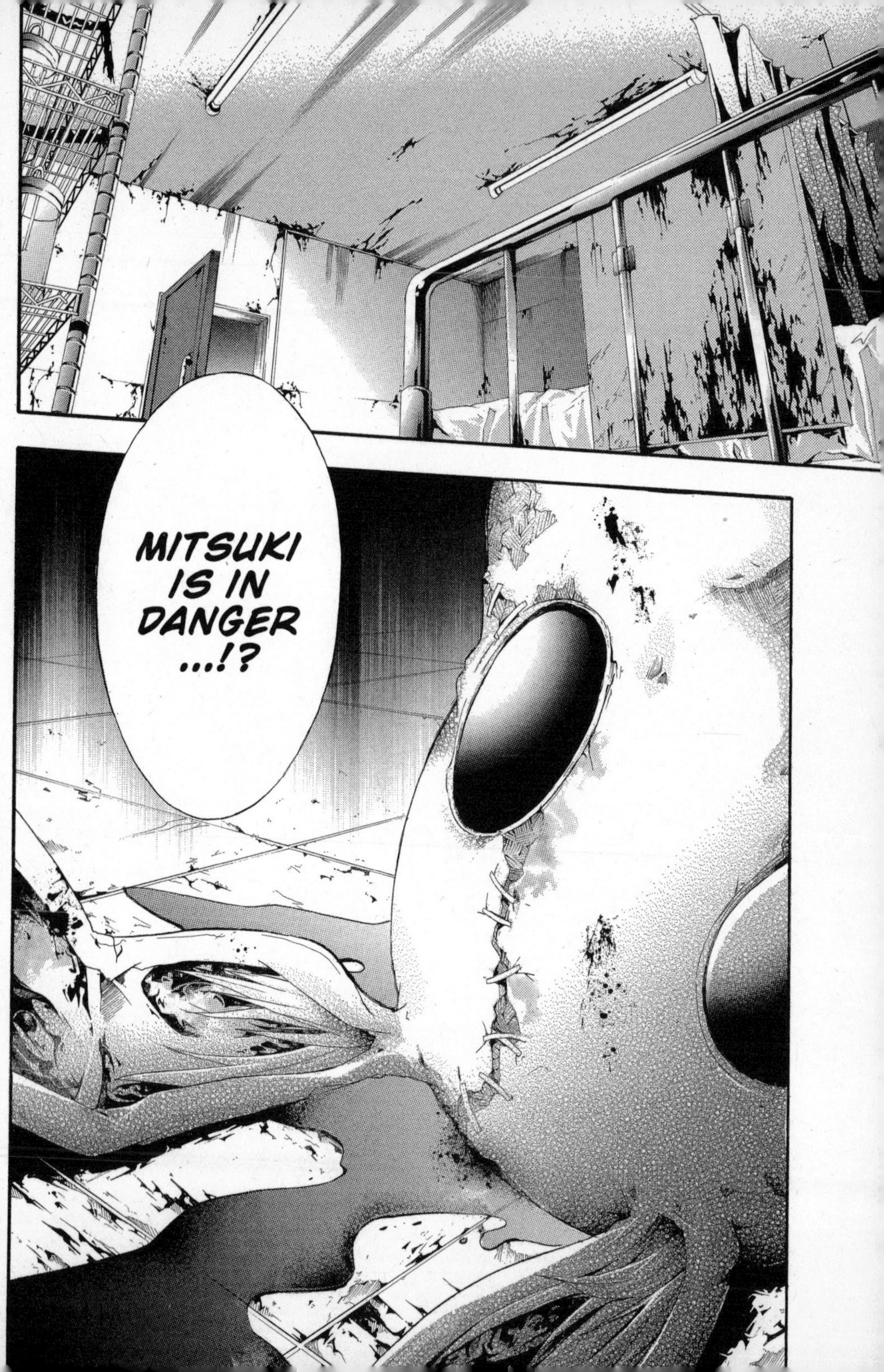
MITSUKI IS IN DANGER ...!?

REI

EIJI

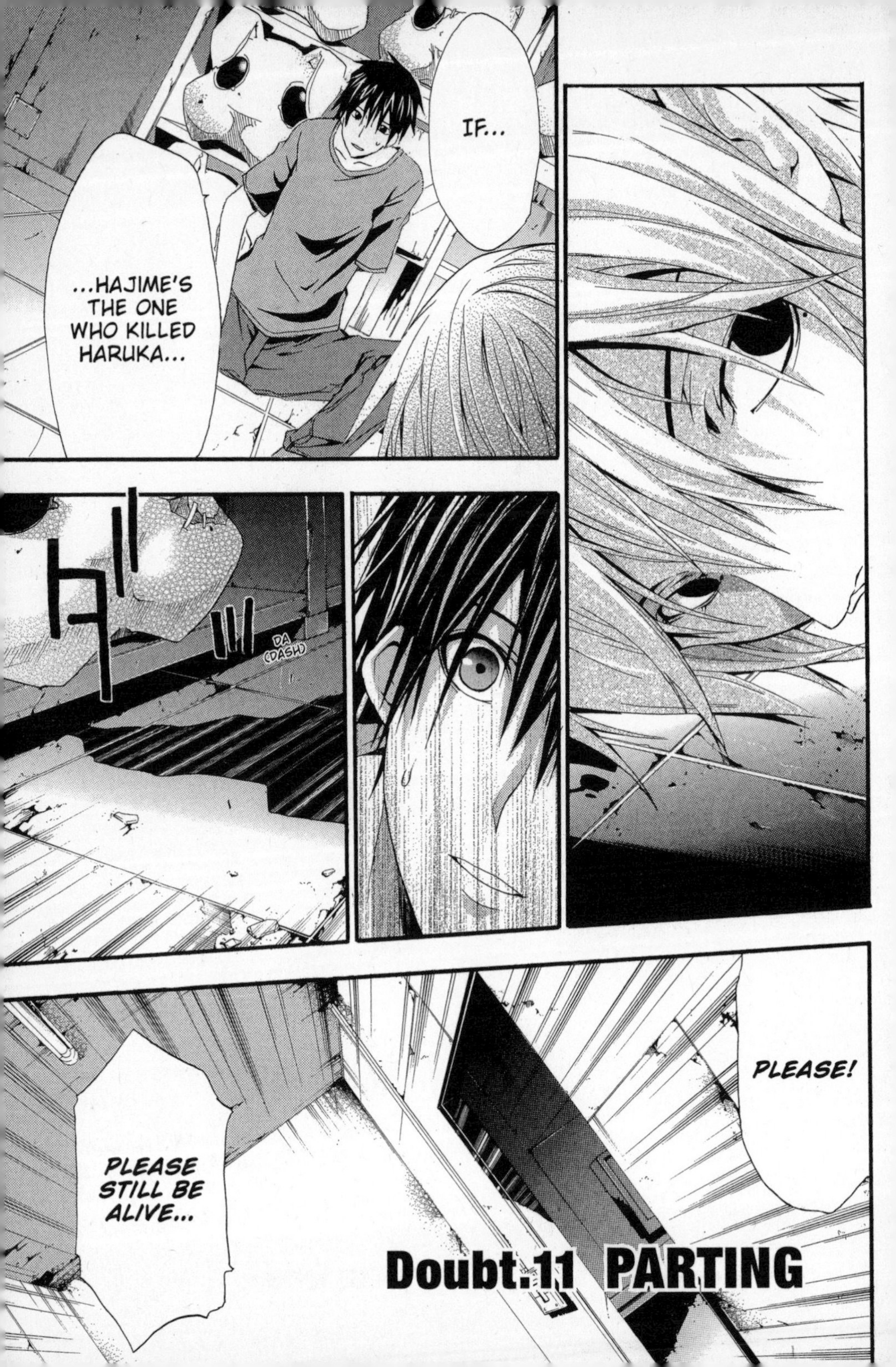
IF...
...HAJIME'S THE ONE WHO KILLED HARUKA...
DA (DASH)
PLEASE!
PLEASE STILL BE ALIVE...
Doubt.11 PARTING

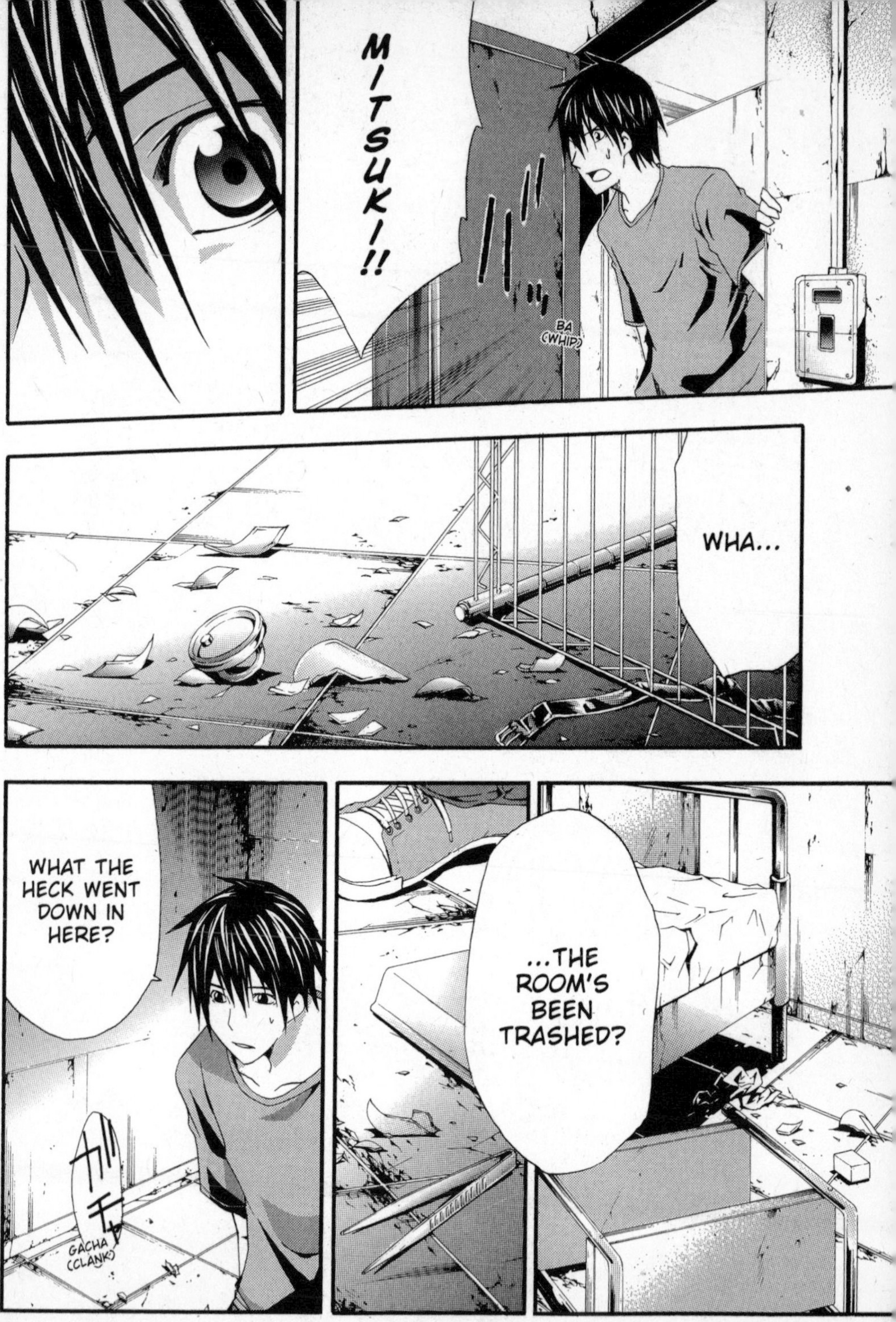
MITSUKI!!
BA (WHIP)
WHA...
...THE ROOM'S BEEN TRASHED?
WHAT THE HECK WENT DOWN IN HERE?
カチャ
GACHA (CLANK)

THESE ARE THE RESTRAINTS I USED ON HAJIME...

HE COULDN'T HAVE...

ZA
(SWSH)

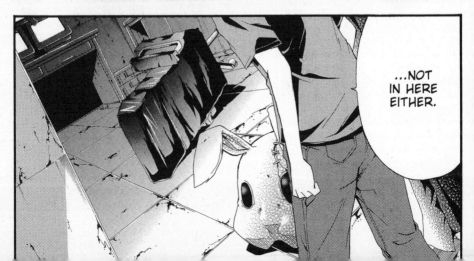

...NOT IN HERE EITHER.

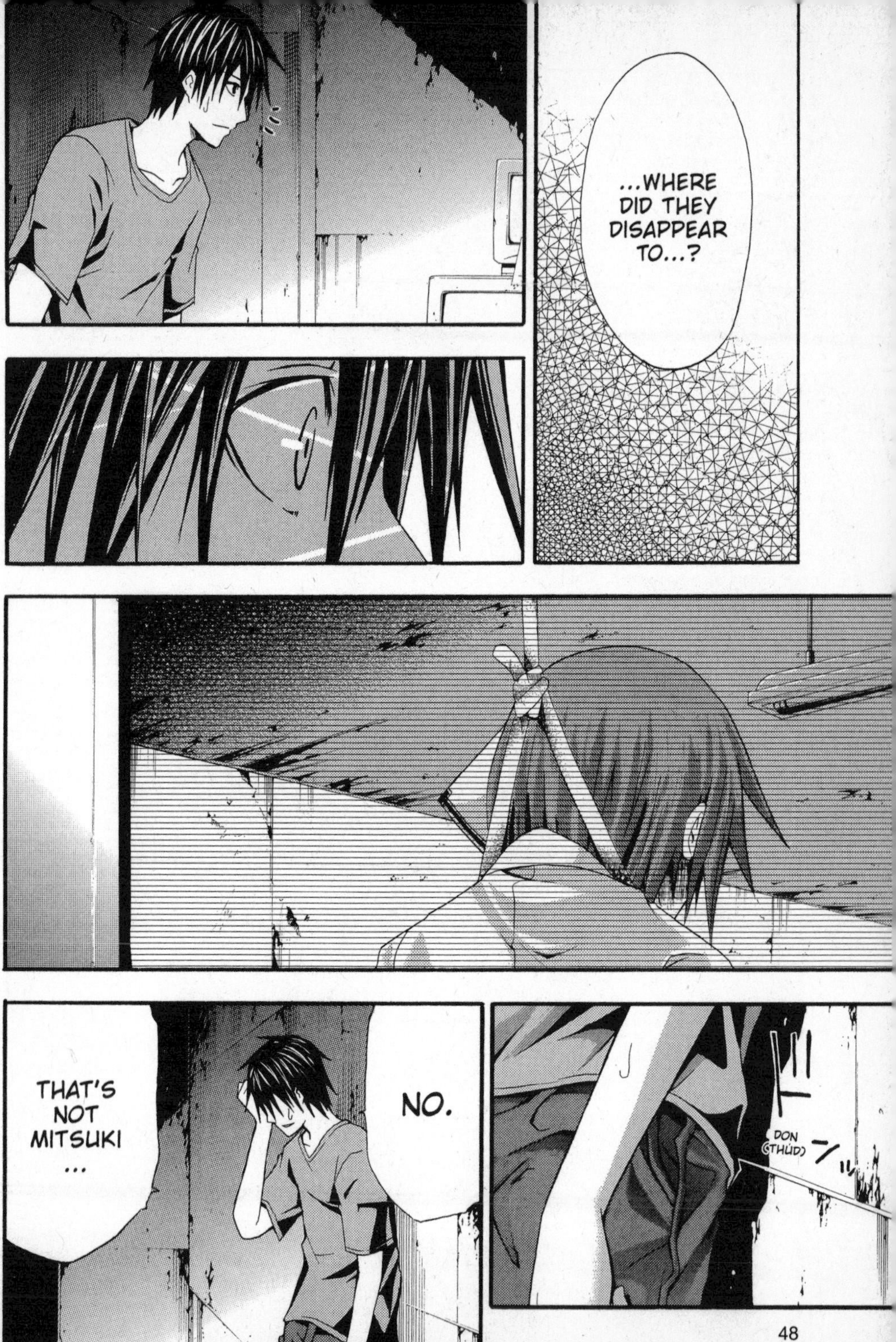
...WHERE DID THEY DISAPPEAR TO...?
DON (THUD)
NO.
THAT'S NOT MITSUKI ...

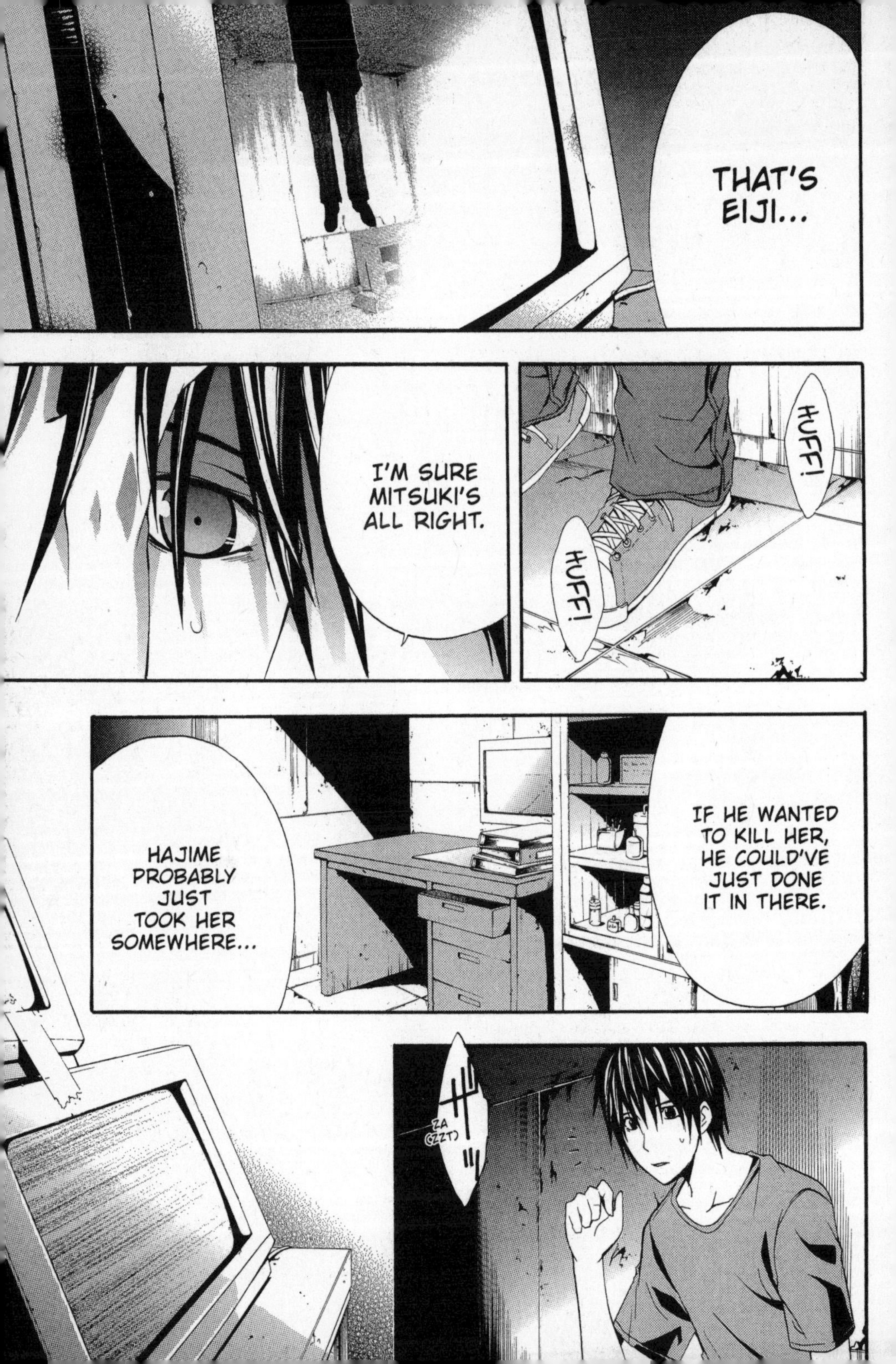
THAT'S EIJI...
HUFF!
HUFF!
I'M SURE MITSUKI'S ALL RIGHT.
IF HE WANTED TO KILL HER, HE COULD'VE JUST DONE IT IN THERE.
HAJIME PROBABLY JUST TOOK HER SOMEWHERE...
ZA (ZZT)

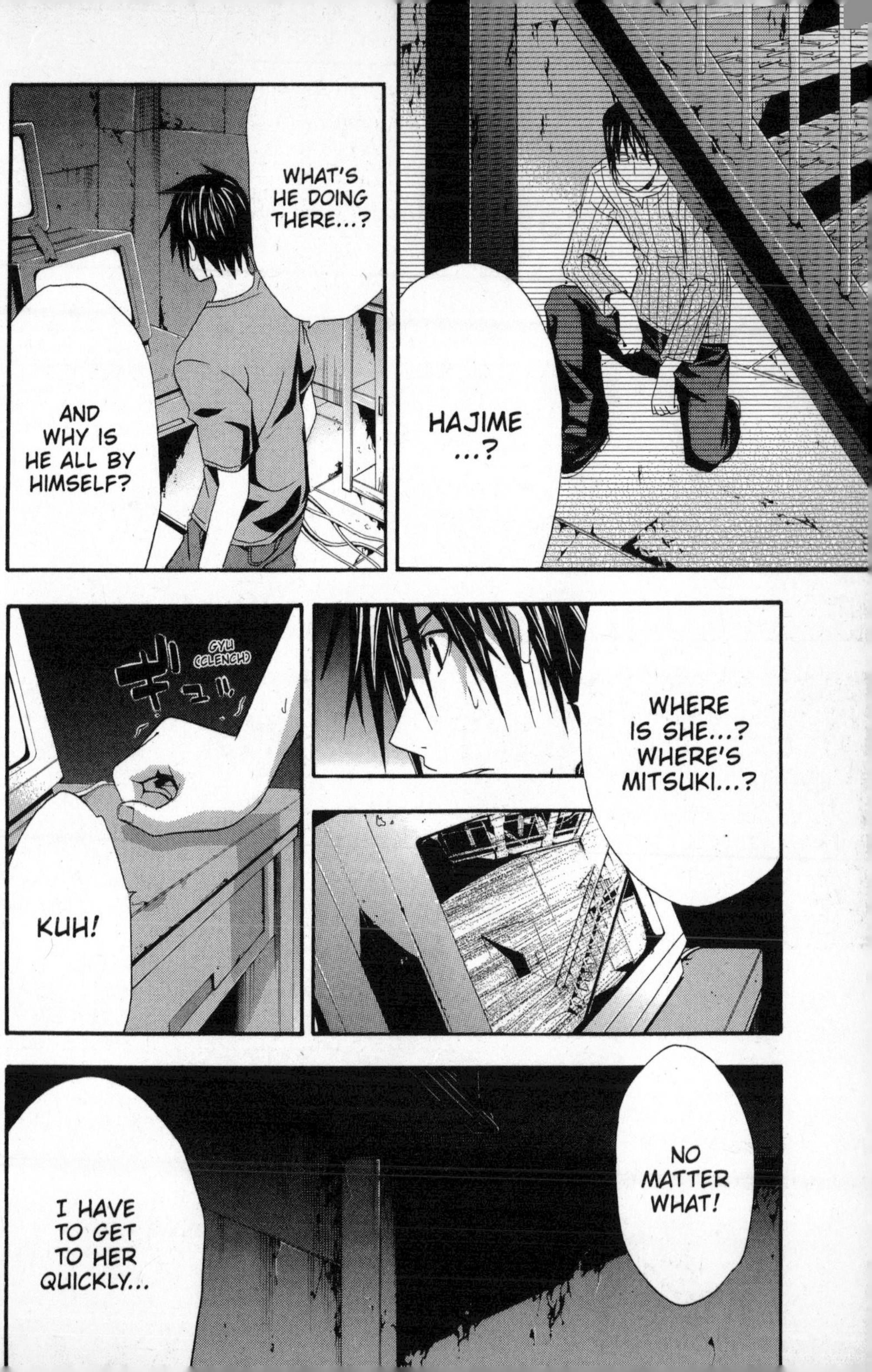
HAJIME ...?
WHAT'S HE DOING THERE...?
AND WHY IS HE ALL BY HIMSELF?
WHERE IS SHE...? WHERE'S MITSUKI...?
GYU (CLENCH)
ギュッ
KUH!
NO MATTER WHAT!
I HAVE TO GET TO HER QUICKLY...

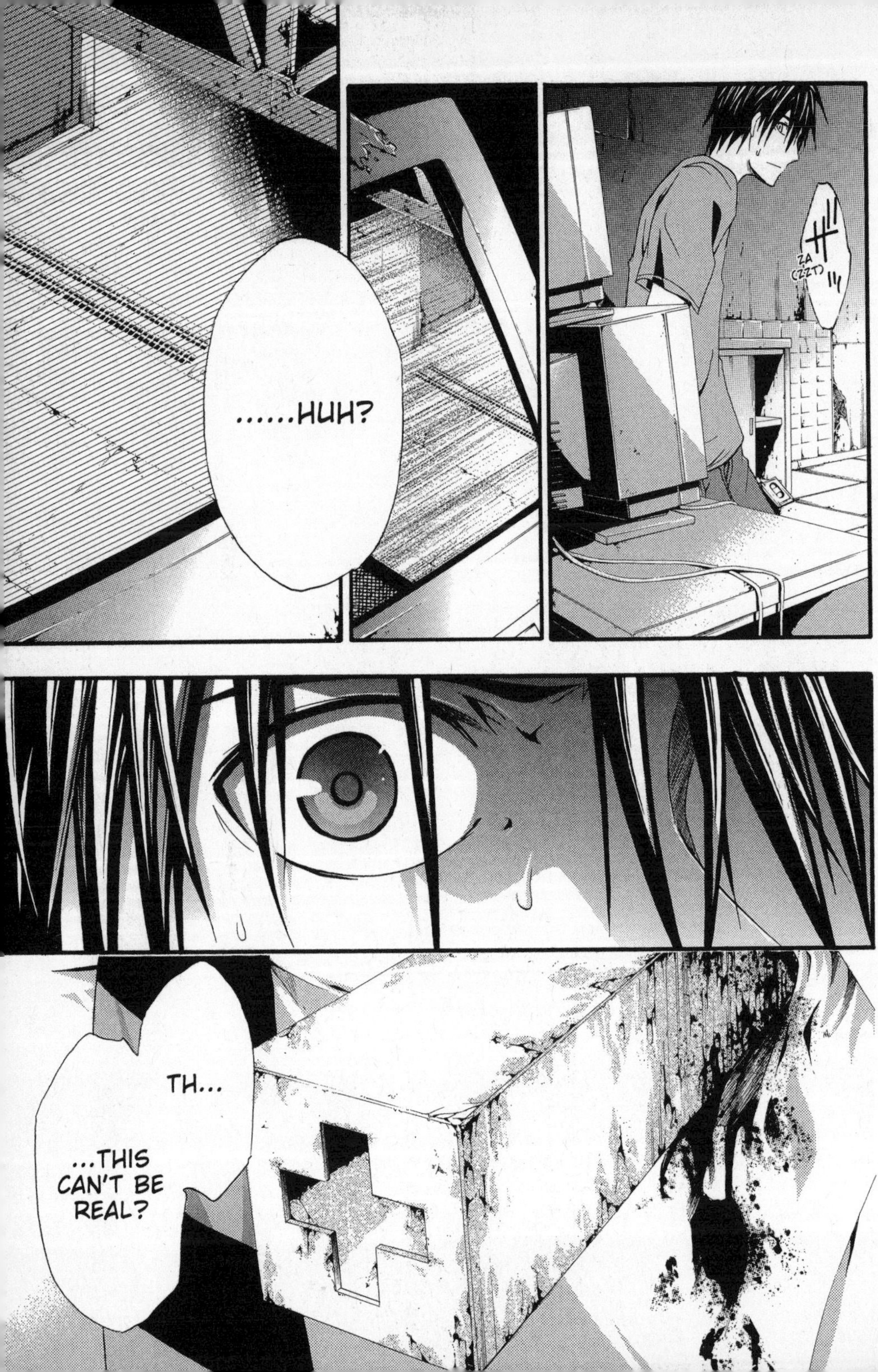
ZA (ZZZT)
......HUH?
TH...
...THIS CAN'T BE REAL?

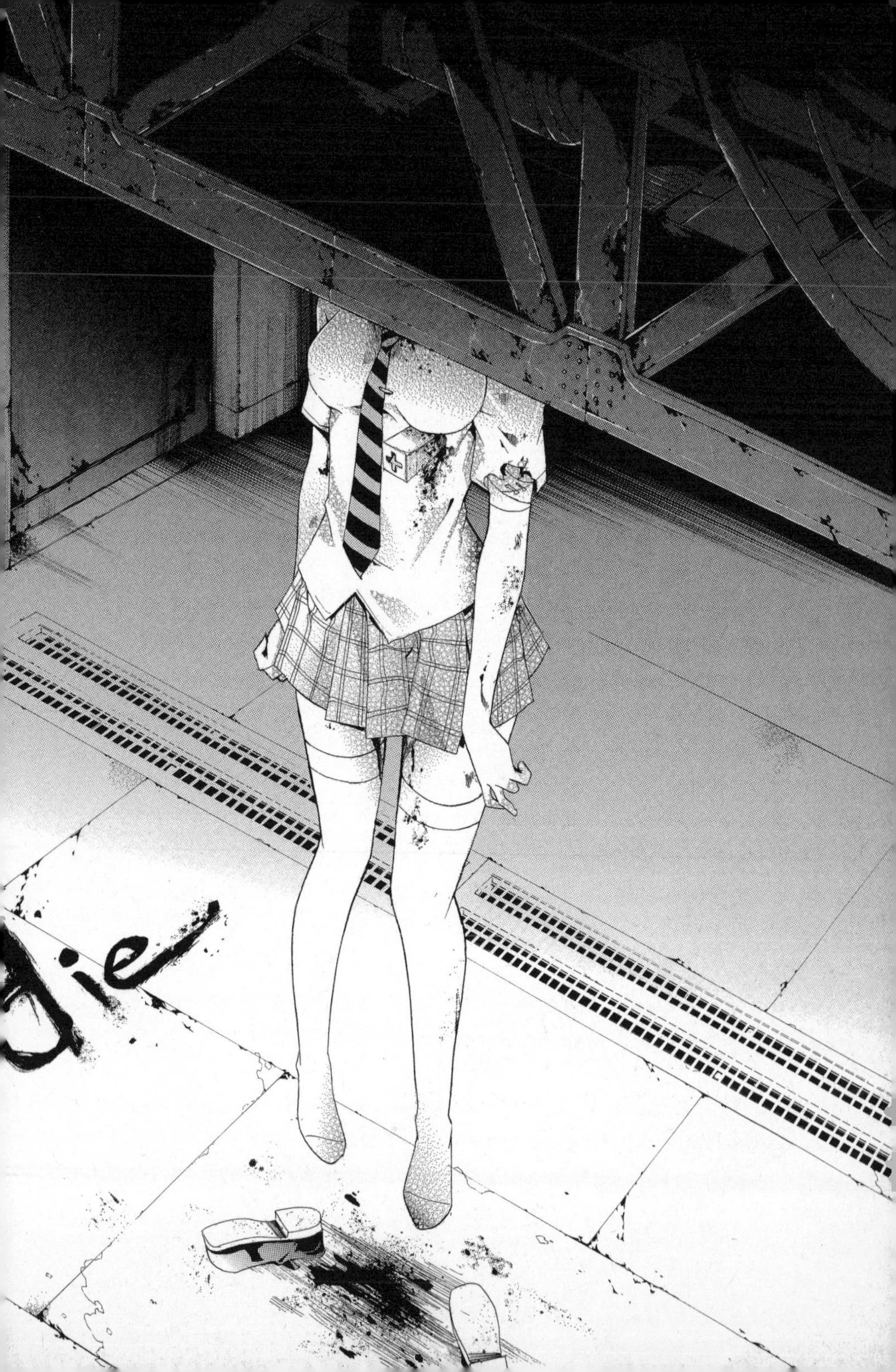

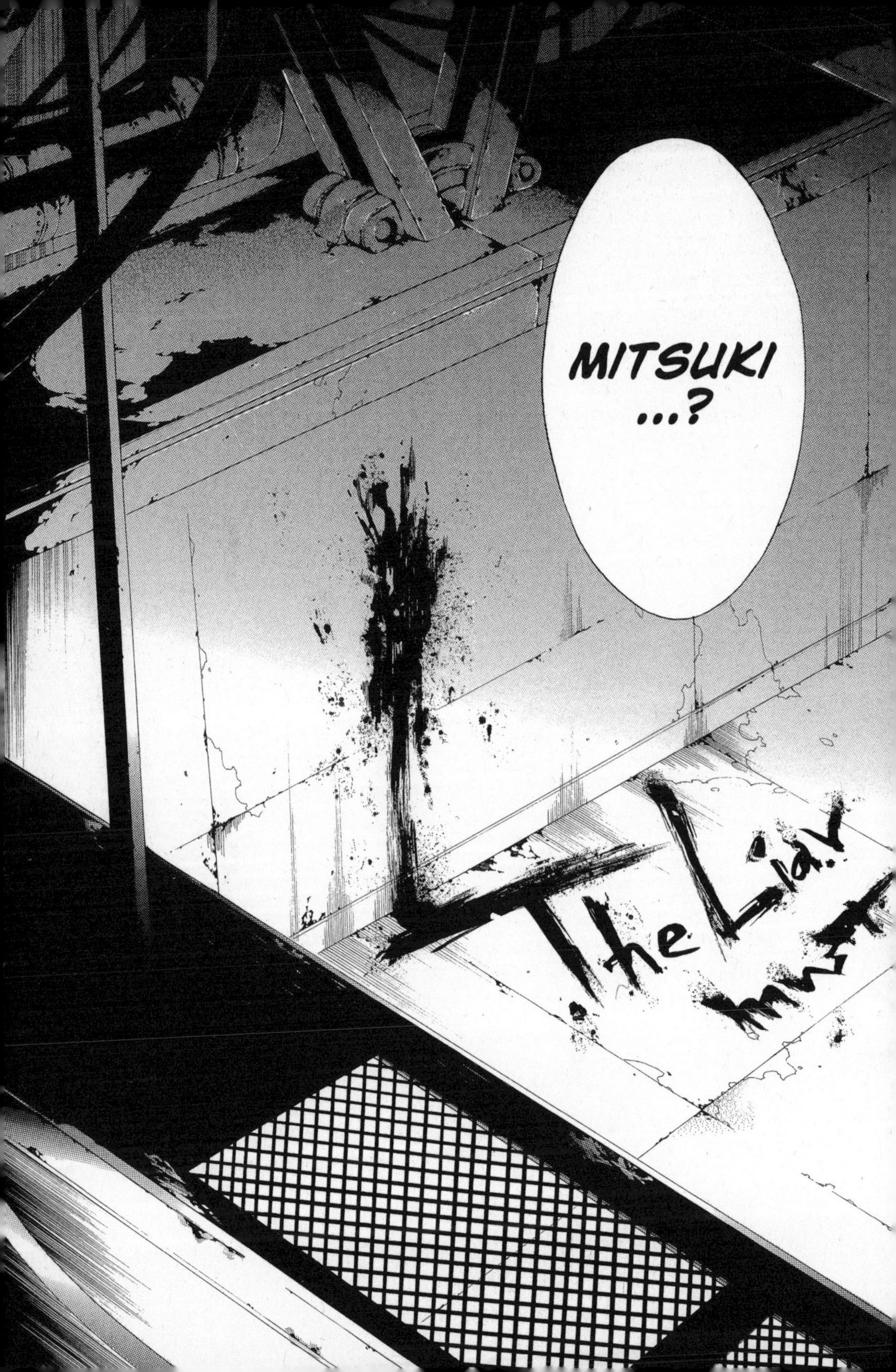
MITSUKI ...?
The Liar

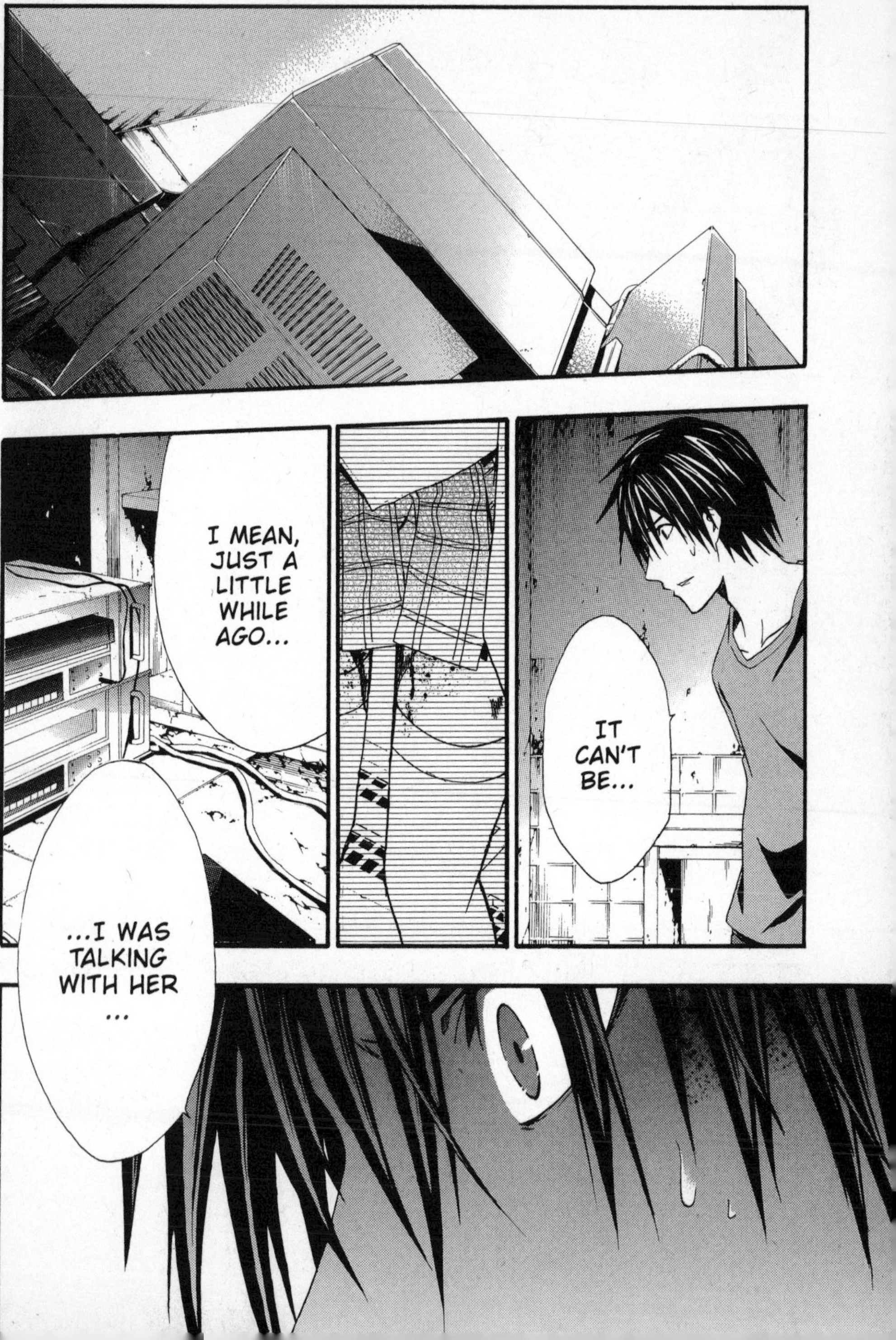
IT CAN'T BE...
I MEAN, JUST A LITTLE WHILE AGO...
...I WAS TALKING WITH HER ...

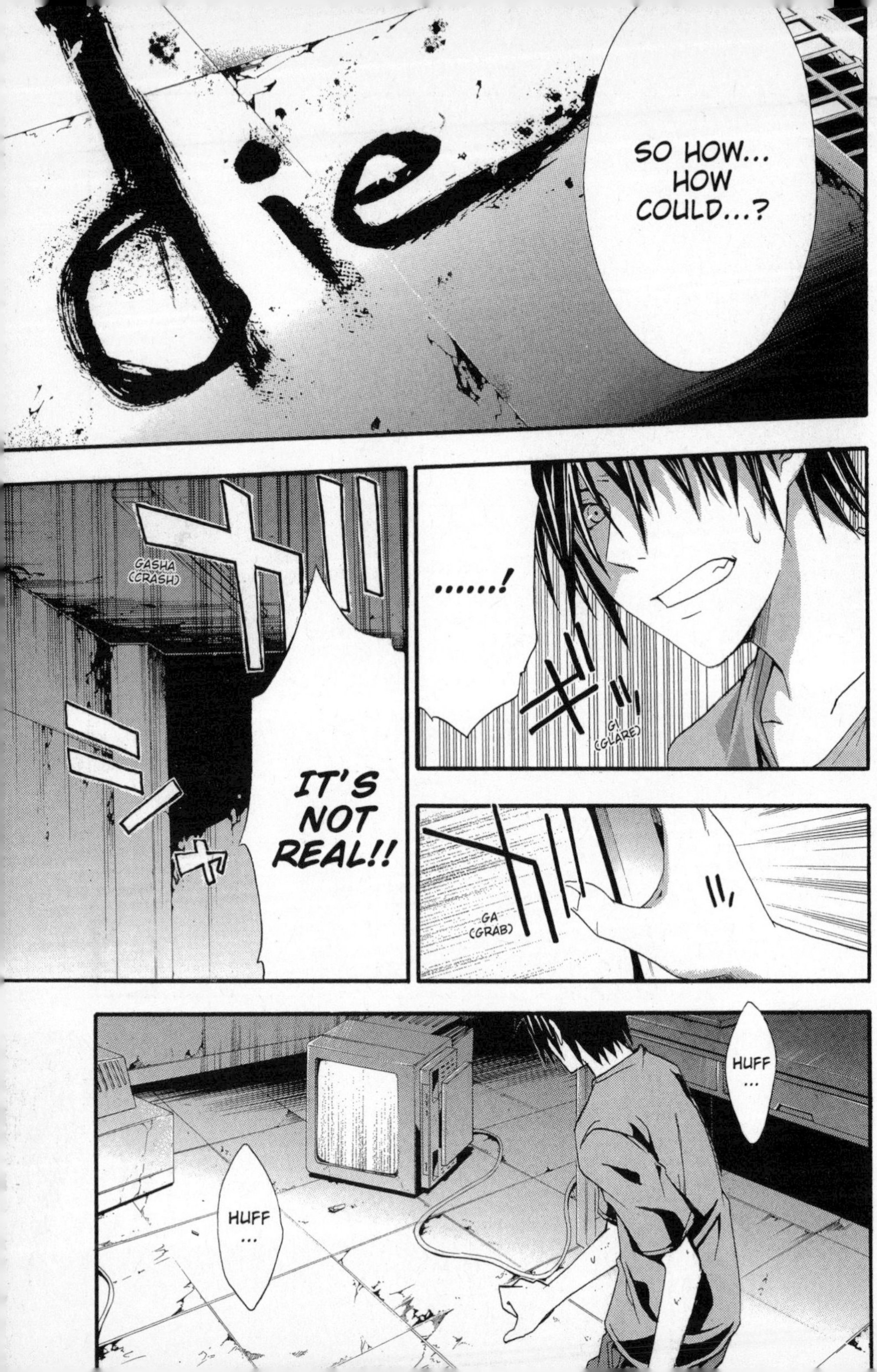
die
SO HOW... HOW COULD...?
......!
GI (GLARE)
GA (GRAB)
GASHA (CRASH)
IT'S NOT REAL!!
HUFF...
HUFF...

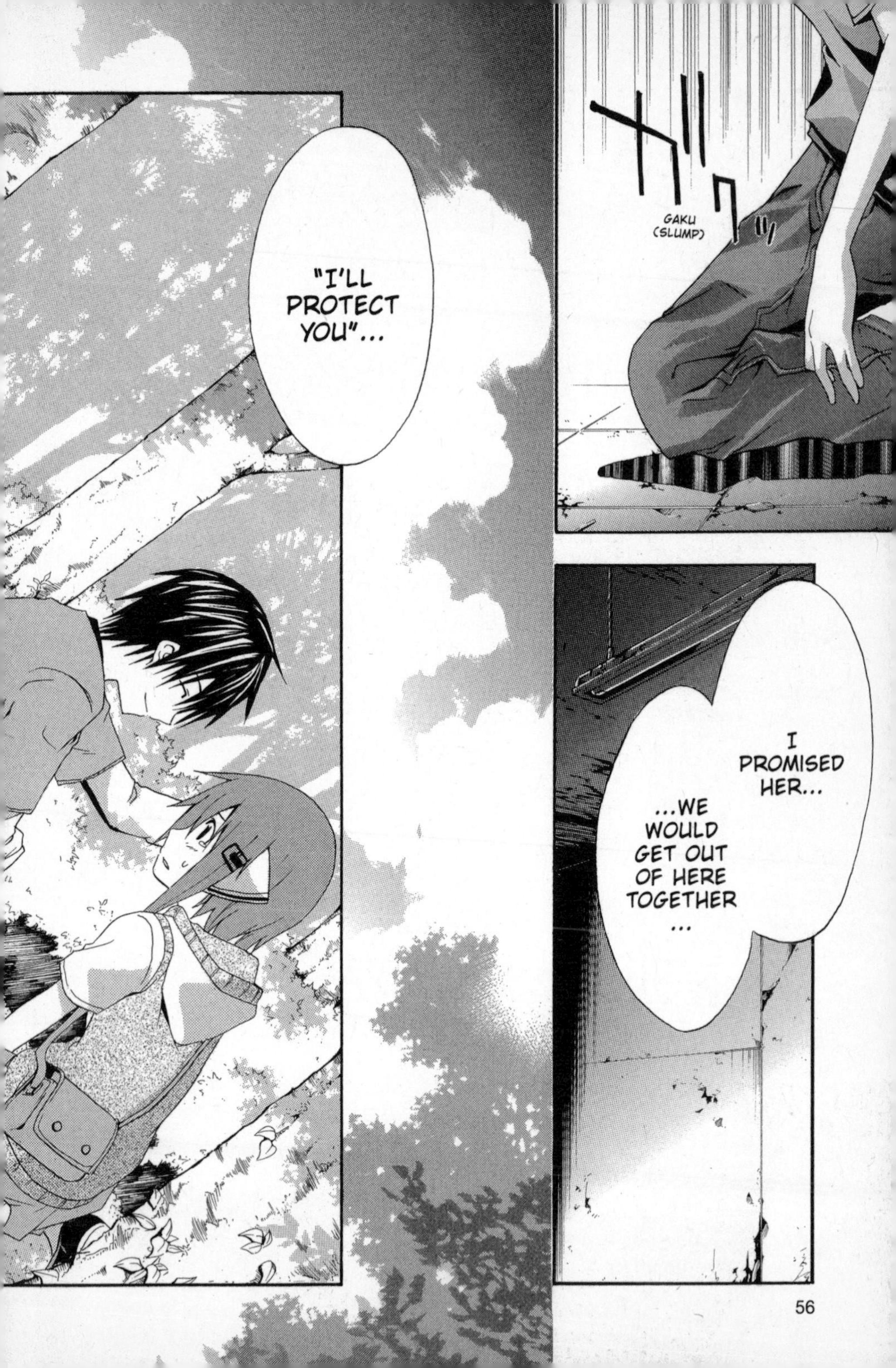
GAKU (SLUMP)
I PROMISED HER...
...WE WOULD GET OUT OF HERE TOGETHER ...
"I'LL PROTECT YOU"...

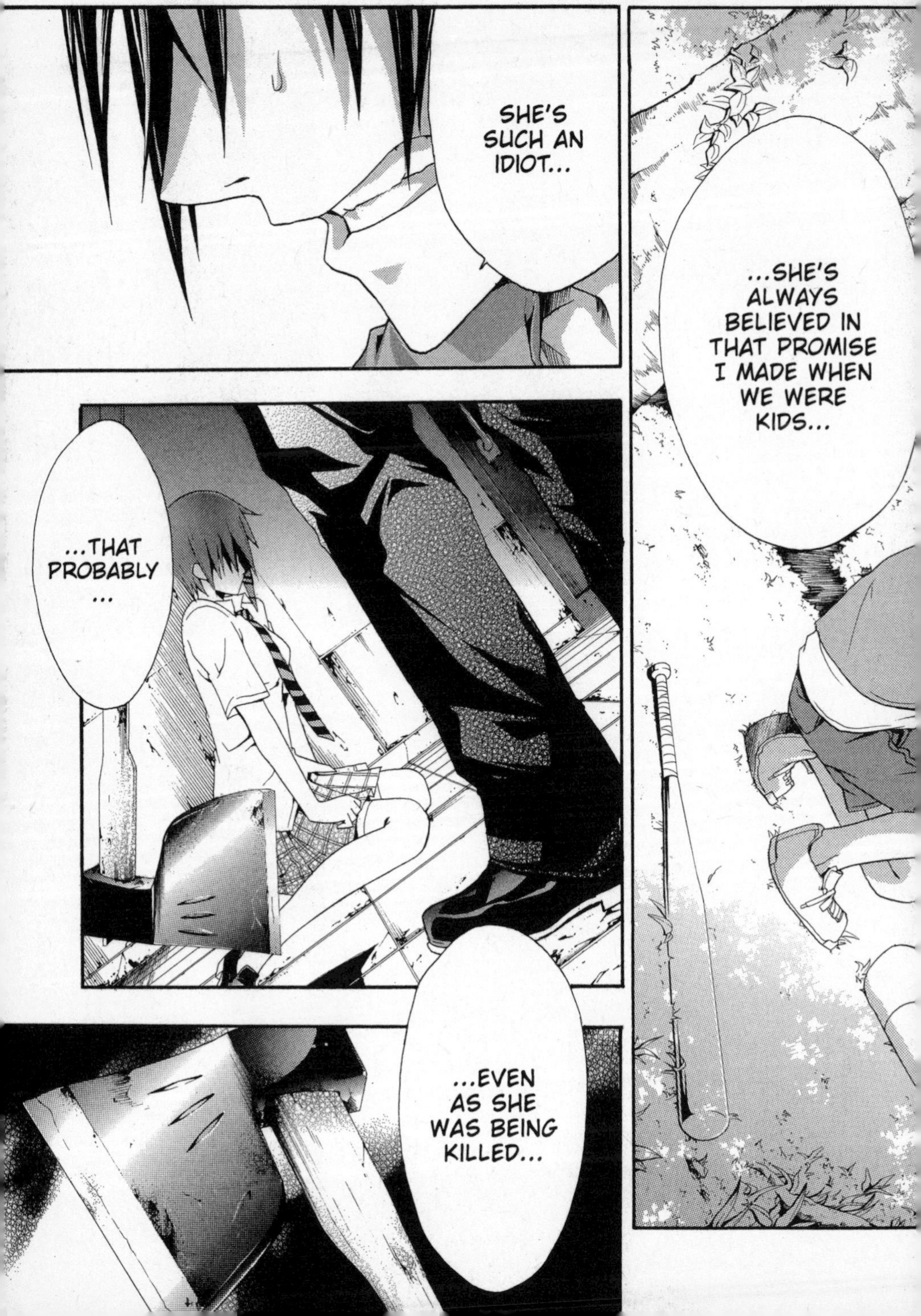
...SHE'S ALWAYS BELIEVED IN THAT PROMISE I MADE WHEN WE WERE KIDS...
SHE'S SUCH AN IDIOT...
...THAT PROBABLY ...
...EVEN AS SHE WAS BEING KILLED...

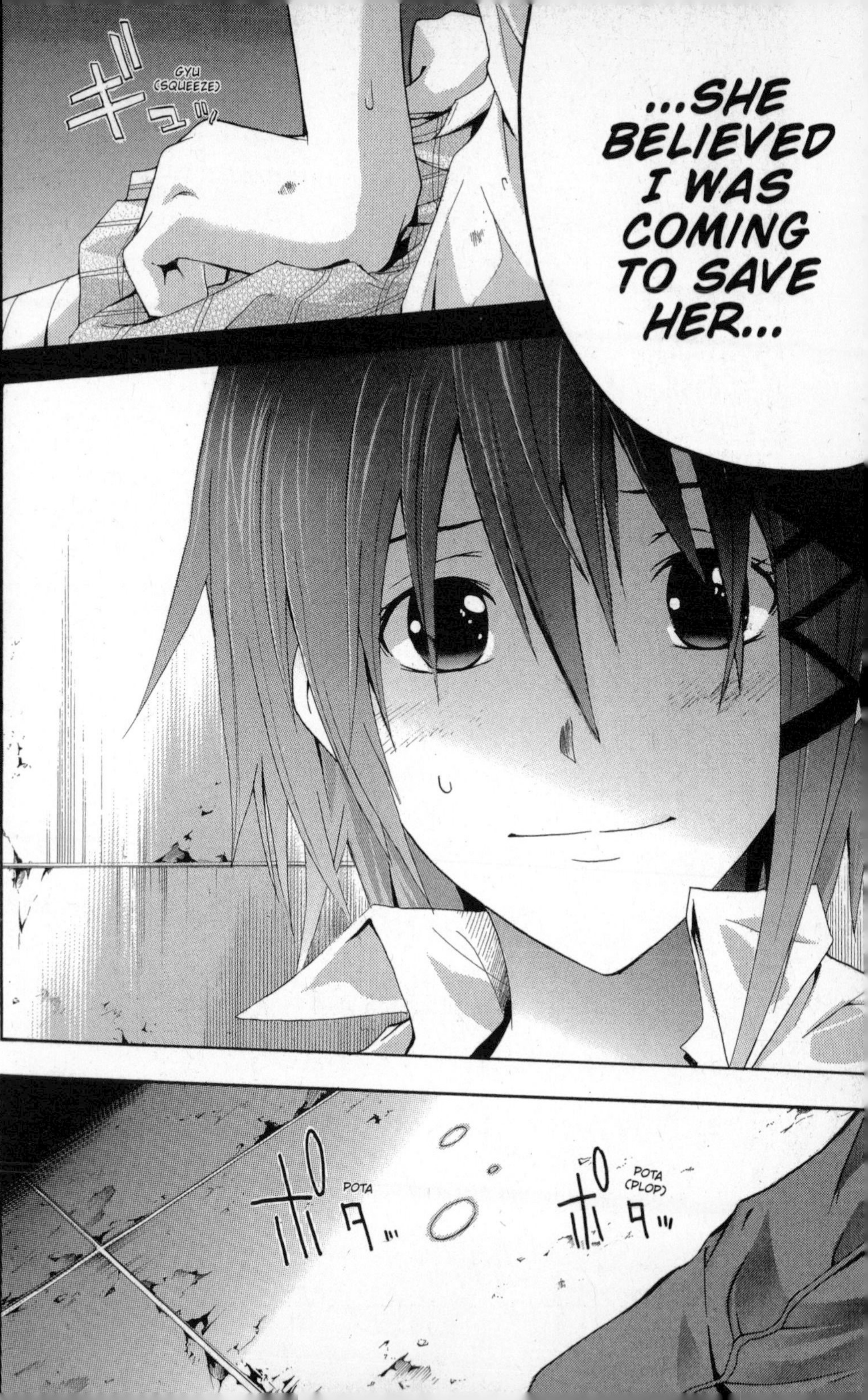
...SHE BELIEVED I WAS COMING TO SAVE HER...
ギュッ
GYU (SQUEEZE)
ポタッ
POTA (PLOP)
ポタッ
POTA

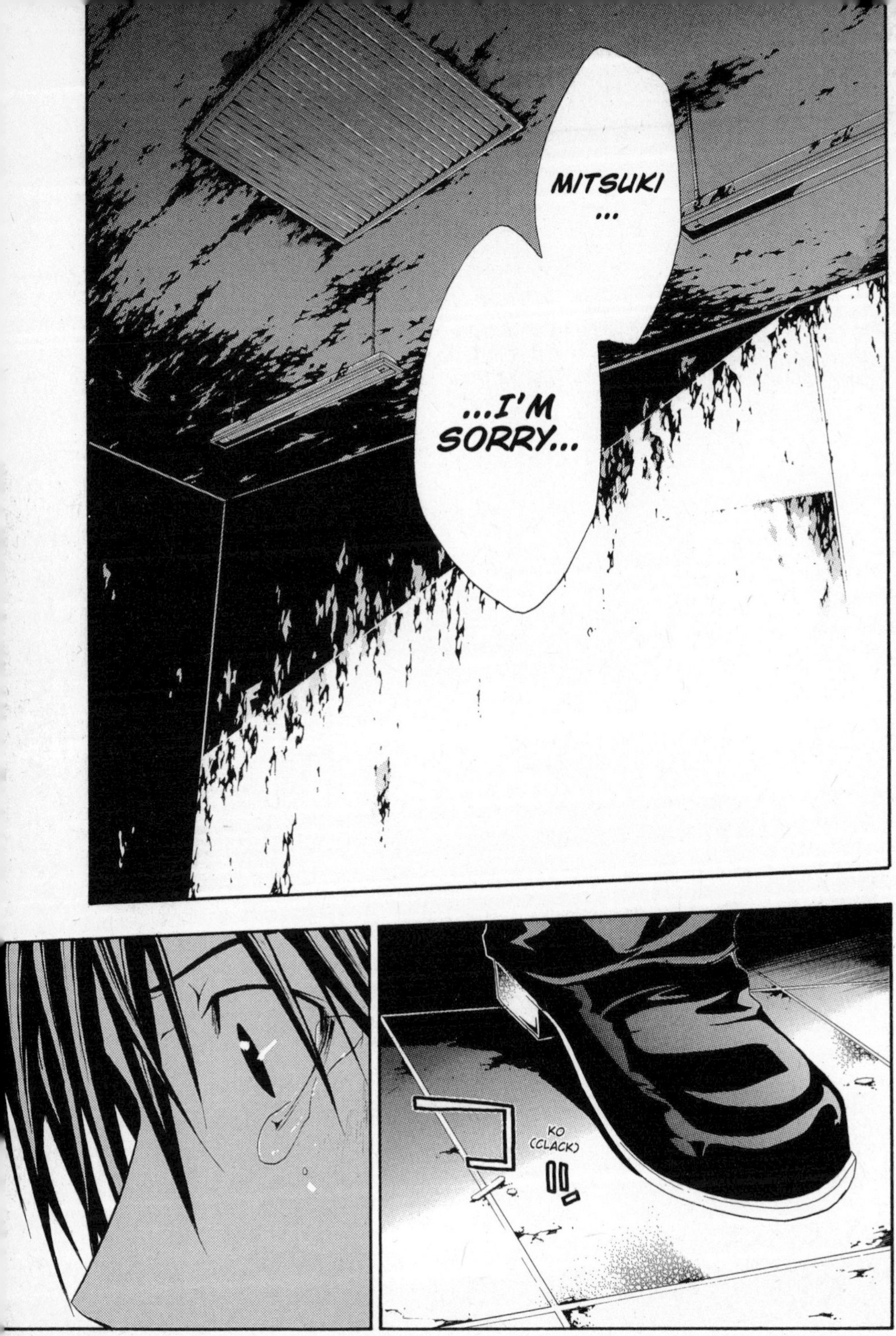
MITSUKI ...
...I'M SORRY...
KO (CLACK)

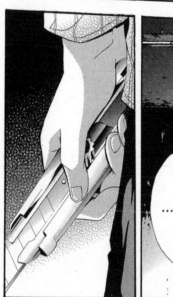

....

HAJIME...

IT...

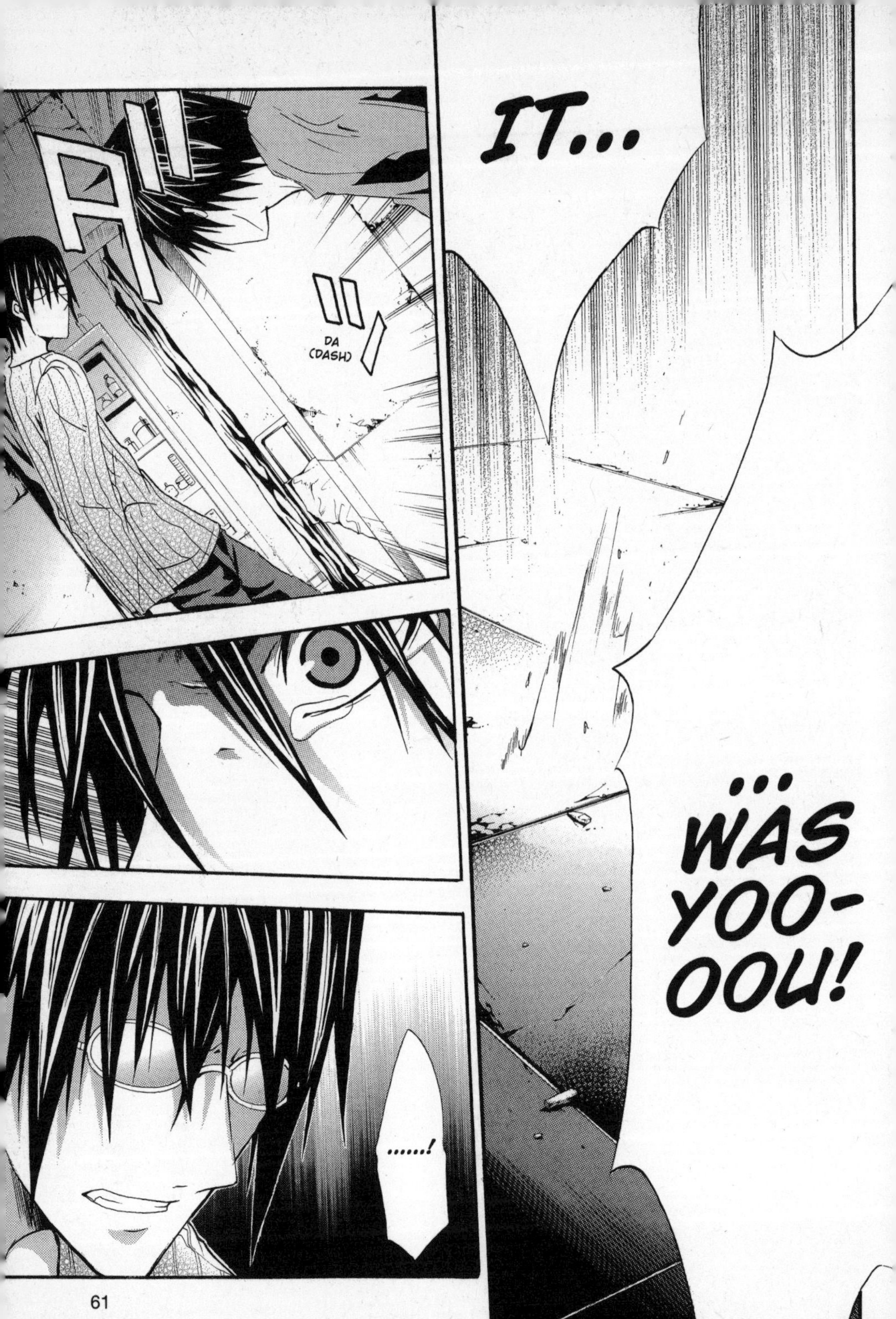
IT...
...WÄS YOO-OOU!
A!!
DA (DASH)
......!

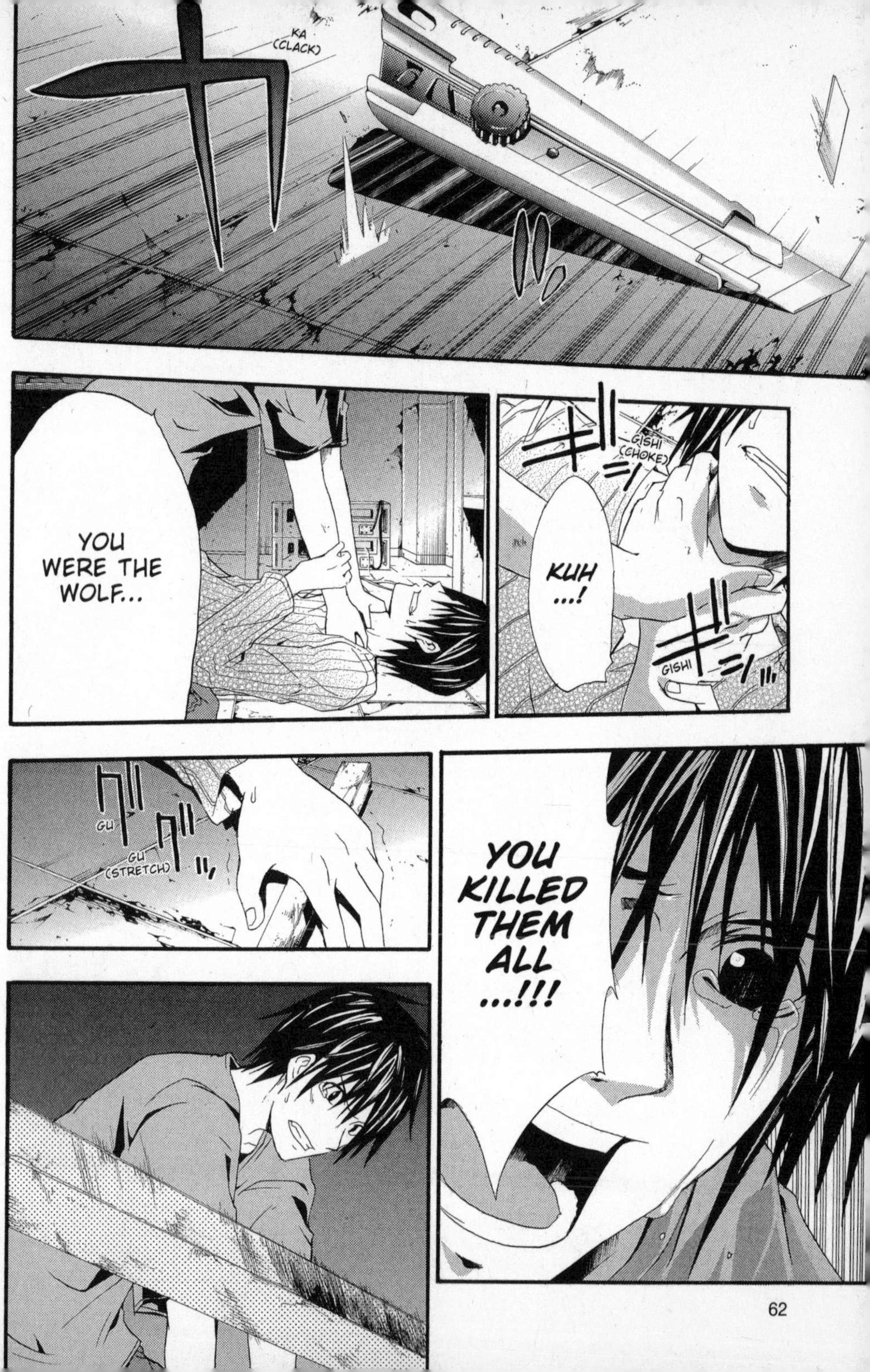
KA (CLACK)
GISHI (CHOKE)
KUH ...!
GISHI
YOU WERE THE WOLF...
YOU KILLED THEM ALL ...!!!
GU
GU (STRETCH)

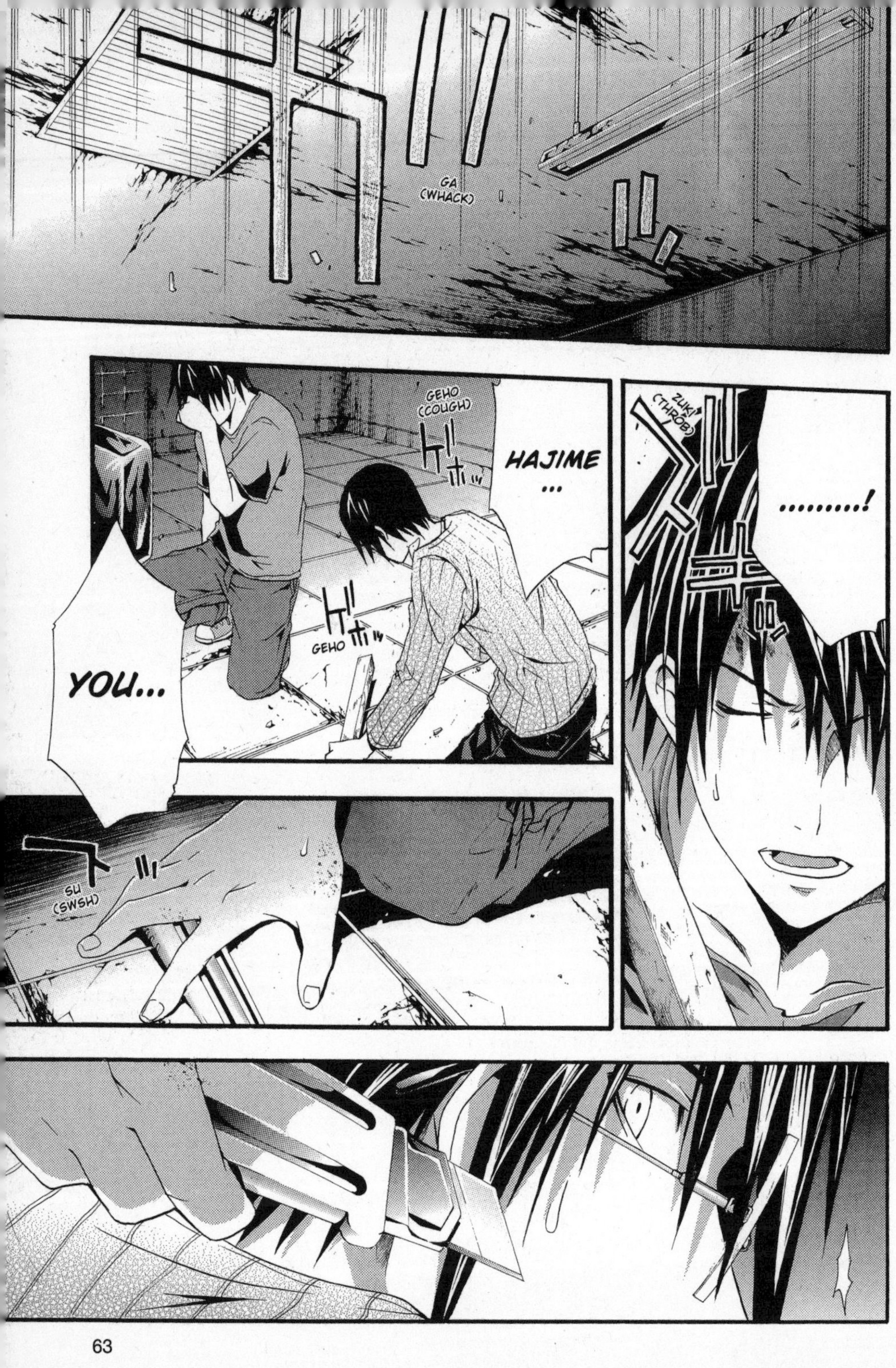
GA (WHACK)
ZUKI (THROB)
.........!
HAJIME ...
GEHO (COUGH)
GEHO
YOU...
SU (SWSH)

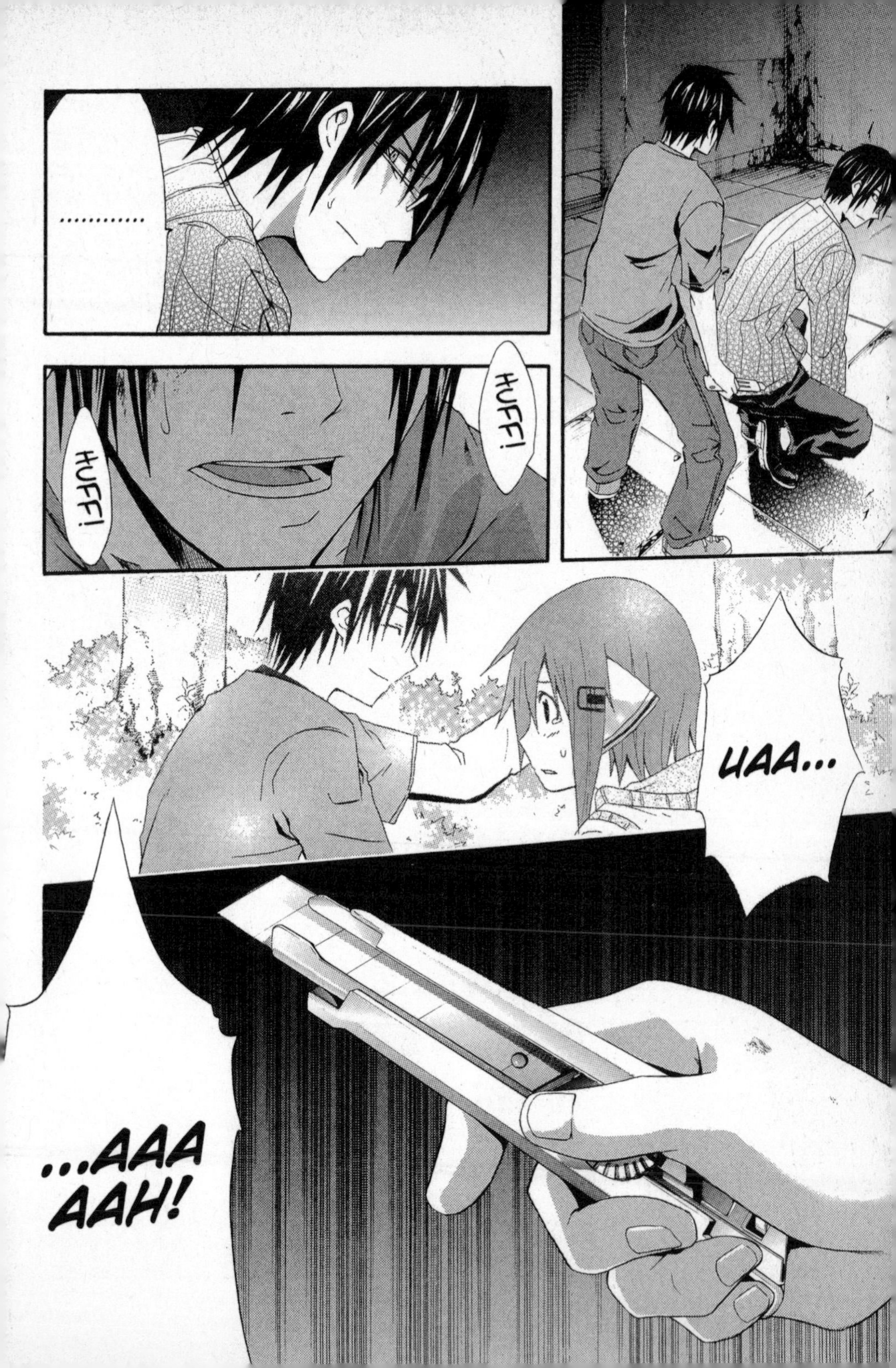

....
HUFF!
HUFF!
UAA...
...AAA AAH!

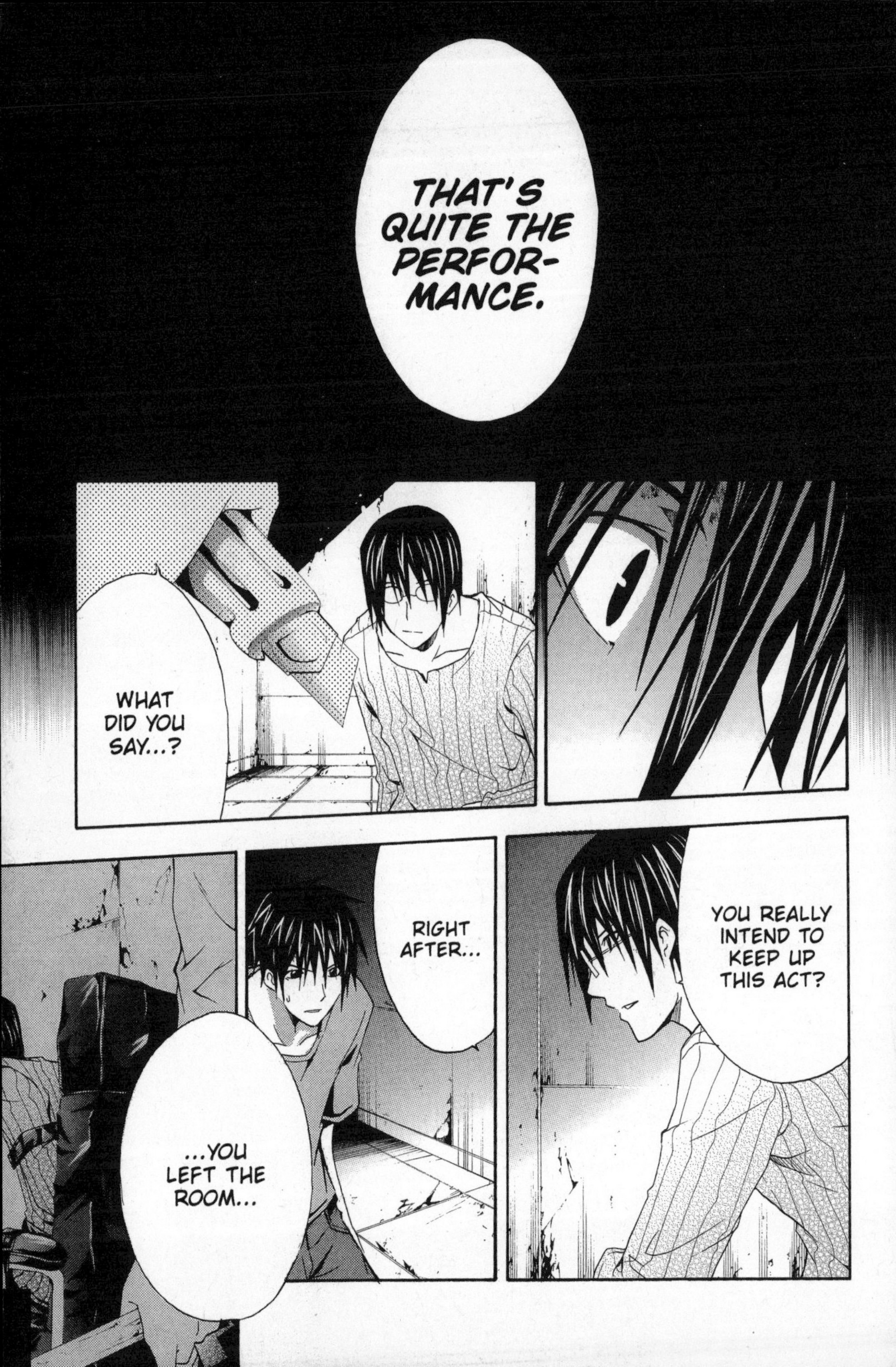
THAT'S QUITE THE PERFORMANCE.
WHAT DID YOU SAY...?
YOU REALLY INTEND TO KEEP UP THIS ACT?
RIGHT AFTER...
...YOU LEFT THE ROOM...

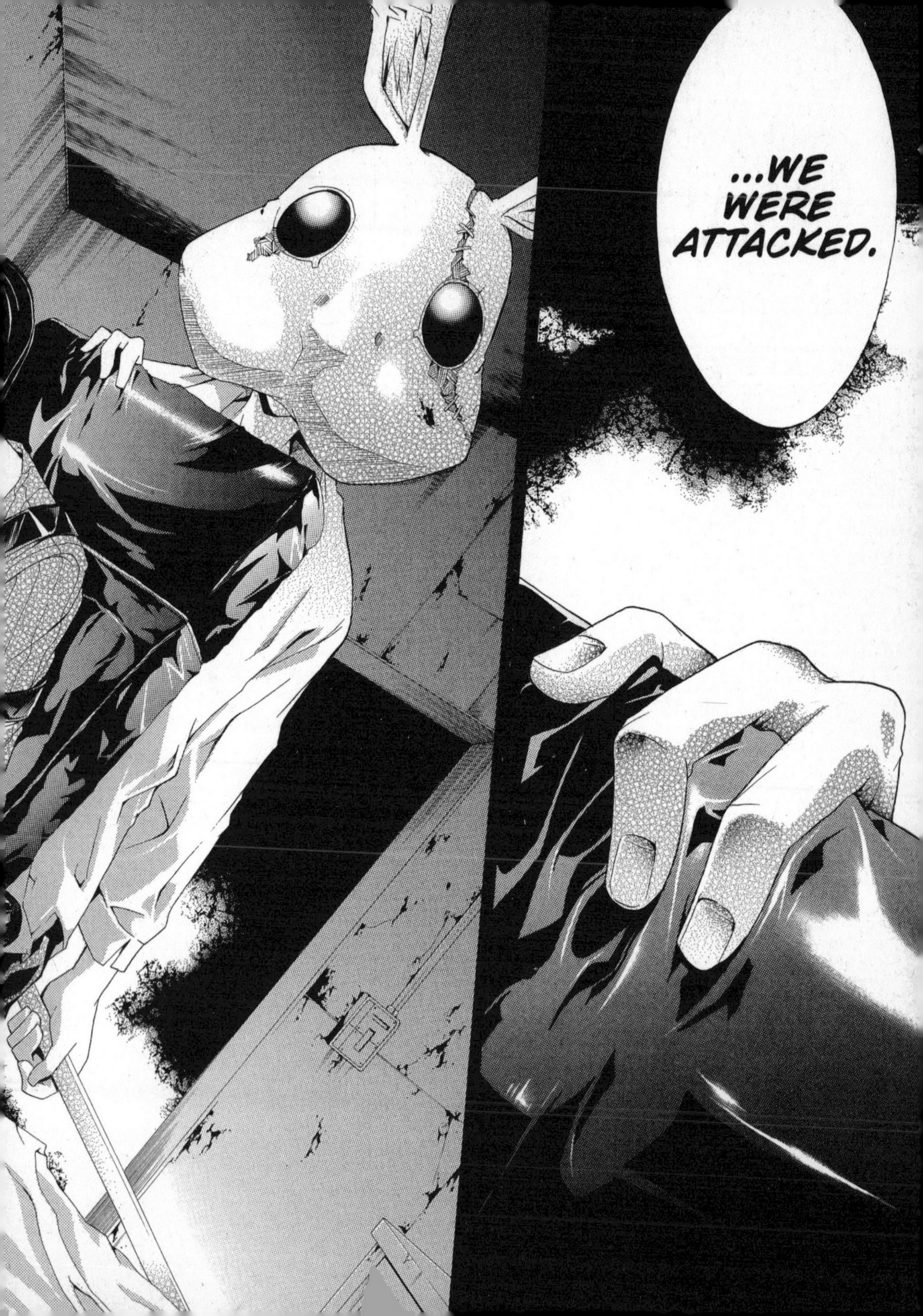
...WE WERE ATTACKED.

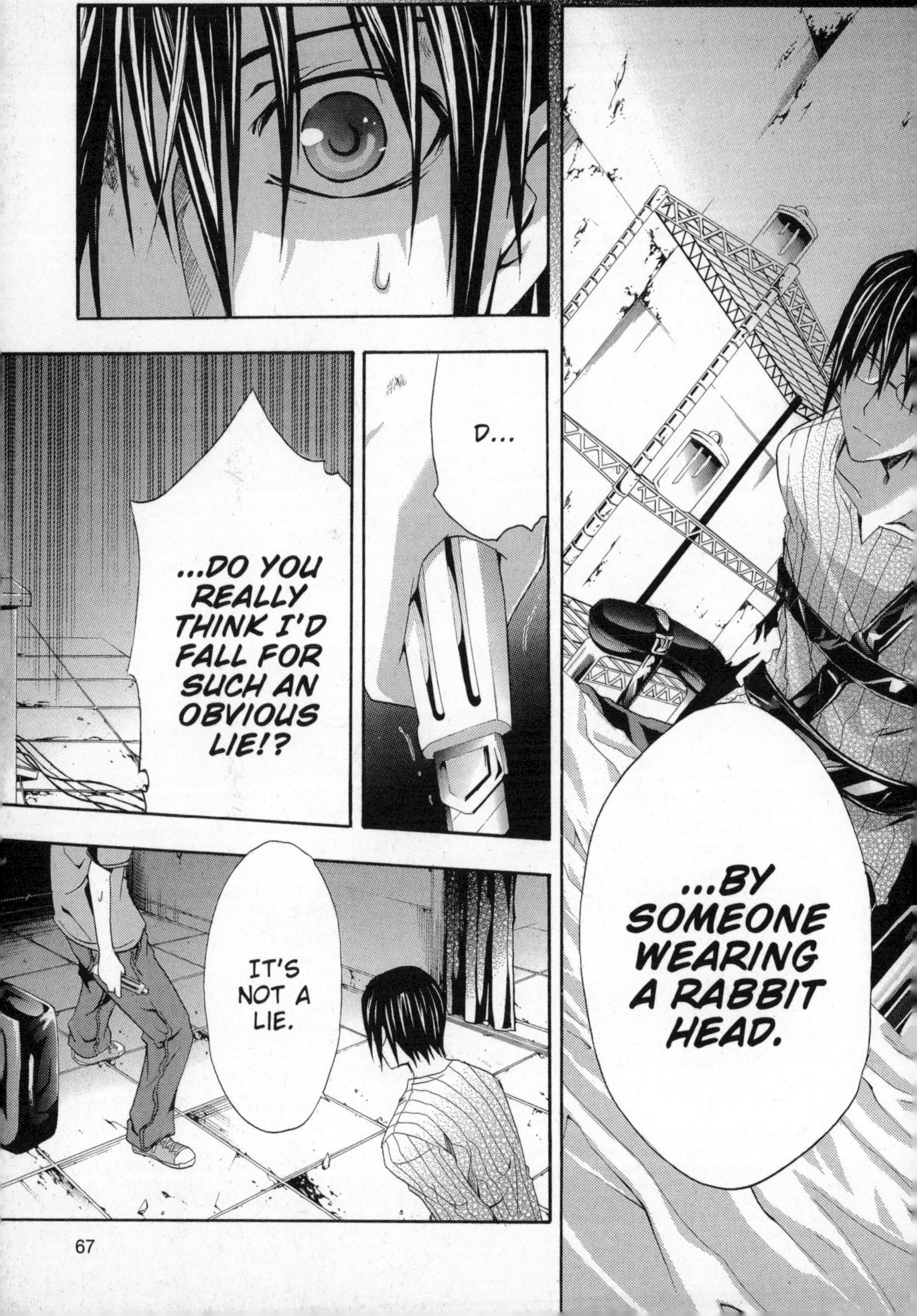
...BY SOMEONE WEARING A RABBIT HEAD.
D...
...DO YOU REALLY THINK I'D FALL FOR SUCH AN OBVIOUS LIE!?
IT'S NOT A LIE.

I GOT ATTACKED...

...AND SHE WAS TAKEN AWAY...

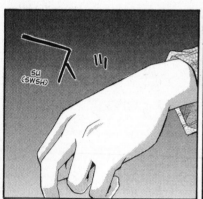

SU (SWSH)

THERE WERE ONLY THREE PEOPLE LEFT IN THIS BUILDING...

......

...SO THE EXPLA-NATION'S OBVIOUS.

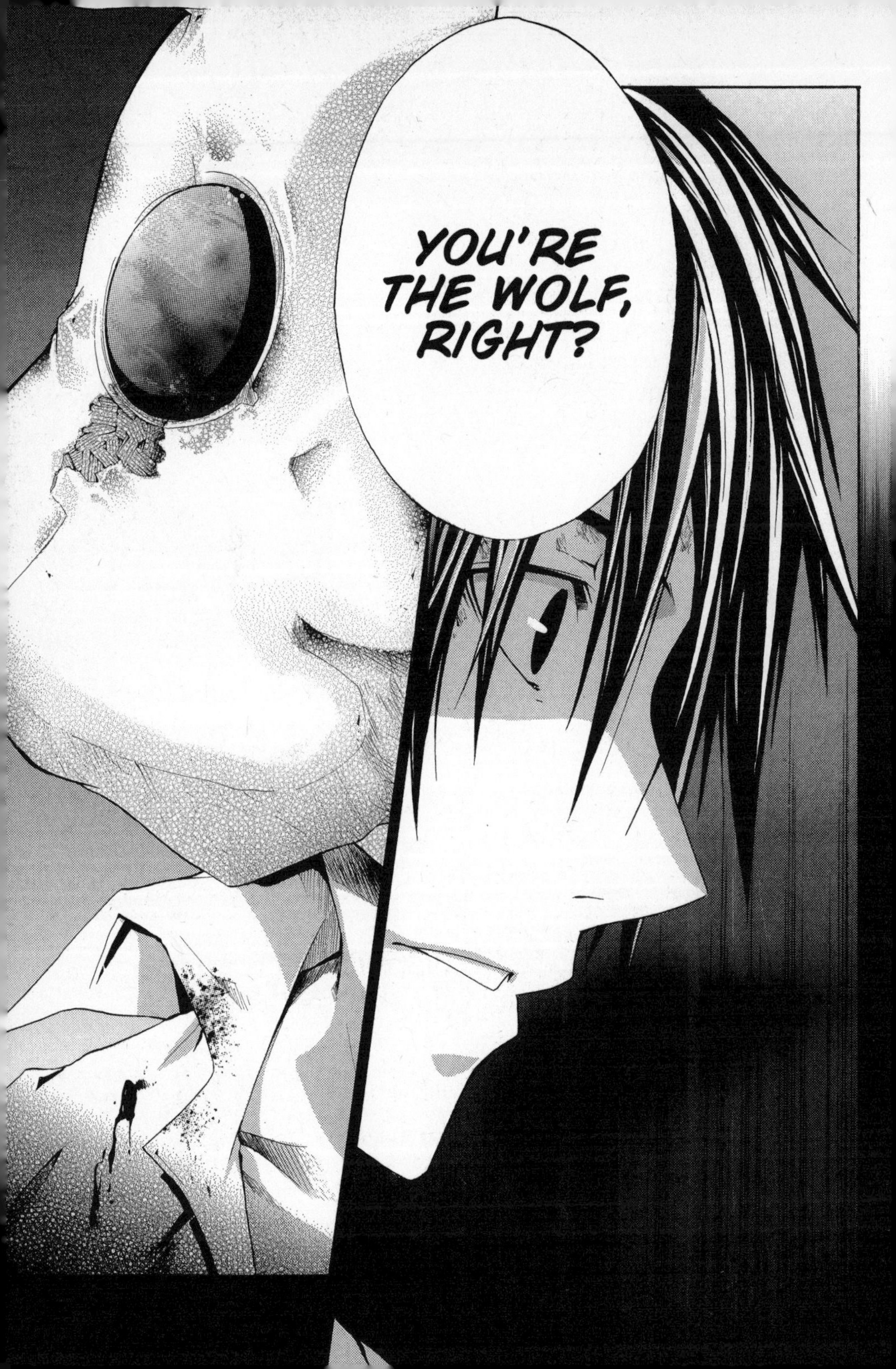
YOU'RE THE WOLF, RIGHT?

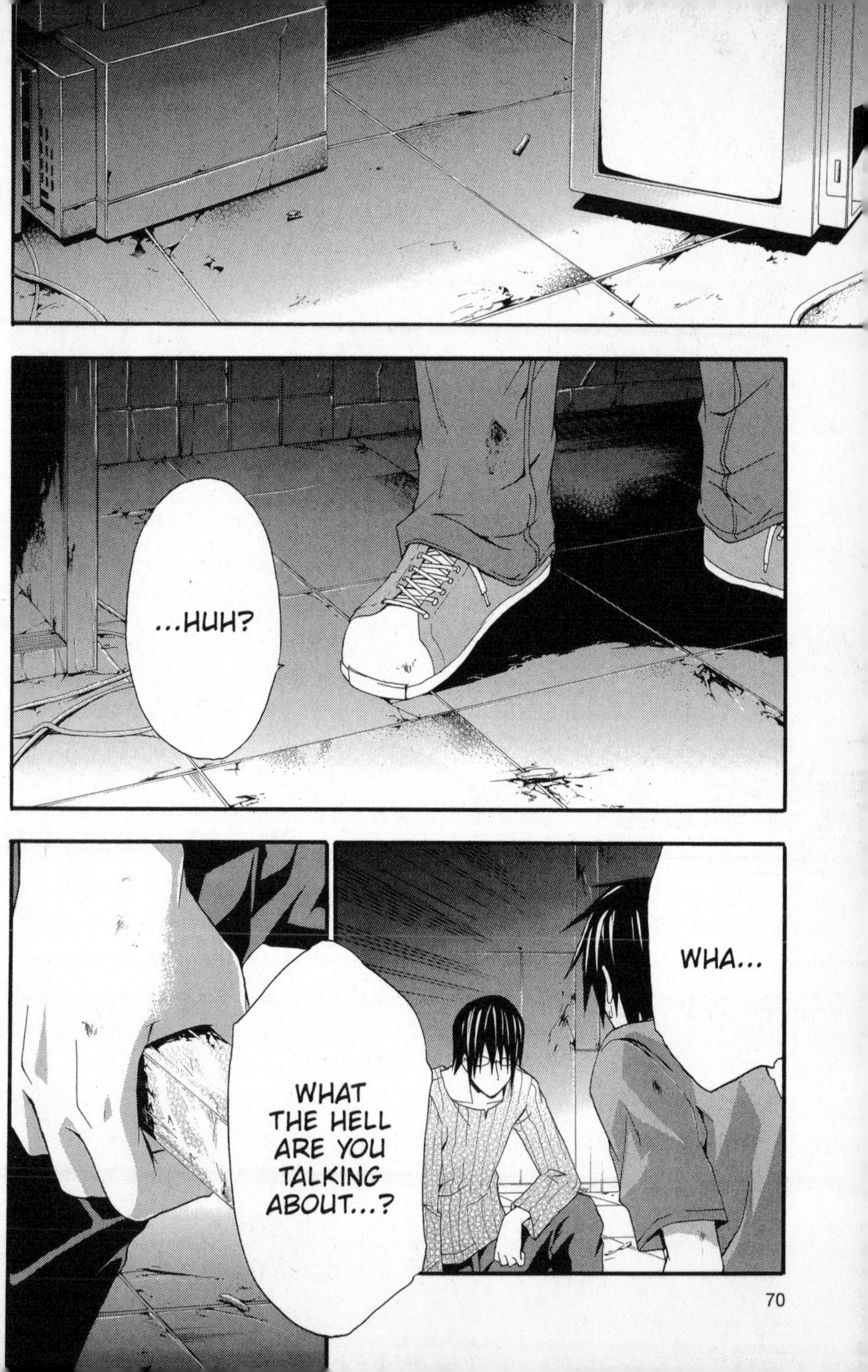
...HUH?
WHA...
WHAT THE HELL ARE YOU TALKING ABOUT...?

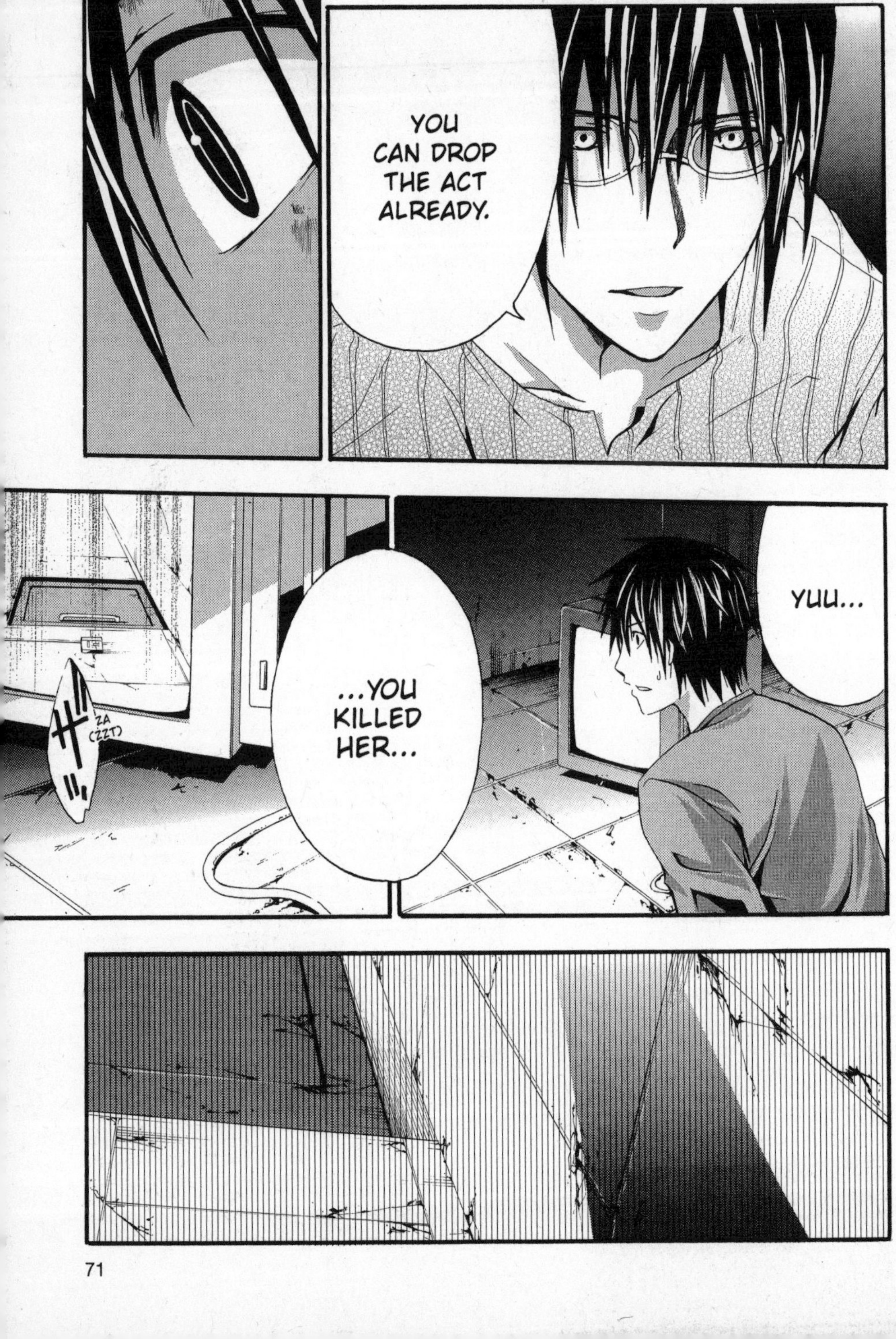
YOU CAN DROP THE ACT ALREADY.
YUU...
...YOU KILLED HER...
ZA (ZZT)

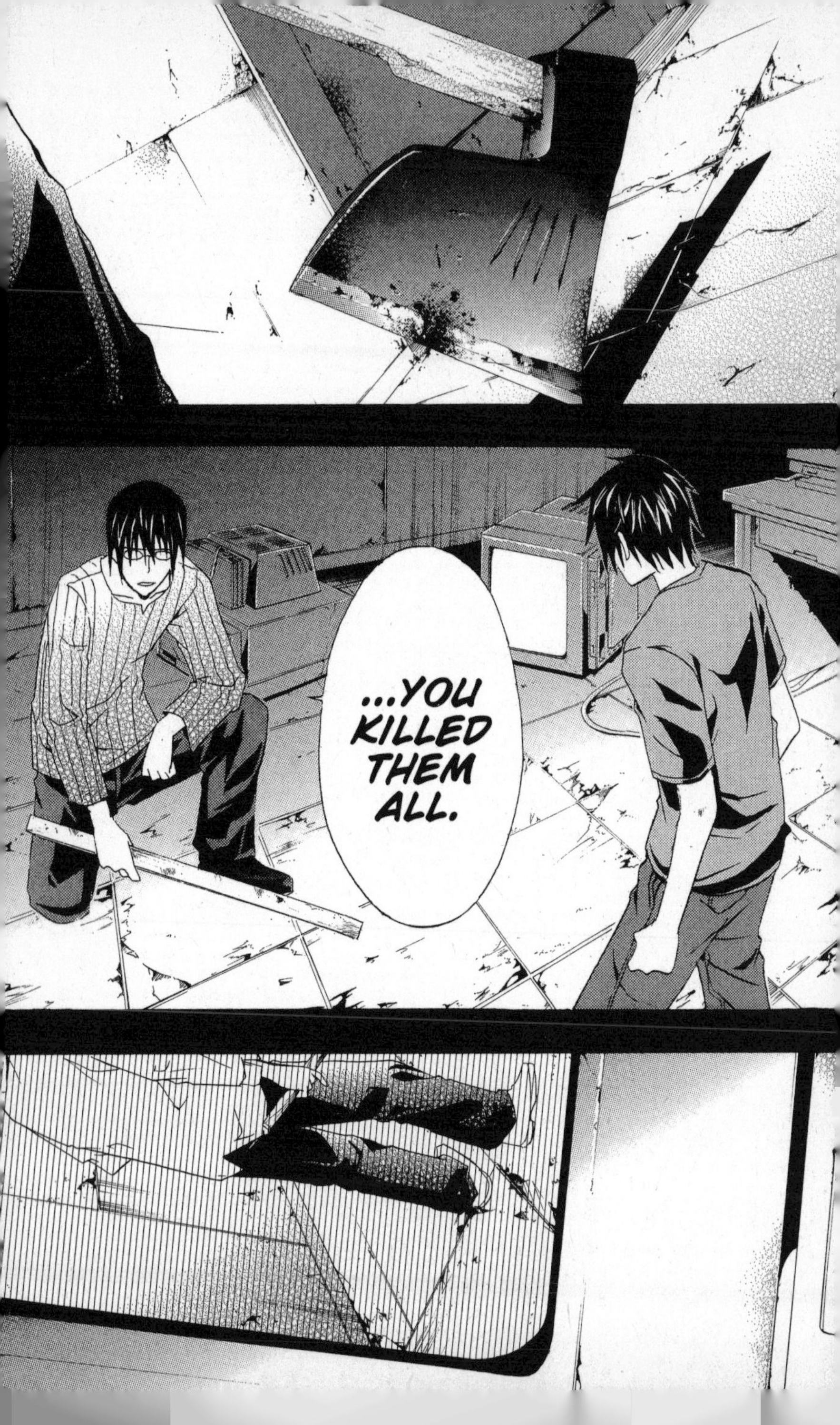
...YOU KILLED THEM ALL.

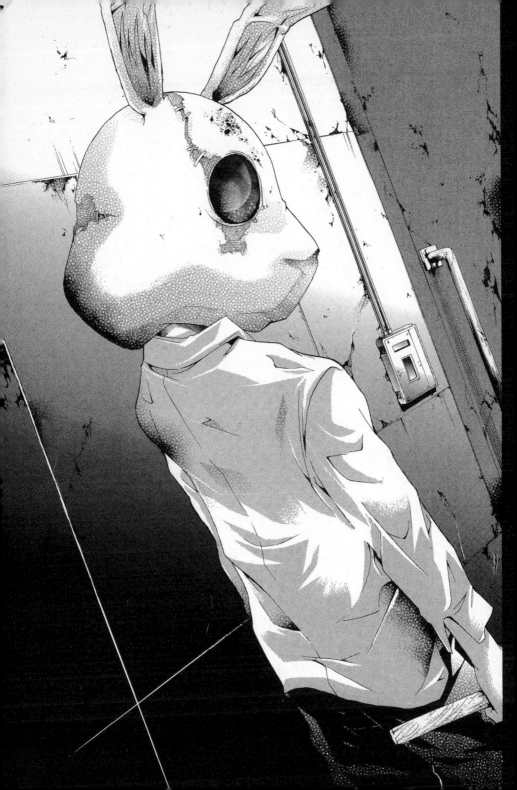

HA
RUKA

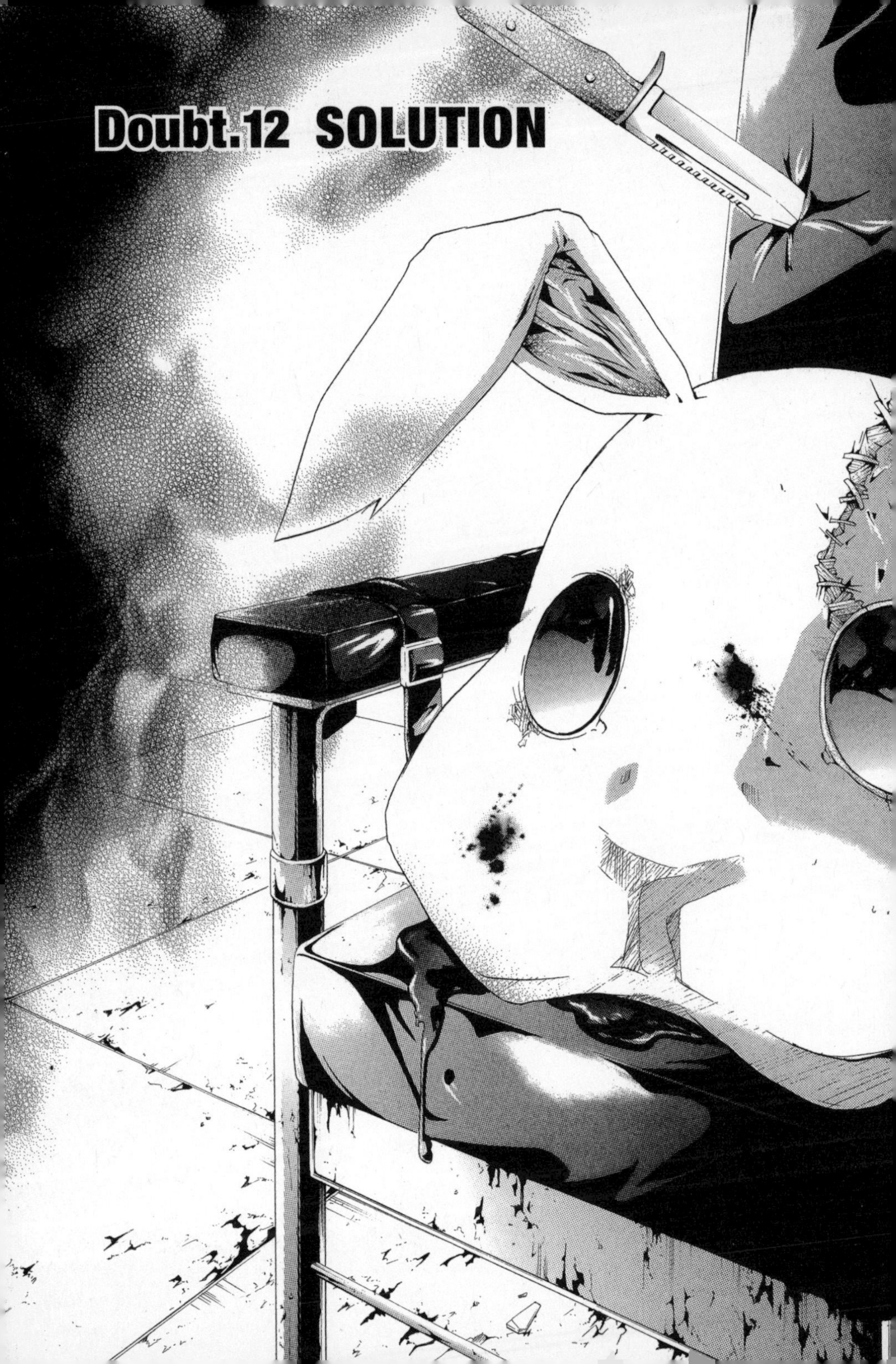
Doubt.12 SOLUTION

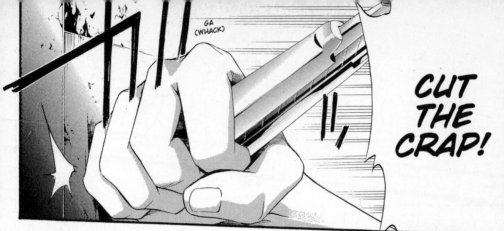

GA
(WHACK)

**CUT
THE
CRAP!**

THERE'S
NO WAY I'D
EVER KILL
MITSUKI!

TH...

GU
(GRIP)

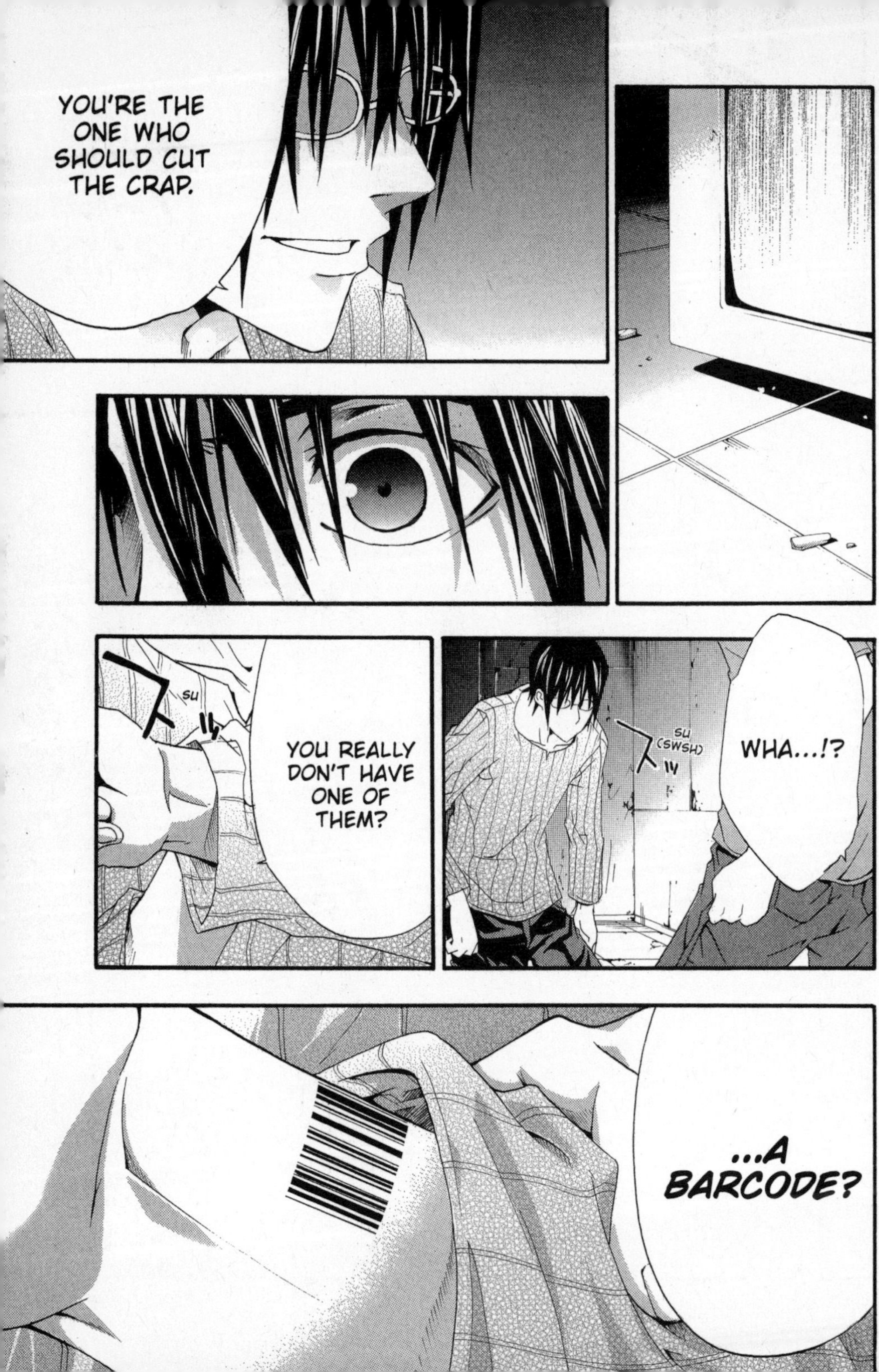
YOU'RE THE ONE WHO SHOULD CUT THE CRAP.
WHA...!?
SU (SWSH)
SU
YOU REALLY DON'T HAVE ONE OF THEM?
...A BARCODE?

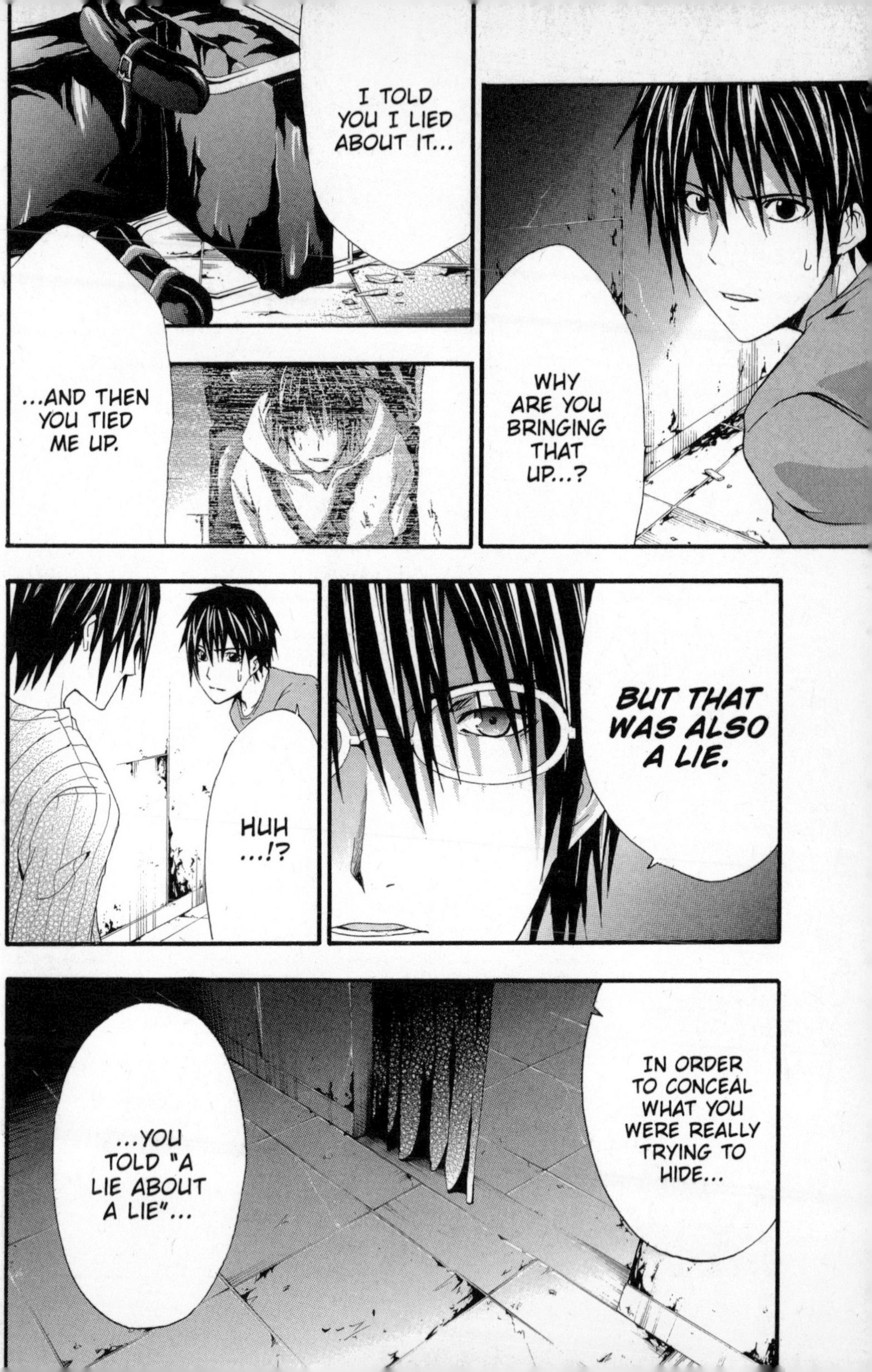
WHY ARE YOU BRINGING THAT UP...?
I TOLD YOU I LIED ABOUT IT...
...AND THEN YOU TIED ME UP.
BUT THAT WAS ALSO A LIE.
HUH ...!?
IN ORDER TO CONCEAL WHAT YOU WERE REALLY TRYING TO HIDE...
...YOU TOLD "A LIE ABOUT A LIE"...

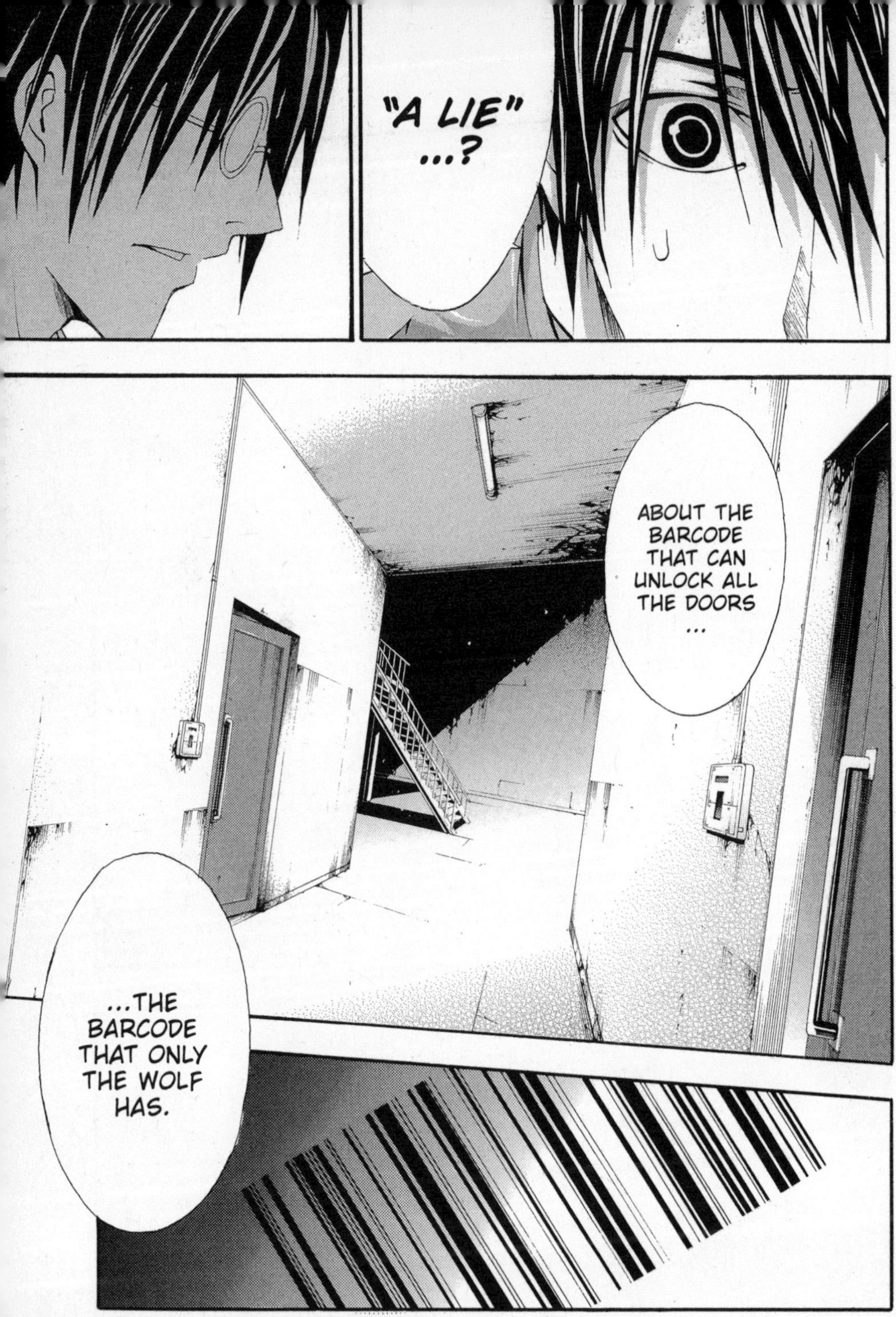
"A LIE" ...?
ABOUT THE BARCODE THAT CAN UNLOCK ALL THE DOORS ...
...THE BARCODE THAT ONLY THE WOLF HAS.

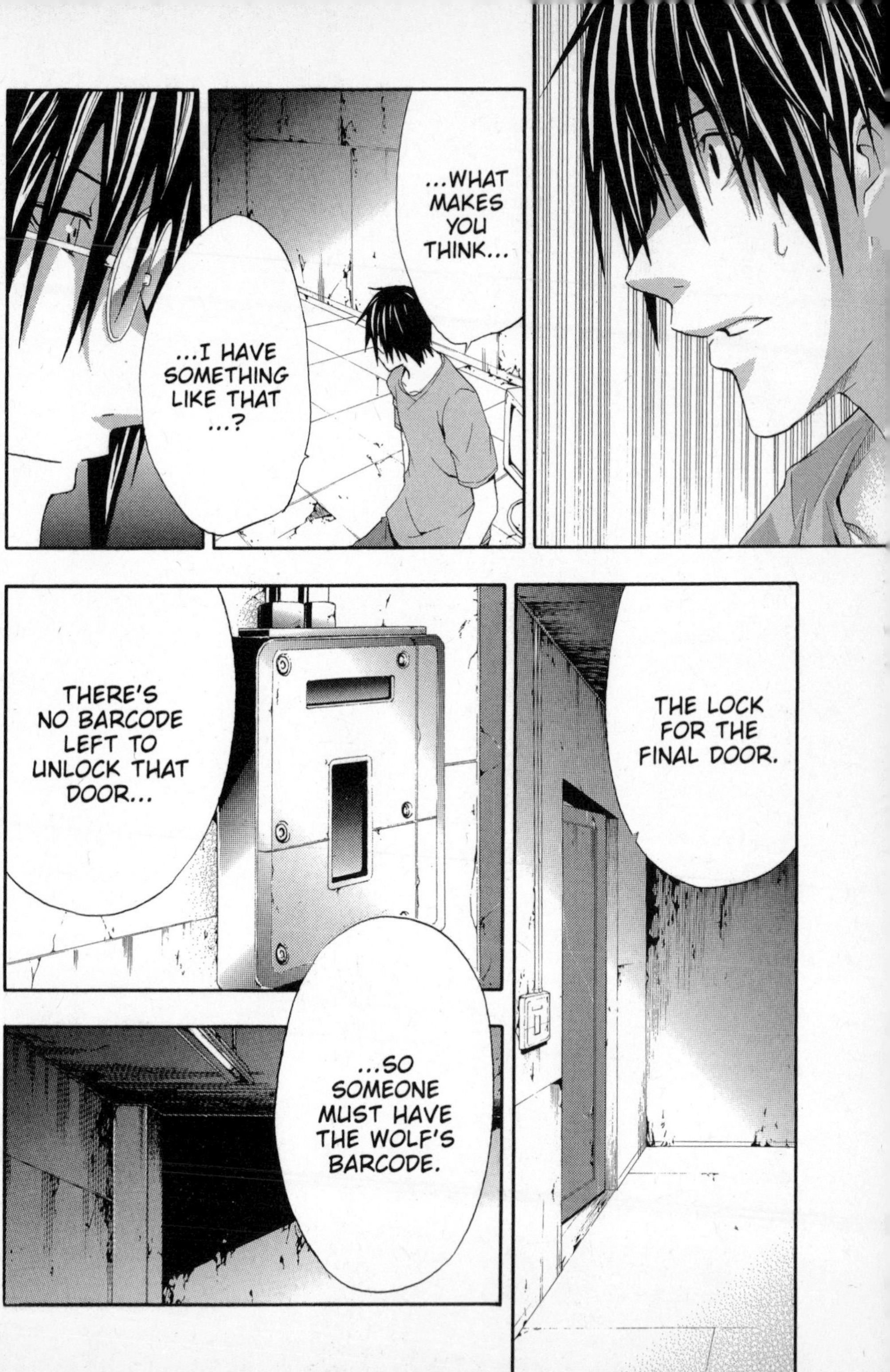
...WHAT MAKES YOU THINK...
...I HAVE SOMETHING LIKE THAT ...?
THE LOCK FOR THE FINAL DOOR.
THERE'S NO BARCODE LEFT TO UNLOCK THAT DOOR...
...SO SOMEONE MUST HAVE THE WOLF'S BARCODE.

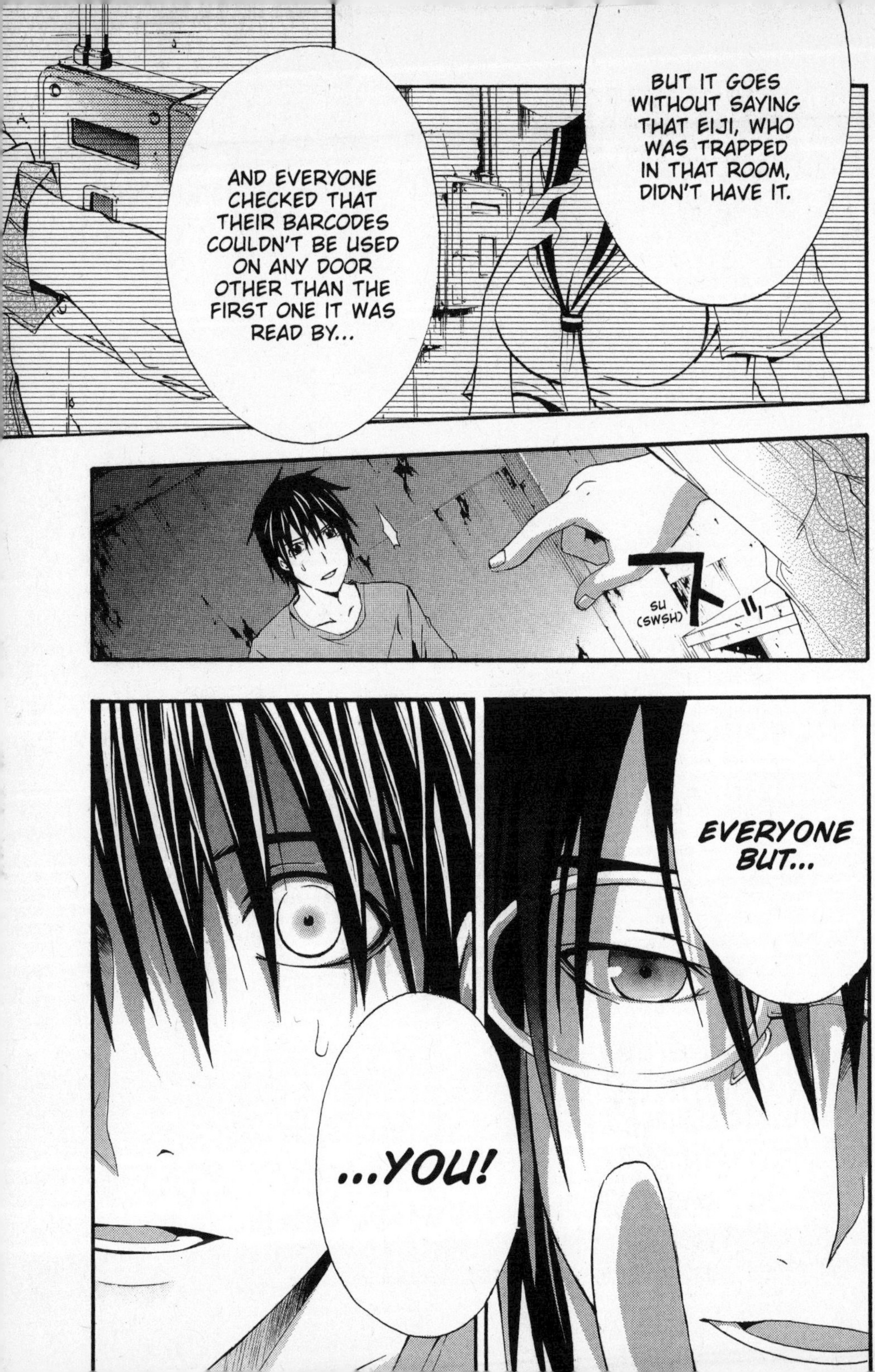
BUT IT GOES WITHOUT SAYING THAT EIJI, WHO WAS TRAPPED IN THAT ROOM, DIDN'T HAVE IT.
AND EVERYONE CHECKED THAT THEIR BARCODES COULDN'T BE USED ON ANY DOOR OTHER THAN THE FIRST ONE IT WAS READ BY...
SU (SWSH)
EVERYONE BUT...
...YOU!

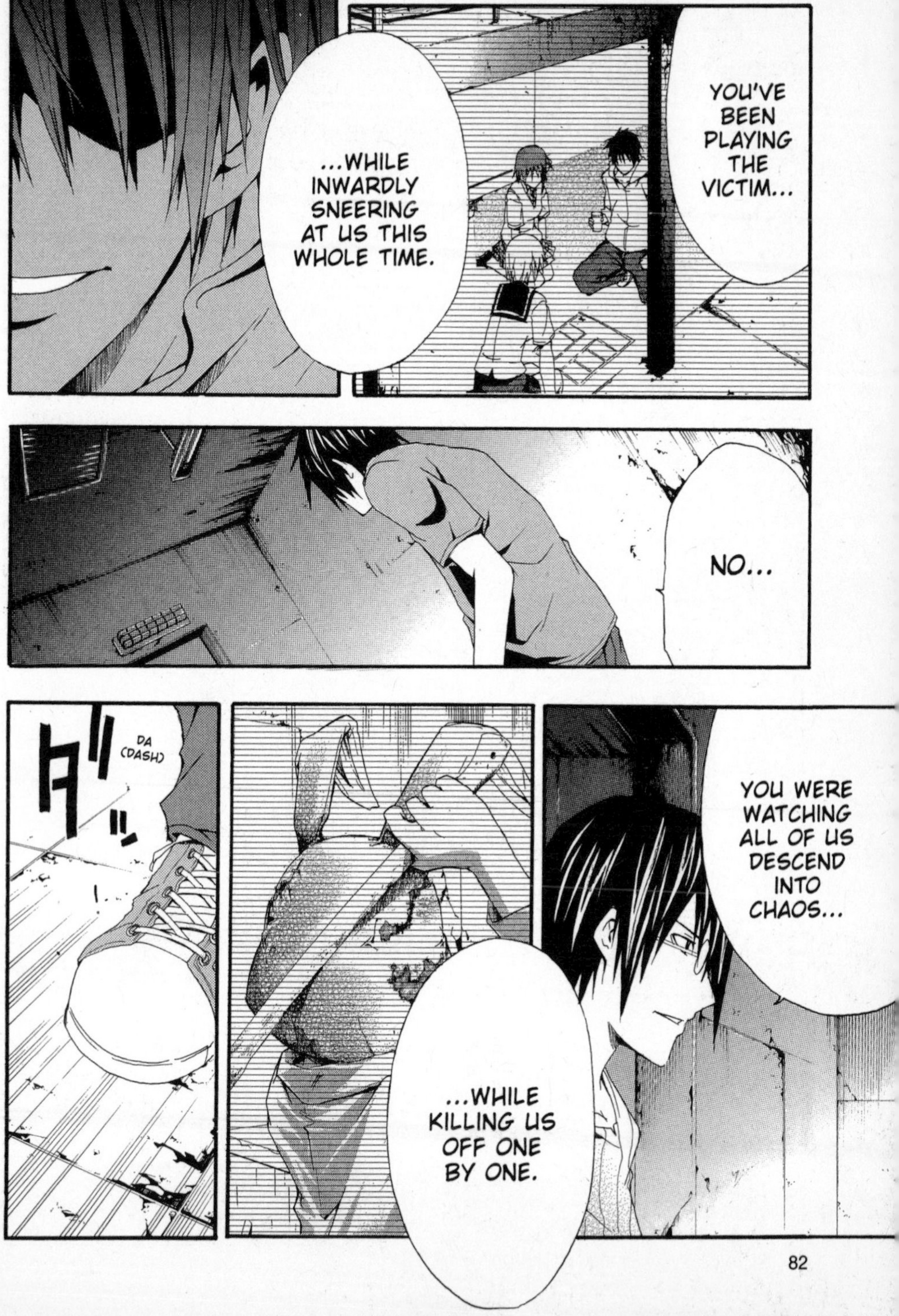
YOU'VE BEEN PLAYING THE VICTIM...
...WHILE INWARDLY SNEERING AT US THIS WHOLE TIME.
NO...
YOU WERE WATCHING ALL OF US DESCEND INTO CHAOS...
...WHILE KILLING US OFF ONE BY ONE.
DA (DASH)

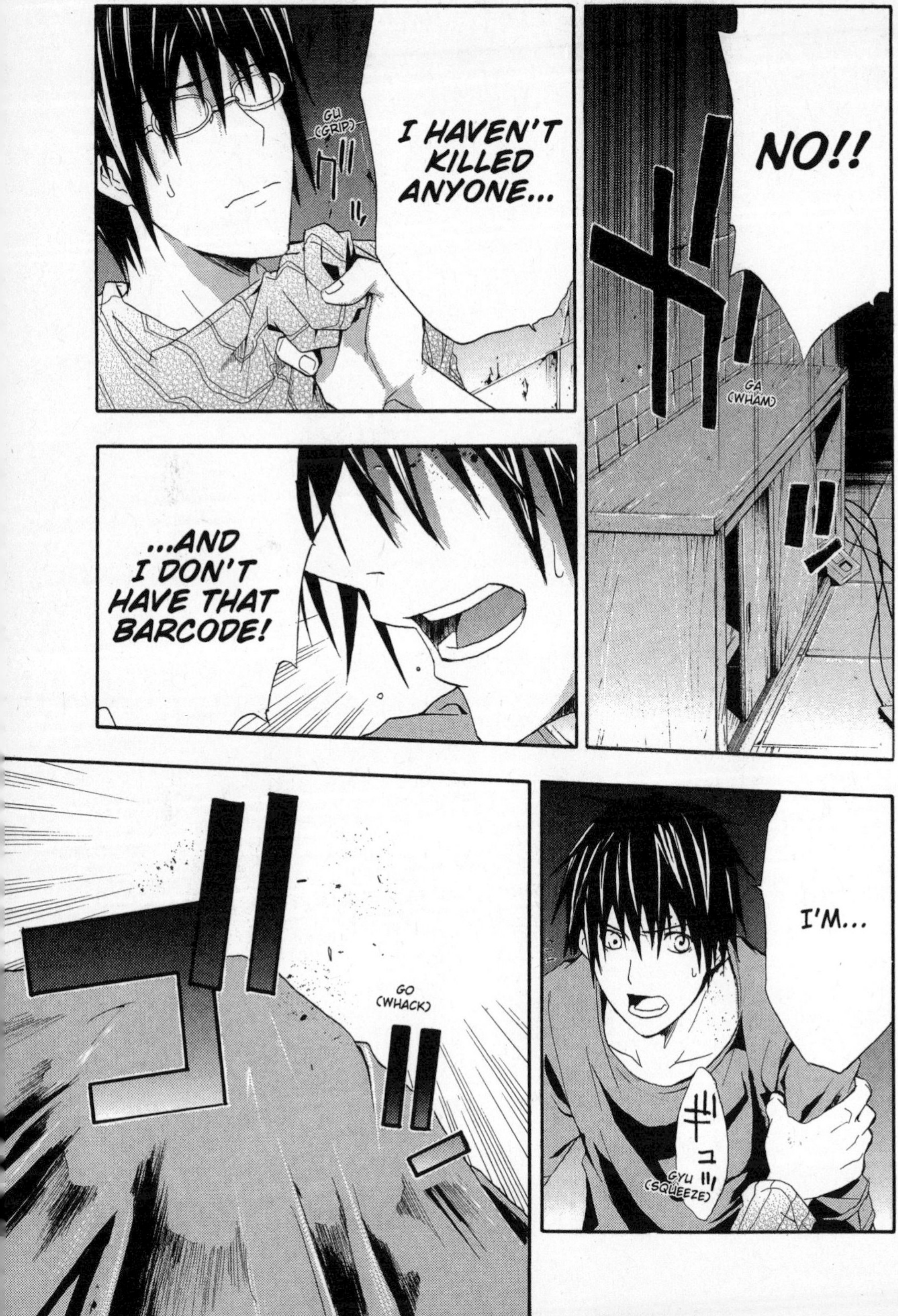
NO!!
GA (WHAM)
GU (GRIP)
I HAVEN'T KILLED ANYONE...
...AND I DON'T HAVE THAT BARCODE!
I'M...
GYU (SQUEEZE)
GO (WHACK)

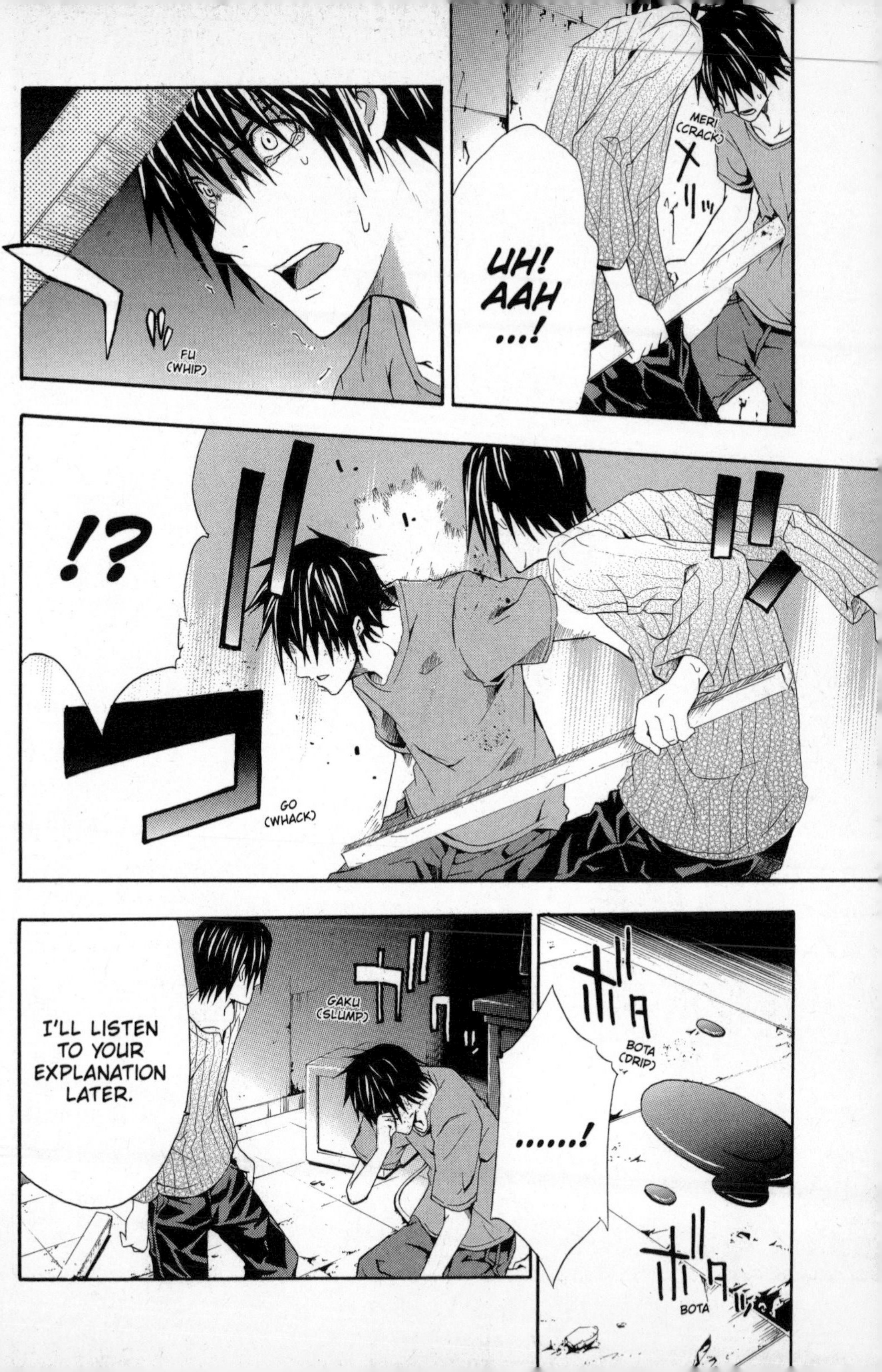
MERI (CRACK)
UH! AAH ...!
FU (WHIP)
!?
GO (WHACK)
BOTA (DRIP)
......!
BOTA
I'LL LISTEN TO YOUR EXPLANATION LATER.
GAKU (SLUMP)

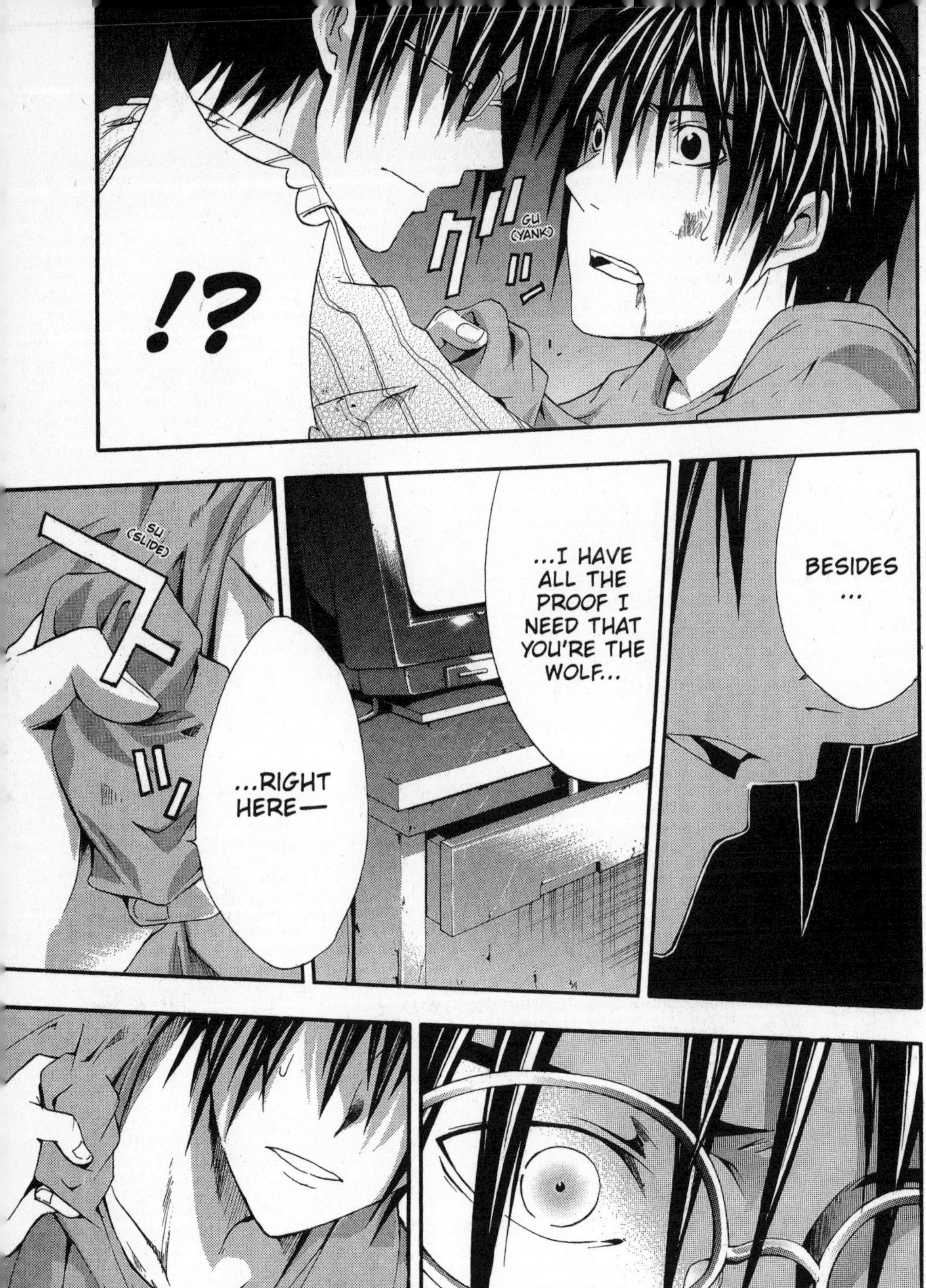
GU (YANK)
!?
BESIDES ...
...I HAVE ALL THE PROOF I NEED THAT YOU'RE THE WOLF...
...RIGHT HERE—
SU (SLIDE)

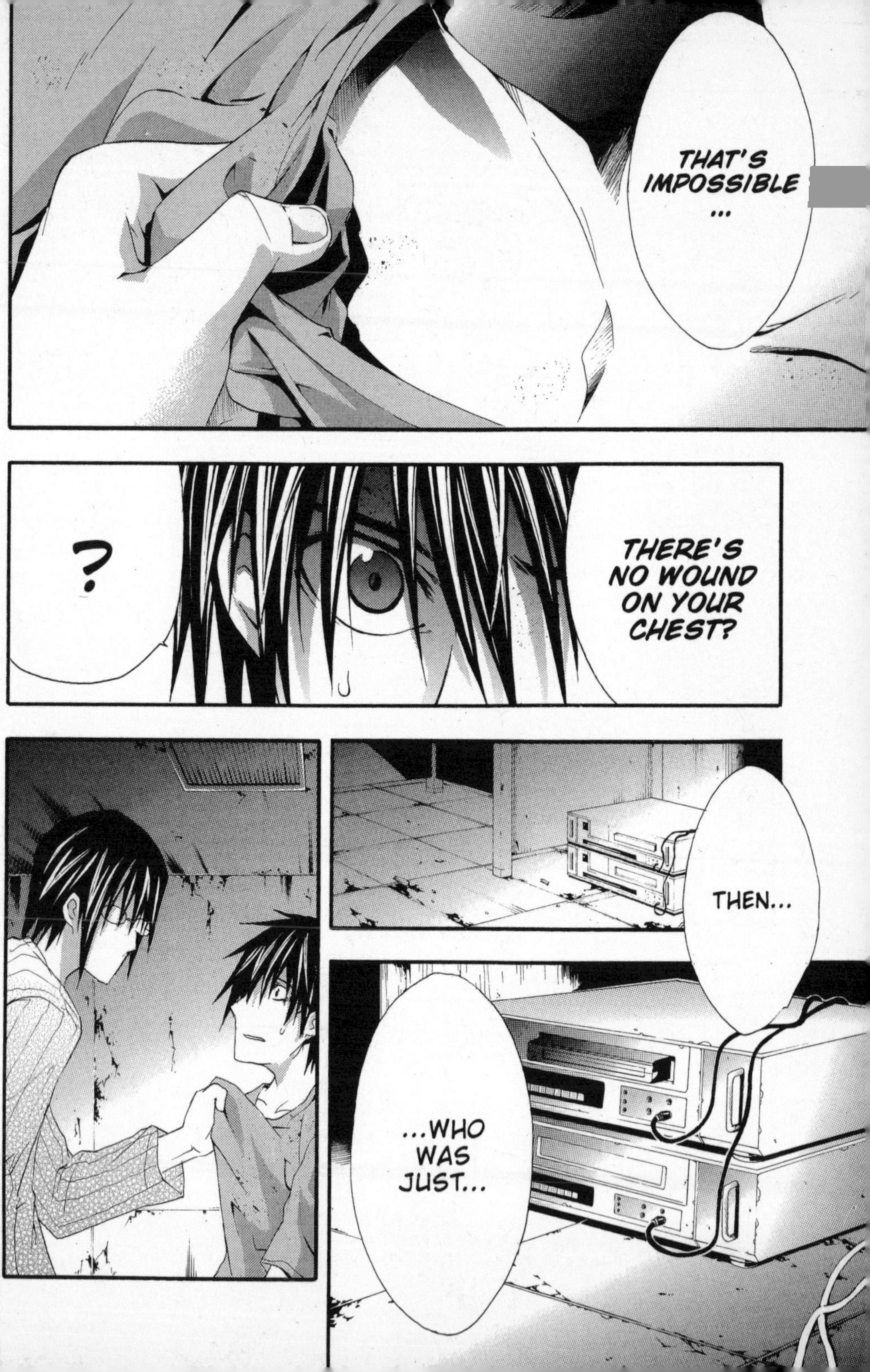
THAT'S IMPOSSIBLE ...
THERE'S NO WOUND ON YOUR CHEST?
?
THEN...
...WHO WAS JUST...

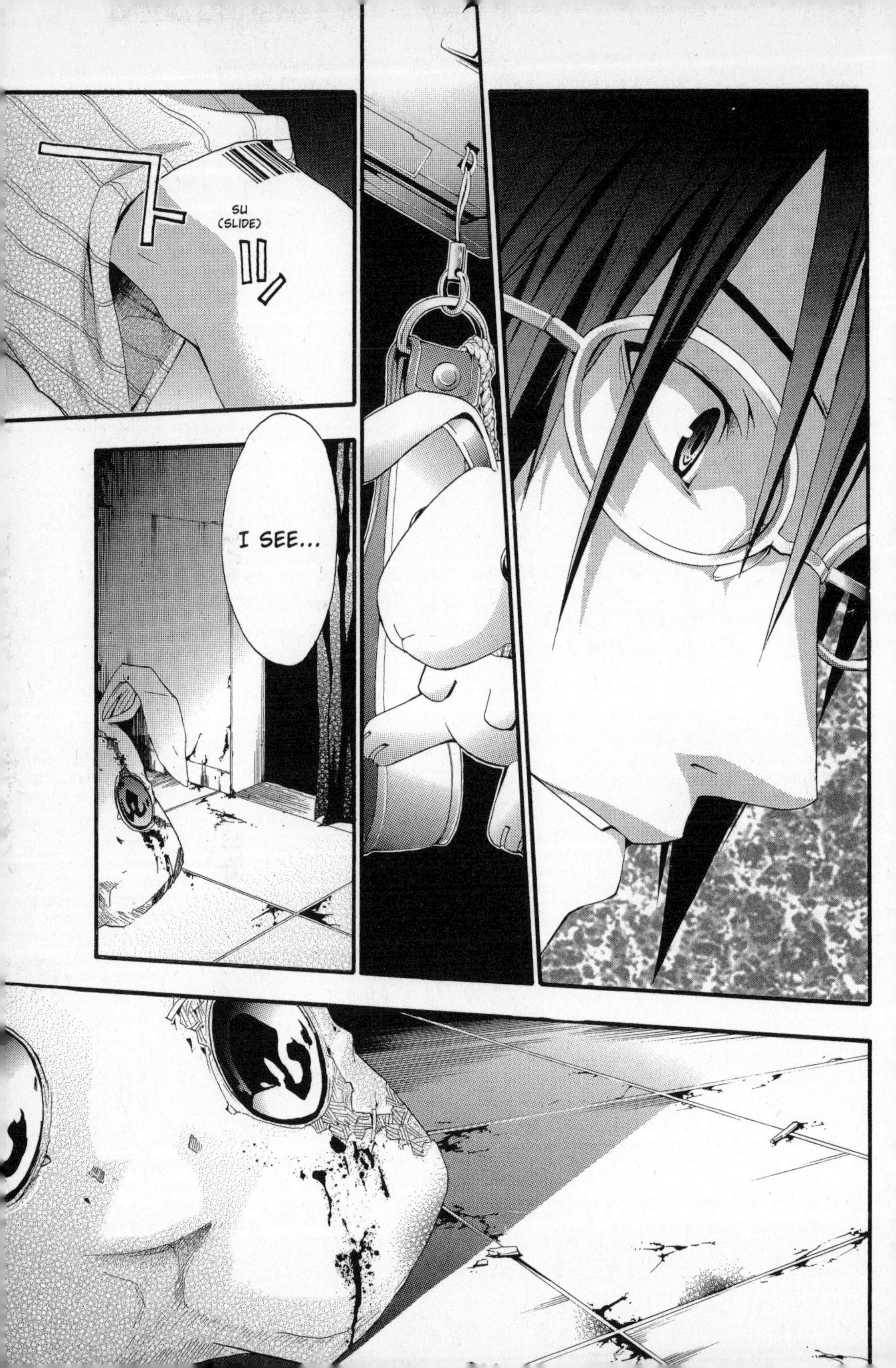
SU
(SLIDE)
I SEE...

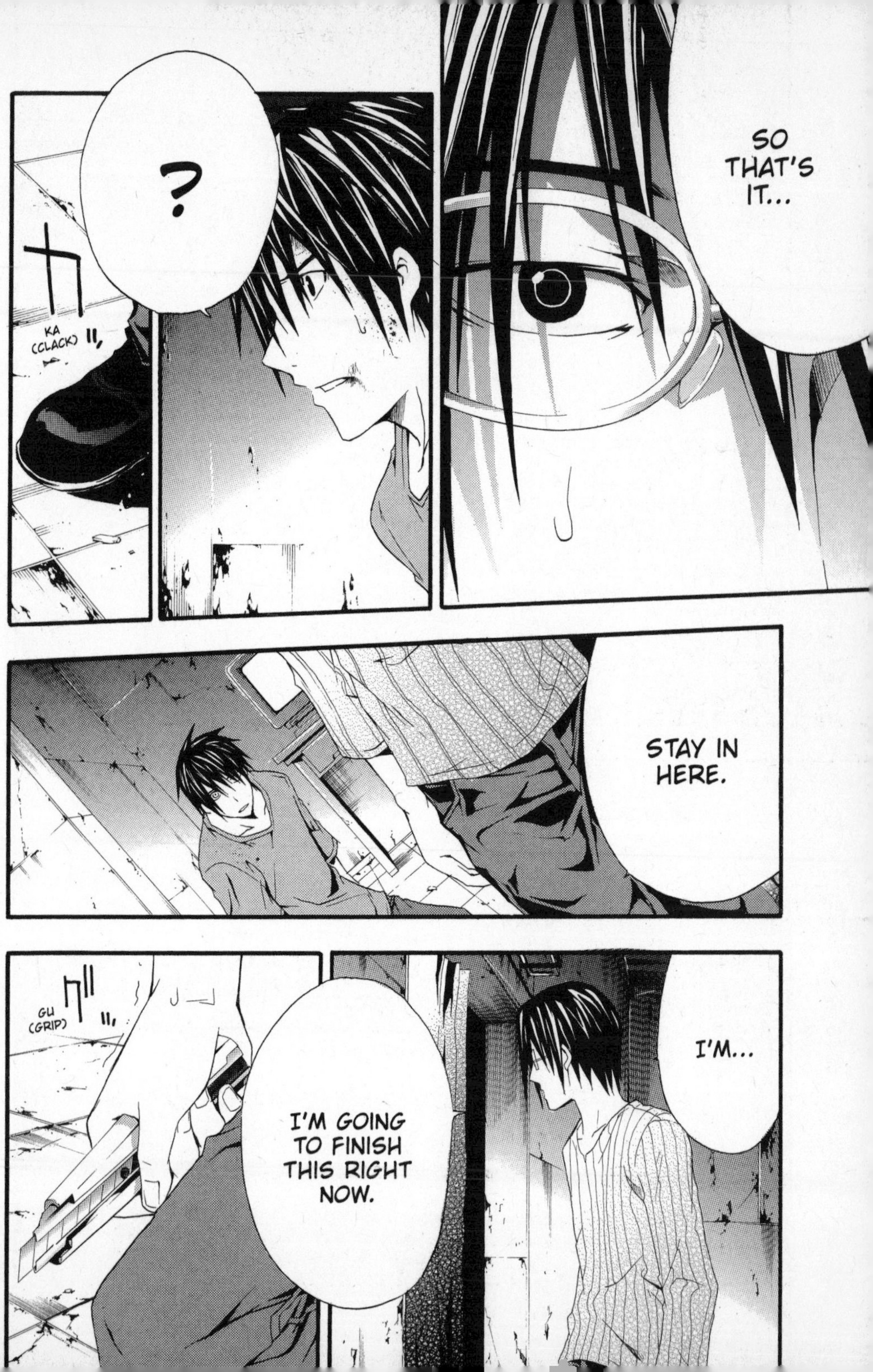
SO THAT'S IT...
?
KA (CLACK)
STAY IN HERE.
I'M...
I'M GOING TO FINISH THIS RIGHT NOW.
GU (GRIP)

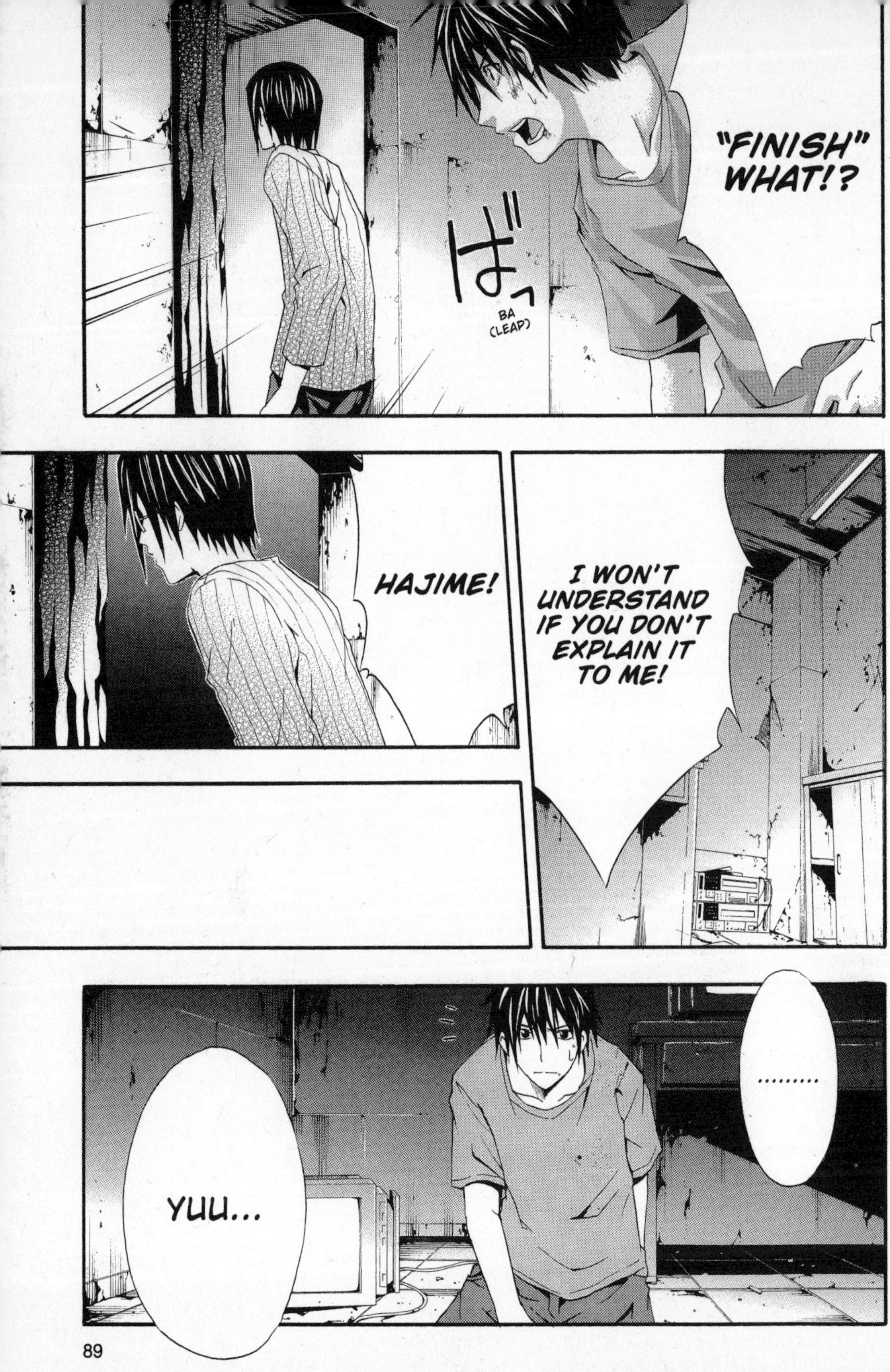
"FINISH" WHAT!?
ばっ
BA (LEAP)
I WON'T UNDERSTAND IF YOU DON'T EXPLAIN IT TO ME!
HAJIME!
....
YUU...

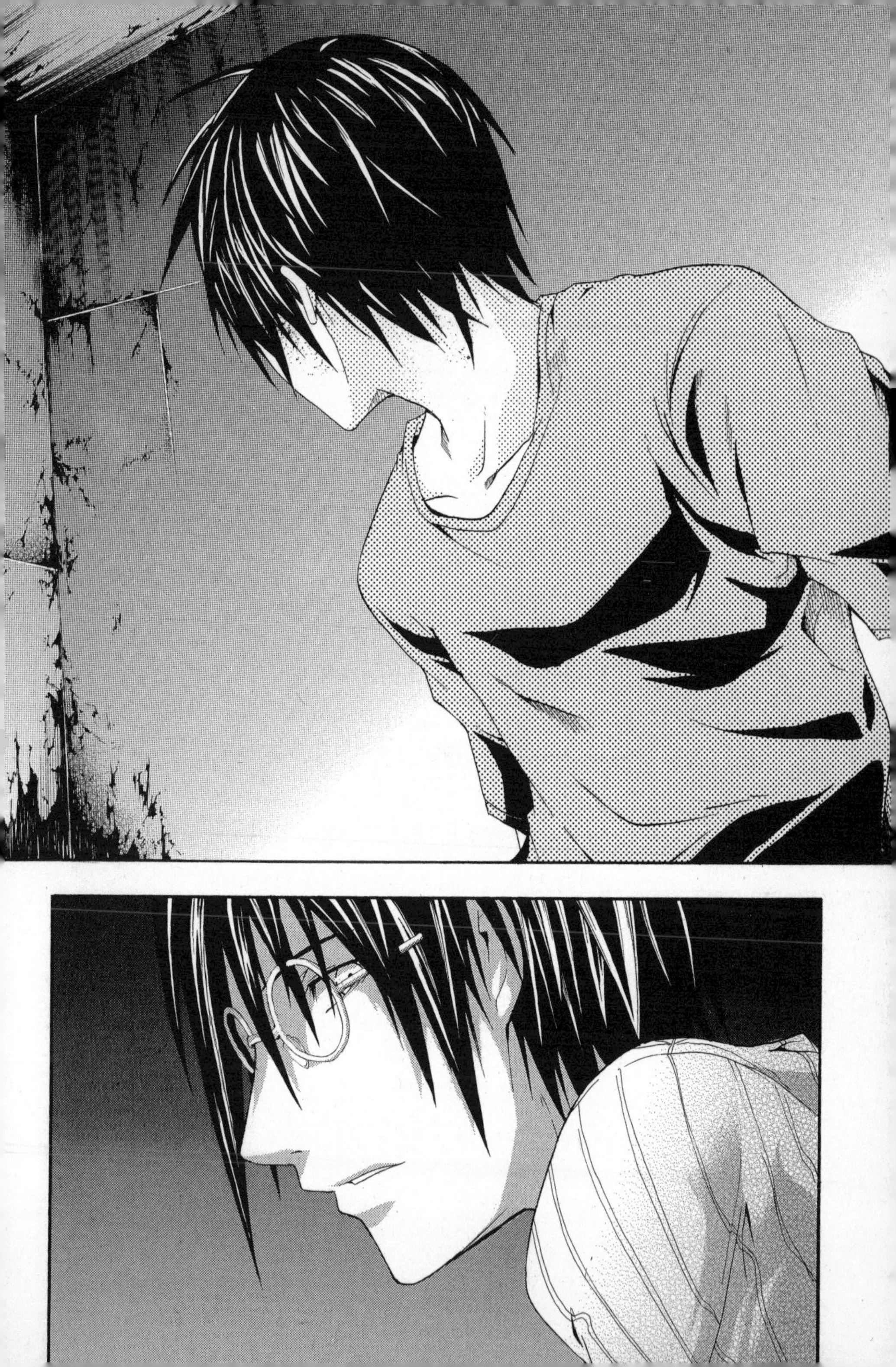

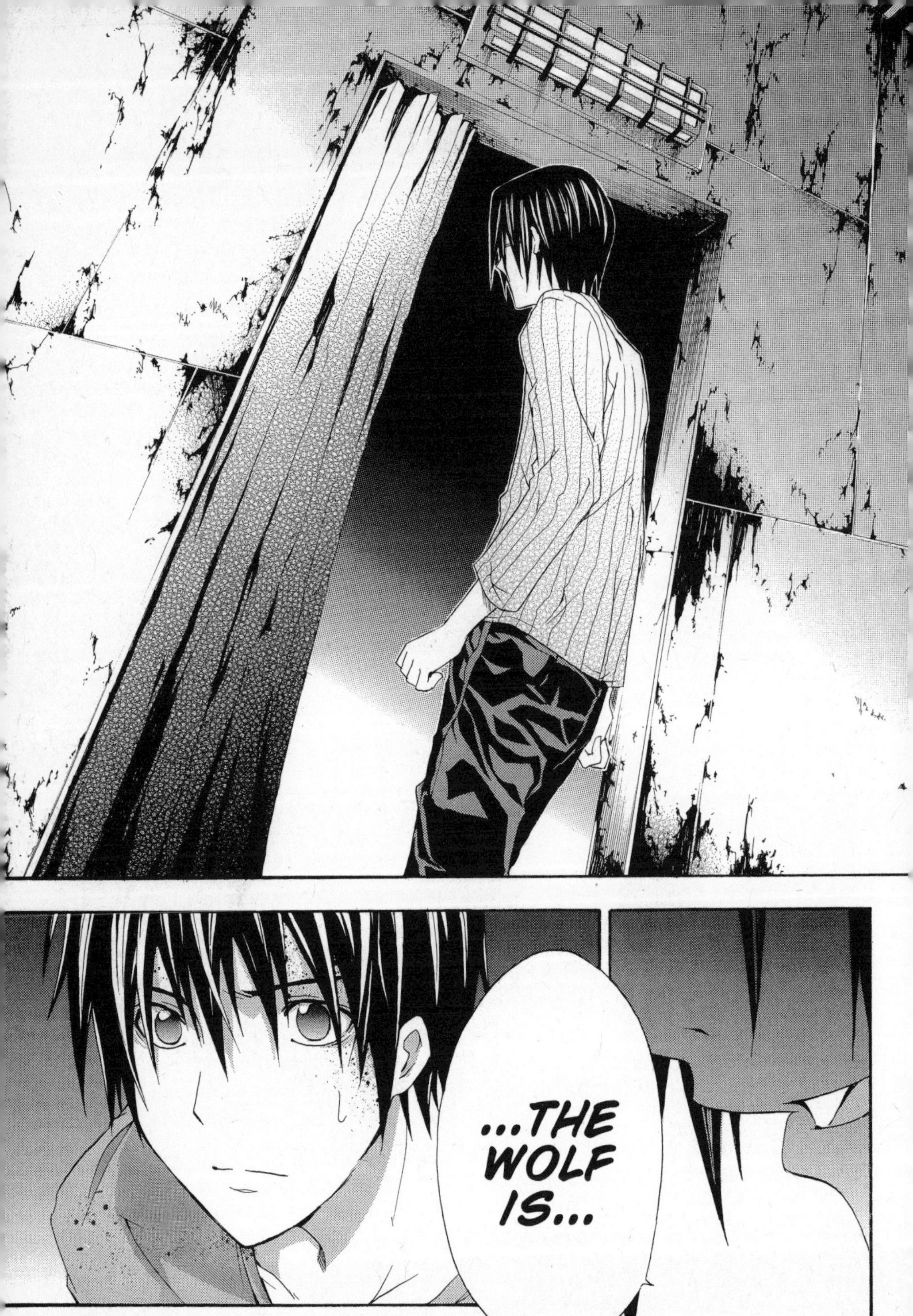
...THE WOLF IS...

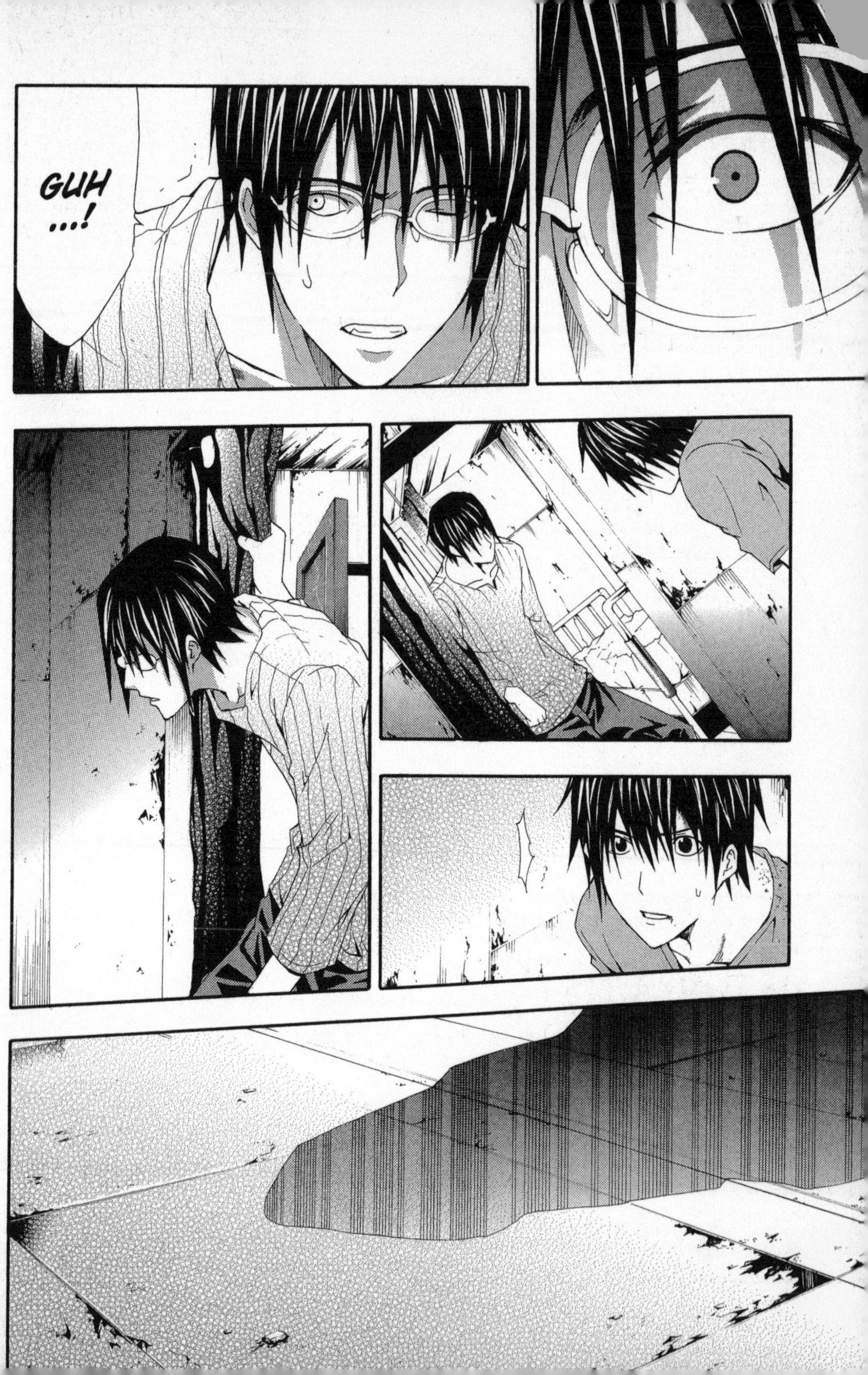
GUH ...!

...HUH?

DOSA
(THUD)

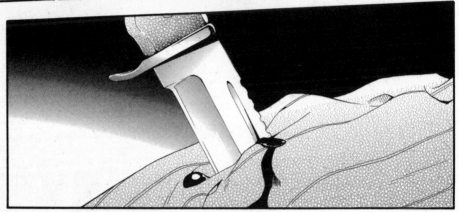

BA
(LUNGE)

WHAT HAP- PENED!?

HAJIME!!

93

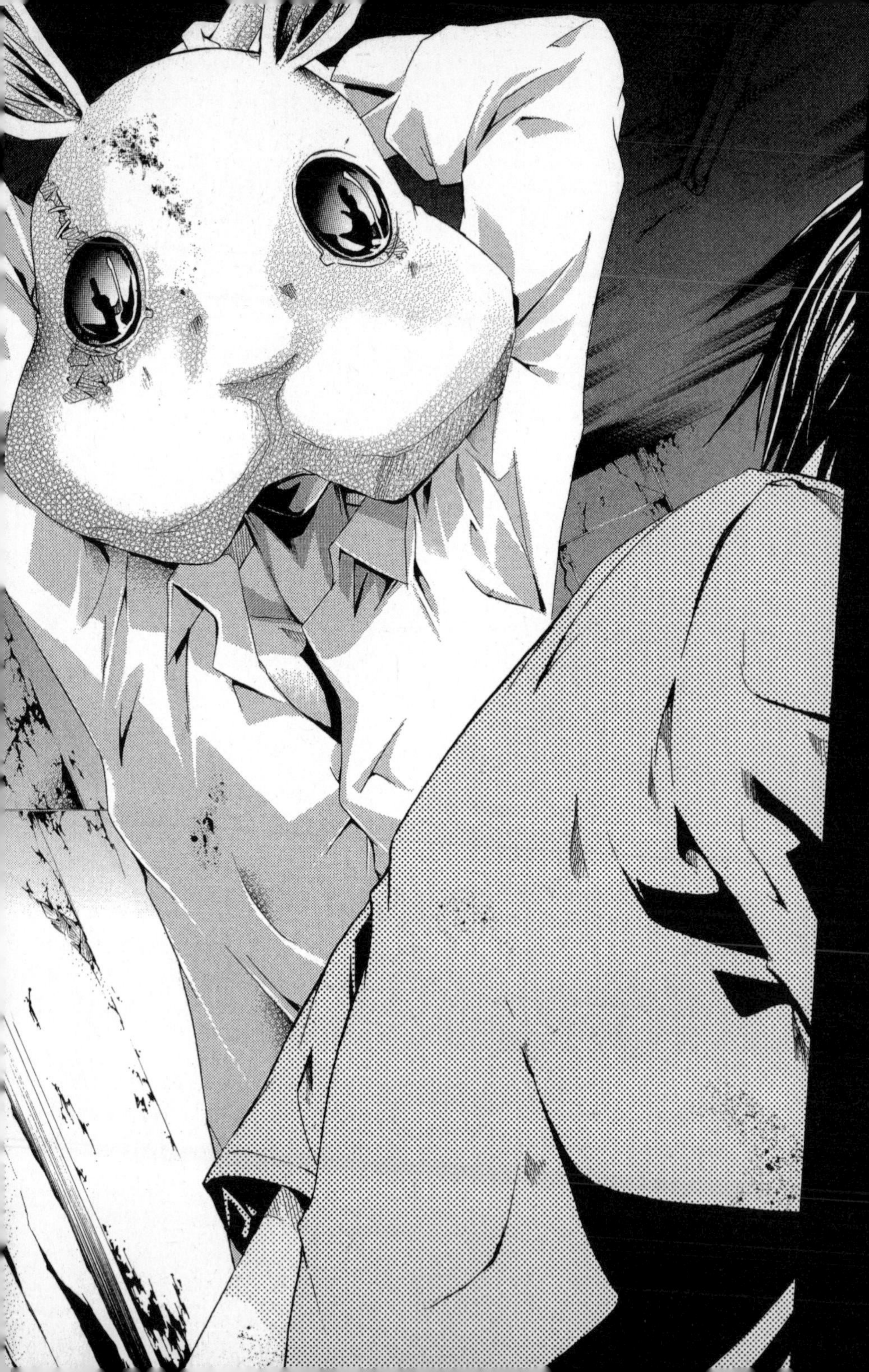

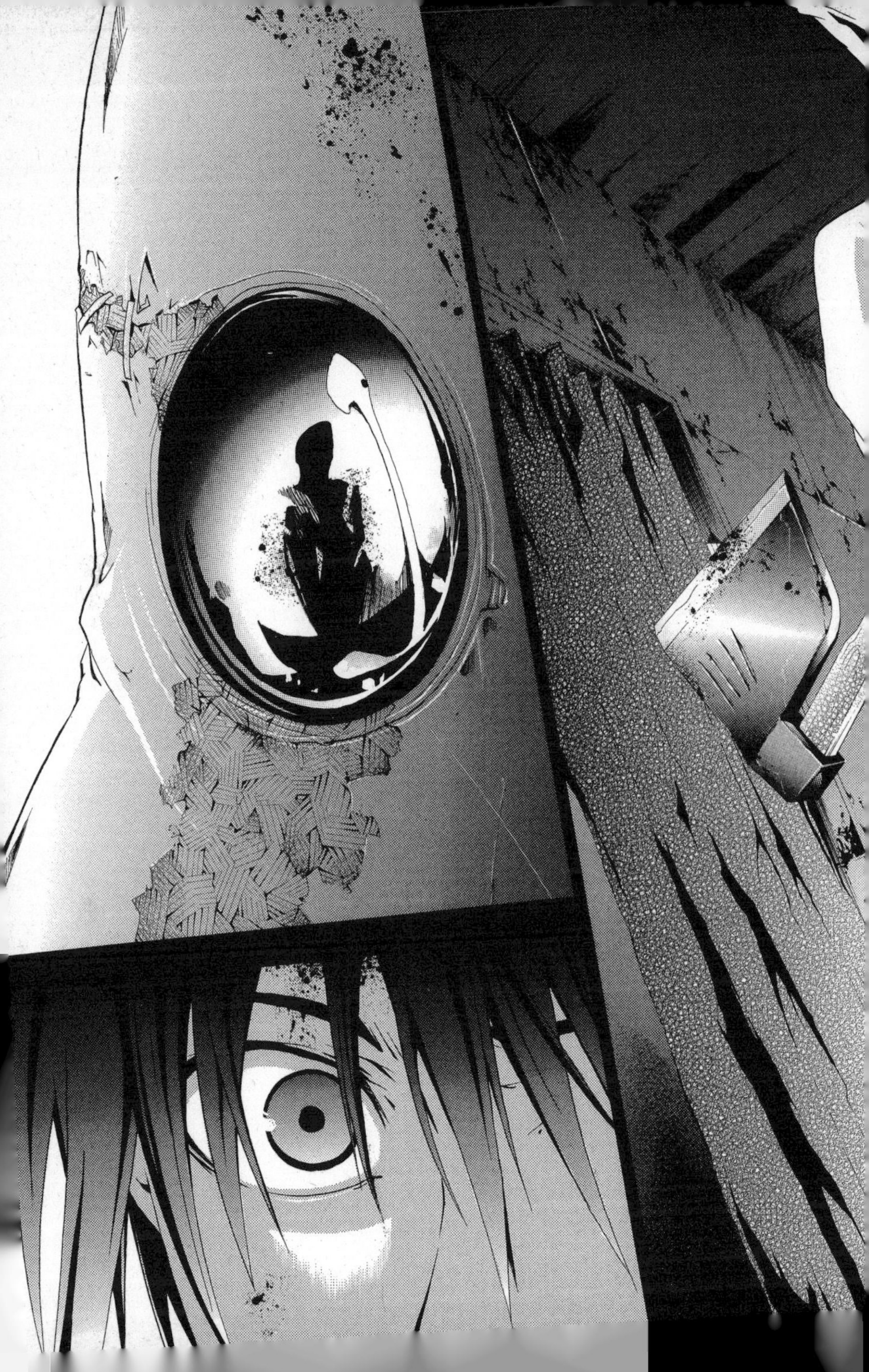

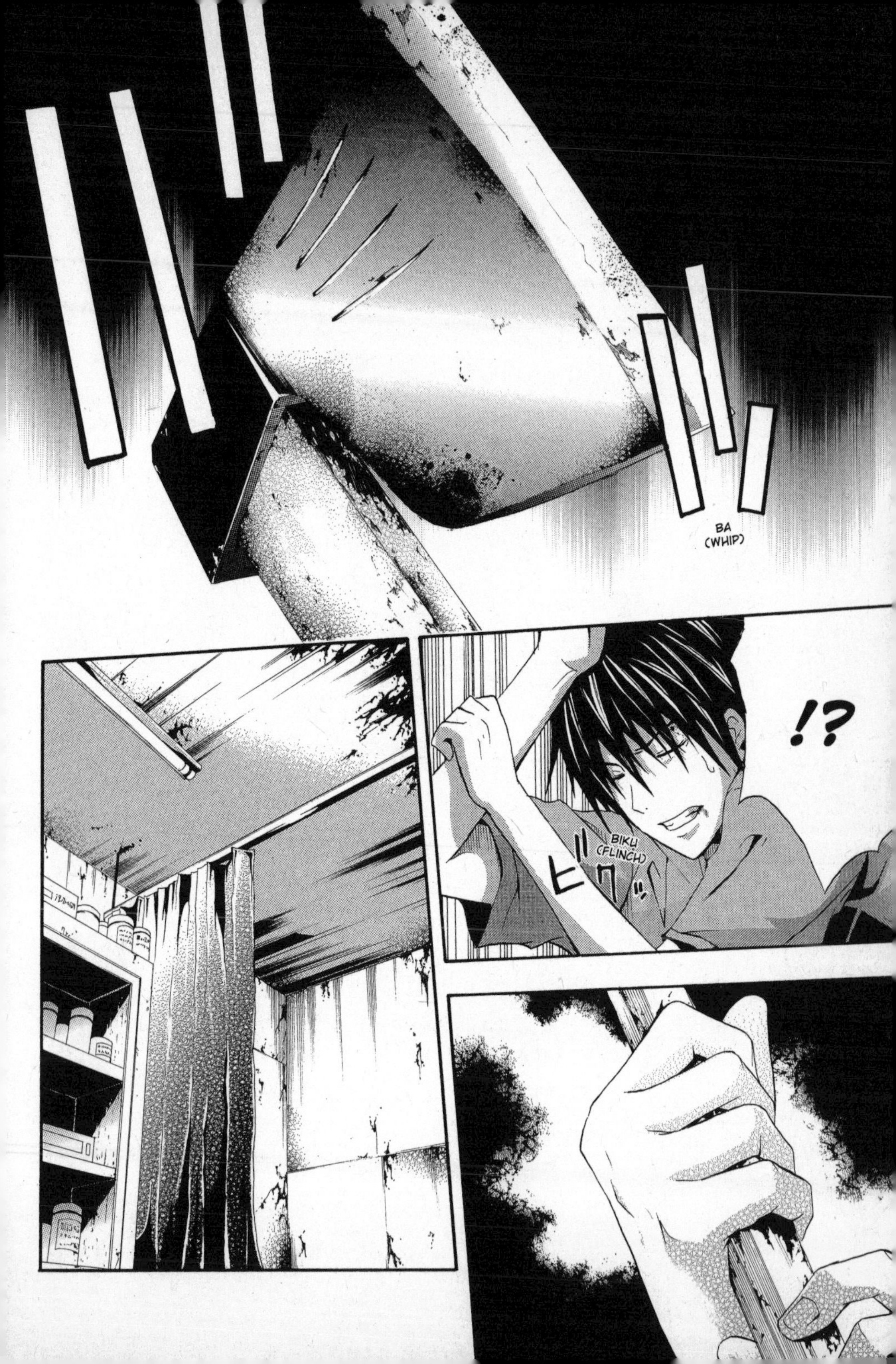
BA
(WHIP)
!?
BIKU
(FLINCH)

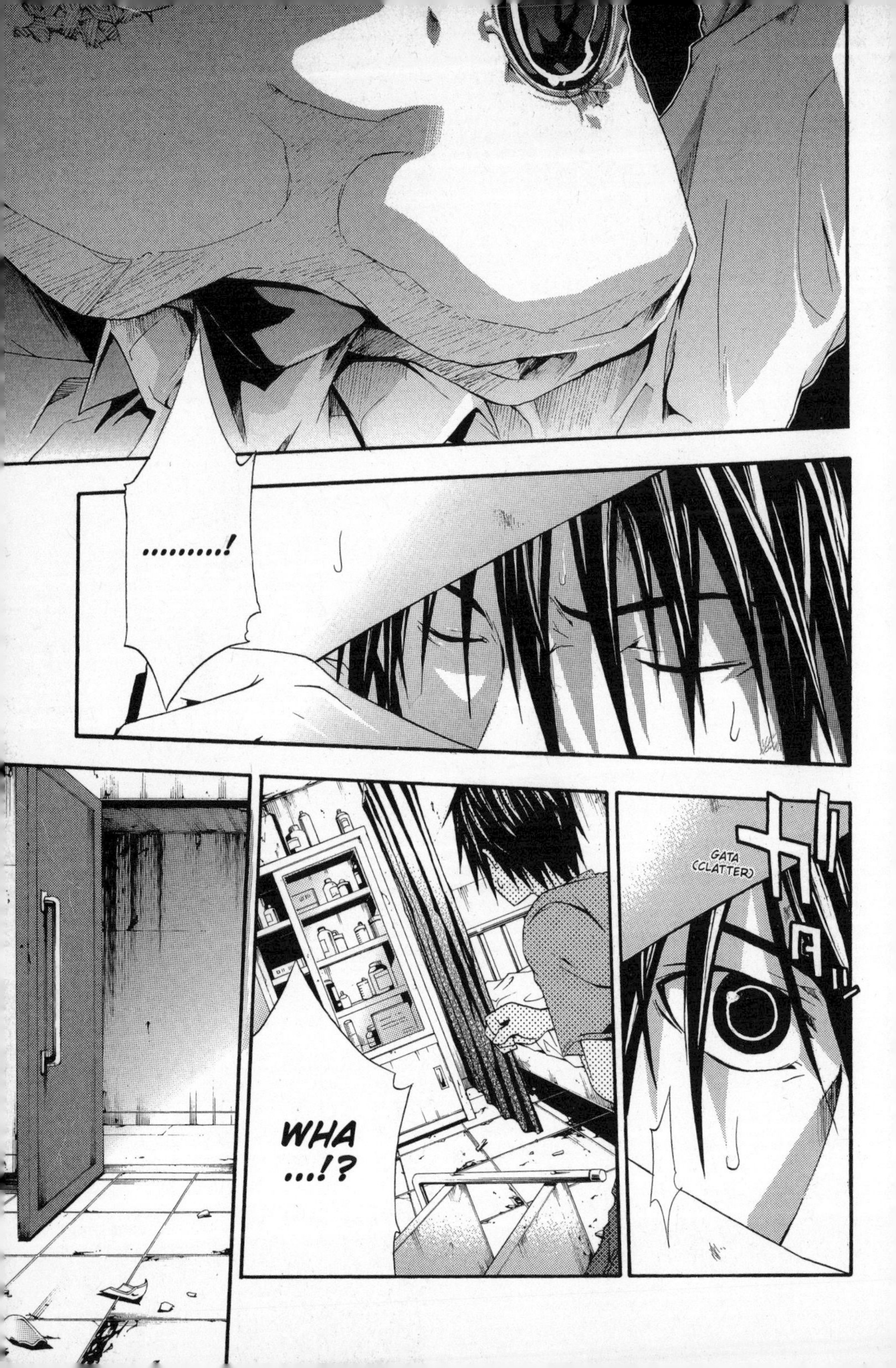
........!
GATA (CLATTER)
WHA ...!?

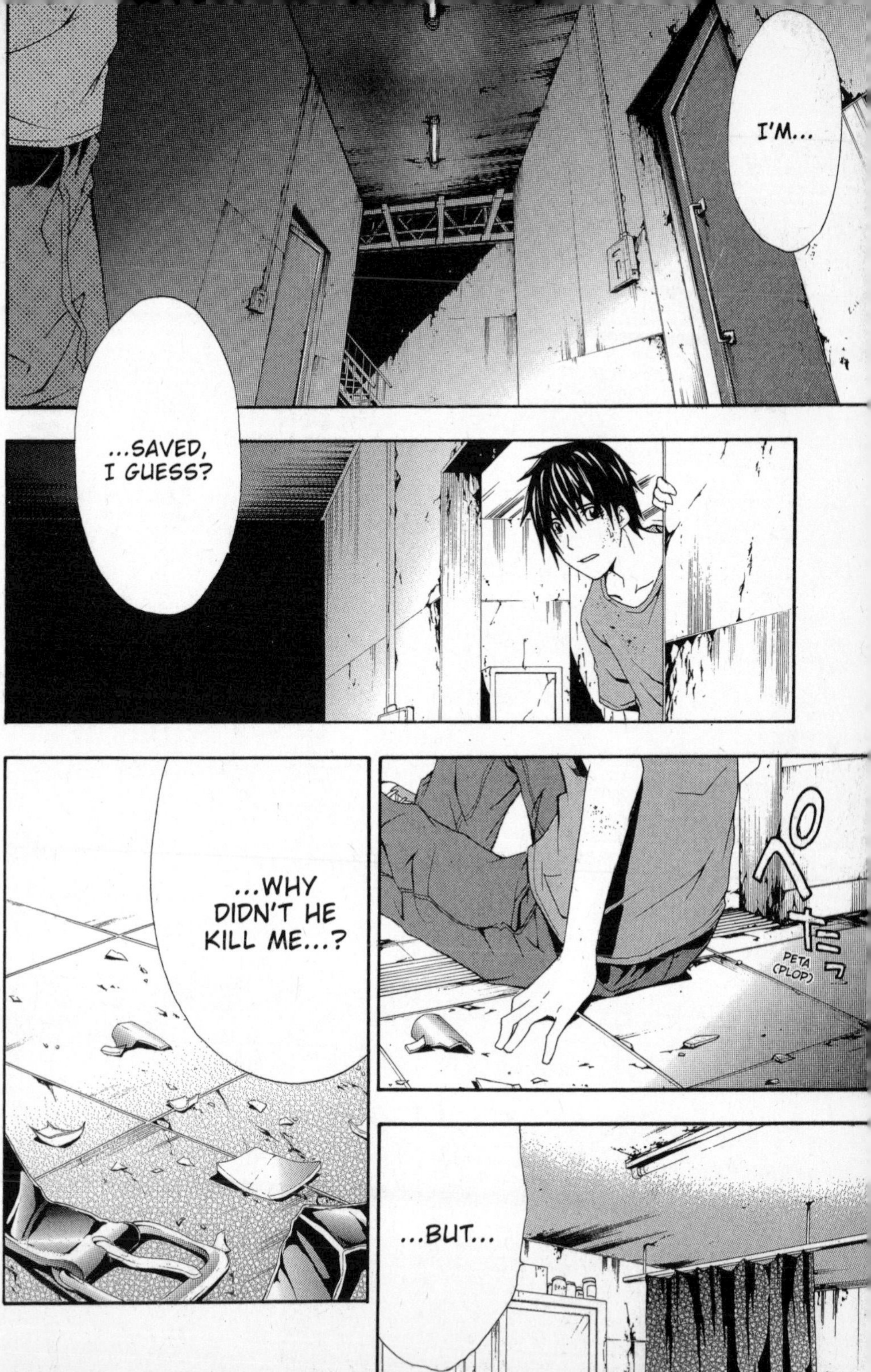
I'M...
...SAVED, I GUESS?
PETA (PLOP)
...BUT...
...WHY DIDN'T HE KILL ME...?

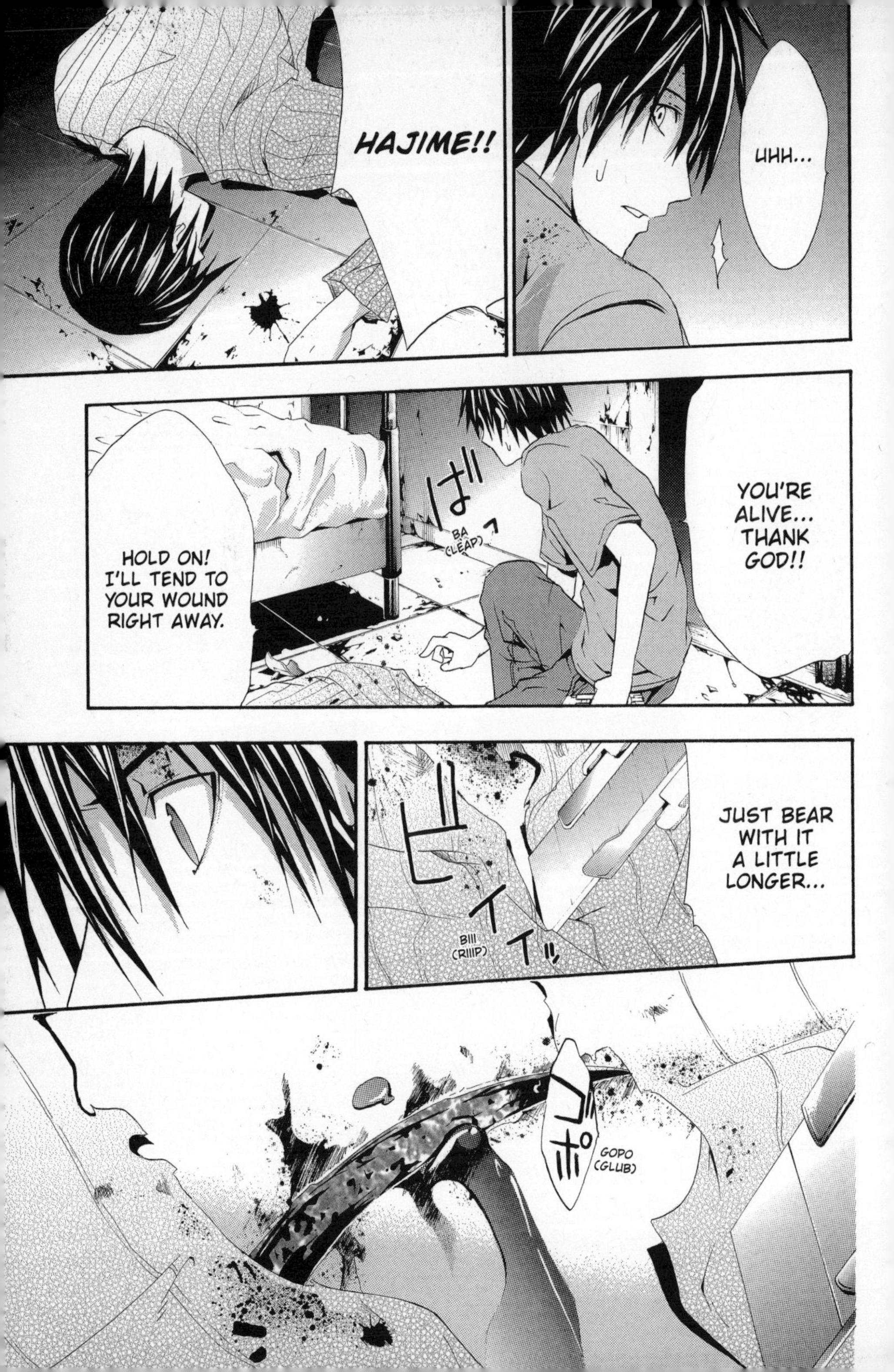
UHH...
HAJIME!!
YOU'RE ALIVE... THANK GOD!!
ば
BA (LEAP)
HOLD ON! I'LL TEND TO YOUR WOUND RIGHT AWAY.
JUST BEAR WITH IT A LITTLE LONGER...
ビイイッ
BIII (RIIIP)
ゴポ
GOPO (GLUB)

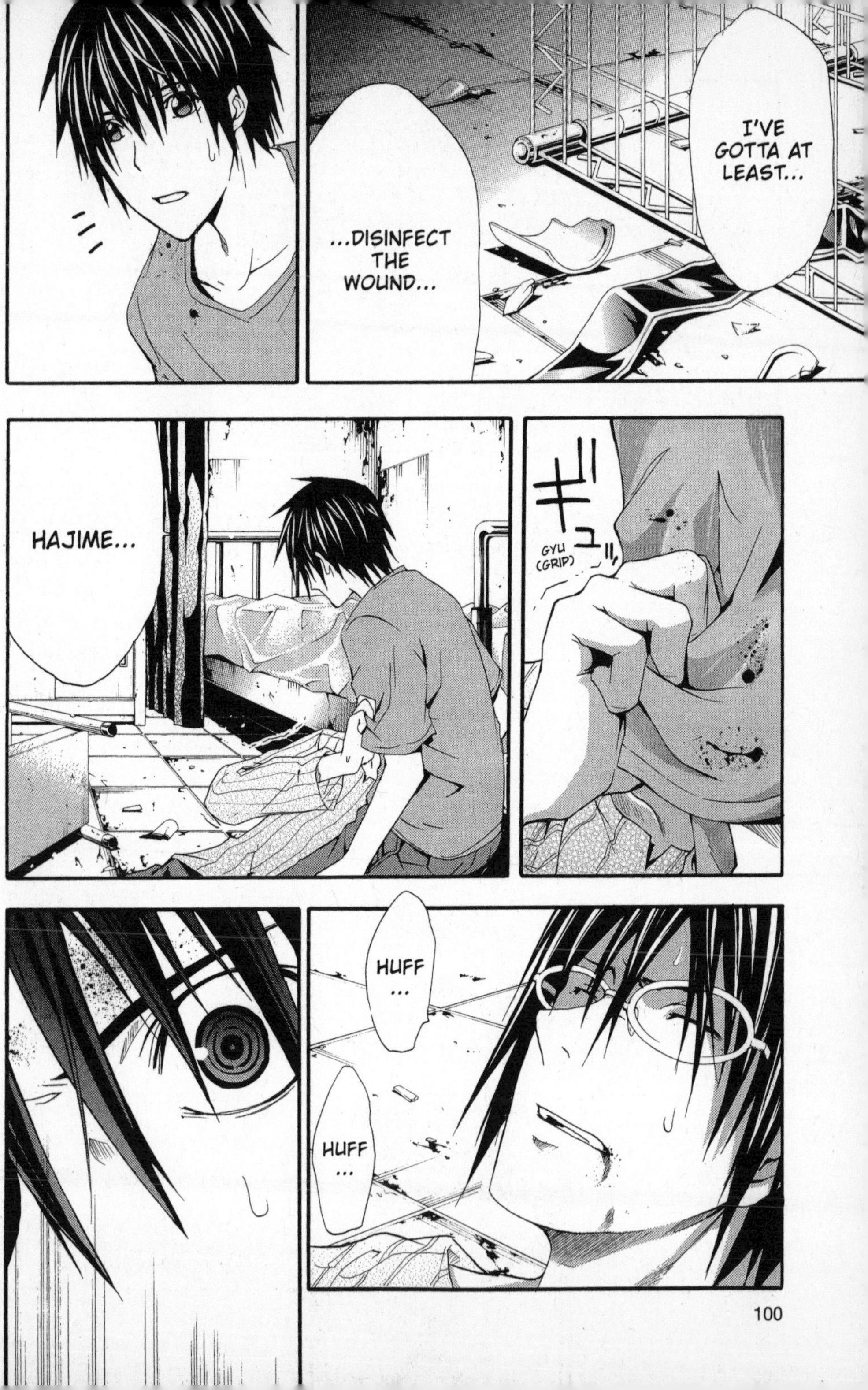
I'VE GOTTA AT LEAST...
...DISINFECT THE WOUND...
ギュッ
GYU (GRIP)
HAJIME...
HUFF ...
HUFF ...

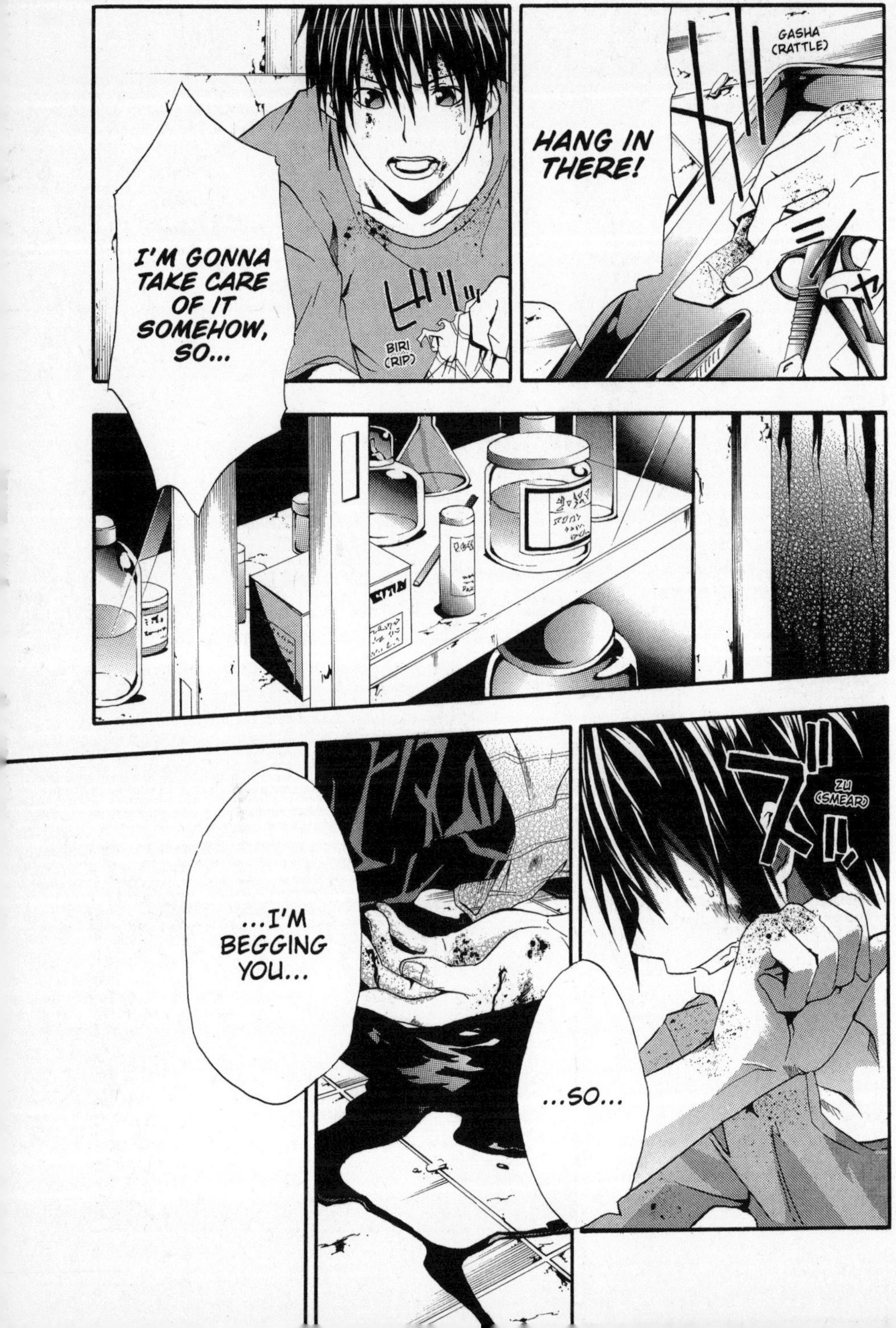
GASHA (RATTLE)
HANG IN THERE!
I'M GONNA TAKE CARE OF IT SOMEHOW, SO...
BIRI (RIP)
ZU (SMEAR)
...SO...
...I'M BEGGING YOU...

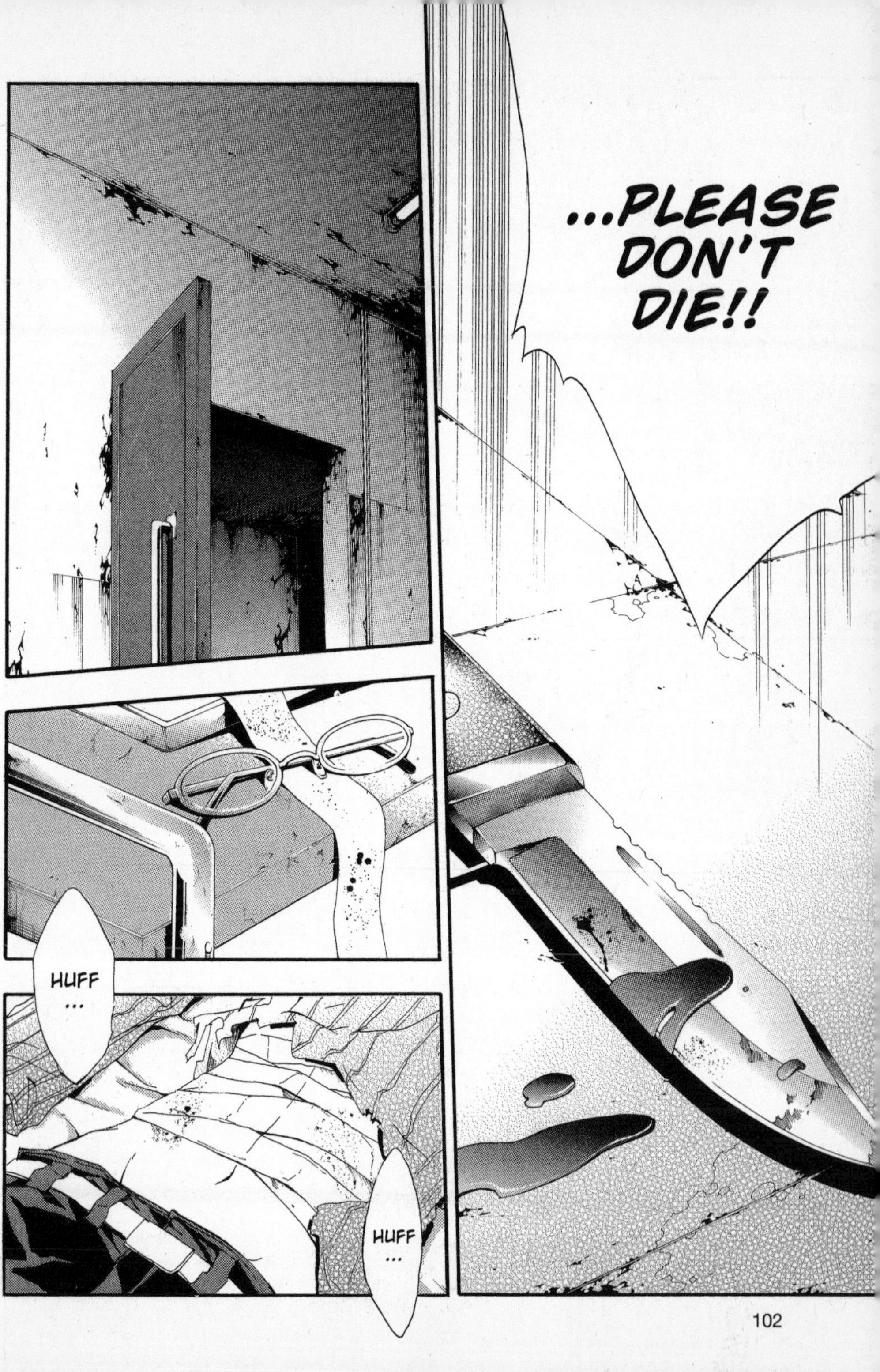
...PLEASE DON'T DIE!!
HUFF ...
HUFF ...

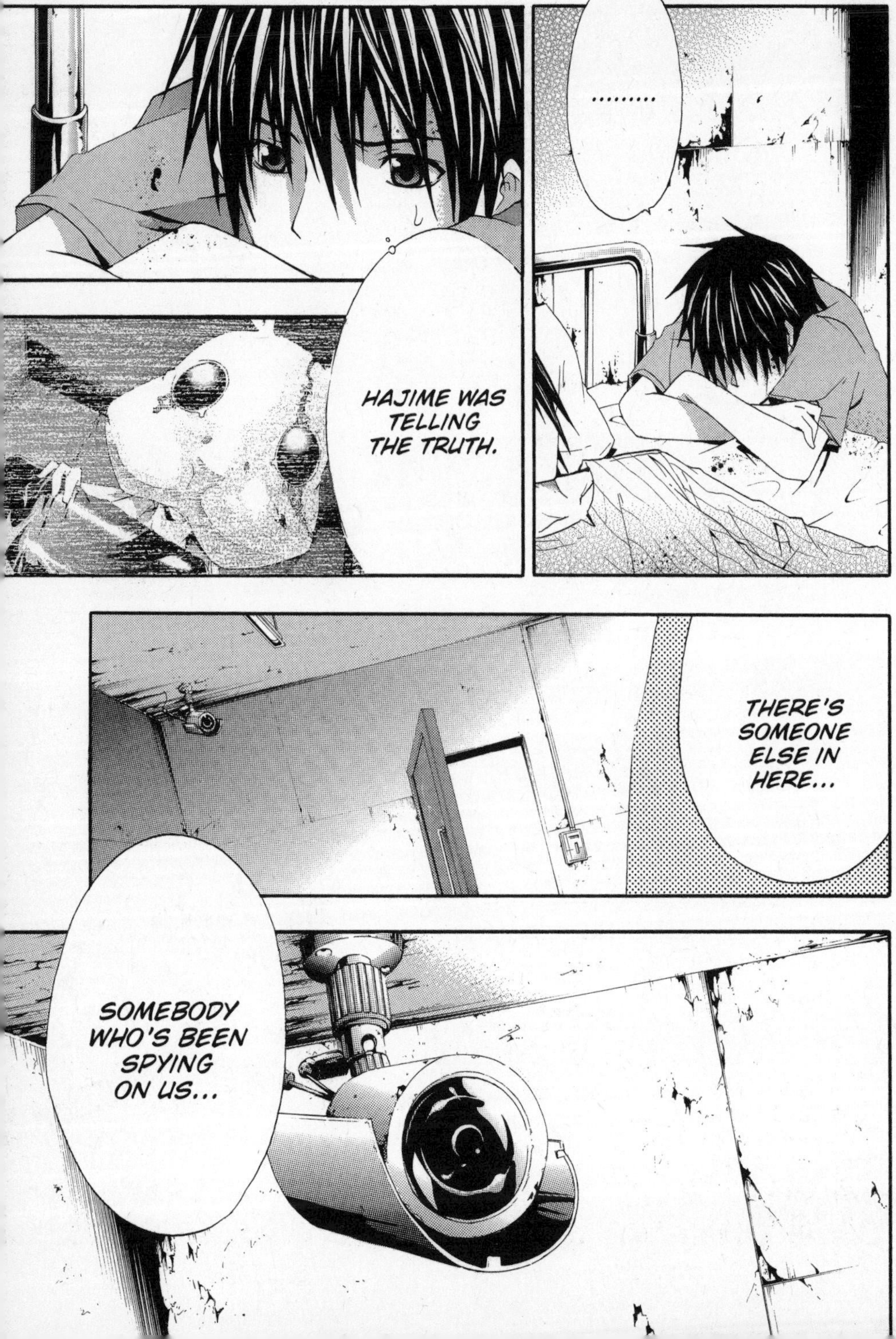
....
HAJIME WAS TELLING THE TRUTH.
THERE'S SOMEONE ELSE IN HERE...
SOMEBODY WHO'S BEEN SPYING ON US...

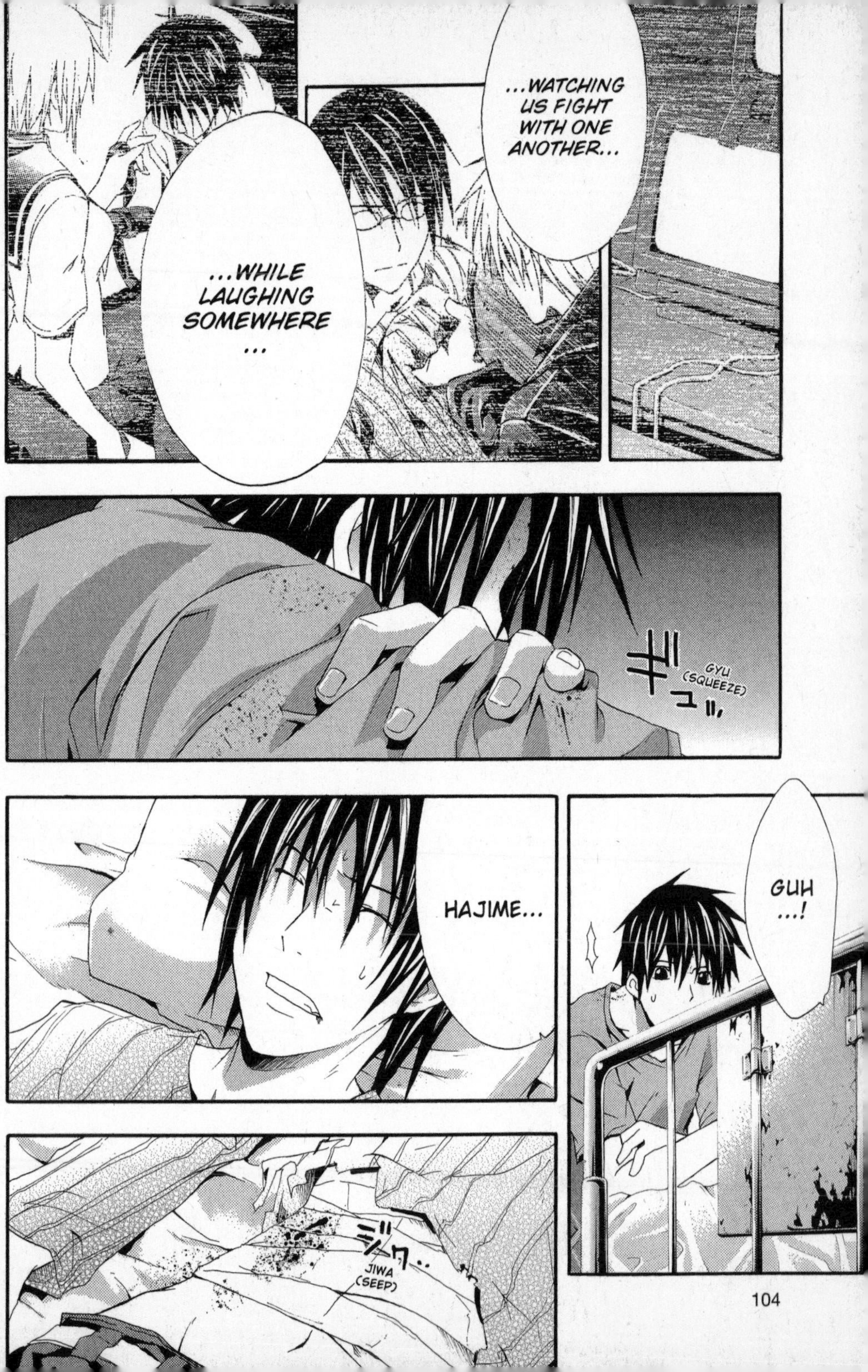
...WATCHING US FIGHT WITH ONE ANOTHER...
...WHILE LAUGHING SOMEWHERE ...
ギュッ
GYU (SQUEEZE)
GUH ...!
HAJIME...
ジワ..
JIWA (SEEP)

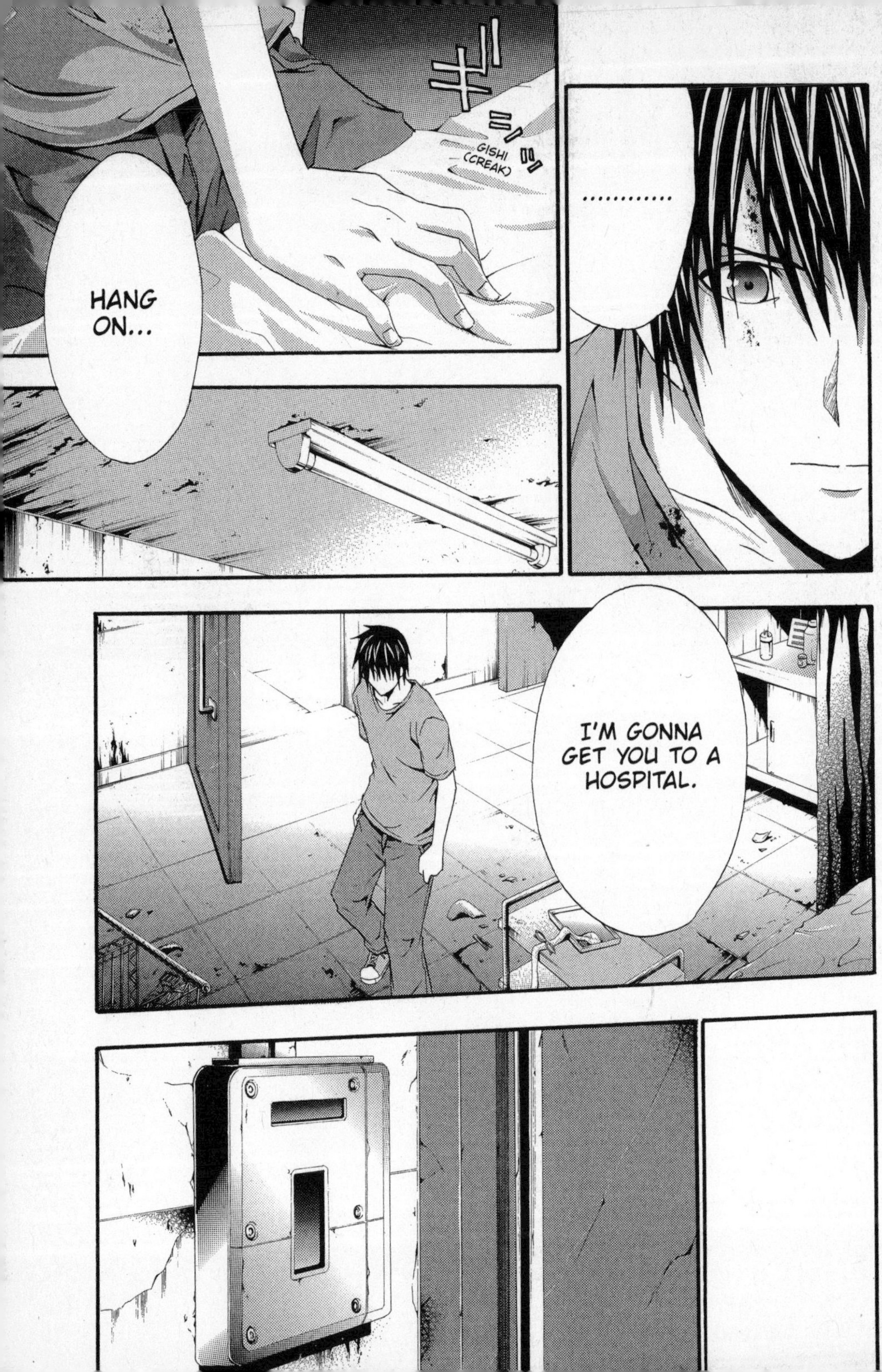
....
GISHI (CREAK)
HANG ON...
I'M GONNA GET YOU TO A HOSPITAL.

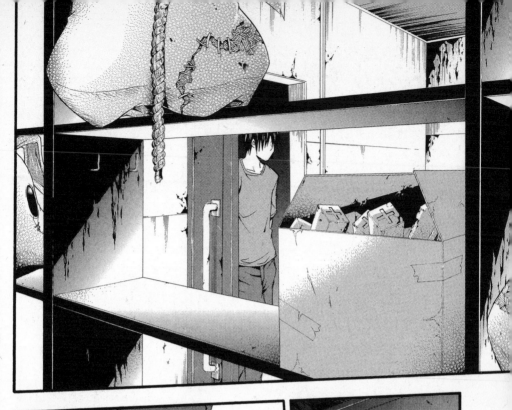

I'M
SURE...

...I SAW IT
AROUND HERE
EARLIER...

GACHA
(CLANK)

GACHA

....

PIKU
(TWITCH)

!

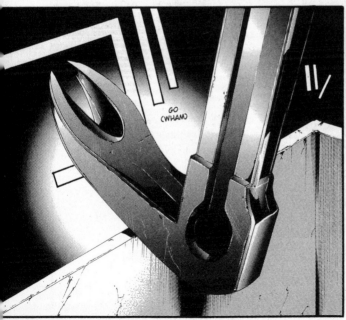

GO
(WHAM)

...THERE
IT IS.

GARA
(RATTLE)

I'M GONNA HUNT THIS GUY DOWN AND TAKE HIS KEY...

NOW IT'S A ONE-ON-ONE MATCH.

JARA

JARA (JANGLE)

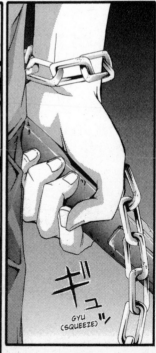

I'M GONNA...

GYU (SQUEEZE)

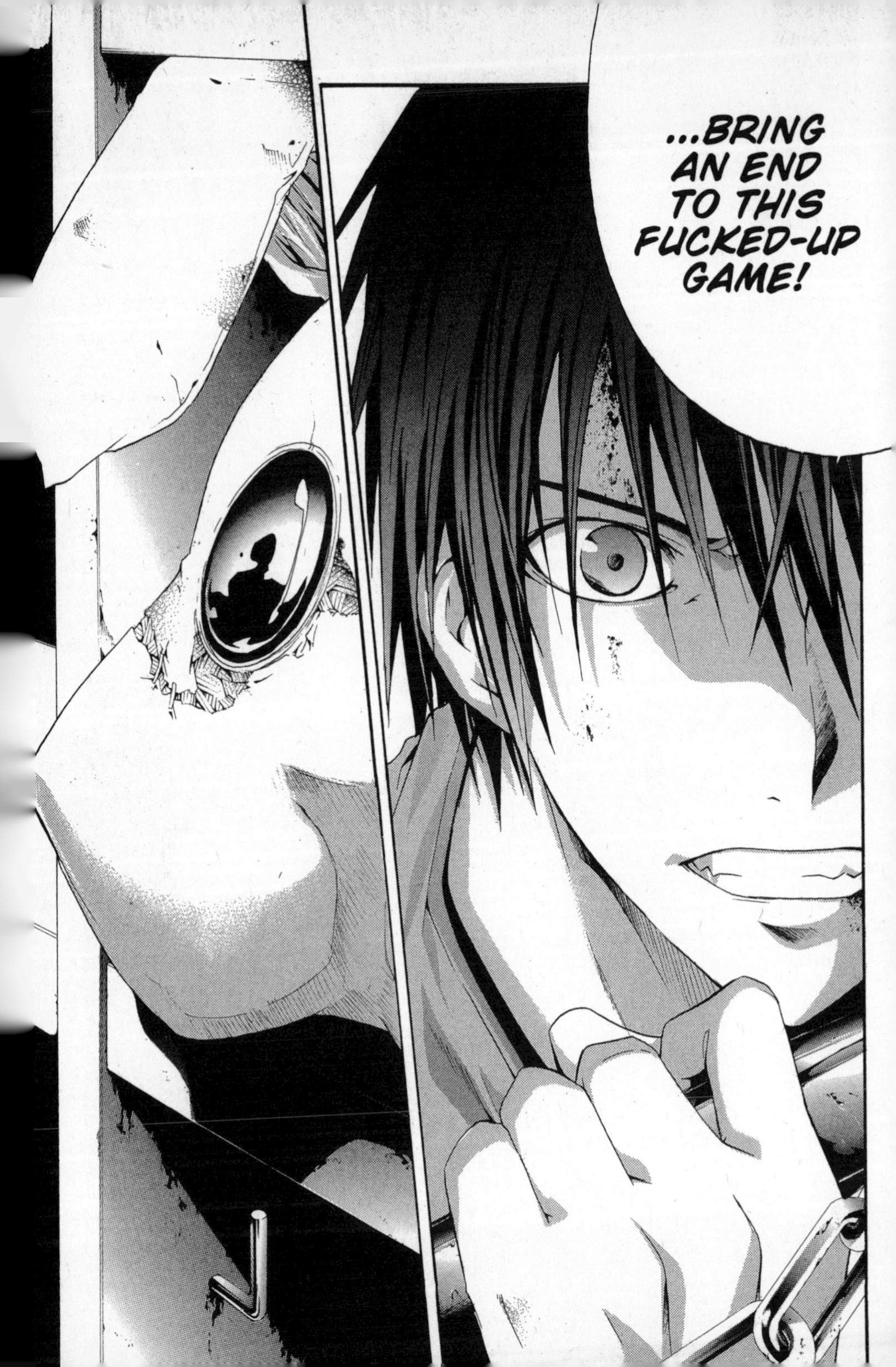
...BRING AN END TO THIS FUCKED-UP GAME!

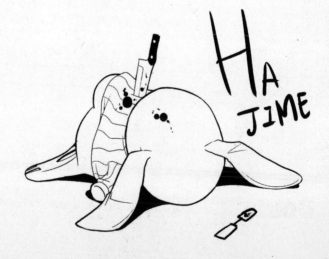

HA
JIME

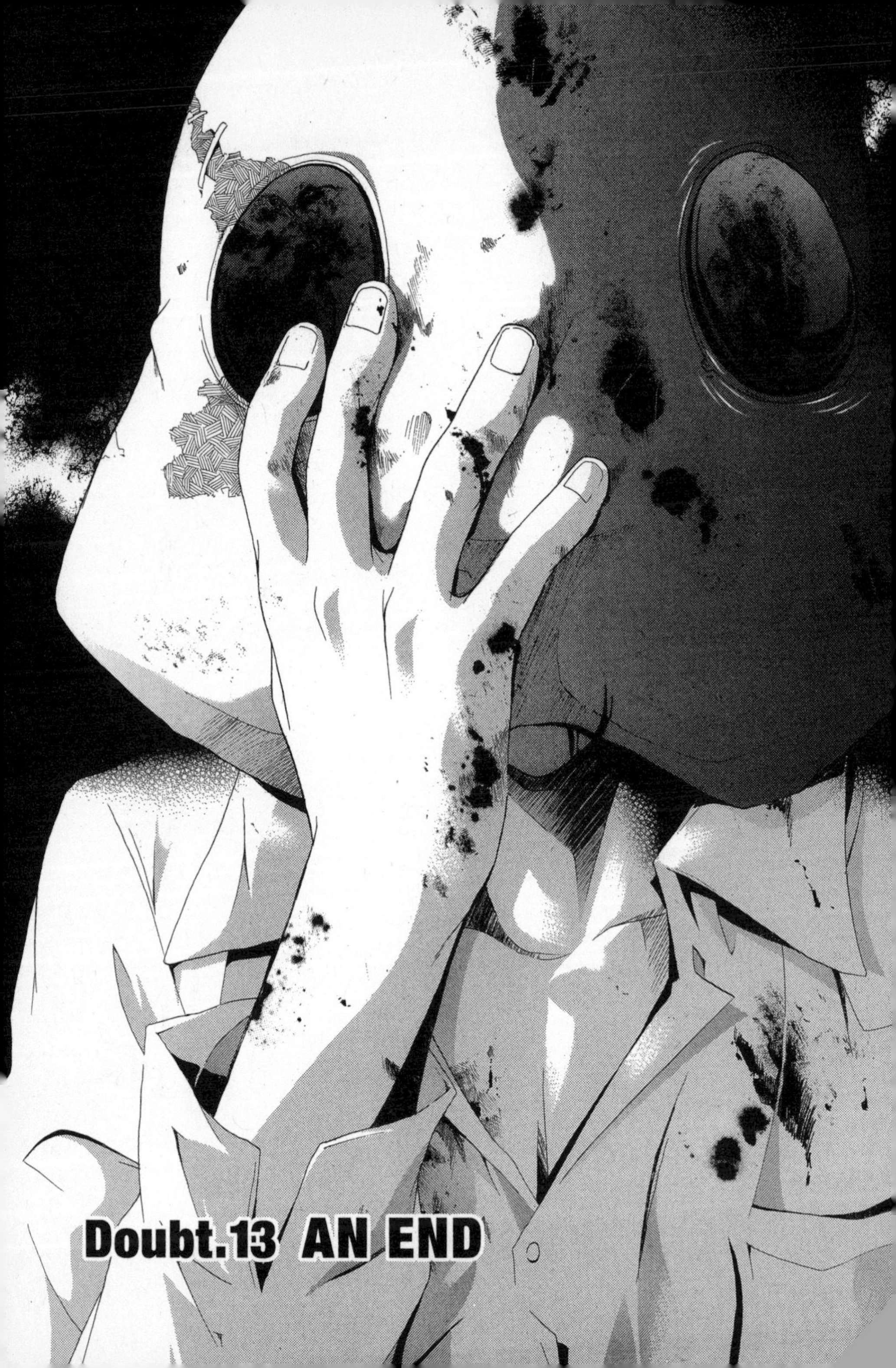
Doubt.13 AN END

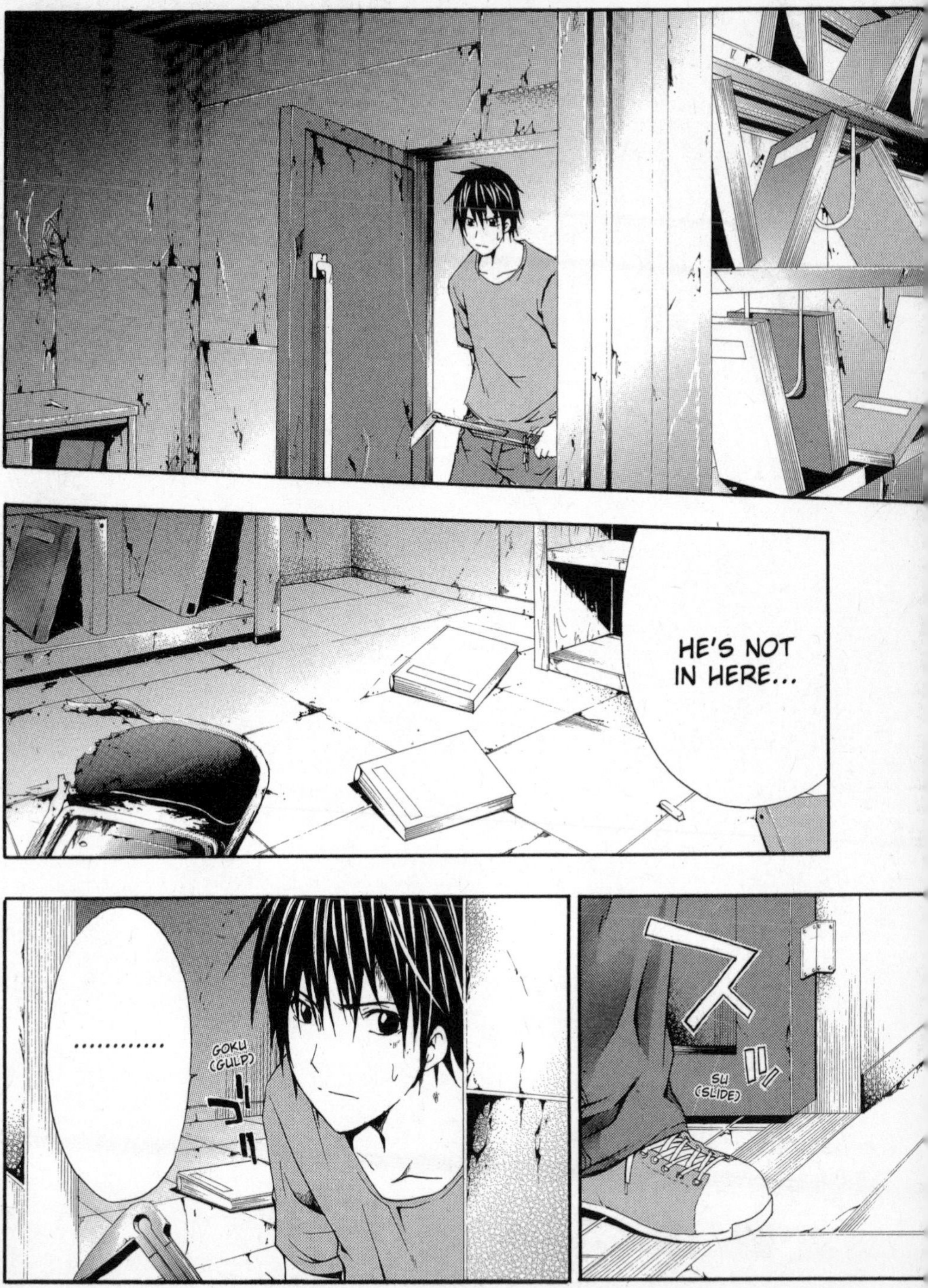
HE'S NOT IN HERE...
SU (SLIDE)
....
GOKU (GULP)

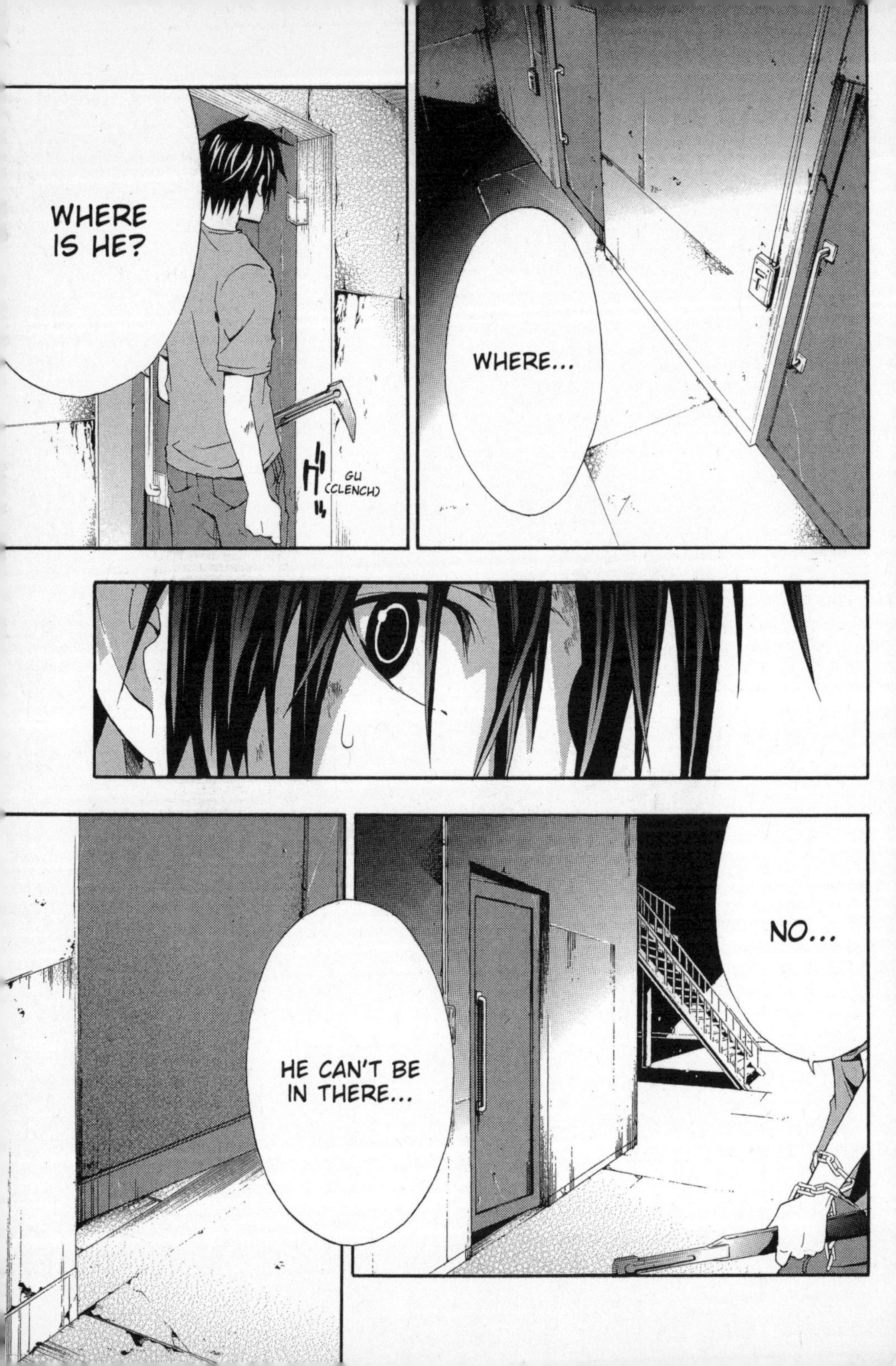
WHERE...
WHERE IS HE?
GU (CLENCH)
NO...
HE CAN'T BE IN THERE...

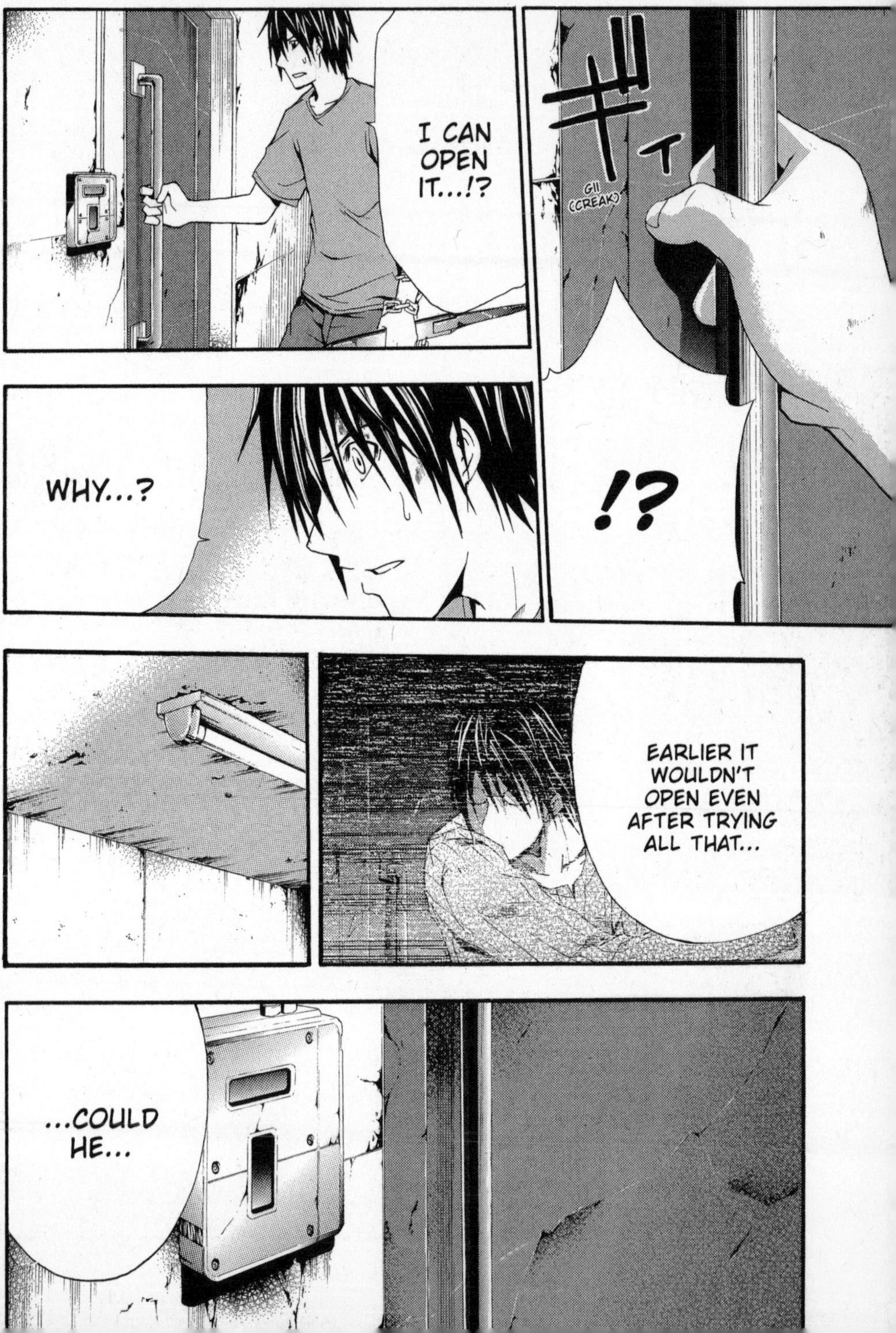
ギィ
GII (CREAK)
!?
I CAN OPEN IT...!?
WHY...?
EARLIER IT WOULDN'T OPEN EVEN AFTER TRYING ALL THAT...
...COULD HE...

...BE
INSIDE
HERE...?

....

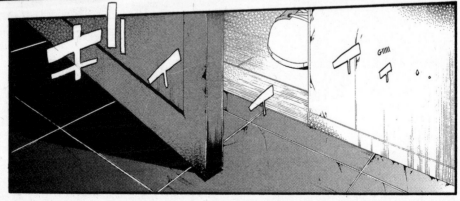

GIIIII

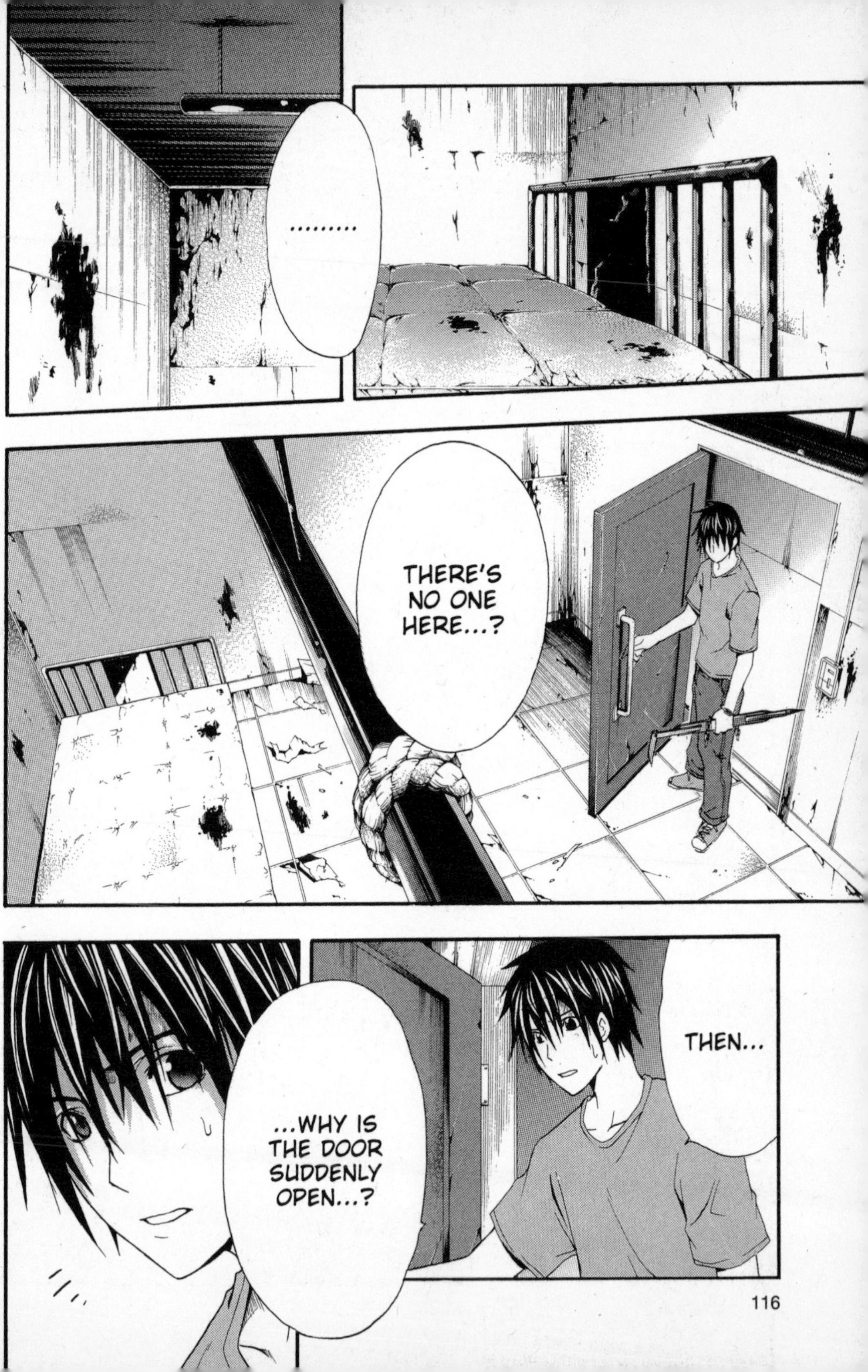
....
THERE'S NO ONE HERE...?
THEN...
...WHY IS THE DOOR SUDDENLY OPEN...?

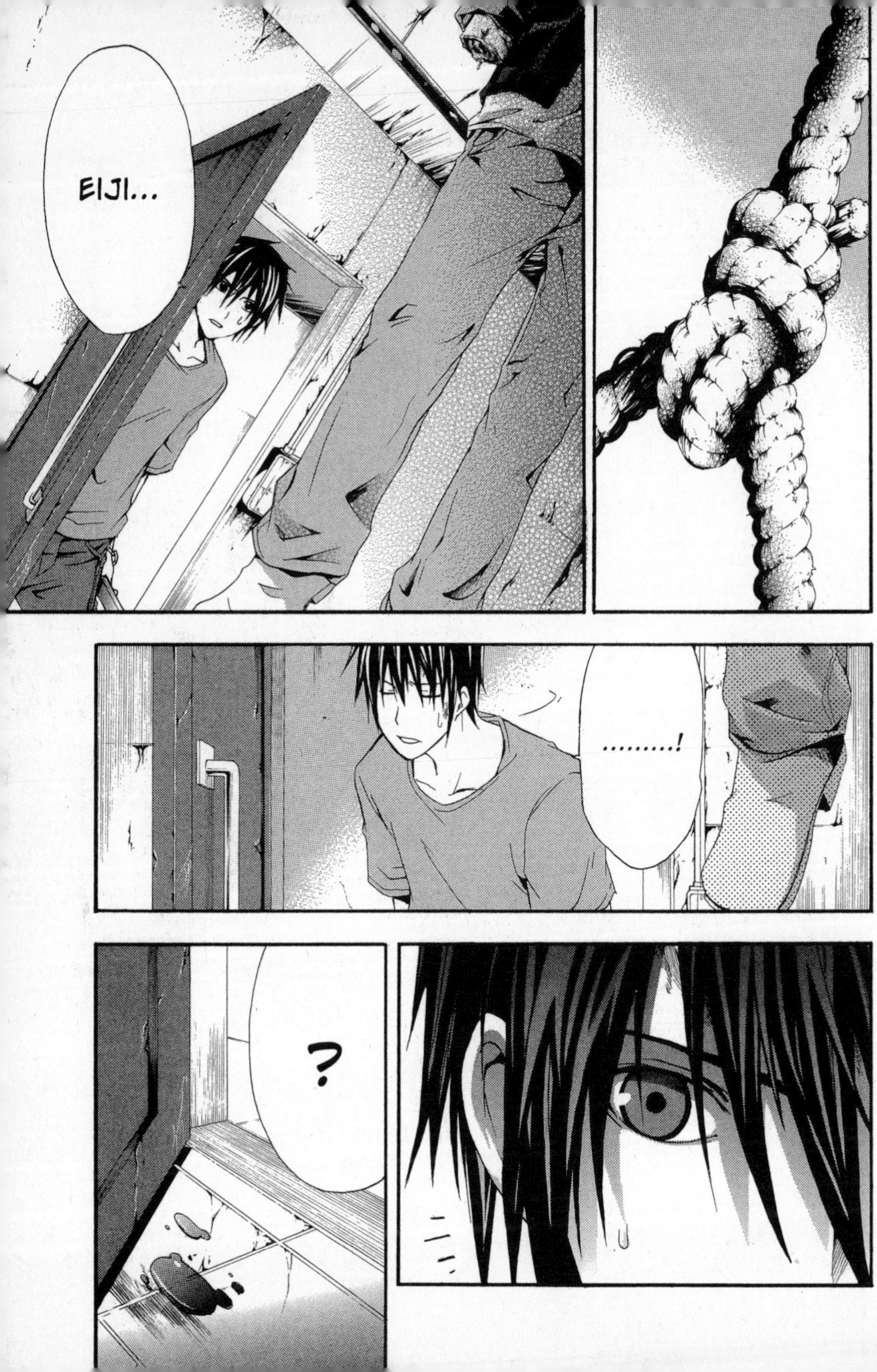
EIJI...
..........!
?

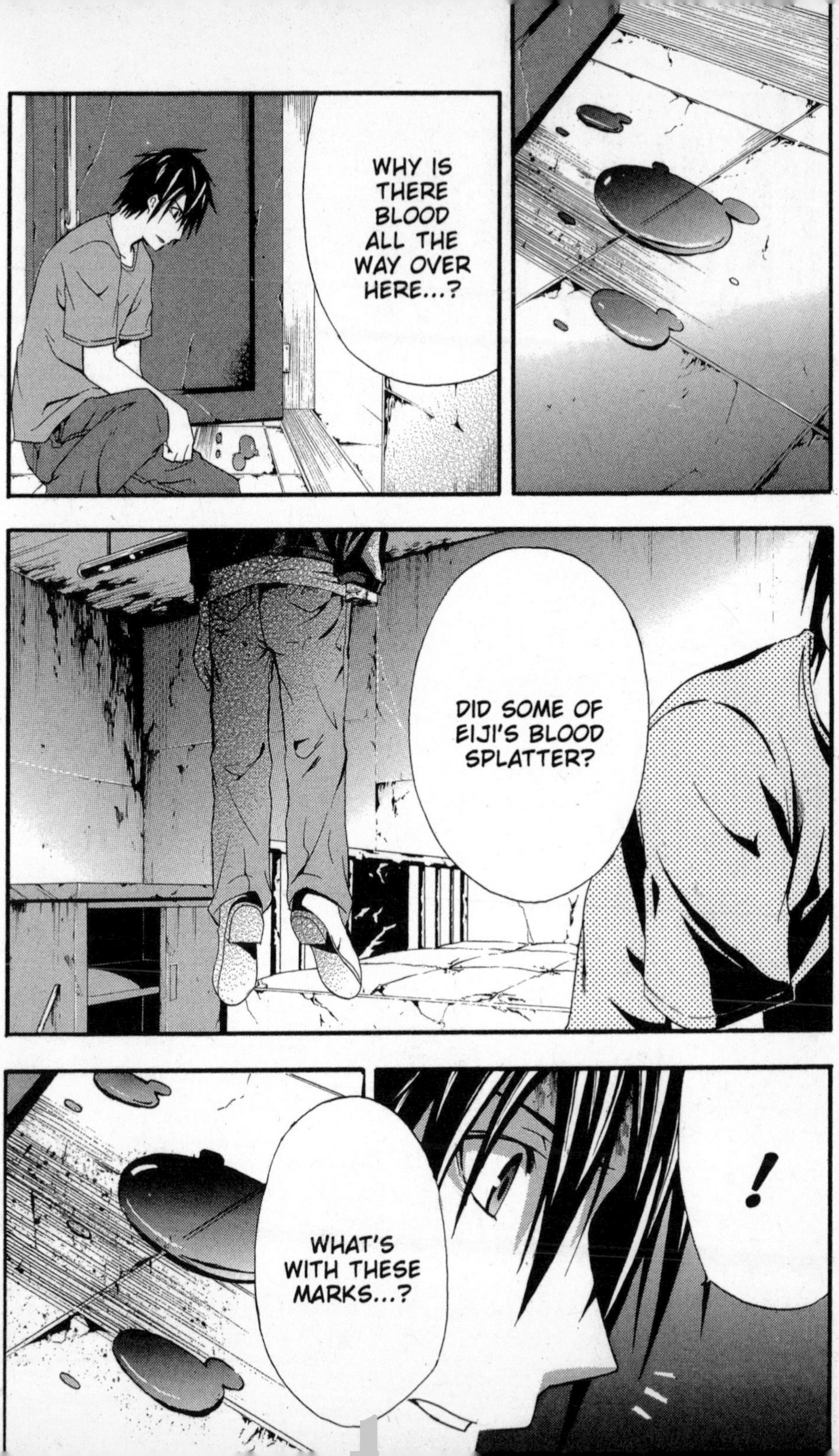
WHY IS THERE BLOOD ALL THE WAY OVER HERE...?
DID SOME OF EIJI'S BLOOD SPLATTER?
!
WHAT'S WITH THESE MARKS...?

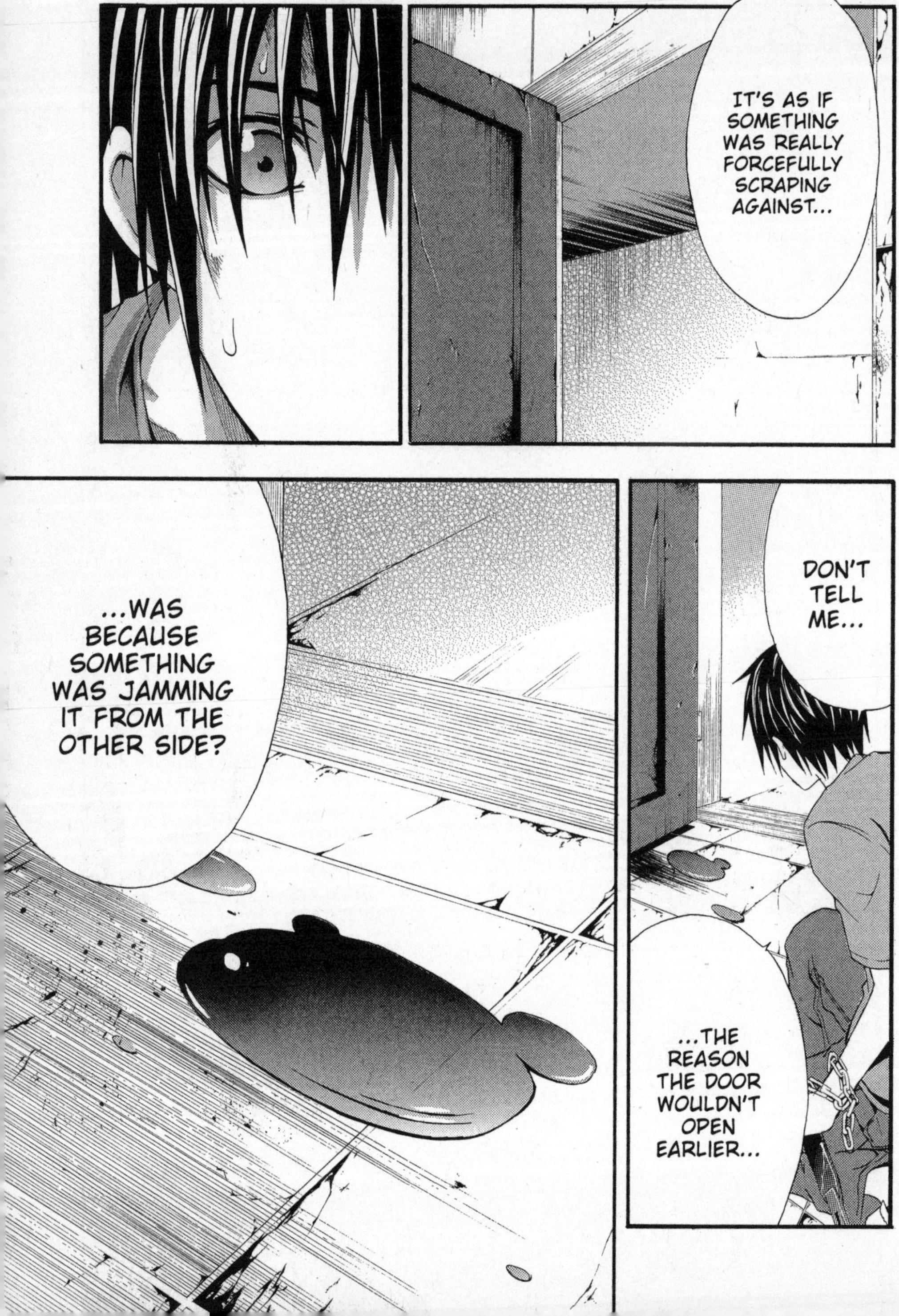
IT'S AS IF SOMETHING WAS REALLY FORCEFULLY SCRAPING AGAINST...
DON'T TELL ME...
...THE REASON THE DOOR WOULDN'T OPEN EARLIER...
...WAS BECAUSE SOMETHING WAS JAMMING IT FROM THE OTHER SIDE?

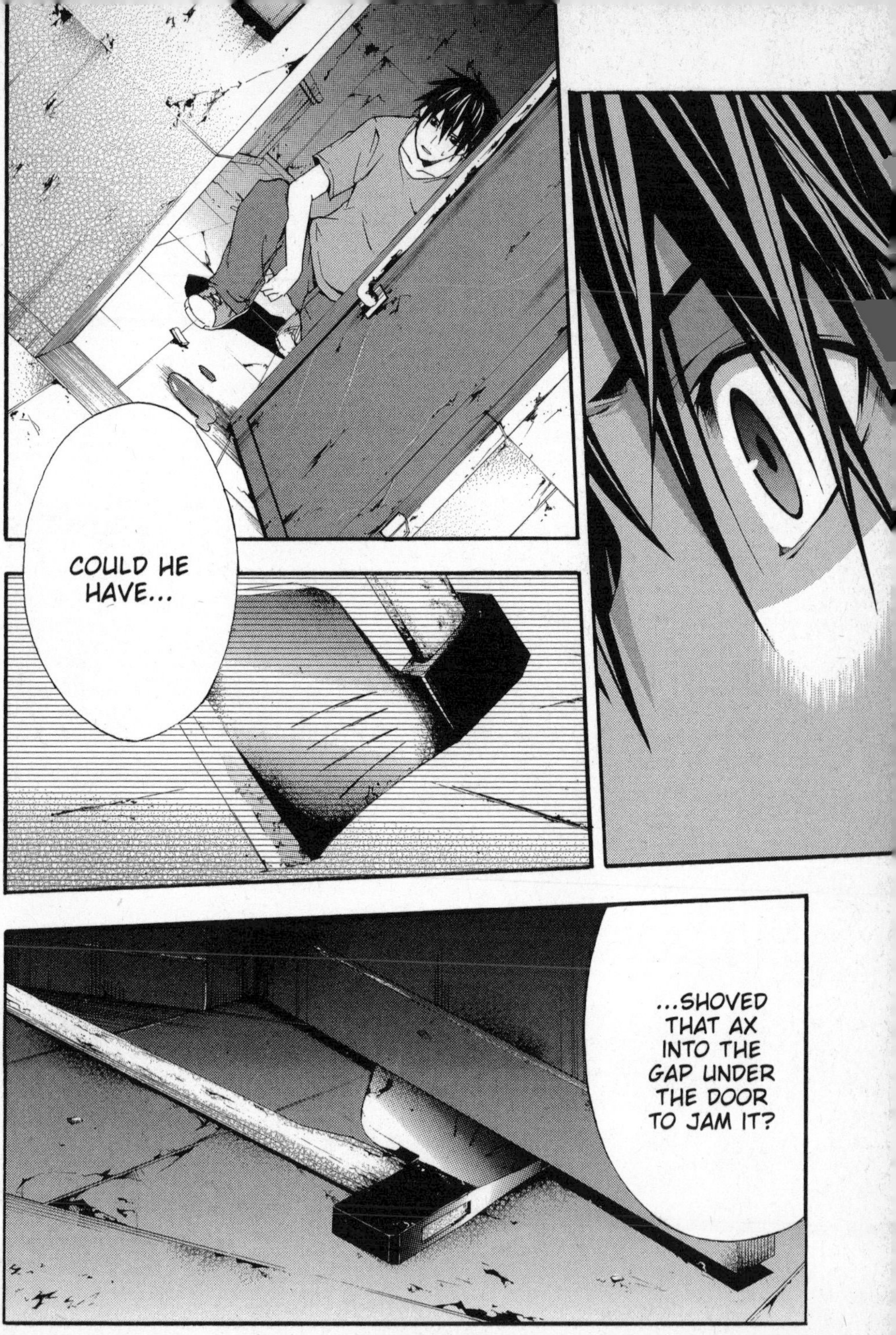
COULD HE HAVE...
...SHOVED THAT AX INTO THE GAP UNDER THE DOOR TO JAM IT?

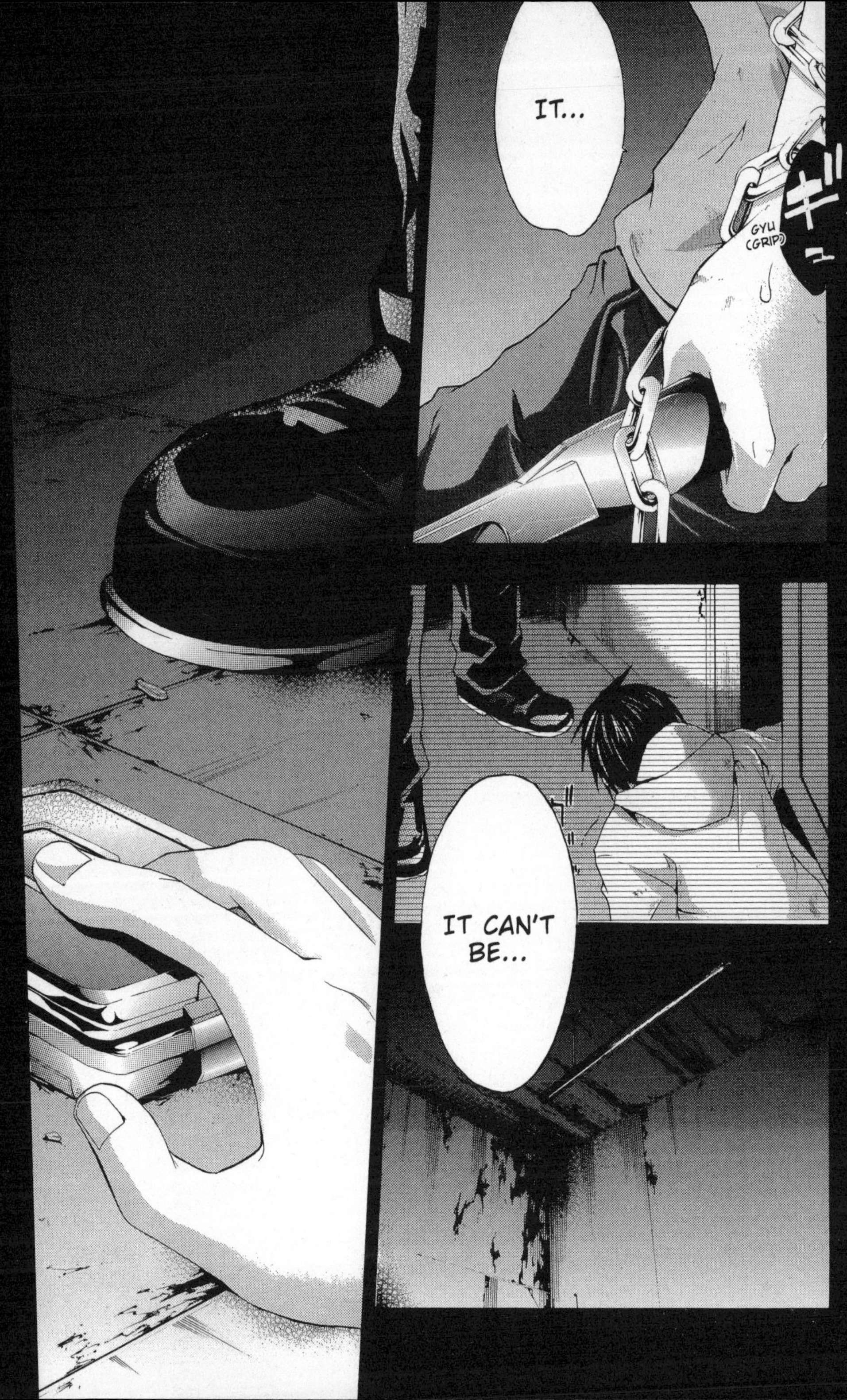
IT...
GYU
(GRIP)
IT CAN'T BE...

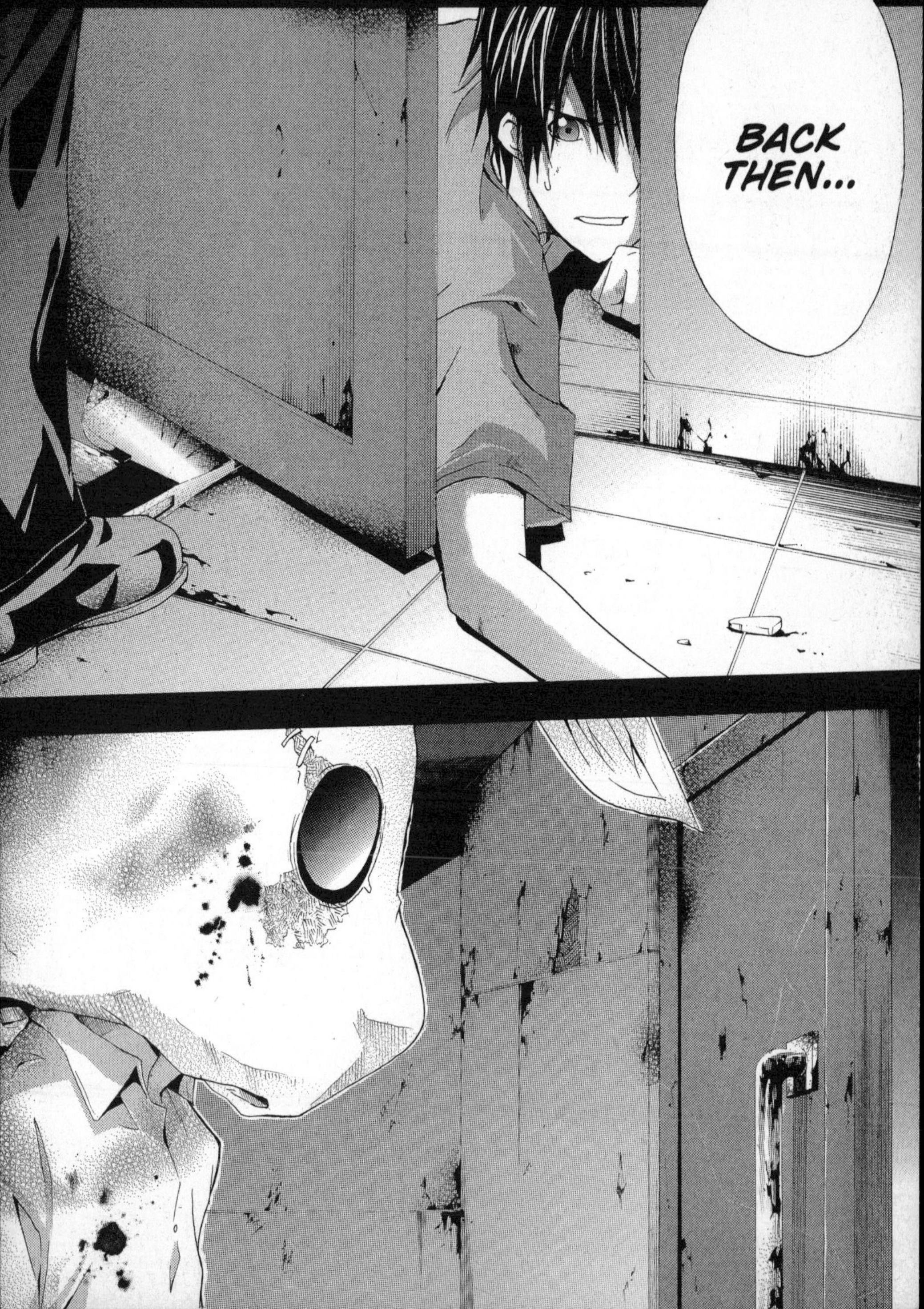
BACK THEN...

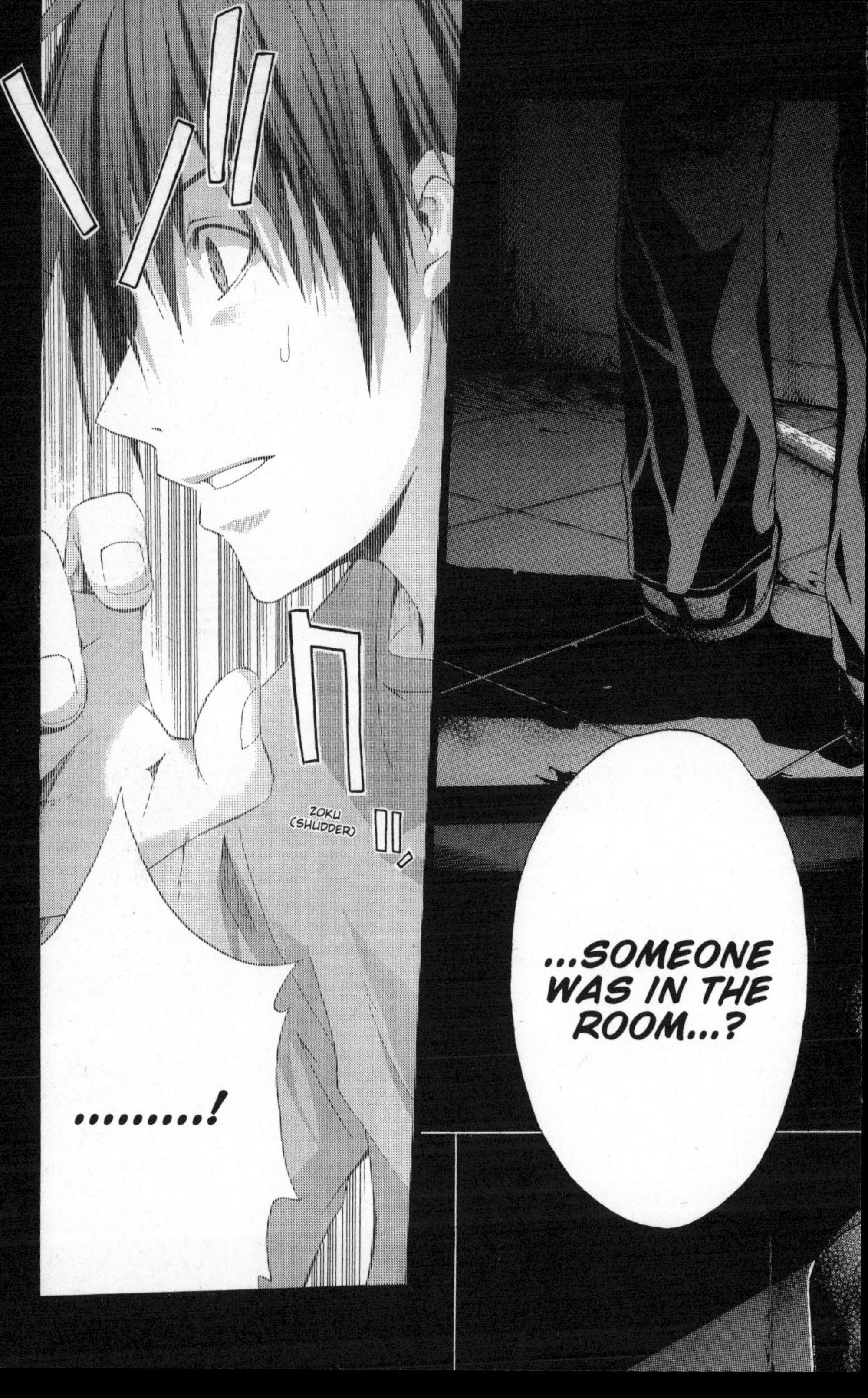
...SOMEONE WAS IN THE ROOM...?
ZOKU (SHUDDER)
.........!

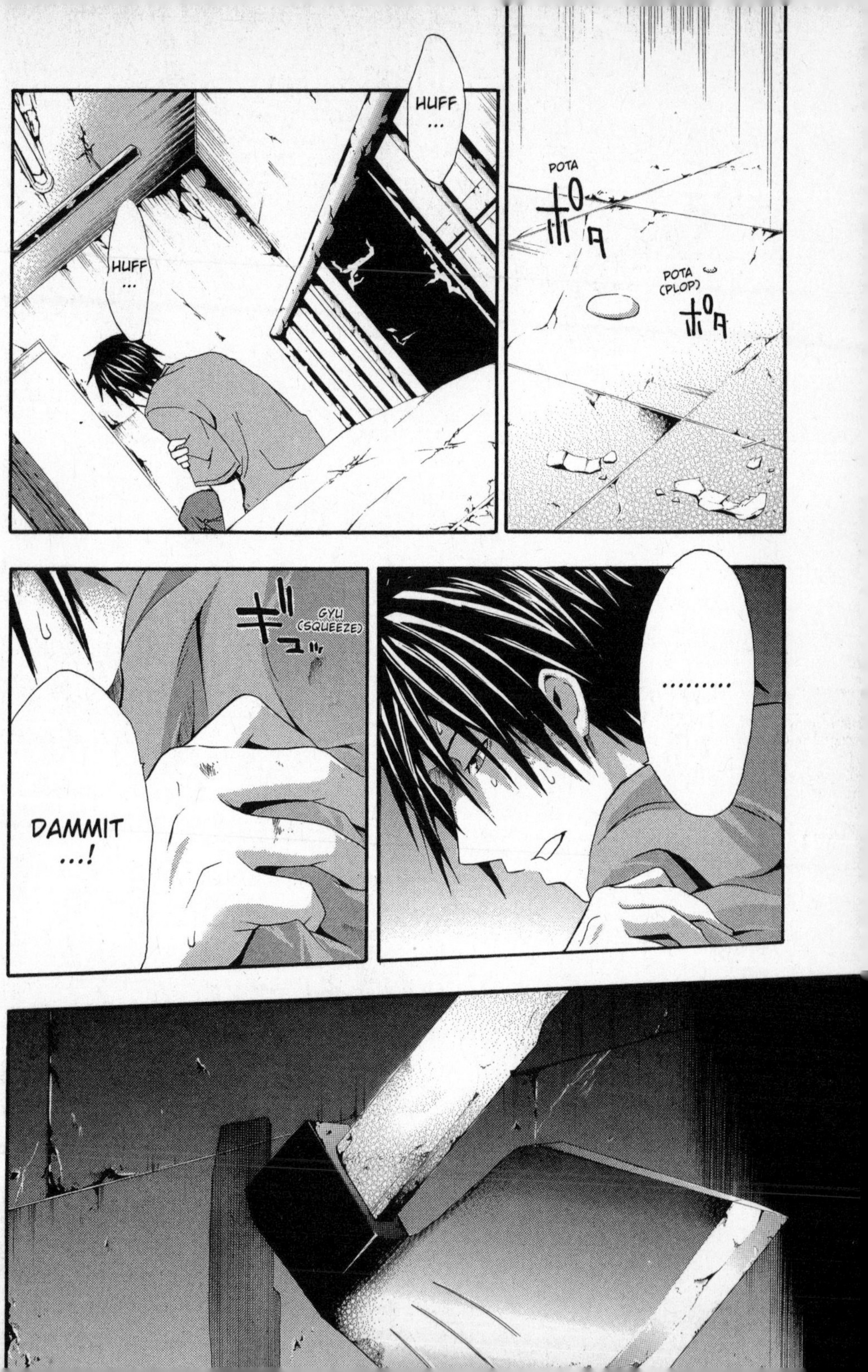
ポタ
POTA
ポタ
POTA
(PLOP)
HUFF
...
HUFF
...
....
ギュ
GYU
(SQUEEZE)
DAMMIT
...!

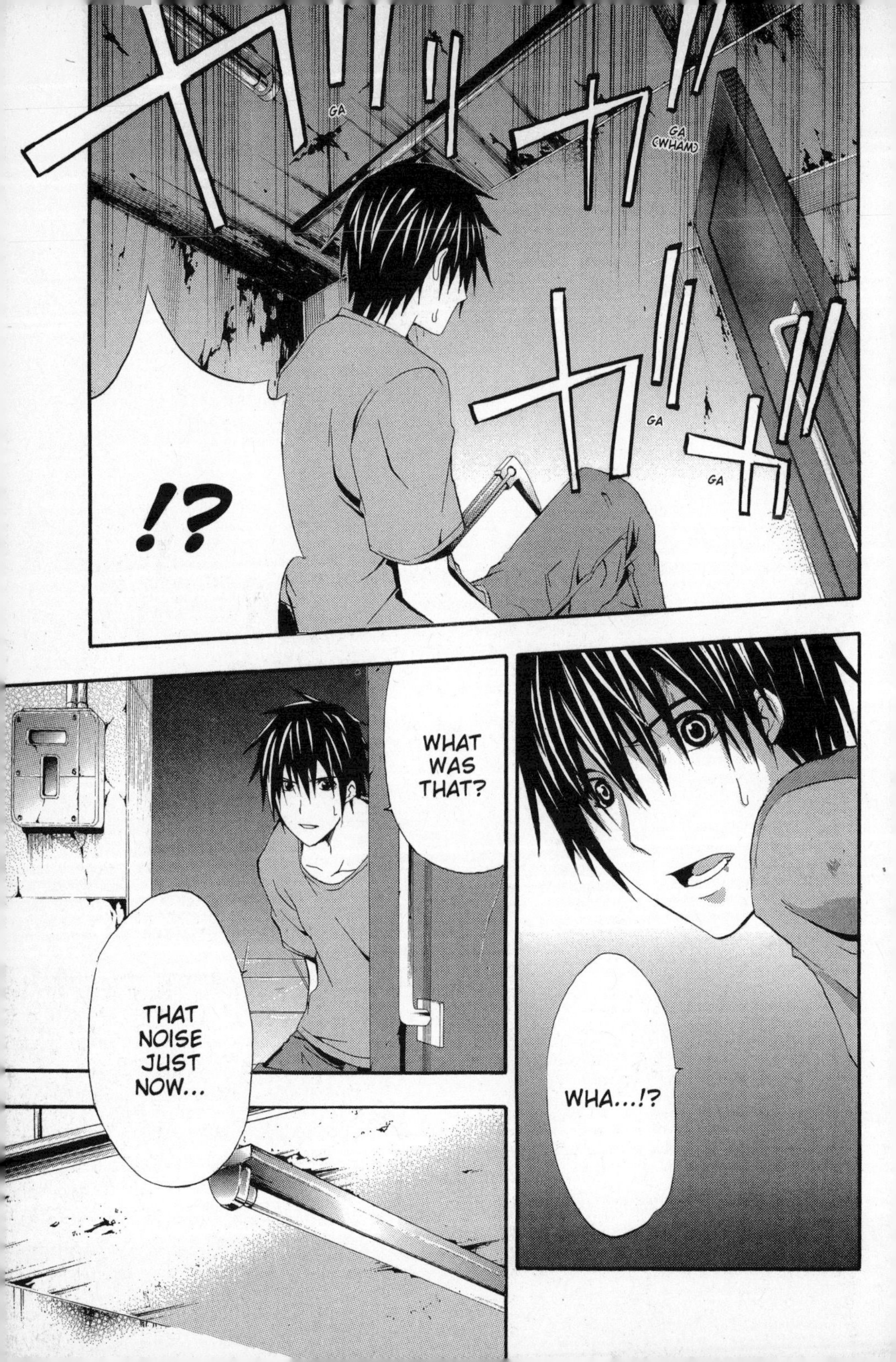
GA (WHAM)
GA
GA
GA
!?
WHA...!?
WHAT WAS THAT?
THAT NOISE JUST NOW...

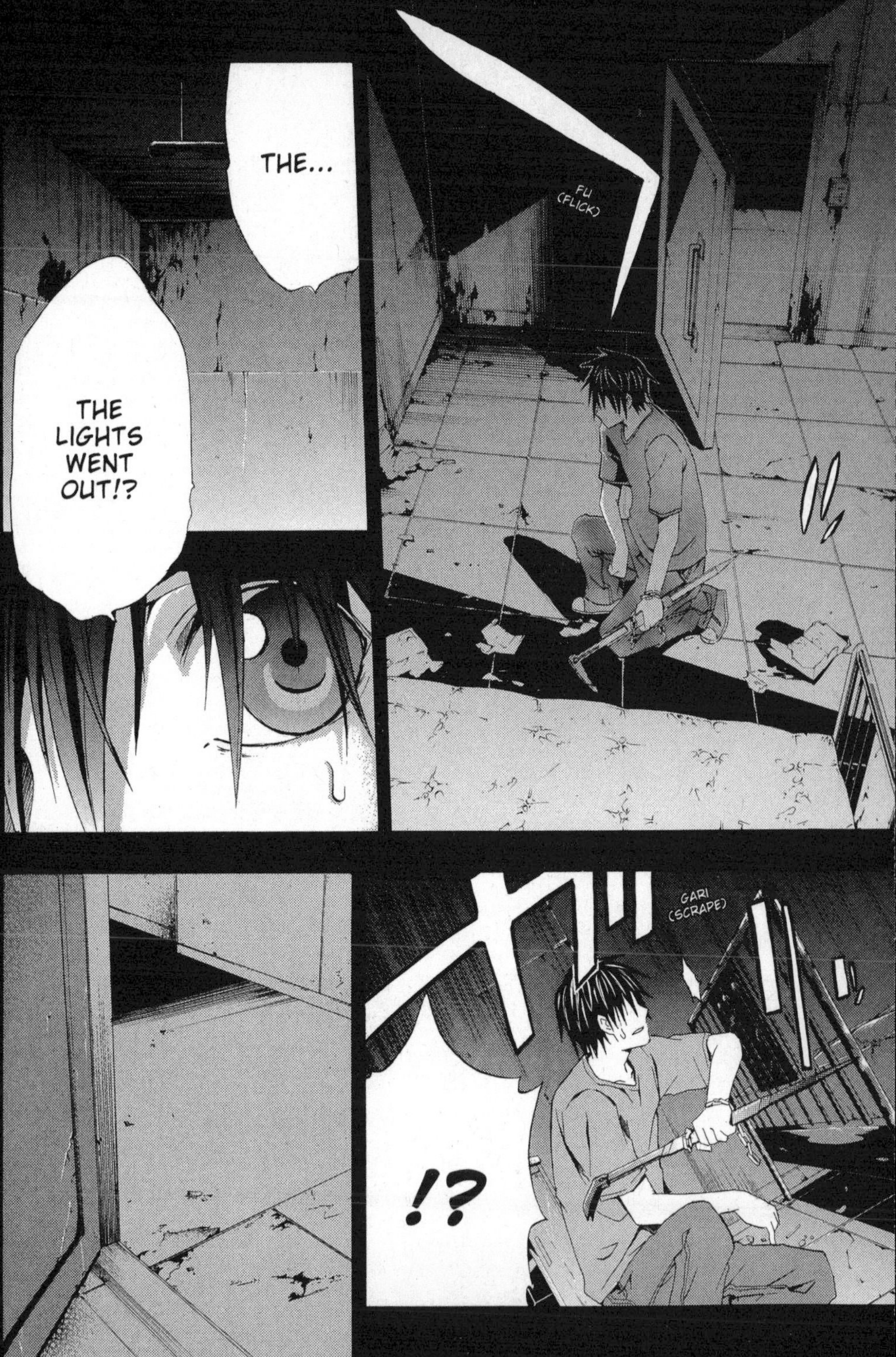
FU (FLICK)
THE...
THE LIGHTS WENT OUT!?
GARI (SCRAPE)
!?

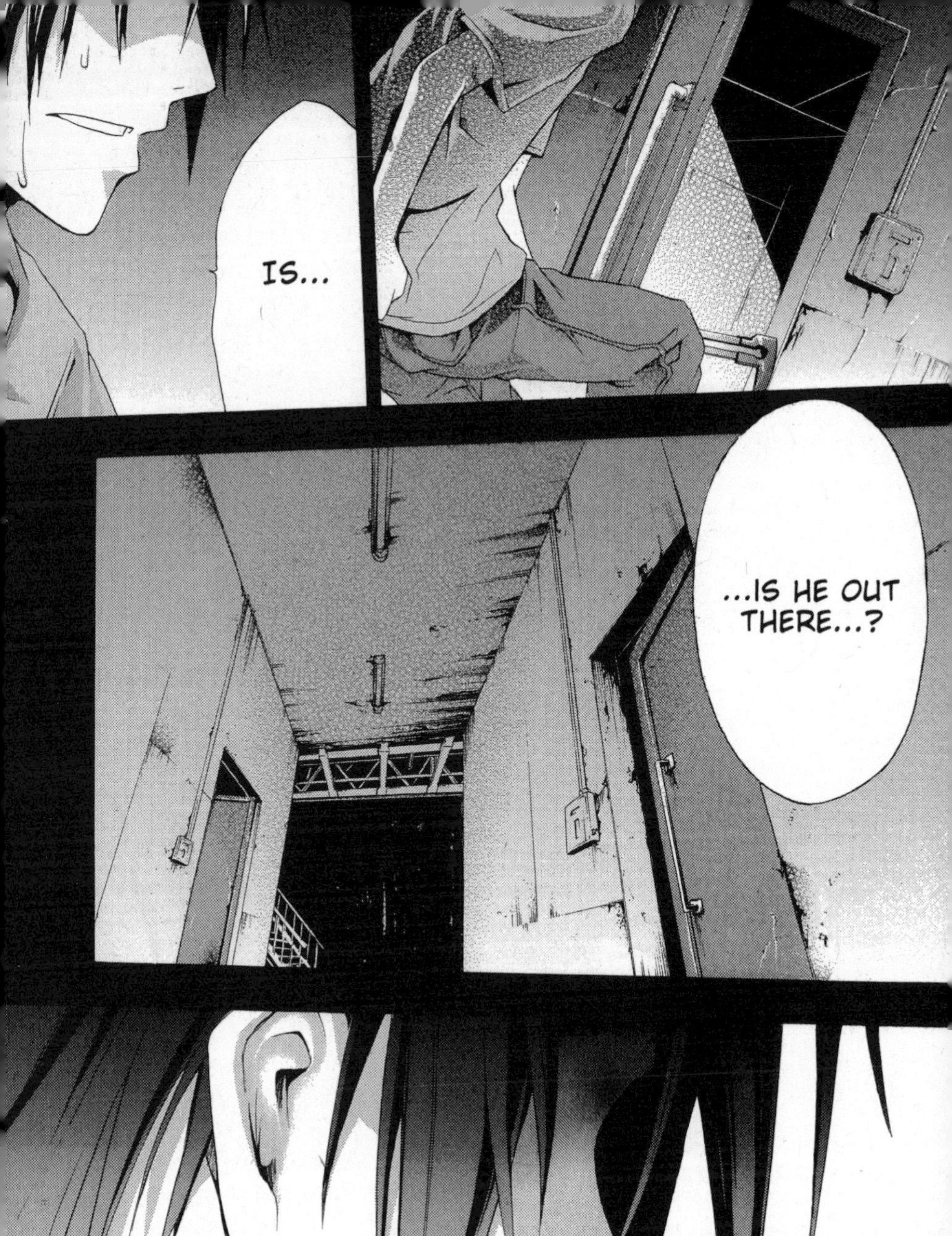
IS...
...IS HE OUT THERE...?

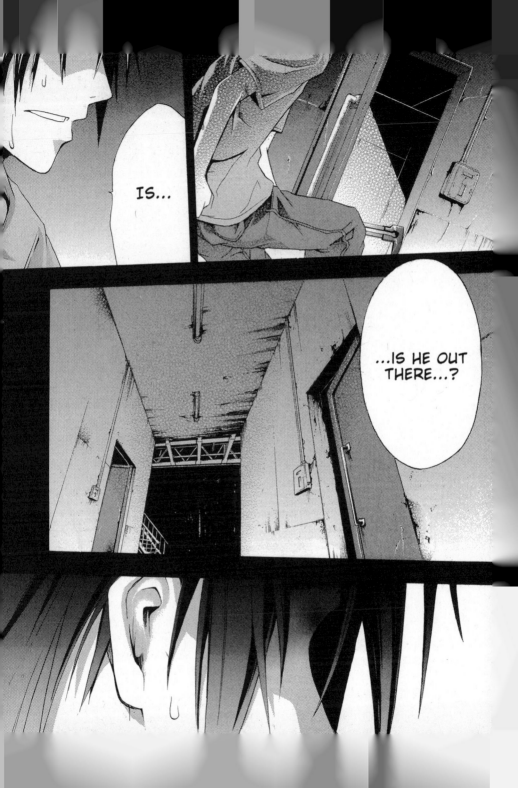

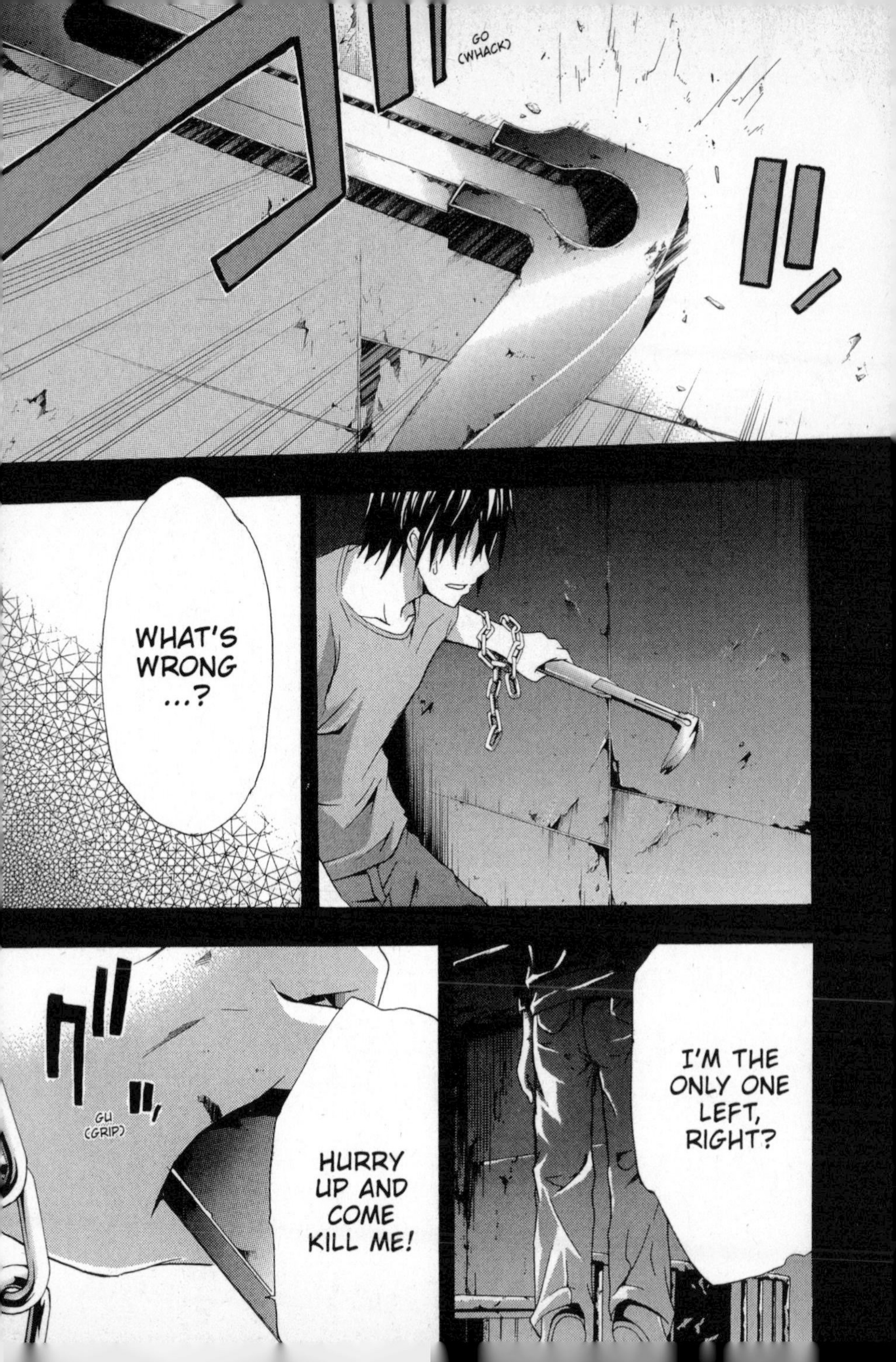
GO (WHACK)
WHAT'S WRONG ...?
I'M THE ONLY ONE LEFT, RIGHT?
GU (GRIP)
HURRY UP AND COME KILL ME!

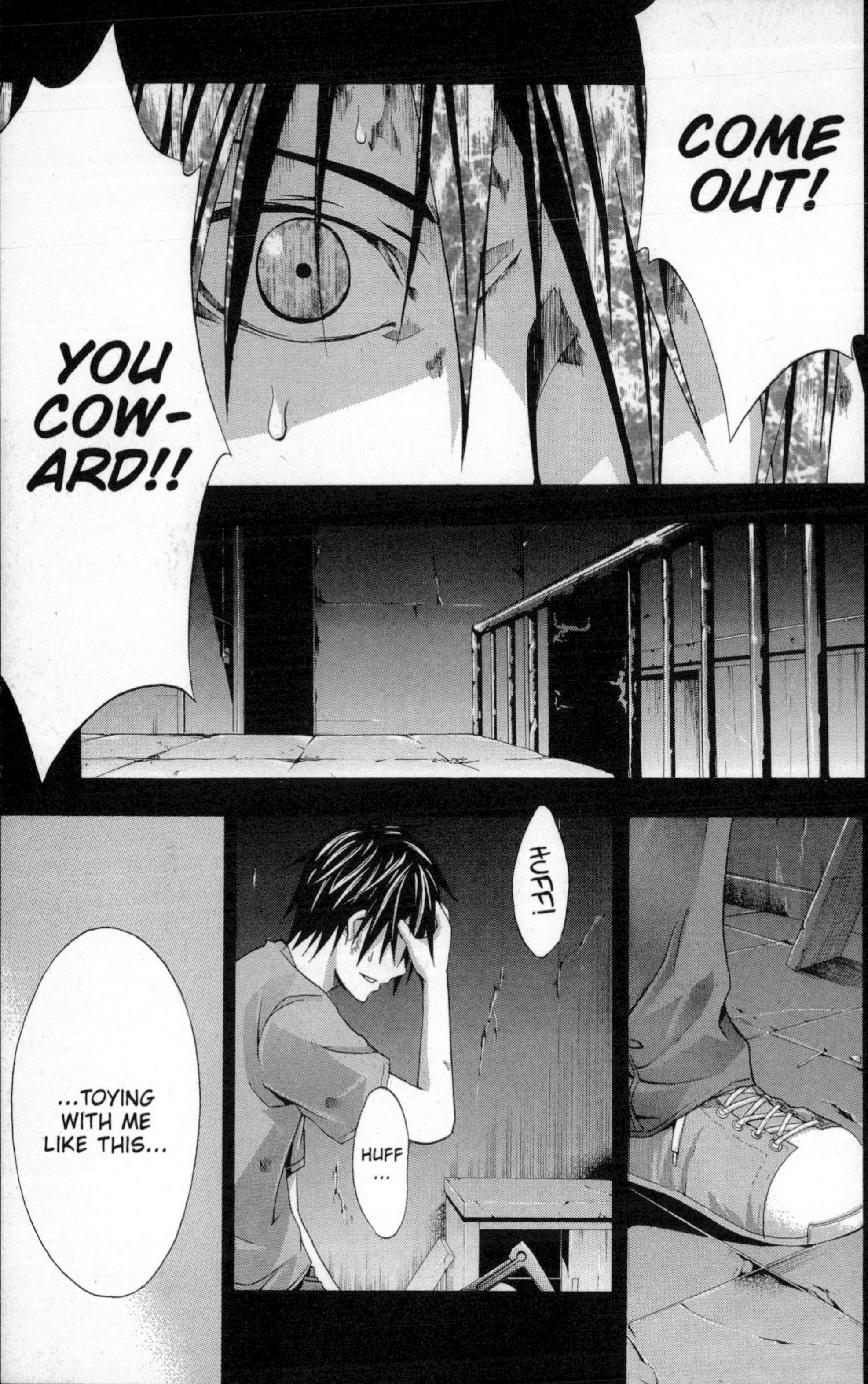
COME OUT!
YOU COW-ARD!!
HUFF!
HUFF ...
...TOYING WITH ME LIKE THIS...

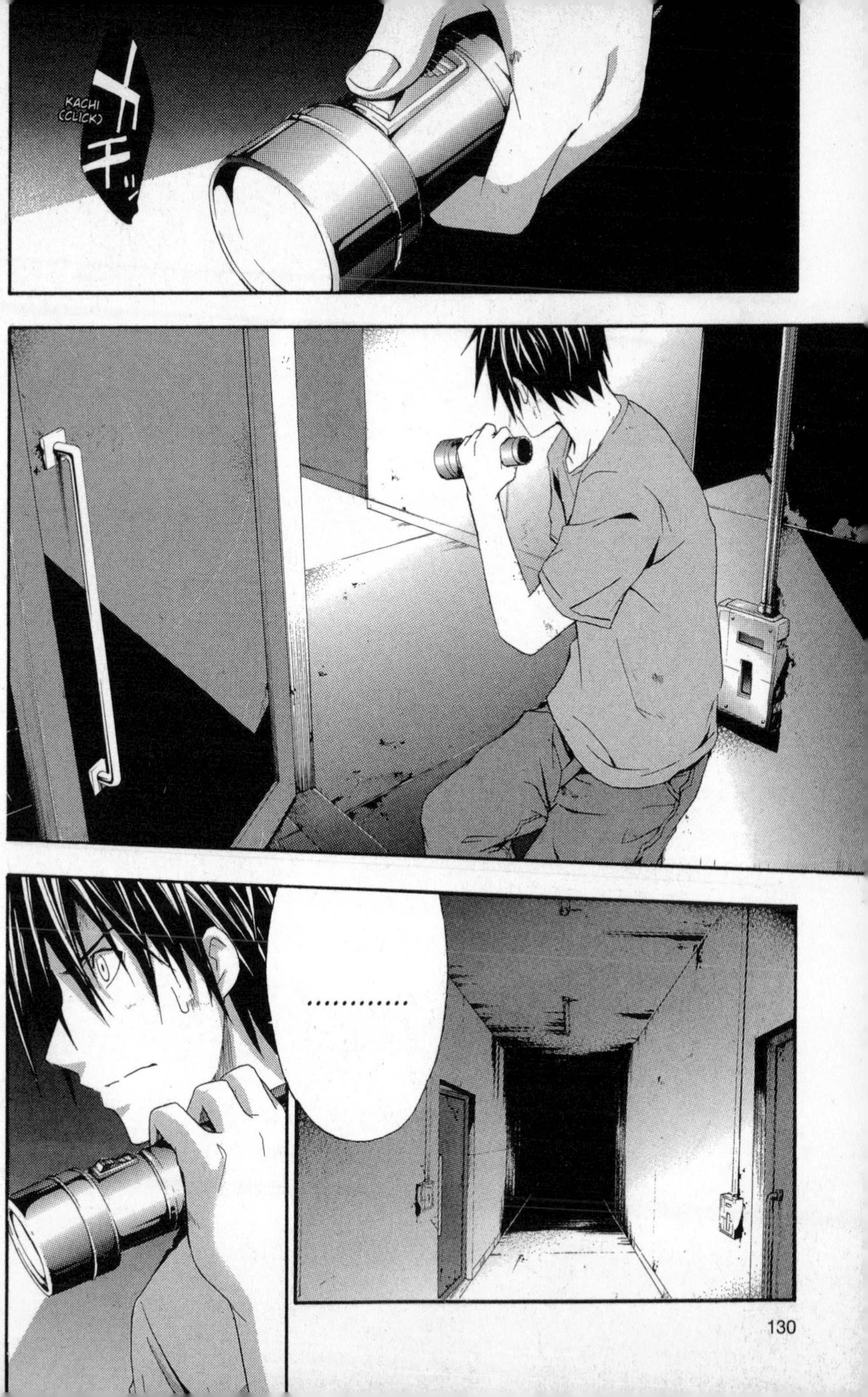
カチッ
KACHI (CLICK)
....

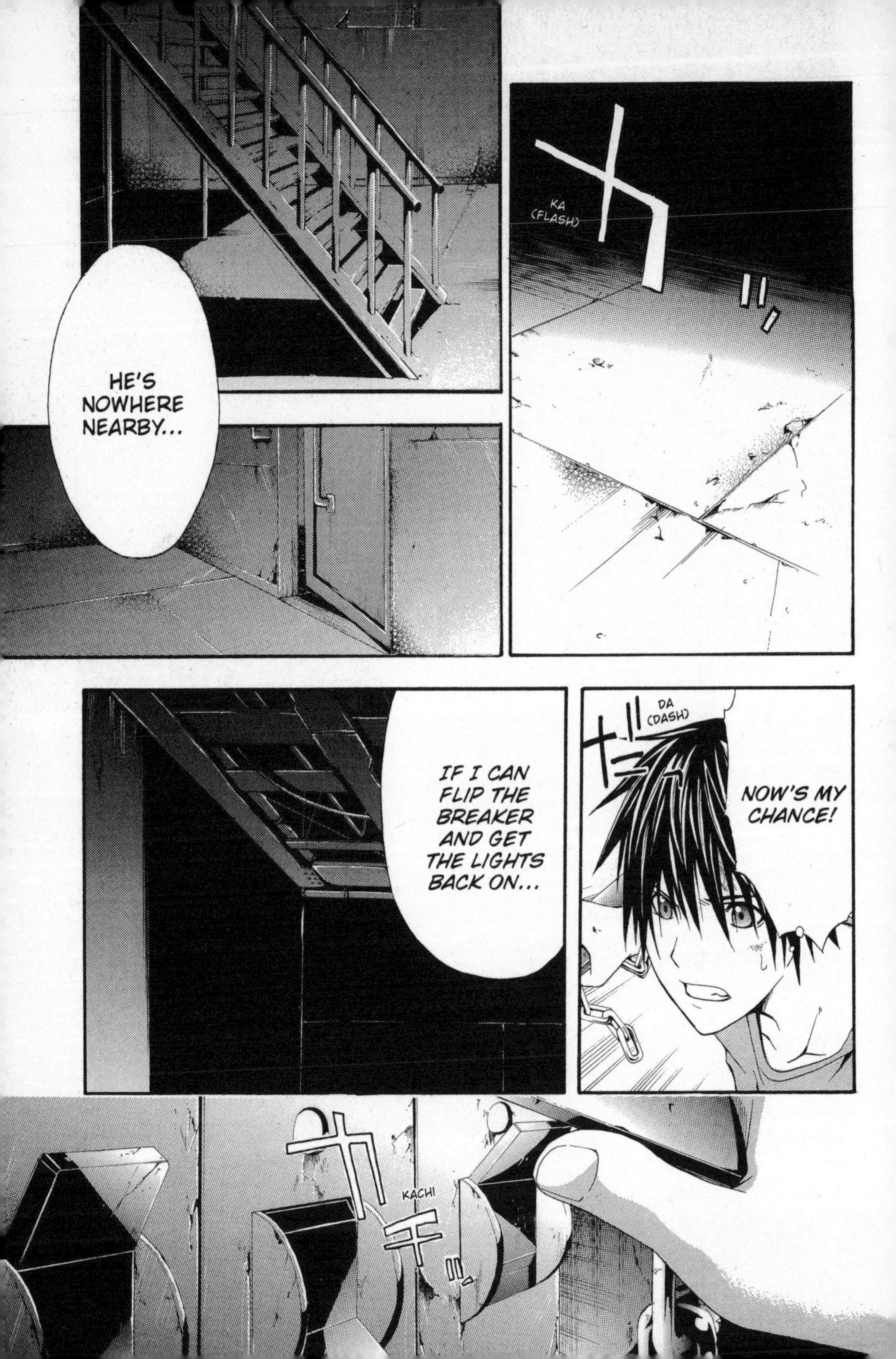
KA
(FLASH)
HE'S NOWHERE NEARBY...
DA
(DASH)
NOW'S MY CHANCE!
IF I CAN FLIP THE BREAKER AND GET THE LIGHTS BACK ON...
KACHI

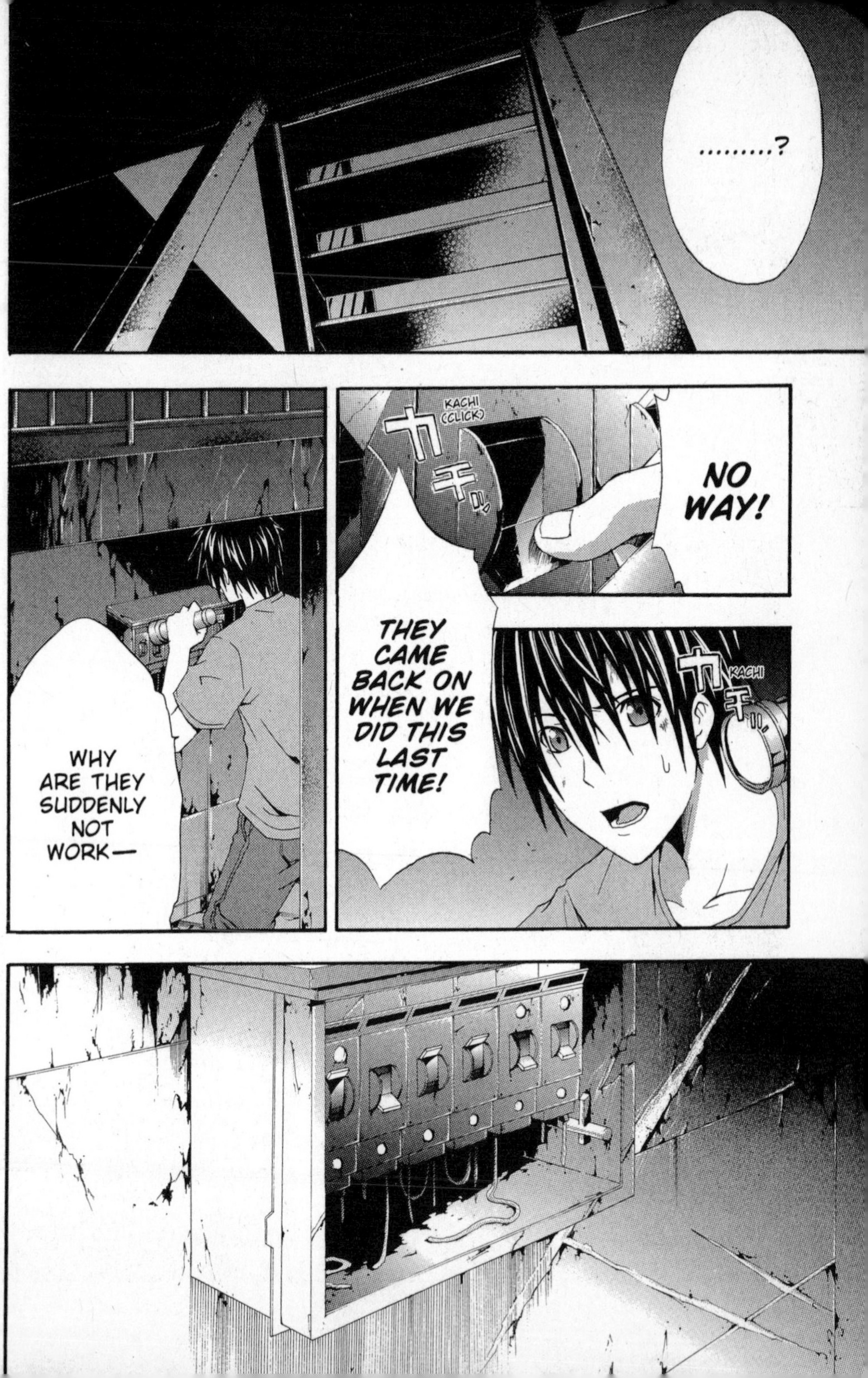
........?
KACHI (CLICK)
NO WAY!
KACHI
THEY CAME BACK ON WHEN WE DID THIS LAST TIME!
WHY ARE THEY SUDDENLY NOT WORK—

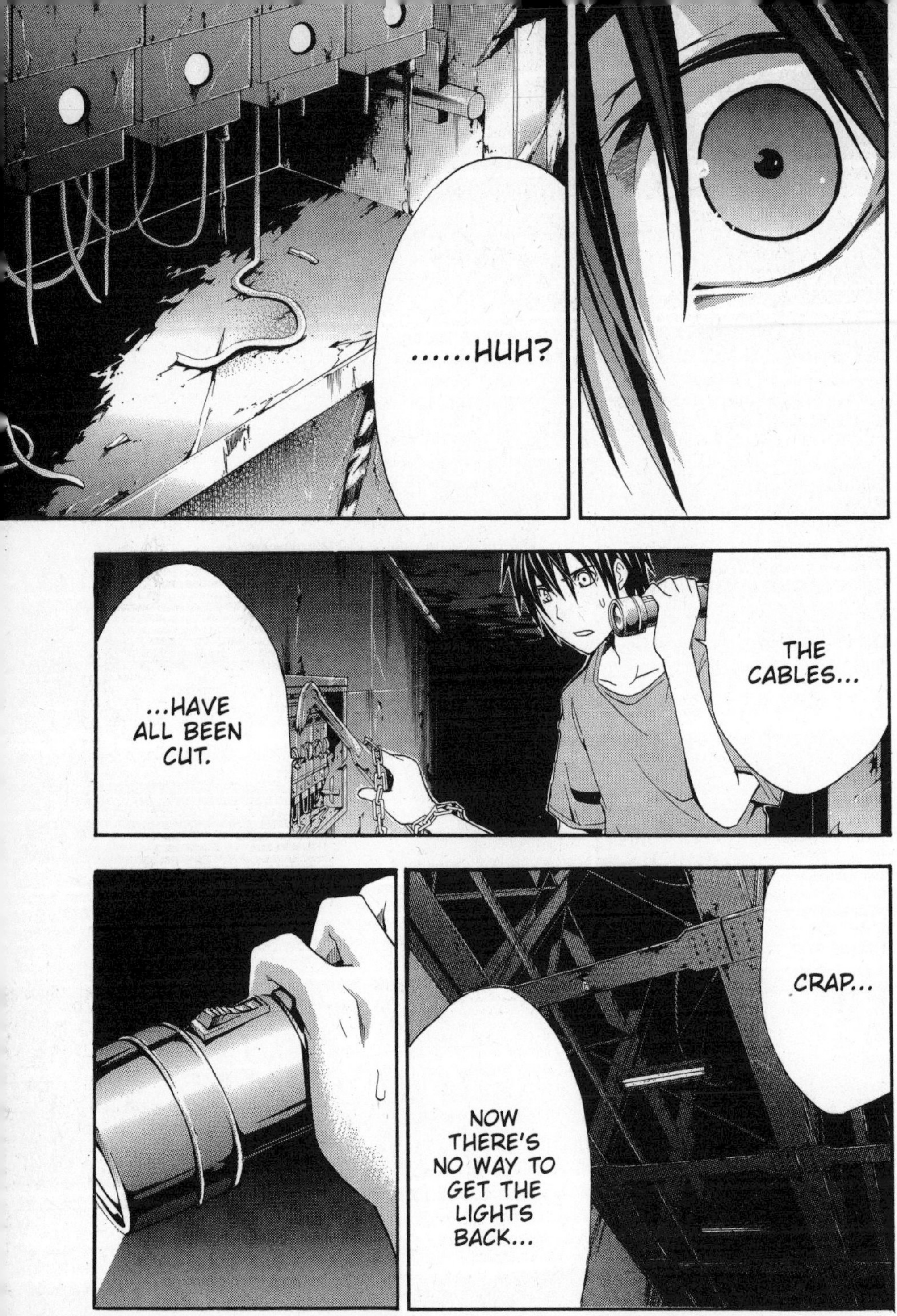
......HUH?
THE CABLES...
...HAVE ALL BEEN CUT.
CRAP...
NOW THERE'S NO WAY TO GET THE LIGHTS BACK...

BIKU
(FLINCH)

WHY GO OUT OF YOUR WAY...DOING SOMETHING LIKE THIS...?

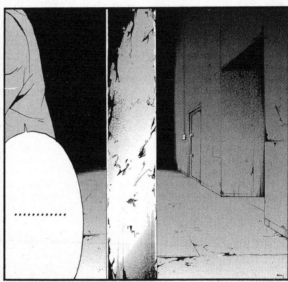

....

ARE YOU HIDING SOMEWHERE?

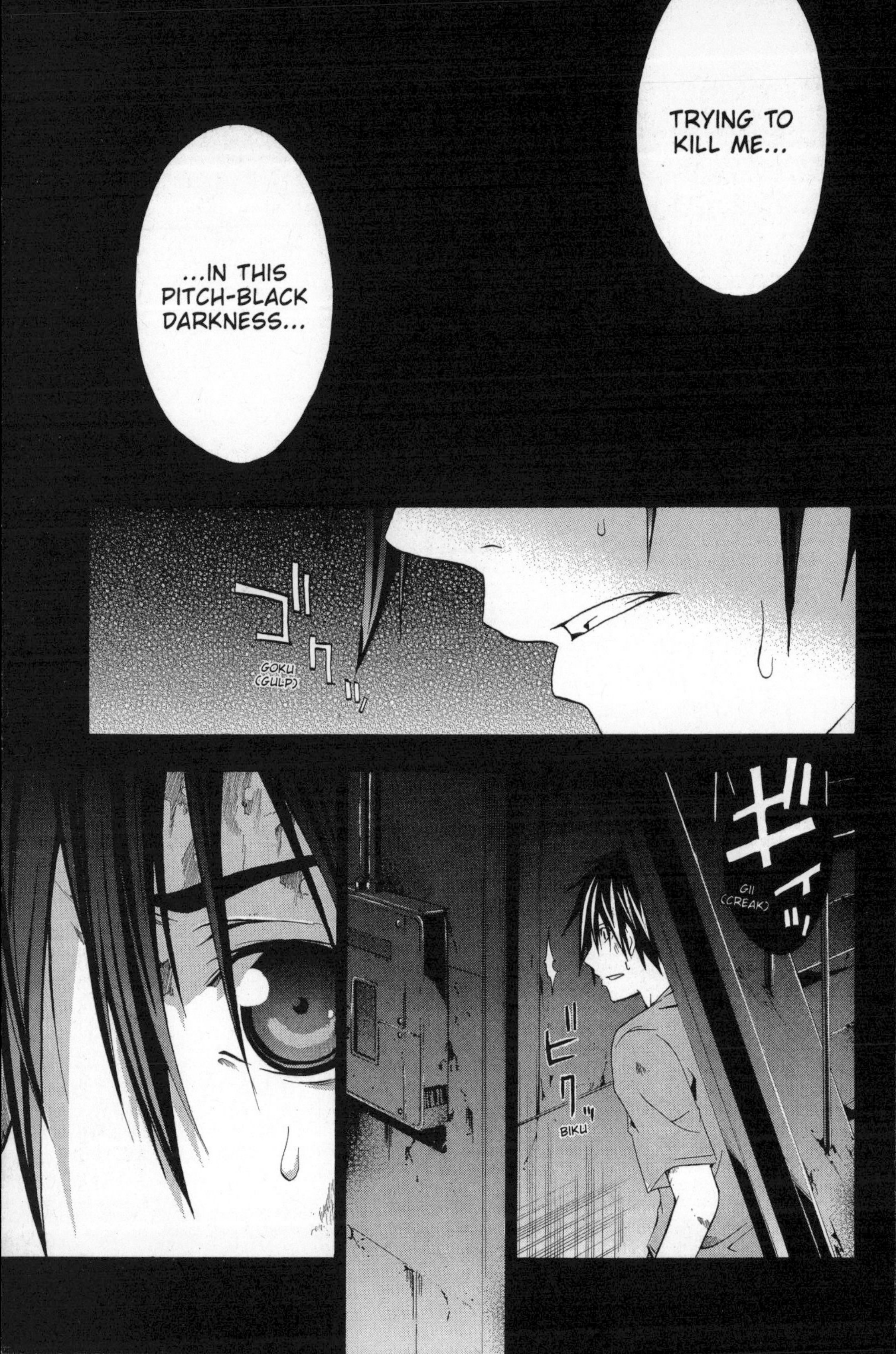
TRYING TO KILL ME...
...IN THIS PITCH-BLACK DARKNESS...
GOKU (GULP)
GII (CREAK)
BIKU

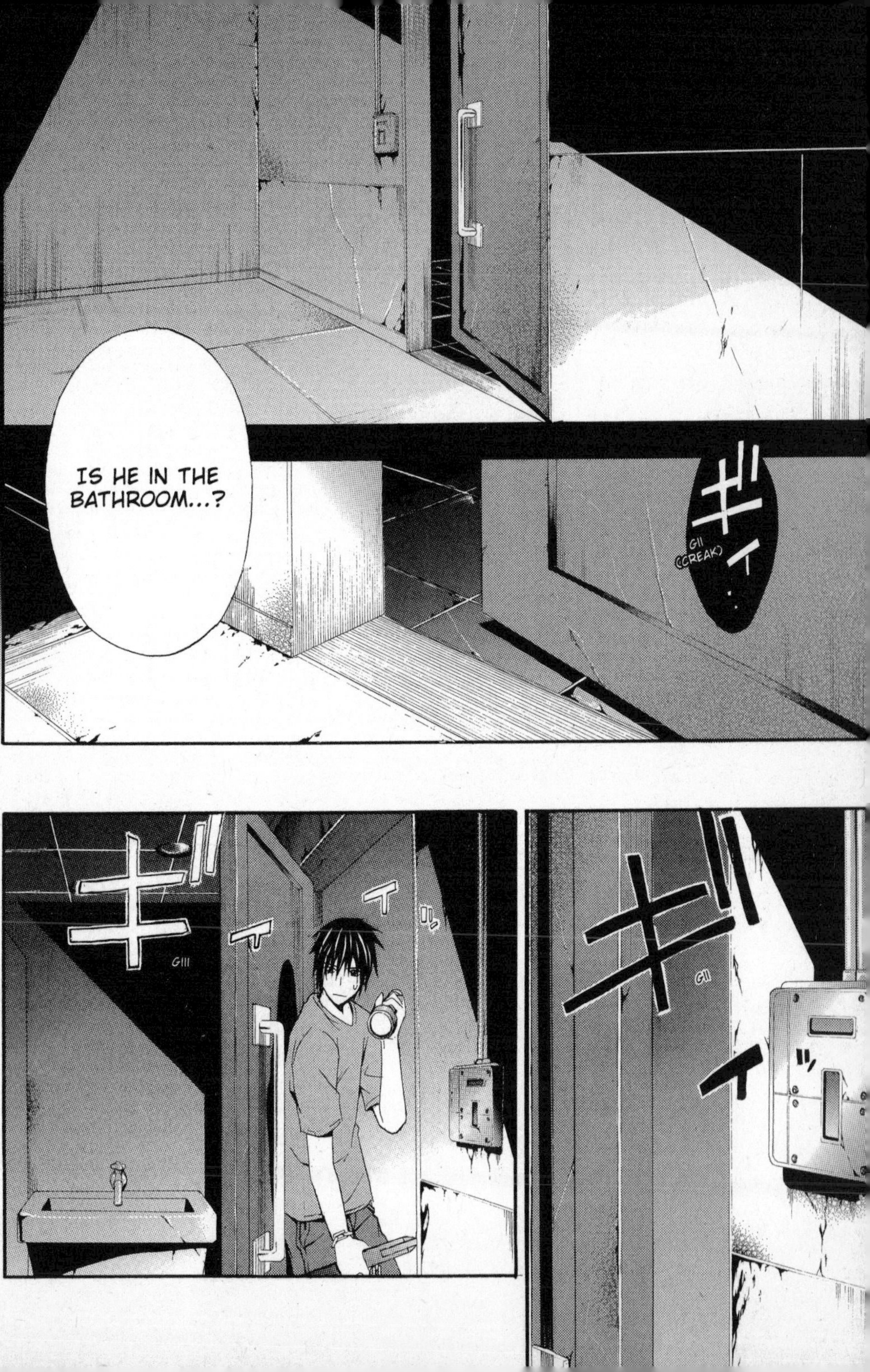
IS HE IN THE BATHROOM...?
GII (CREAK)
GII
GIII

HE'S NOT HERE...

HE MUST BE IN ONE OF THE STALLS!

...NO!

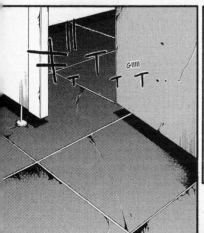

GIIIII
TT...

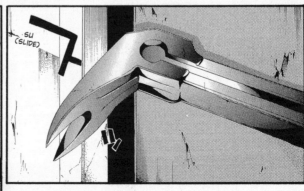

·SU
(SLIDE)

WHICH JUST LEAVES...

...NOT HERE.

HUFF!

HUFF!

SHIT!

AT A TIME LIKE THIS!

GATA

GATA (SHAKE)

!?

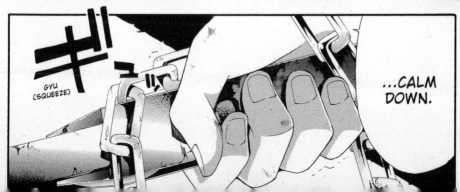

GYU (SQUEEZE)

...CALM DOWN.

HE'S...

...IN THERE...

DA
(DASH)

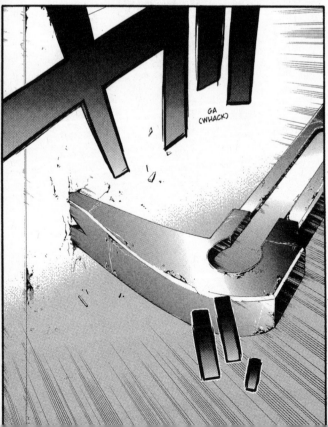

GA
(WHACK)

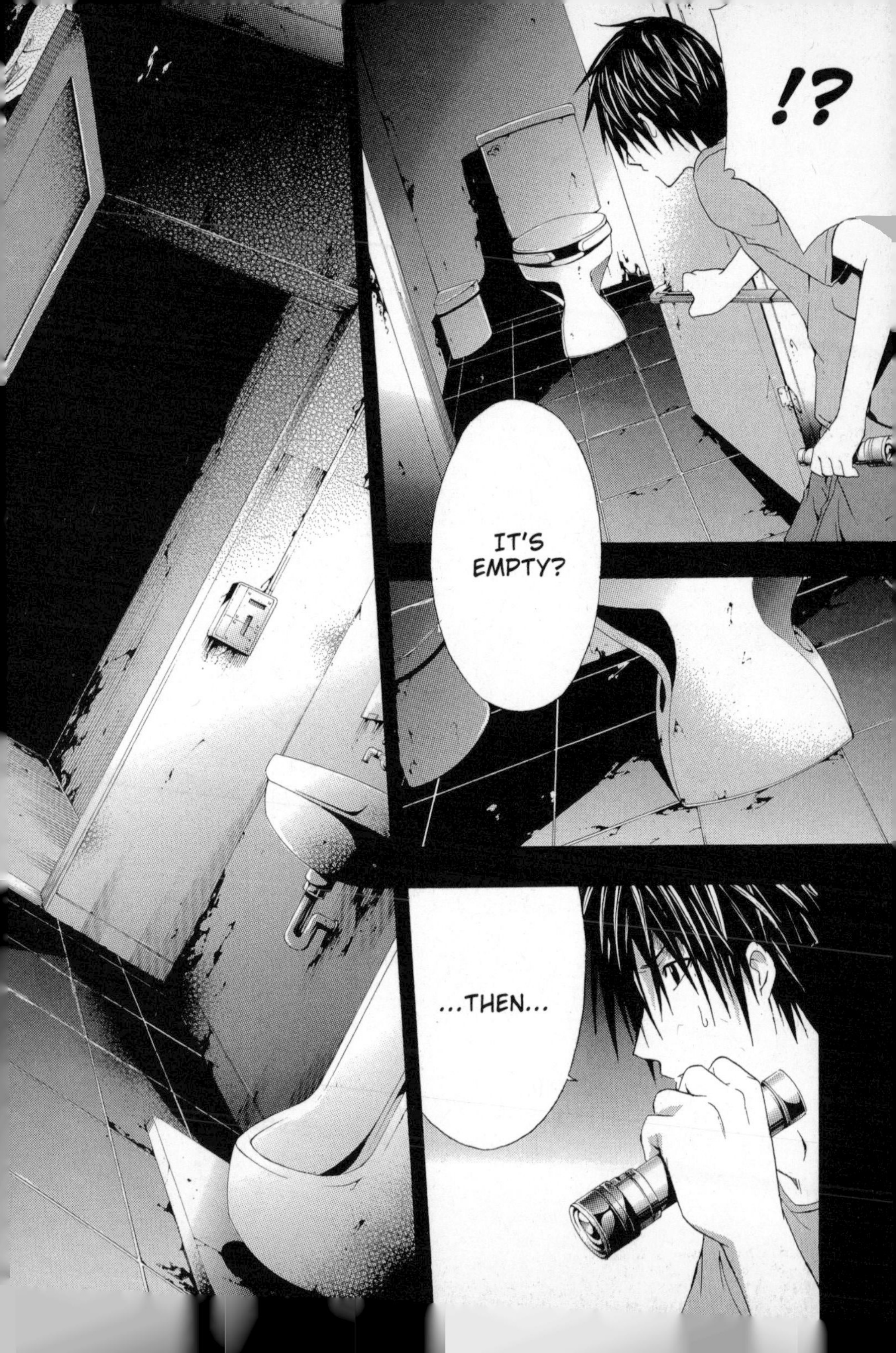
!?
IT'S EMPTY?
...THEN...

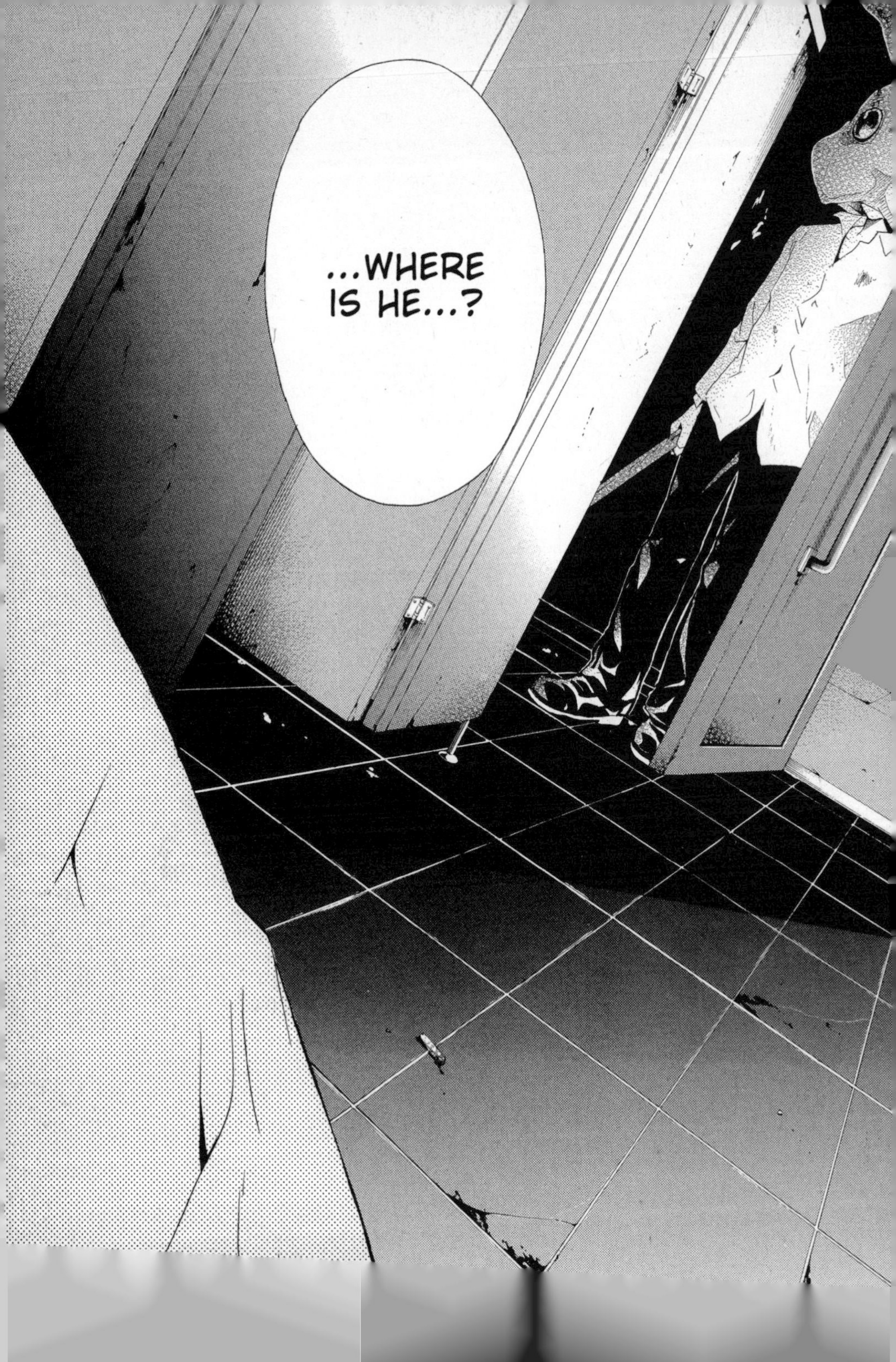
...WHERE IS HE...?

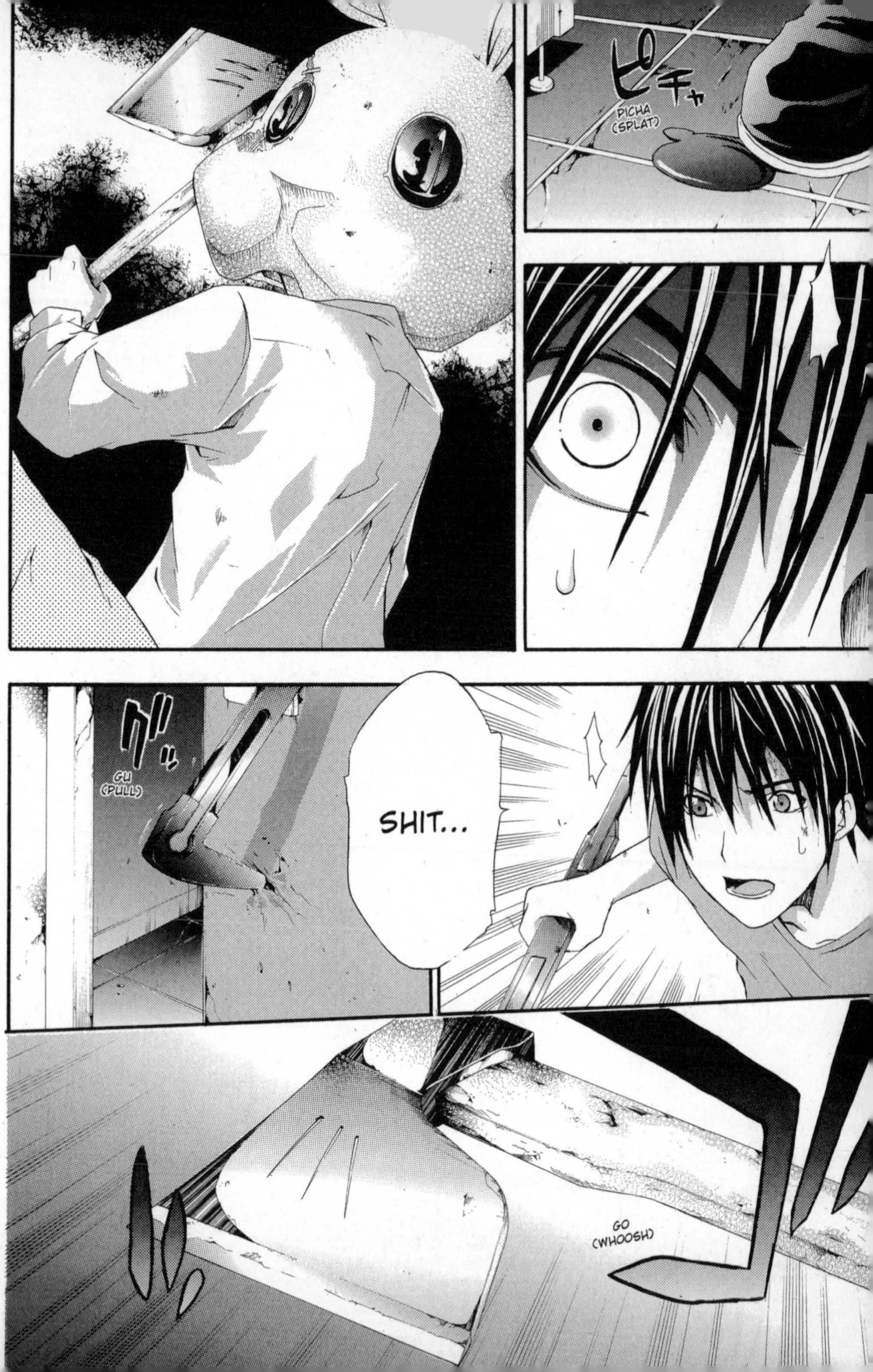
ピチャ
PICHA (SPLAT)
SHIT...
グッ
GU (PULL)
GO (WHOOSH)

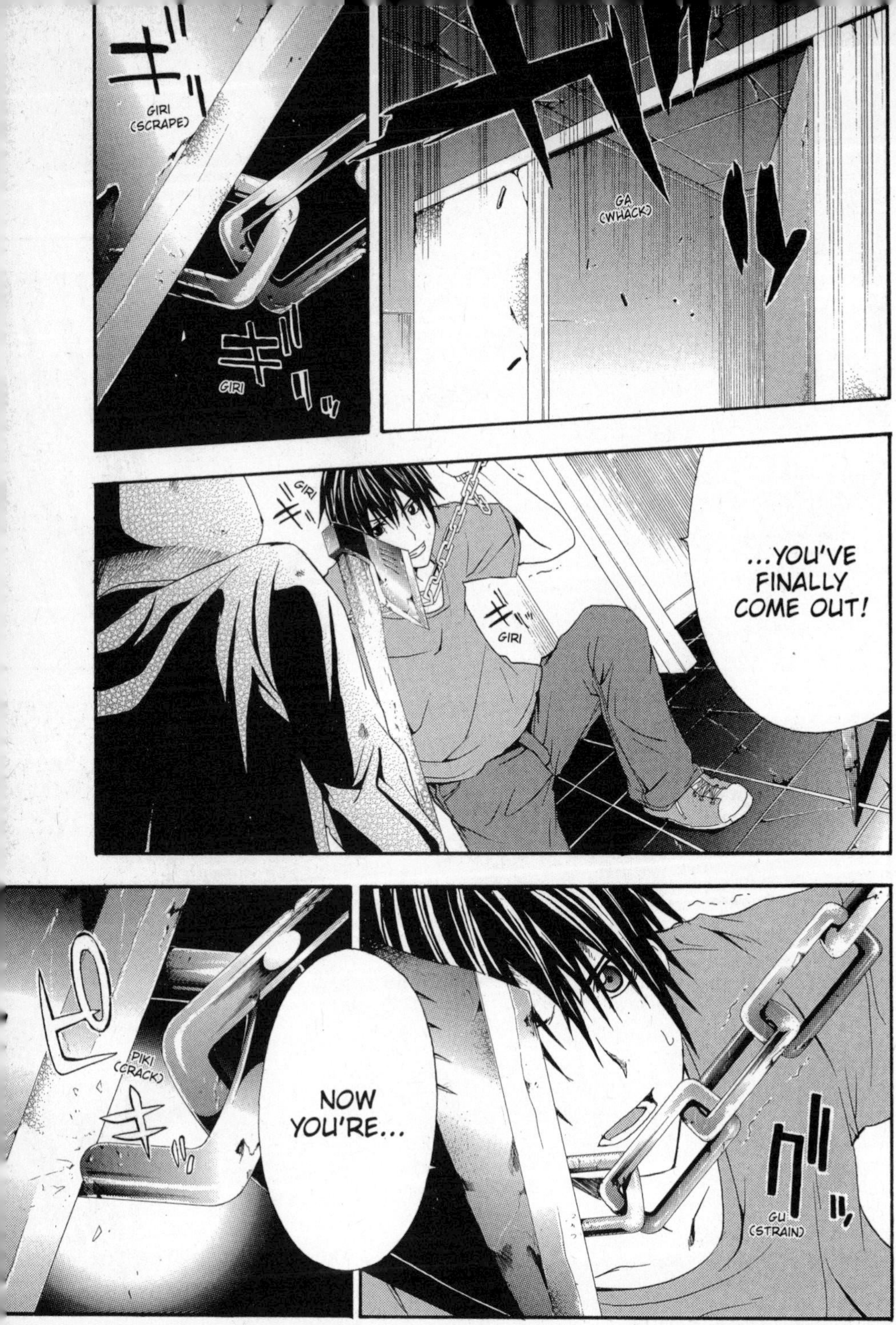
GA (WHACK)
GIRI (SCRAPE)
GIRI
...YOU'VE FINALLY COME OUT!
GIRI
GIRI
GU (STRAIN)
NOW YOU'RE...
PIKI (CRACK)

GA
(WHACK)

!!

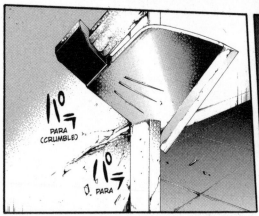

パラ
PARA
(CRUMBLE)

パラ
PARA

KUH
...!

YORO
(WOBBLE)

ヨロ

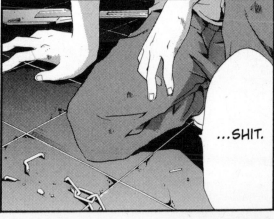

...SHIT.

144

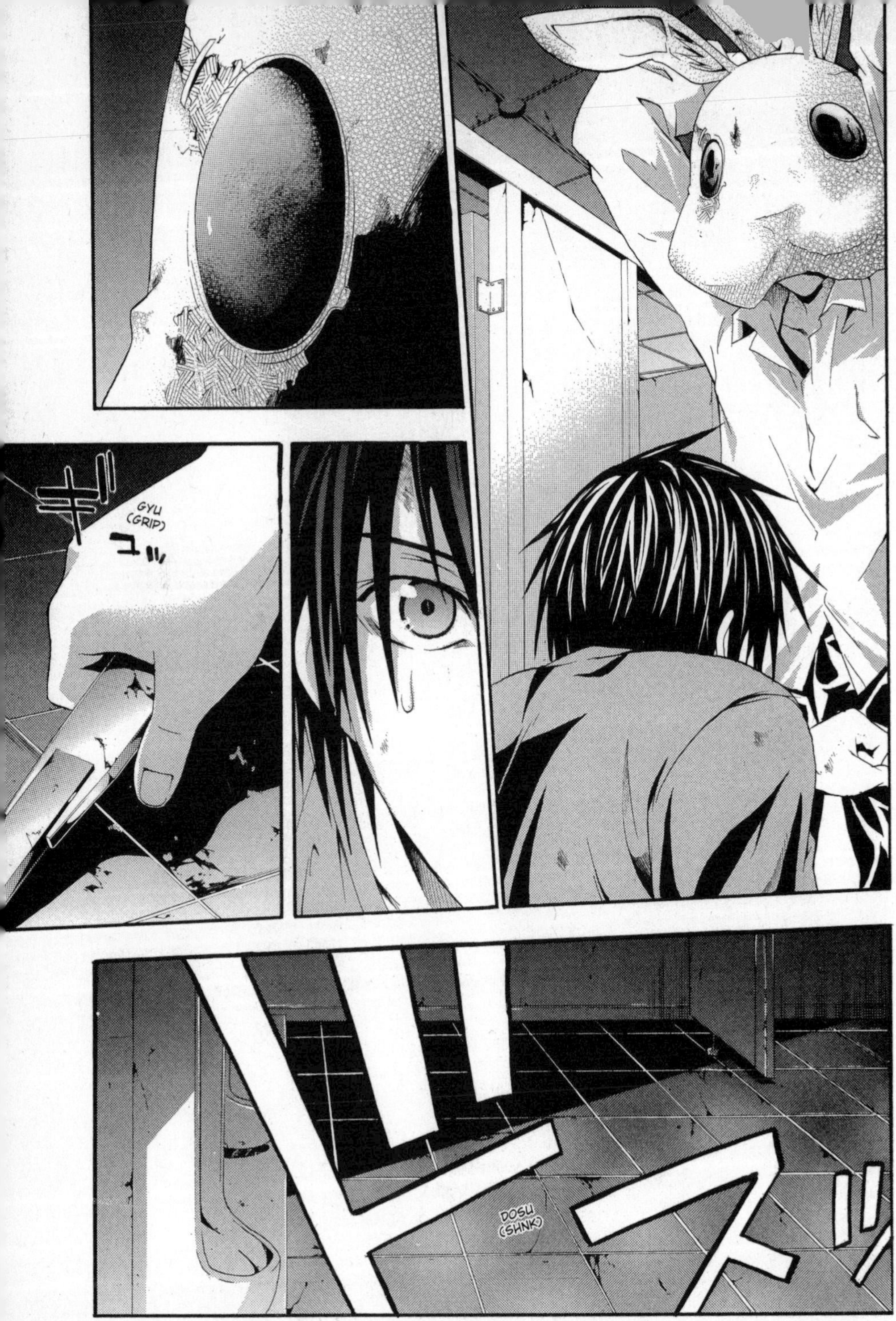
ギュッ
GYU (GRIP)
ドスッ
DOSU (SHNK)

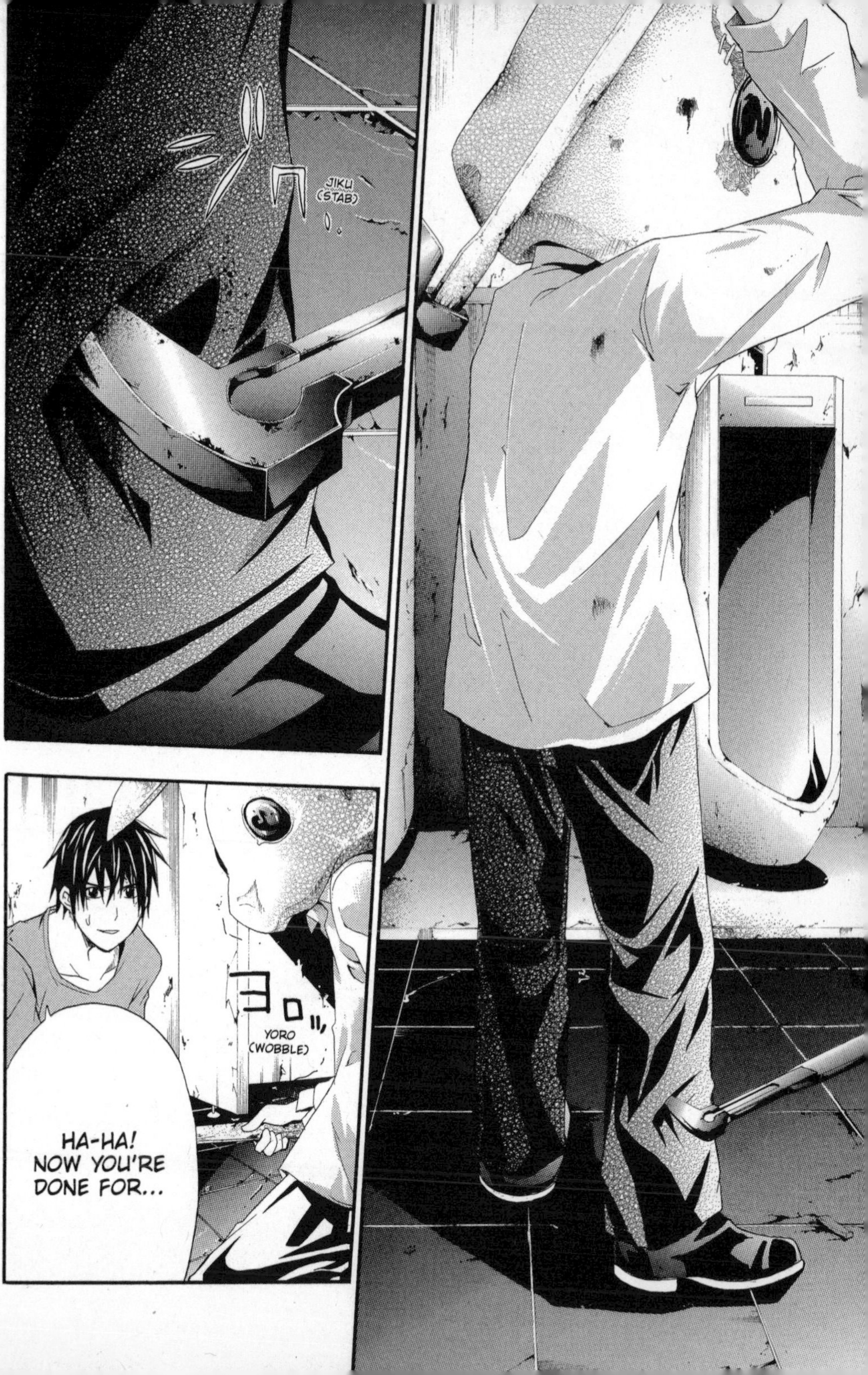
JIKU
(STAB)
YORO
(WOBBLE)
HA-HA!
NOW YOU'RE
DONE FOR...

!?

GO
(WHAM)

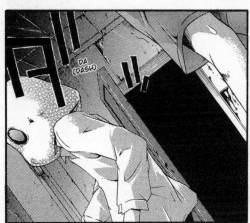

DA
(DASH)

AGH...

JIRI
(SCRAPE)

W...

WAIT!!

GU
(STRAIN)

GU

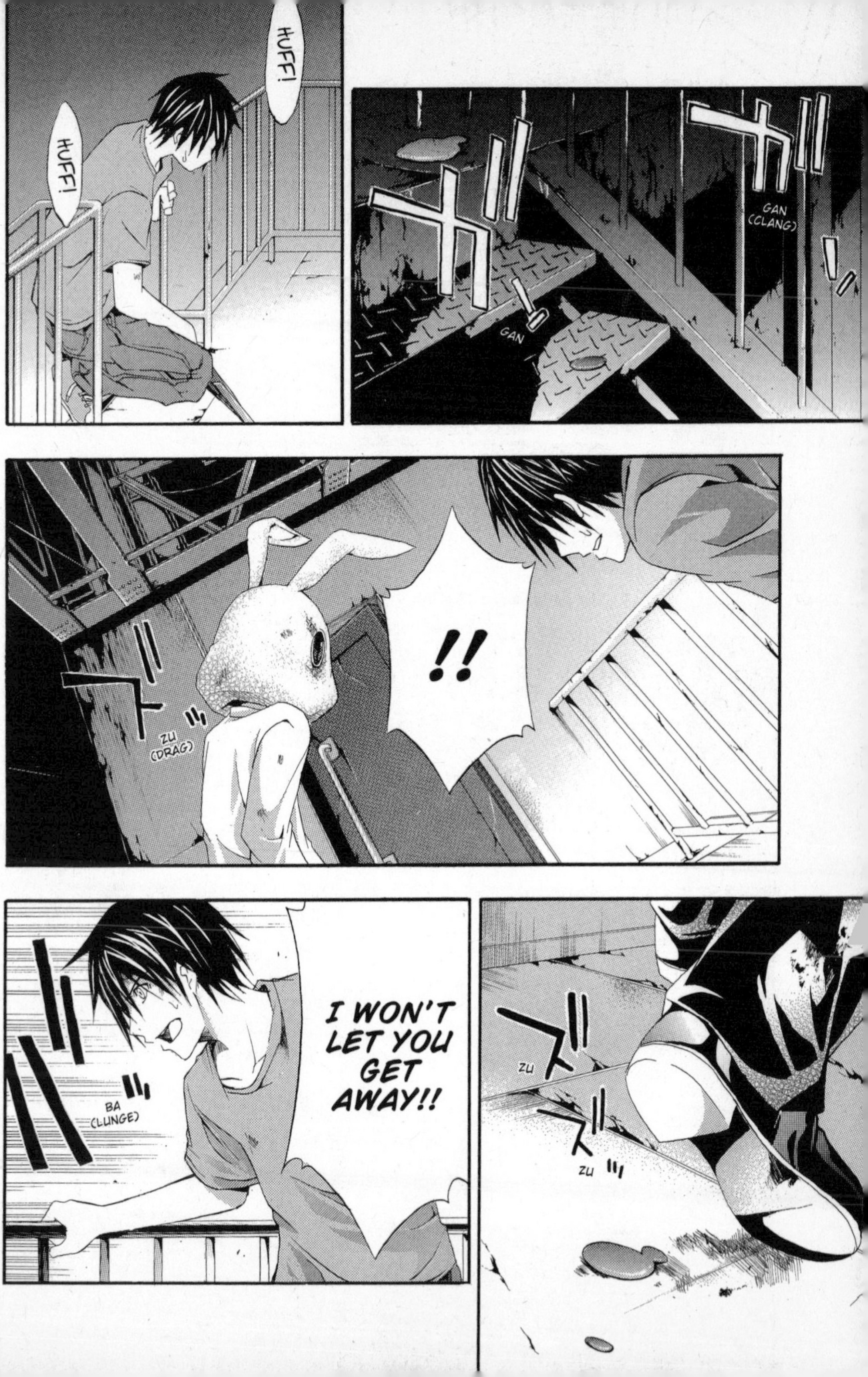
GAN (CLANG)
GAN
HUFF!
HUFF!
!!
ZU (DRAG)
ZU
ZU
I WON'T LET YOU GET AWAY!!
BA (LUNGE)

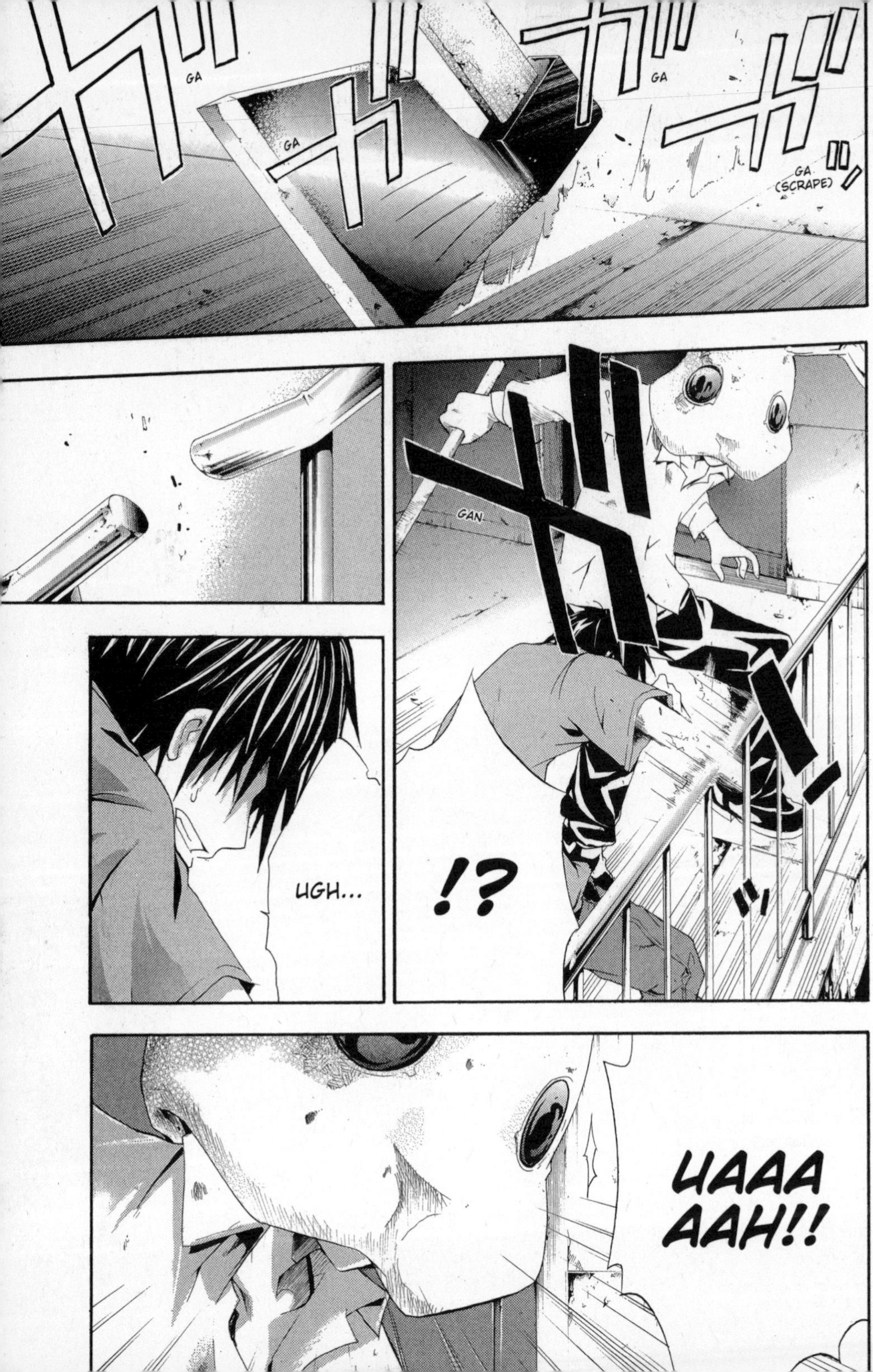
GA (SCRAPE)
GA
GA
GA
GAN
!?
UGH...
UAAAAAH!!

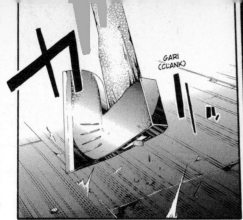

GARI
(CLANK)

DOGA
(THUNK)

I'VE
CAUGHT
YOU...

YOU'RE THE ONE WHO KILLED EVERY-ONE...

....

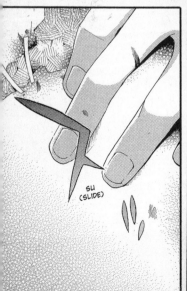

SU
(SLIDE)

GOKU
(GULP)

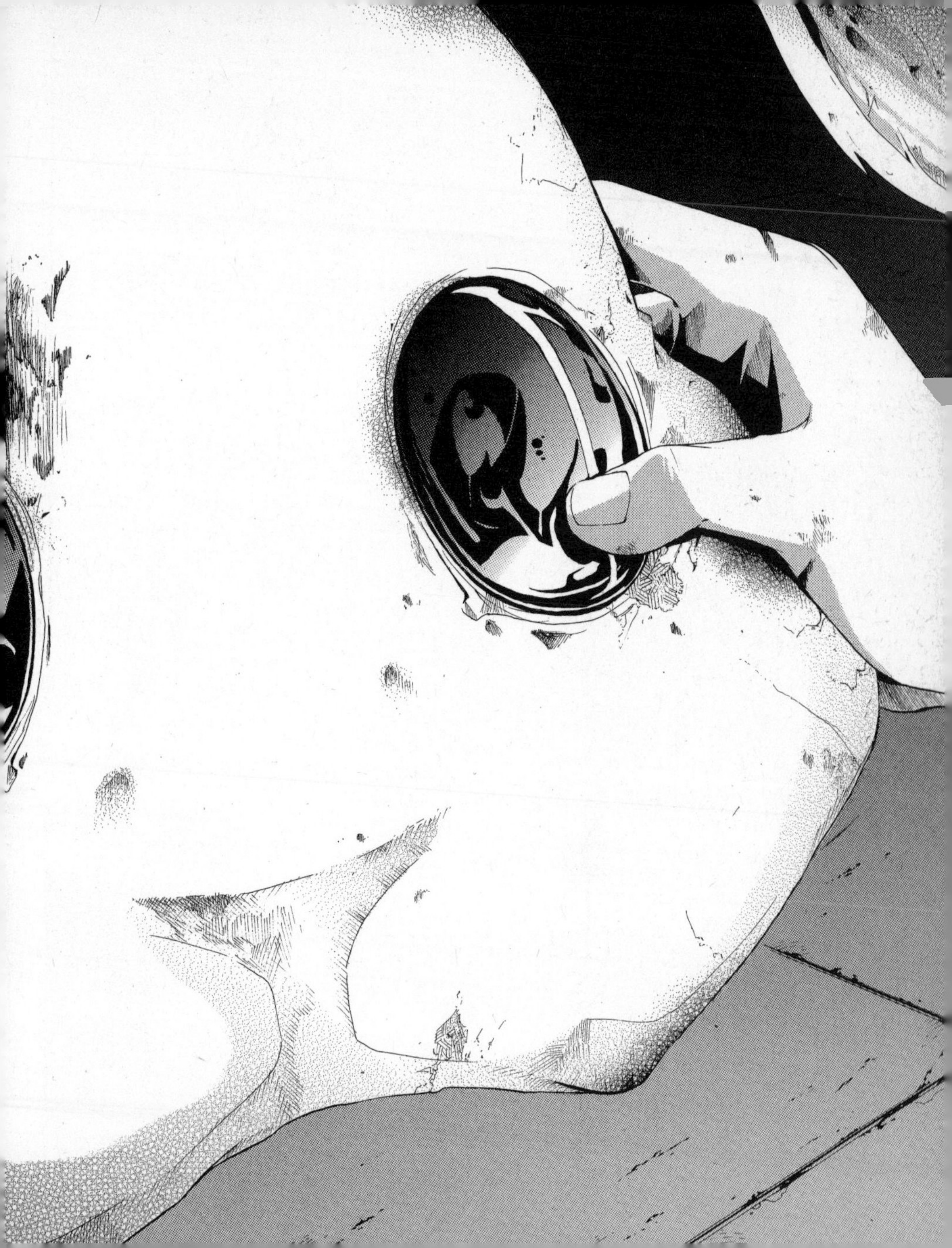

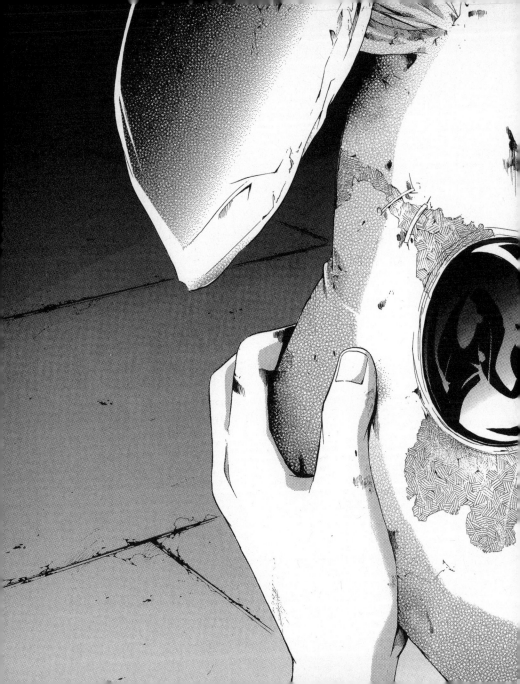

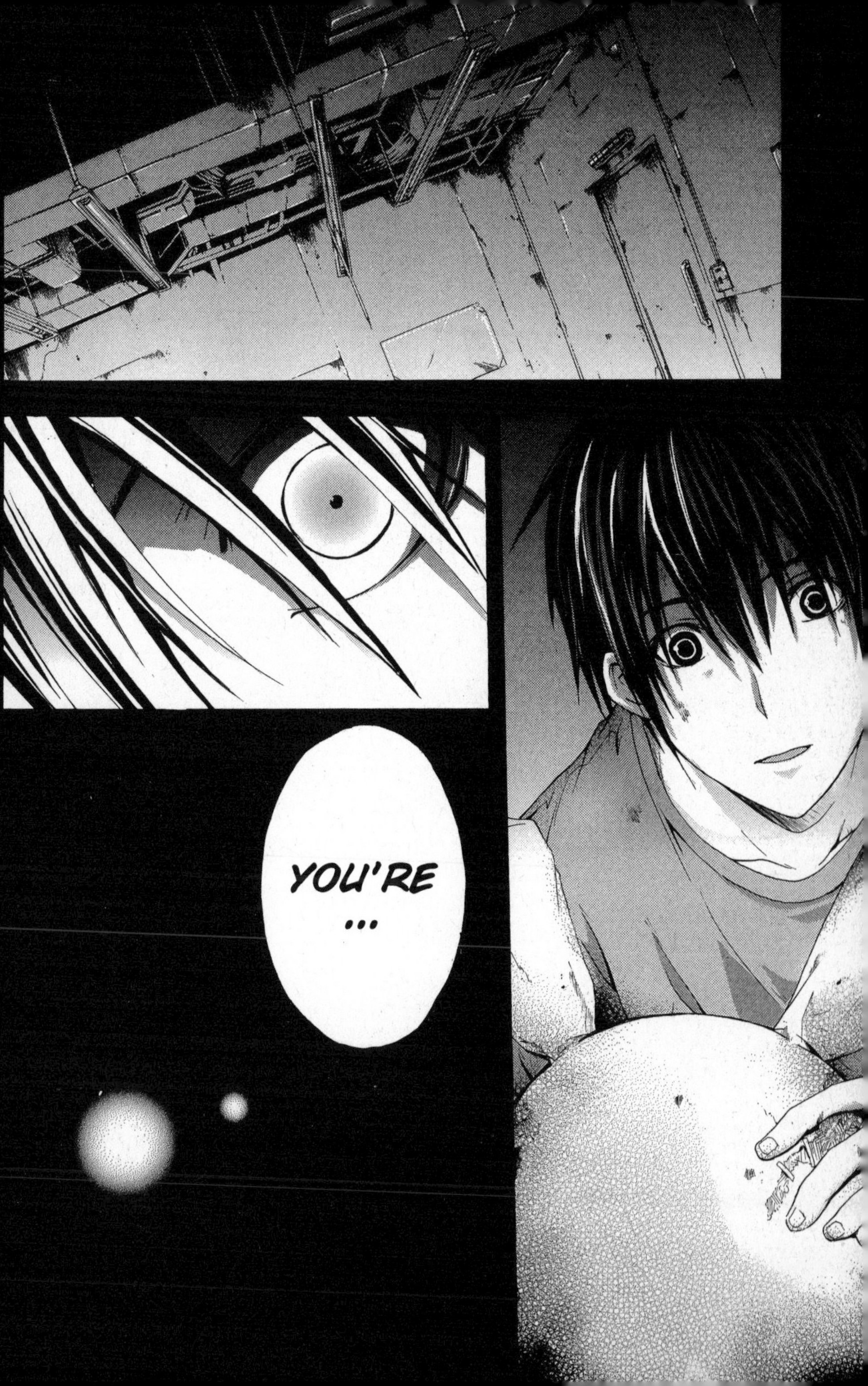
YOU'RE
...

Doubt.14 REASON

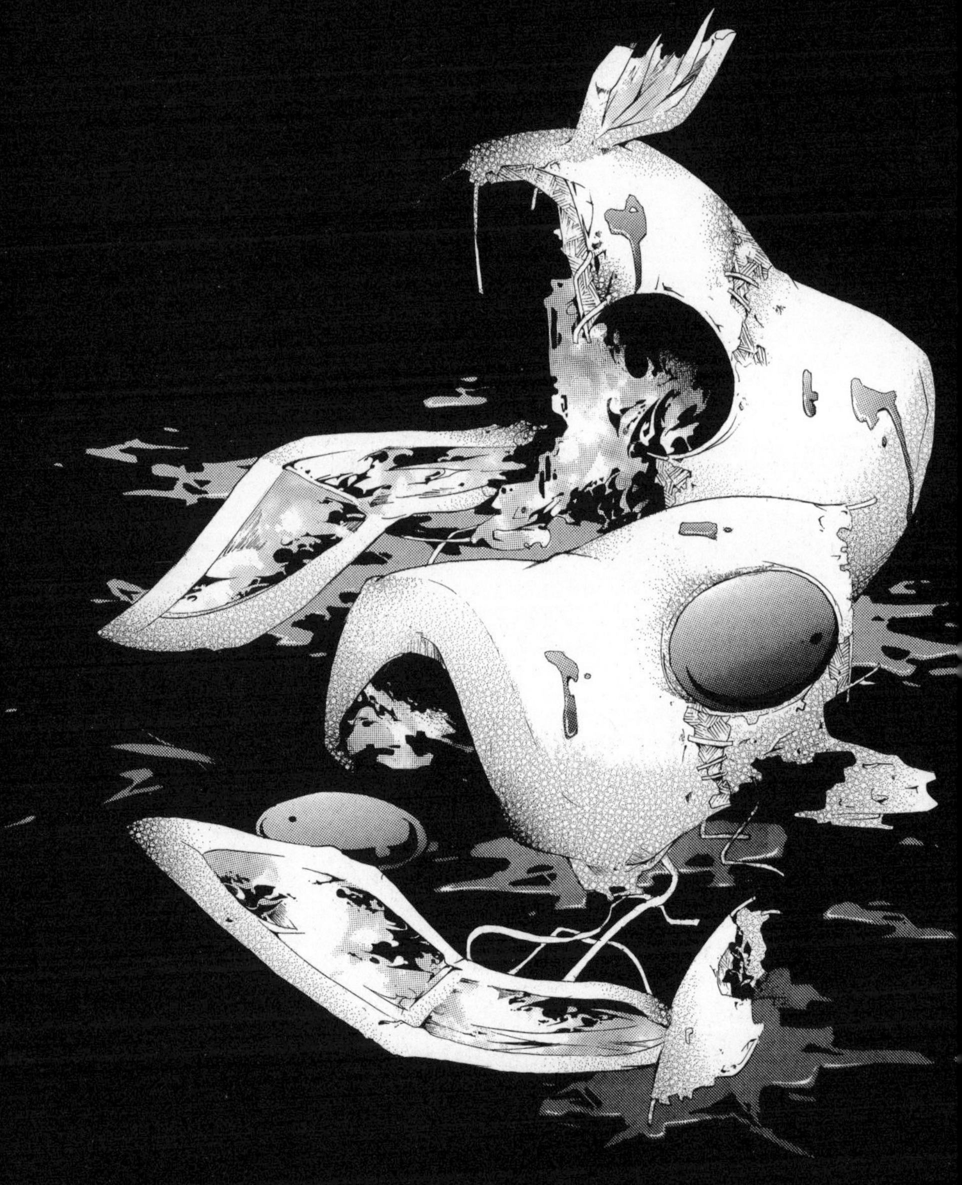

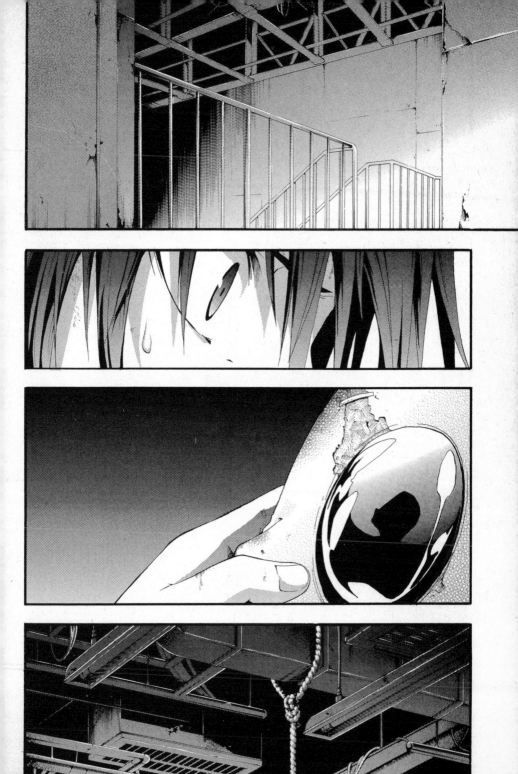

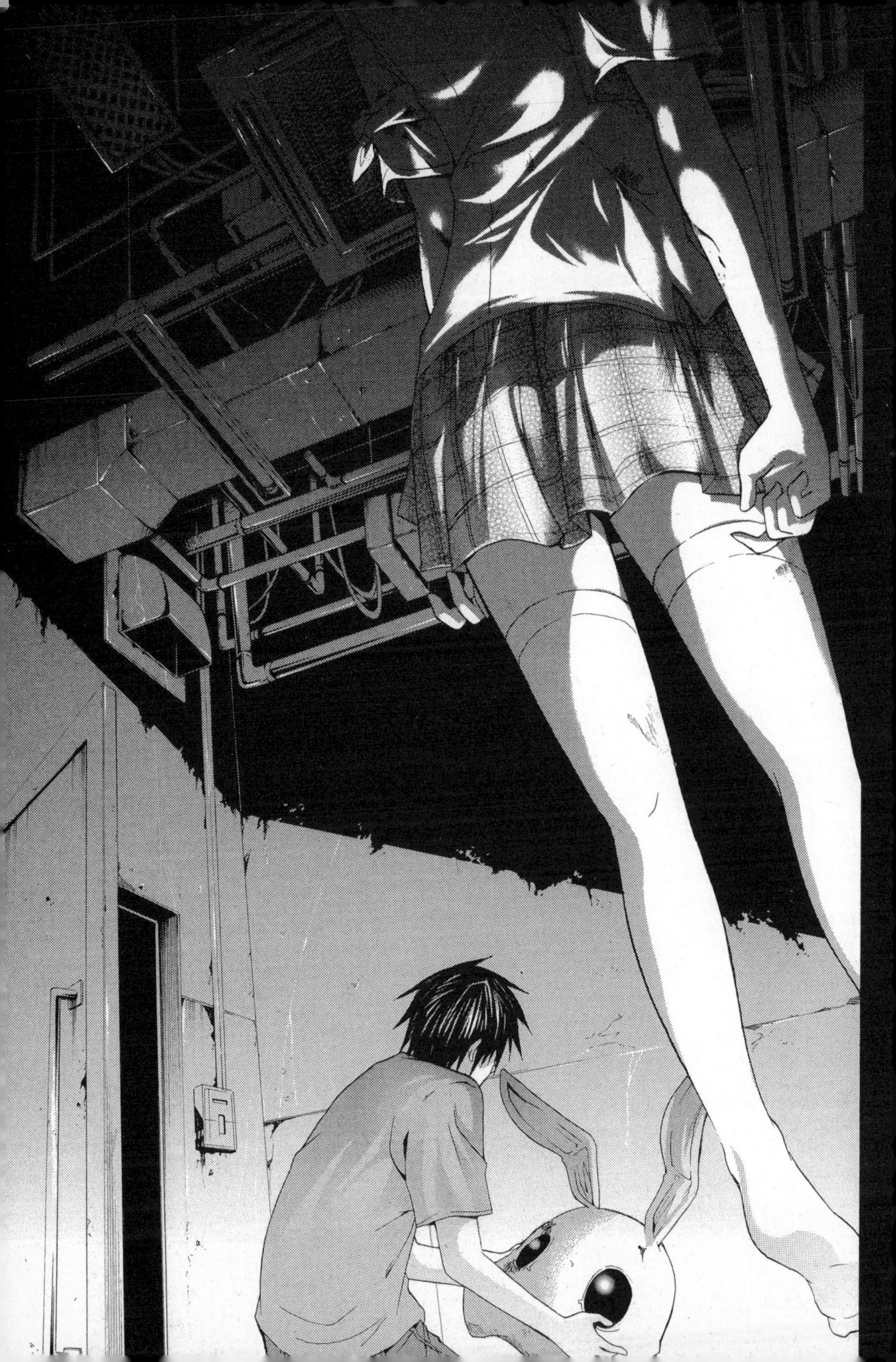

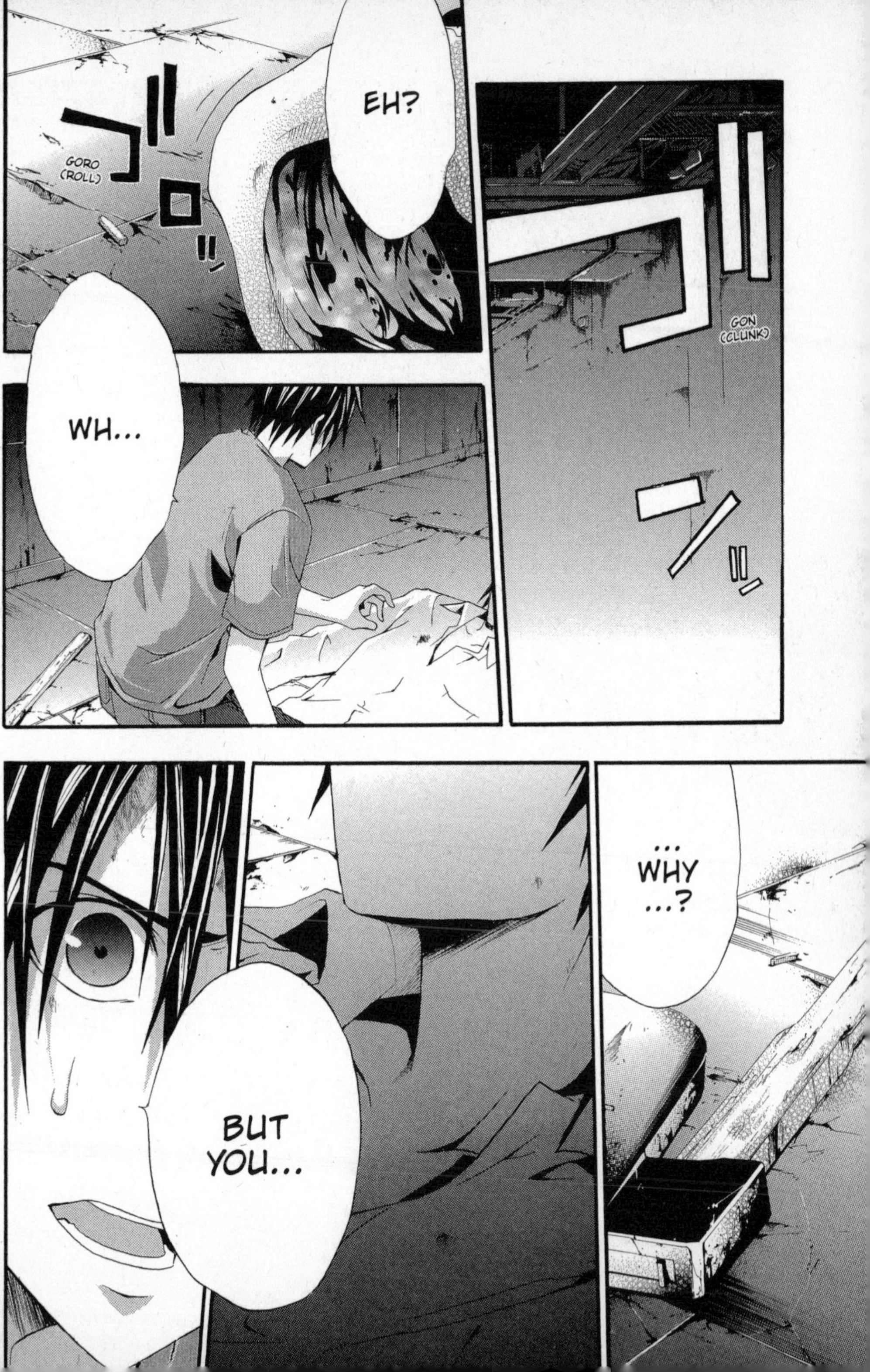
GON
(CLUNK)
EH?
GORO
(ROLL)
WH...
... WHY ...?
BUT YOU...

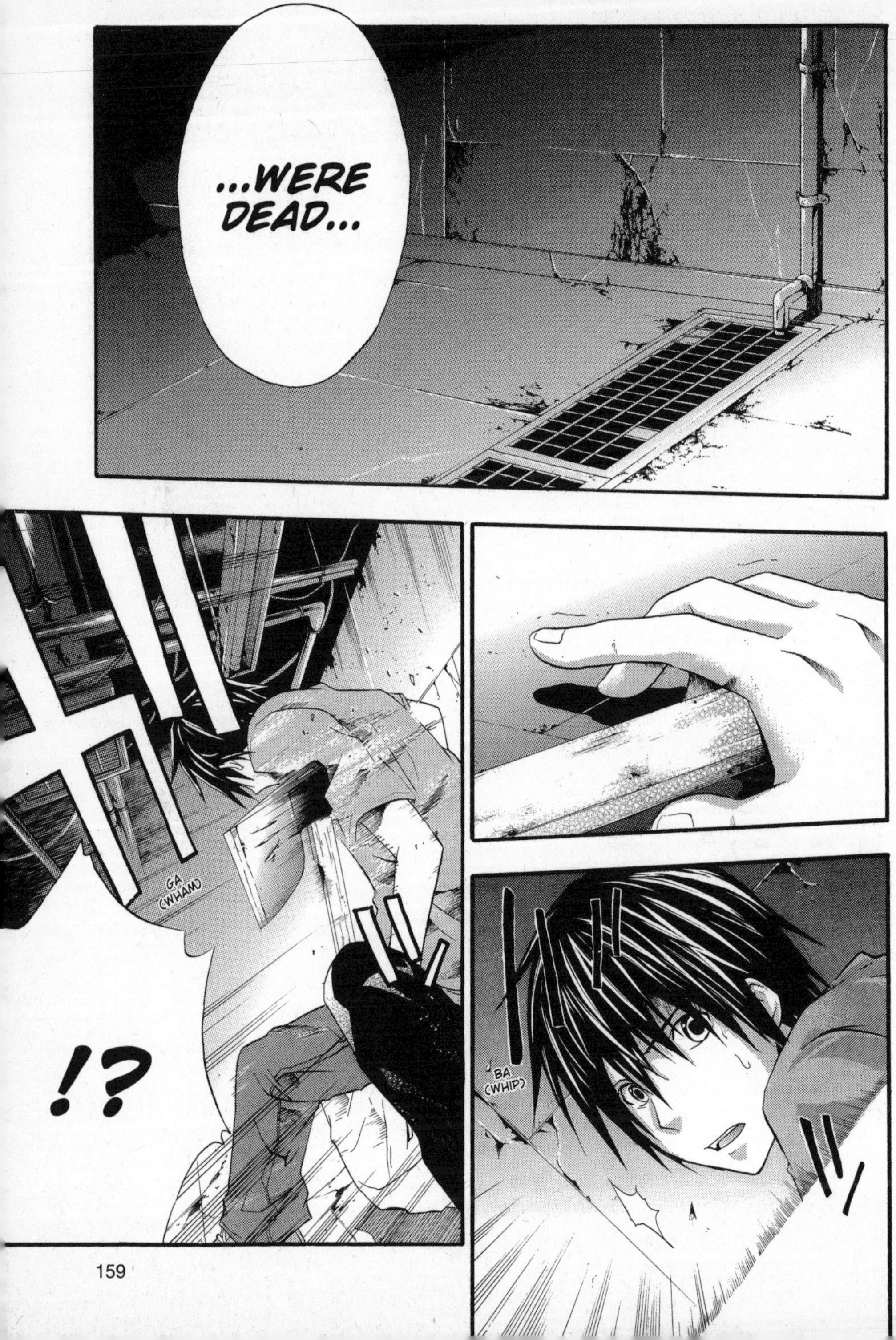
...WERE DEAD...
BA (WHIP)
GA (WHAM)
!?

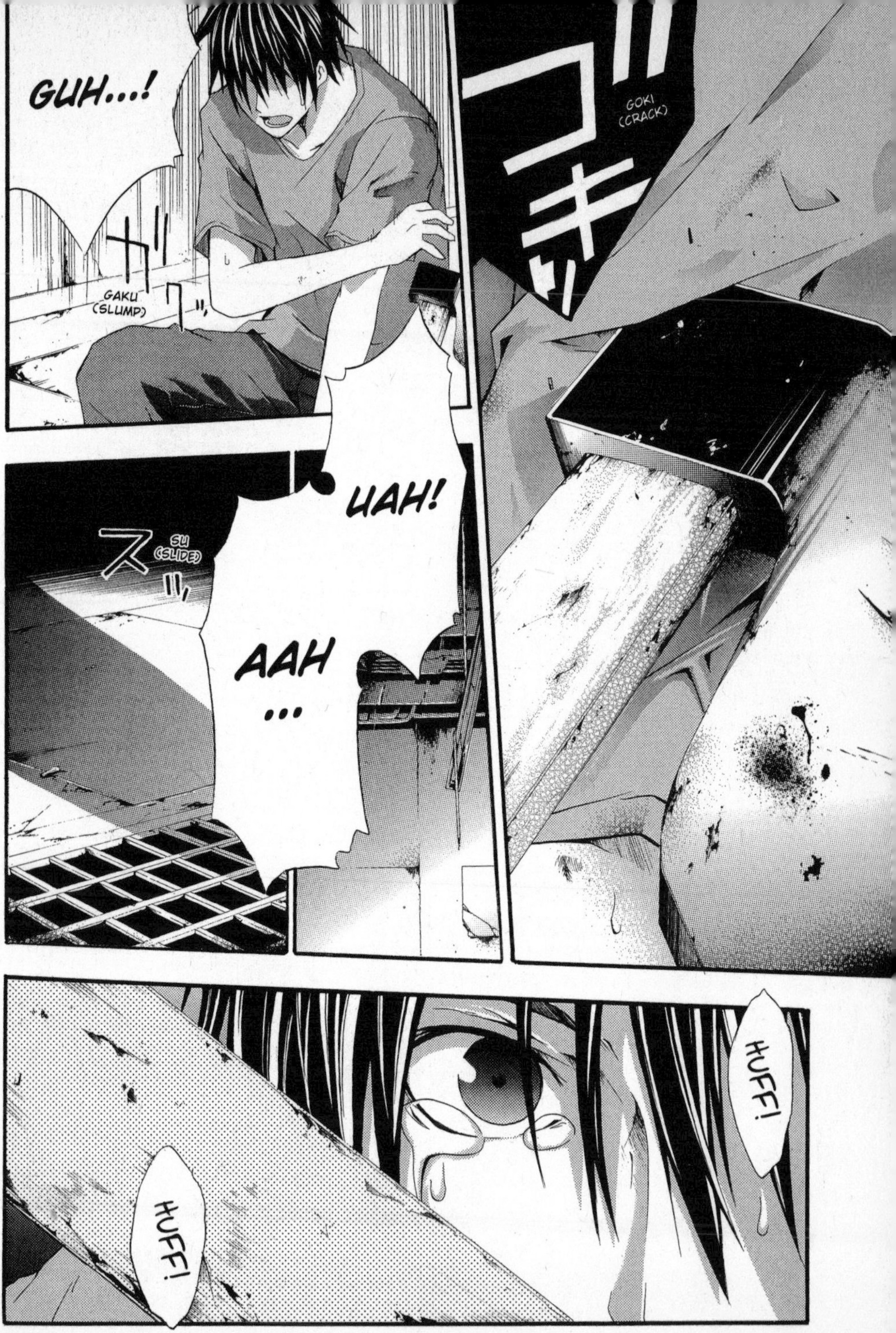
GOKI (CRACK)
GUH...!
GAKU (SLUMP)
UAH!
AAH ...
SU (SLIDE)
HUFF!
HUFF!

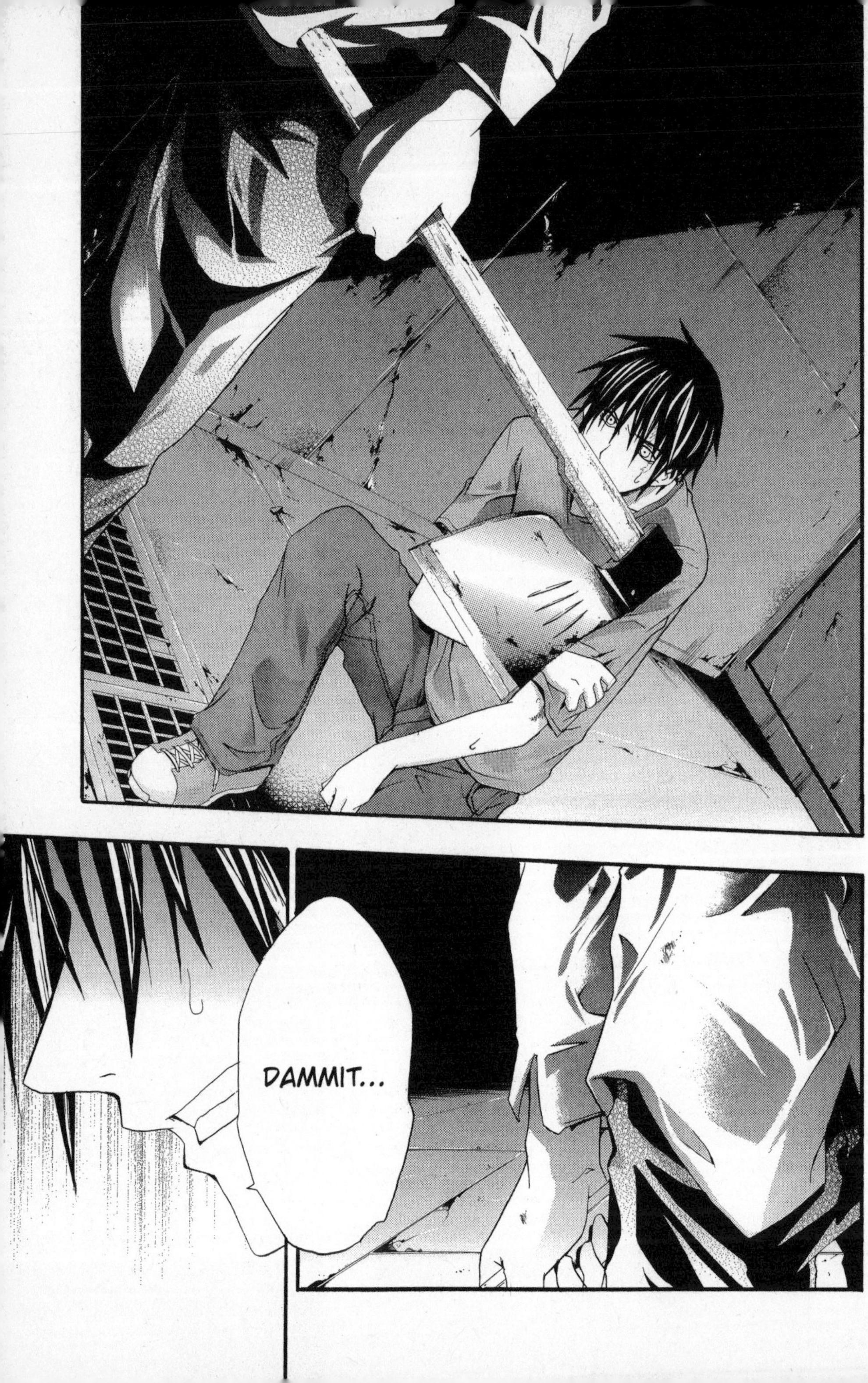
DAMMIT...

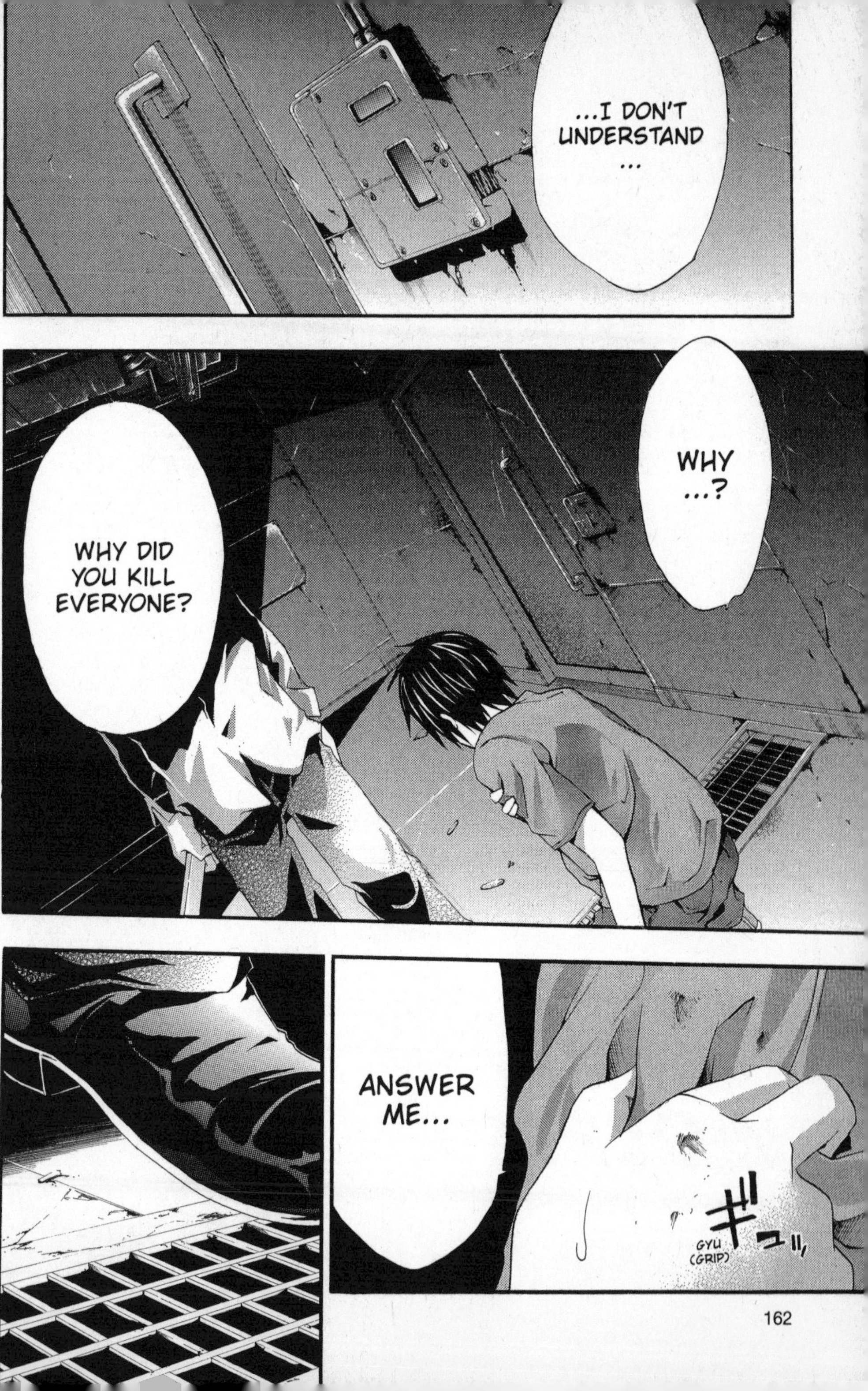

...I DON'T UNDERSTAND ...
WHY ...?
WHY DID YOU KILL EVERYONE?
ANSWER ME...
ギュッ
GYU (GRIP)

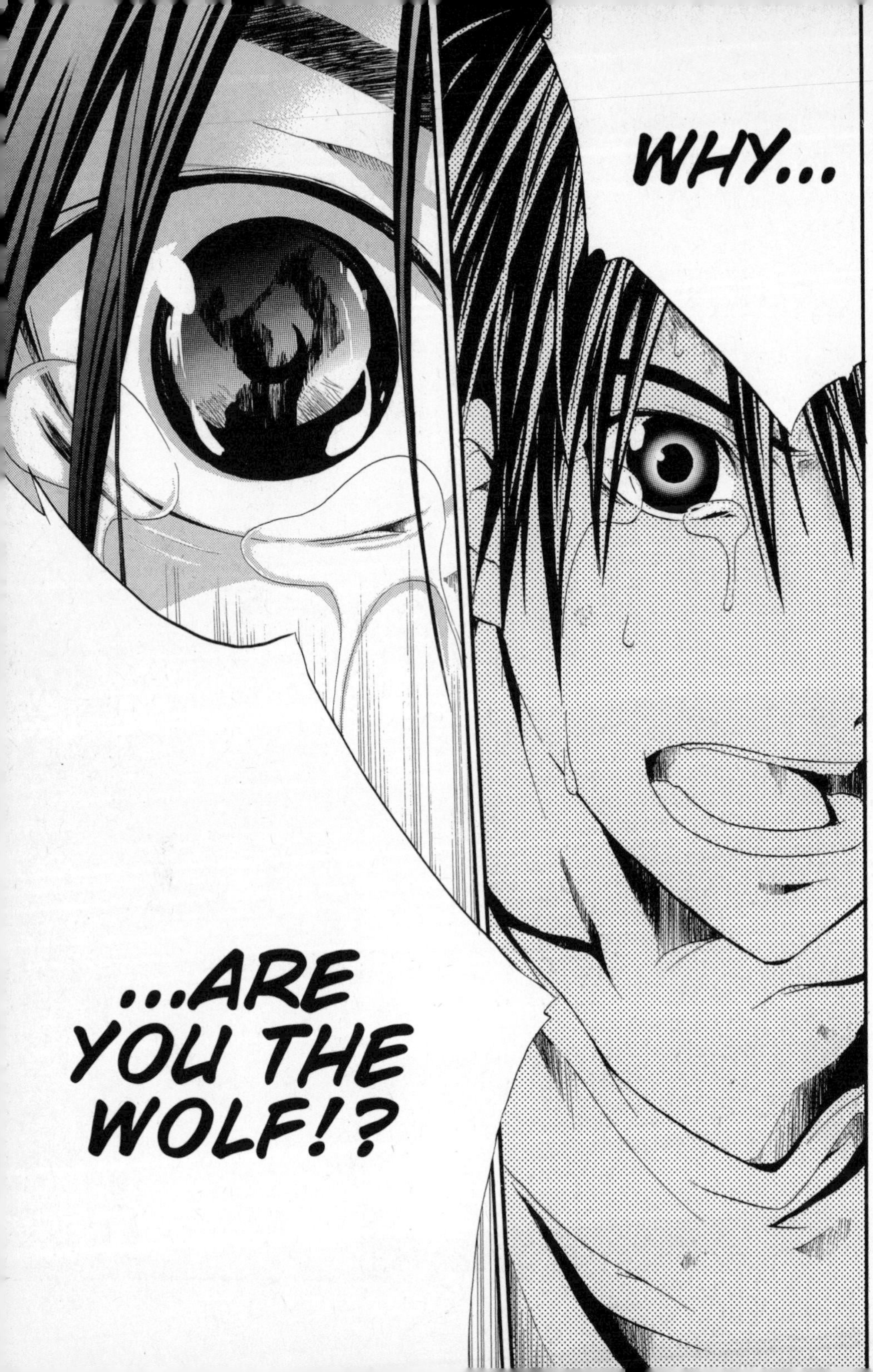
WHY...
...ARE YOU THE WOLF!?

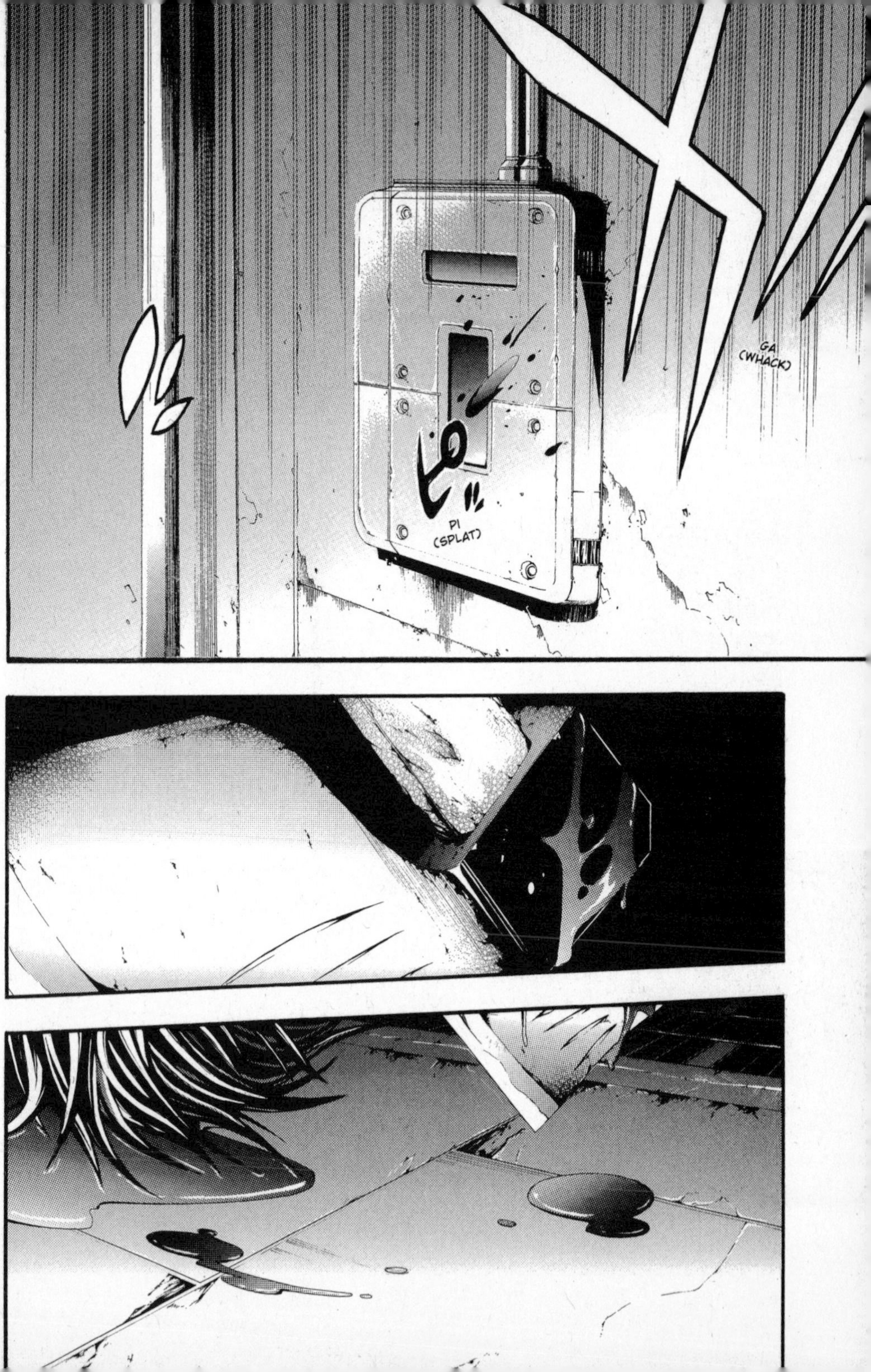
GA
(WHACK)
PI
(SPLAT)

GASHA
(CLANK)

GU
(GRAB)

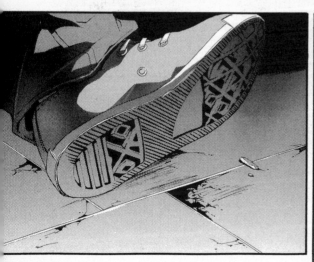

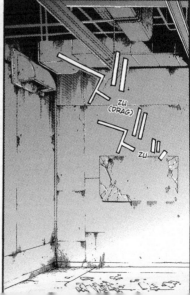

ZU
(DRAG)

ZU

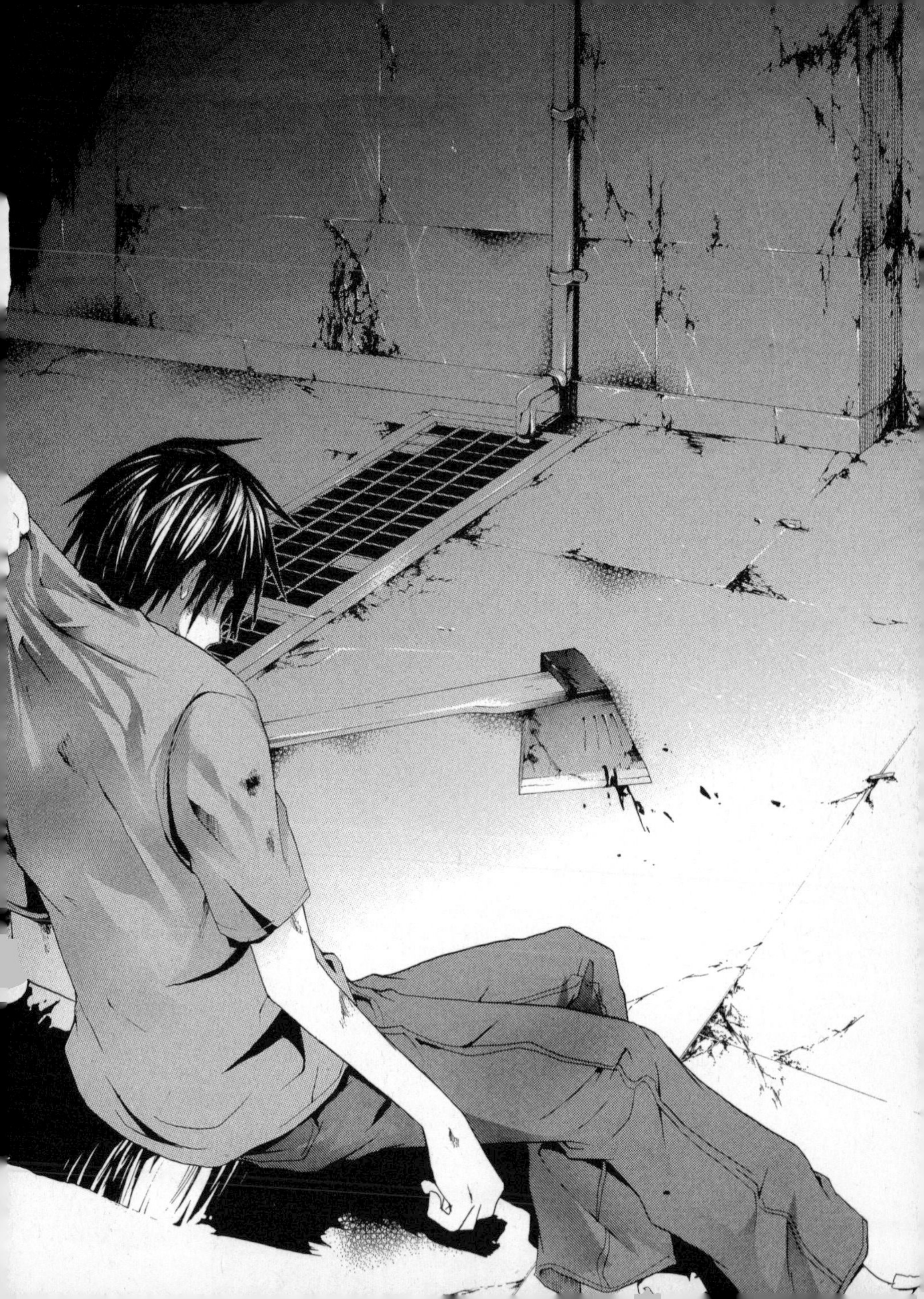

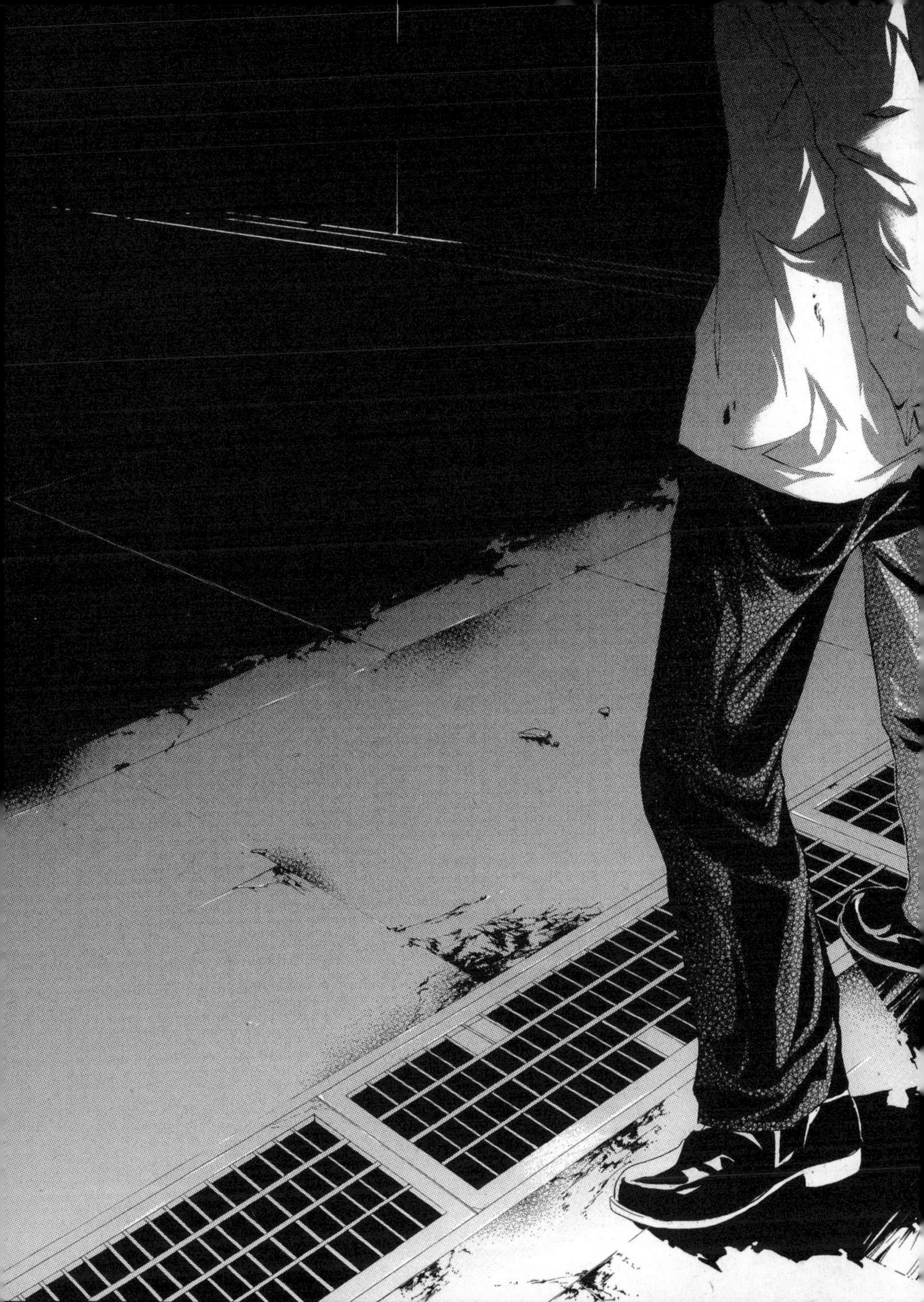

ZU
(DRAG)

ZU

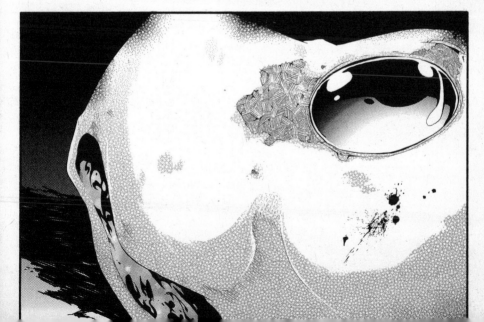

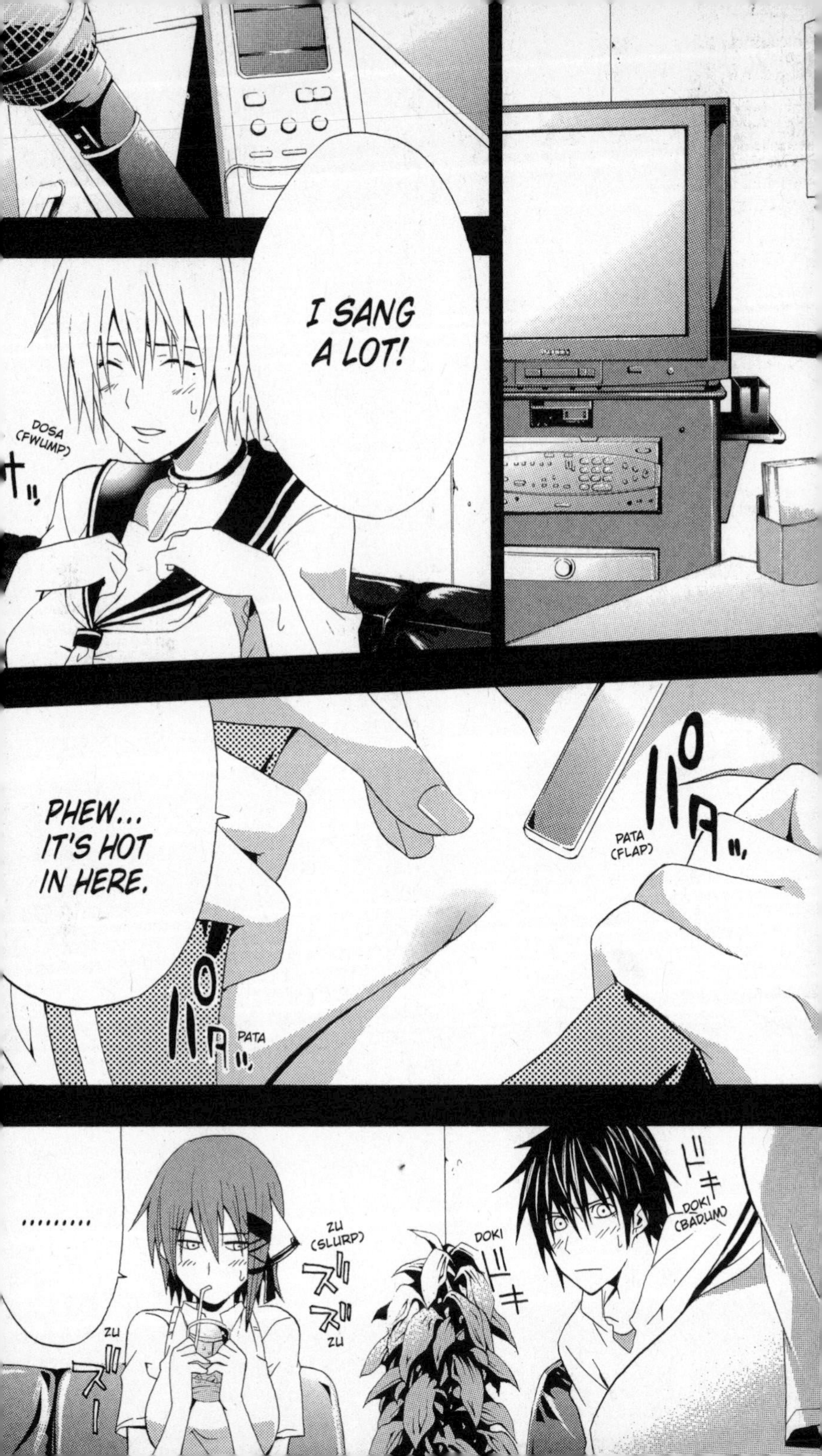
I SANG A LOT!
DOSA (FWUMP)
パタッ
PATA (FLAP)
PHEW... IT'S HOT IN HERE.
パタッ
PATA
ドキ
DOKI (BADUM)
DOKI
ドキ
ZU (SLURP)
ズズ
ZU
....
ZU
ズー

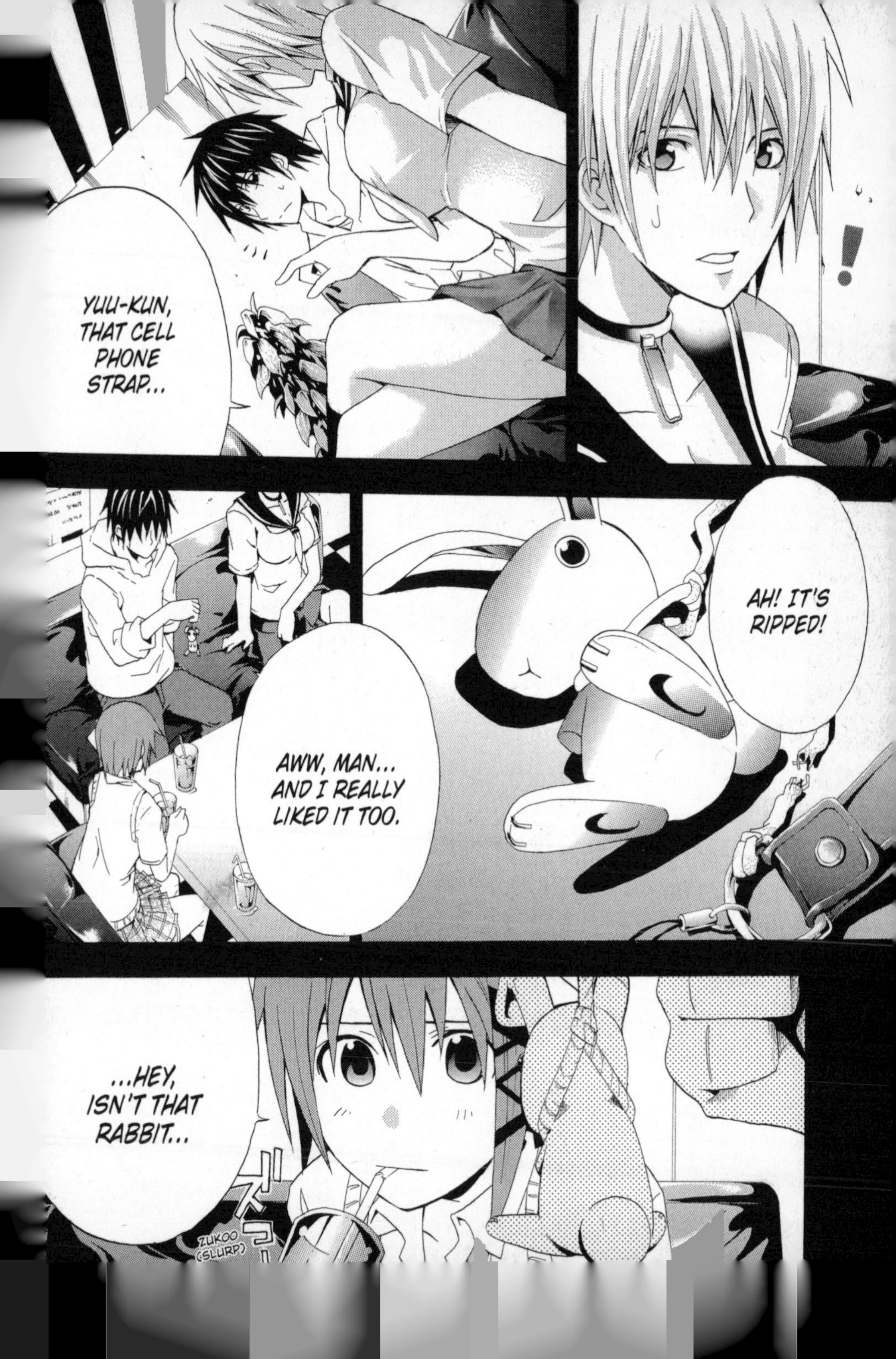
!
YUU-KUN, THAT CELL PHONE STRAP...
AH! IT'S RIPPED!
AWW, MAN... AND I REALLY LIKED IT TOO.
...HEY, ISN'T THAT RABBIT...
ZUKOO (SLURP)

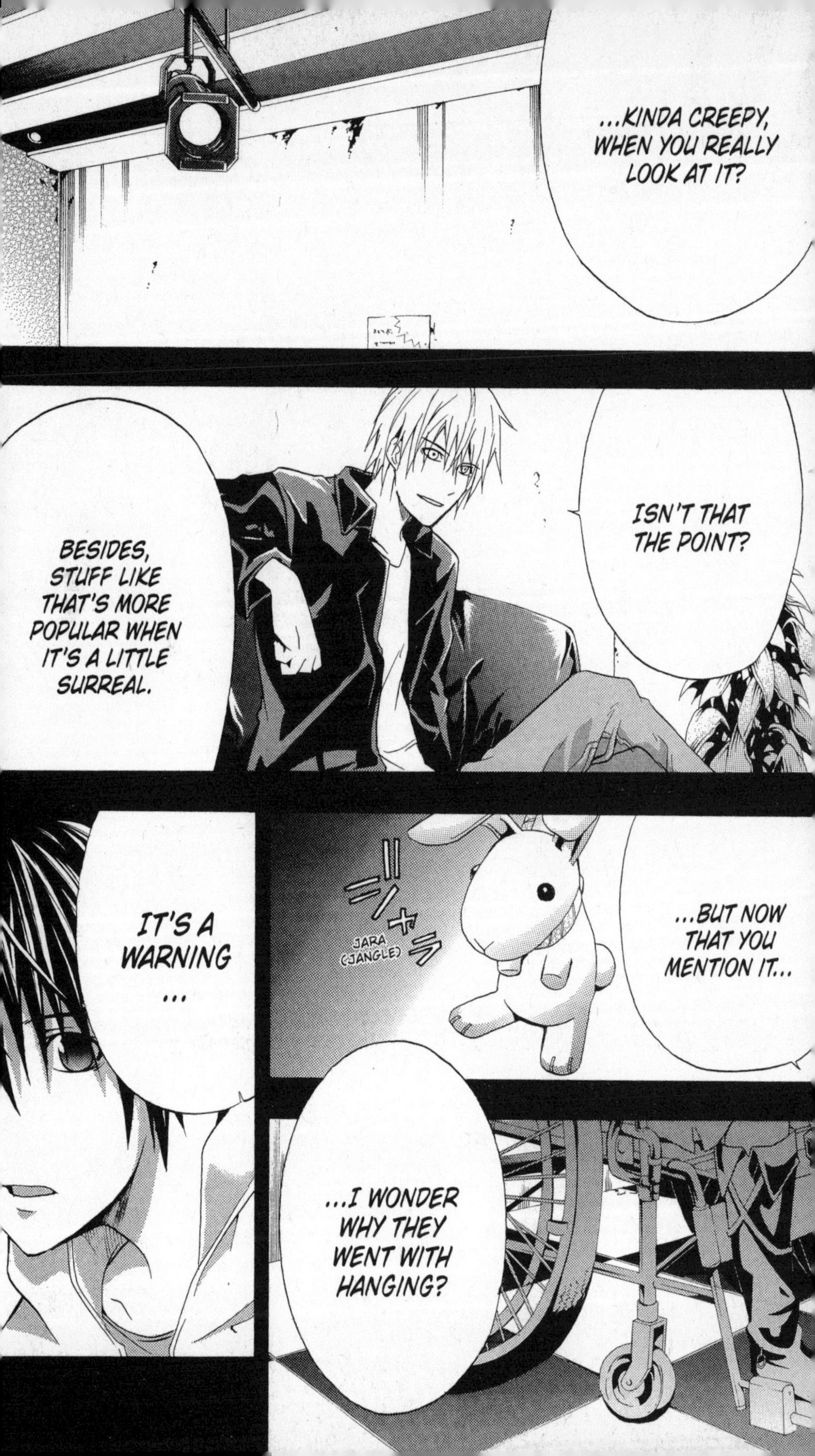
...KINDA CREEPY, WHEN YOU REALLY LOOK AT IT?
ISN'T THAT THE POINT?
BESIDES, STUFF LIKE THAT'S MORE POPULAR WHEN IT'S A LITTLE SURREAL.
ジャラ
JARA (JANGLE)
...BUT NOW THAT YOU MENTION IT...
...I WONDER WHY THEY WENT WITH HANGING?
IT'S A WARNING ...

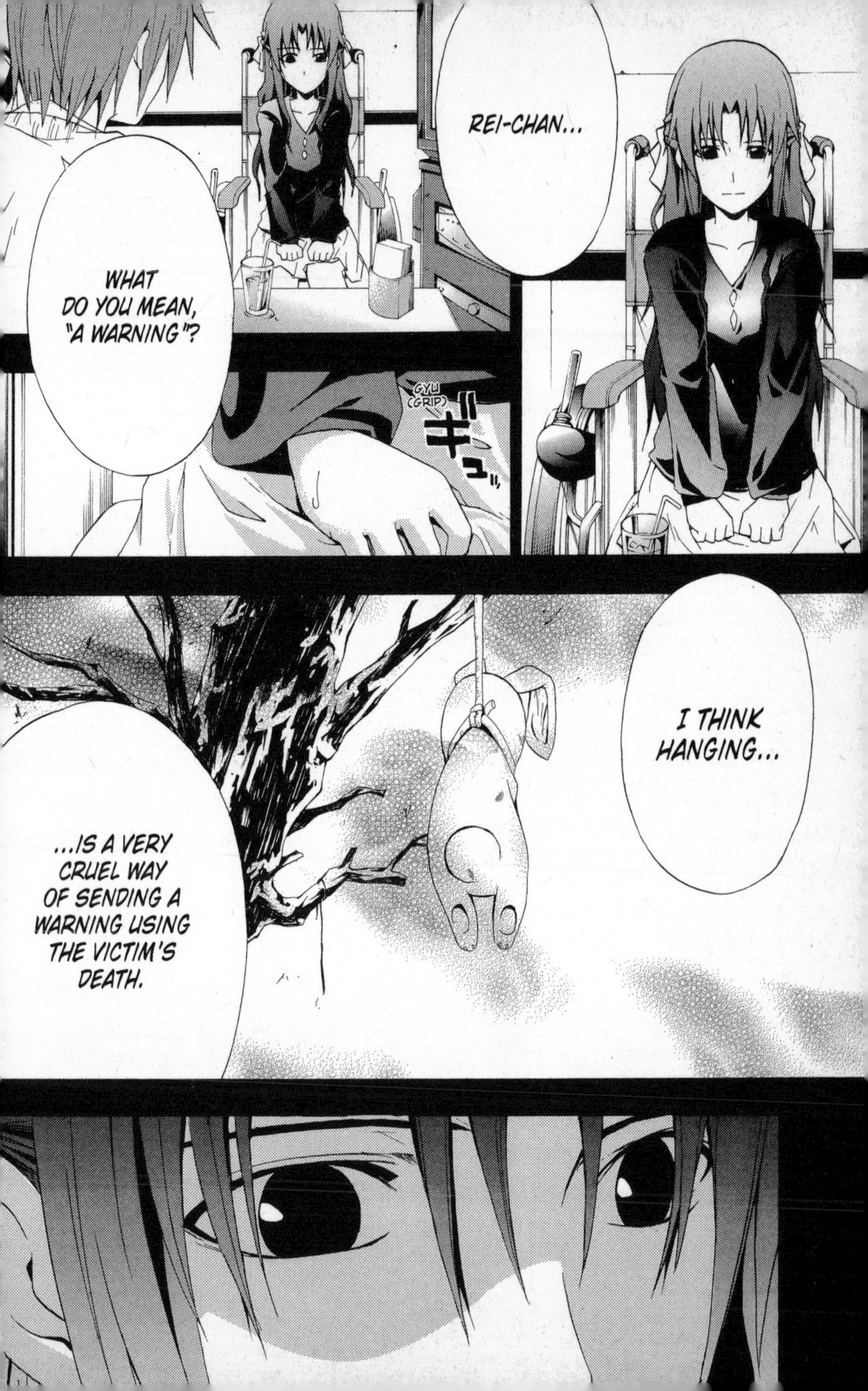
REI-CHAN...
WHAT DO YOU MEAN, "A WARNING"?
GYU (GRIP)
I THINK HANGING...
...IS A VERY CRUEL WAY OF SENDING A WARNING USING THE VICTIM'S DEATH.

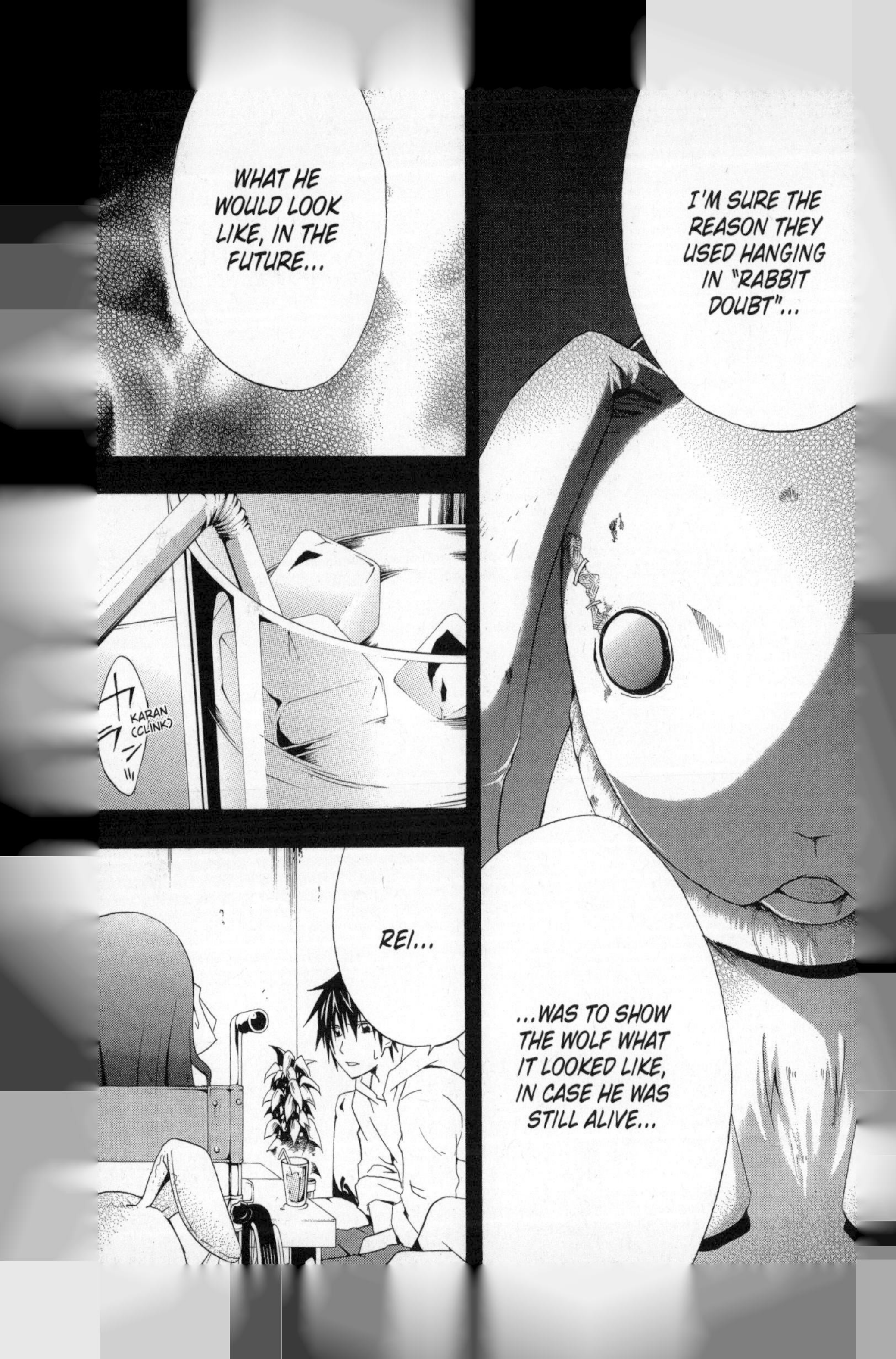
I'M SURE THE REASON THEY USED HANGING IN "RABBIT DOUBT"...
...WAS TO SHOW THE WOLF WHAT IT LOOKED LIKE, IN CASE HE WAS STILL ALIVE...
WHAT HE WOULD LOOK LIKE, IN THE FUTURE...
KARAN (CLINK)
REI...

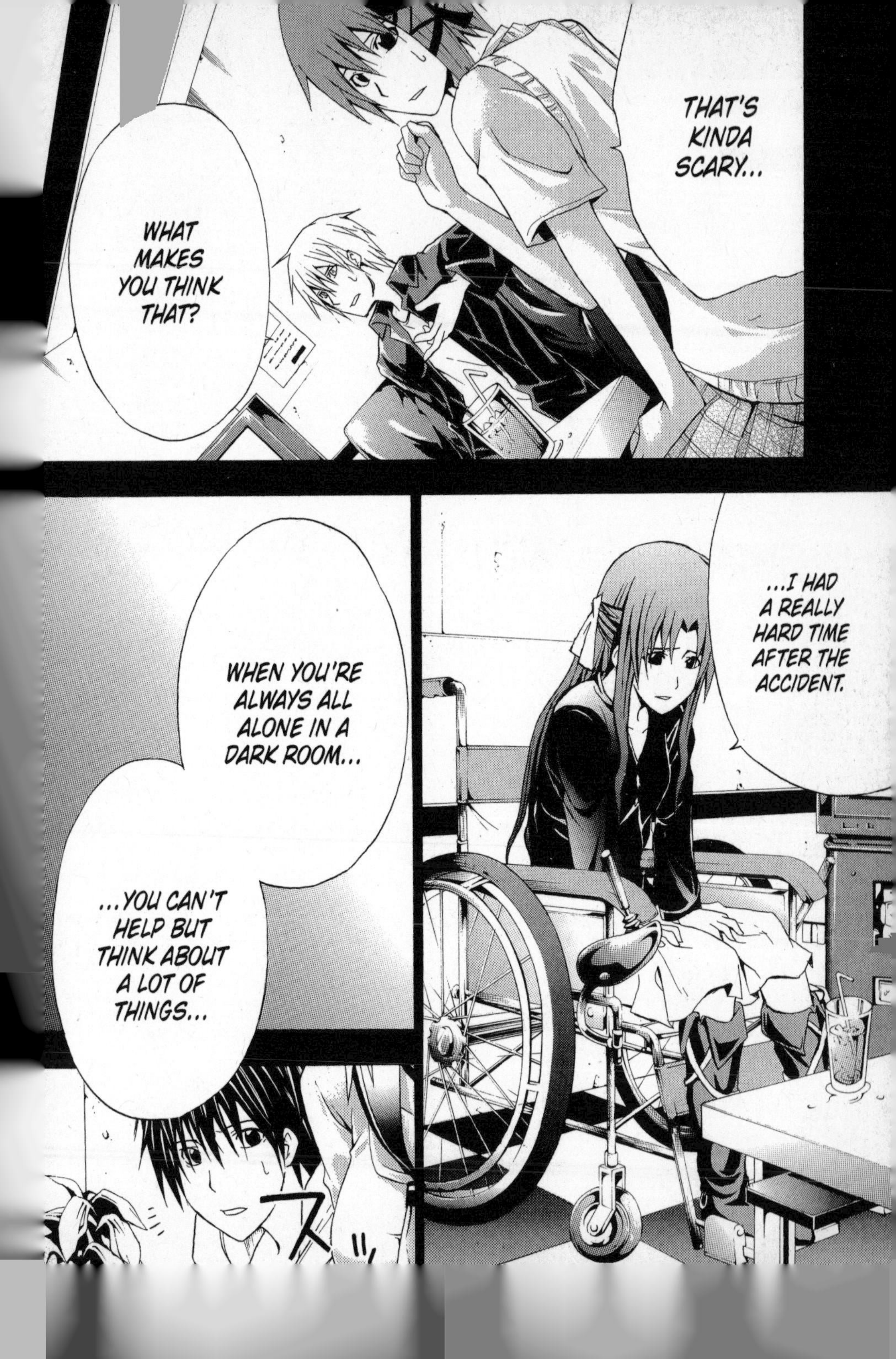
THAT'S KINDA SCARY...
WHAT MAKES YOU THINK THAT?
...I HAD A REALLY HARD TIME AFTER THE ACCIDENT.
WHEN YOU'RE ALWAYS ALL ALONE IN A DARK ROOM...
...YOU CAN'T HELP BUT THINK ABOUT A LOT OF THINGS...

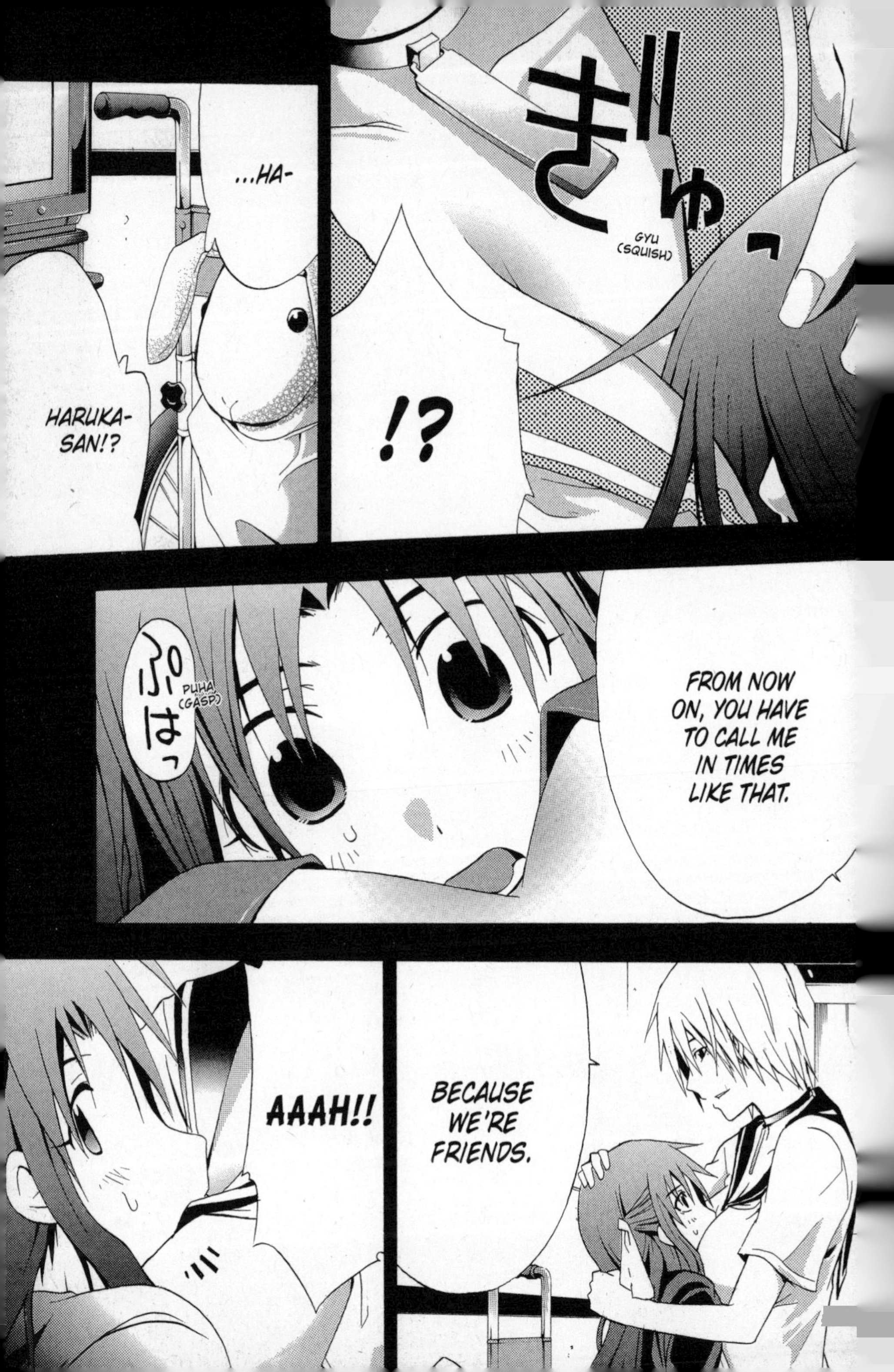

ぎゅっ
GYU (SQUISH)
!?
...HA-
HARUKA-SAN!?
FROM NOW ON, YOU HAVE TO CALL ME IN TIMES LIKE THAT.
ぷはっ
PUHA (GASP)
BECAUSE WE'RE FRIENDS.
AAAH!!

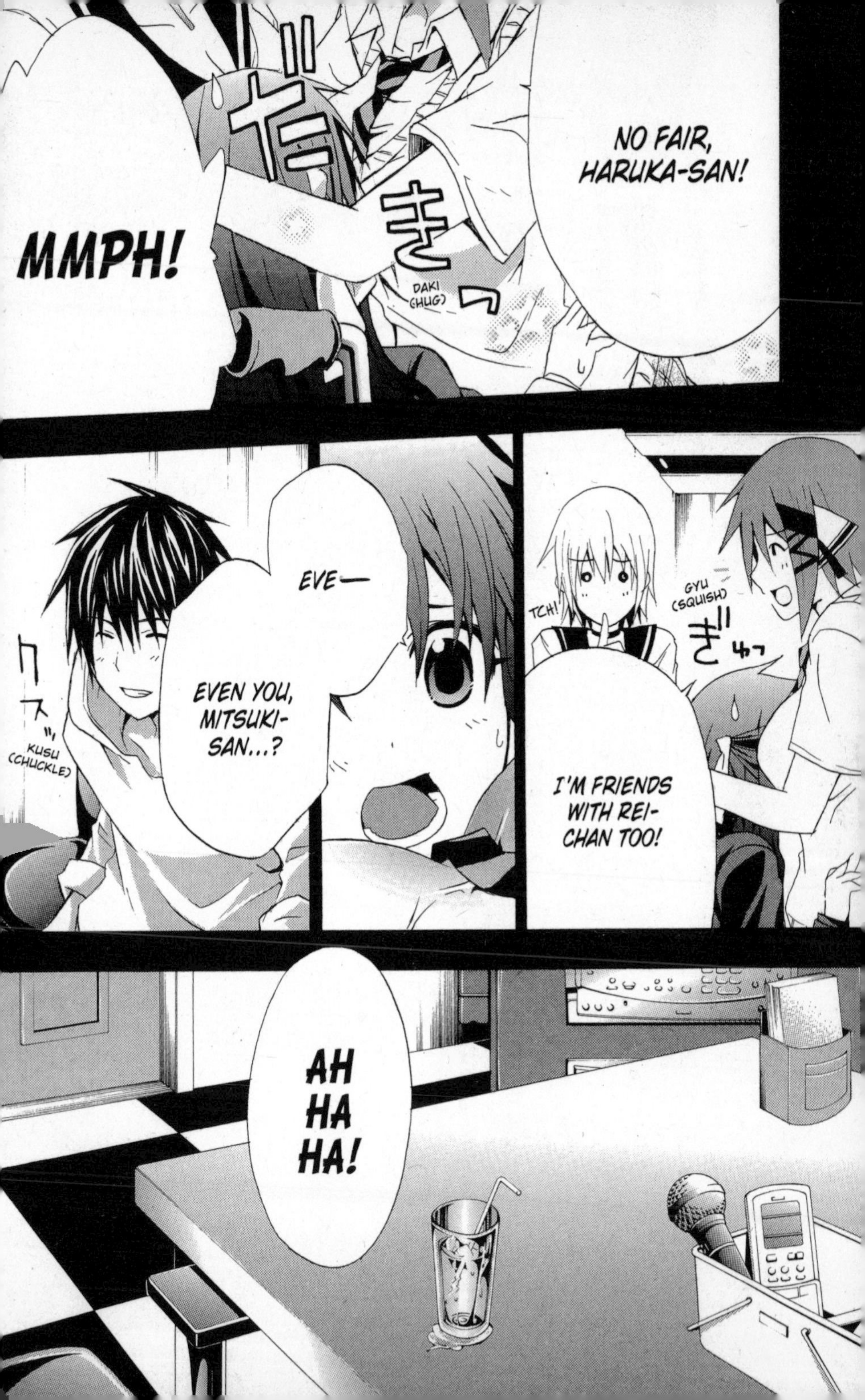
NO FAIR, HARUKA-SAN!
だきっ
DAKI (HUG)
MMPH!
TCH!
ぎゅっ
GYU (SQUISH)
I'M FRIENDS WITH REI-CHAN TOO!
EVE—
EVEN YOU, MITSUKI-SAN...?
クスッ
KUSU (CHUCKLE)
AH HA HA!

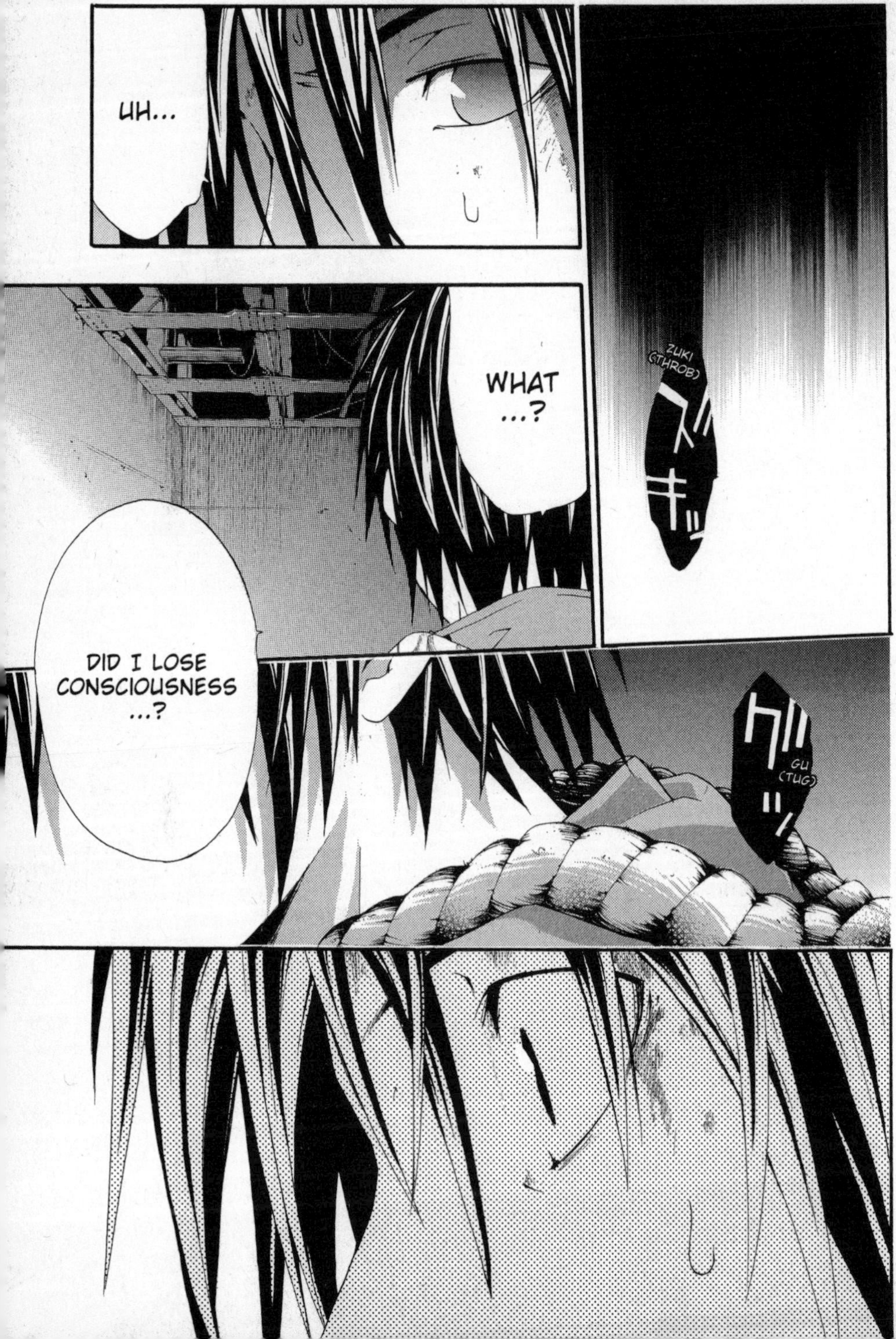
ZUKI (THROB)
UH...
WHAT ...?
DID I LOSE CONSCIOUSNESS ...?
GU (TUG)

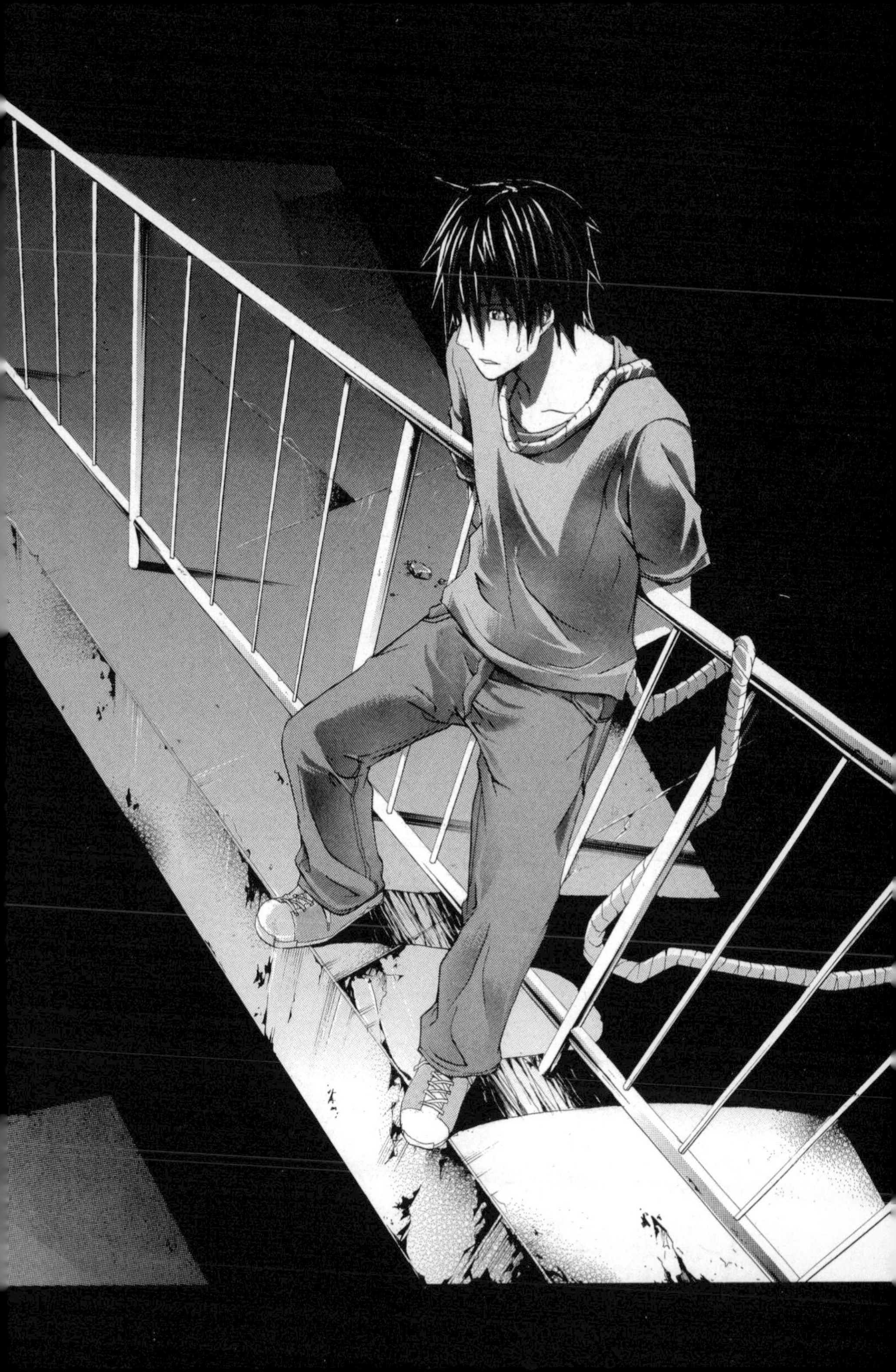

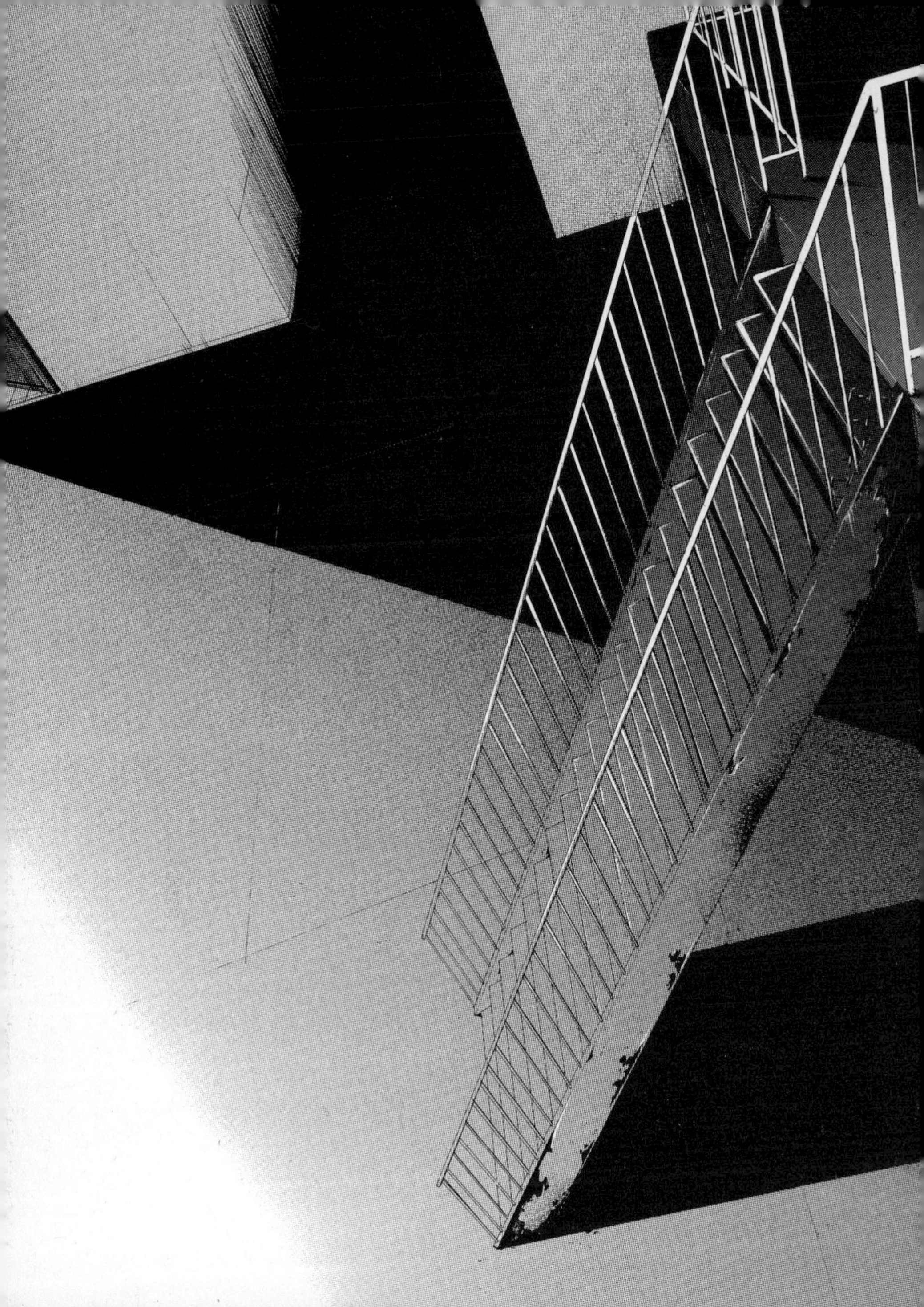

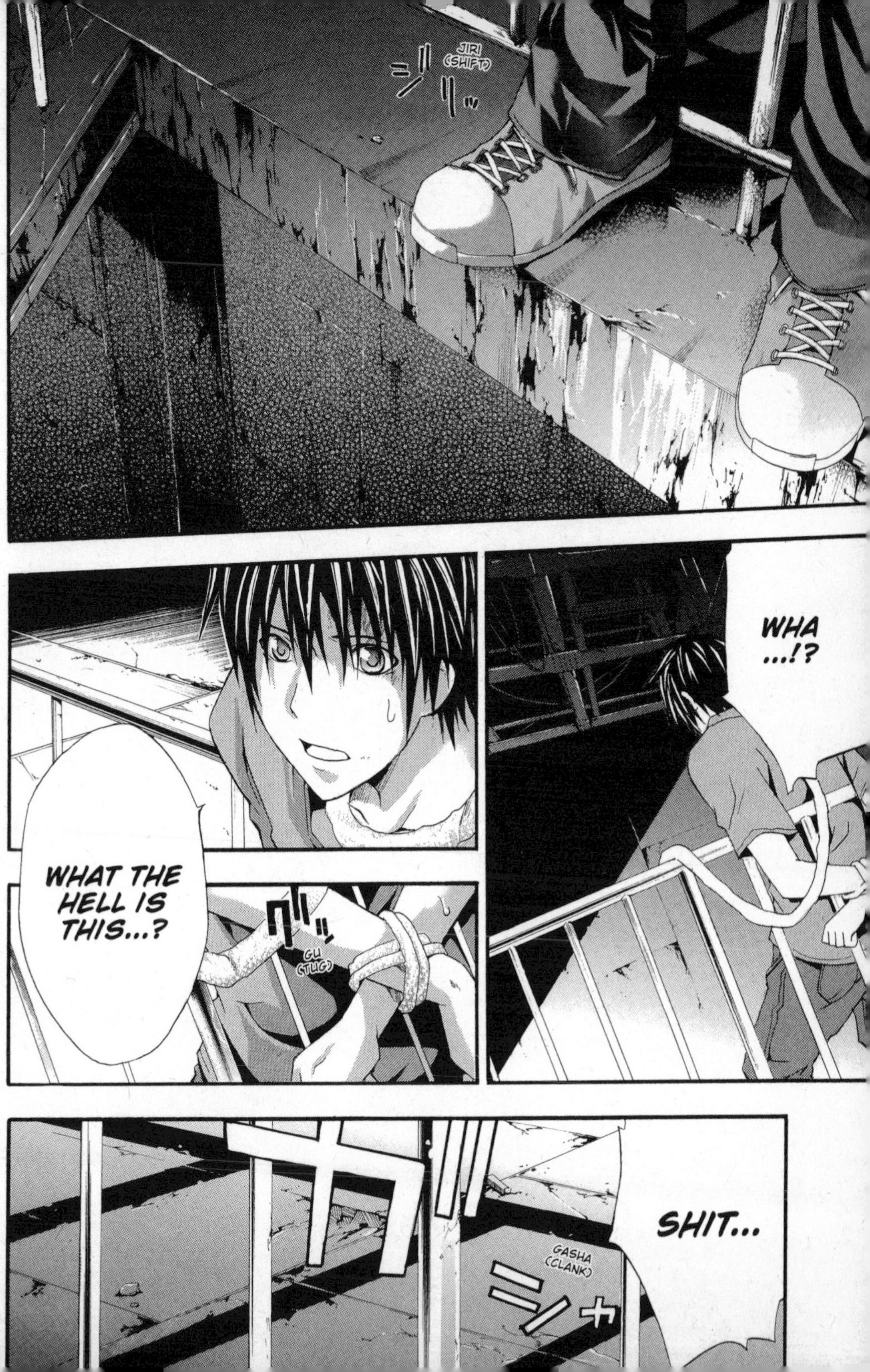
JIRI
(SHIFT)
WHA
...!?
WHAT THE HELL IS THIS...?
GU
(TUG)
SHIT...
GASHA
(CLANK)

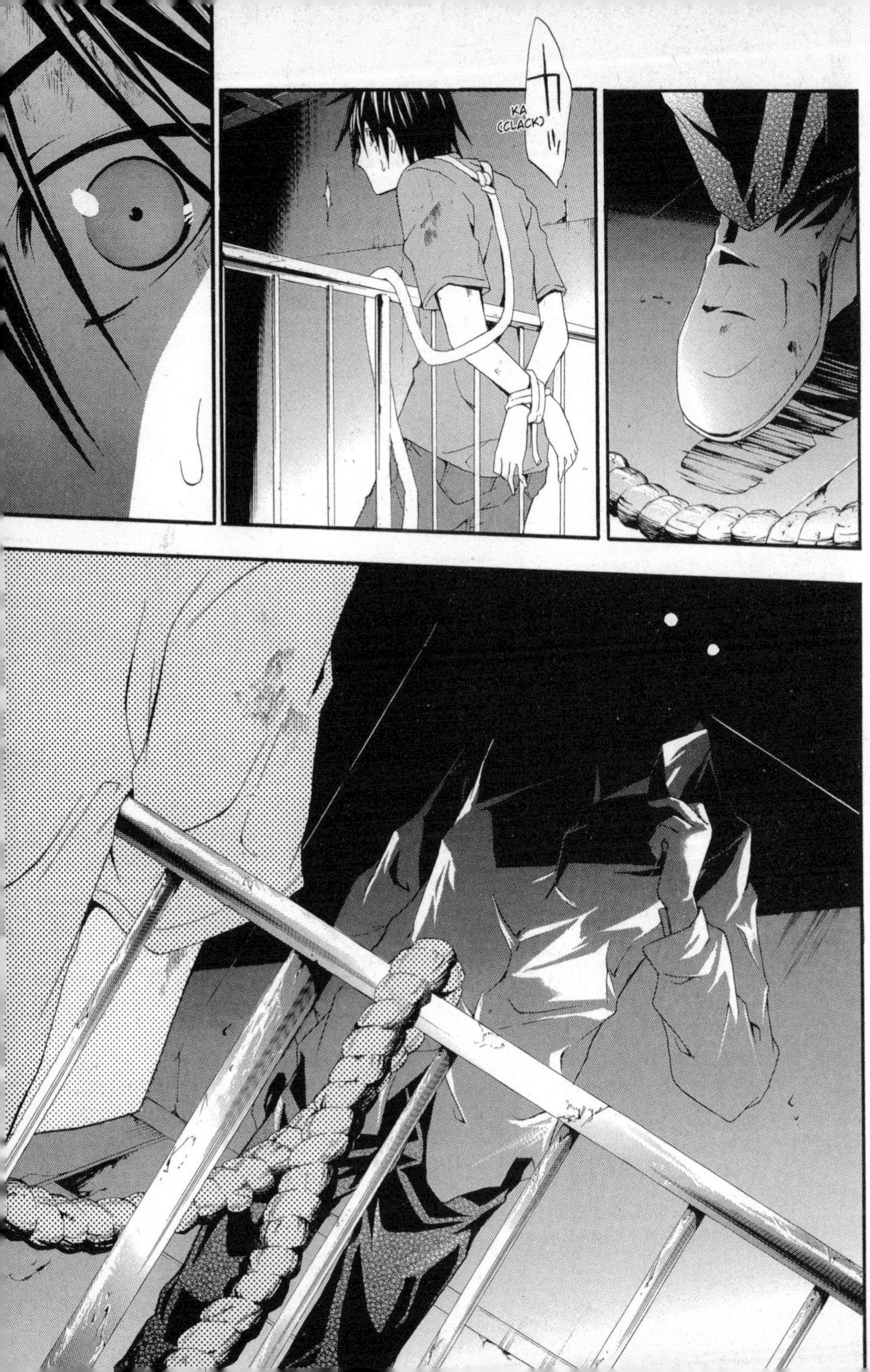
KA
(CLACK)

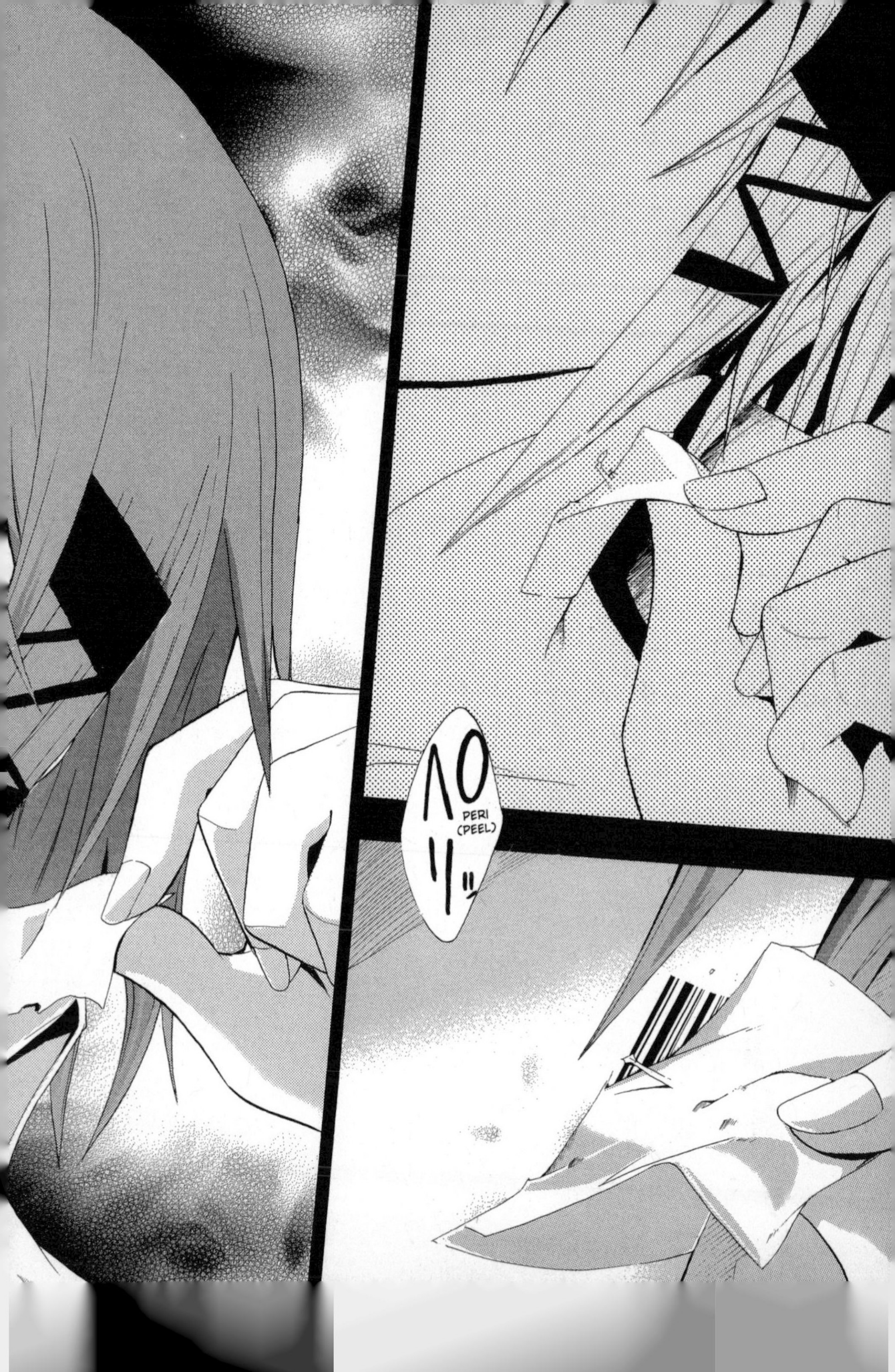
PERI
(PEEL)

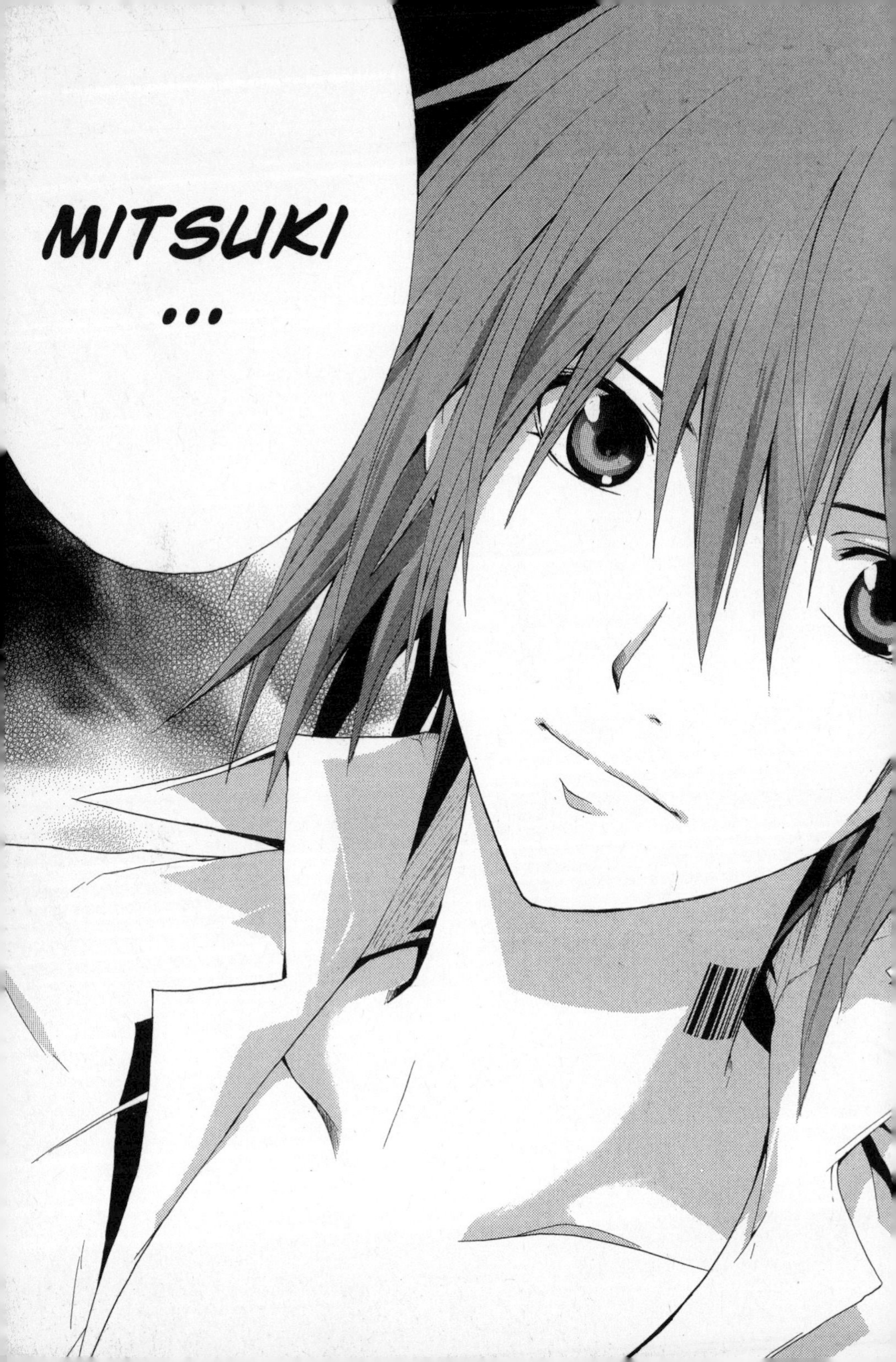
MITSUKI ...

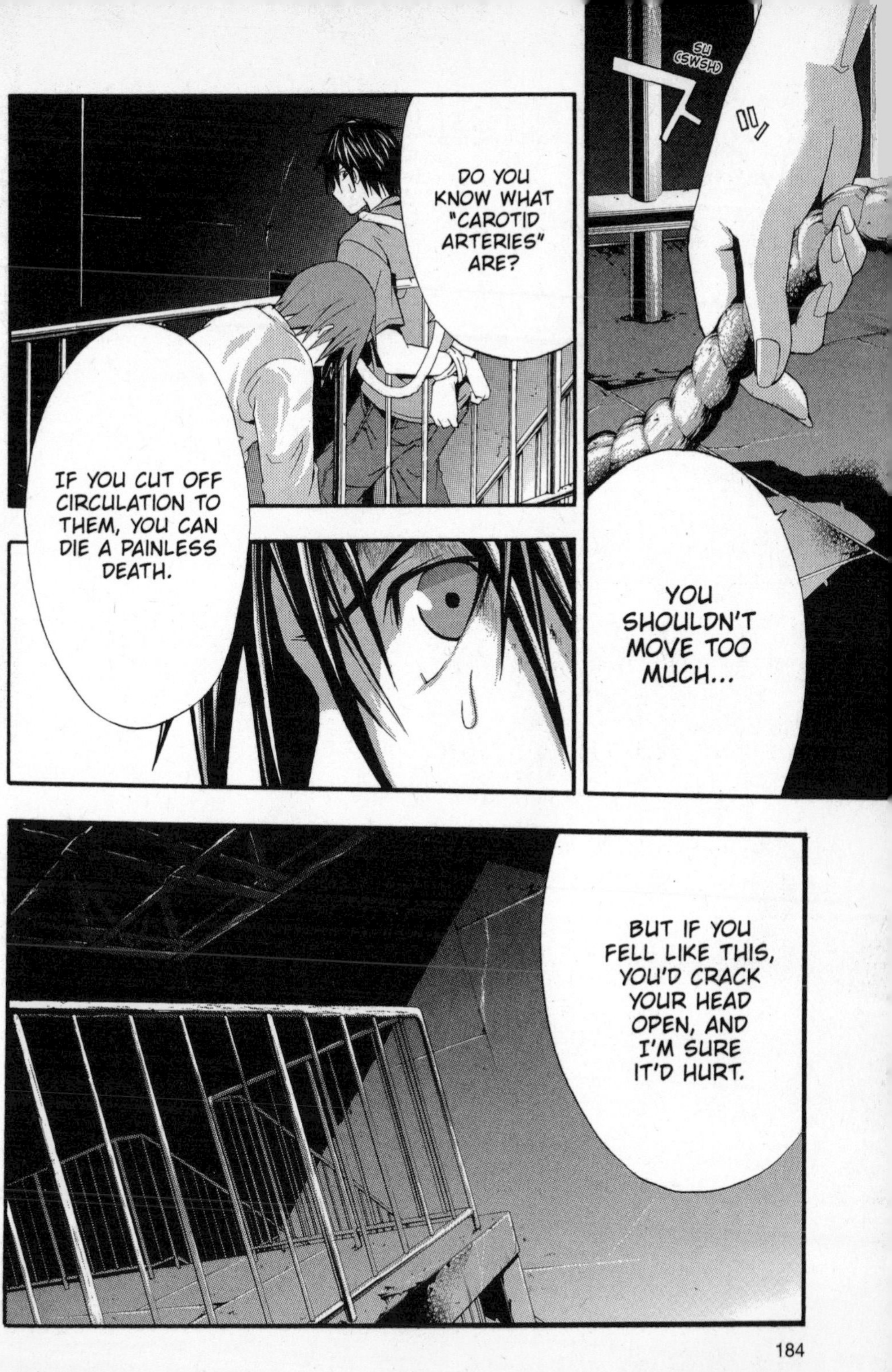
SU
(SWSH)
YOU SHOULDN'T MOVE TOO MUCH...
DO YOU KNOW WHAT "CAROTID ARTERIES" ARE?
IF YOU CUT OFF CIRCULATION TO THEM, YOU CAN DIE A PAINLESS DEATH.
BUT IF YOU FELL LIKE THIS, YOU'D CRACK YOUR HEAD OPEN, AND I'M SURE IT'D HURT.

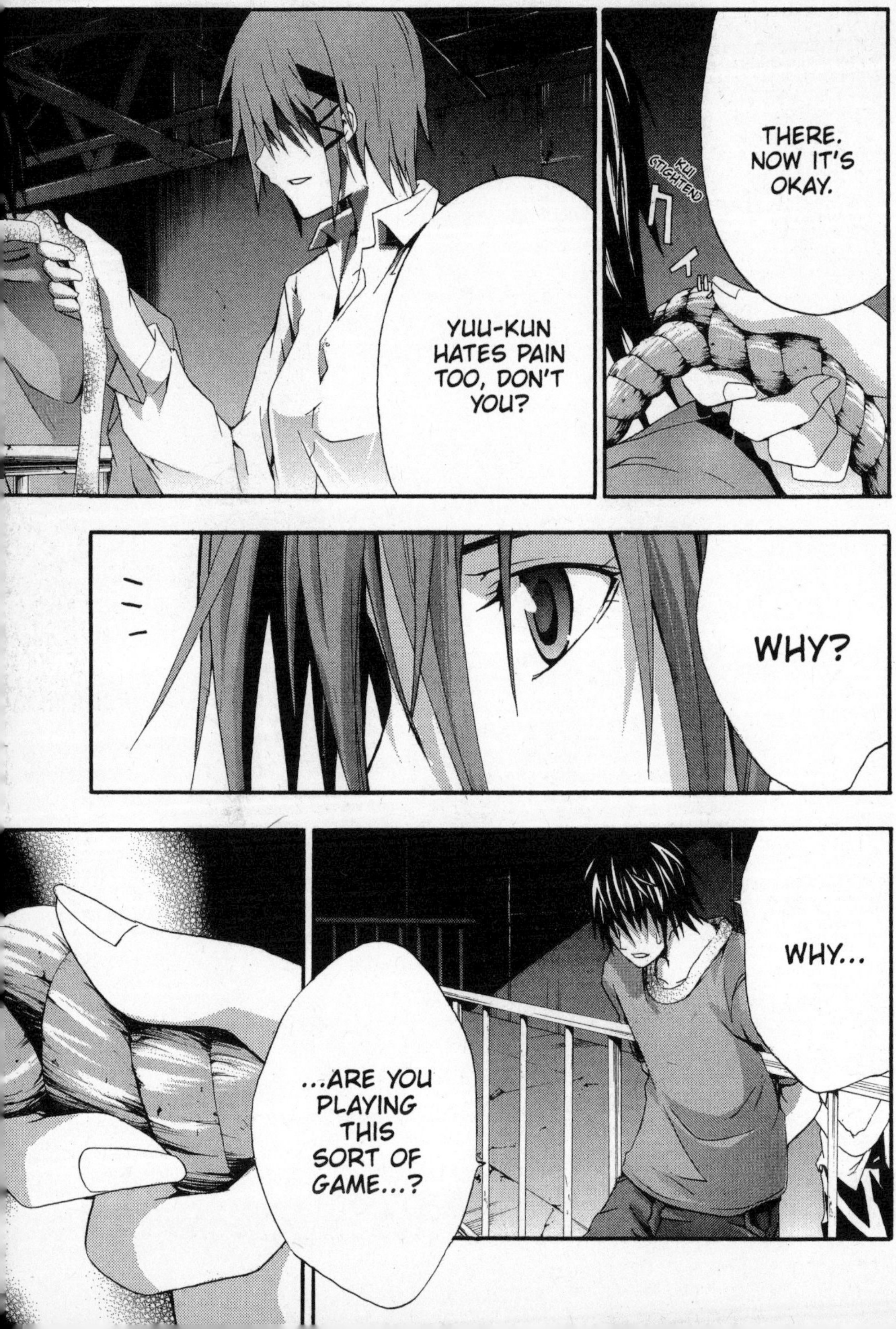
KUI (TIGHTEN)
THERE. NOW IT'S OKAY.
YUU-KUN HATES PAIN TOO, DON'T YOU?
WHY?
WHY...
...ARE YOU PLAYING THIS SORT OF GAME...?

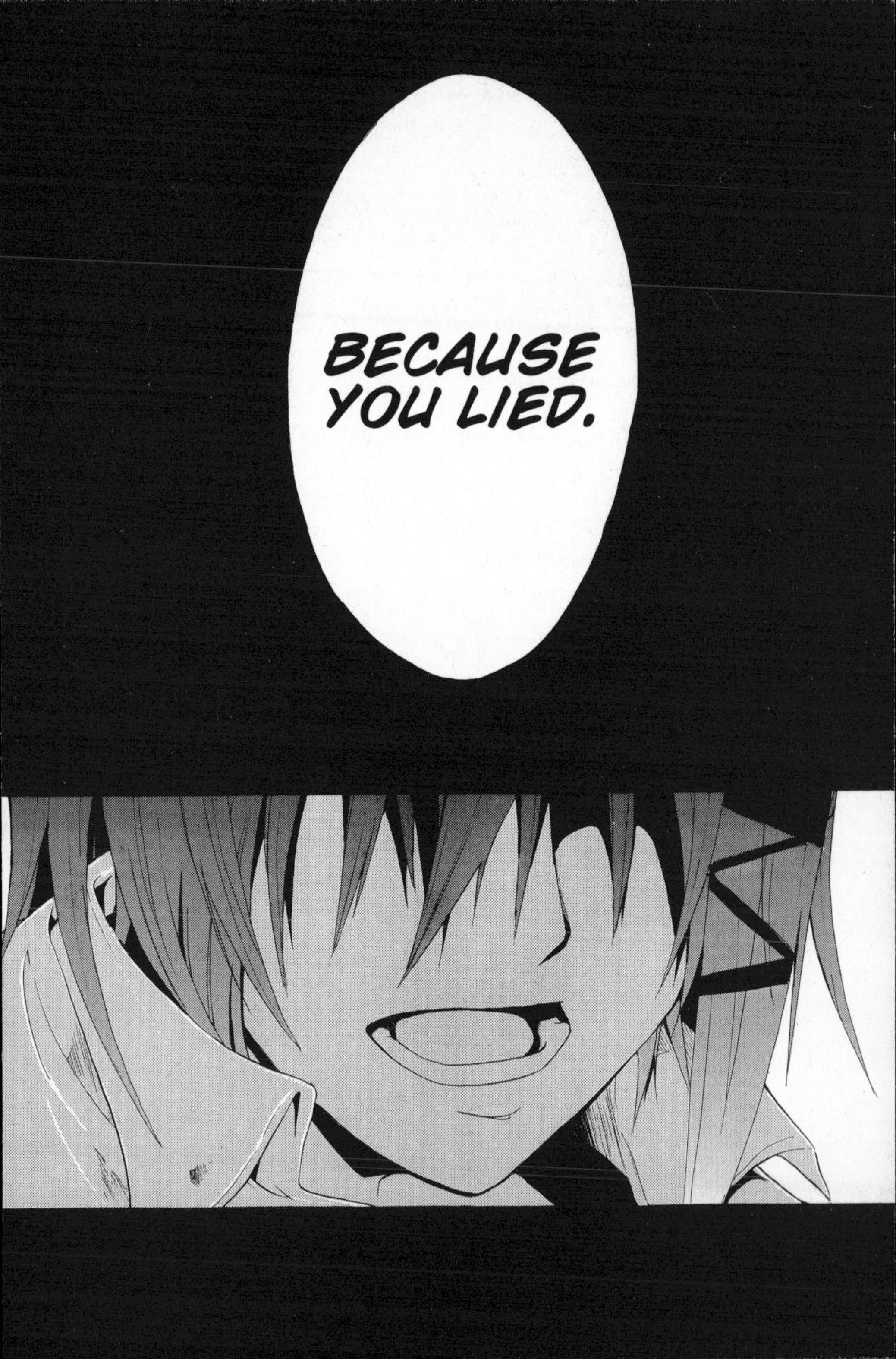
BECAUSE YOU LIED.

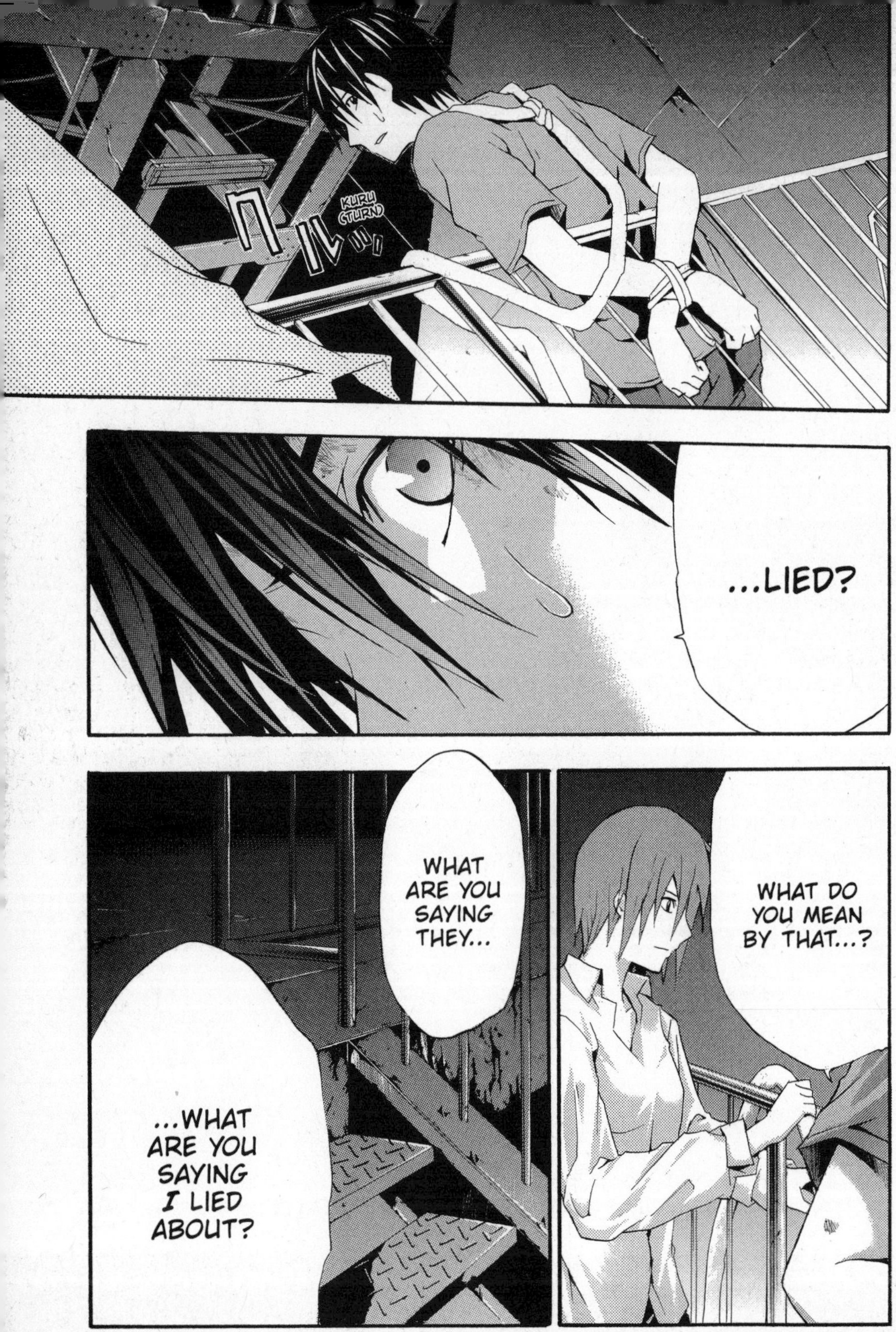
KURU (TURN)
...LIED?
WHAT DO YOU MEAN BY THAT...?
WHAT ARE YOU SAYING THEY...
...WHAT ARE YOU SAYING I LIED ABOUT?

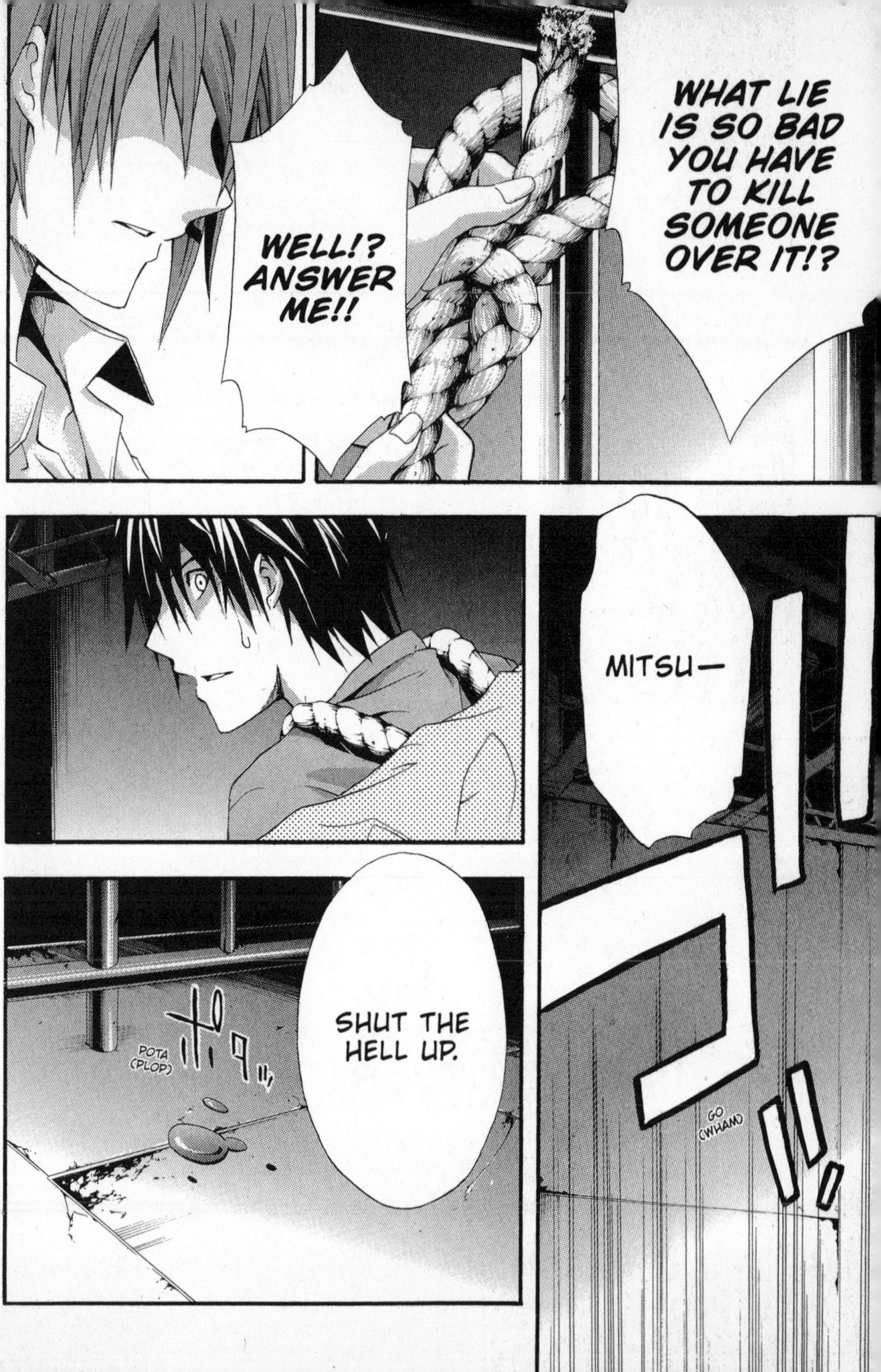
WHAT LIE IS SO BAD YOU HAVE TO KILL SOMEONE OVER IT!?
WELL!? ANSWER ME!!
MITSU—
GO (WHAM)
SHUT THE HELL UP.
POTA (PLOP)

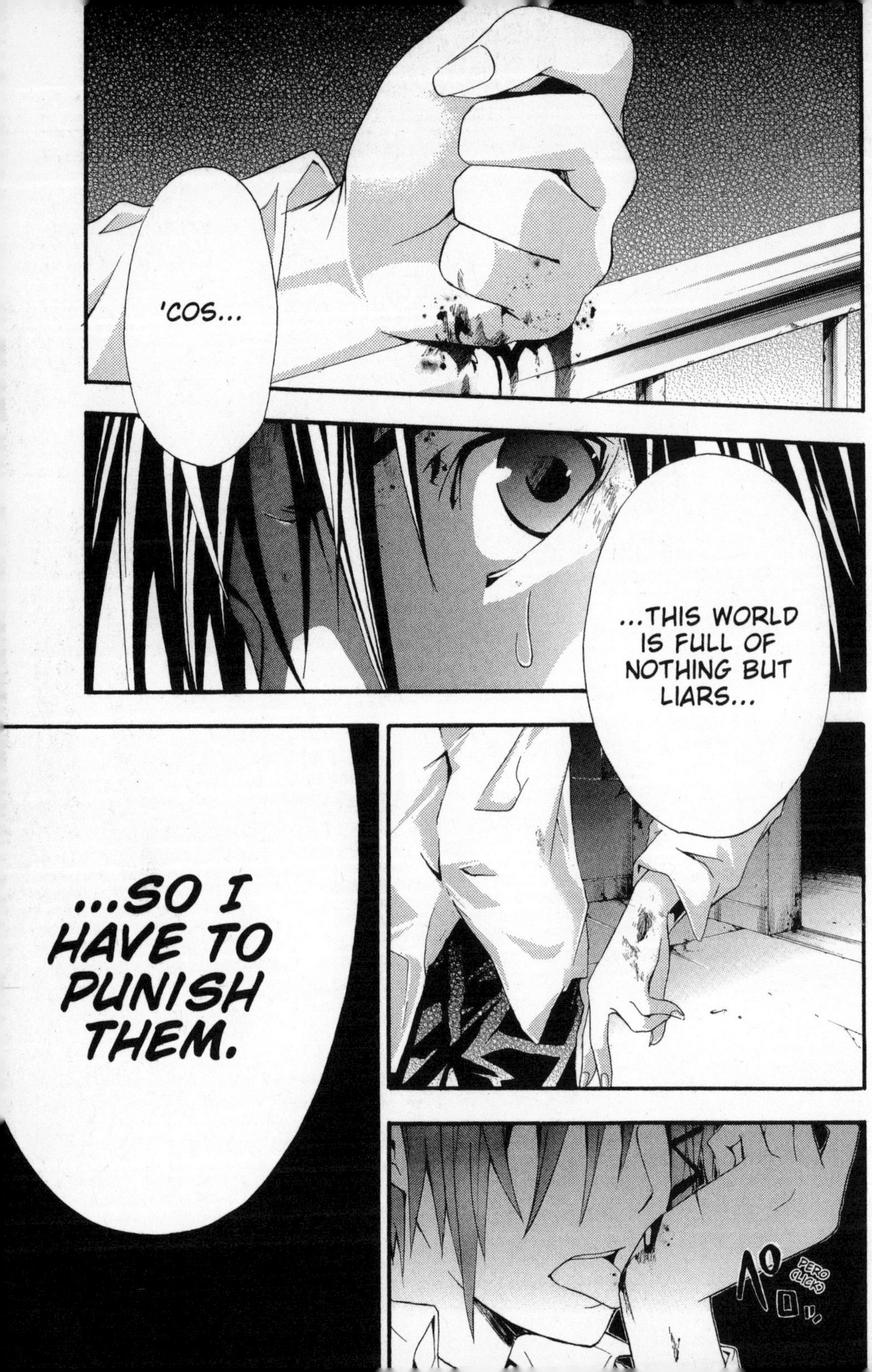
'COS...
...THIS WORLD IS FULL OF NOTHING BUT LIARS...
...SO I HAVE TO PUNISH THEM.
PERO (CLICK)

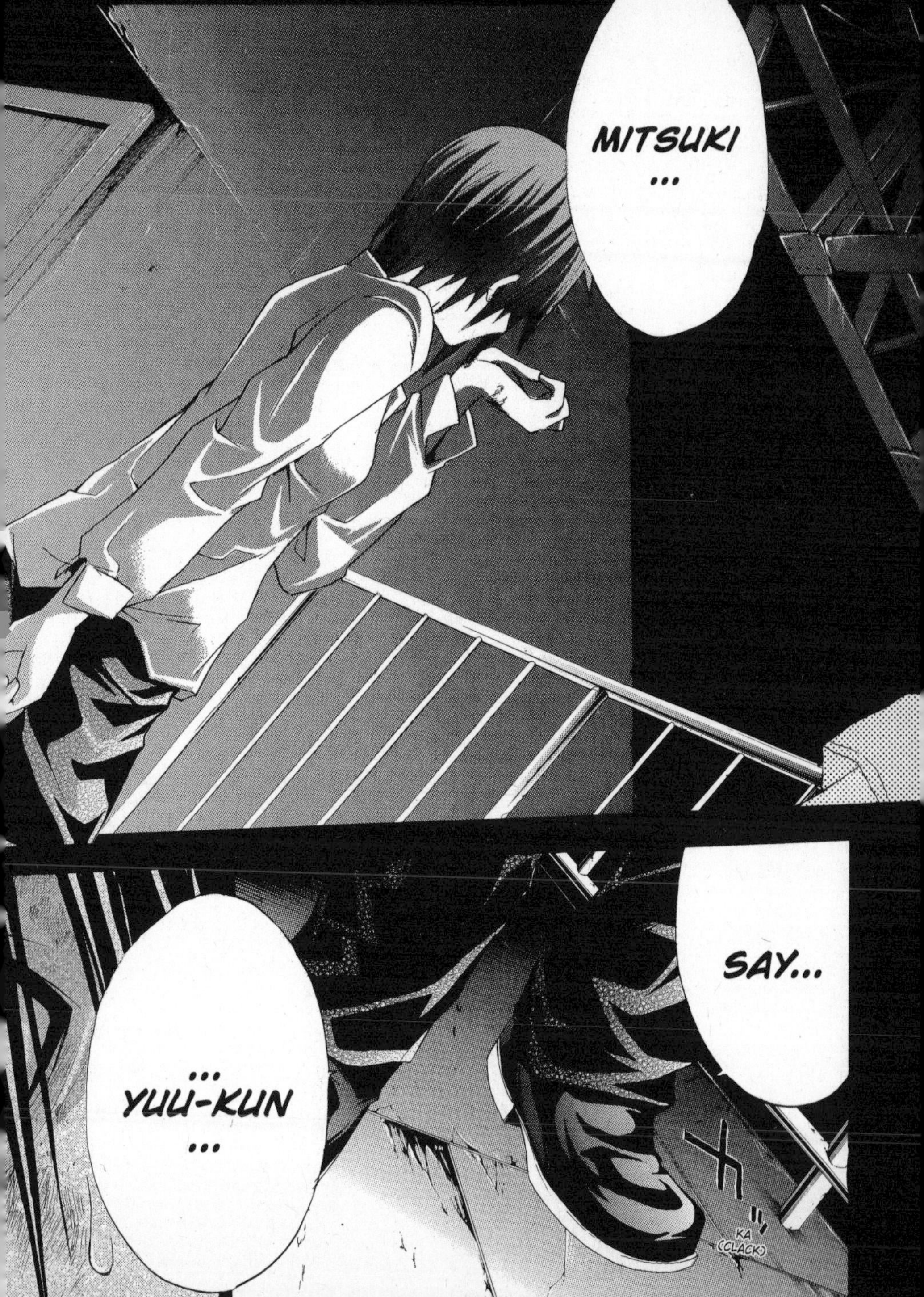
MITSUKI ...
SAY...
... YUU-KUN ...
KA (CLACK)

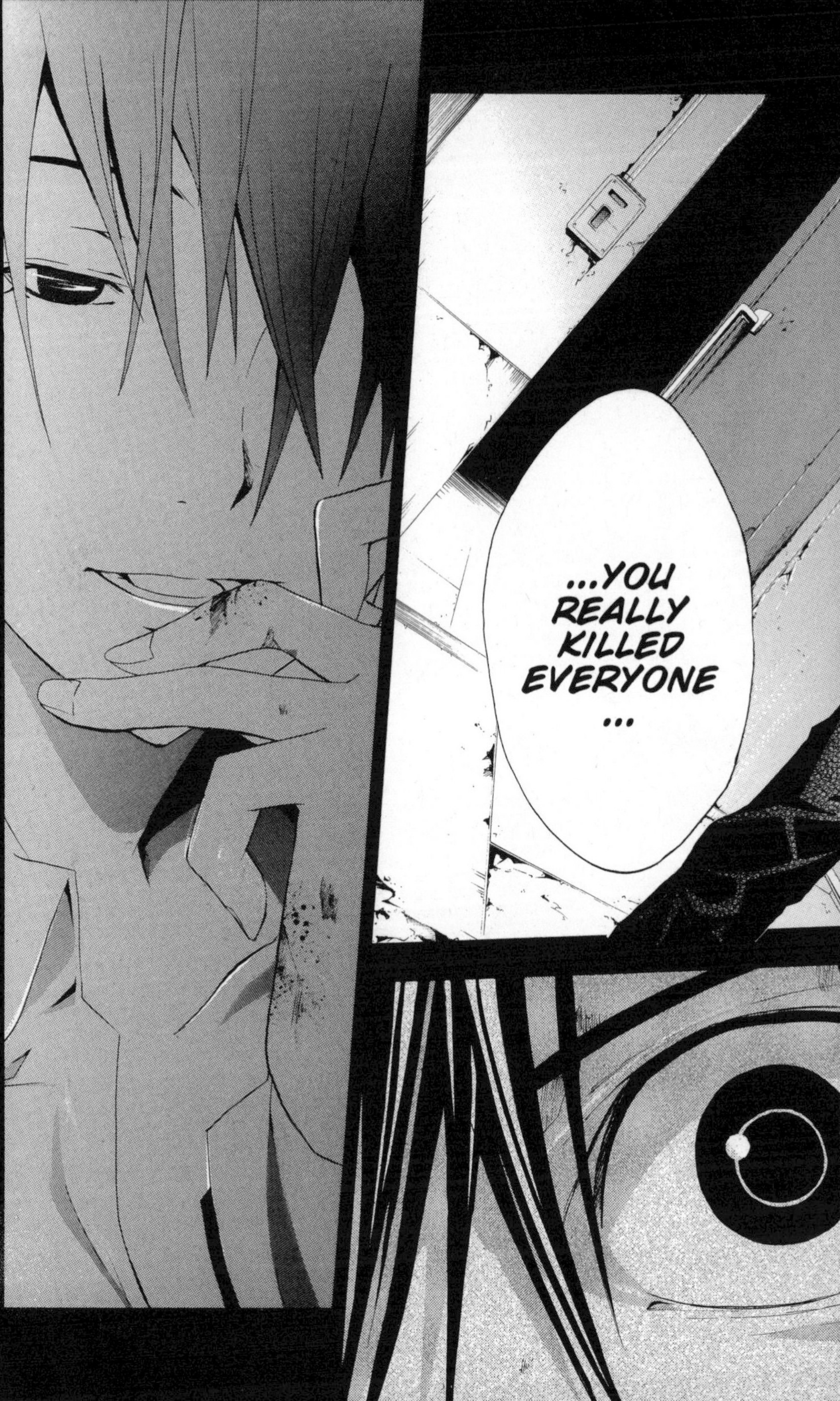
...YOU REALLY KILLED EVERYONE ...

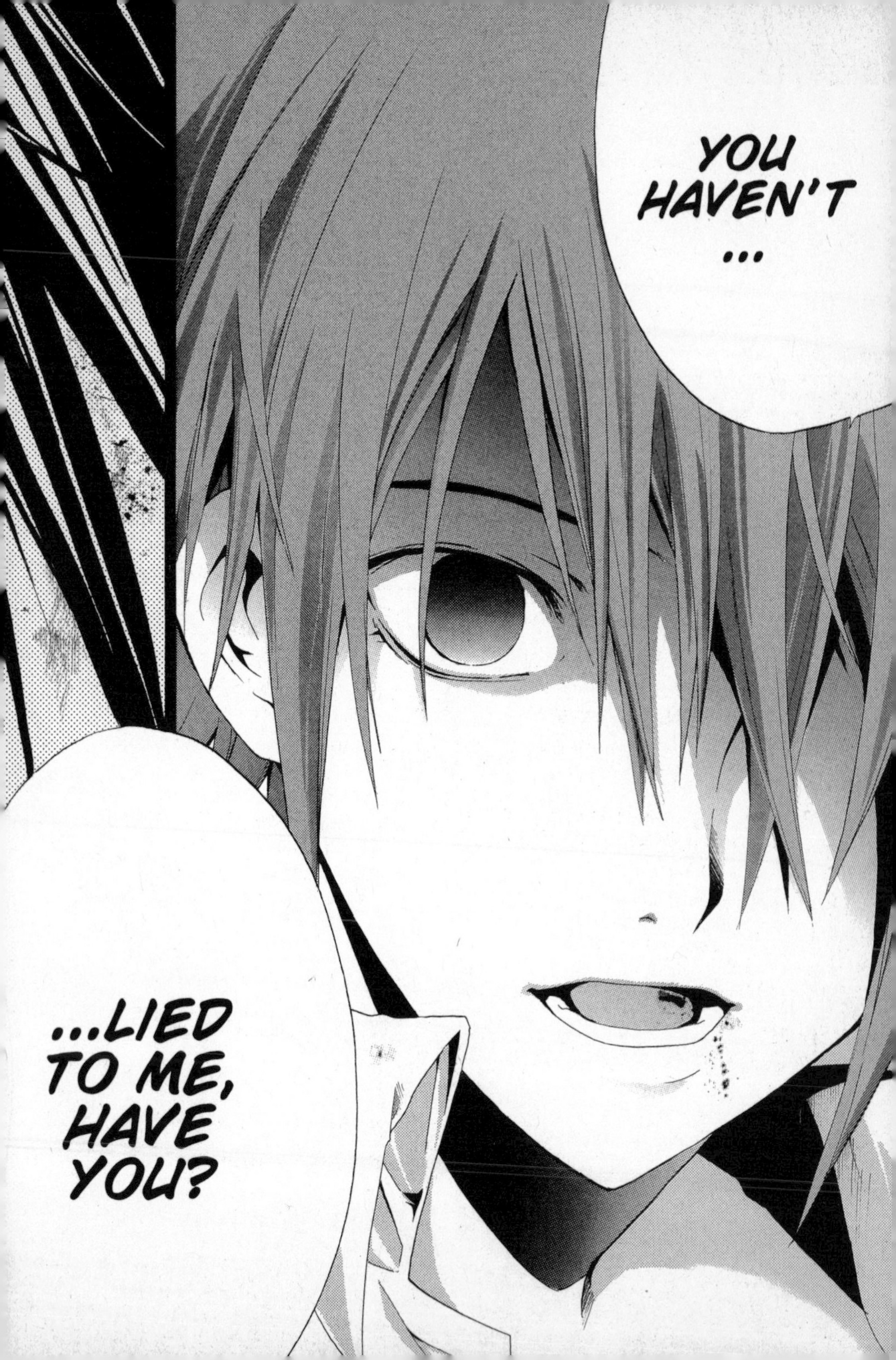
YOU HAVEN'T ...
...LIED TO ME, HAVE YOU?

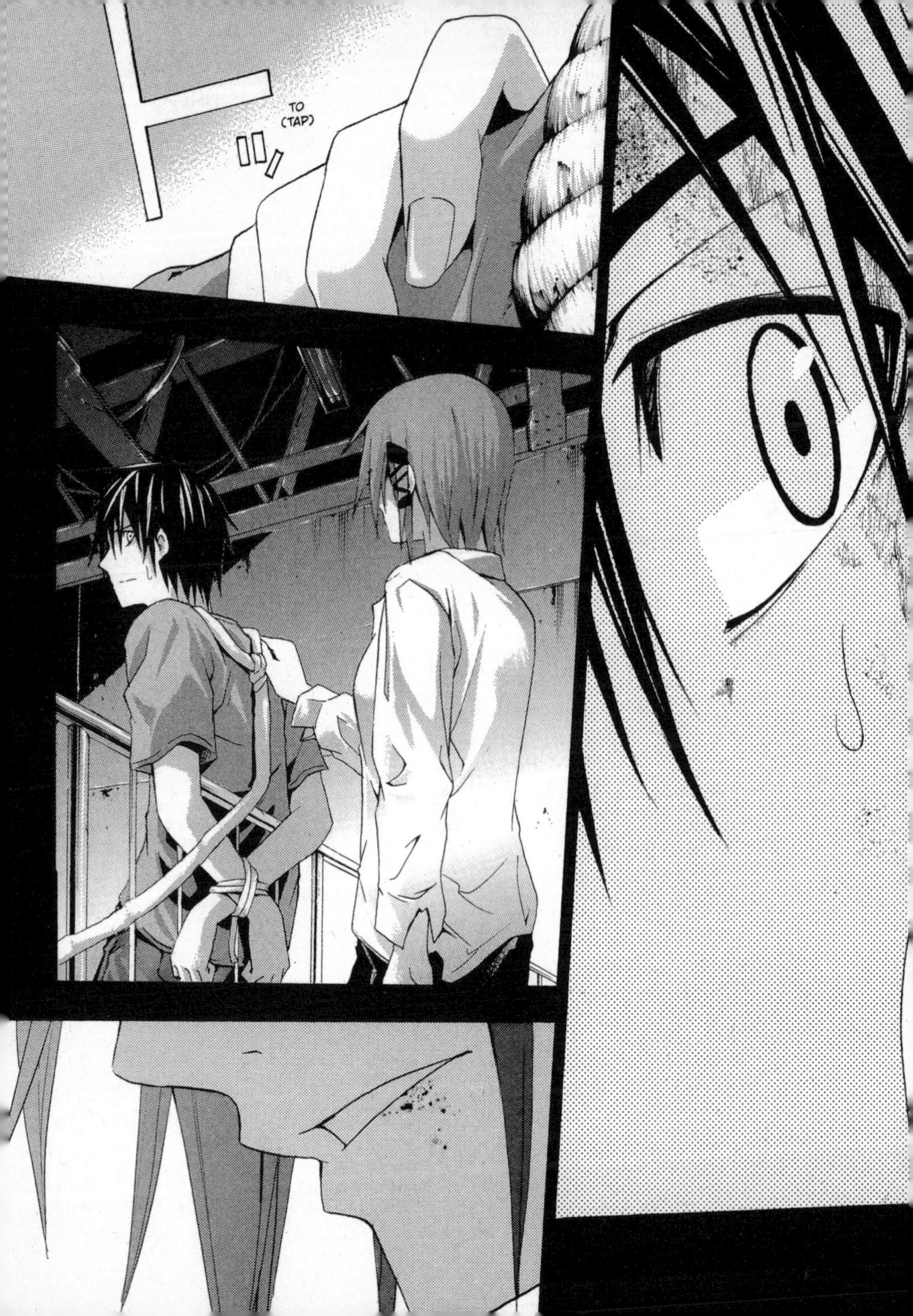
TO
(TAP)

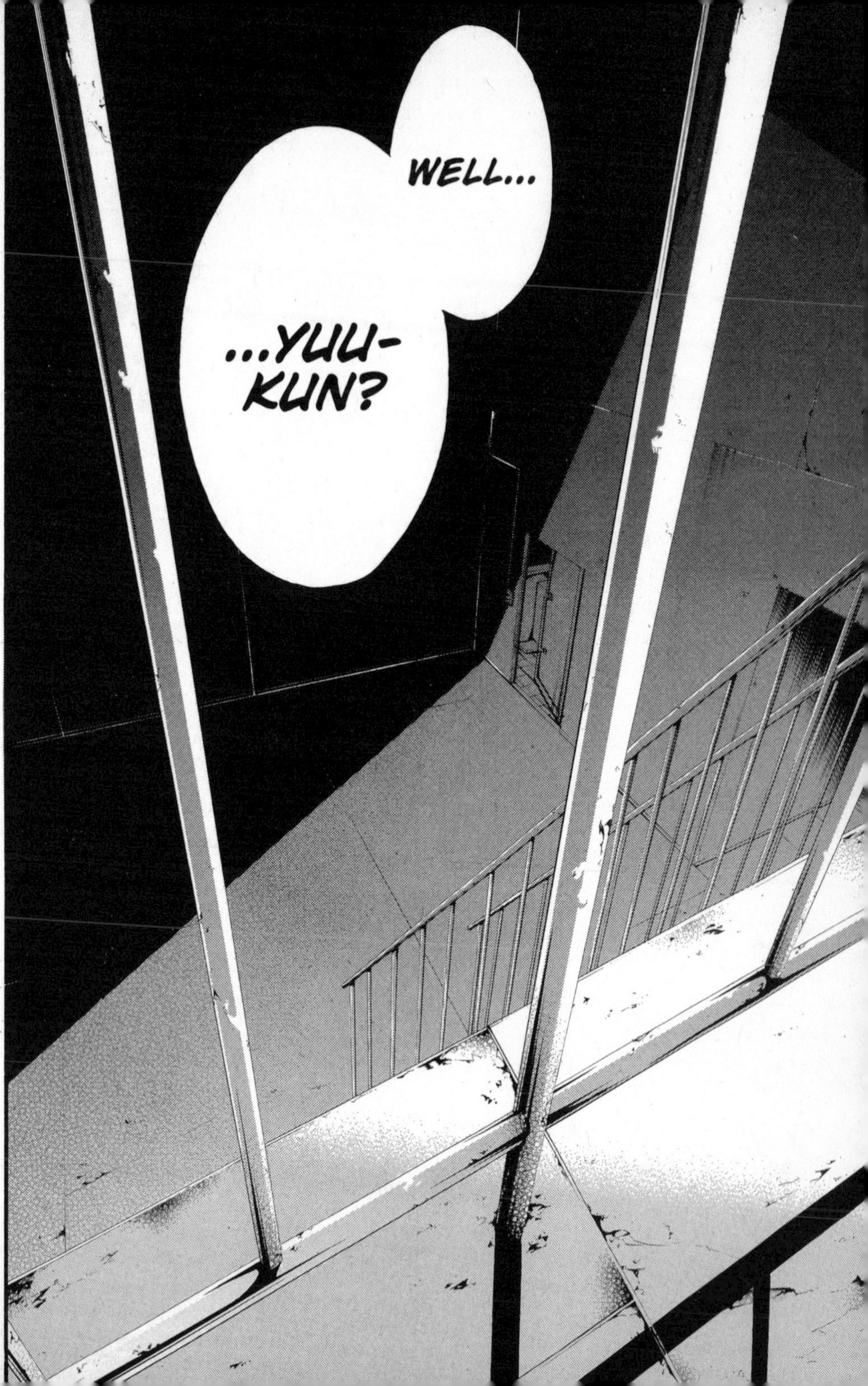
WELL...
...YUU-KUN?

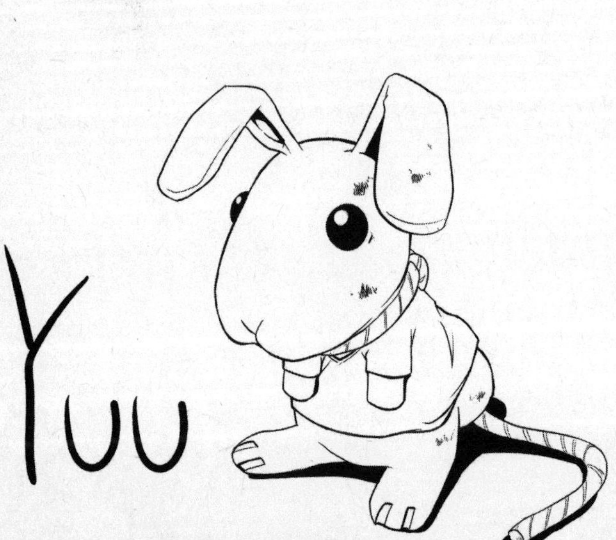
Yuu

MI
TSUKI

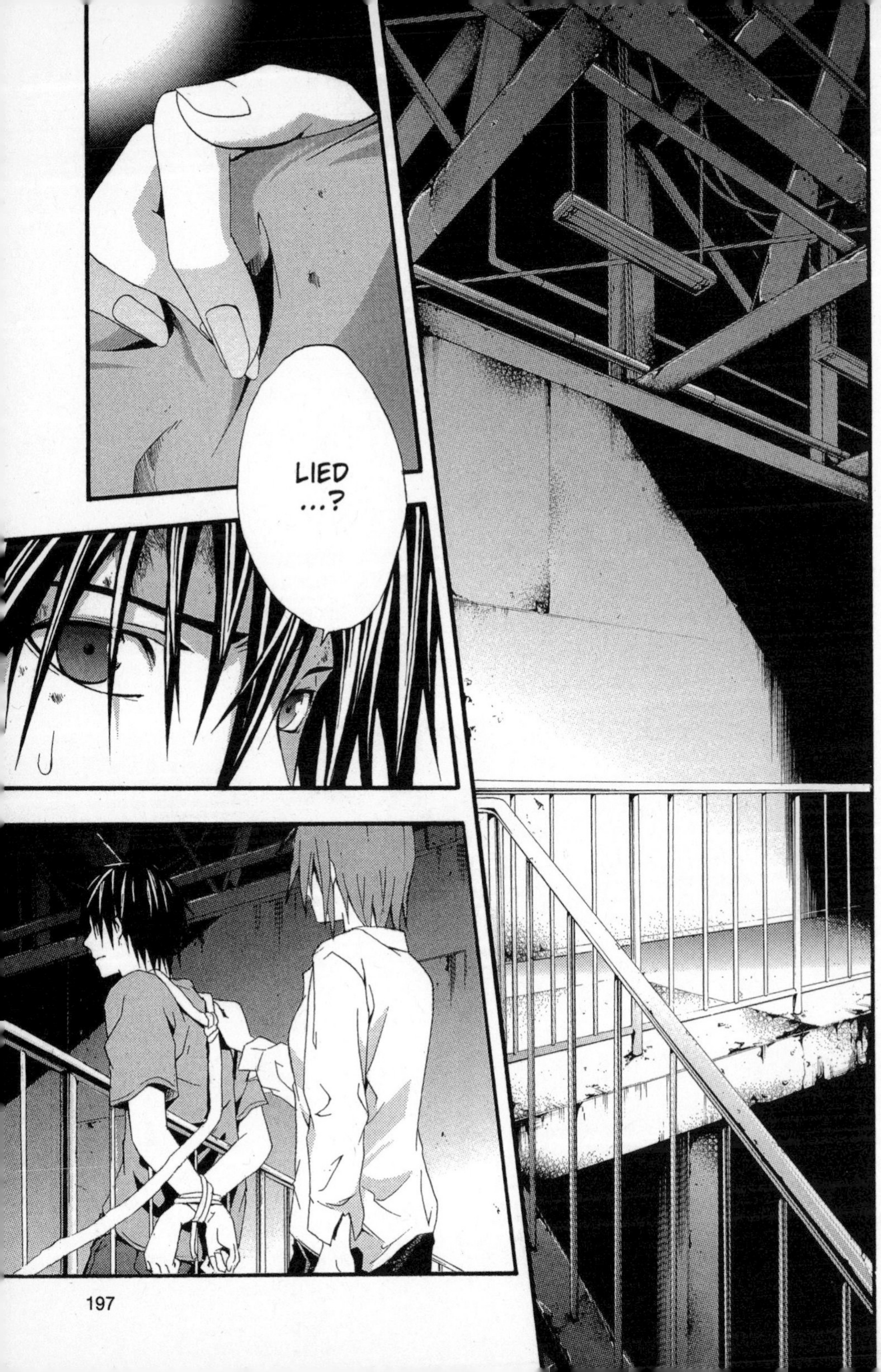
LIED ...?

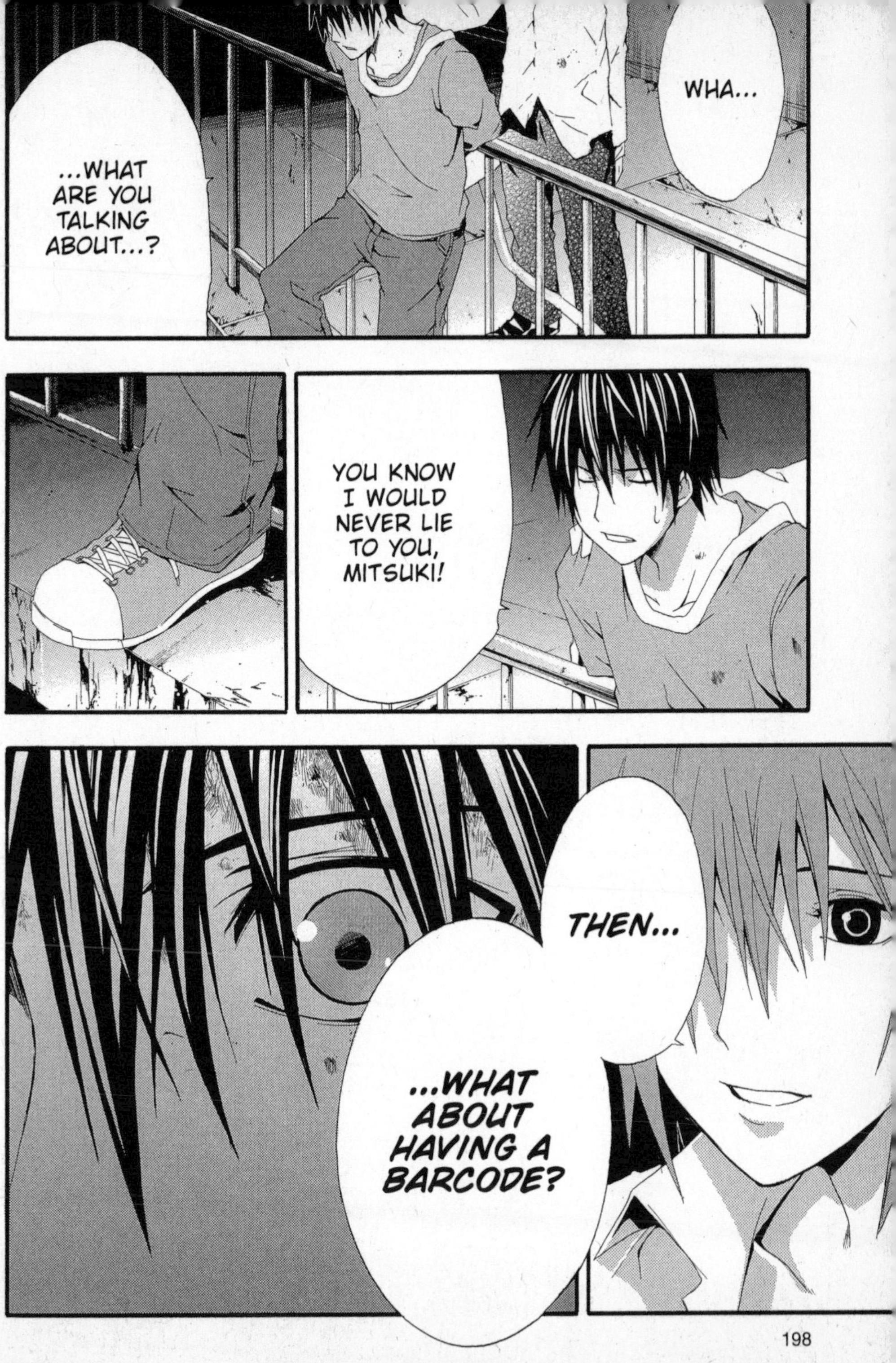
WHA...
...WHAT ARE YOU TALKING ABOUT...?
YOU KNOW I WOULD NEVER LIE TO YOU, MITSUKI!
THEN...
...WHAT ABOUT HAVING A BARCODE?

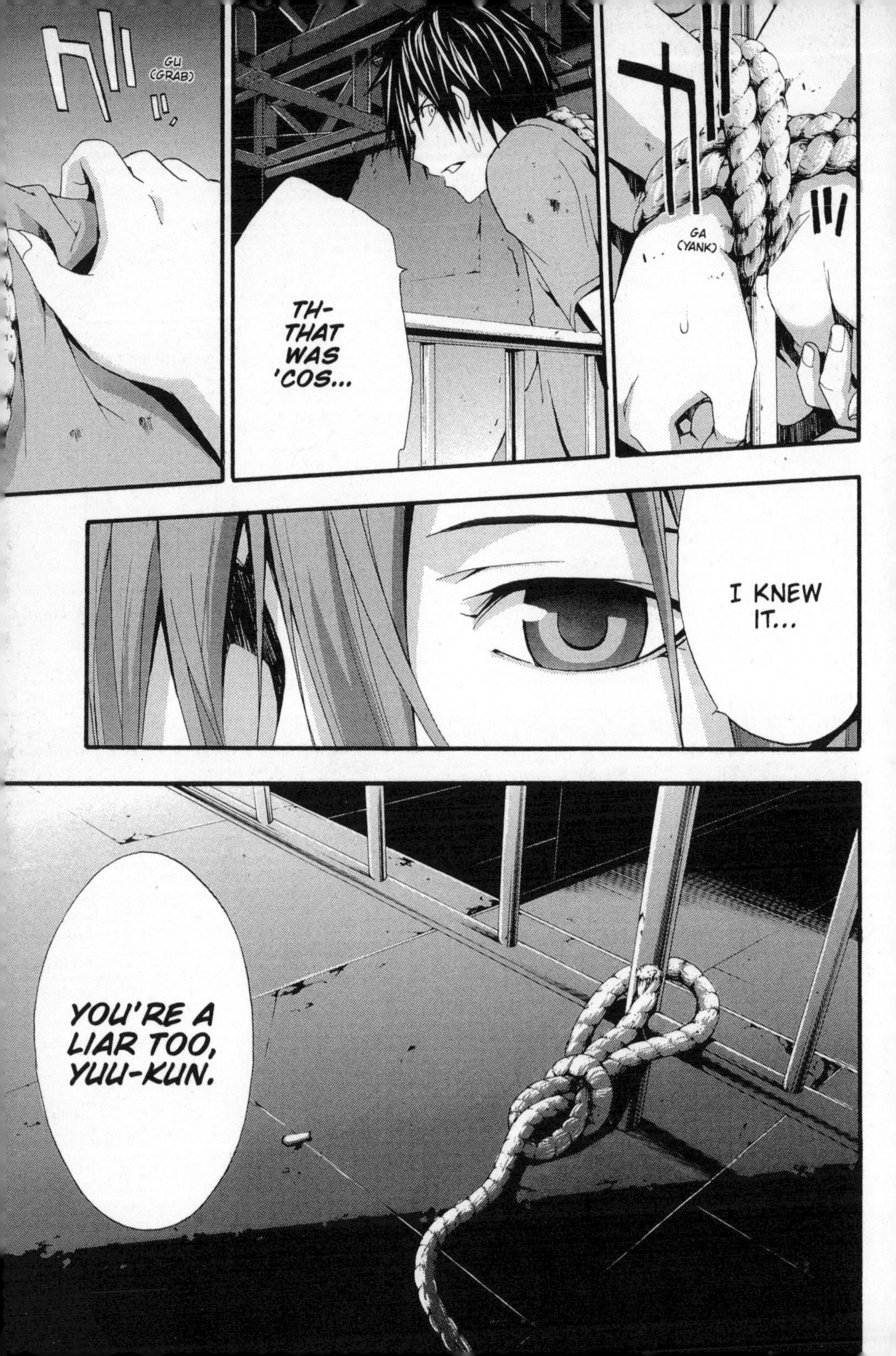
GA (YANK)
I...
...
TH- THAT WAS 'COS...
GU (GRAB)
I KNEW IT...
YOU'RE A LIAR TOO, YUU-KUN.

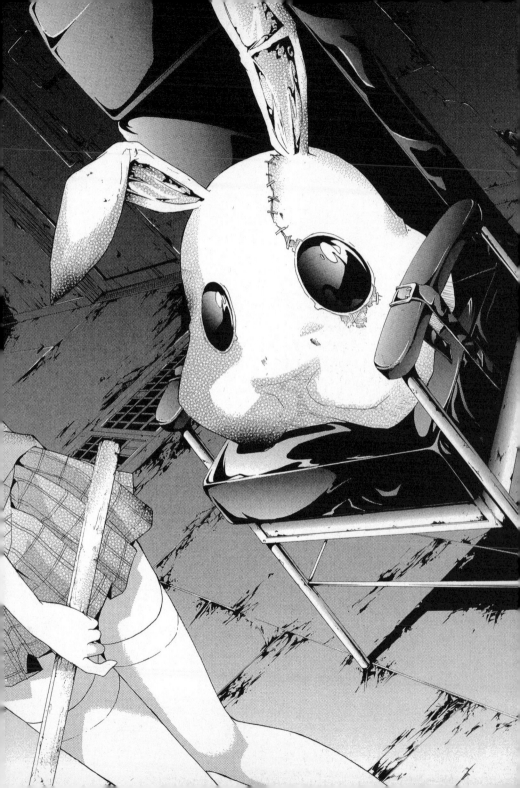

Doubt.15 LAST CHANCE

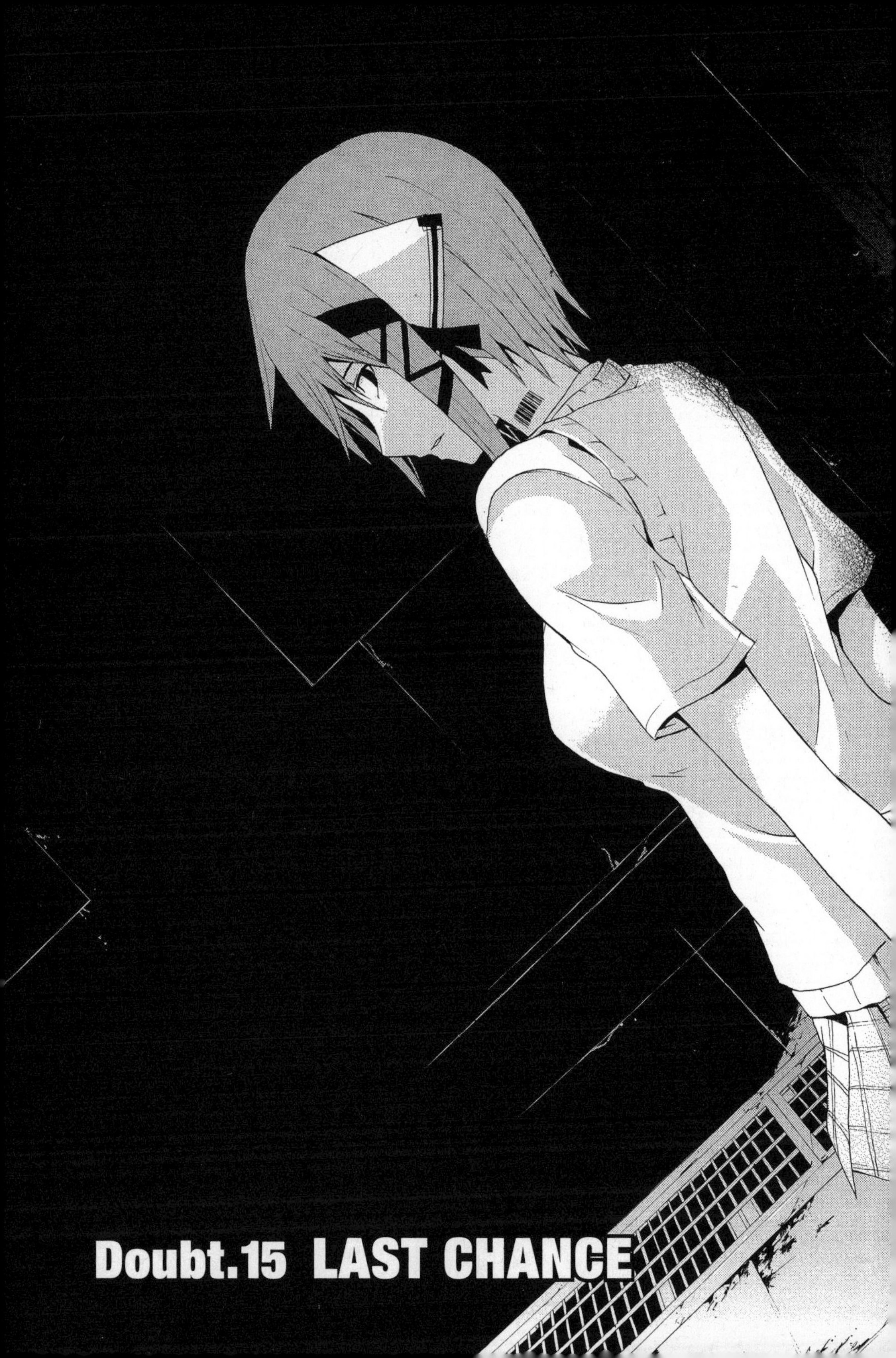

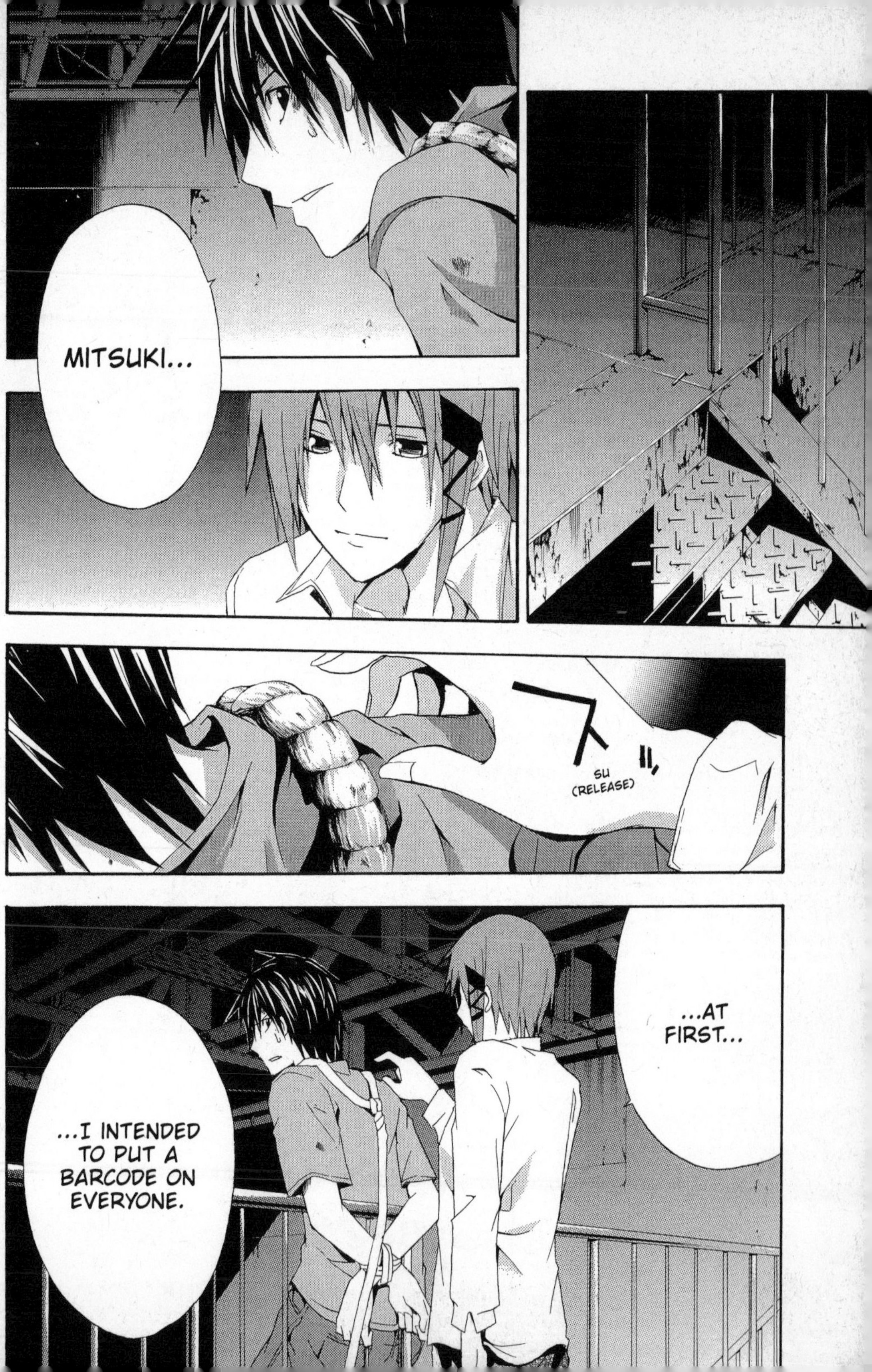
MITSUKI...
SU (RELEASE)
...AT FIRST...
...I INTENDED TO PUT A BARCODE ON EVERYONE.

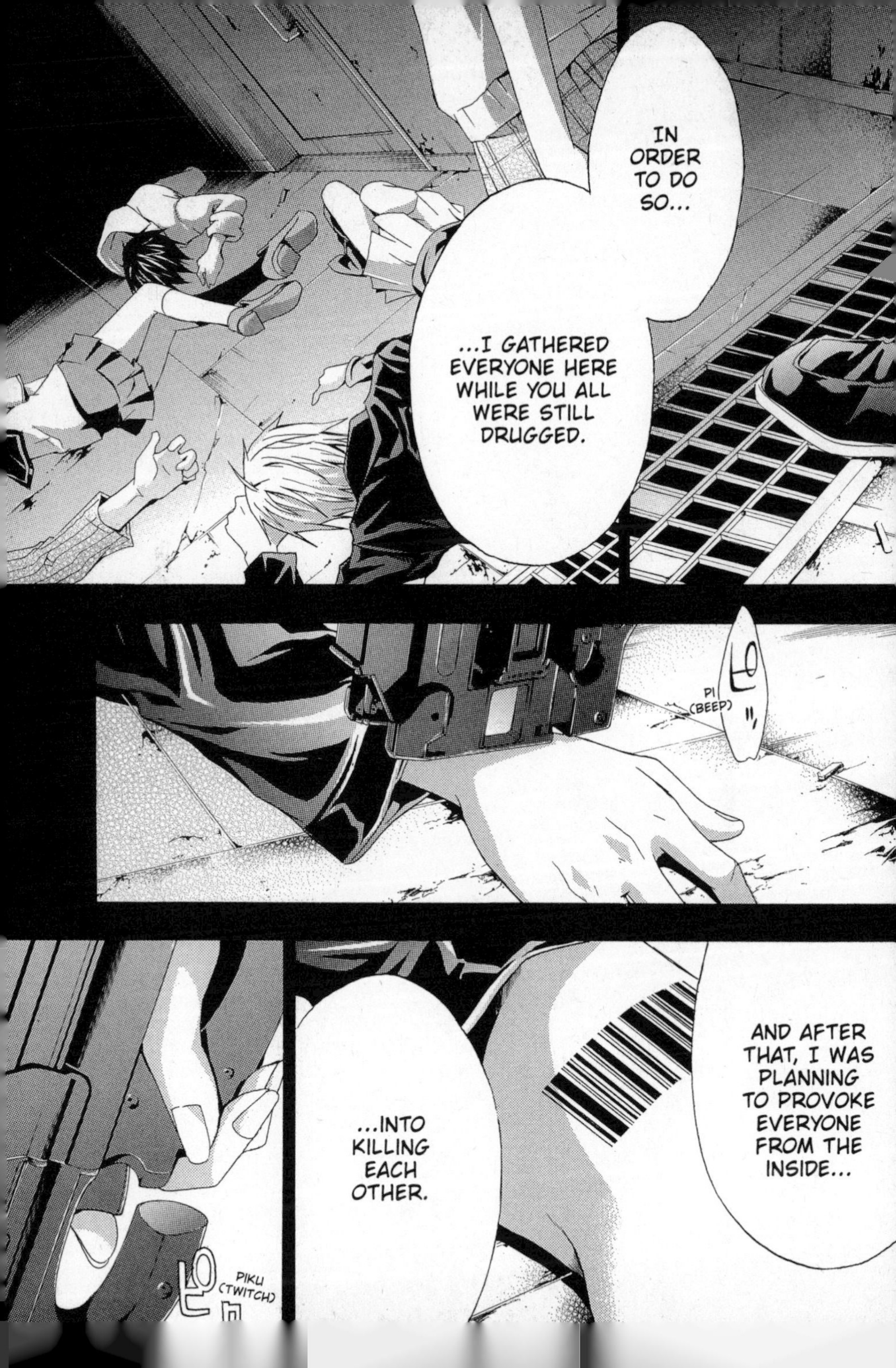
IN ORDER TO DO SO...
...I GATHERED EVERYONE HERE WHILE YOU ALL WERE STILL DRUGGED.
PI (BEEP)
AND AFTER THAT, I WAS PLANNING TO PROVOKE EVERYONE FROM THE INSIDE...
...INTO KILLING EACH OTHER.
PIKU (TWITCH)

...BUT...

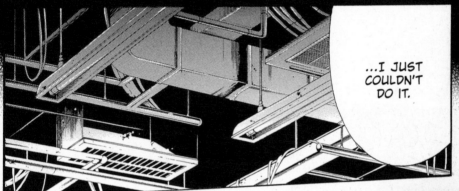

...I JUST COULDN'T DO IT.

I THOUGHT IF YOU WERE THE ONLY ONE WHO DIDN'T HAVE A BARCODE...

...YOU'D BE THE VERY FIRST PERSON THEY'D SUSPECT.

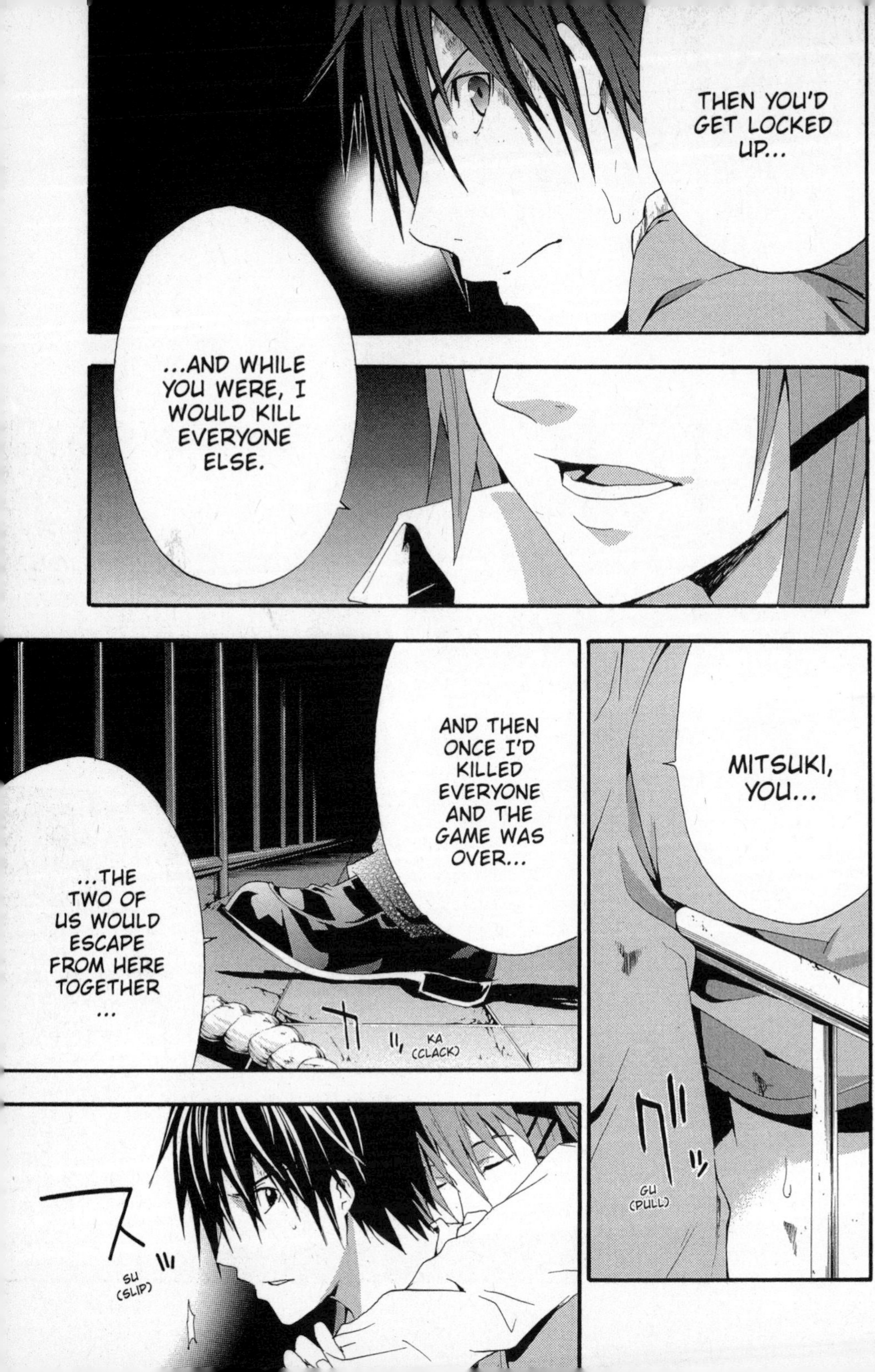
THEN YOU'D GET LOCKED UP...
...AND WHILE YOU WERE, I WOULD KILL EVERYONE ELSE.
MITSUKI, YOU...
GU (PULL)
AND THEN ONCE I'D KILLED EVERYONE AND THE GAME WAS OVER...
...THE TWO OF US WOULD ESCAPE FROM HERE TOGETHER ...
KA (CLACK)
SU (SLIP)

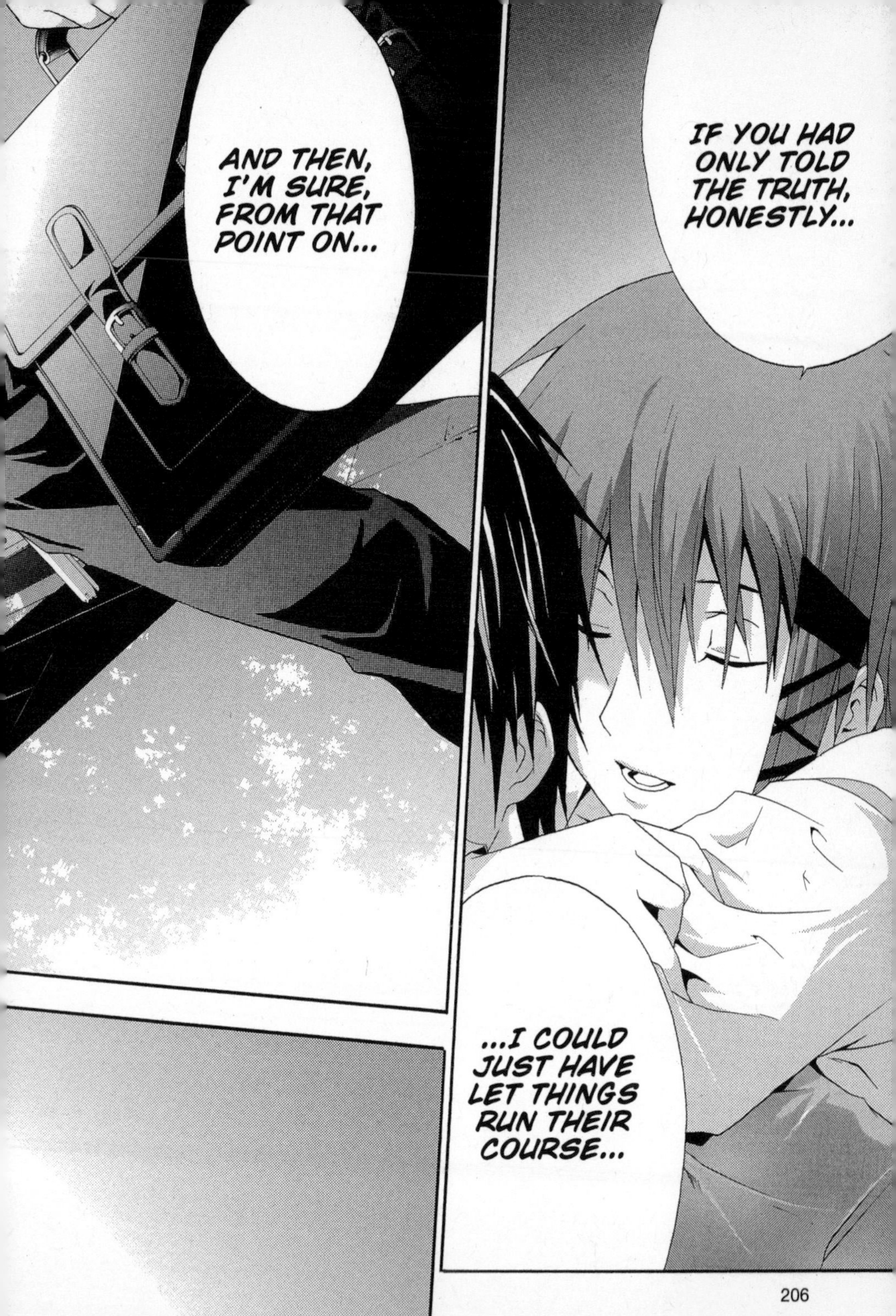
IF YOU HAD ONLY TOLD THE TRUTH, HONESTLY...
...I COULD JUST HAVE LET THINGS RUN THEIR COURSE...
AND THEN, I'M SURE, FROM THAT POINT ON...

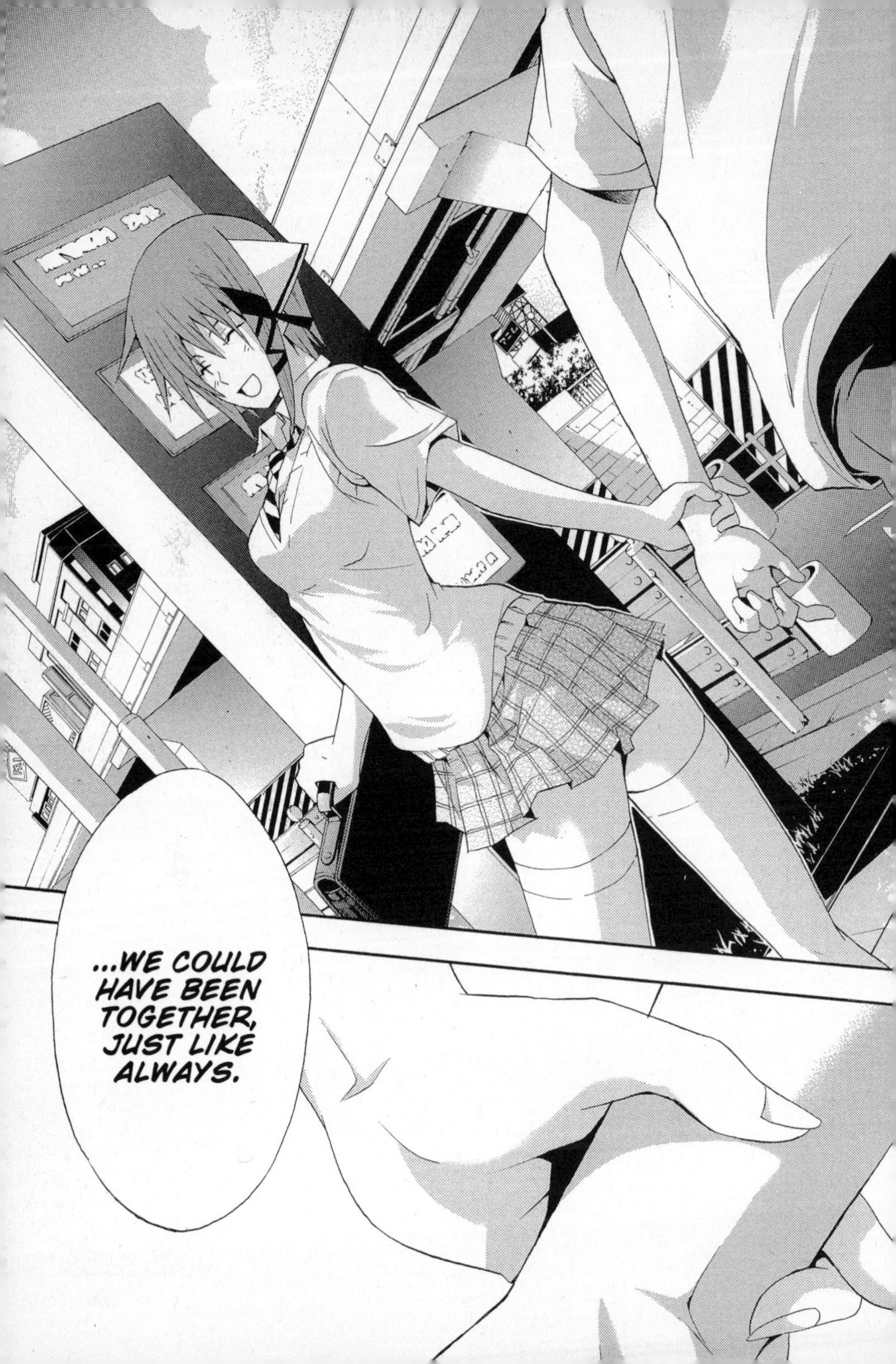
...WE COULD HAVE BEEN TOGETHER, JUST LIKE ALWAYS.

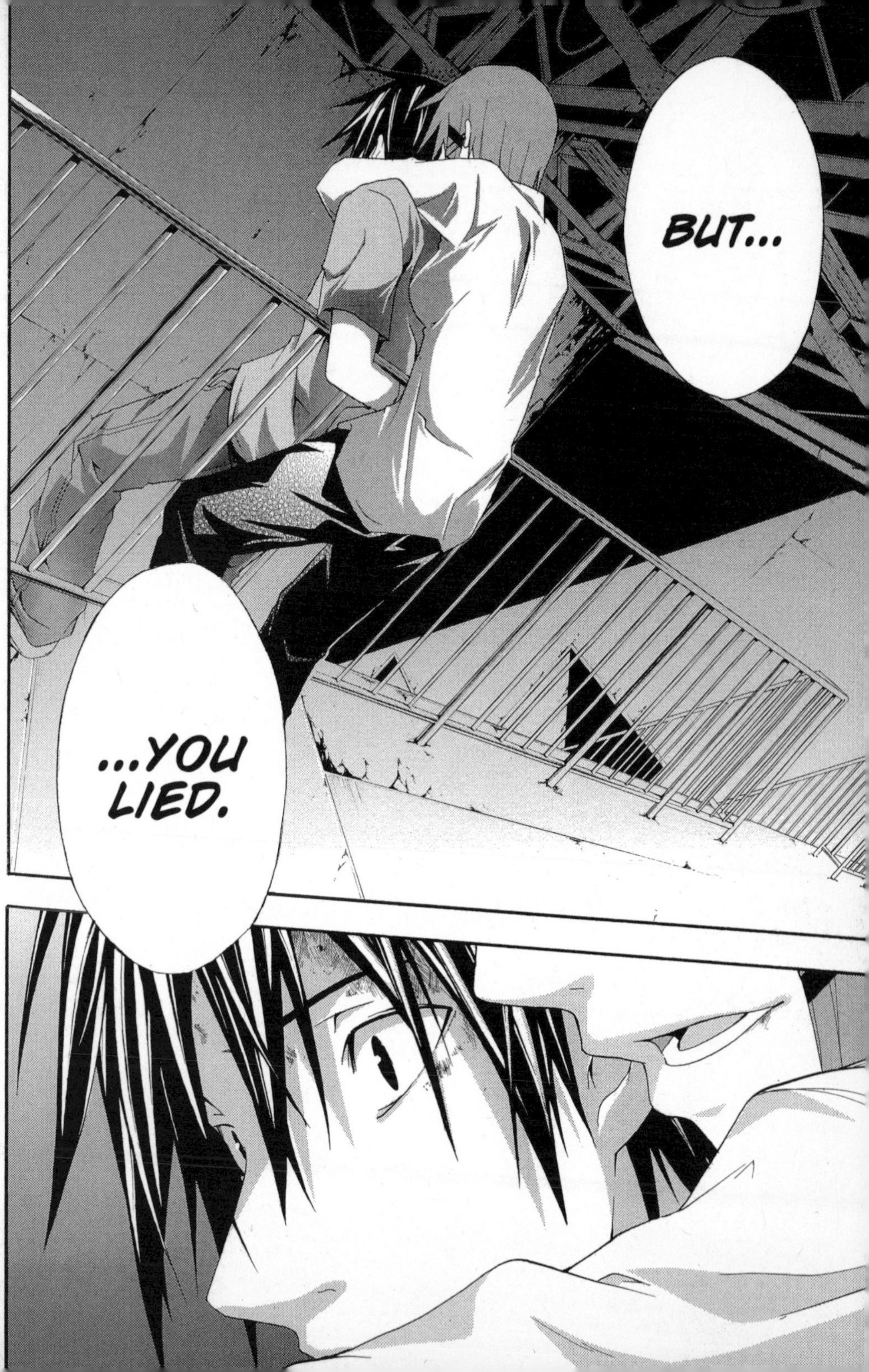
BUT...
...YOU LIED.

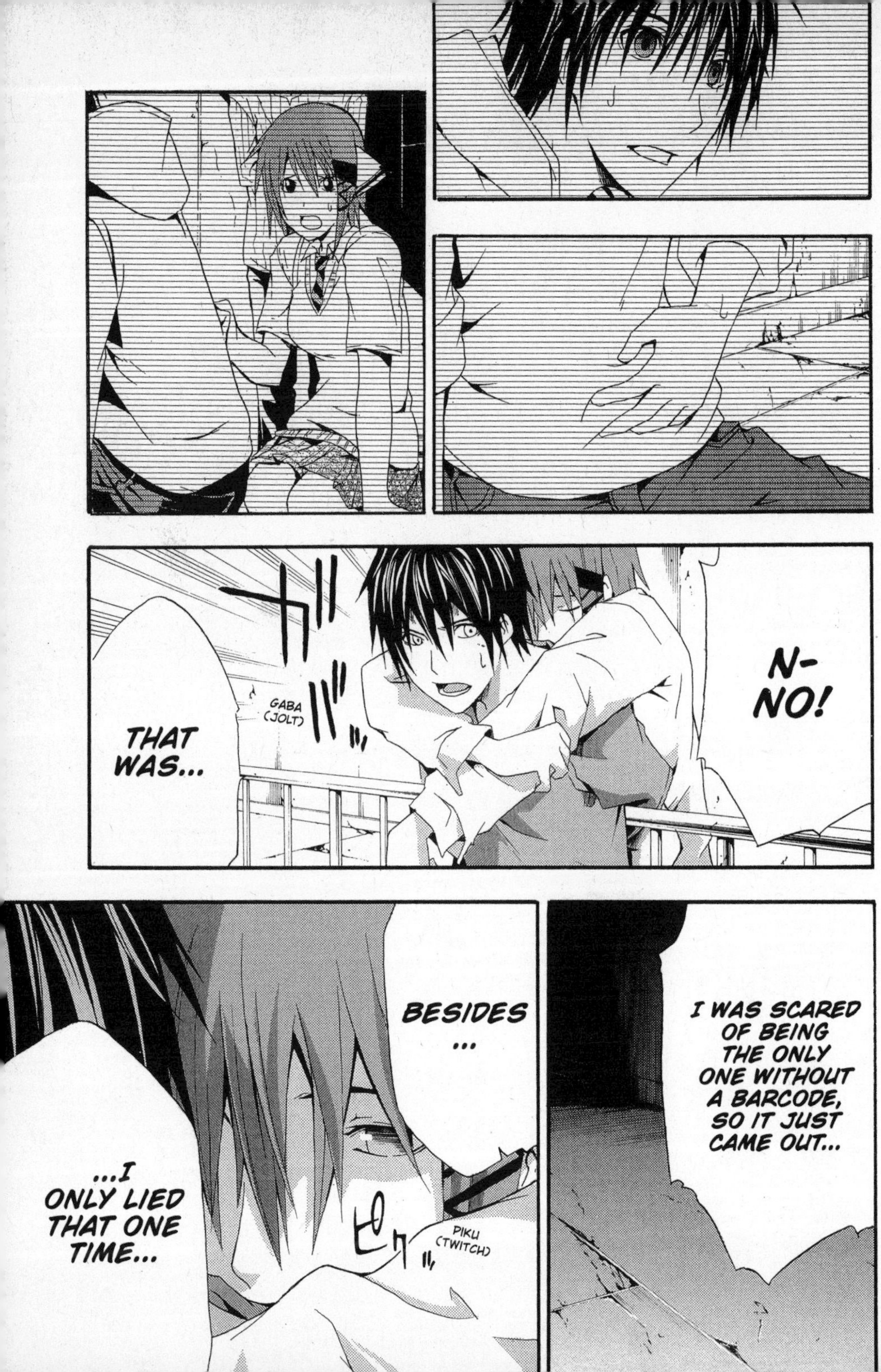
N-NO!
GABA (JOLT)
THAT WAS...
I WAS SCARED OF BEING THE ONLY ONE WITHOUT A BARCODE, SO IT JUST CAME OUT...
BESIDES ...
...I ONLY LIED THAT ONE TIME...
PIKU (TWITCH)

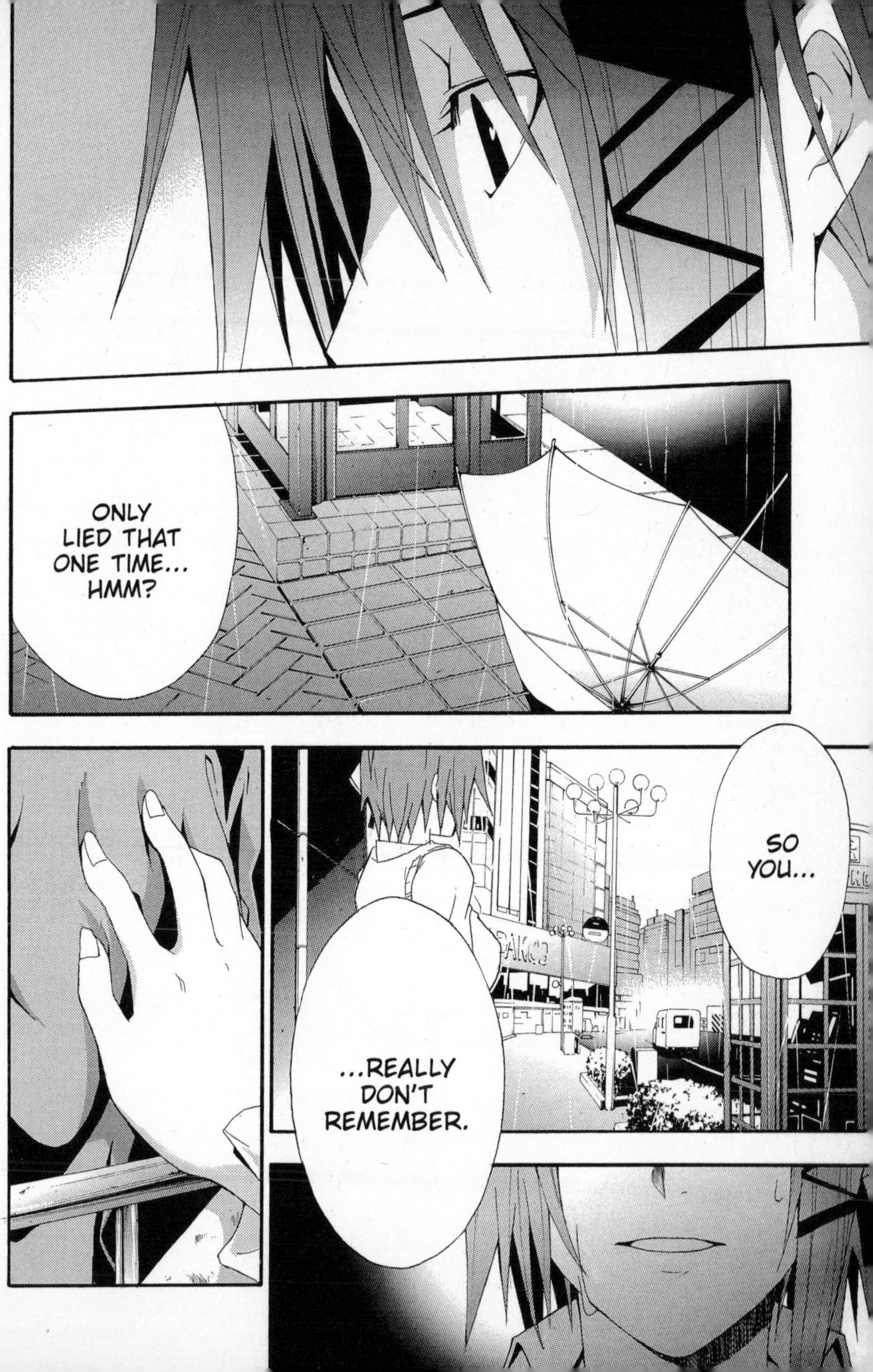
ONLY LIED THAT ONE TIME... HMM?
SO YOU...
...REALLY DON'T REMEMBER.

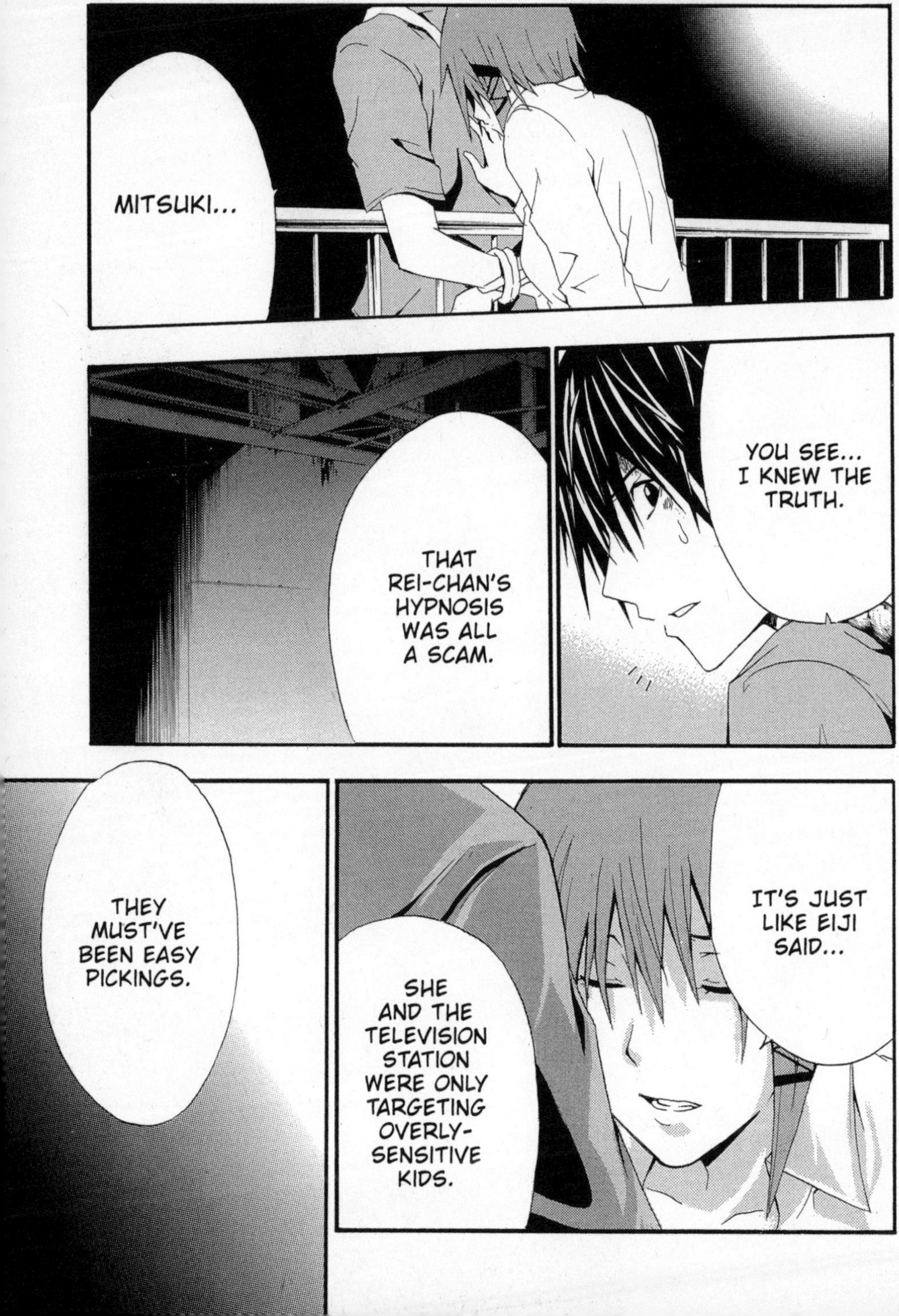
MITSUKI...
YOU SEE... I KNEW THE TRUTH.
THAT REI-CHAN'S HYPNOSIS WAS ALL A SCAM.
IT'S JUST LIKE EIJI SAID...
SHE AND THE TELEVISION STATION WERE ONLY TARGETING OVERLY-SENSITIVE KIDS.
THEY MUST'VE BEEN EASY PICKINGS.

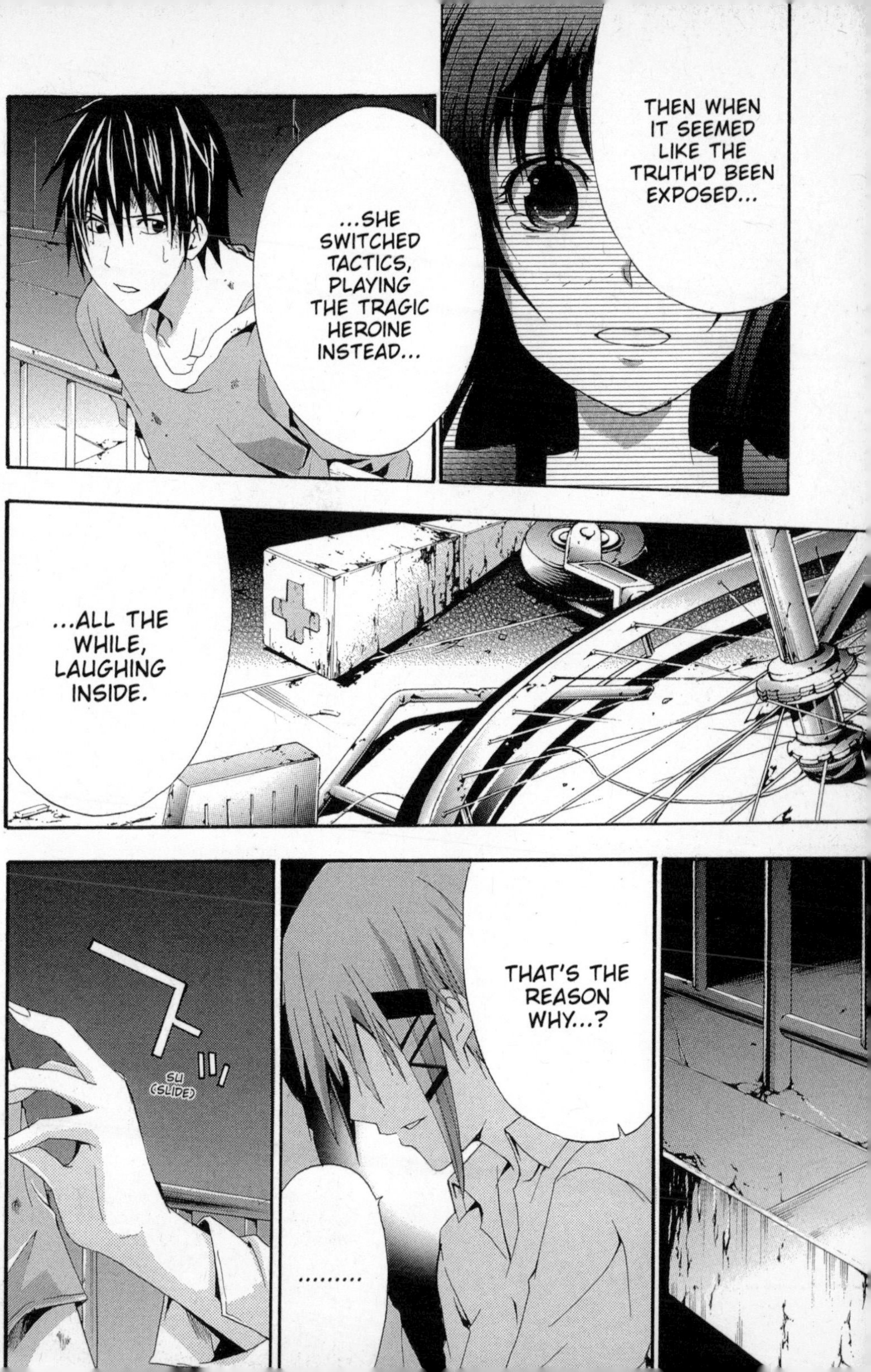
THEN WHEN IT SEEMED LIKE THE TRUTH'D BEEN EXPOSED...
...SHE SWITCHED TACTICS, PLAYING THE TRAGIC HEROINE INSTEAD...
...ALL THE WHILE, LAUGHING INSIDE.
THAT'S THE REASON WHY...?
....
SU (SLIDE)

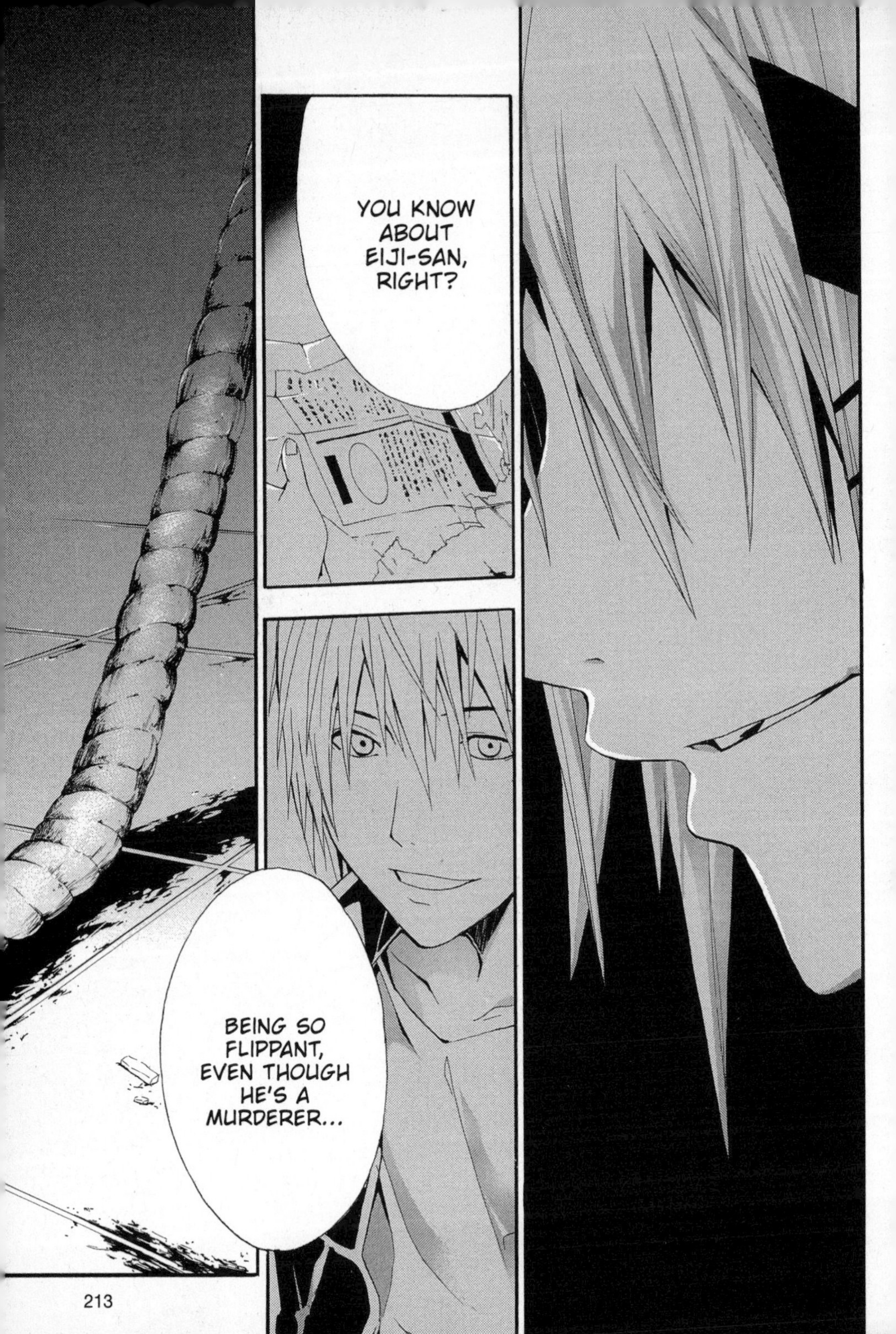
YOU KNOW ABOUT EIJI-SAN, RIGHT?
BEING SO FLIPPANT, EVEN THOUGH HE'S A MURDERER...

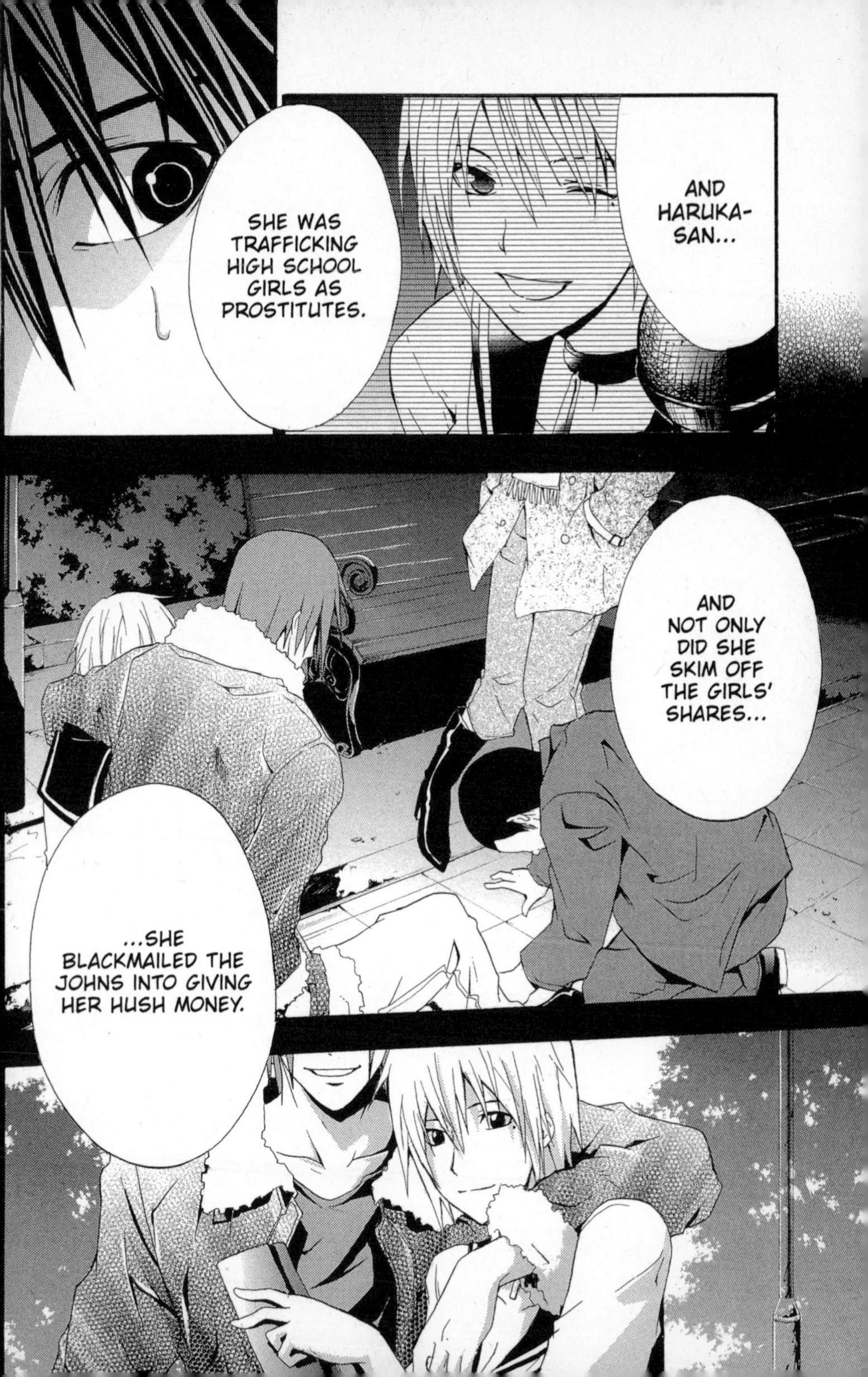
AND HARUKA-SAN...
SHE WAS TRAFFICKING HIGH SCHOOL GIRLS AS PROSTITUTES.
AND NOT ONLY DID SHE SKIM OFF THE GIRLS' SHARES...
...SHE BLACKMAILED THE JOHNS INTO GIVING HER HUSH MONEY.

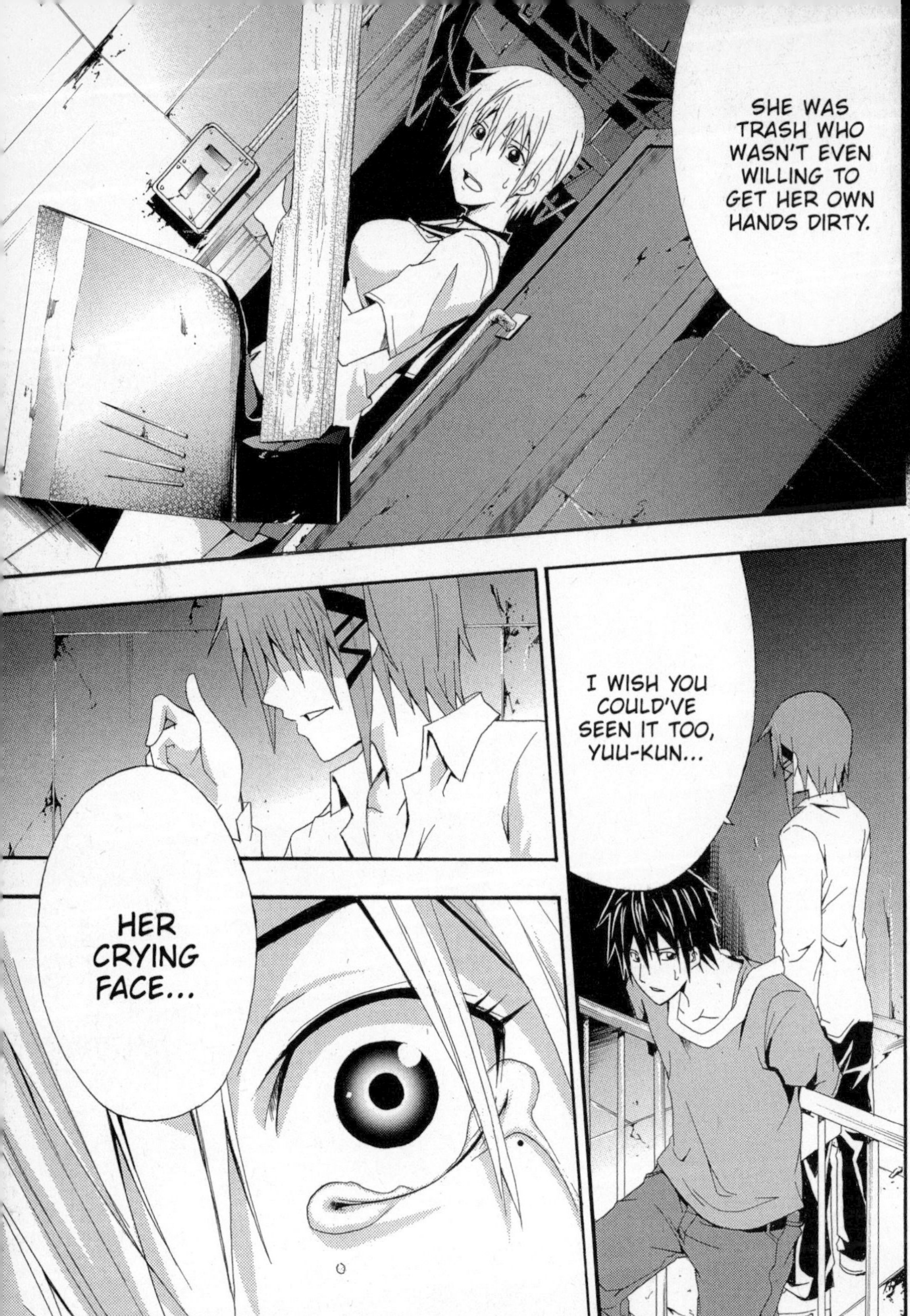
SHE WAS TRASH WHO WASN'T EVEN WILLING TO GET HER OWN HANDS DIRTY.
I WISH YOU COULD'VE SEEN IT TOO, YUU-KUN...
HER CRYING FACE...

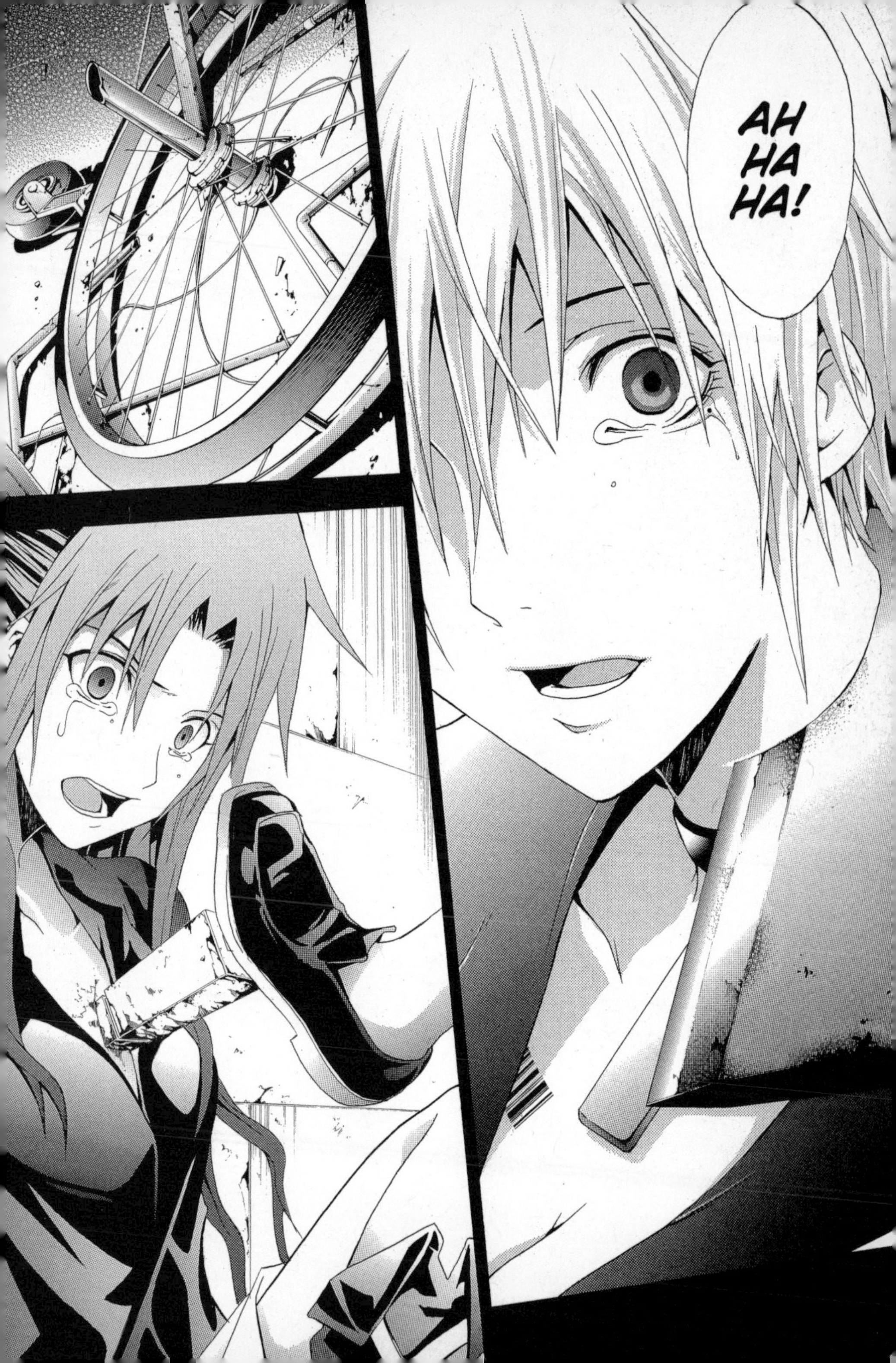
AH HA HA!

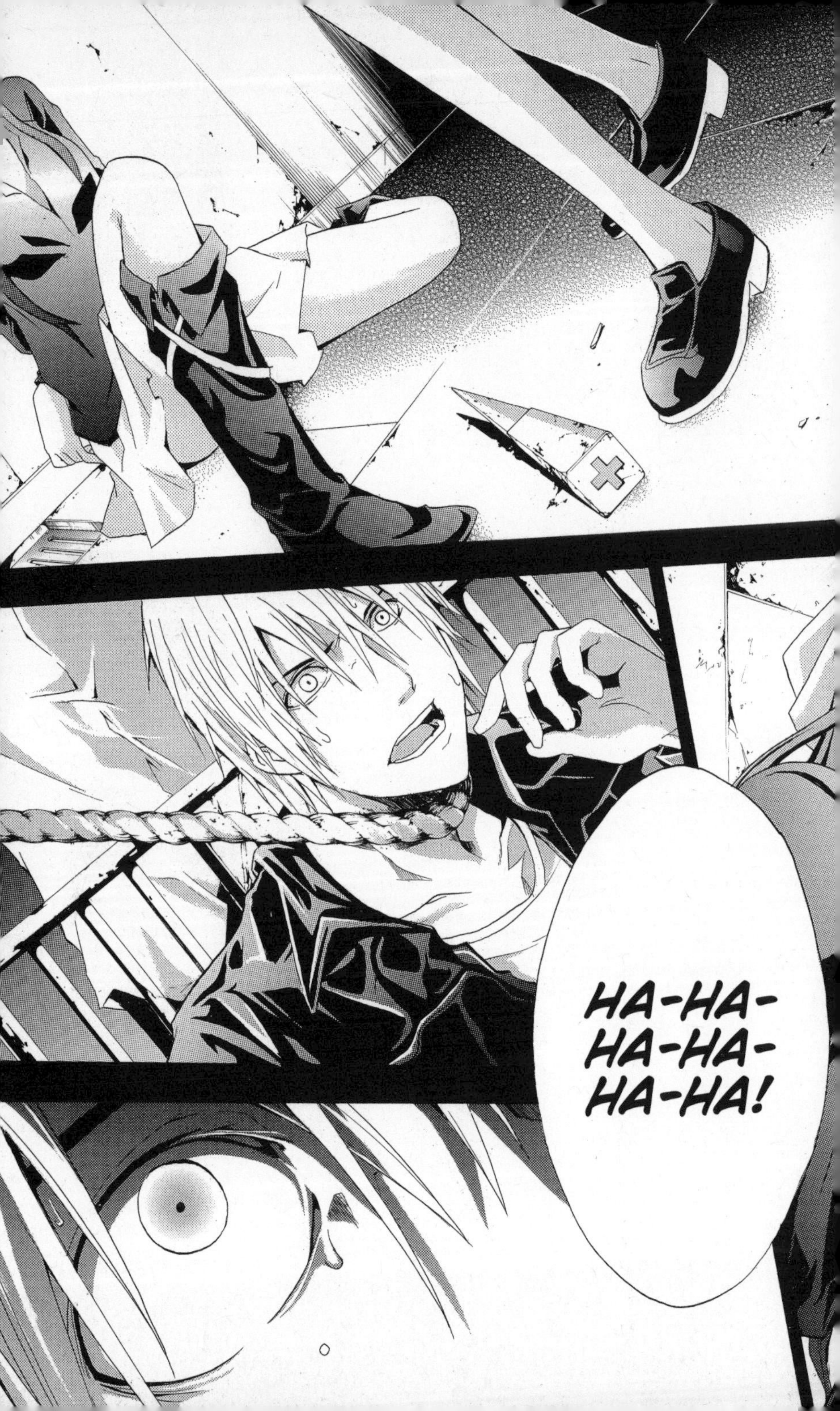
HA-HA-HA-HA-HA-HA!

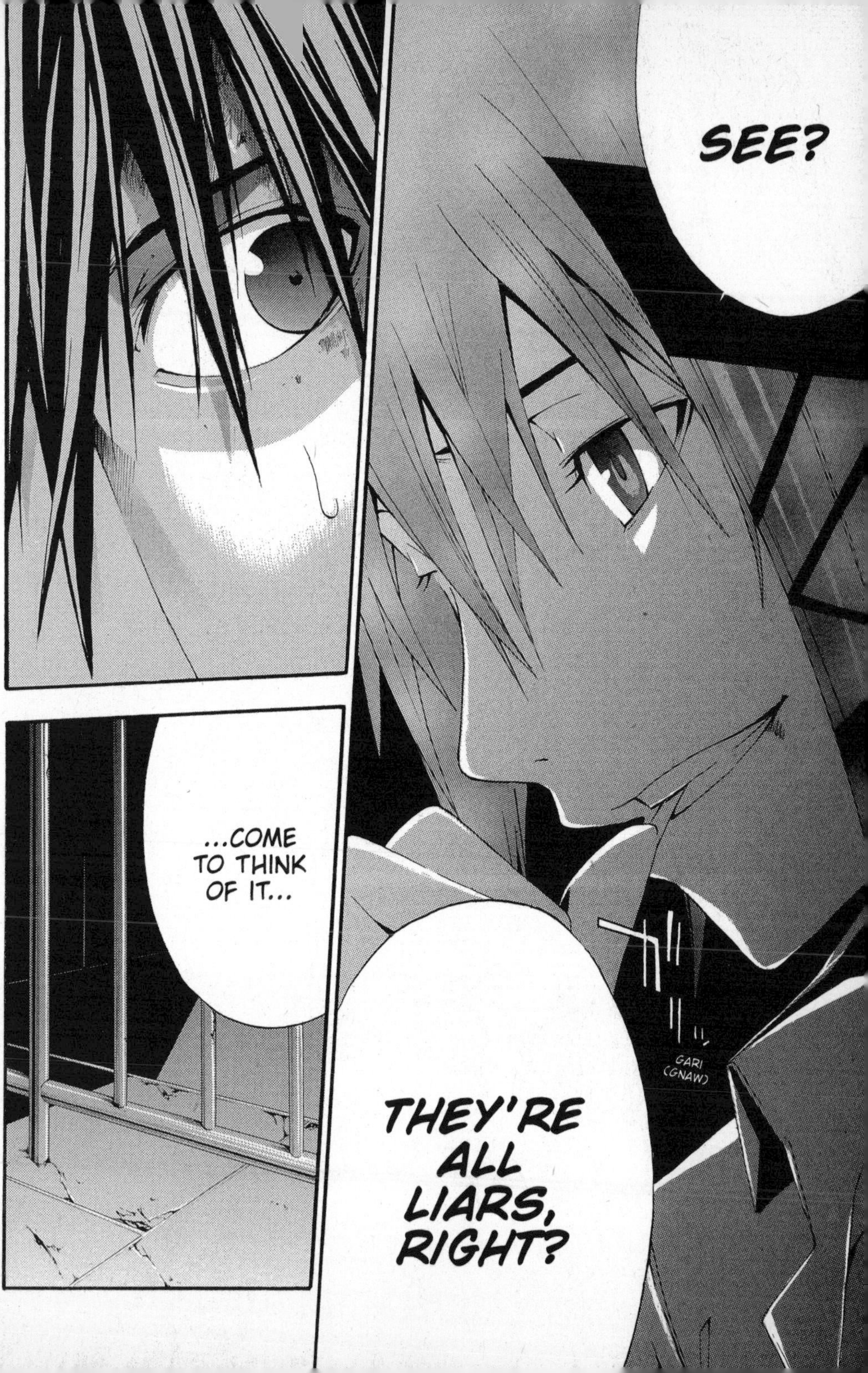
SEE?
GARI (GNAW)
THEY'RE ALL LIARS, RIGHT?
...COME TO THINK OF IT...

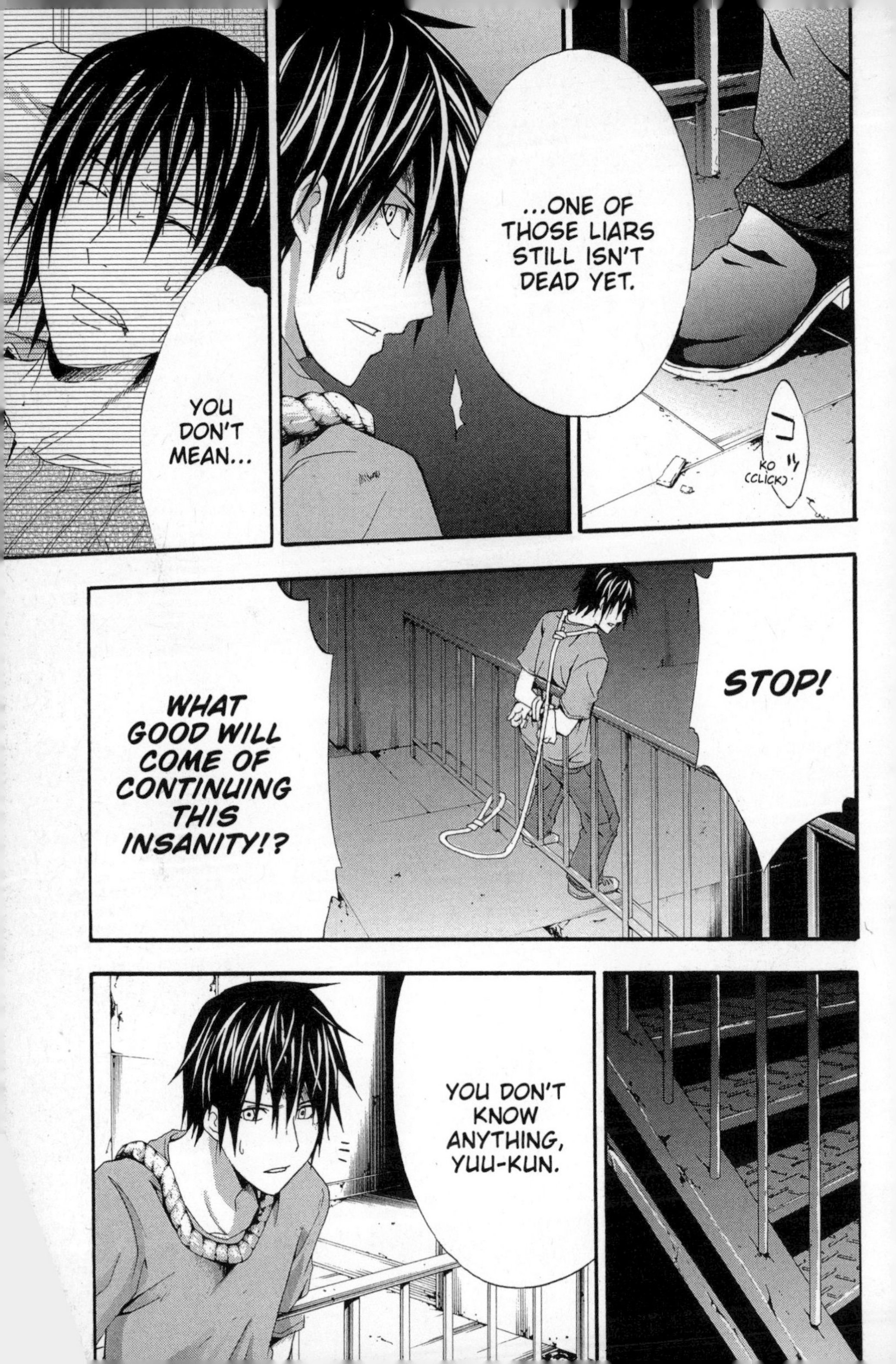
KO (CLICK)
...ONE OF THOSE LIARS STILL ISN'T DEAD YET.
YOU DON'T MEAN...
STOP!
WHAT GOOD WILL COME OF CONTINUING THIS INSANITY!?
YOU DON'T KNOW ANYTHING, YUU-KUN.

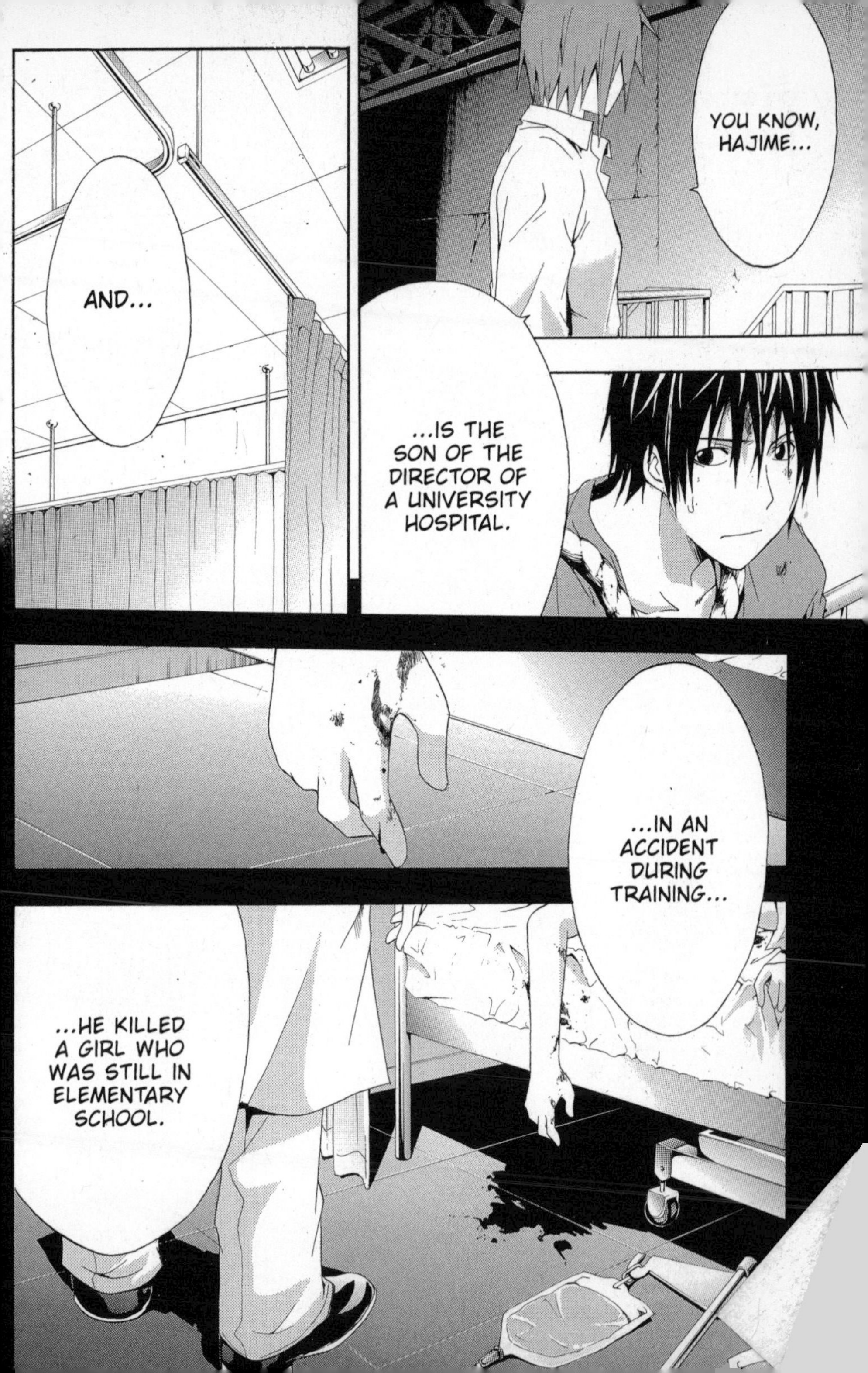
YOU KNOW, HAJIME...
...IS THE SON OF THE DIRECTOR OF A UNIVERSITY HOSPITAL.
AND...
...IN AN ACCIDENT DURING TRAINING...
...HE KILLED A GIRL WHO WAS STILL IN ELEMENTARY SCHOOL.

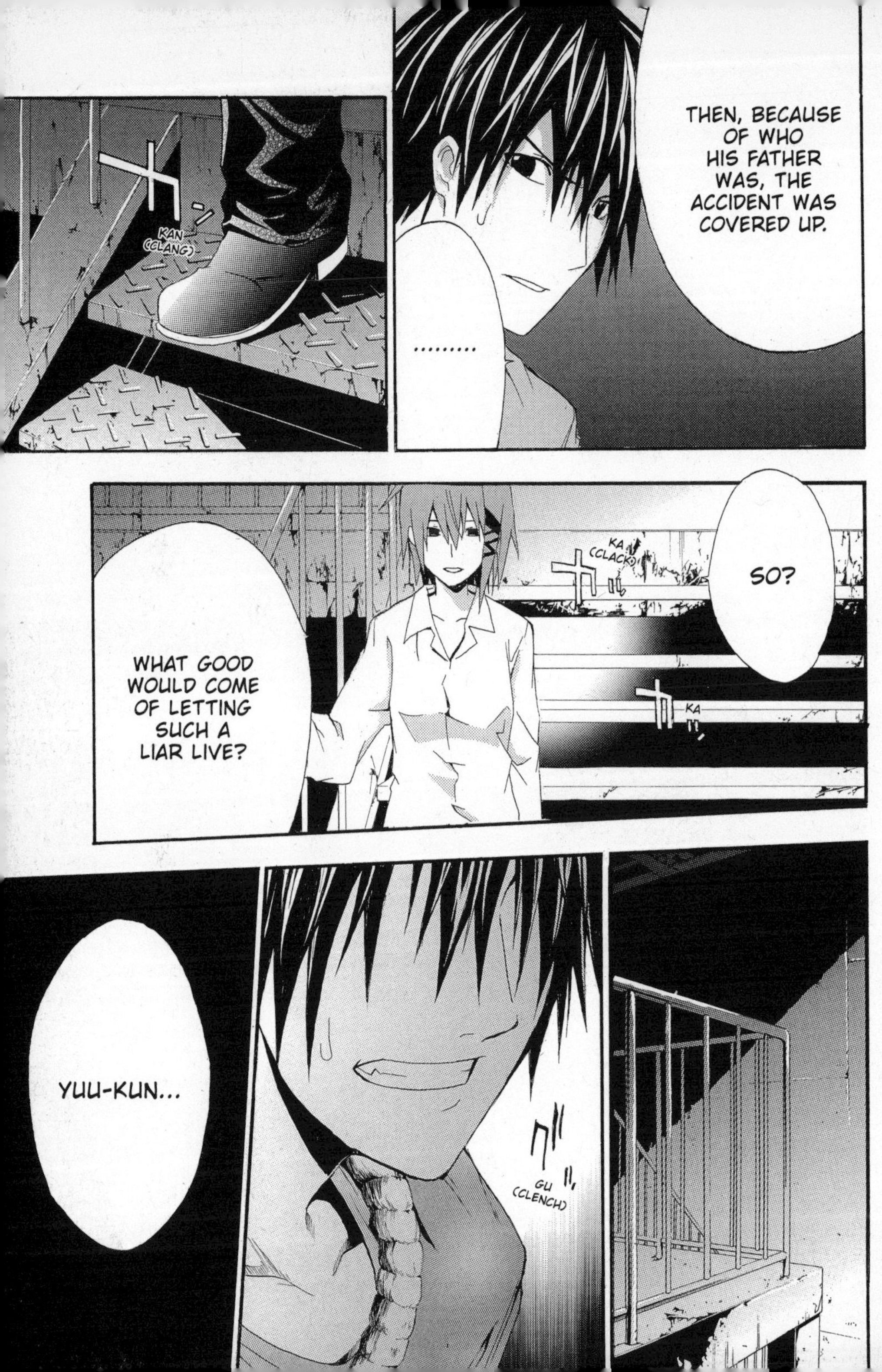
THEN, BECAUSE OF WHO HIS FATHER WAS, THE ACCIDENT WAS COVERED UP.
....
KAN (CLANG)
SO?
KA (CLACK)
KA
WHAT GOOD WOULD COME OF LETTING SUCH A LIAR LIVE?
GU (CLENCH)
YUU-KUN...

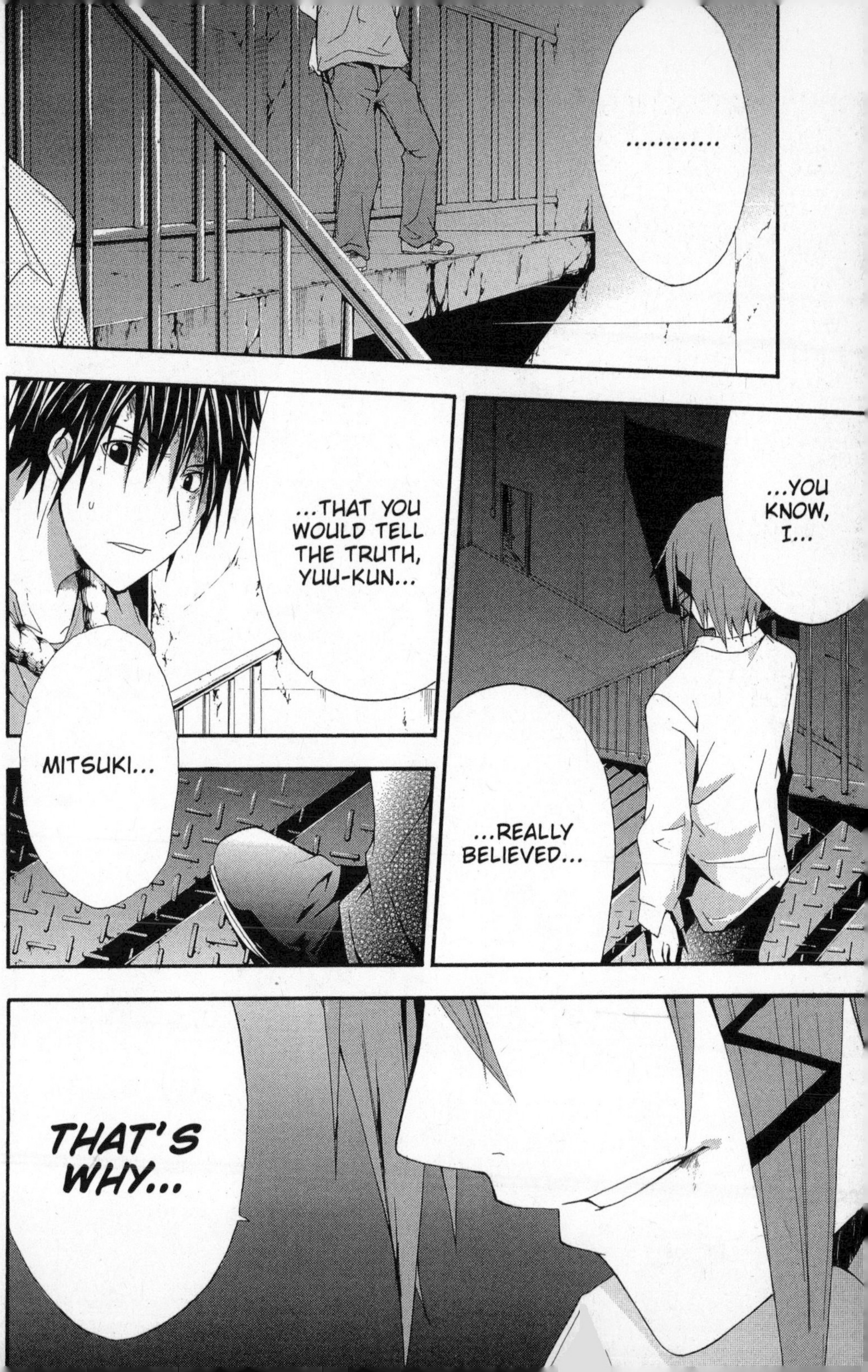
....
...YOU KNOW, I...
...REALLY BELIEVED...
...THAT YOU WOULD TELL THE TRUTH, YUU-KUN...
MITSUKI...
THAT'S WHY...

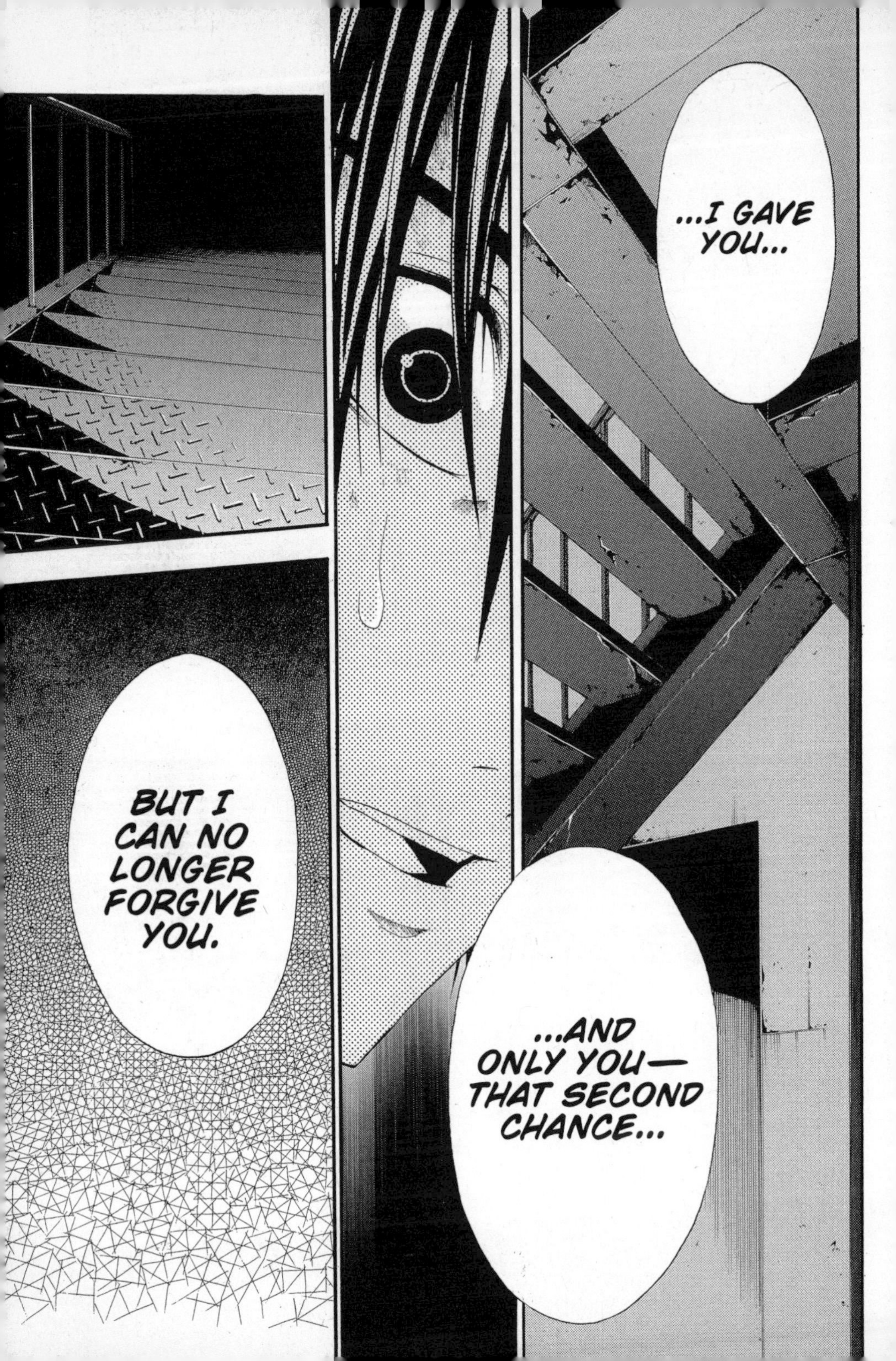
...I GAVE YOU...
...AND ONLY YOU— THAT SECOND CHANCE...
BUT I CAN NO LONGER FORGIVE YOU.

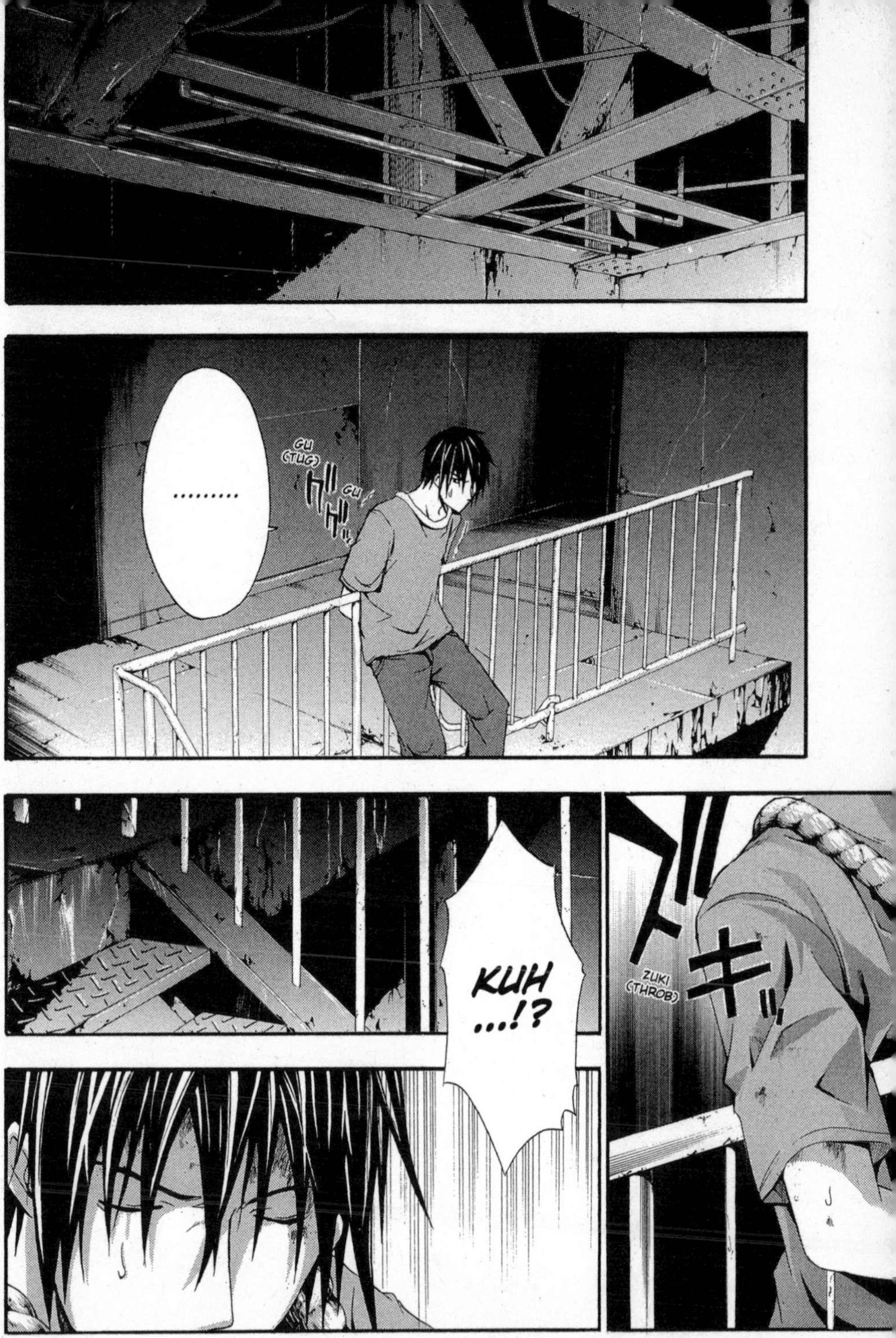
....
GU
(TUG)
GU
ZUKI
(THROB)
KUH
...!?

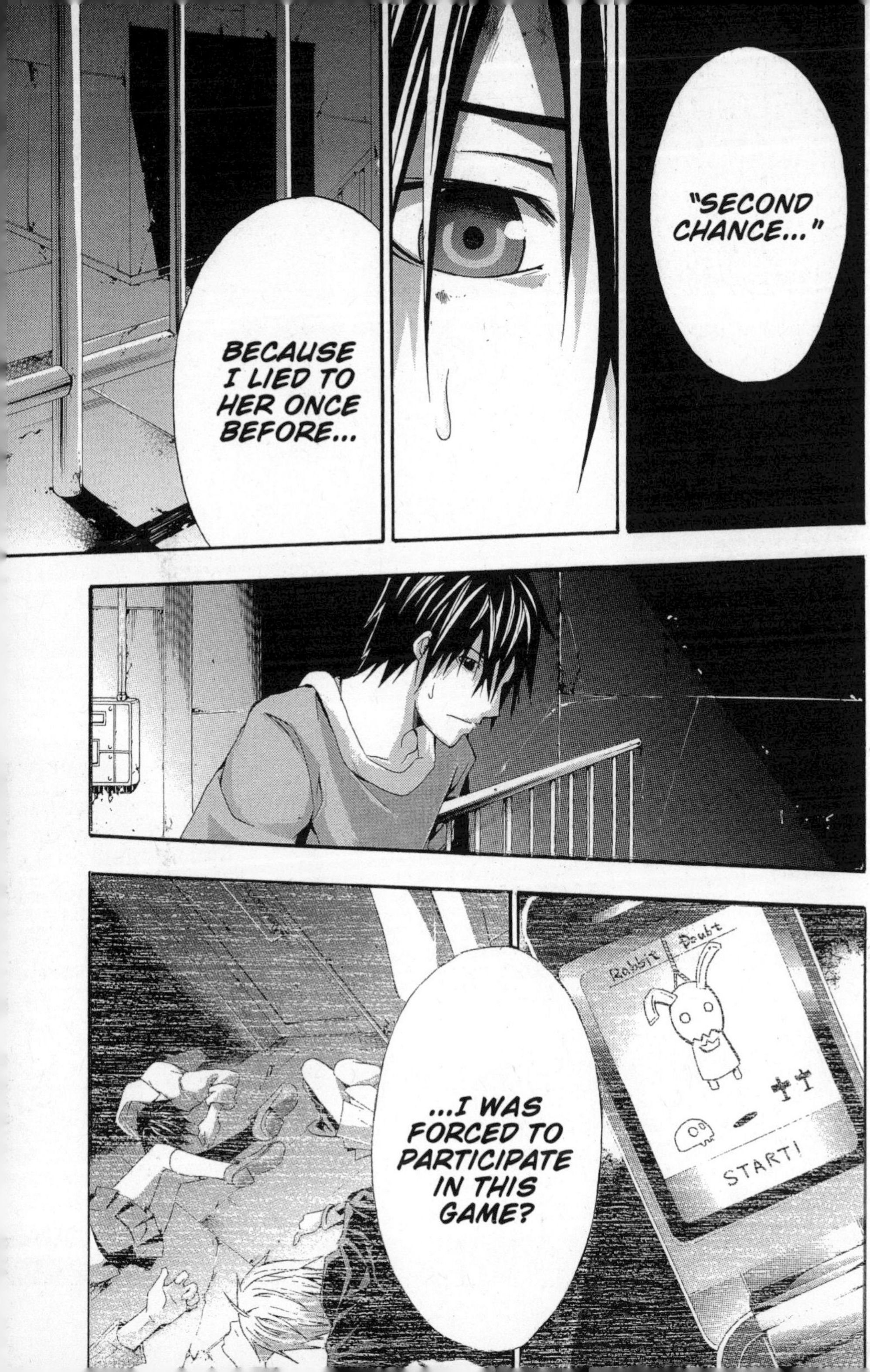
"SECOND CHANCE..."
BECAUSE I LIED TO HER ONCE BEFORE...
Rabbit Doubt
START!
...I WAS FORCED TO PARTICIPATE IN THIS GAME?

I TOLD...

....

...A LIE...

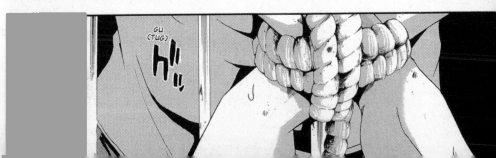

GU
(TUG)

WHAT LIE COULD I HAVE TOLD...

...TO TURN YOU INTO THIS?

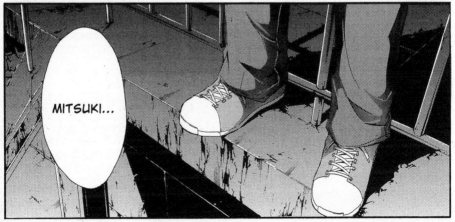

MITSUKI...

YEAH.

....

YEAH.

GOT IT...

MITSUKI?

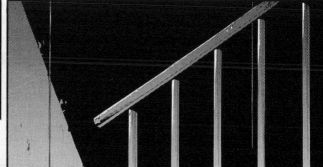

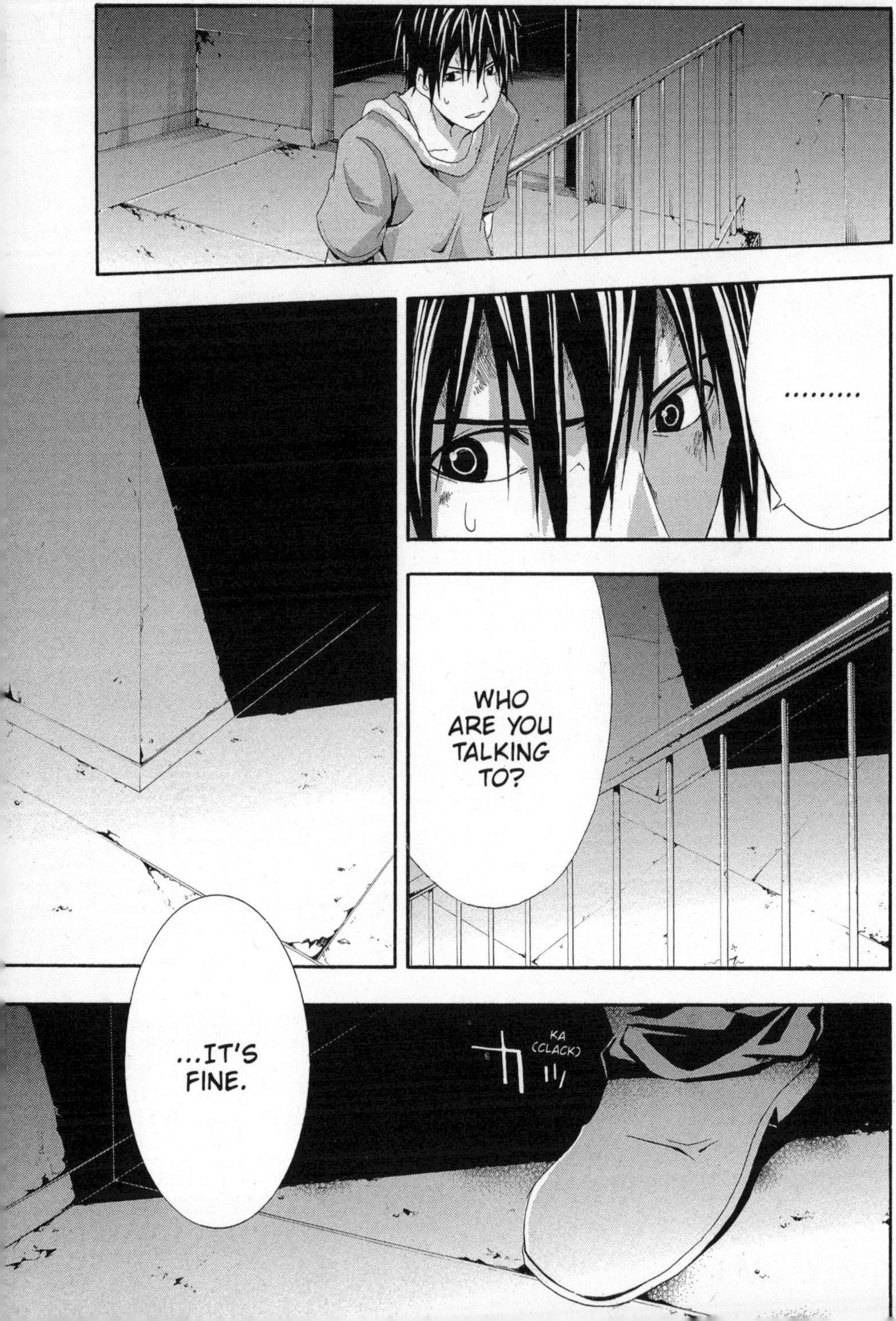
....
WHO ARE YOU TALKING TO?
...IT'S FINE.
KA (CLACK)

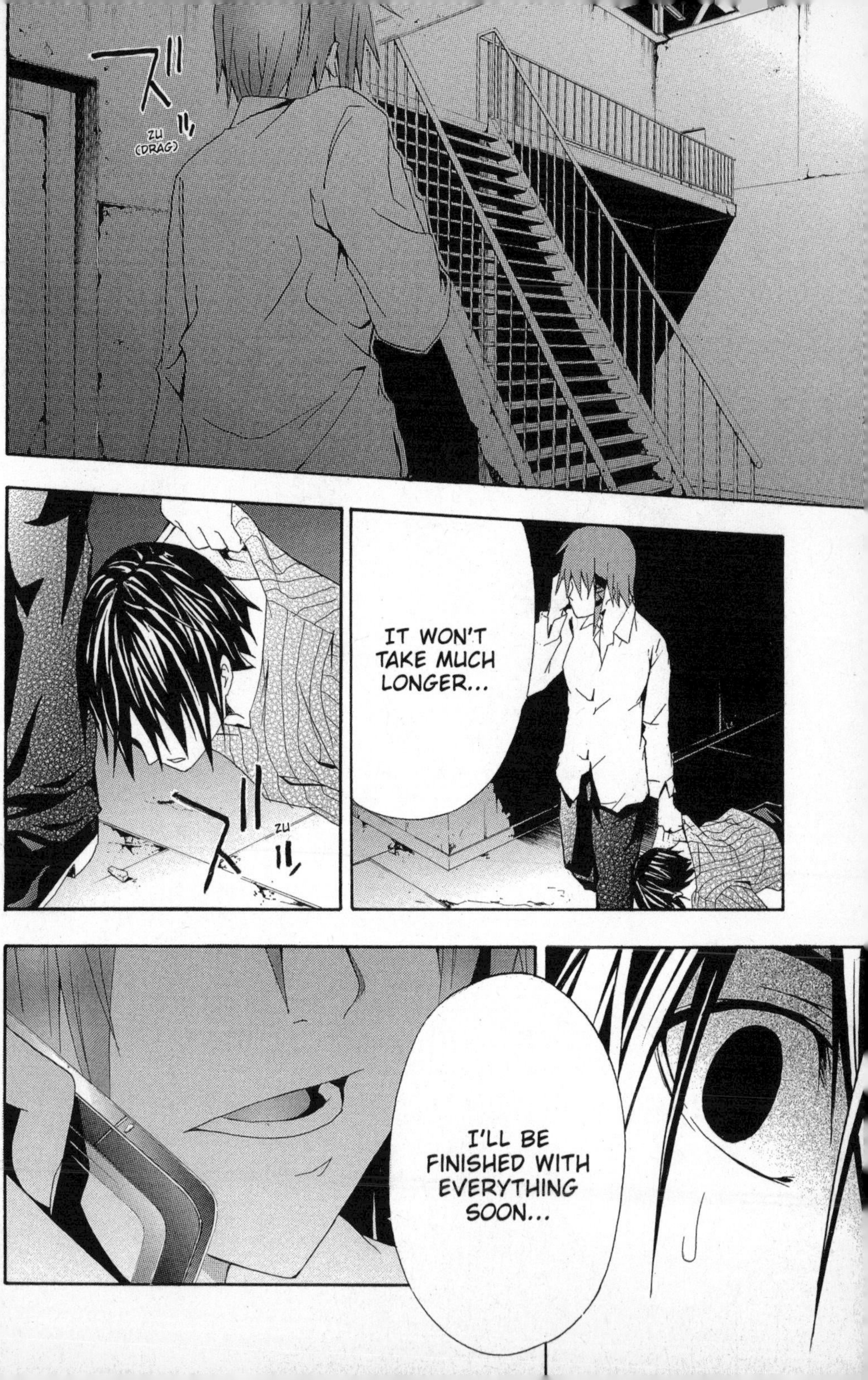
ズ ル
ZU
(DRAG)
ZU
IT WON'T TAKE MUCH LONGER...
I'LL BE FINISHED WITH EVERYTHING SOON...

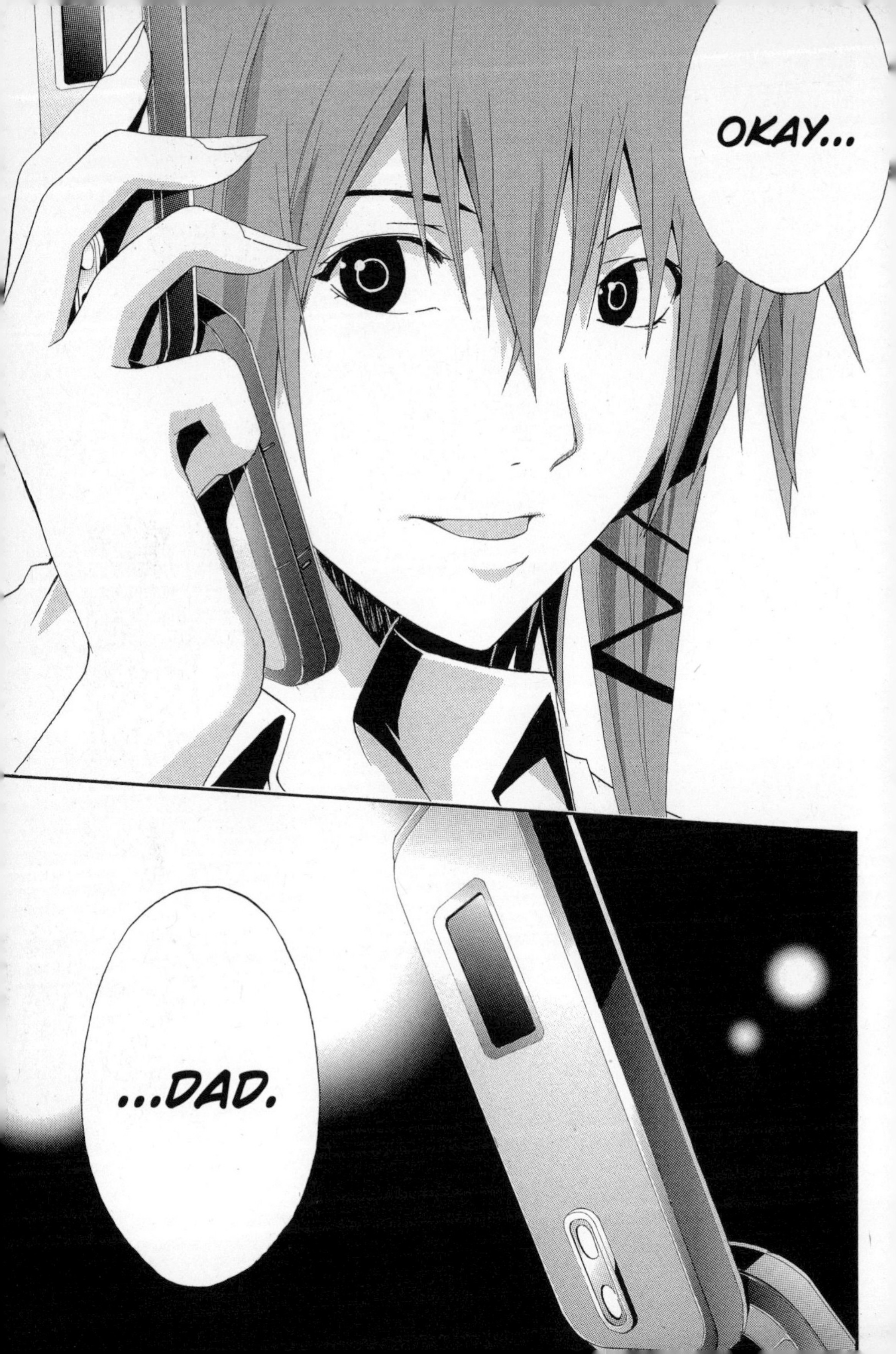
OKAY...
...DAD.

CARTON: MILK

Doubt.16 AVENGER

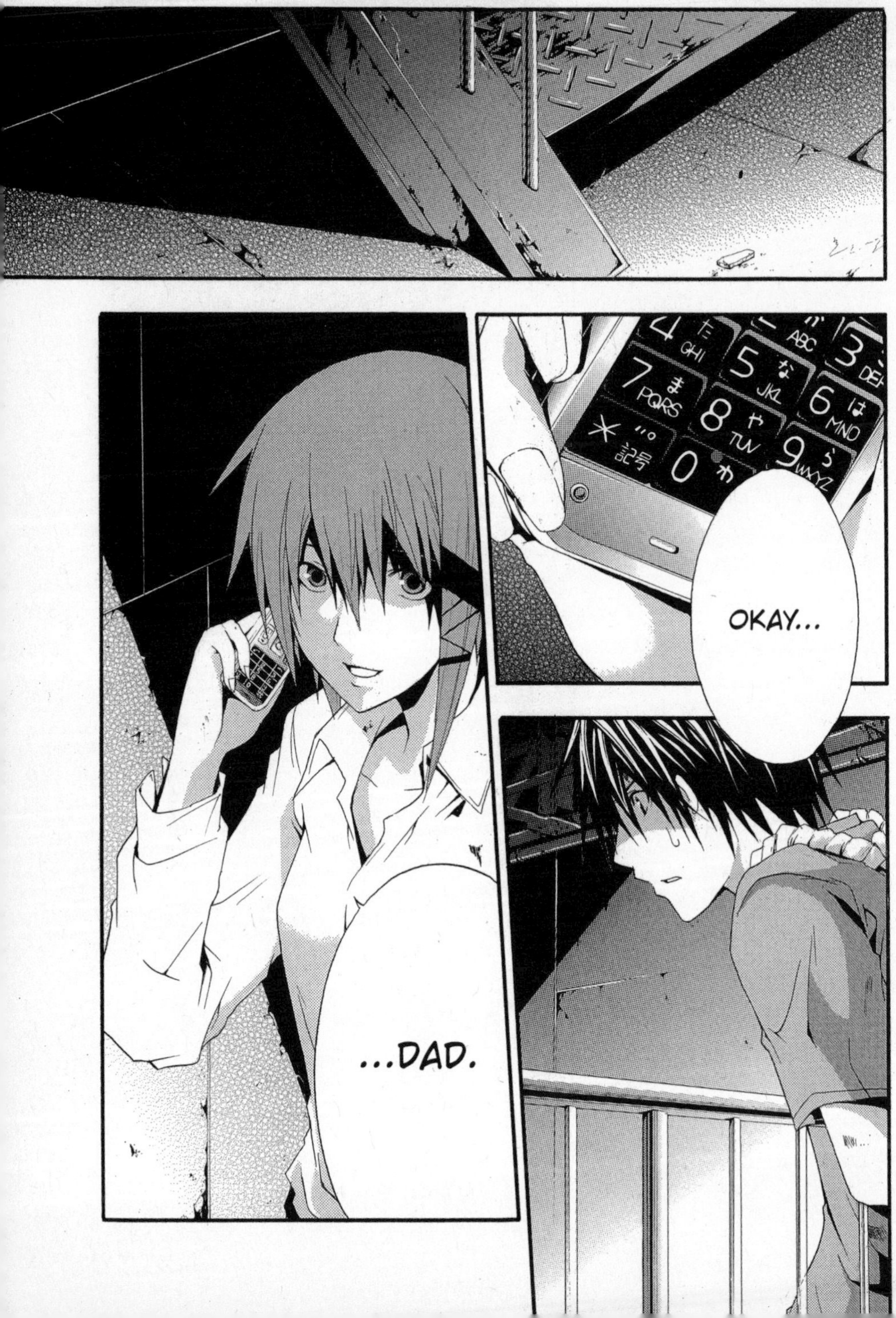

OKAY...
...DAD.

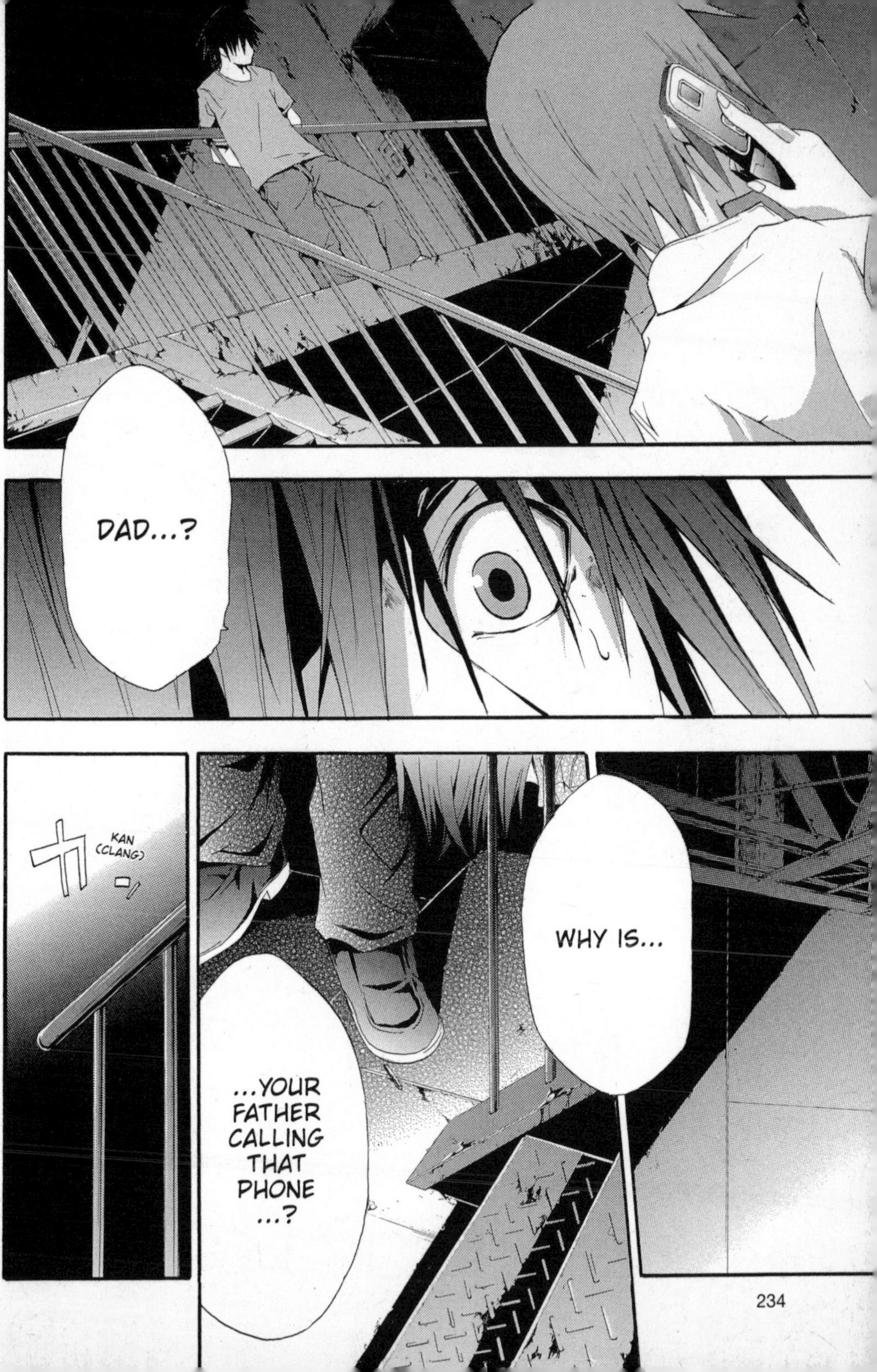
DAD...?
WHY IS...
...YOUR FATHER CALLING THAT PHONE ...?
KAN (CLANG)

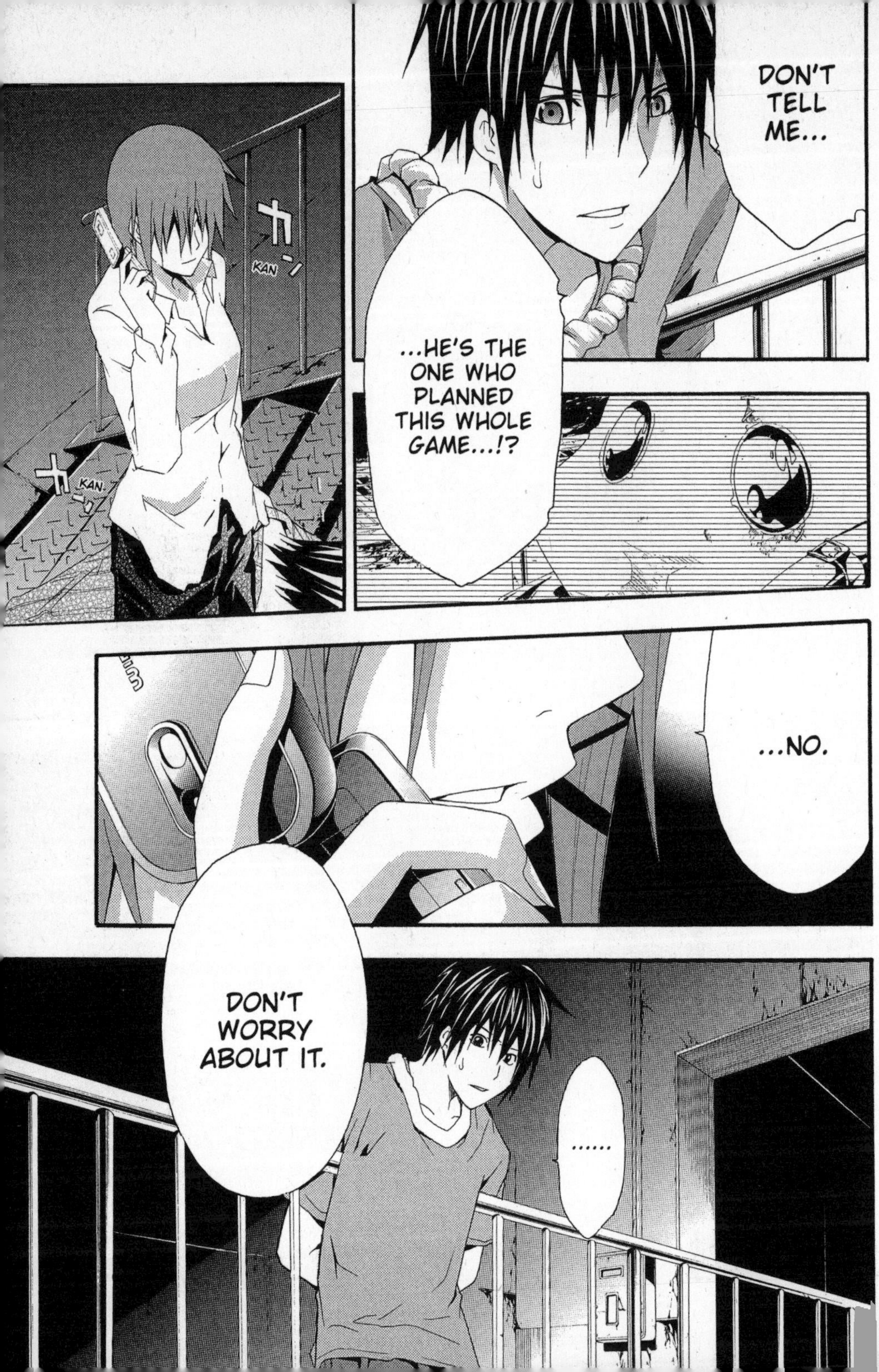

DON'T TELL ME...
...HE'S THE ONE WHO PLANNED THIS WHOLE GAME...!?
KAN
KAN
...NO.
DON'T WORRY ABOUT IT.
......

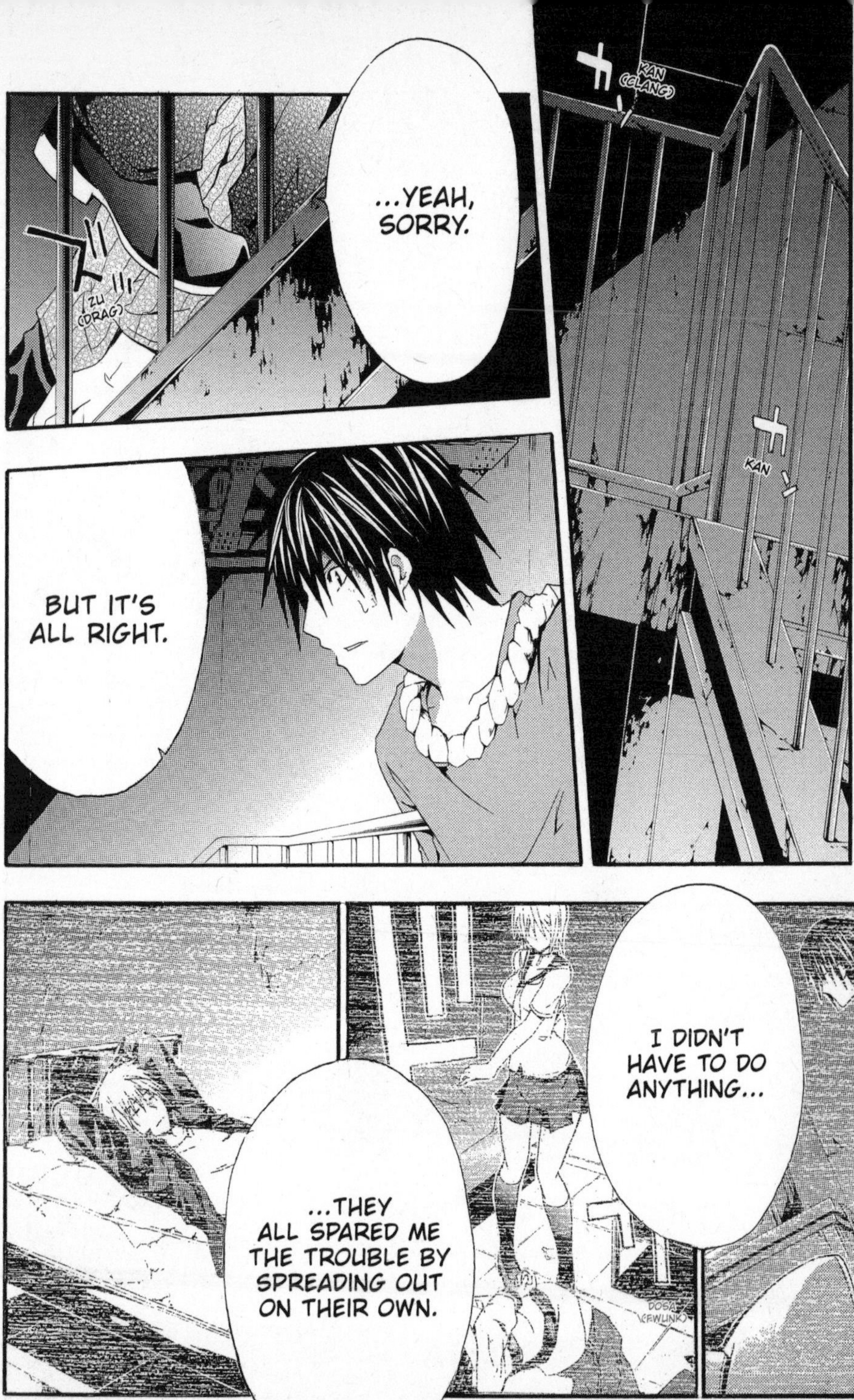
KAN (CLANG)
KAN
...YEAH, SORRY.
ZU (DRAG)
BUT IT'S ALL RIGHT.
I DIDN'T HAVE TO DO ANYTHING...
...THEY ALL SPARED ME THE TROUBLE BY SPREADING OUT ON THEIR OWN.
DOSA (FWUNK)

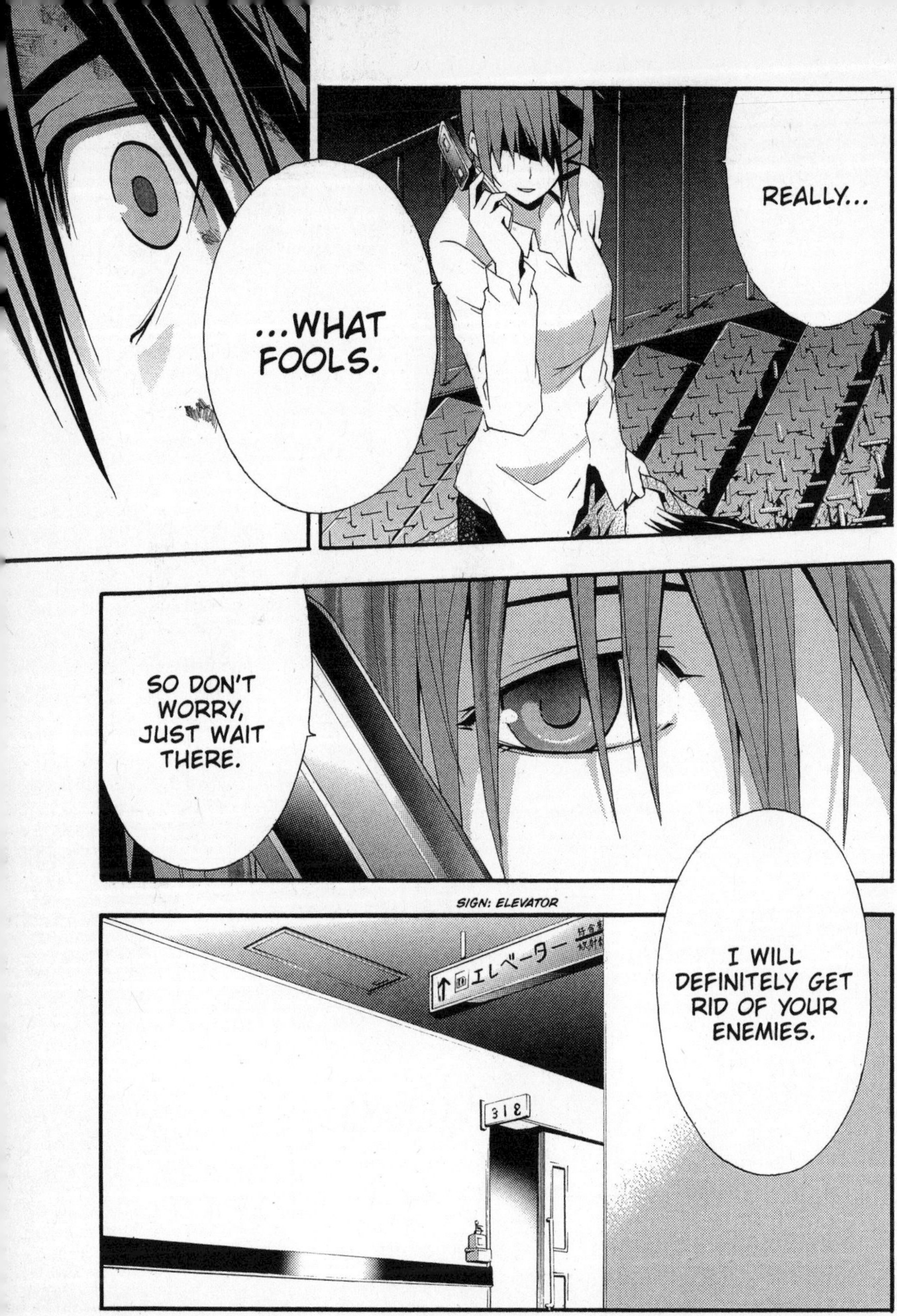
REALLY...
...WHAT FOOLS.
SO DON'T WORRY, JUST WAIT THERE.
I WILL DEFINITELY GET RID OF YOUR ENEMIES.
SIGN: ELEVATOR
エレベーター
318

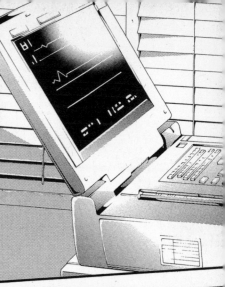

THE ONES WHO PUT YOU IN SUCH A STATE...

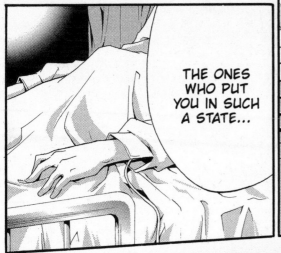

...THE LIARS... I'LL KILL THEM AND COME HOME.

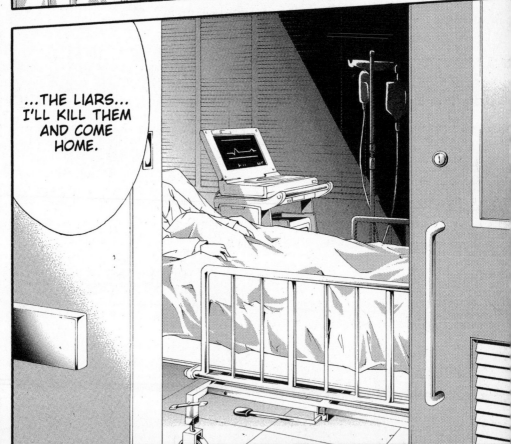

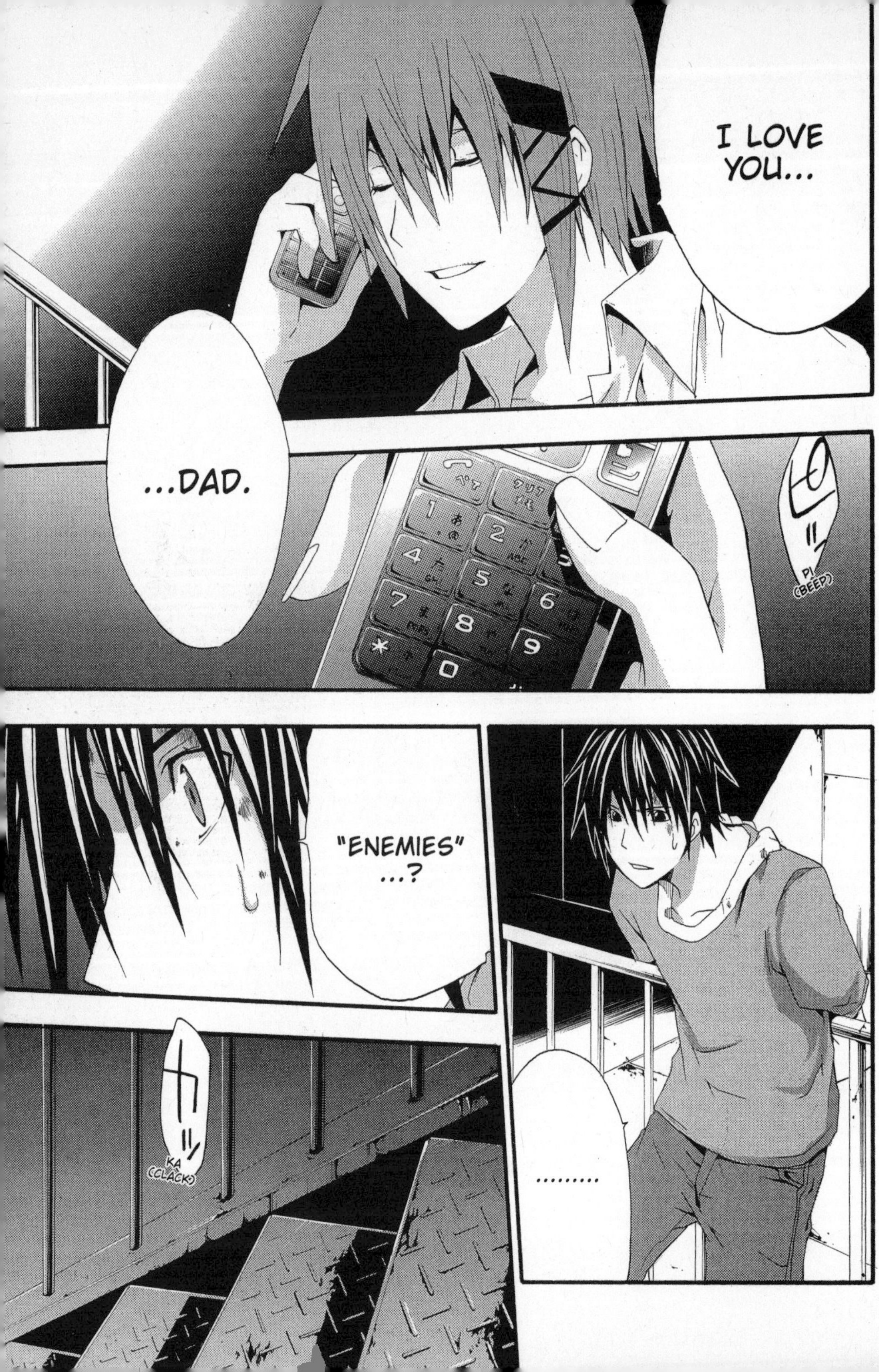
I LOVE YOU...
...DAD.
PI (BEEP)
....
"ENEMIES" ...?
KA (CLACK)

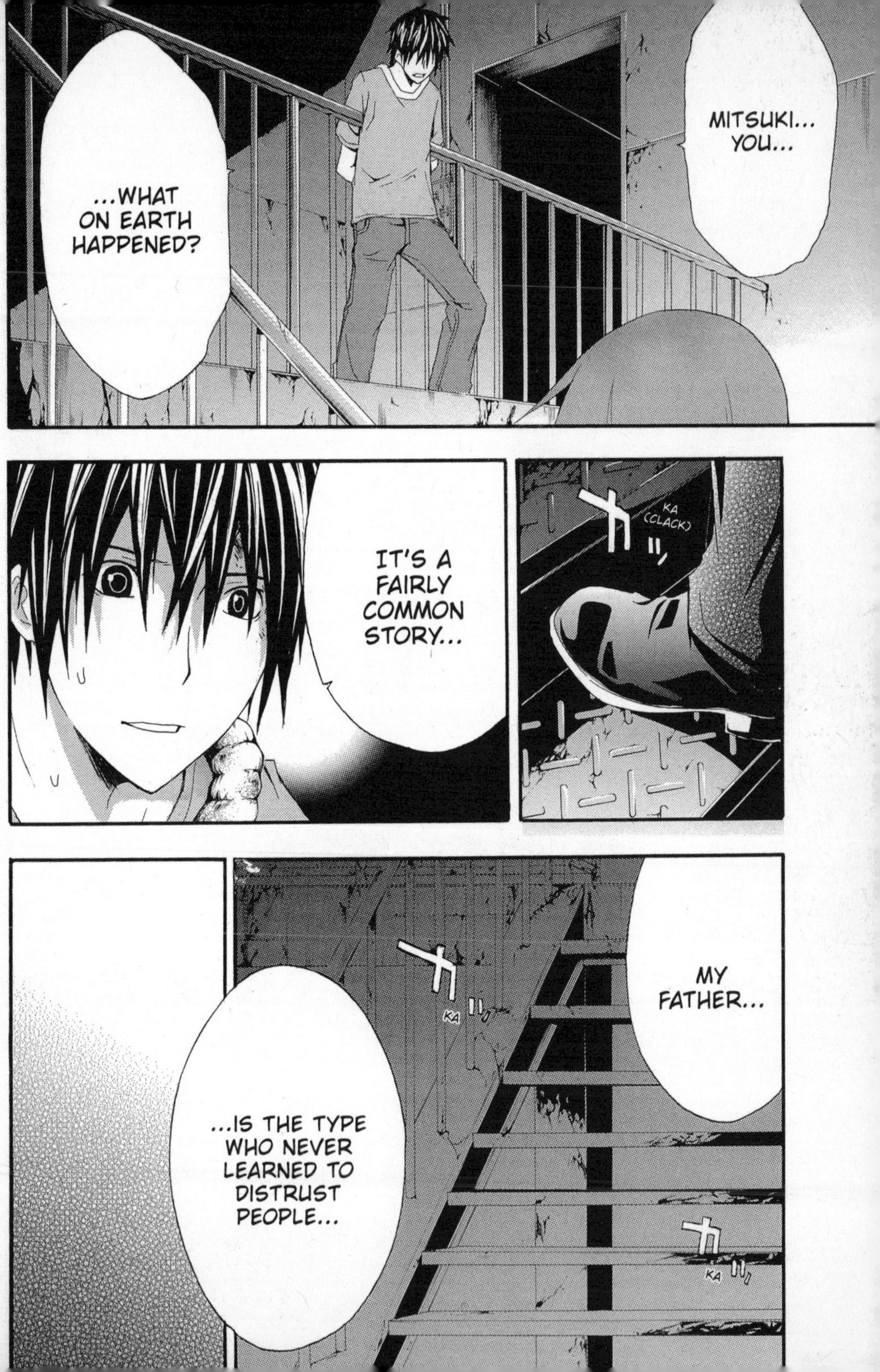
MITSUKI... YOU...
...WHAT ON EARTH HAPPENED?
KA (CLACK)
IT'S A FAIRLY COMMON STORY...
MY FATHER...
KA
...IS THE TYPE WHO NEVER LEARNED TO DISTRUST PEOPLE...
KA

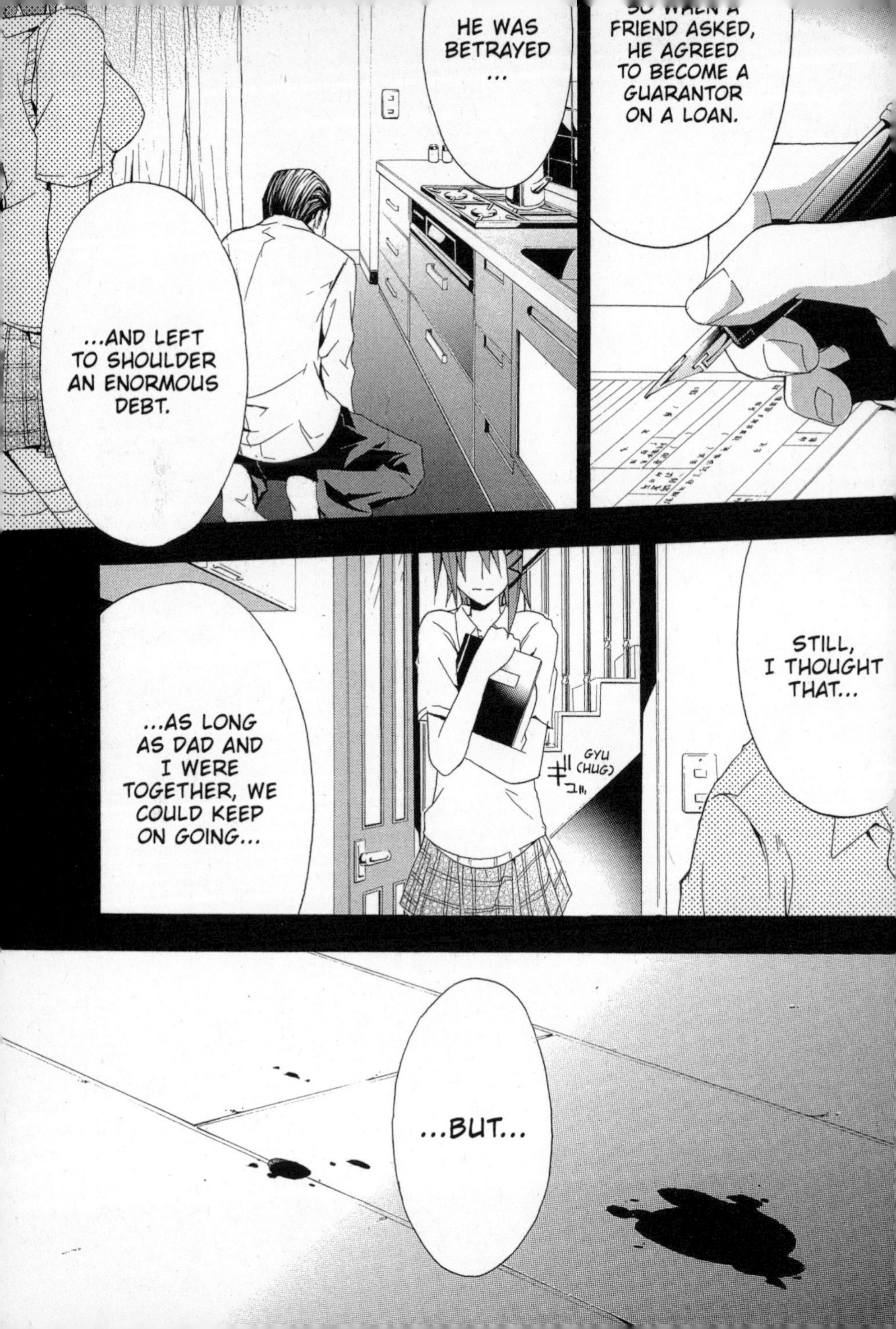
FRIEND ASKED, HE AGREED TO BECOME A GUARANTOR ON A LOAN.
HE WAS BETRAYED ...
...AND LEFT TO SHOULDER AN ENORMOUS DEBT.
STILL, I THOUGHT THAT...
GYU (HUG)
...AS LONG AS DAD AND I WERE TOGETHER, WE COULD KEEP ON GOING...
...BUT...

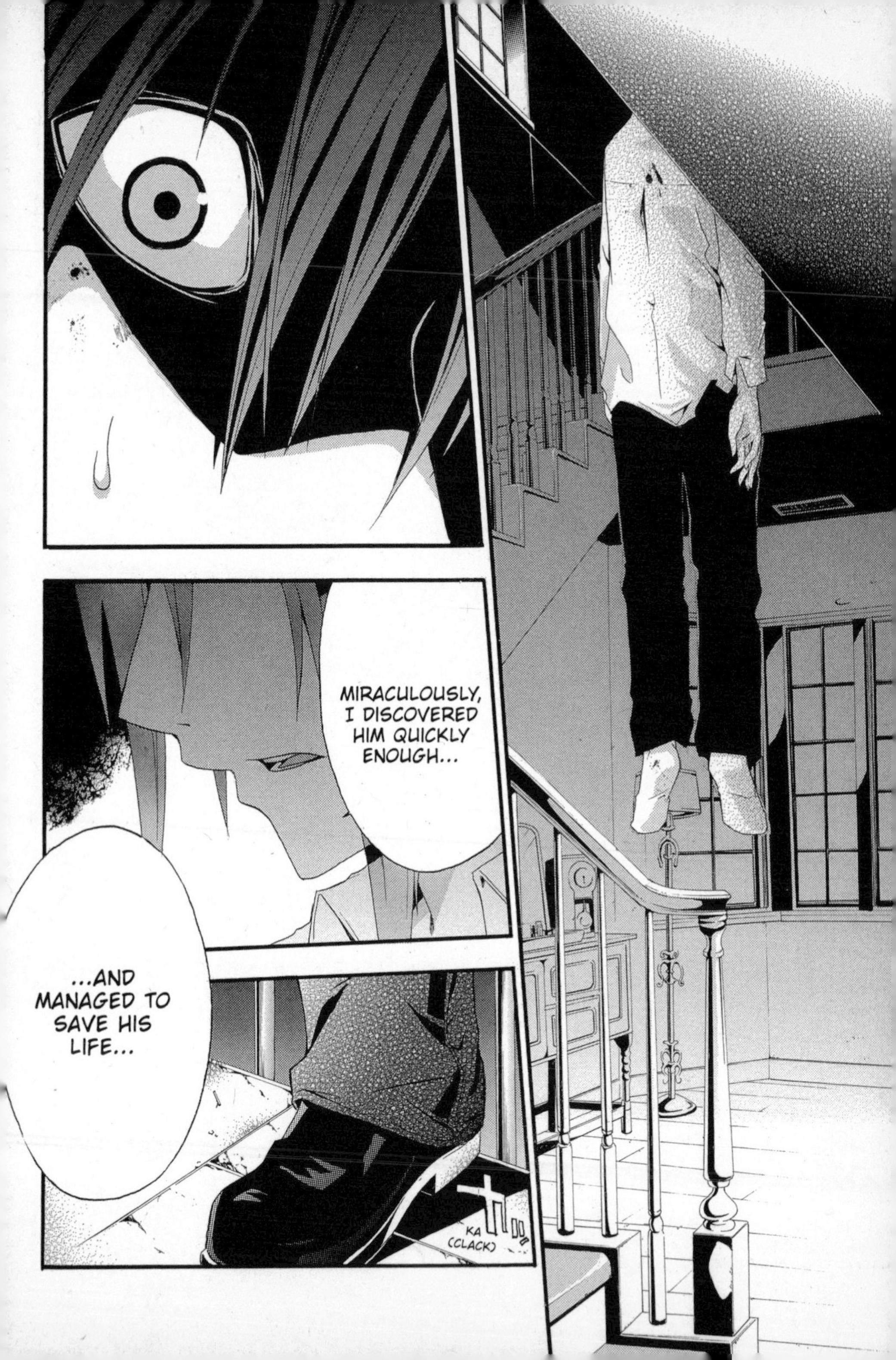
MIRACULOUSLY, I DISCOVERED HIM QUICKLY ENOUGH...
...AND MANAGED TO SAVE HIS LIFE...
KA (CLACK)

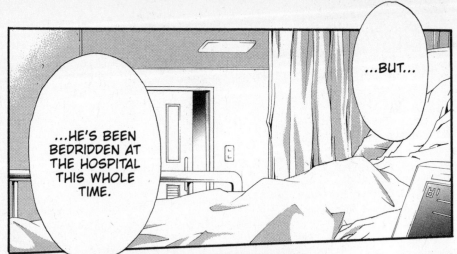

...BUT...

...HE'S BEEN BEDRIDDEN AT THE HOSPITAL THIS WHOLE TIME.

MY DAD WAS TOO NICE...

EVEN SO...

...TO GO ON LIVING IN THIS WORLD FULL OF LIARS.

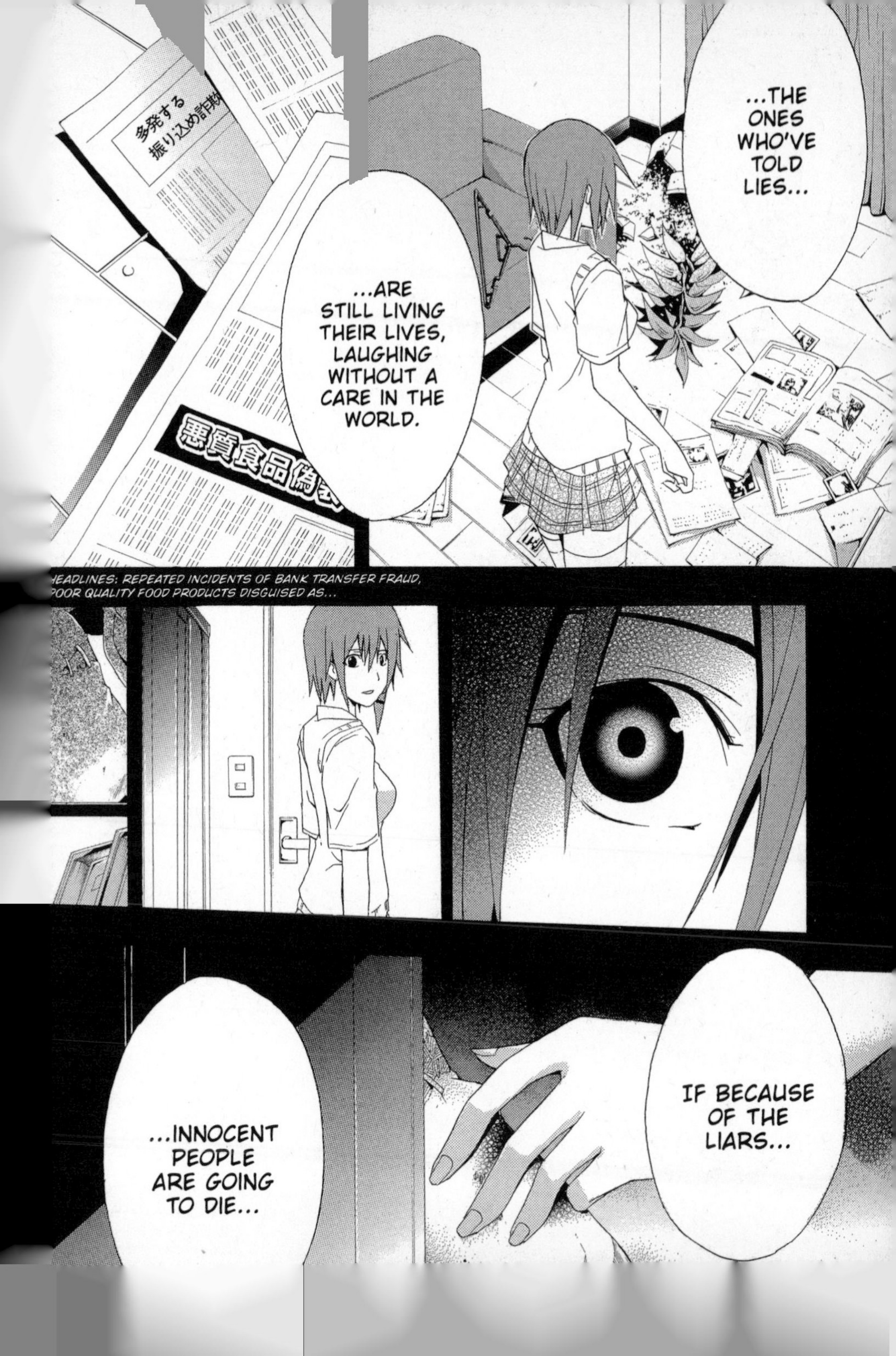
...THE ONES WHO'VE TOLD LIES...
...ARE STILL LIVING THEIR LIVES, LAUGHING WITHOUT A CARE IN THE WORLD.
多発する
HEADLINES: REPEATED INCIDENTS OF BANK TRANSFER FRAUD, POOR QUALITY FOOD PRODUCTS DISGUISED AS...
IF BECAUSE OF THE LIARS...
...INNOCENT PEOPLE ARE GOING TO DIE...

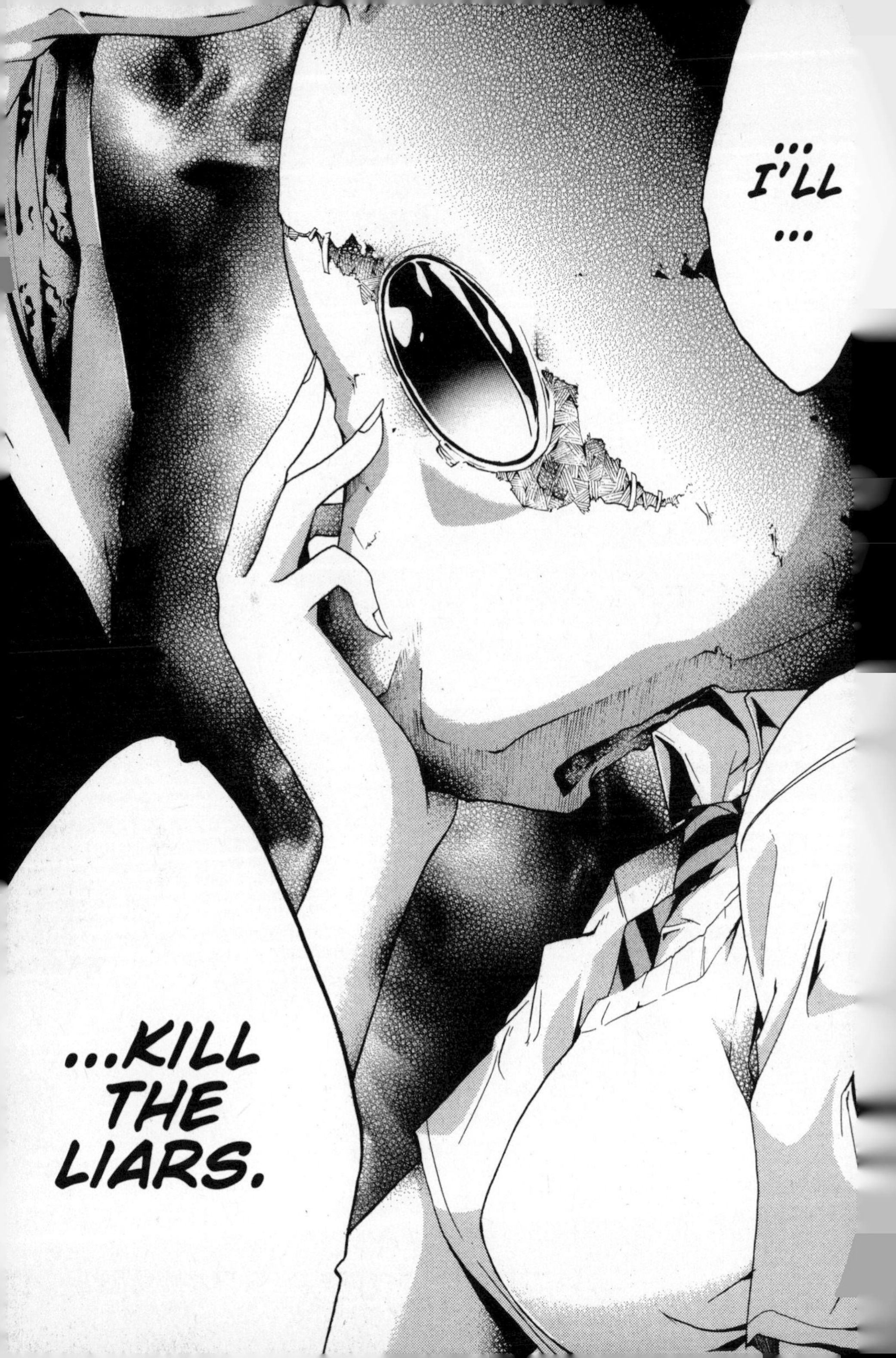
...I'LL ...
...KILL THE LIARS.

SO THAT DAD
CAN LIVE HIS
LIFE HAPPILY...

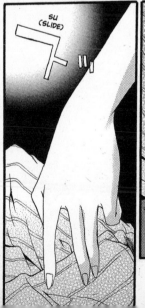

SU
(SLIDE)

IF THIS IS
ALL THE ROPE
THERE IS,
IT WON'T BE
ENOUGH.

AH...!

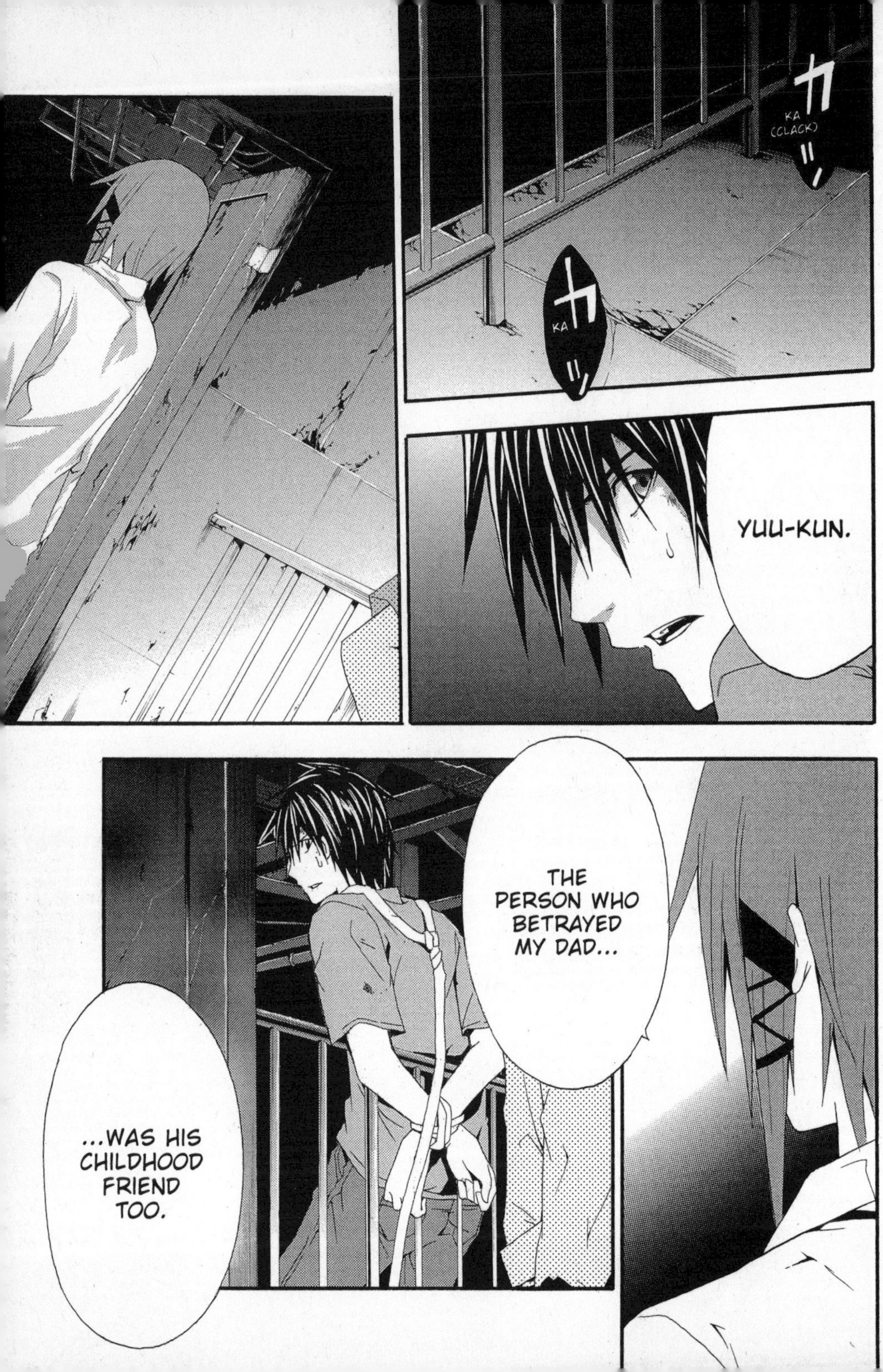
カッ
KA (CLACK)
カッ
KA
YUU-KUN.
THE PERSON WHO BETRAYED MY DAD...
...WAS HIS CHILDHOOD FRIEND TOO.

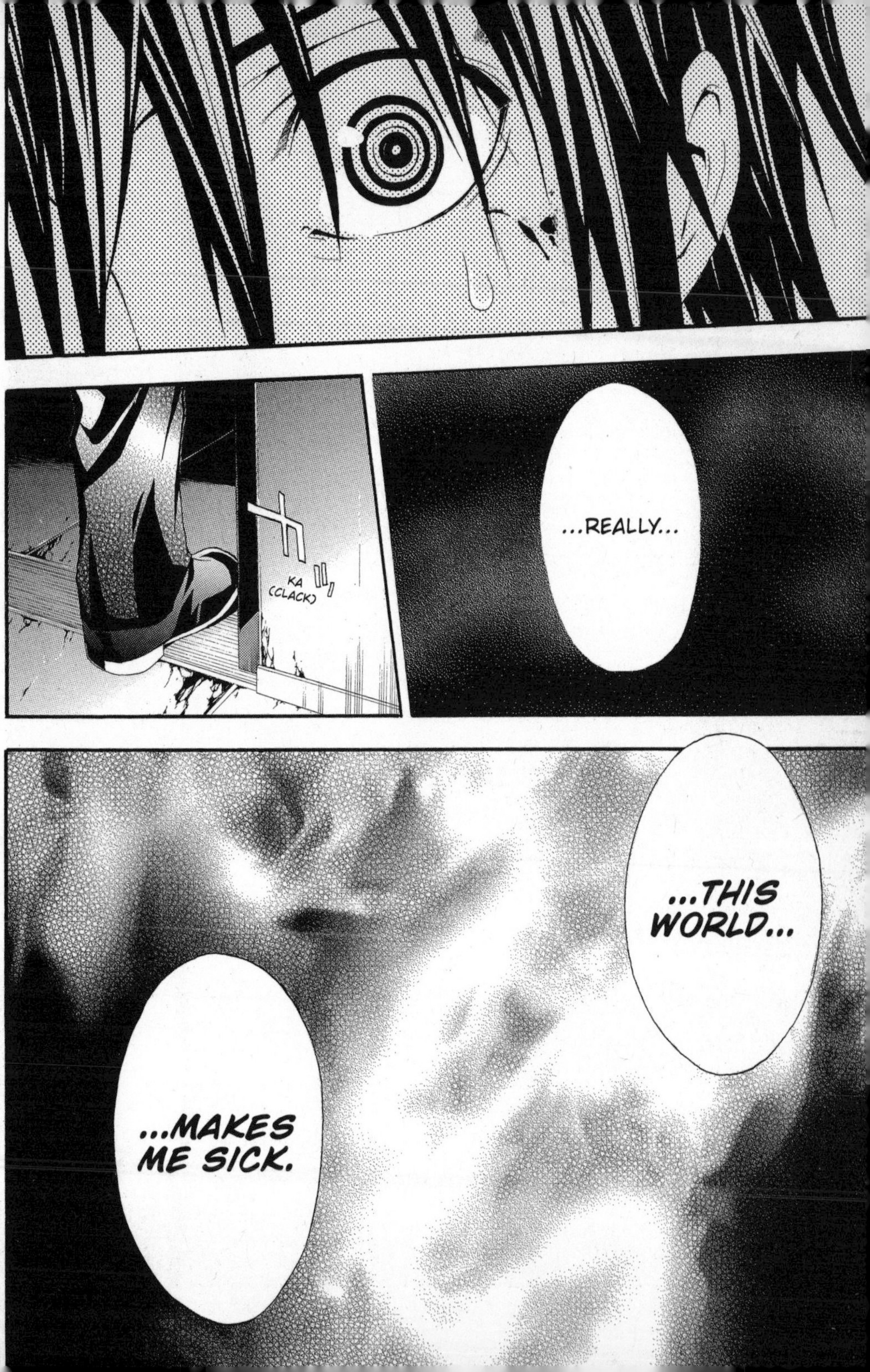
...REALLY...
KA (CLACK)
...THIS WORLD...
...MAKES ME SICK.

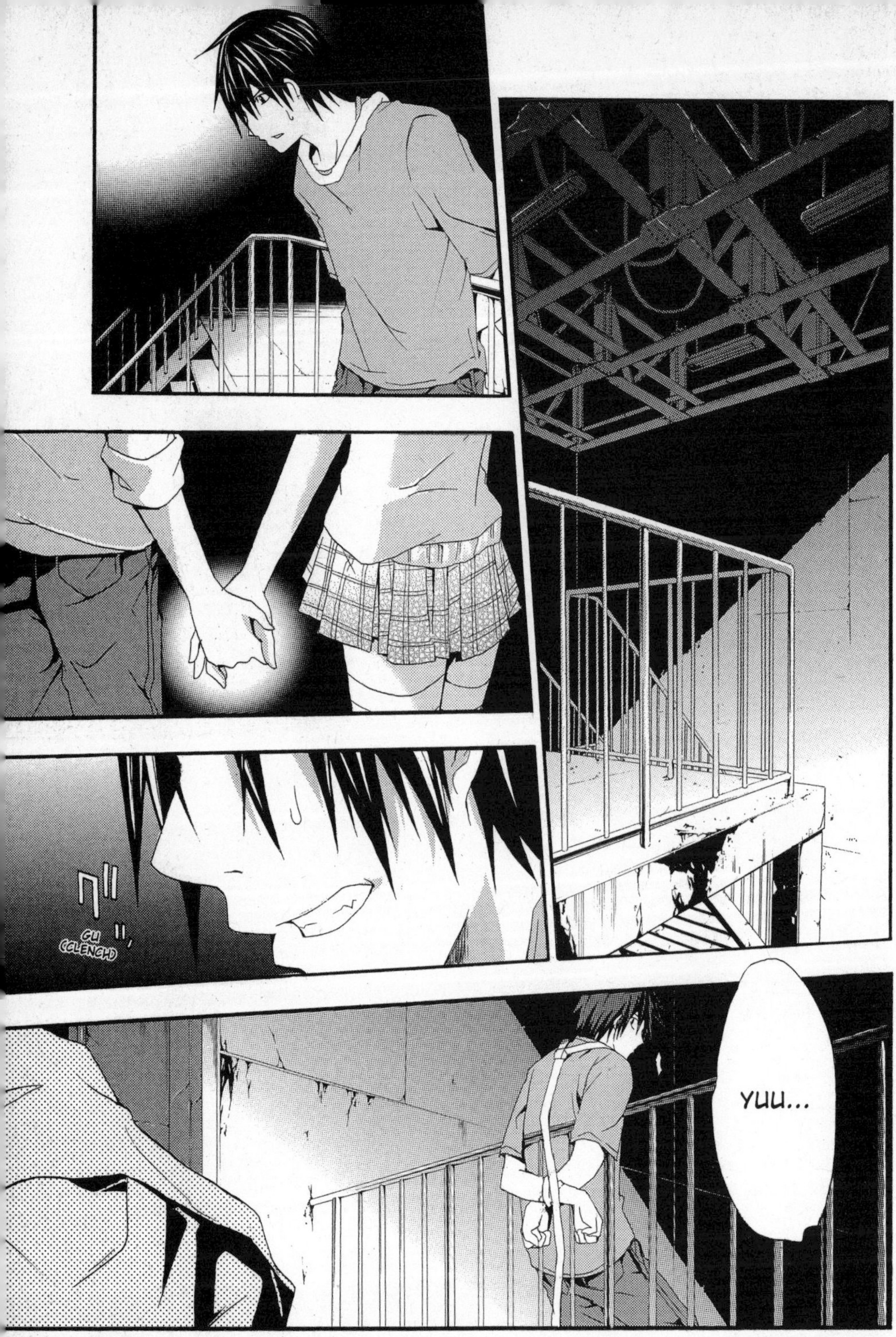
グ
GU
(CLENCH)
YUU...

HAJIME...!?

I'M SORRY...

YOU...

...YOU WERE AWAKE ALL THIS TIME!?

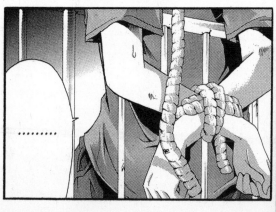

....

PIKU (TWITCH)

I HEARD PART OF IT...

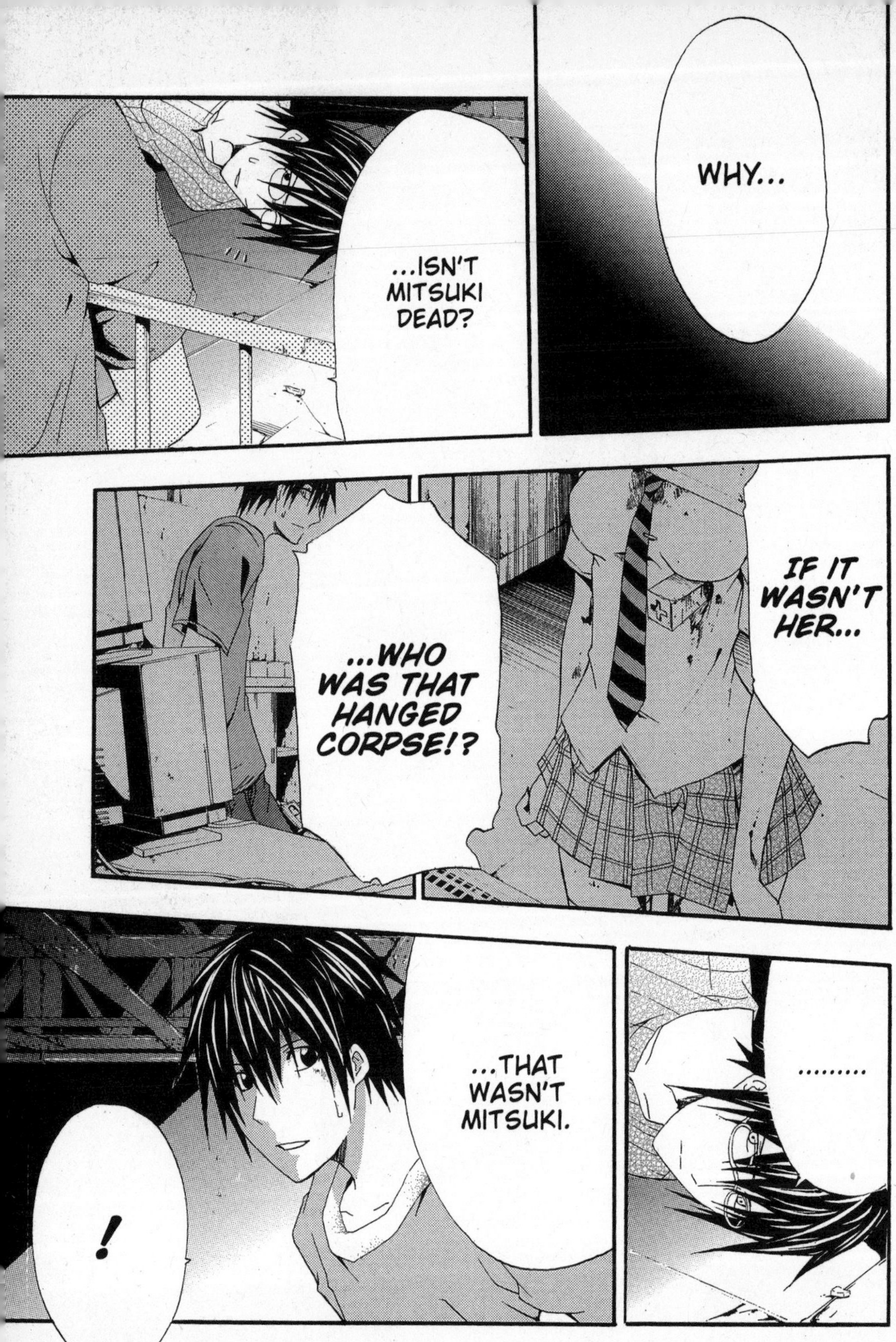
WHY...
...ISN'T MITSUKI DEAD?
IF IT WASN'T HER...
...WHO WAS THAT HANGED CORPSE!?
....
...THAT WASN'T MITSUKI.
!

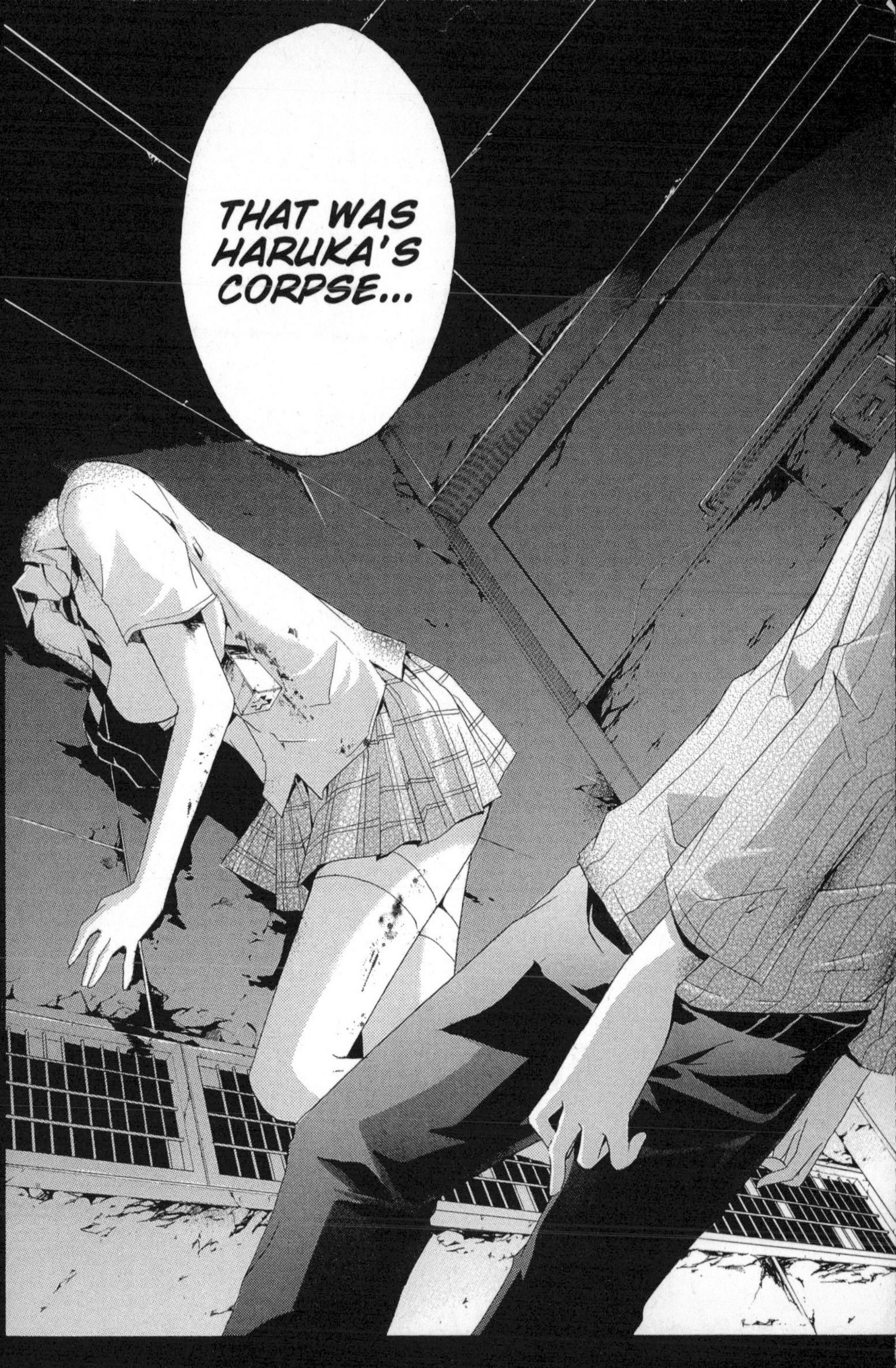
THAT WAS HARUKA'S CORPSE...

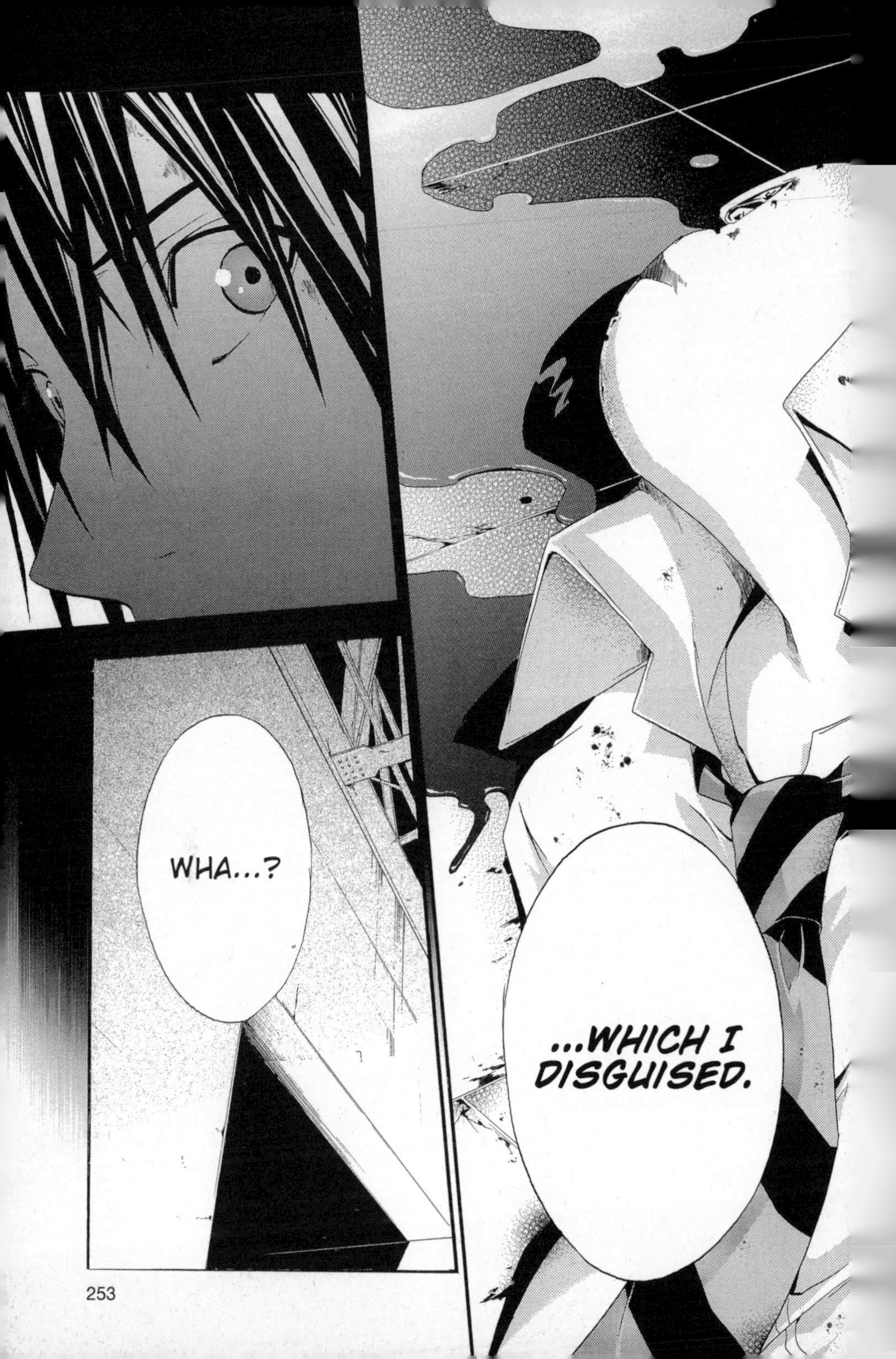
...WHICH I DISGUISED.
WHA...?

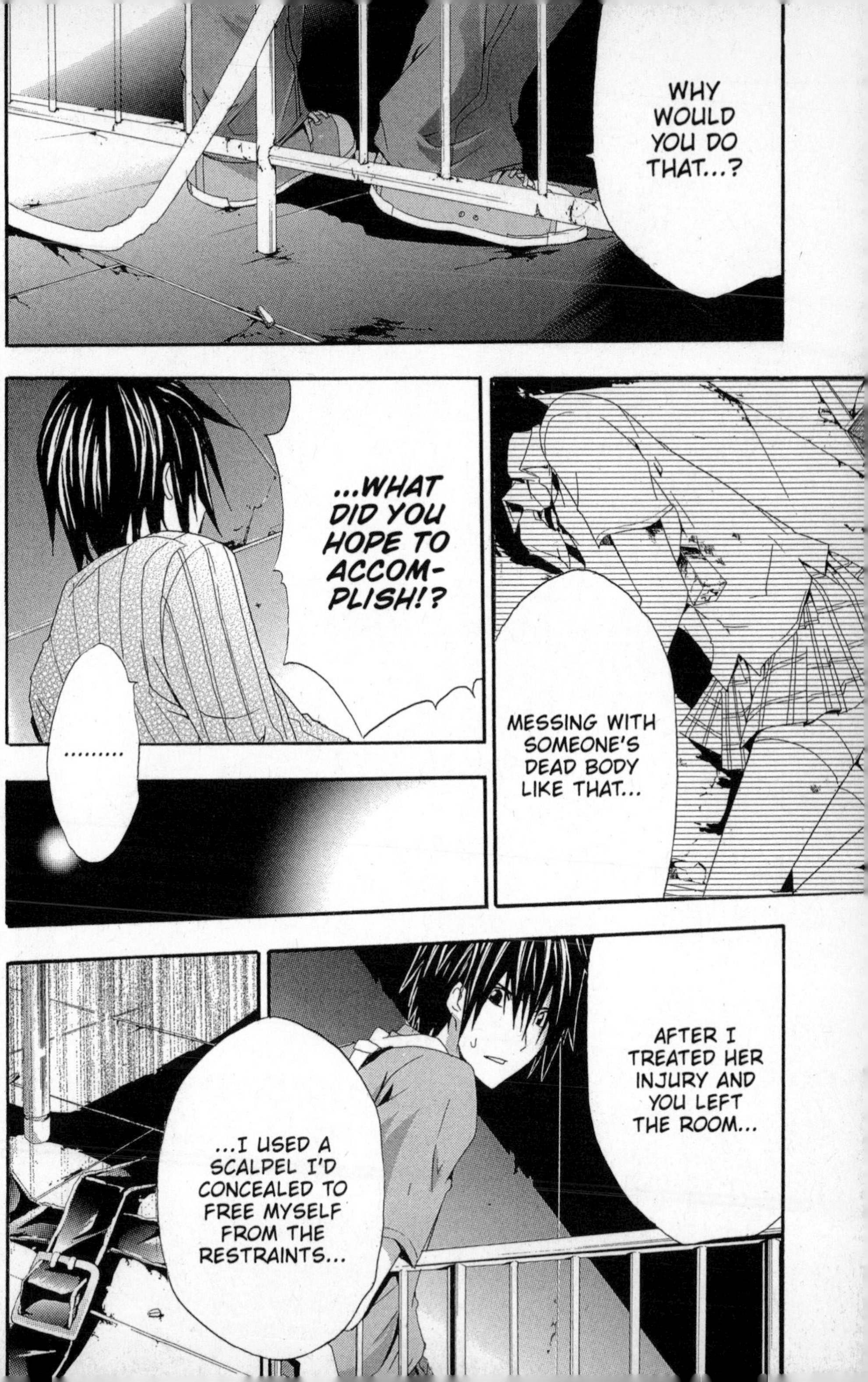
WHY WOULD YOU DO THAT...?
MESSING WITH SOMEONE'S DEAD BODY LIKE THAT...
...WHAT DID YOU HOPE TO ACCOMPLISH!?
....
AFTER I TREATED HER INJURY AND YOU LEFT THE ROOM...
...I USED A SCALPEL I'D CONCEALED TO FREE MYSELF FROM THE RESTRAINTS...

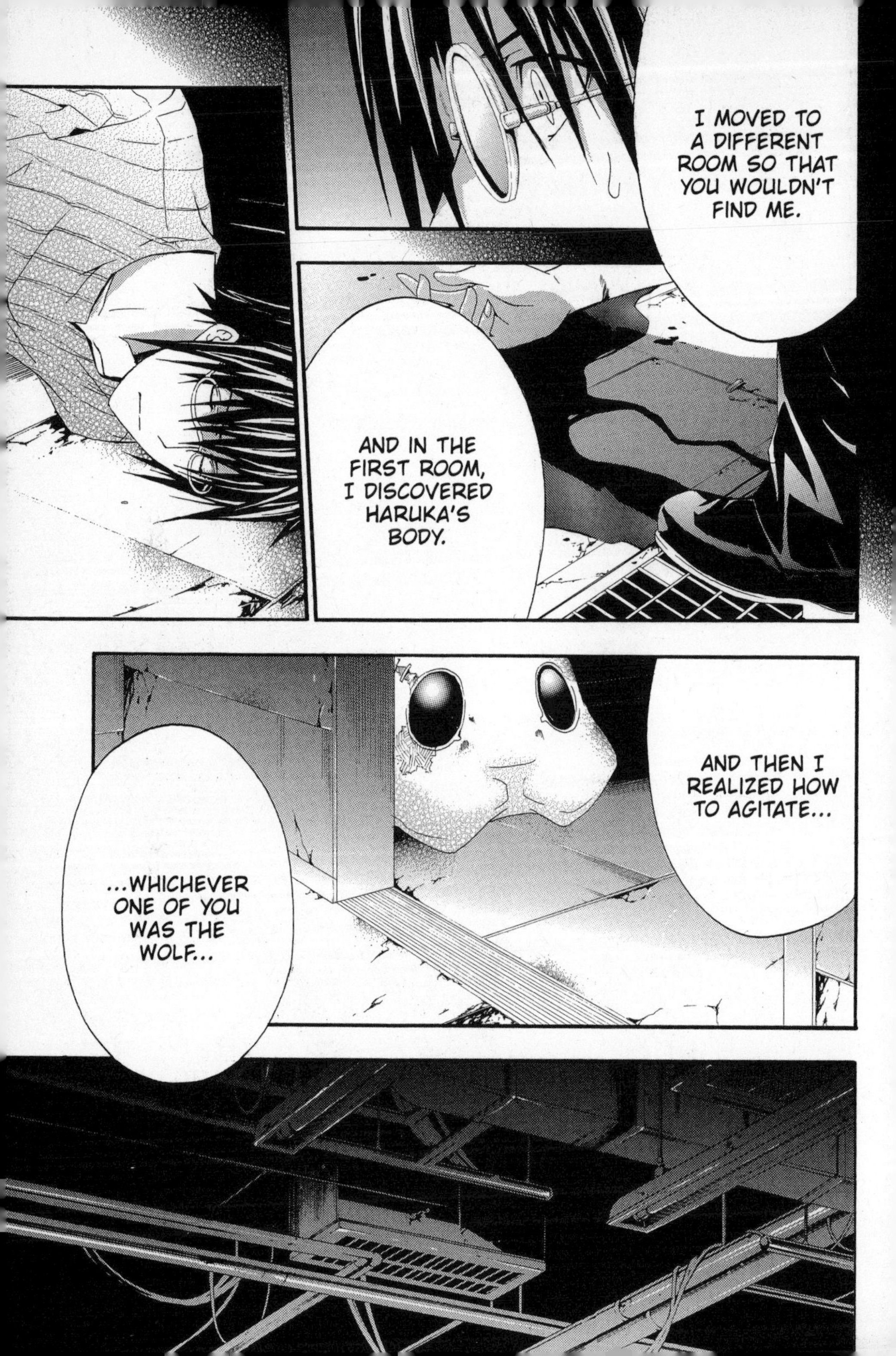
I MOVED TO A DIFFERENT ROOM SO THAT YOU WOULDN'T FIND ME.
AND IN THE FIRST ROOM, I DISCOVERED HARUKA'S BODY.
AND THEN I REALIZED HOW TO AGITATE...
...WHICHEVER ONE OF YOU WAS THE WOLF...

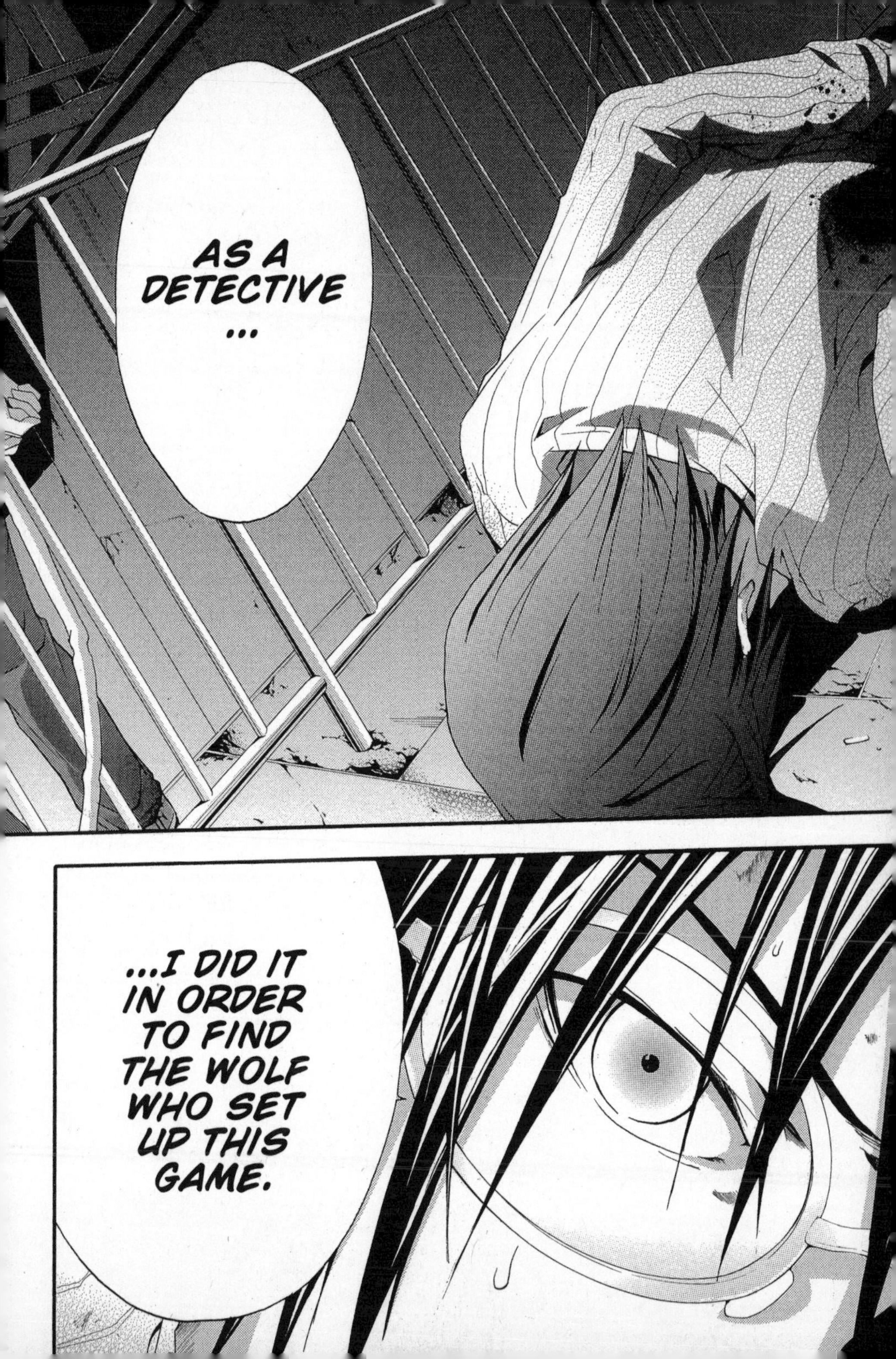
AS A DETECTIVE ...
...I DID IT IN ORDER TO FIND THE WOLF WHO SET UP THIS GAME.

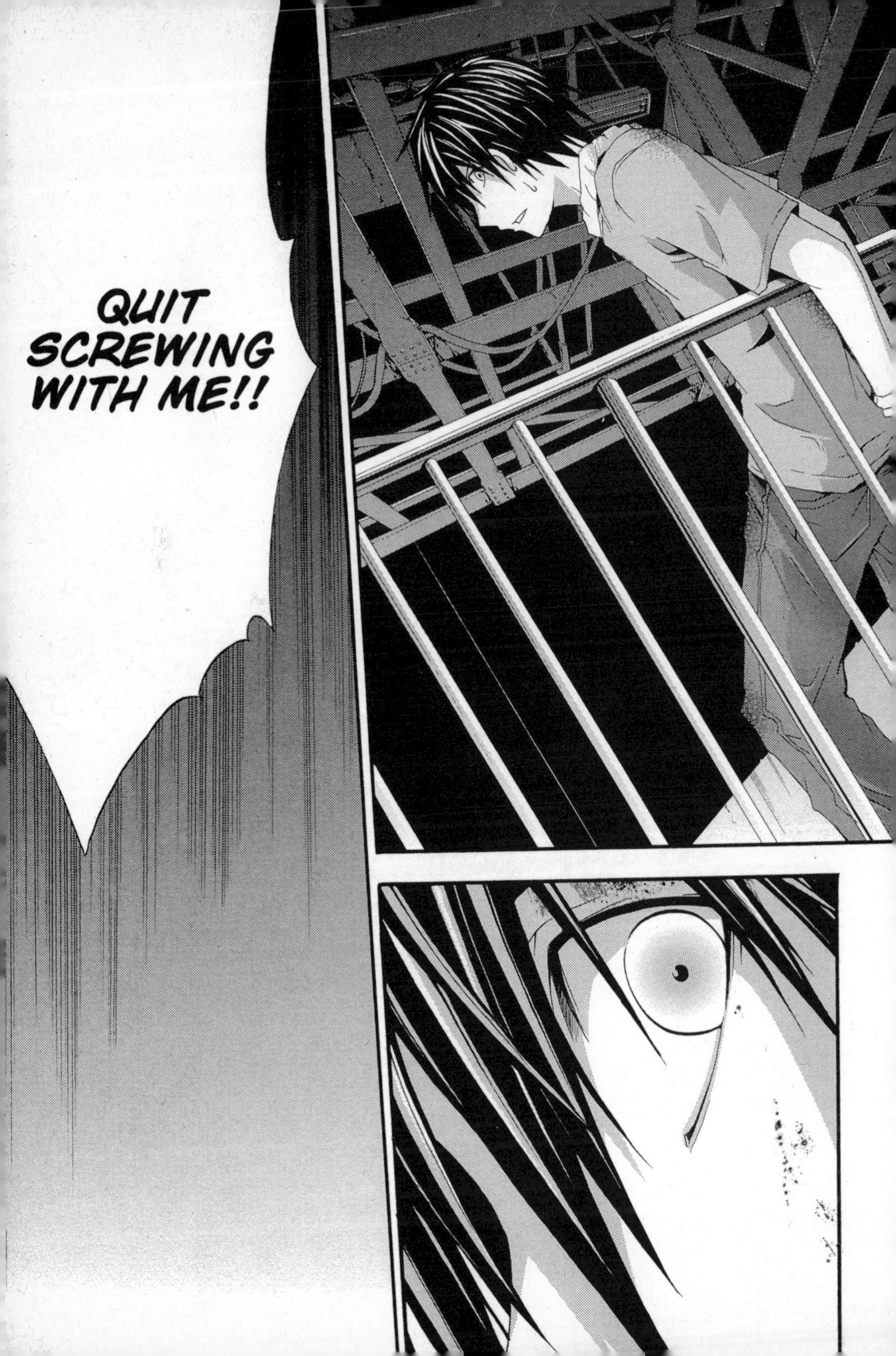
QUIT SCREWING WITH ME!!

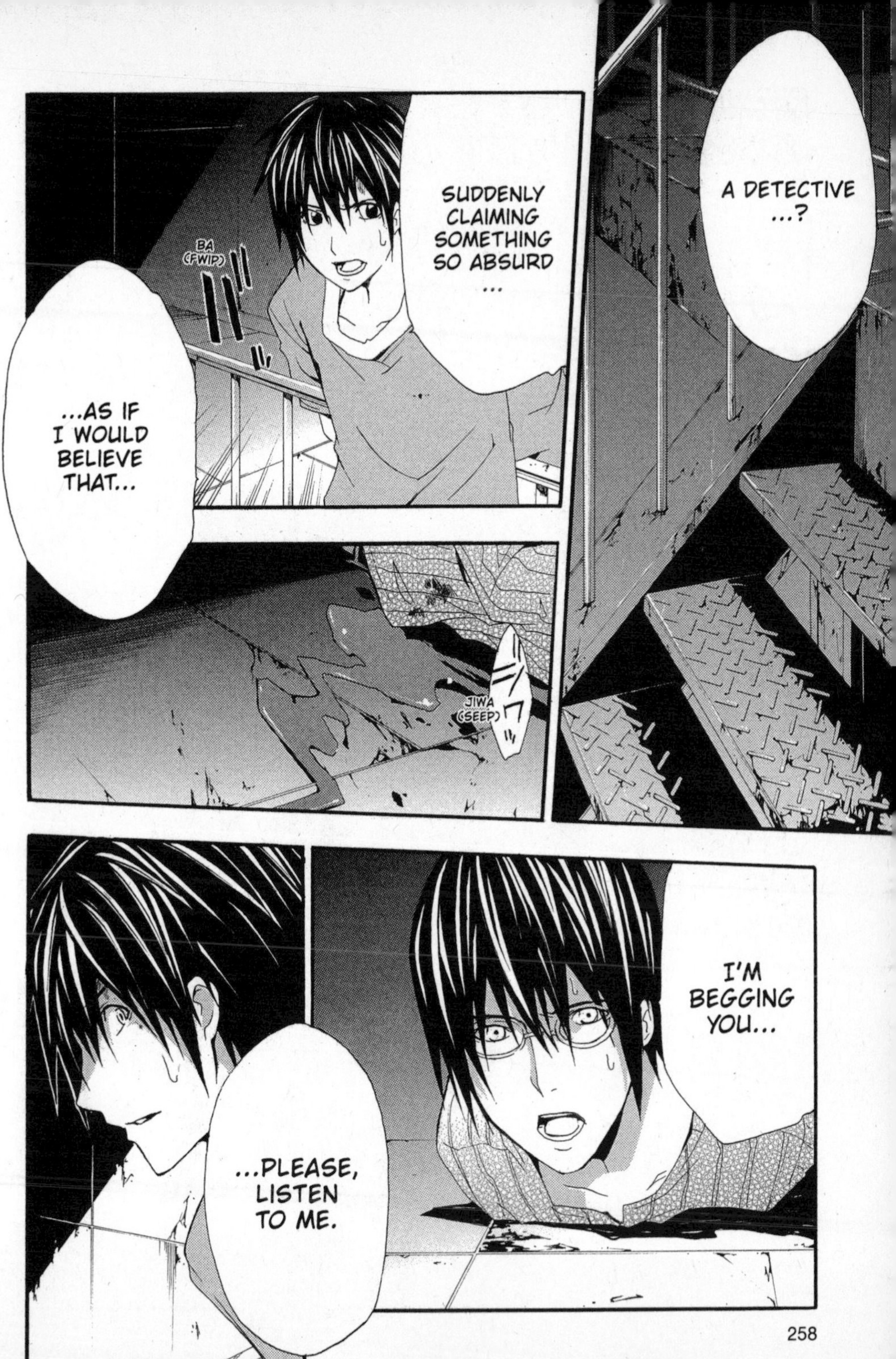
A DETECTIVE ...?
SUDDENLY CLAIMING SOMETHING SO ABSURD ...
BA (FWIP)
...AS IF I WOULD BELIEVE THAT...
JIWA (SEEP)
I'M BEGGING YOU...
...PLEASE, LISTEN TO ME.

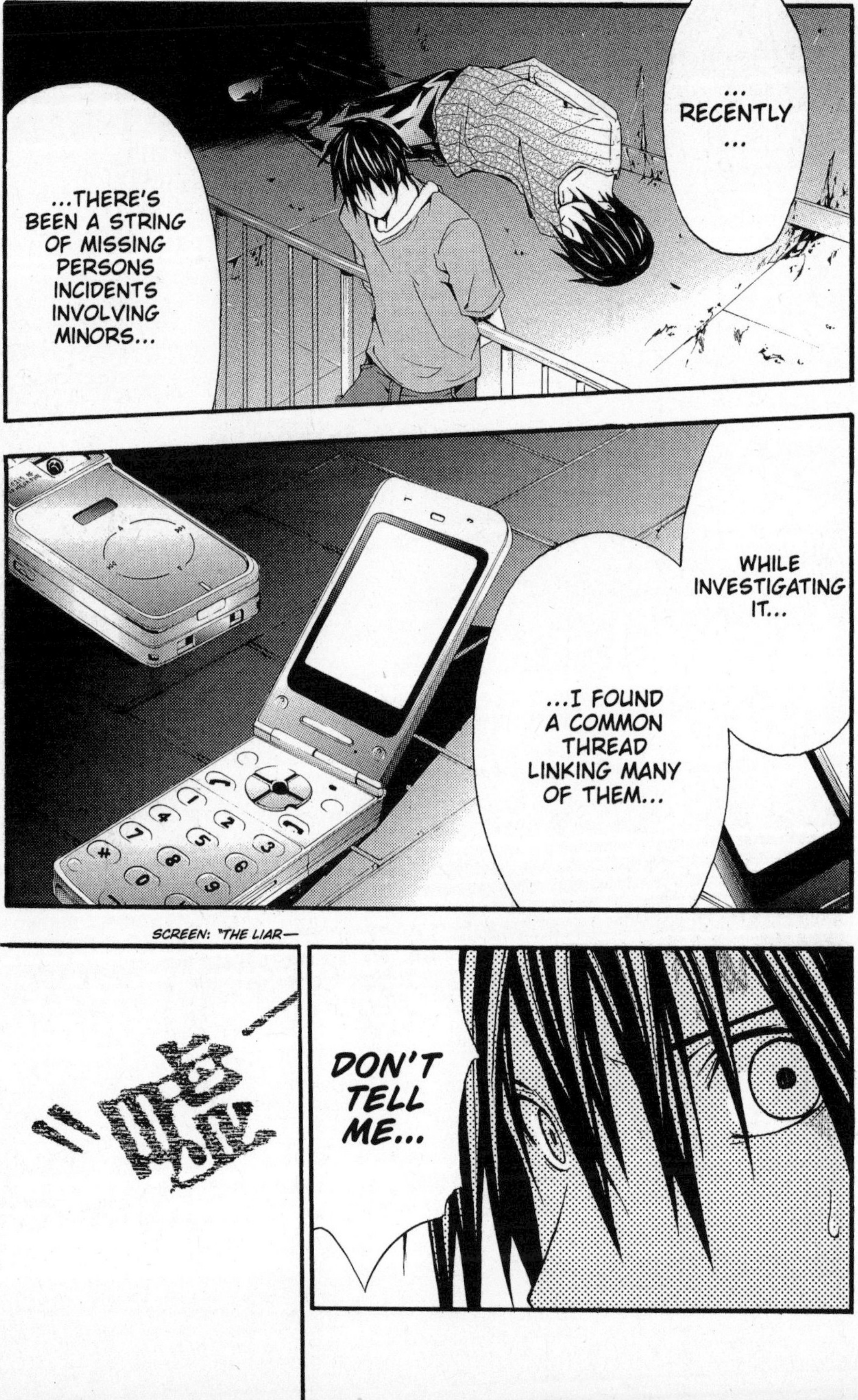
...RECENTLY...
...THERE'S BEEN A STRING OF MISSING PERSONS INCIDENTS INVOLVING MINORS...
WHILE INVESTIGATING IT...
...I FOUND A COMMON THREAD LINKING MANY OF THEM...
DON'T TELL ME...
SCREEN: "THE LIAR—
"嘘—

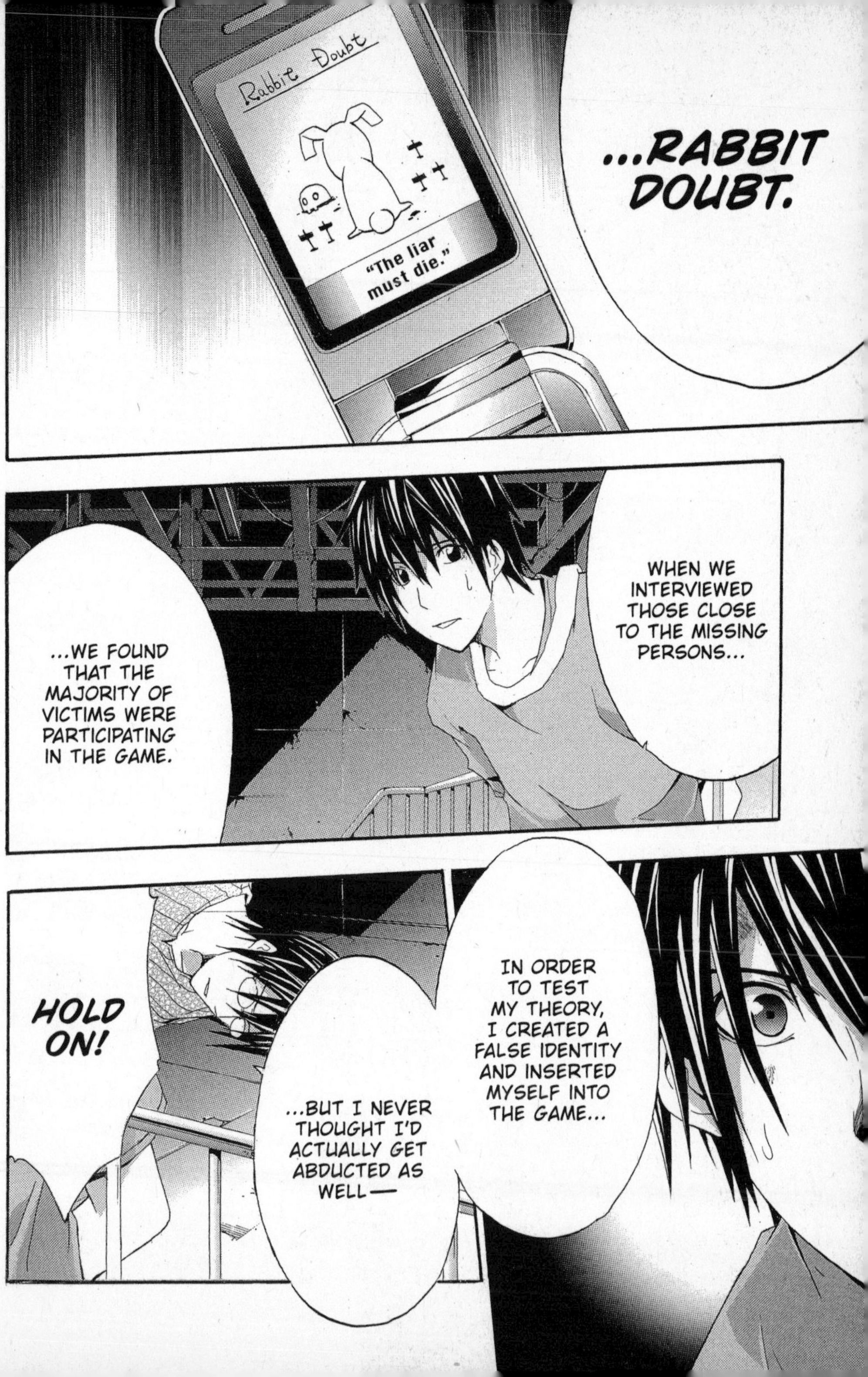
Rabbit Doubt
"The liar must die."
...RABBIT DOUBT.
WHEN WE INTERVIEWED THOSE CLOSE TO THE MISSING PERSONS...
...WE FOUND THAT THE MAJORITY OF VICTIMS WERE PARTICIPATING IN THE GAME.
IN ORDER TO TEST MY THEORY, I CREATED A FALSE IDENTITY AND INSERTED MYSELF INTO THE GAME...
...BUT I NEVER THOUGHT I'D ACTUALLY GET ABDUCTED AS WELL—
HOLD ON!

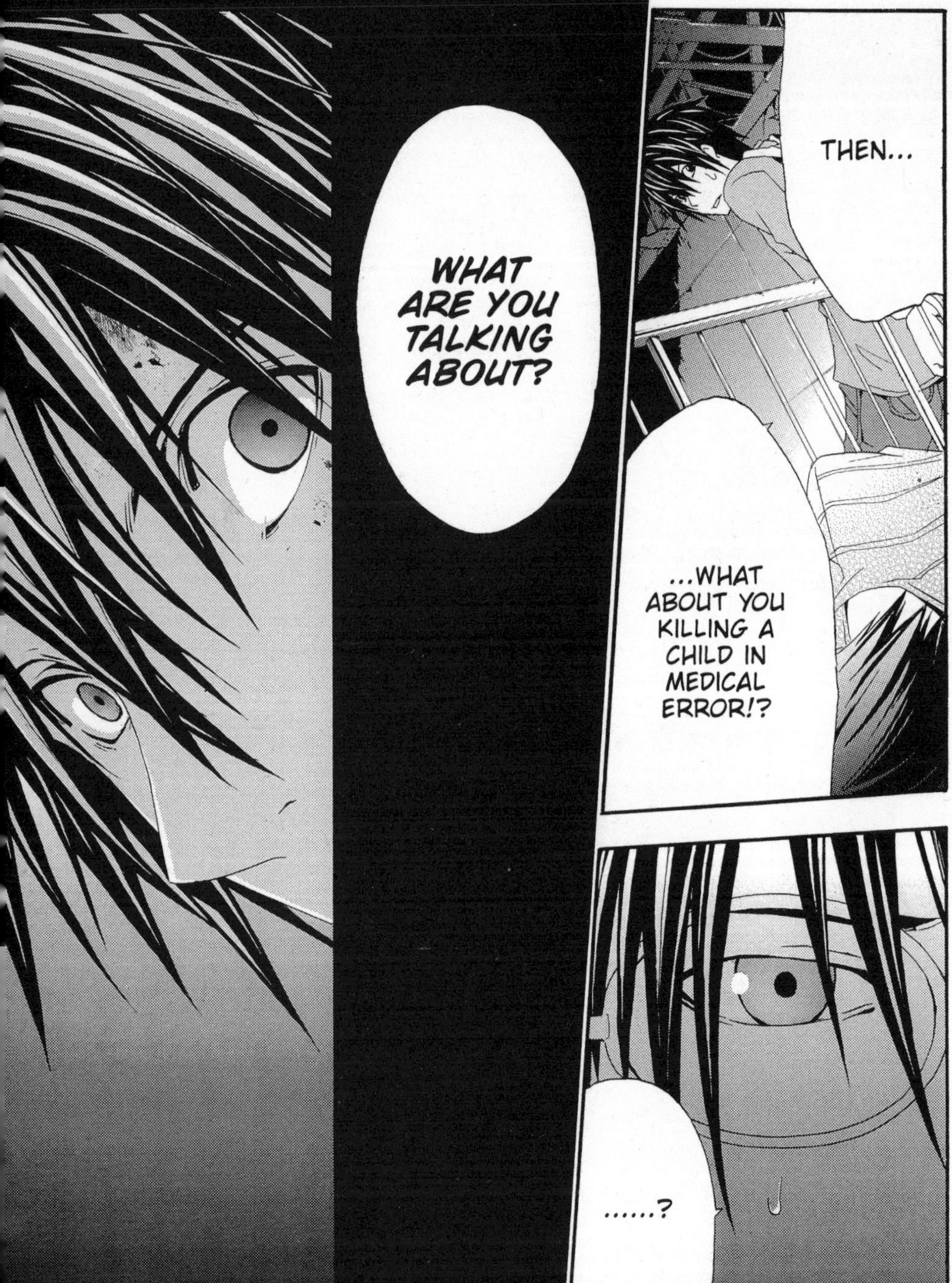
THEN...
...WHAT ABOUT YOU KILLING A CHILD IN MEDICAL ERROR!?
......?
WHAT ARE YOU TALKING ABOUT?

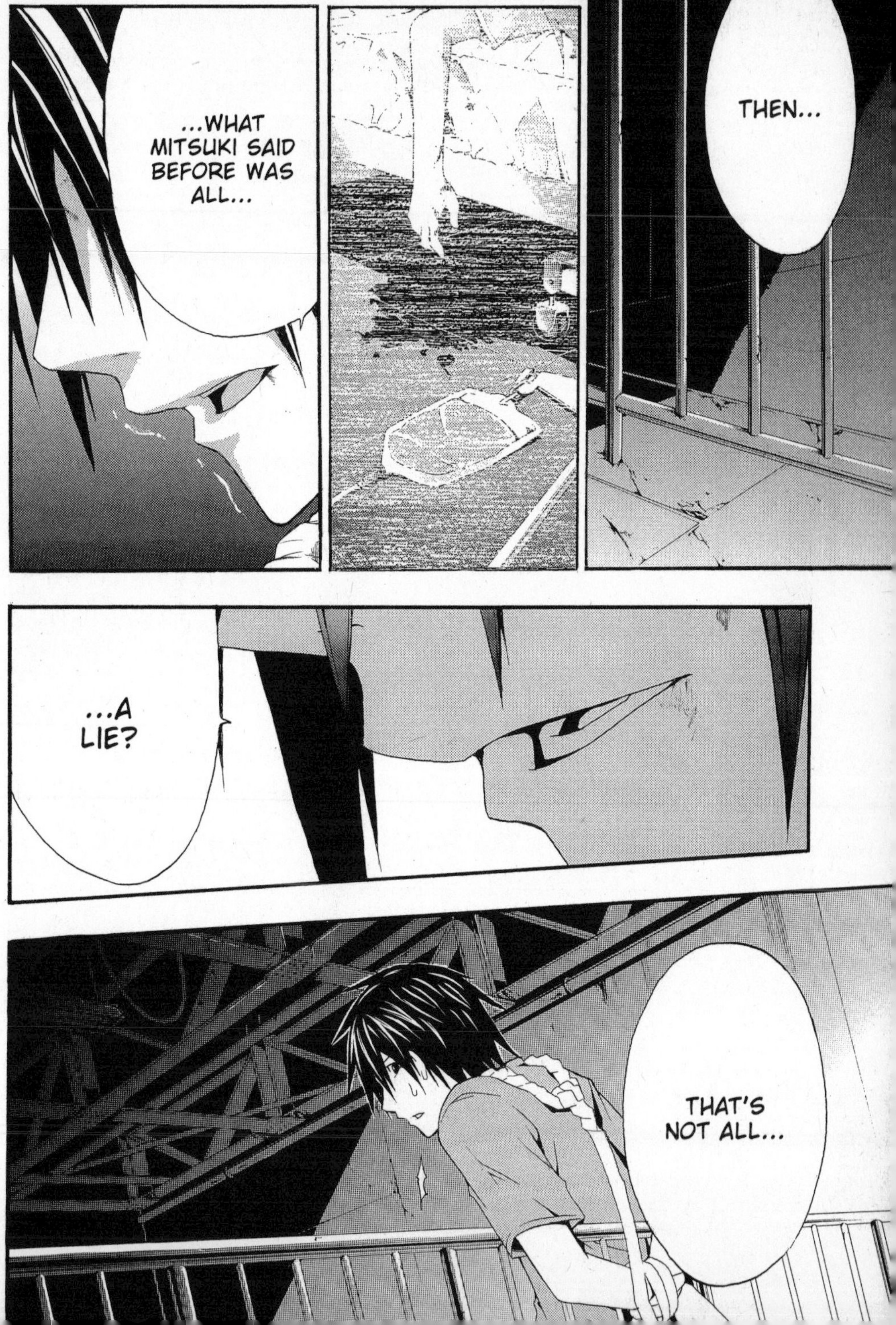
THEN...
...WHAT MITSUKI SAID BEFORE WAS ALL...
...A LIE?
THAT'S NOT ALL...

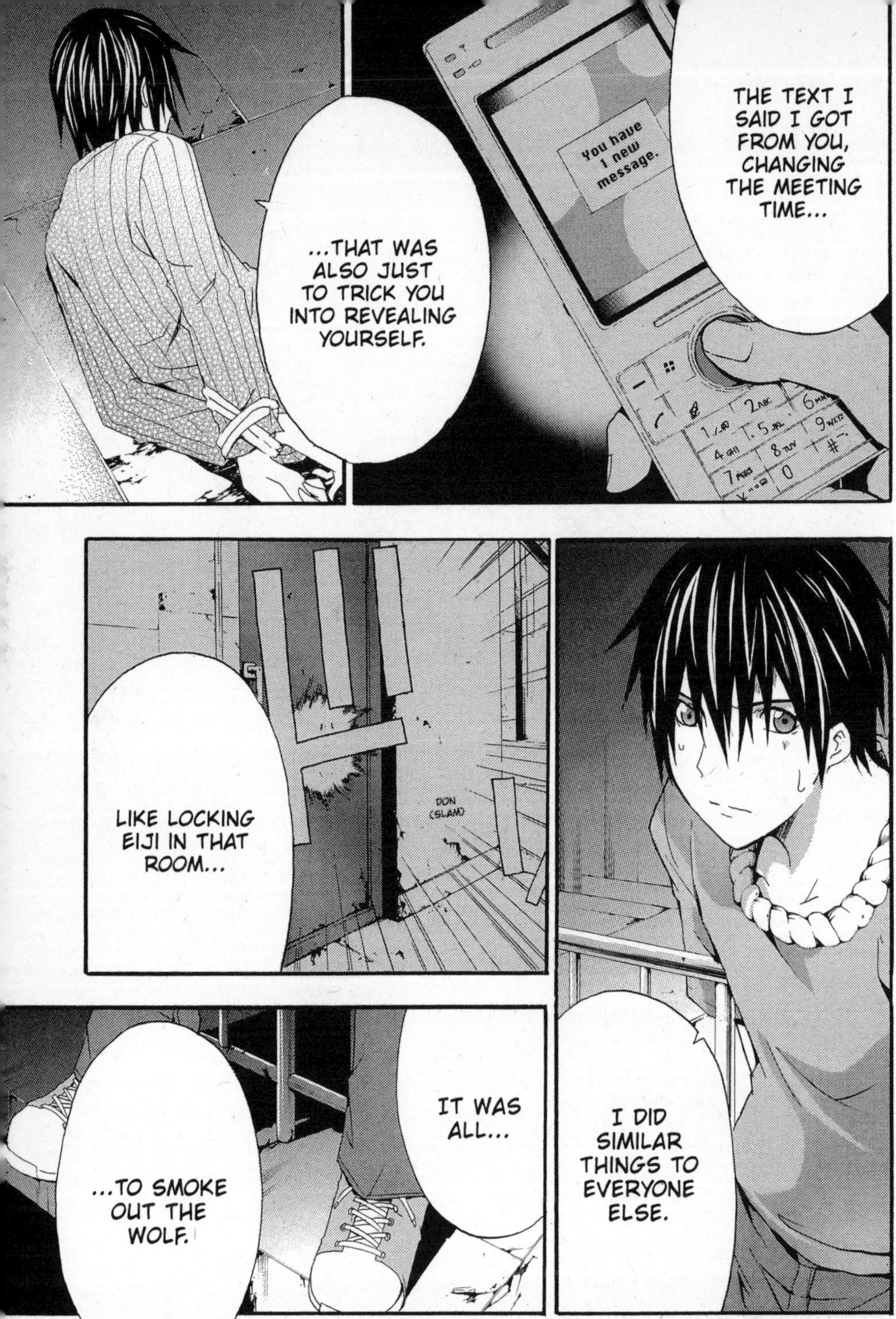
THE TEXT I SAID I GOT FROM YOU, CHANGING THE MEETING TIME...
You have 1 new message.
...THAT WAS ALSO JUST TO TRICK YOU INTO REVEALING YOURSELF.
I DID SIMILAR THINGS TO EVERYONE ELSE.
LIKE LOCKING EIJI IN THAT ROOM...
DON (SLAM)
IT WAS ALL...
...TO SMOKE OUT THE WOLF.

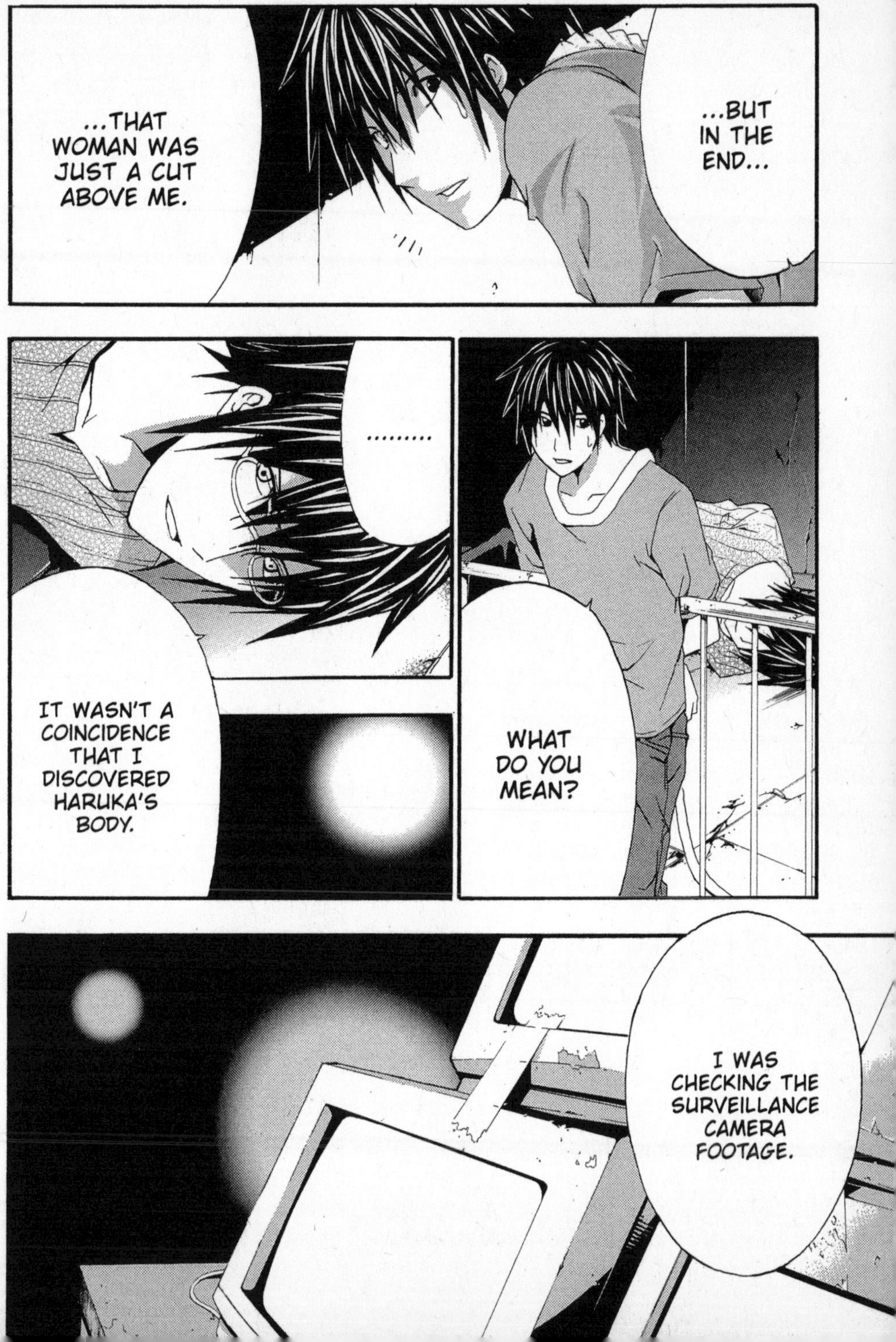
...BUT IN THE END...
...THAT WOMAN WAS JUST A CUT ABOVE ME.
WHAT DO YOU MEAN?
....
IT WASN'T A COINCIDENCE THAT I DISCOVERED HARUKA'S BODY.
I WAS CHECKING THE SURVEILLANCE CAMERA FOOTAGE.

ZU
(DRAG)

.........?

I THOUGHT THERE WAS NOTHING ON THAT TAPE...?

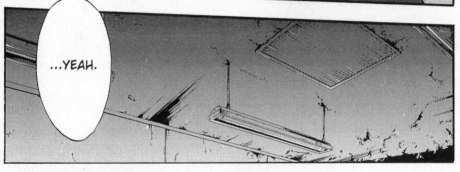

...YEAH.

THAT'S WHY, AFTER I FIRST CHECKED THE TAPE...

...I STARTED A NEW RECORDING FROM THAT POINT ON.

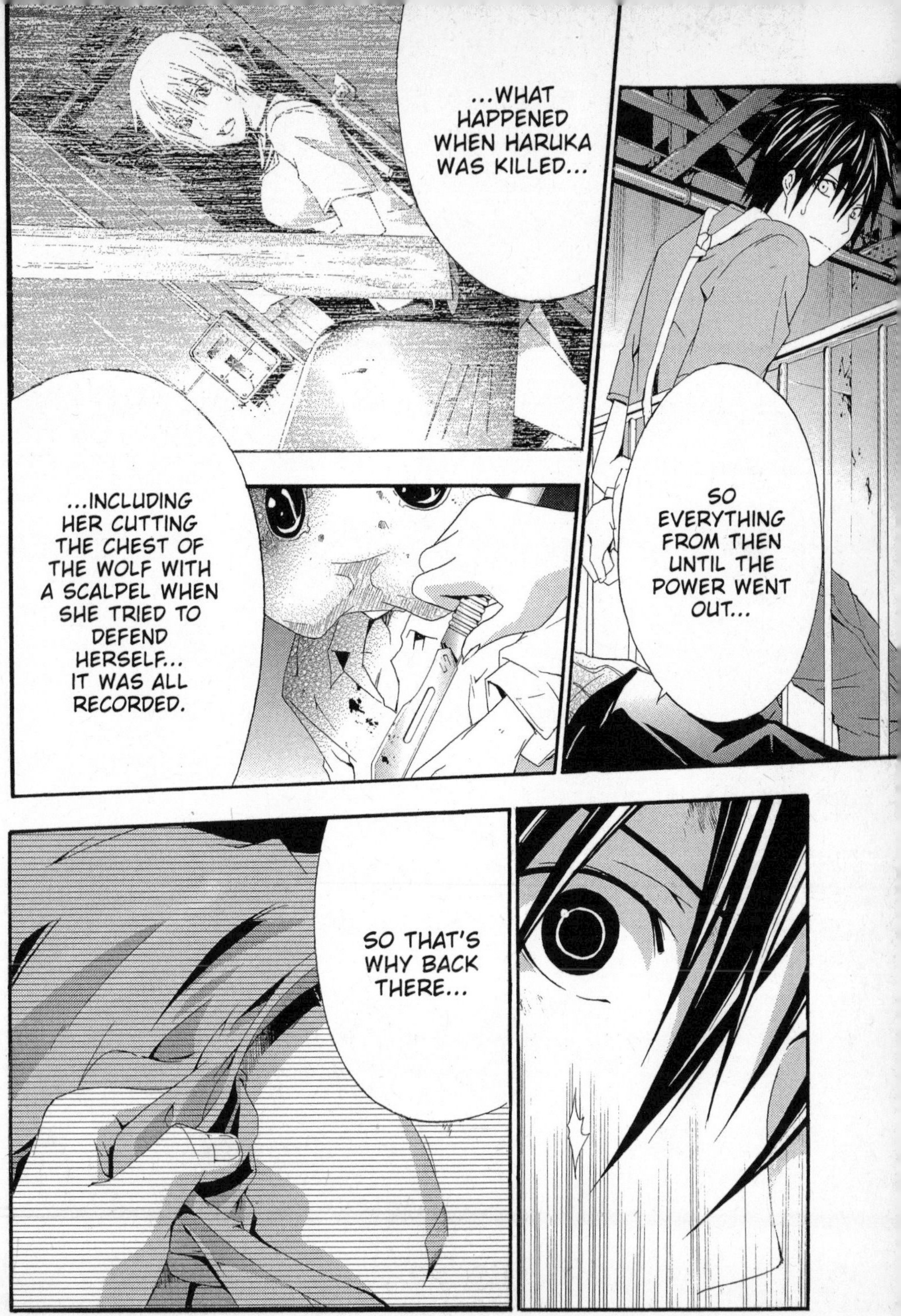
SO EVERYTHING FROM THEN UNTIL THE POWER WENT OUT...
...WHAT HAPPENED WHEN HARUKA WAS KILLED...
...INCLUDING HER CUTTING THE CHEST OF THE WOLF WITH A SCALPEL WHEN SHE TRIED TO DEFEND HERSELF... IT WAS ALL RECORDED.
SO THAT'S WHY BACK THERE...

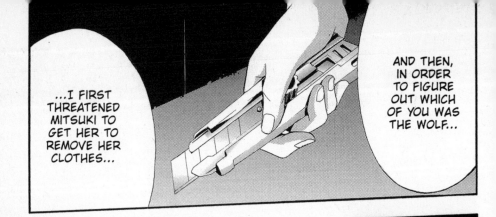

AND THEN, IN ORDER TO FIGURE OUT WHICH OF YOU WAS THE WOLF...

...I FIRST THREATENED MITSUKI TO GET HER TO REMOVE HER CLOTHES...

I GUESS SHE DID A GOOD JOB HIDING IT...

SHE'S REALLY SOMETHING.

...NO.

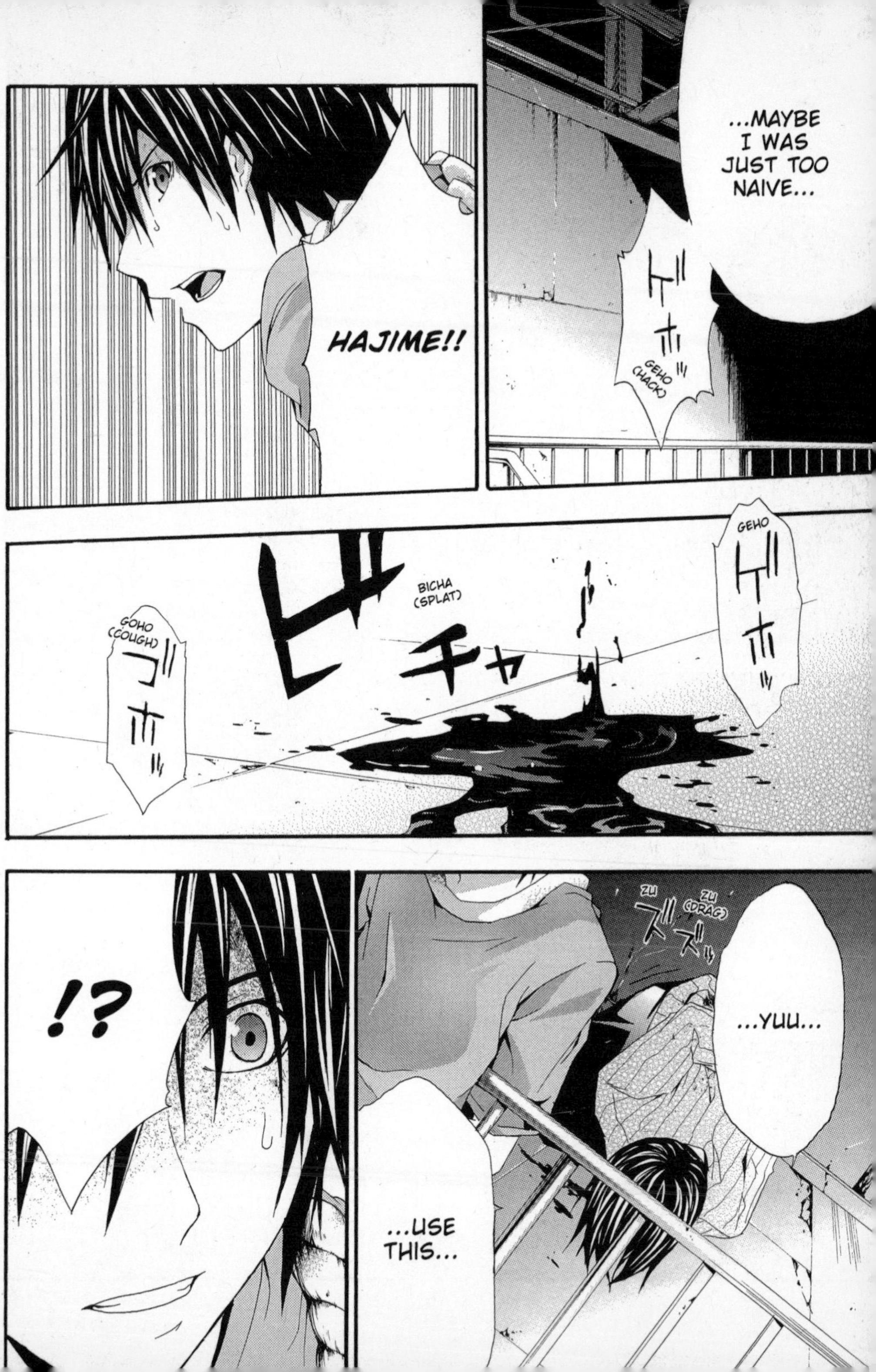
...MAYBE I WAS JUST TOO NAIVE...
ゲホッ
GEHO (HACK)
HAJIME!!
ゲホッ
GEHO
ビチャ
BICHA (SPLAT)
ゴホッ
GOHO (COUGH)
ズズッ
ZU ZU (DRAG)
...YUU...
...USE THIS...
!?

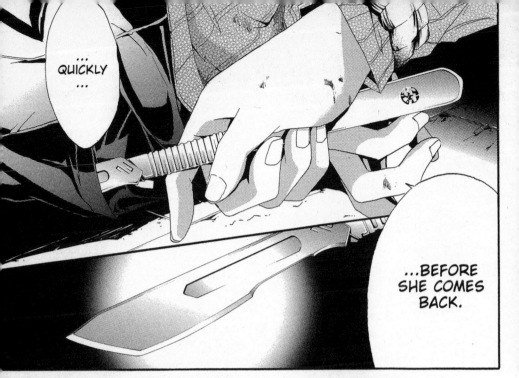

... QUICKLY ...

...BEFORE SHE COMES BACK.

ZU
ZU

HAJIME, ARE YOU...?

I'M BEGGING YOU...

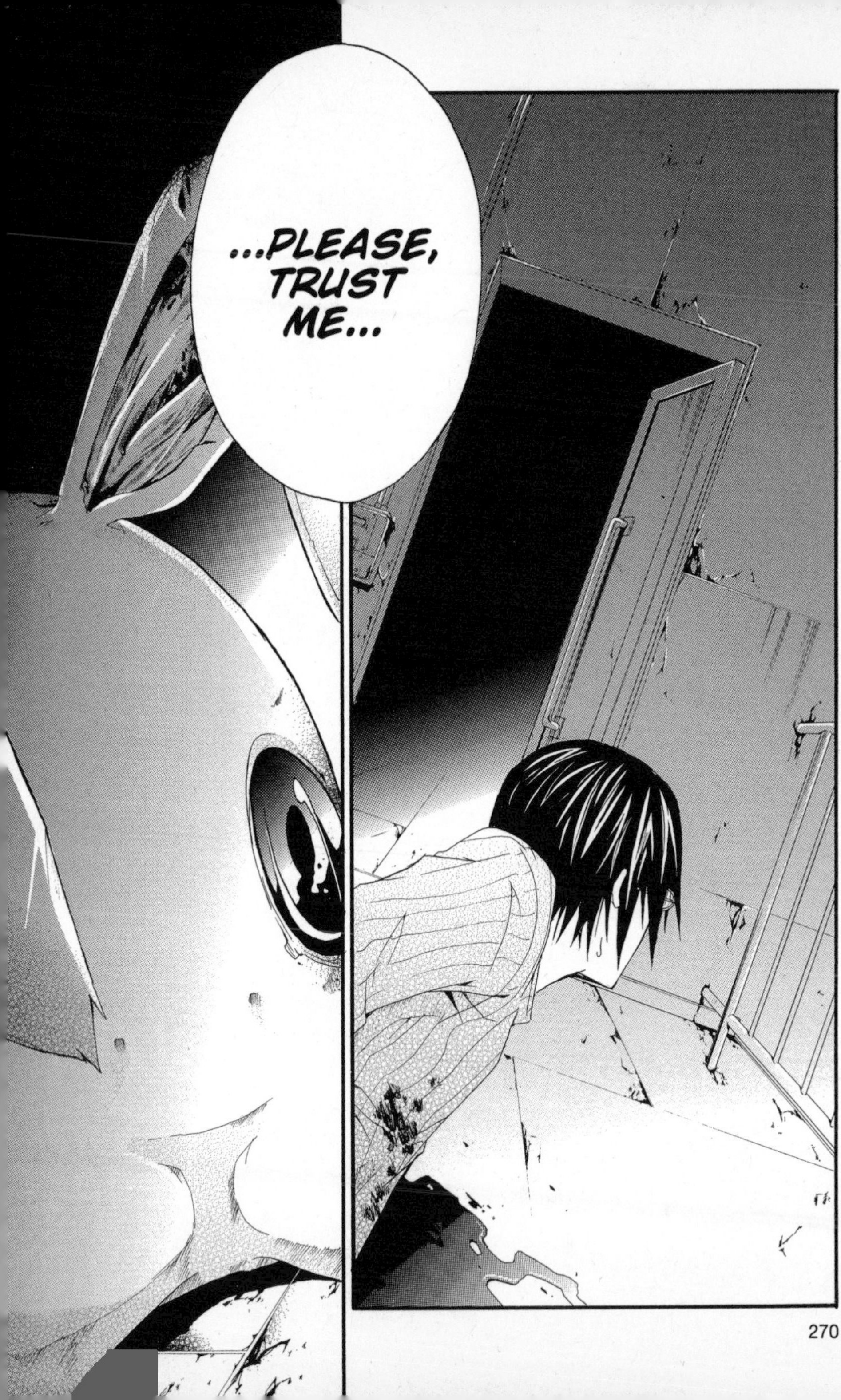
...PLEASE, TRUST ME...

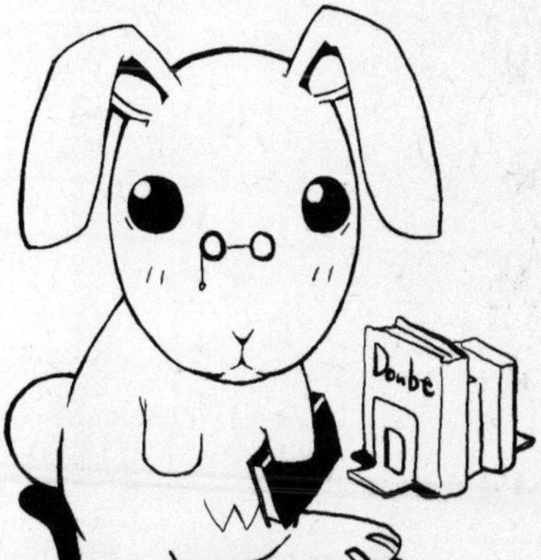
Donbe

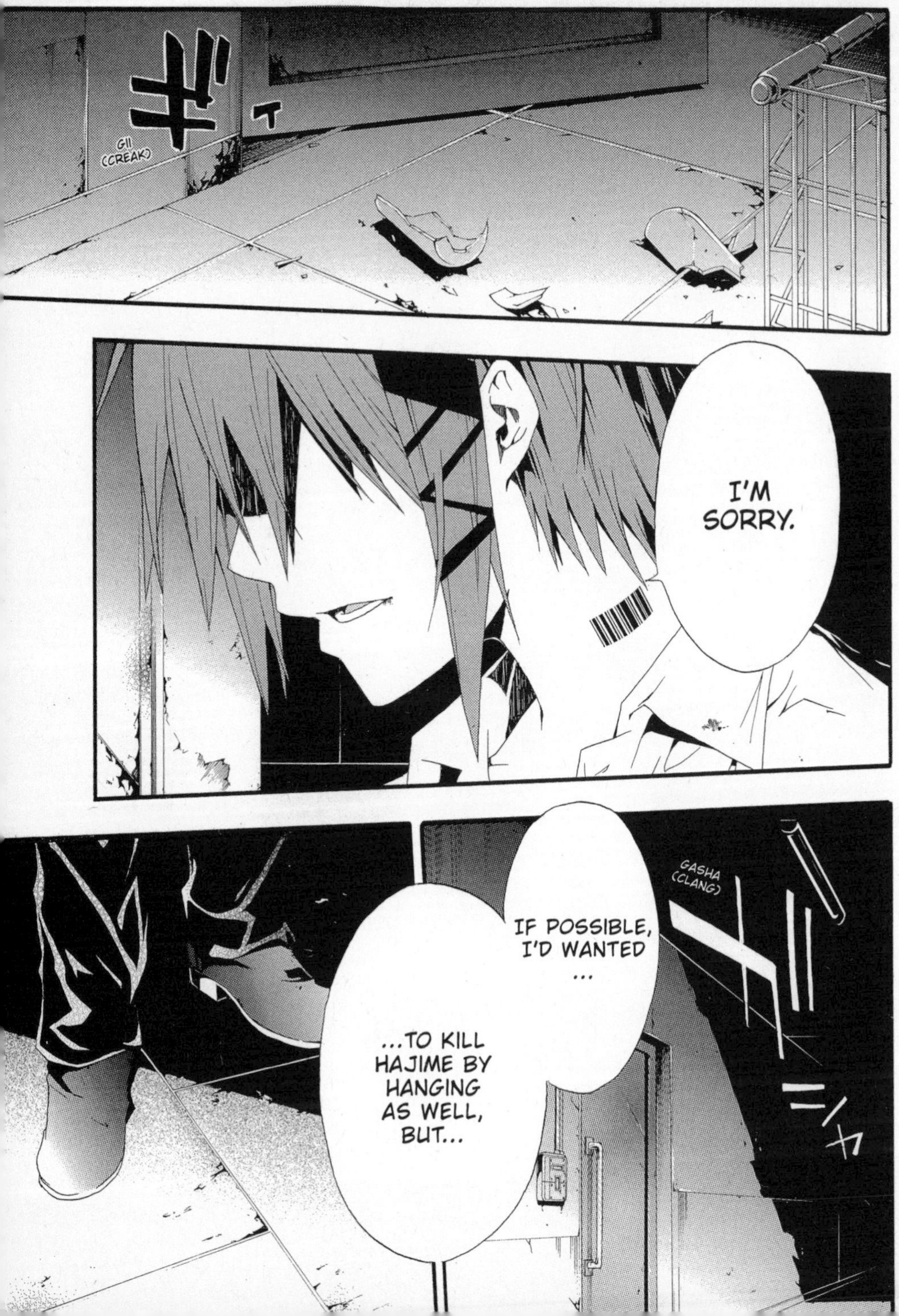
GII (CREAK)
I'M SORRY.
GASHA (CLANG)
IF POSSIBLE, I'D WANTED ...
...TO KILL HAJIME BY HANGING AS WELL, BUT...

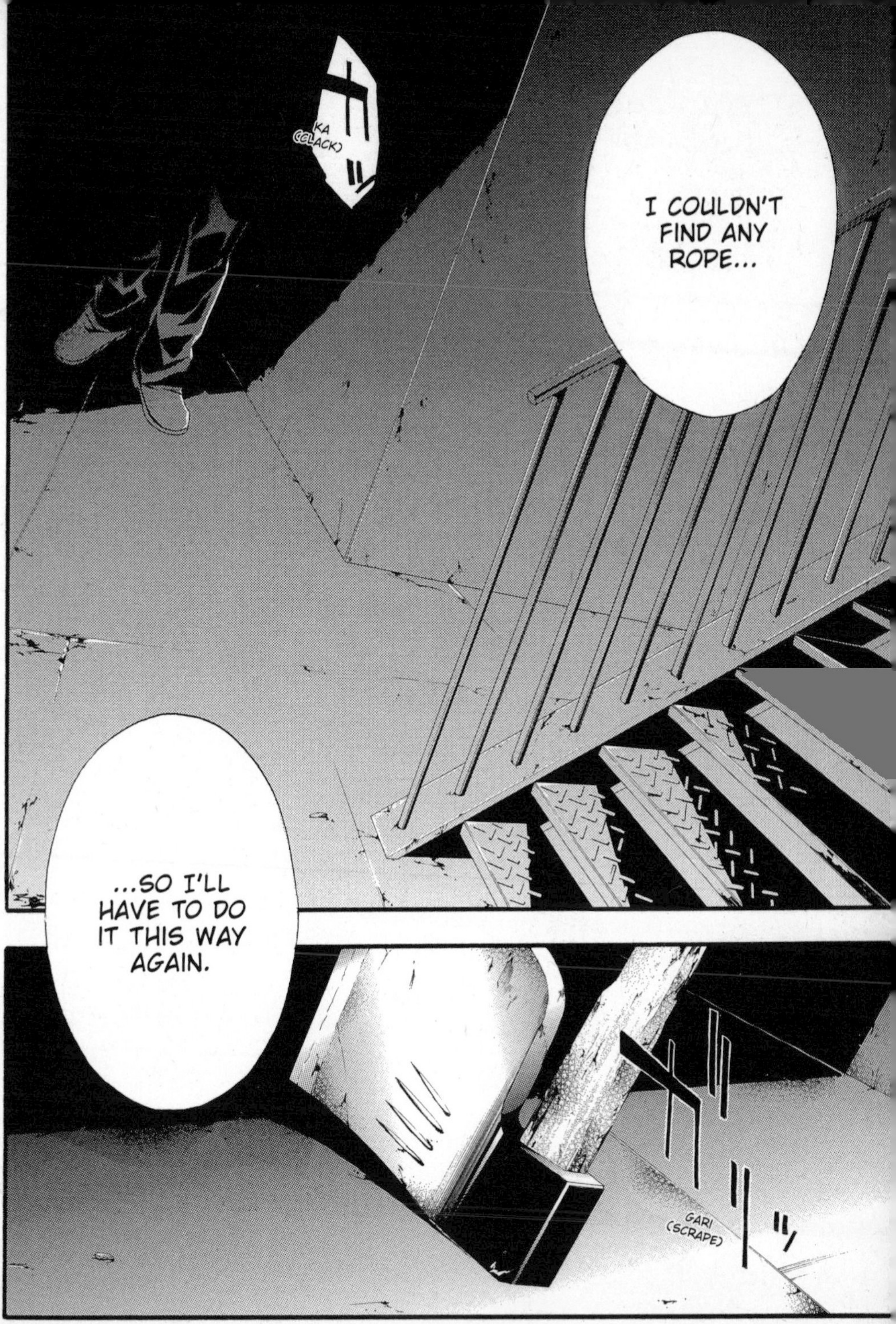
I COULDN'T FIND ANY ROPE...
KA (CLACK)
...SO I'LL HAVE TO DO IT THIS WAY AGAIN.
GARI (SCRAPE)

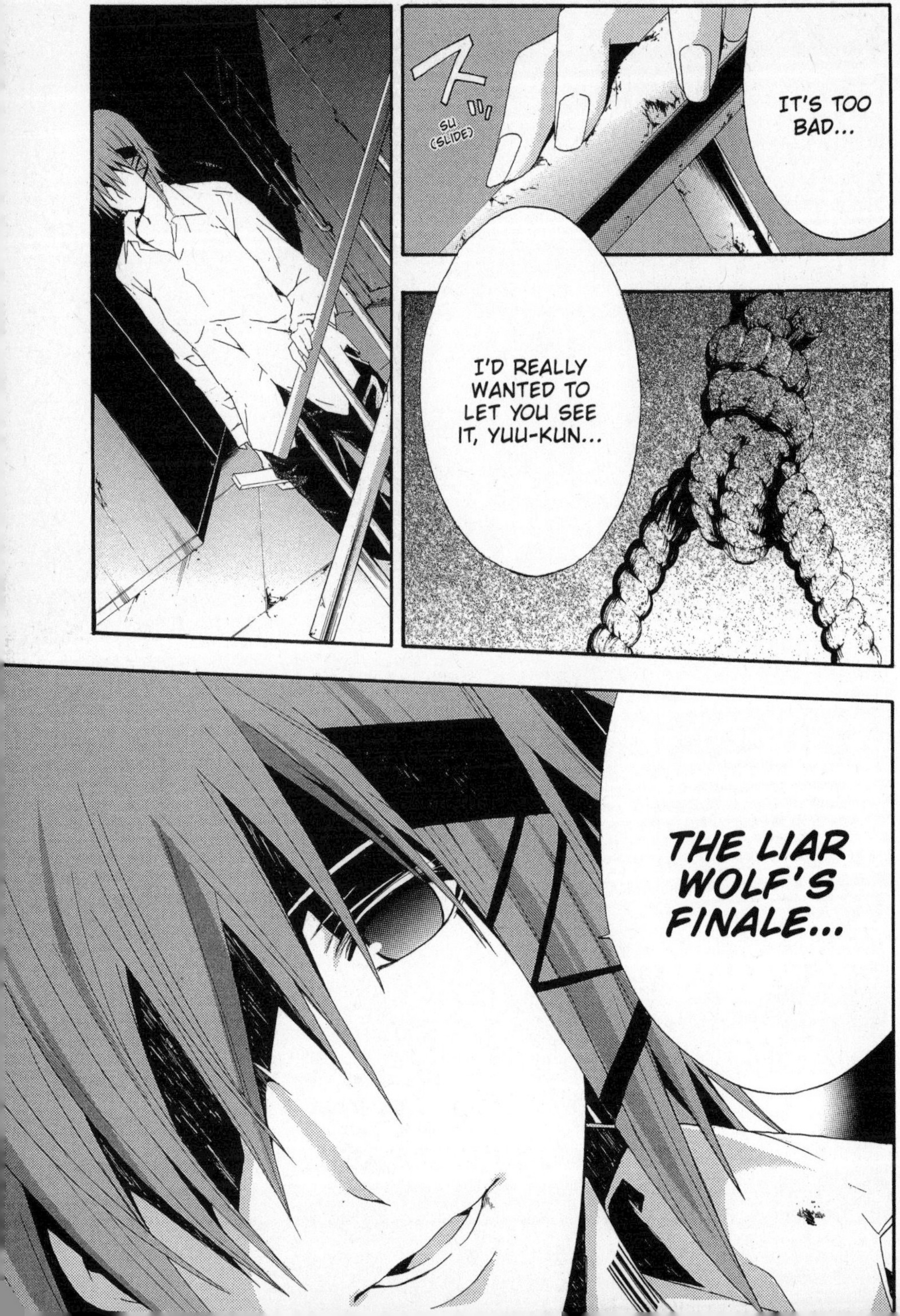
IT'S TOO BAD...
ス
SU (SLIDE)
I'D REALLY WANTED TO LET YOU SEE IT, YUU-KUN...
THE LIAR WOLF'S FINALE...

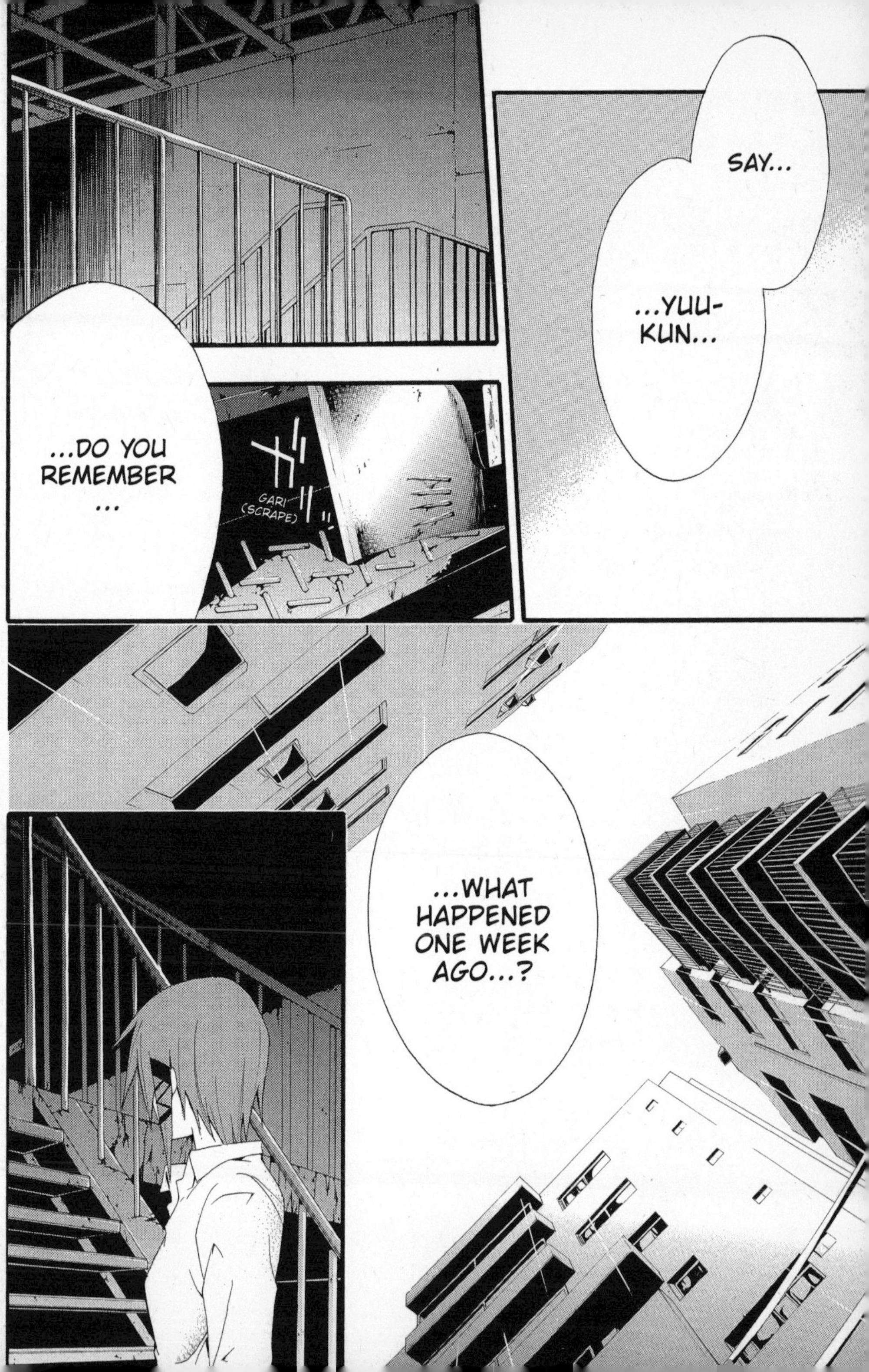
SAY...
...YUU-KUN...
...DO YOU REMEMBER ...
GARI (SCRAPE)
...WHAT HAPPENED ONE WEEK AGO...?

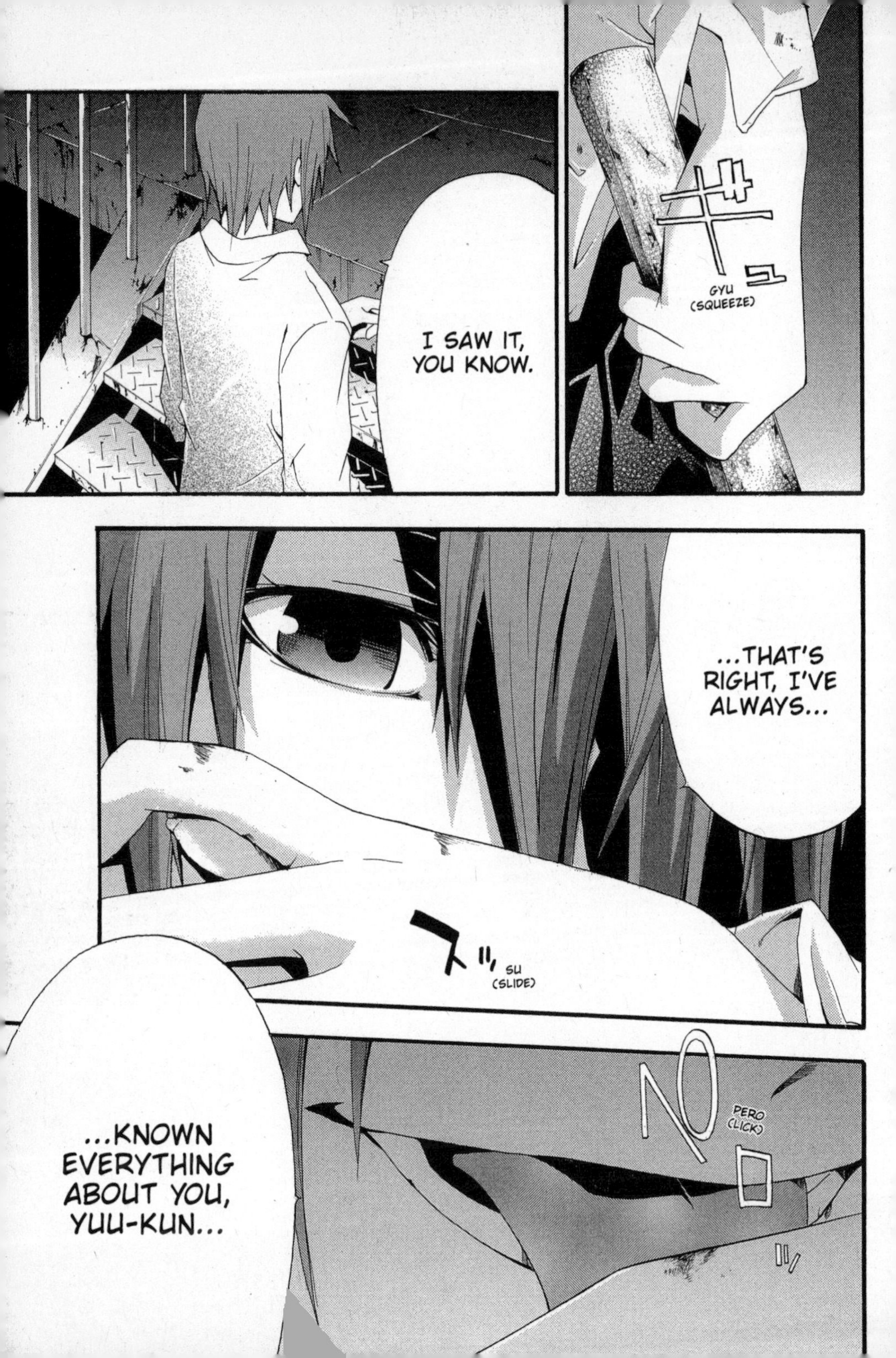
GYU (SQUEEZE)
I SAW IT, YOU KNOW.
...THAT'S RIGHT, I'VE ALWAYS...
SU (SLIDE)
...KNOWN EVERYTHING ABOUT YOU, YUU-KUN...
PERO (LICK)

SO...

...IT'S NO USE PRETENDING ...

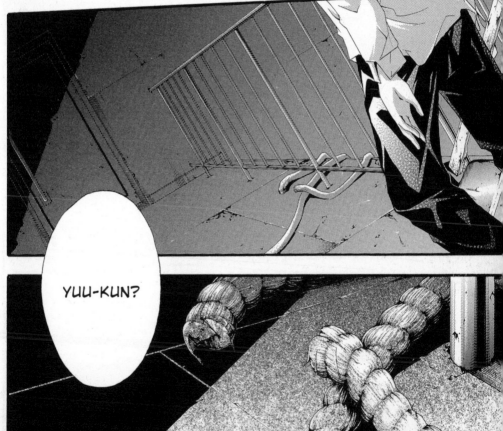

YUU-KUN?

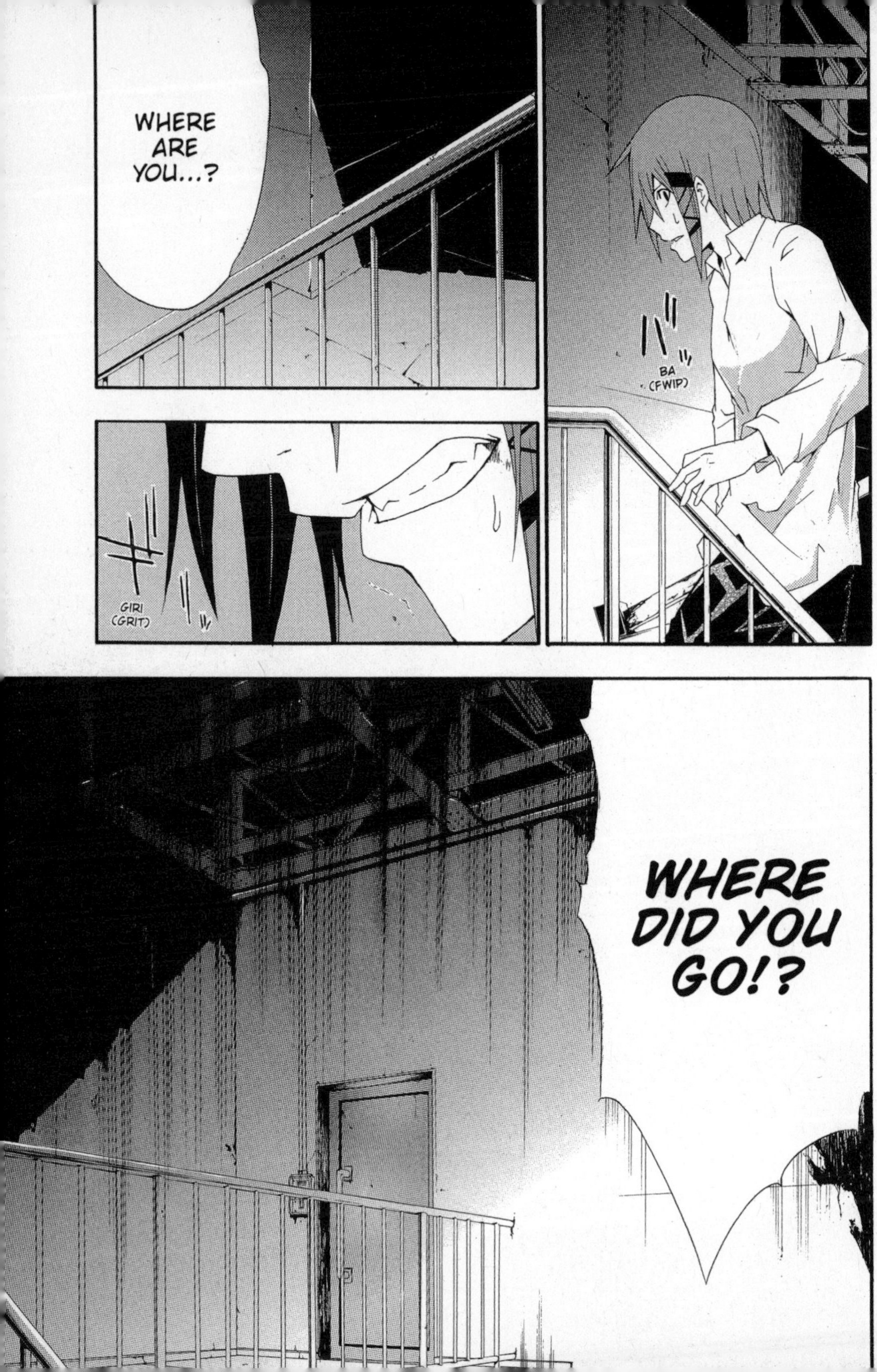
BA
(FWIP)
WHERE ARE YOU...?
GIRI
(GRIT)
WHERE DID YOU GO!?

Doubt.17 PHOTO

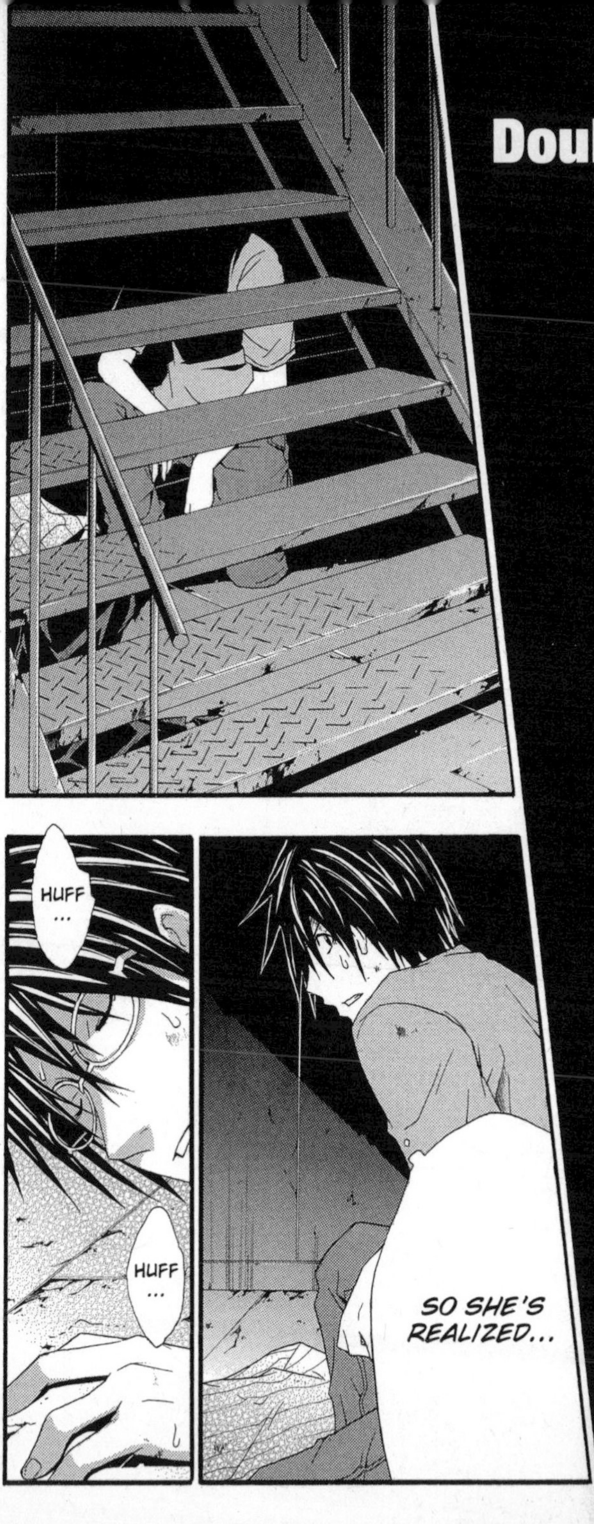
SO SHE'S REALIZED...
HUFF ...
HUFF ...

THERE'S NO MORE TIME...

JIWA
(SEEP)

REGARDLESS OF WHETHER THE THINGS HAJIME SAID ARE TRUE OR NOT...

...I HAVE TO DO SOMETHING TO FORCE MITSUKI TO OPEN THE EXIT.

...BUT...

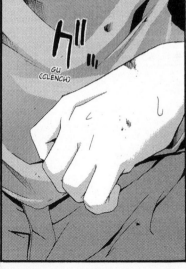

GU
(CLENCH)

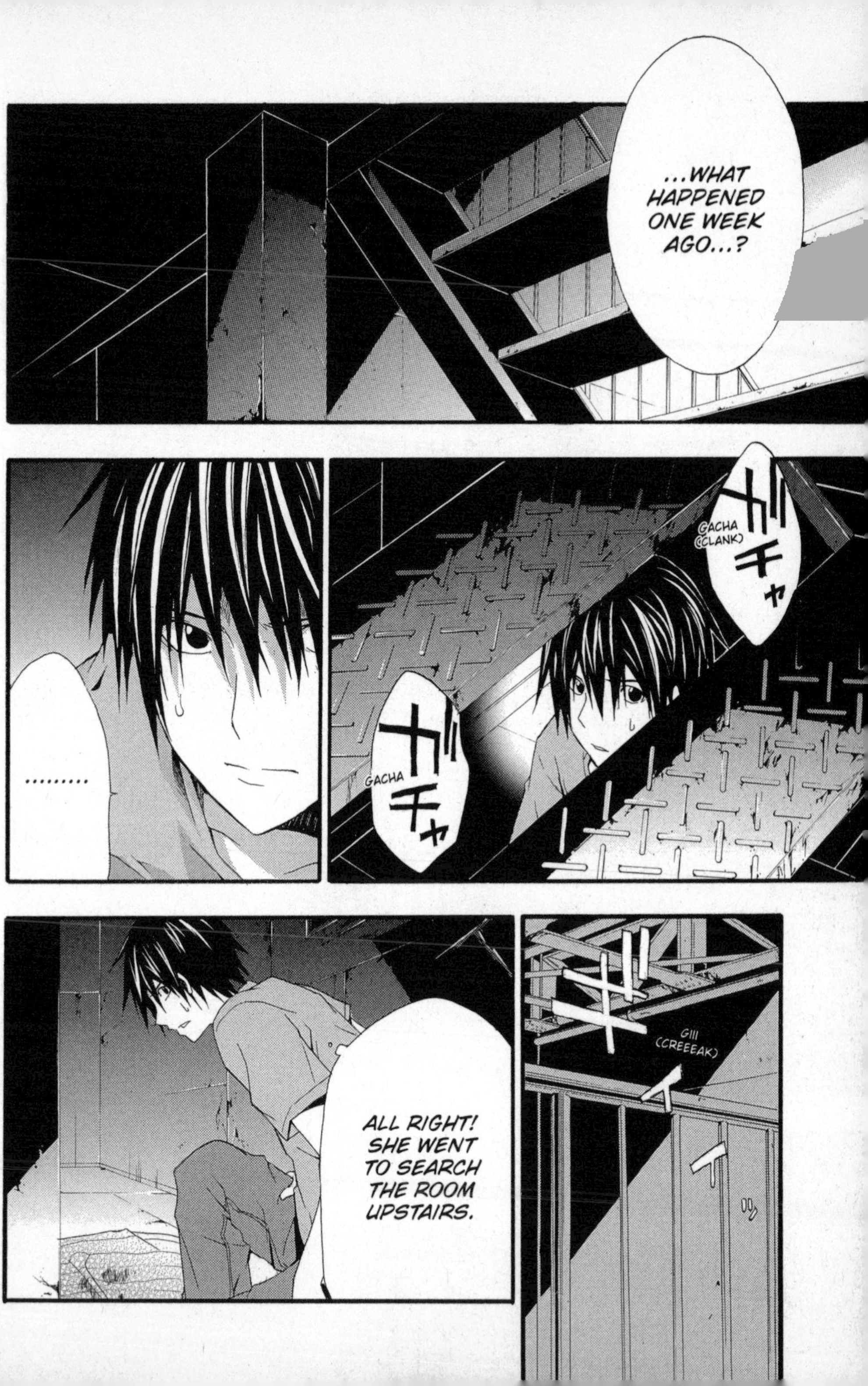
...WHAT HAPPENED ONE WEEK AGO...?
ガチャ
GACHA (CLANK)
ガチャ
GACHA
....
ギィ
GIII (CREEEAK)
ALL RIGHT! SHE WENT TO SEARCH THE ROOM UPSTAIRS.

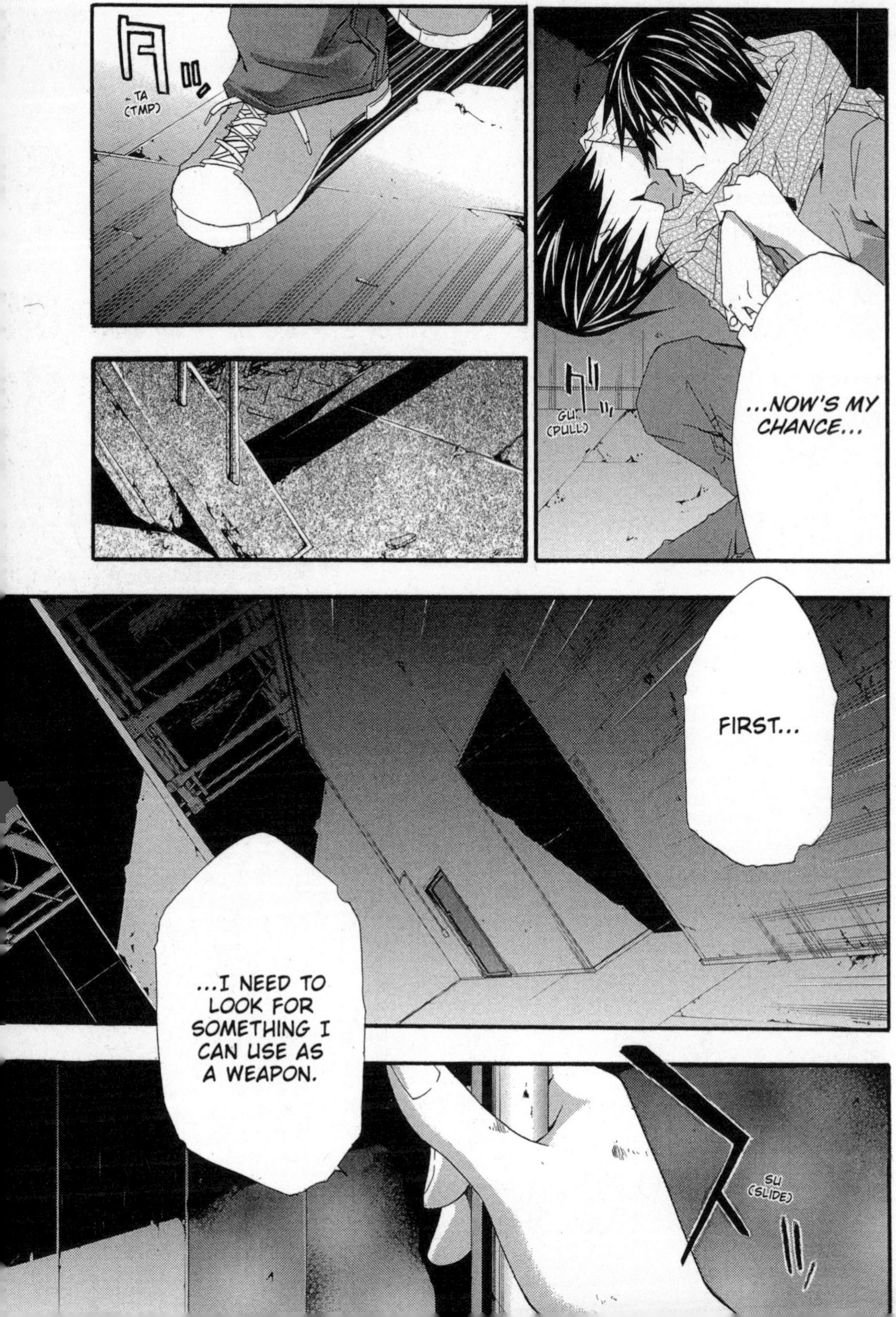
...NOW'S MY CHANCE...
GU (PULL)
TA (TMP)
FIRST...
...I NEED TO LOOK FOR SOMETHING I CAN USE AS A WEAPON.
SU (SLIDE)

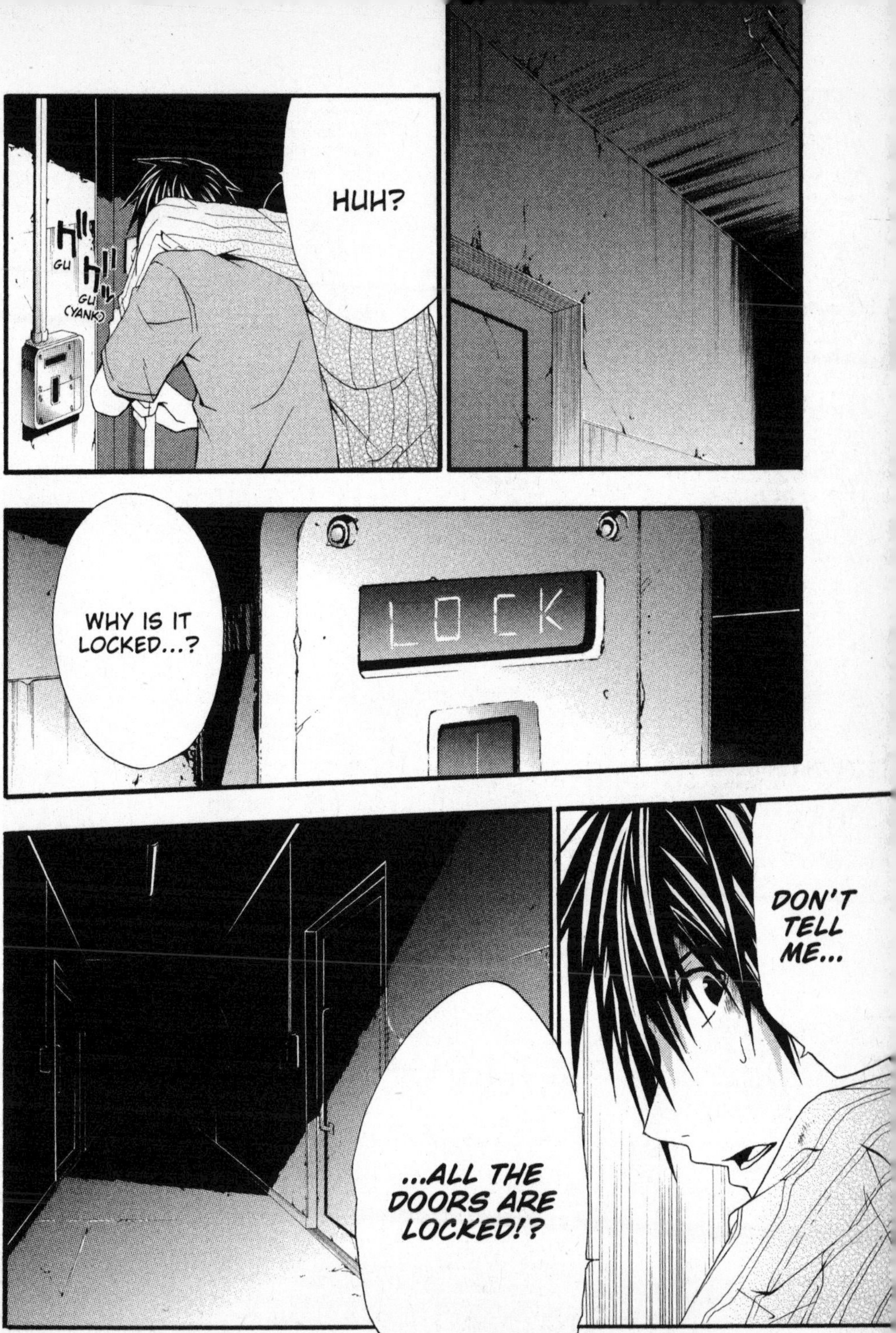

HUH?
ガ GU
ガ GU (YANK)
WHY IS IT LOCKED...?
LOCK
DON'T TELL ME...
...ALL THE DOORS ARE LOCKED!?

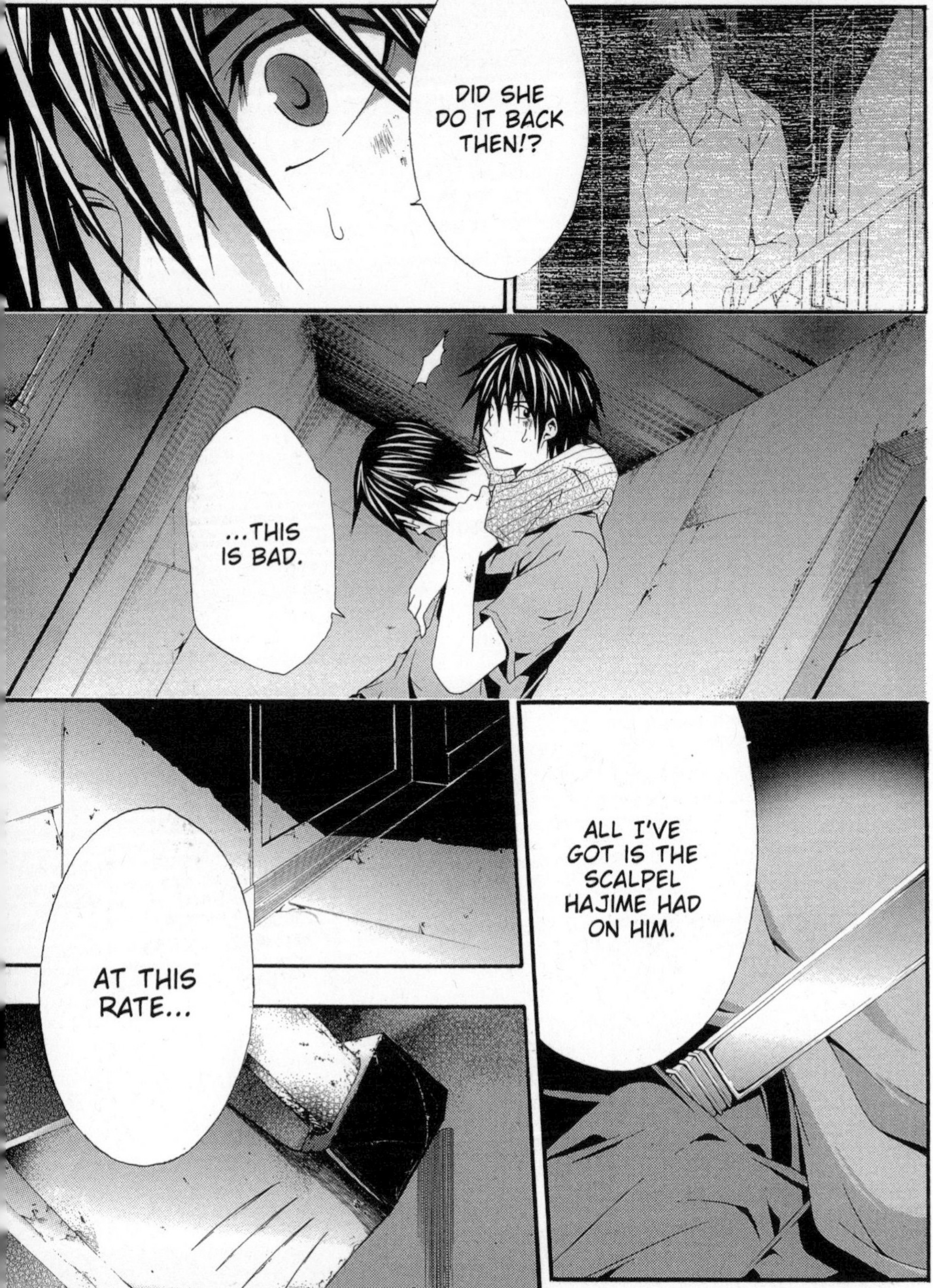
DID SHE DO IT BACK THEN!?
...THIS IS BAD.
ALL I'VE GOT IS THE SCALPEL HAJIME HAD ON HIM.
AT THIS RATE...

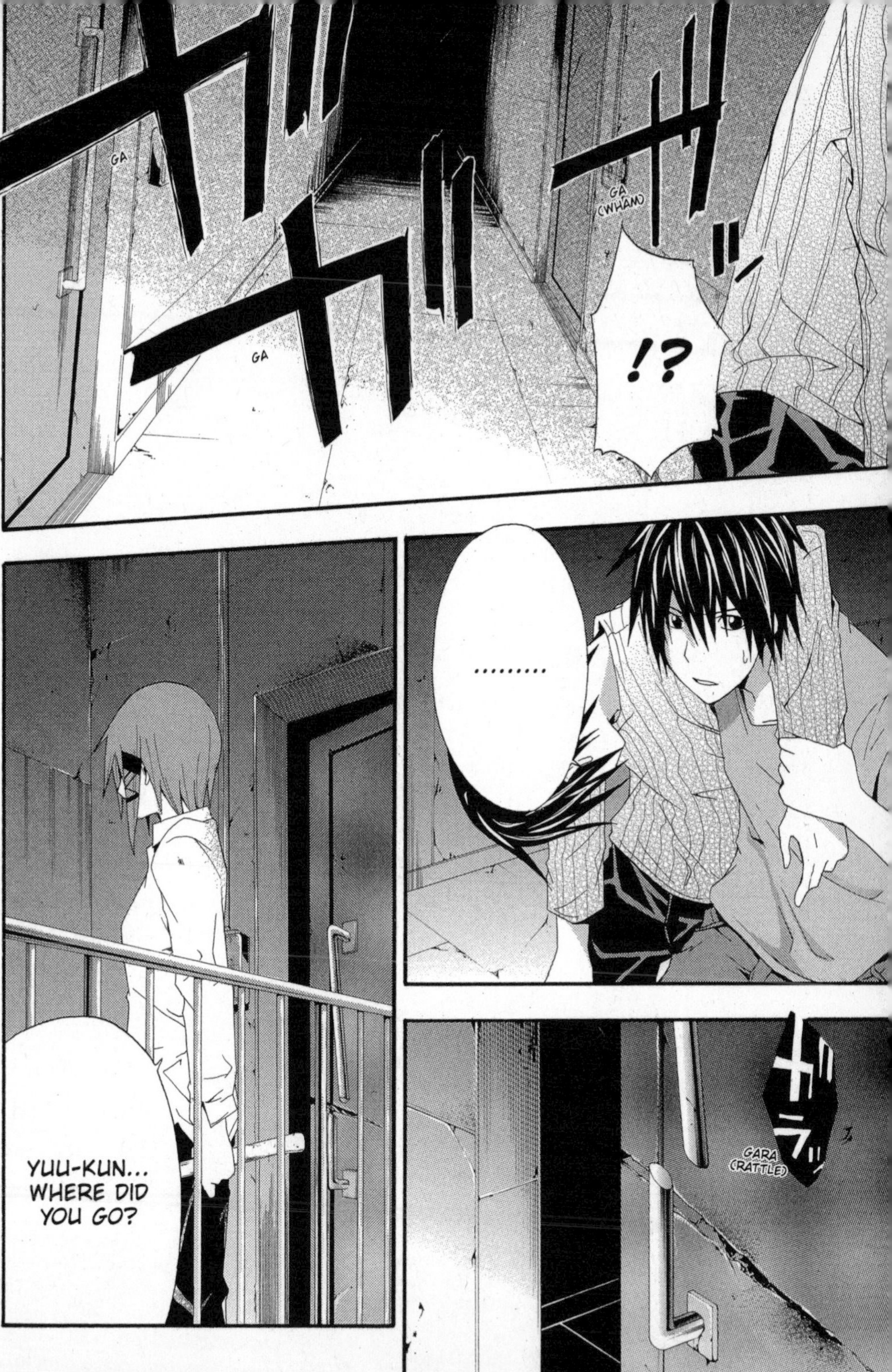
GA
(WHAM)
!?
GA
GA
....
GARA
(RATTLE)
YUU-KUN...
WHERE DID
YOU GO?

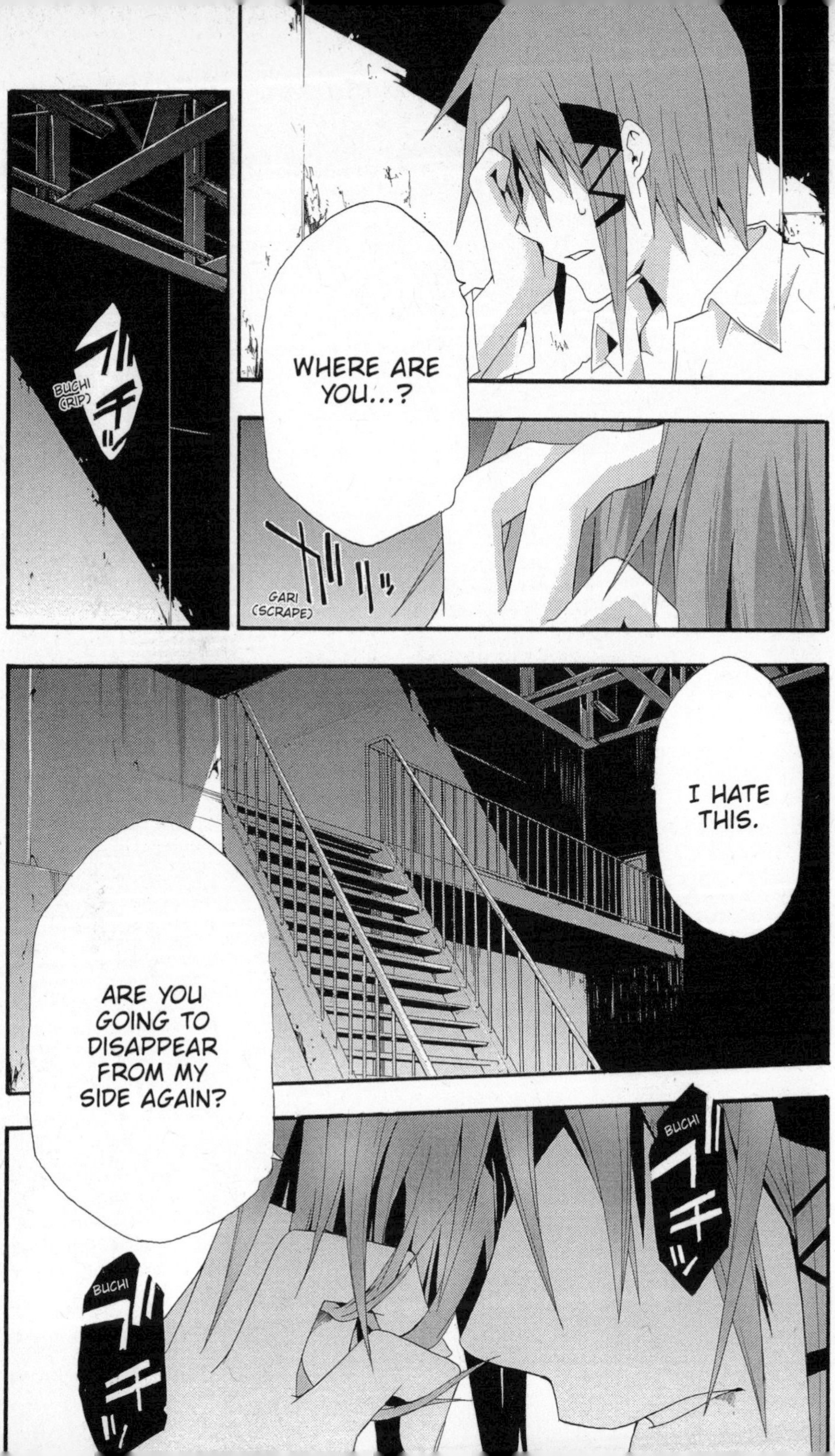
WHERE ARE YOU...?
GARI (SCRAPE)
BUCHI (RIP)
I HATE THIS.
ARE YOU GOING TO DISAPPEAR FROM MY SIDE AGAIN?
BUCHI
BUCHI

COULD IT BE...

...THAT GIRL AGAIN...?

"THAT GIRL"? WHAT IS SHE TALKING ABOUT?

NO...

...THAT'S NOT POSSIBLE.

GACHA (RATTLE)

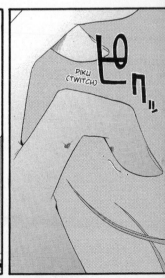

PIKU (TWITCH)

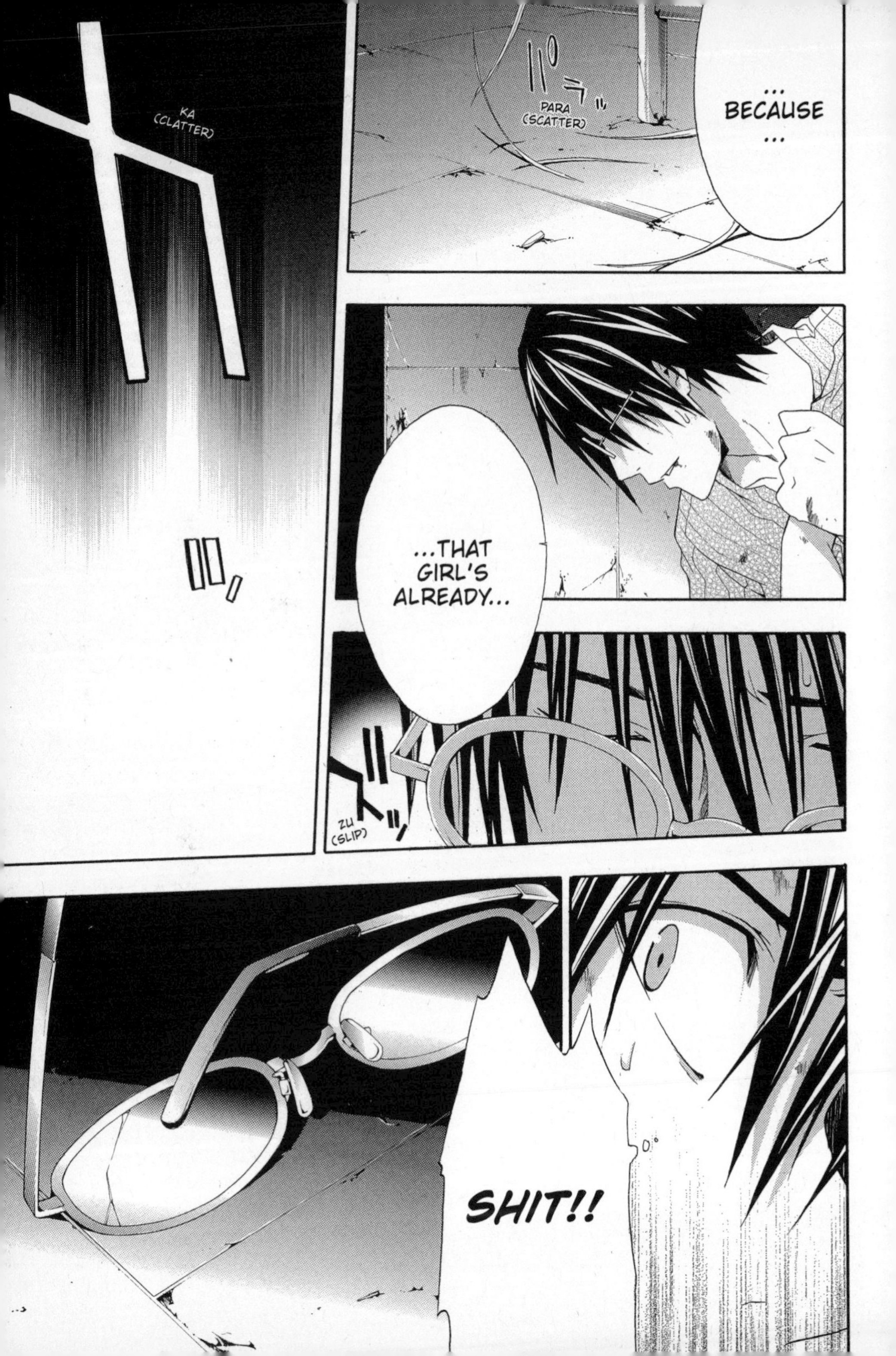
...BECAUSE...
PARA (SCATTER)
...THAT GIRL'S ALREADY...
ZU (SLIP)
KA (CLATTER)
SHIT!!

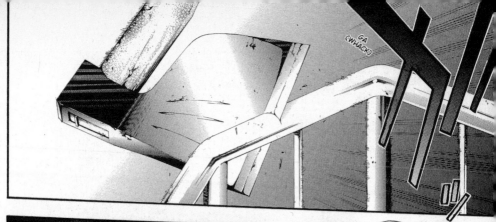

GA
(WHACK)

YUU-KUN...

...ARE YOU
THERE?

....

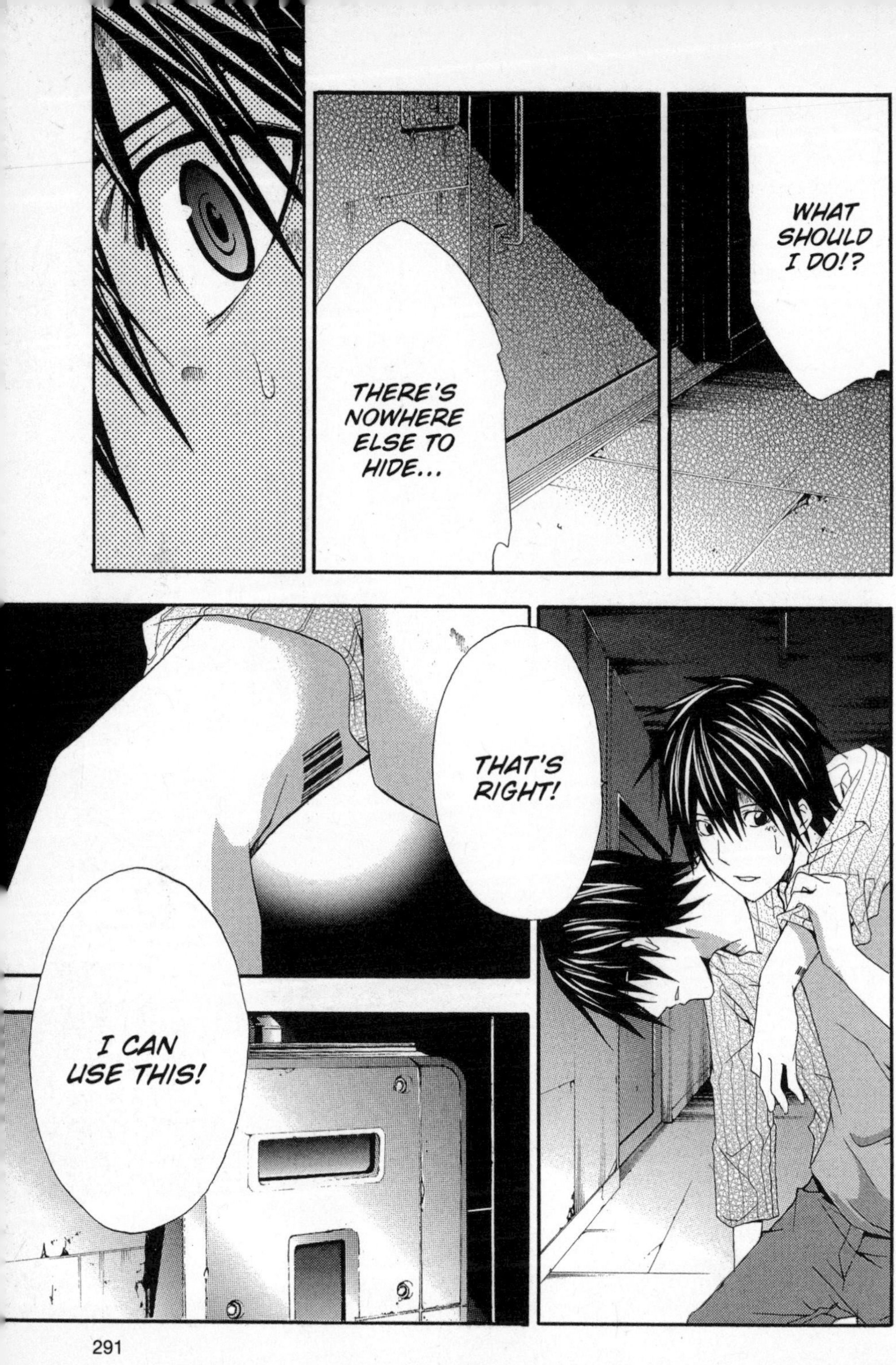
WHAT SHOULD I DO!?
THERE'S NOWHERE ELSE TO HIDE...
THAT'S RIGHT!
I CAN USE THIS!

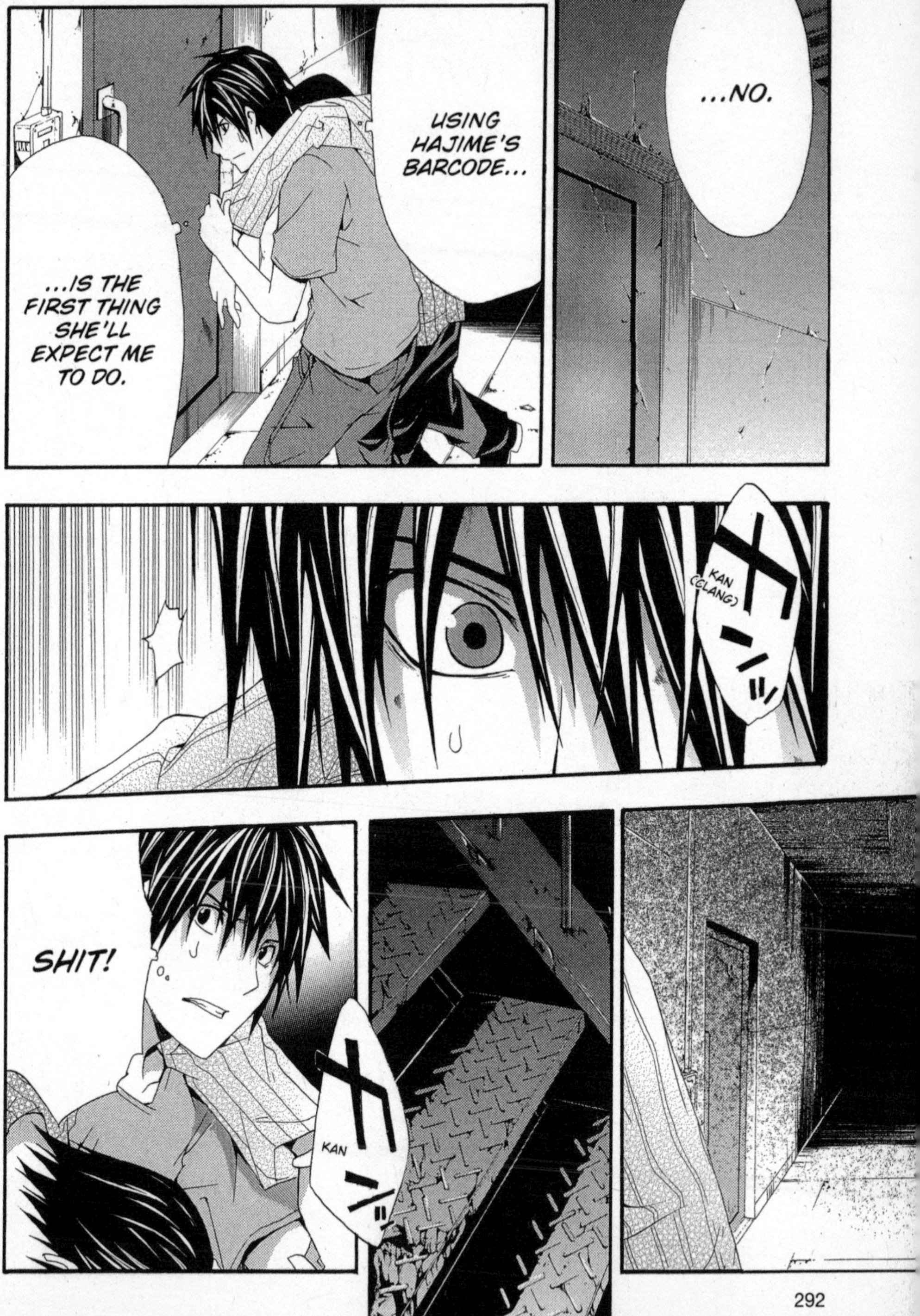
...NO.
USING HAJIME'S BARCODE...
...IS THE FIRST THING SHE'LL EXPECT ME TO DO.
KAN (CLANG)
SHIT!
KAN

WHAT
SHOULD
I DO...

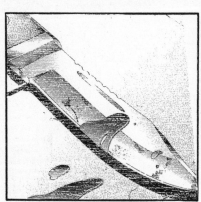

....

NII
(GRIND)

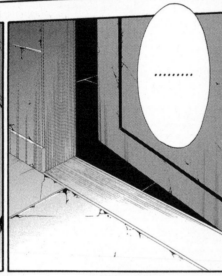

....

YUU-KUN?

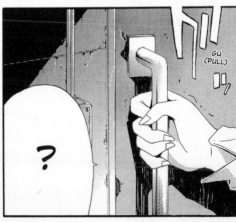

?

GU
(PULL)

PLEASE...

...OPEN THE DOOR.

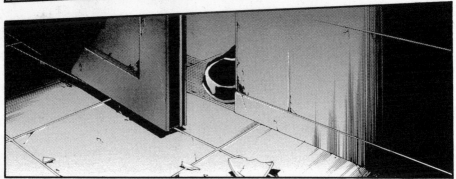

GU (PULL)

IF YOU OPEN UP RIGHT NOW, THEN I'LL SAVE YOU, YUU-KUN!

I KNOW!

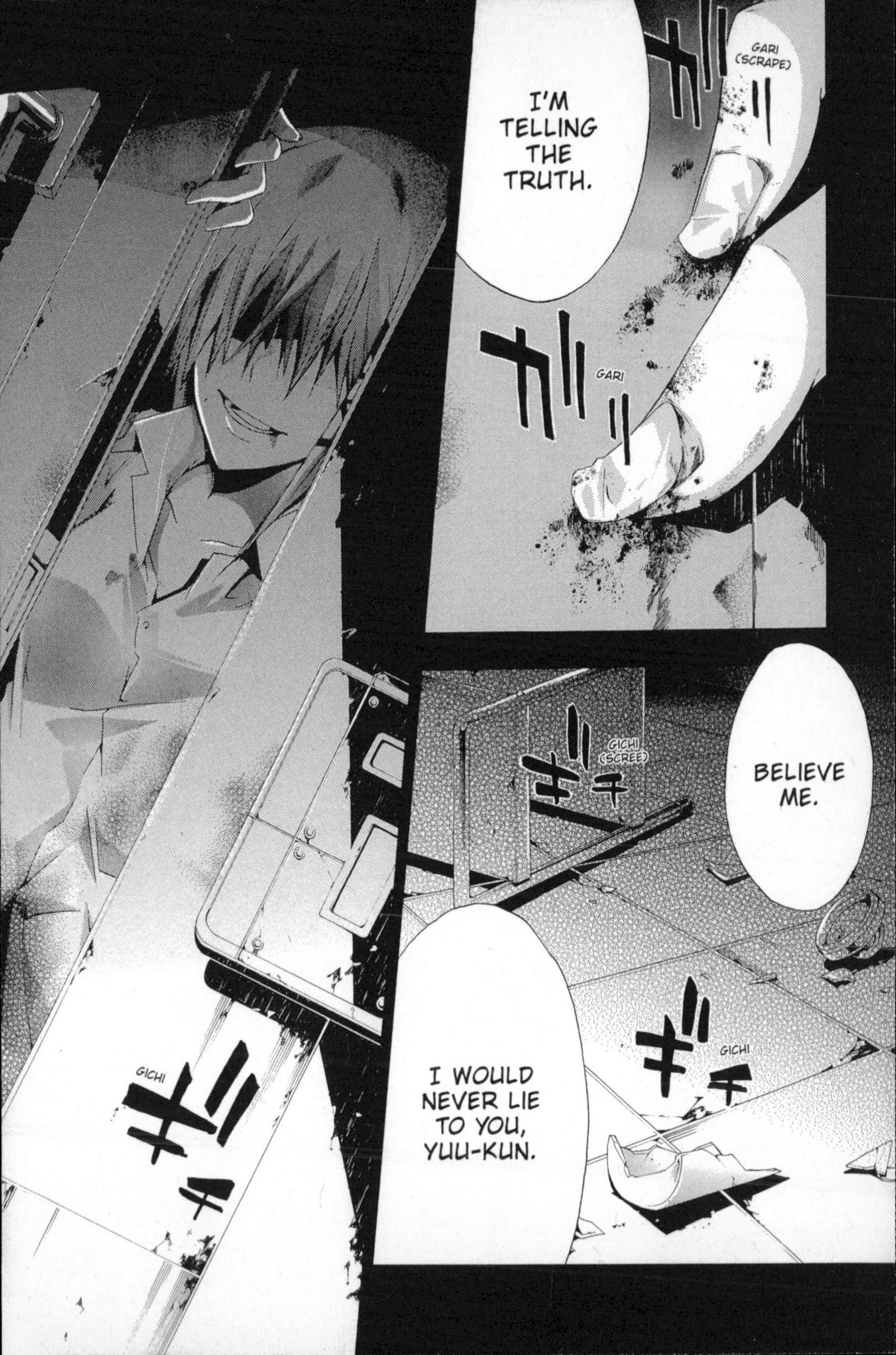
GARI (SCRAPE)
I'M TELLING THE TRUTH.
GARI
BELIEVE ME.
GICHI (SCREE)
GICHI
I WOULD NEVER LIE TO YOU, YUU-KUN.
GICHI

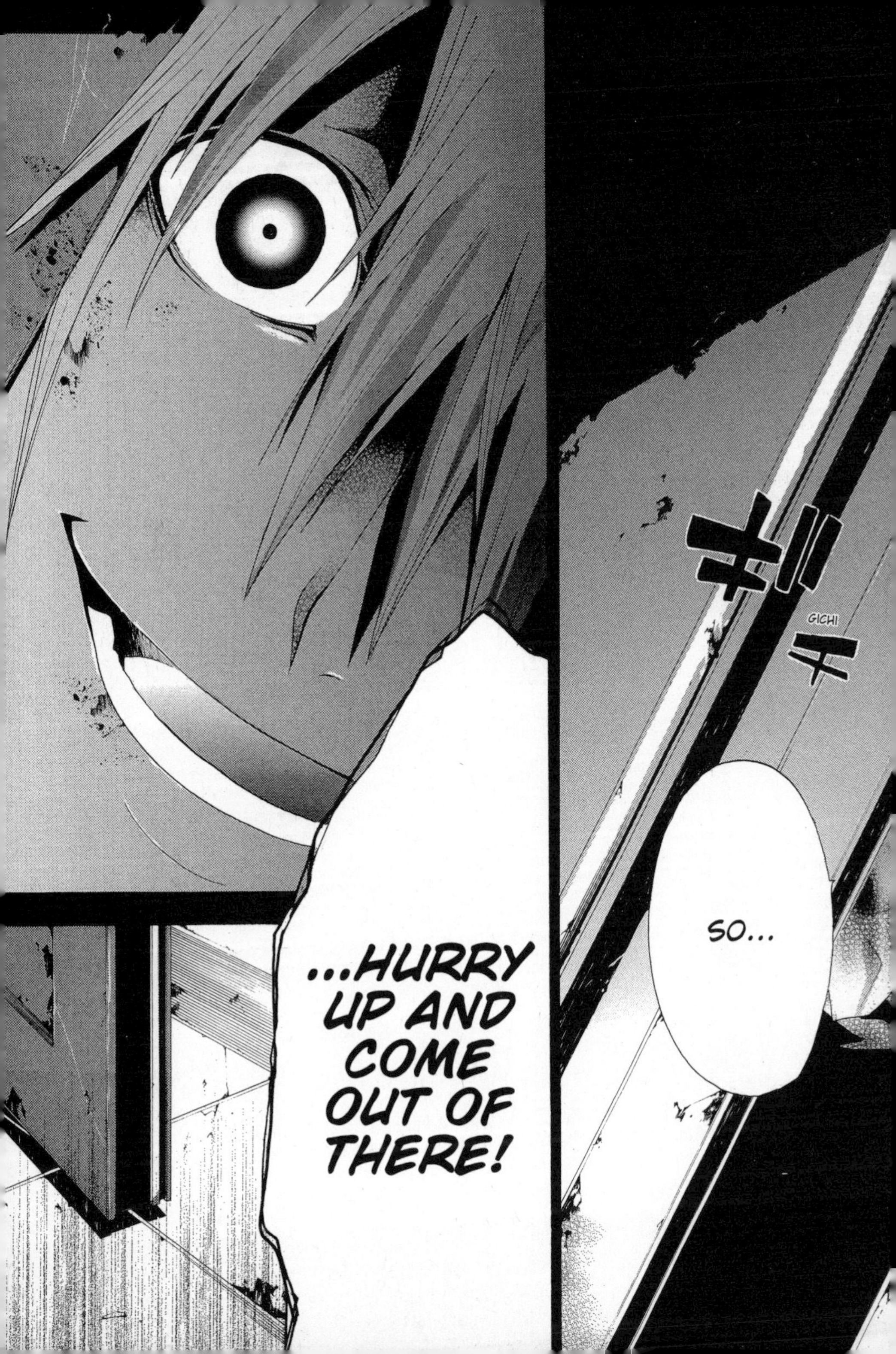
GICHI
SO...
...HURRY UP AND COME OUT OF THERE!

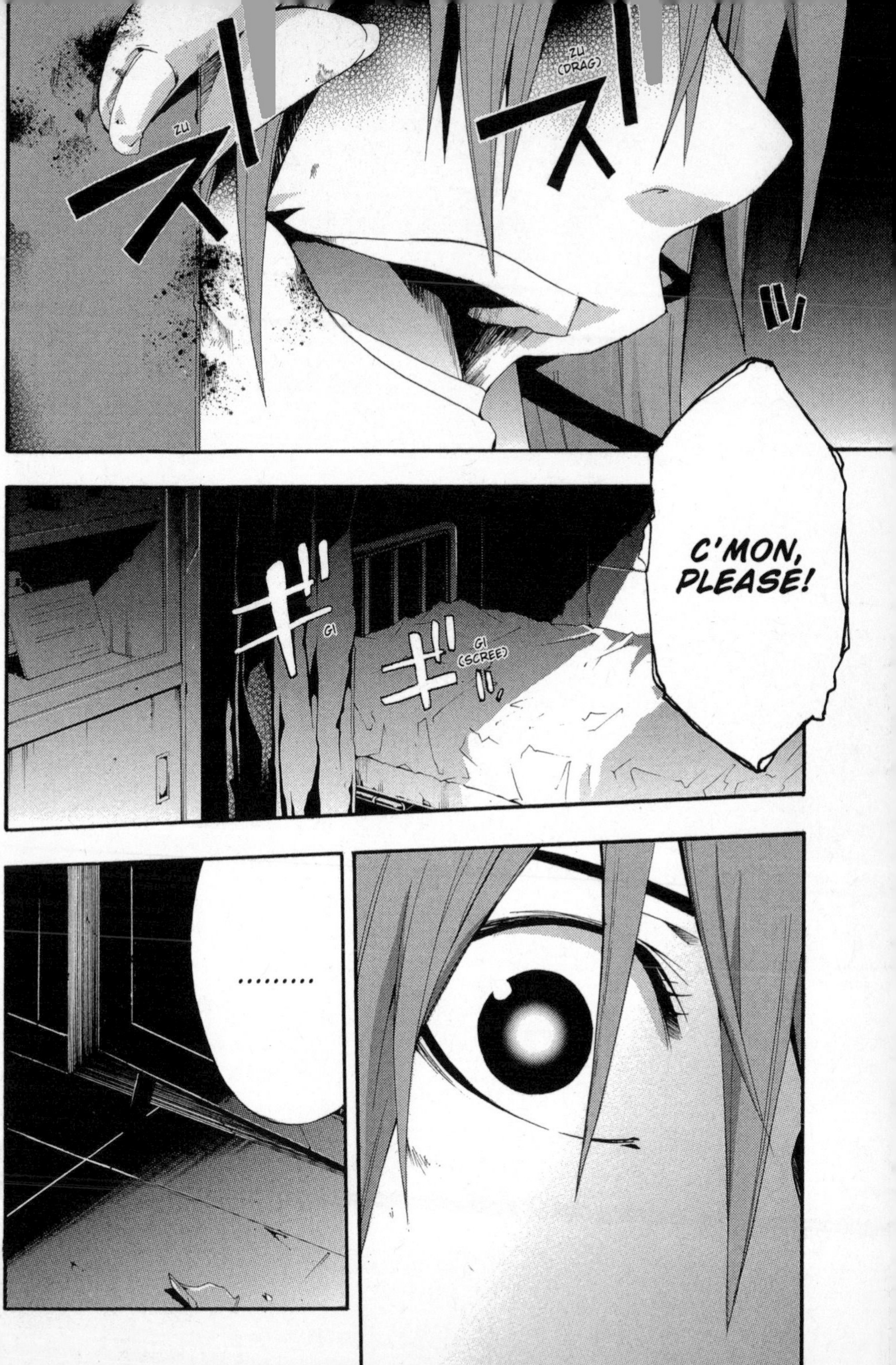
ZU
(DRAG)
ZU
C'MON, PLEASE!
GI
(SCREE)
GI
....

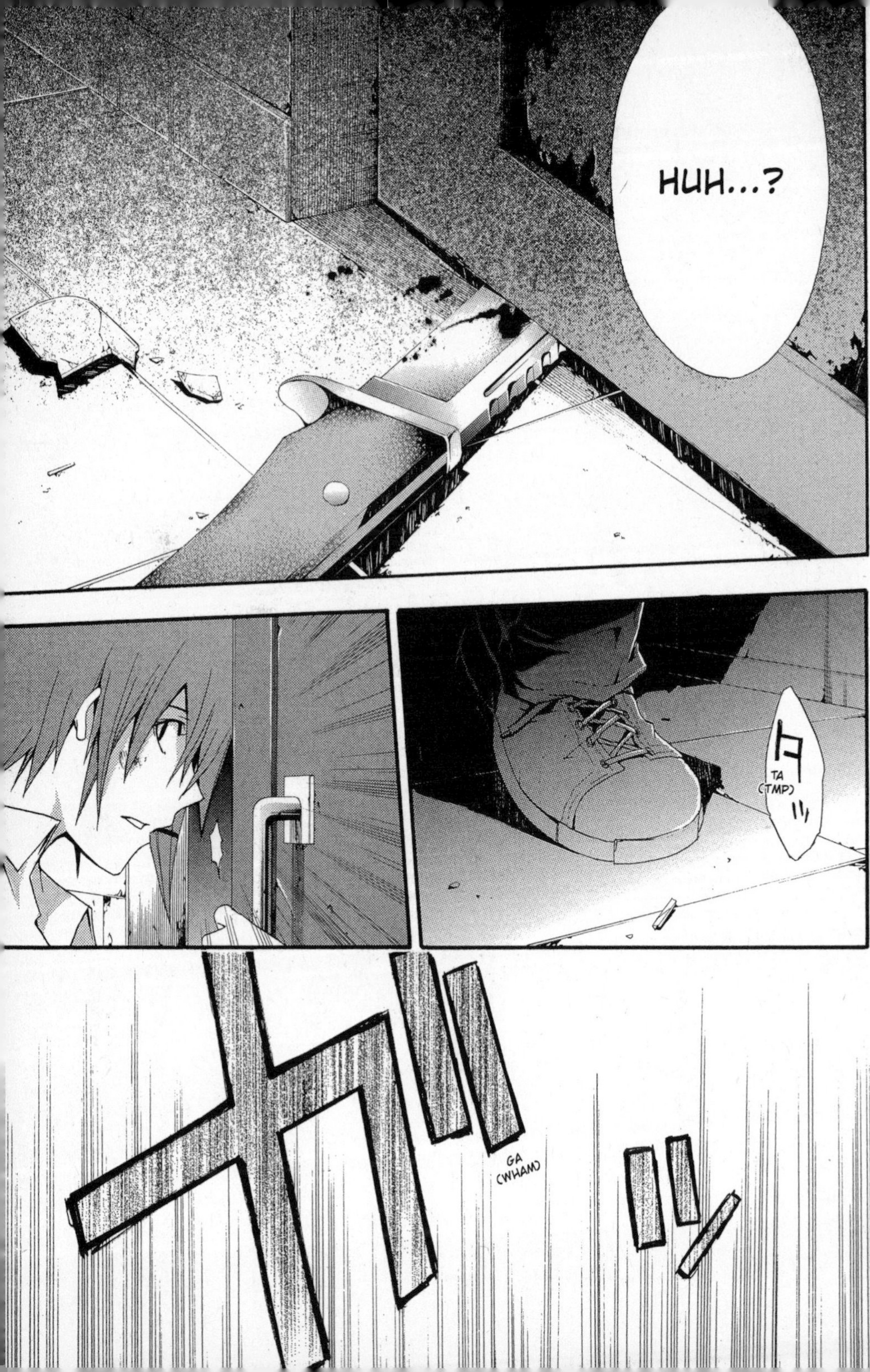
HUH...?
TA
(TMP)
GA
(WHAM)

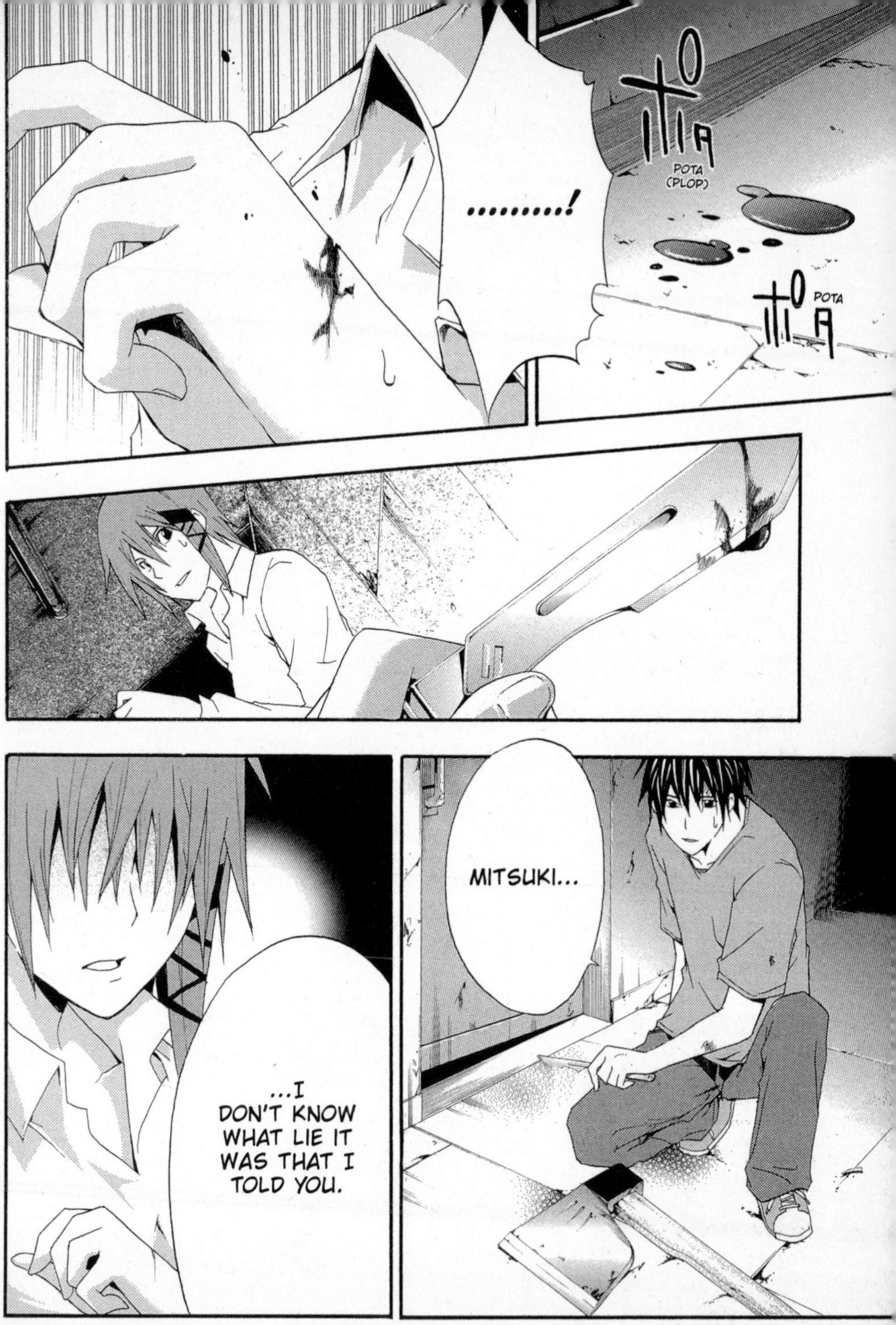
POTA (PLOP)
POTA
.........!
MITSUKI...
...I DON'T KNOW WHAT LIE IT WAS THAT I TOLD YOU.

...NO MATTER WHAT YOUR REASONS WERE...

...I'LL NEVER BE ABLE TO ACCEPT WHAT YOU'VE DONE.

BUT...

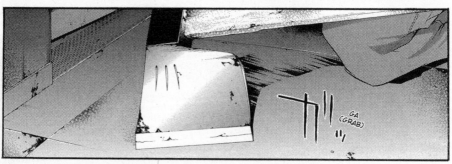

GA
(GRAB)

...EVEN IF I HAVE TO HURT YOU IN THE PROCESS...

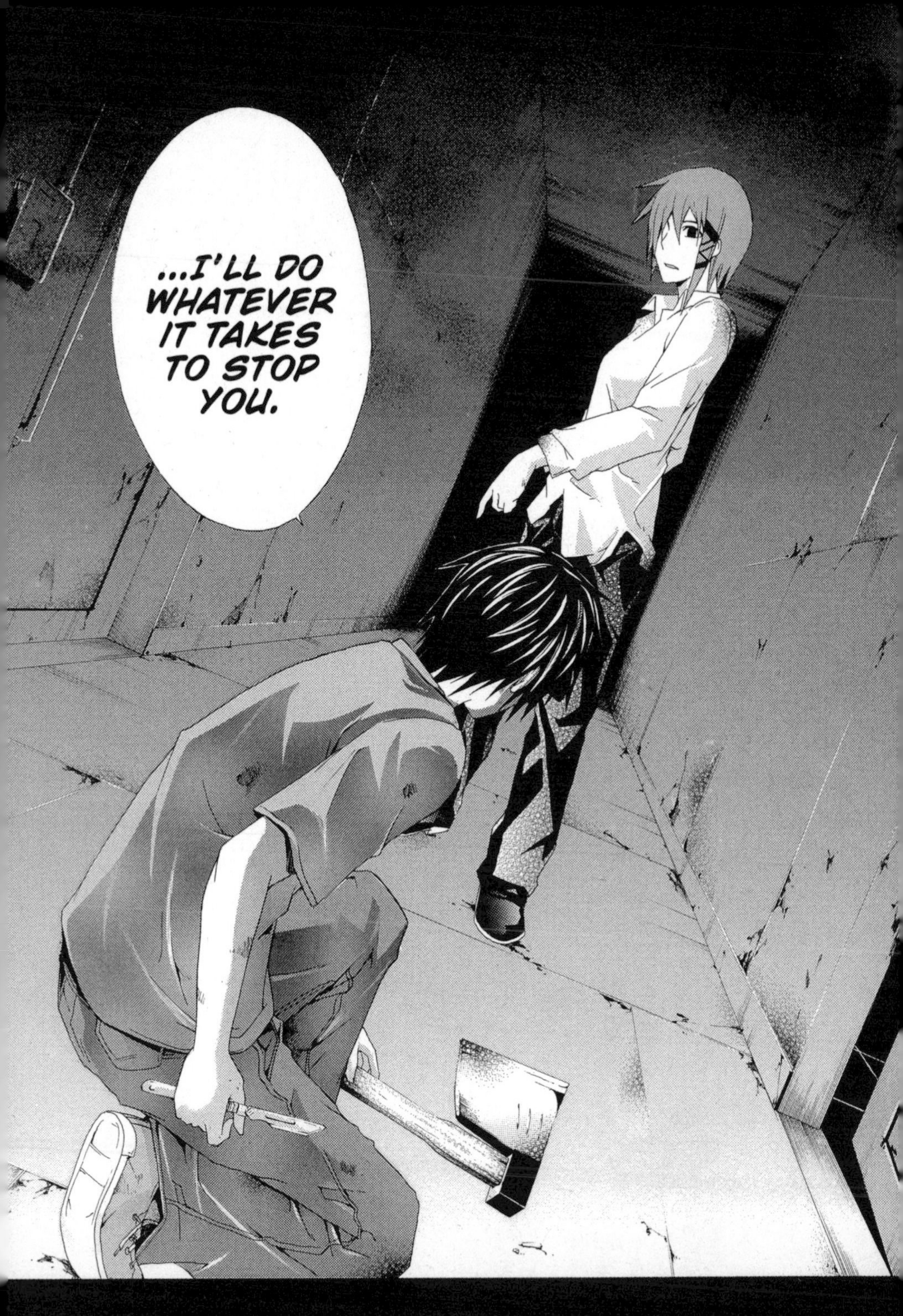
...I'LL DO WHATEVER IT TAKES TO STOP YOU.

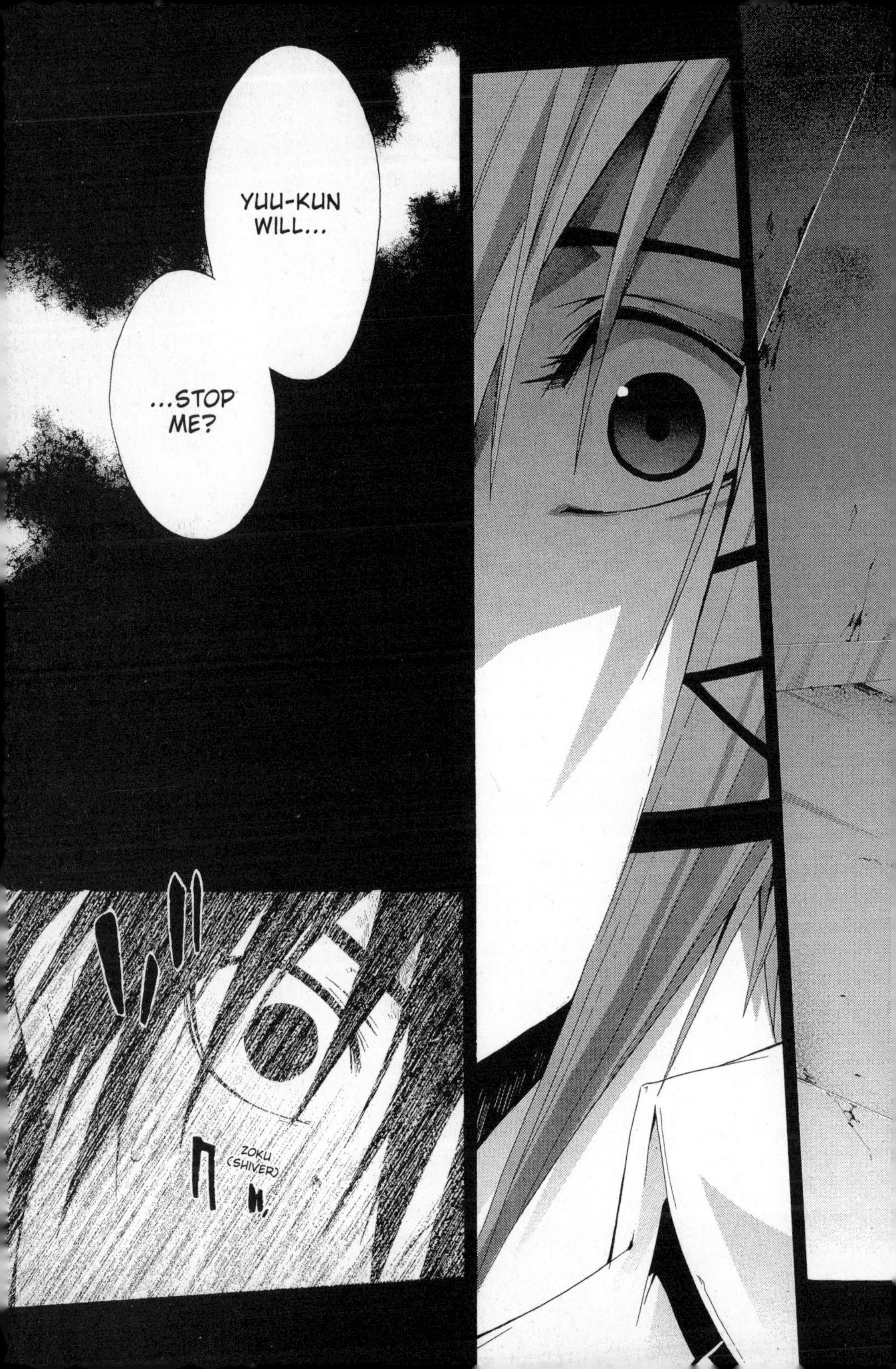
YUU-KUN WILL...
...STOP ME?
ZOKU (SHIVER)

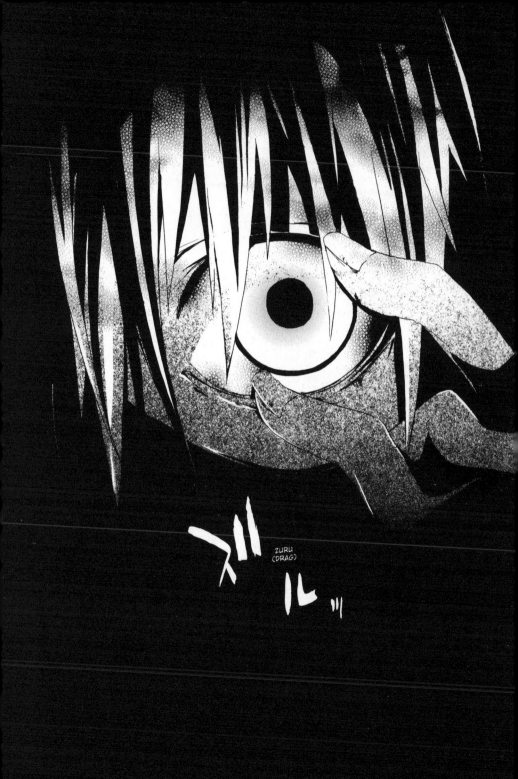

ZURU
(DRAG)

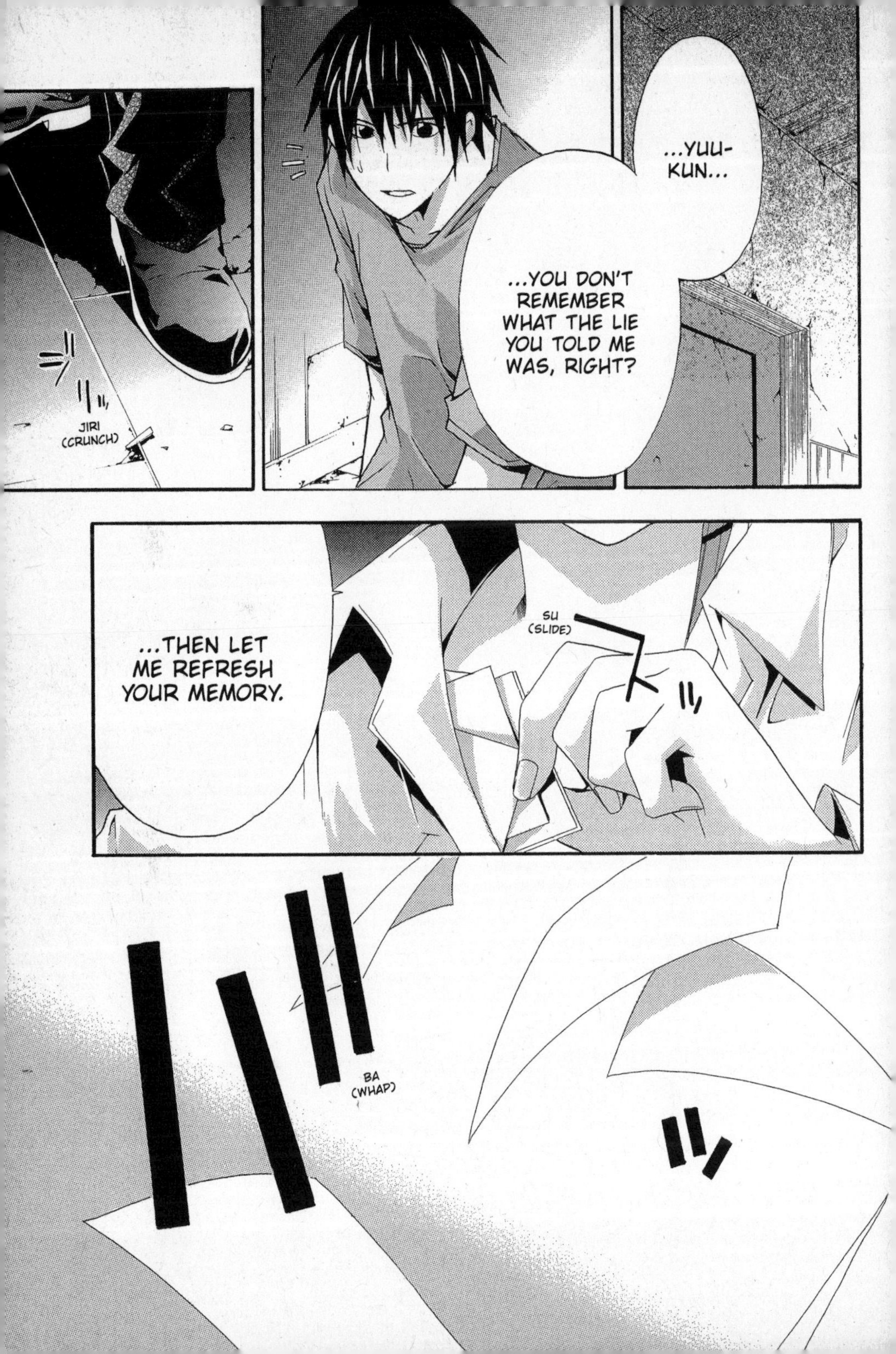
...YUU-KUN...
...YOU DON'T REMEMBER WHAT THE LIE YOU TOLD ME WAS, RIGHT?
JIRI (CRUNCH)
SU (SLIDE)
...THEN LET ME REFRESH YOUR MEMORY.
BA (WHAP)

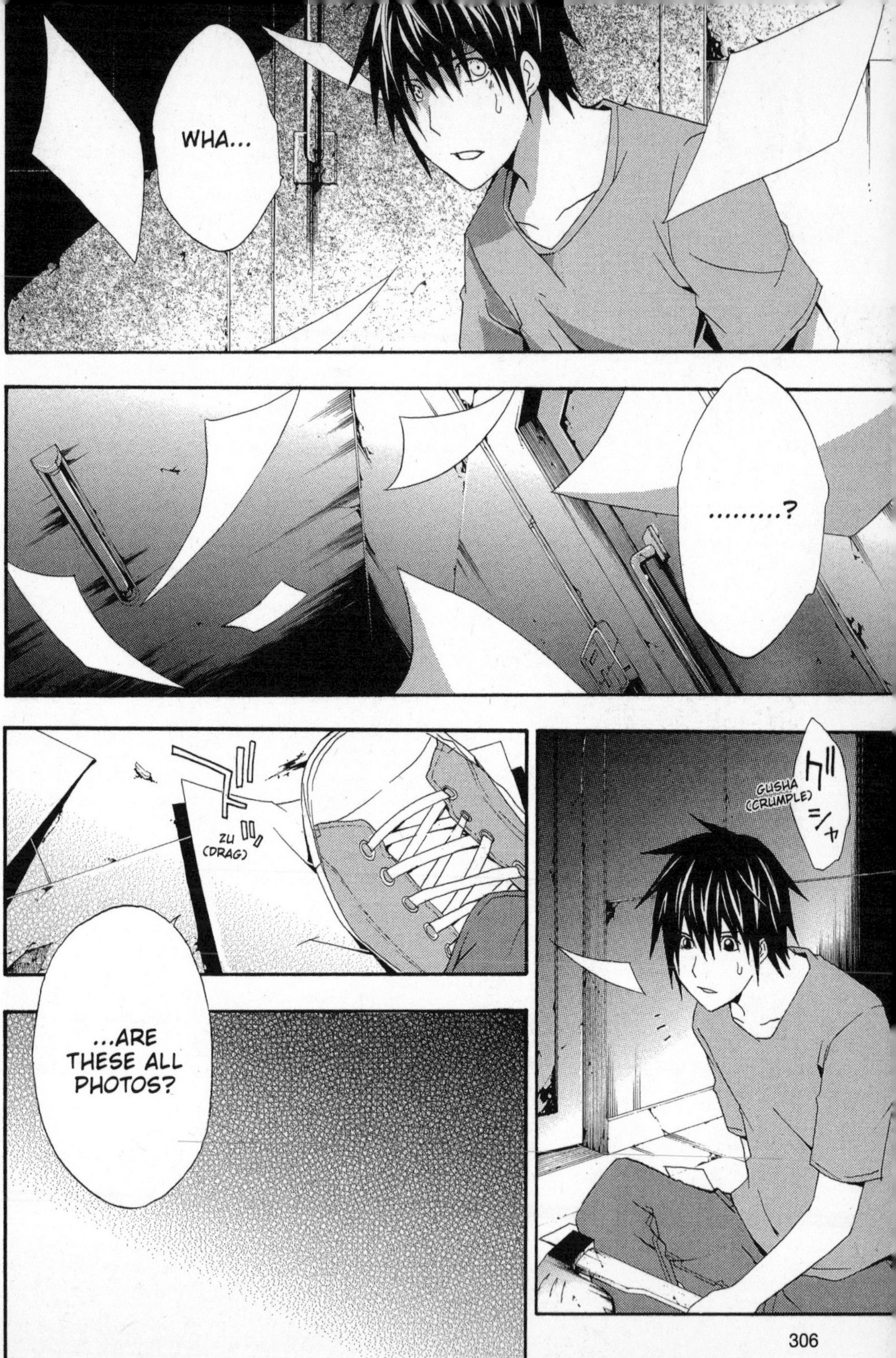
WHA...
.........?
GUSHA (CRUMPLE)
ZU (DRAG)
...ARE THESE ALL PHOTOS?

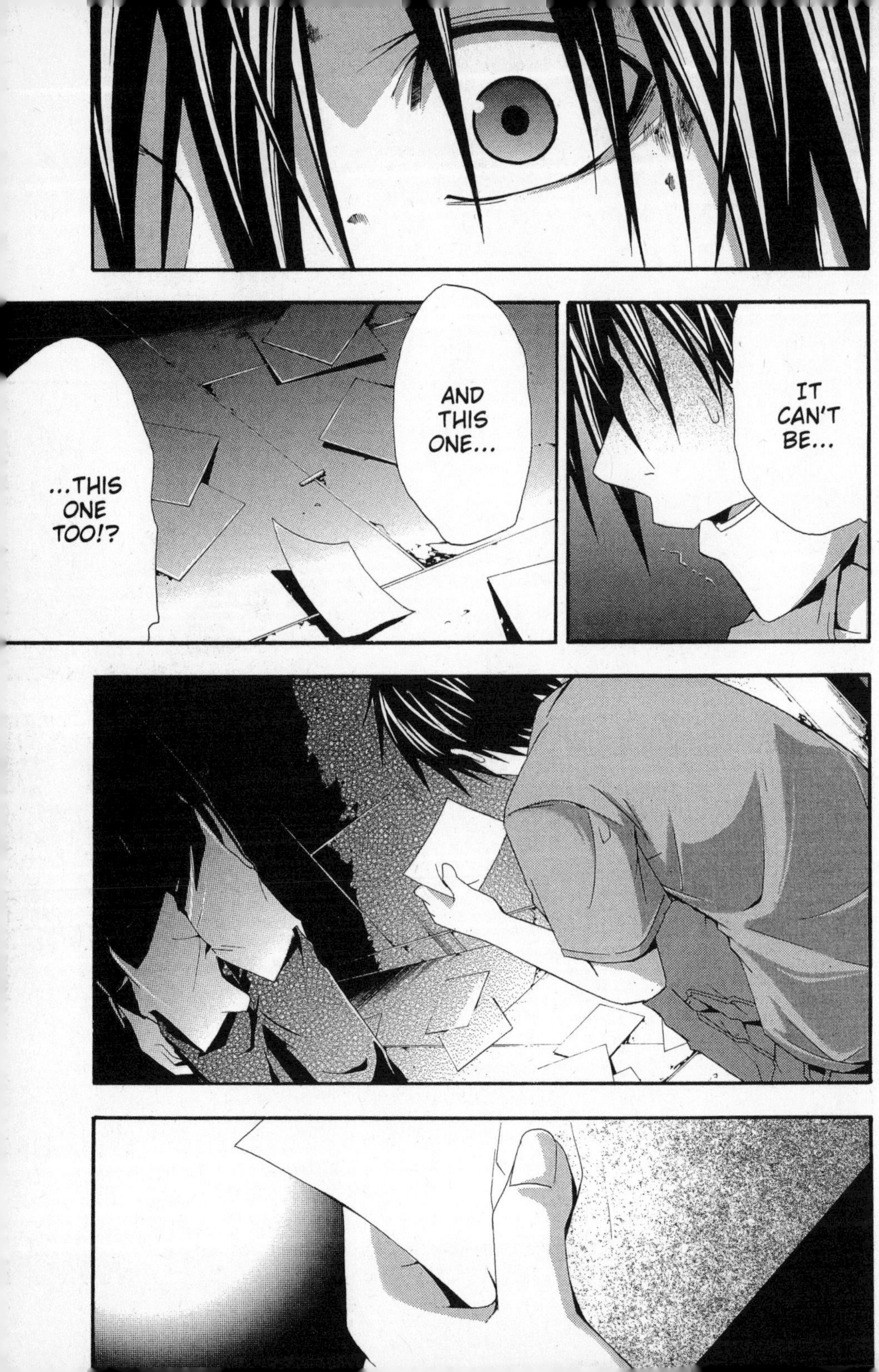
IT CAN'T BE...
AND THIS ONE...
...THIS ONE TOO!?

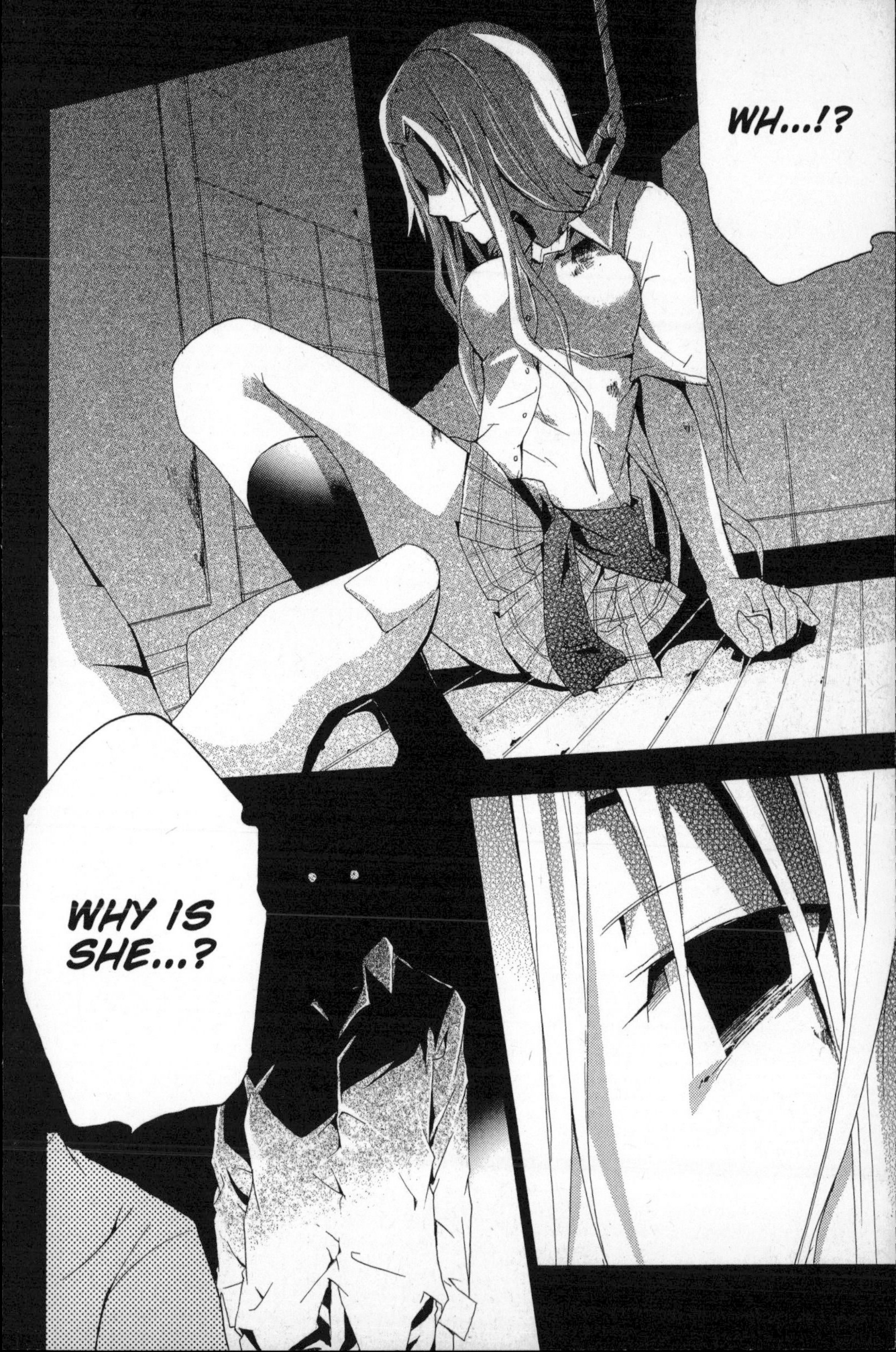
WH...!?
WHY IS SHE...?

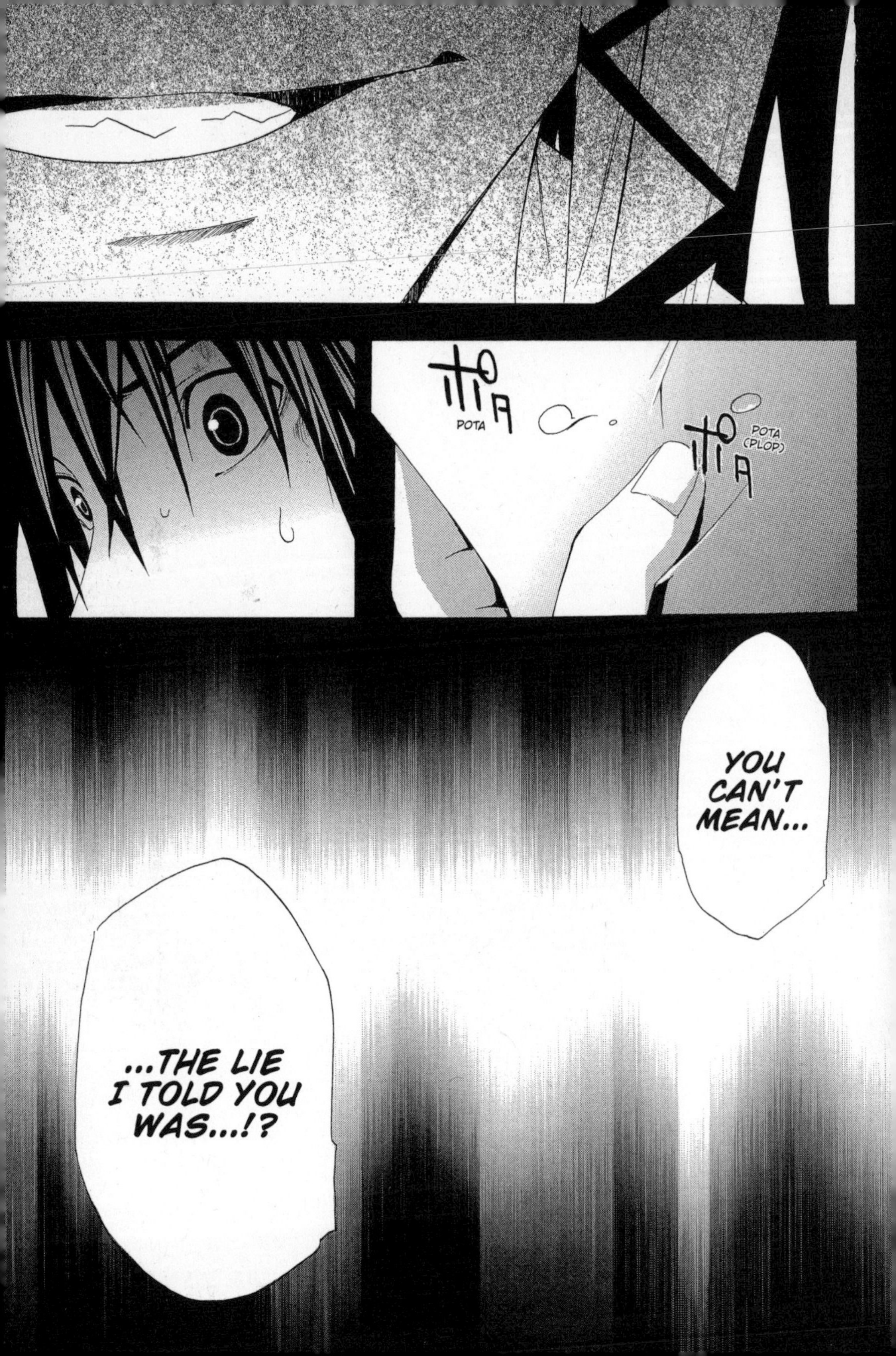
POTA (PLOP)
POTA
YOU CAN'T MEAN...
...THE LIE I TOLD YOU WAS...!?

Doubt.18 LOST

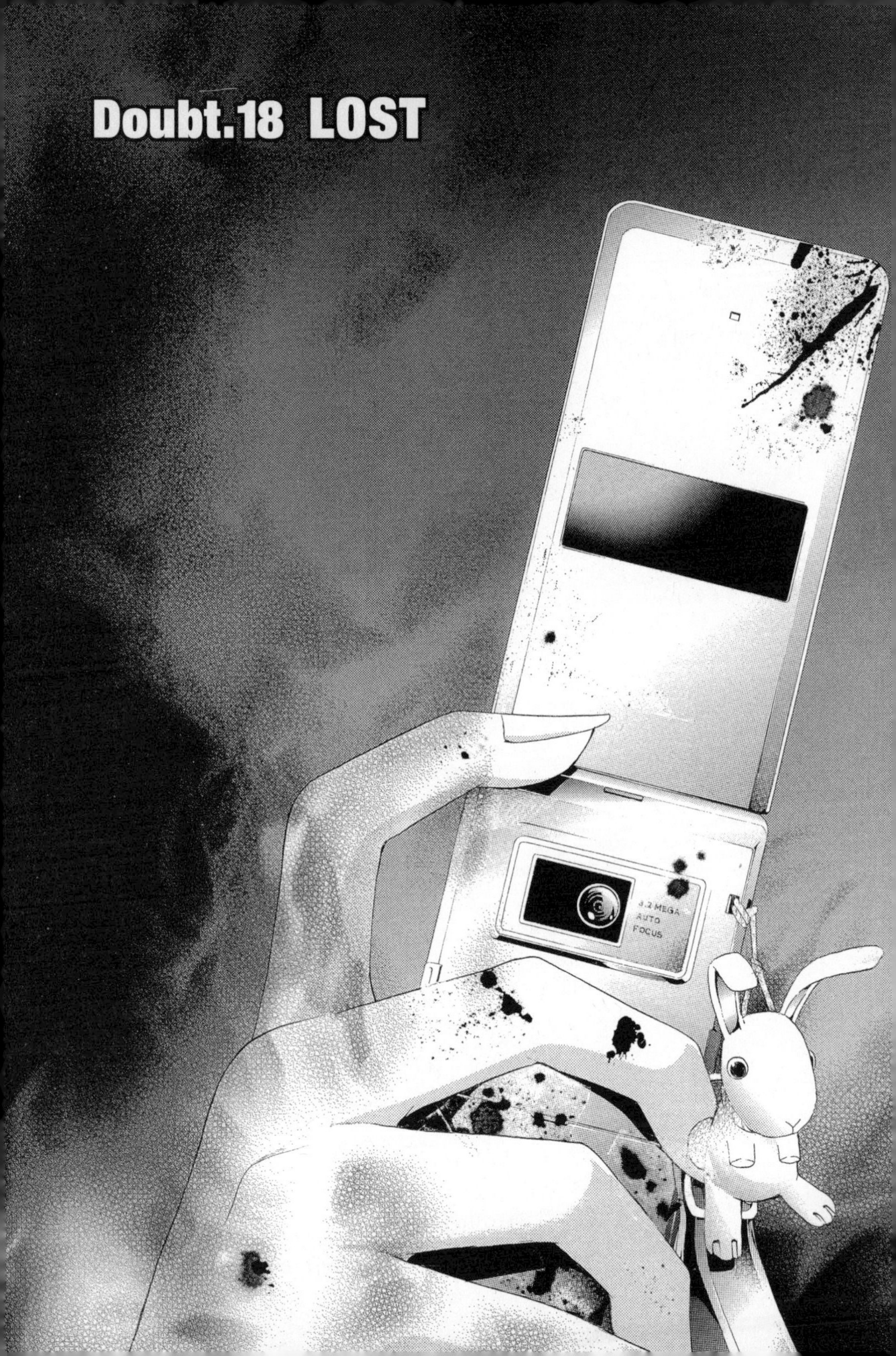
3.2 MEGA
AUTO
FOCUS

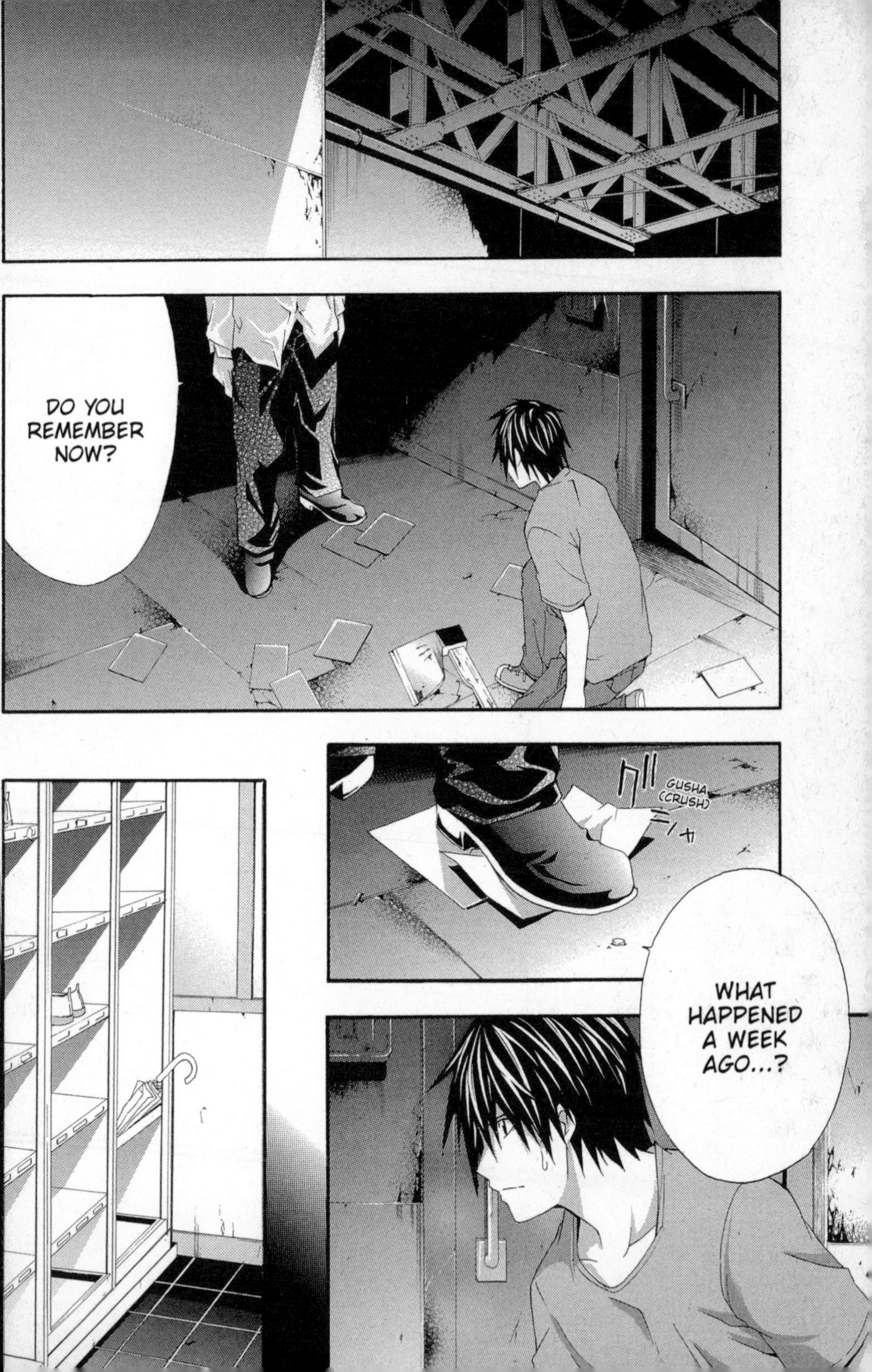
DO YOU REMEMBER NOW?
GUSHA (CRUSH)
WHAT HAPPENED A WEEK AGO...?

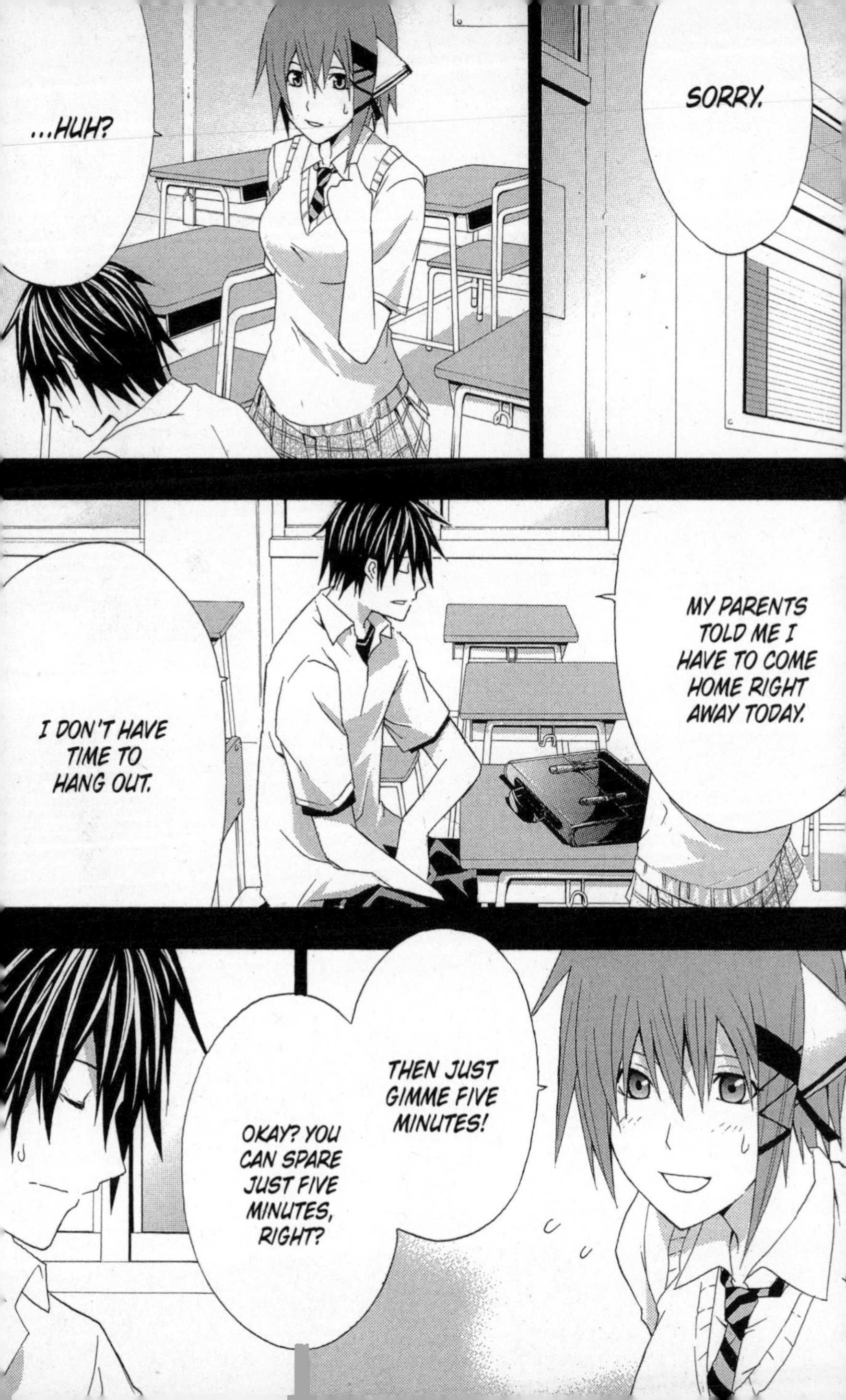
SORRY.
...HUH?
MY PARENTS TOLD ME I HAVE TO COME HOME RIGHT AWAY TODAY.
I DON'T HAVE TIME TO HANG OUT.
THEN JUST GIMME FIVE MINUTES!
OKAY? YOU CAN SPARE JUST FIVE MINUTES, RIGHT?

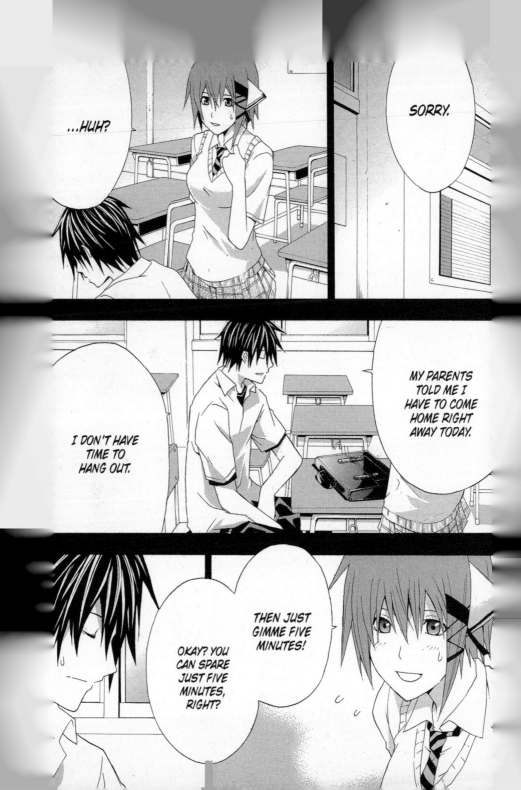

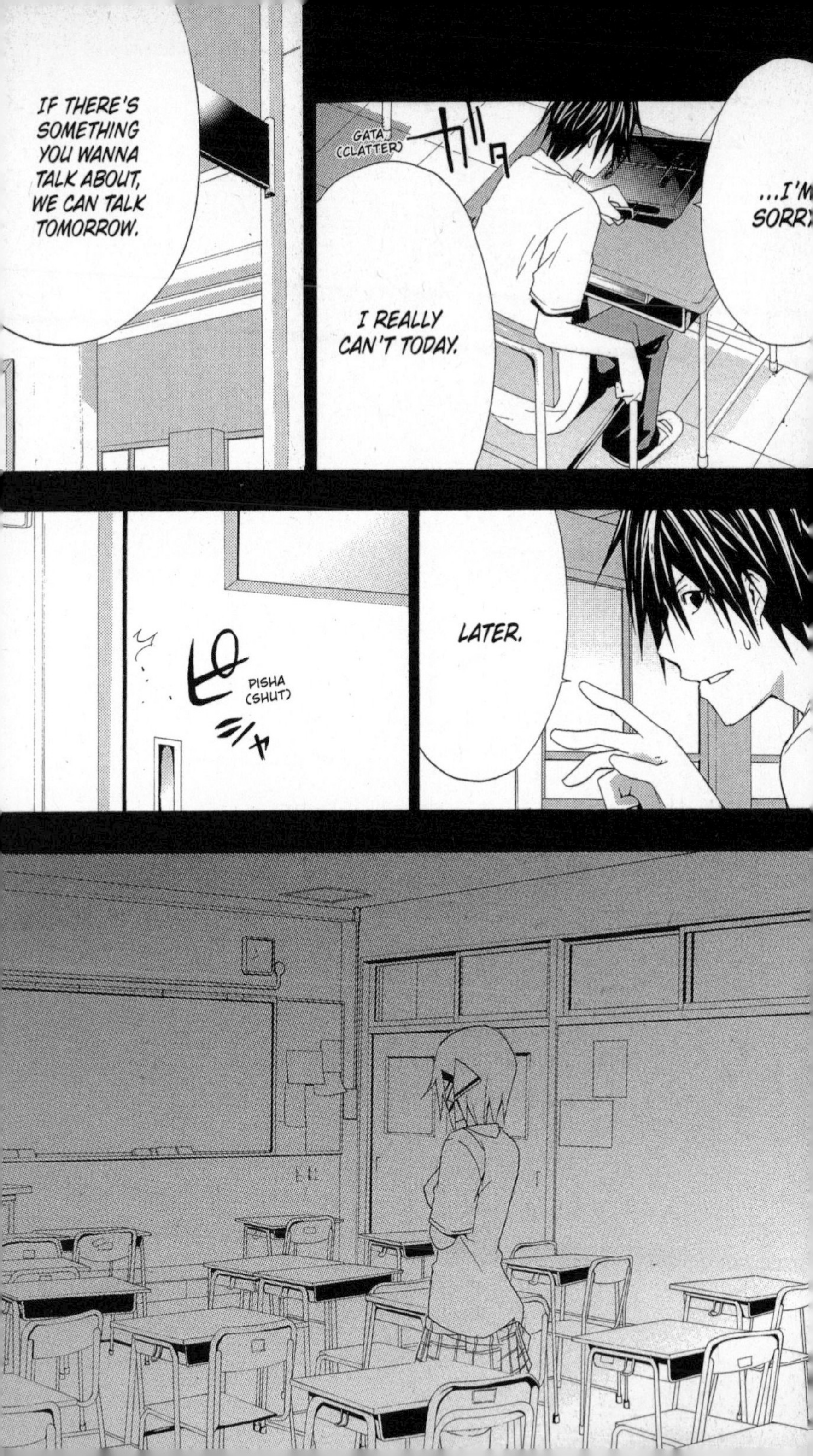
...I'M SORR
GATA (CLATTER)
I REALLY CAN'T TODAY.
IF THERE'S SOMETHING YOU WANNA TALK ABOUT, WE CAN TALK TOMORROW.
LATER.
PISHA (SHUT)

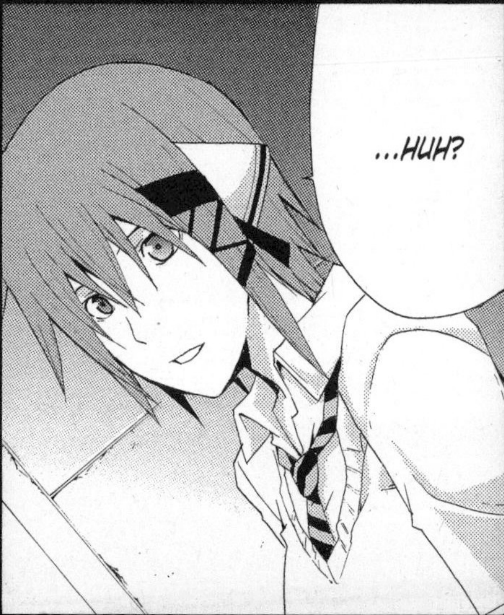
...HUH?
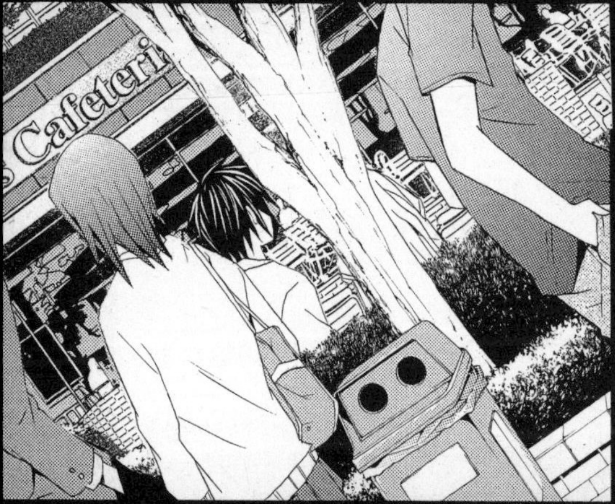
Cafeteri

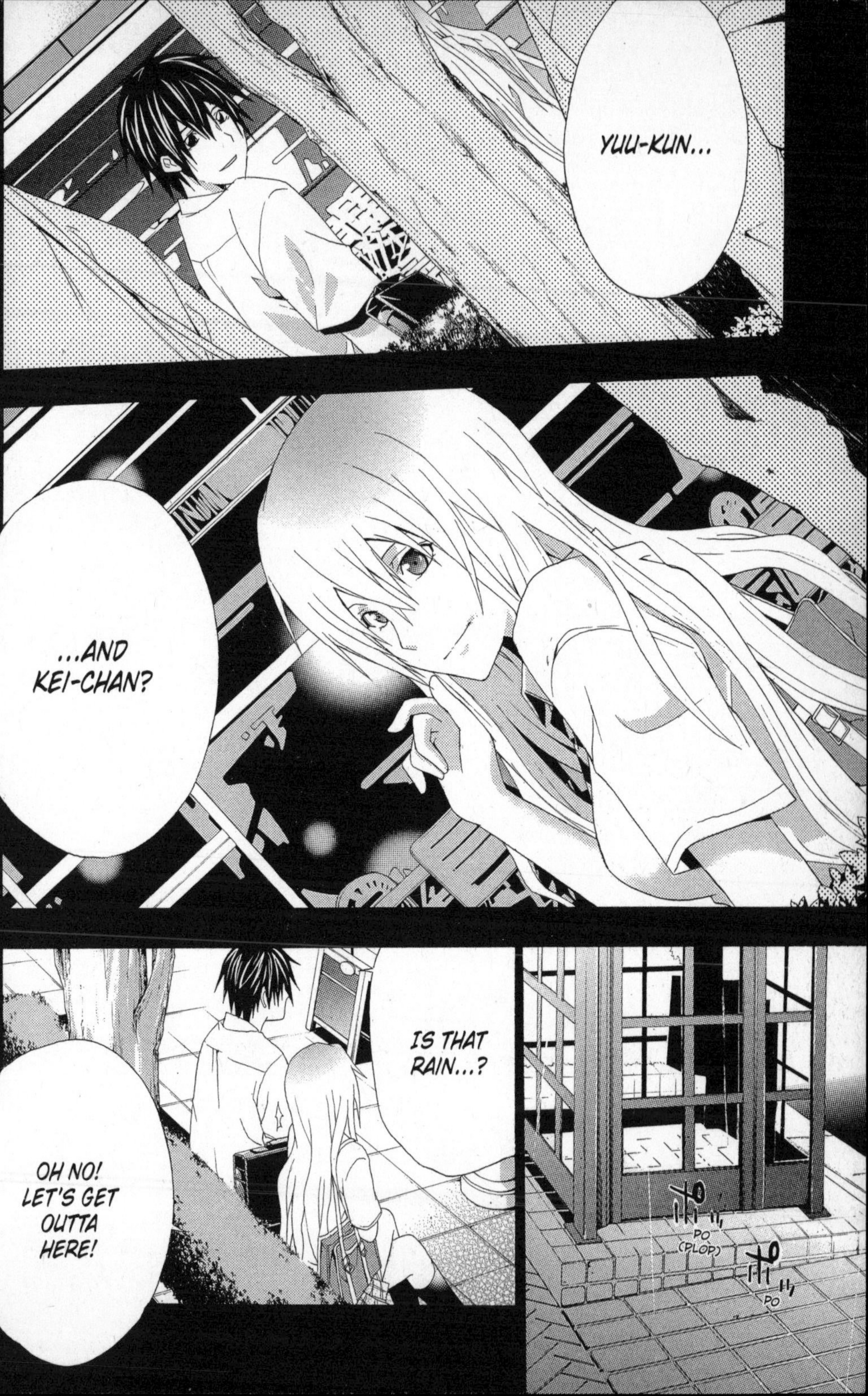
YUU-KUN...
...AND KEI-CHAN?
PO (PLOP)
PO
IS THAT RAIN...?
OH NO! LET'S GET OUTTA HERE!

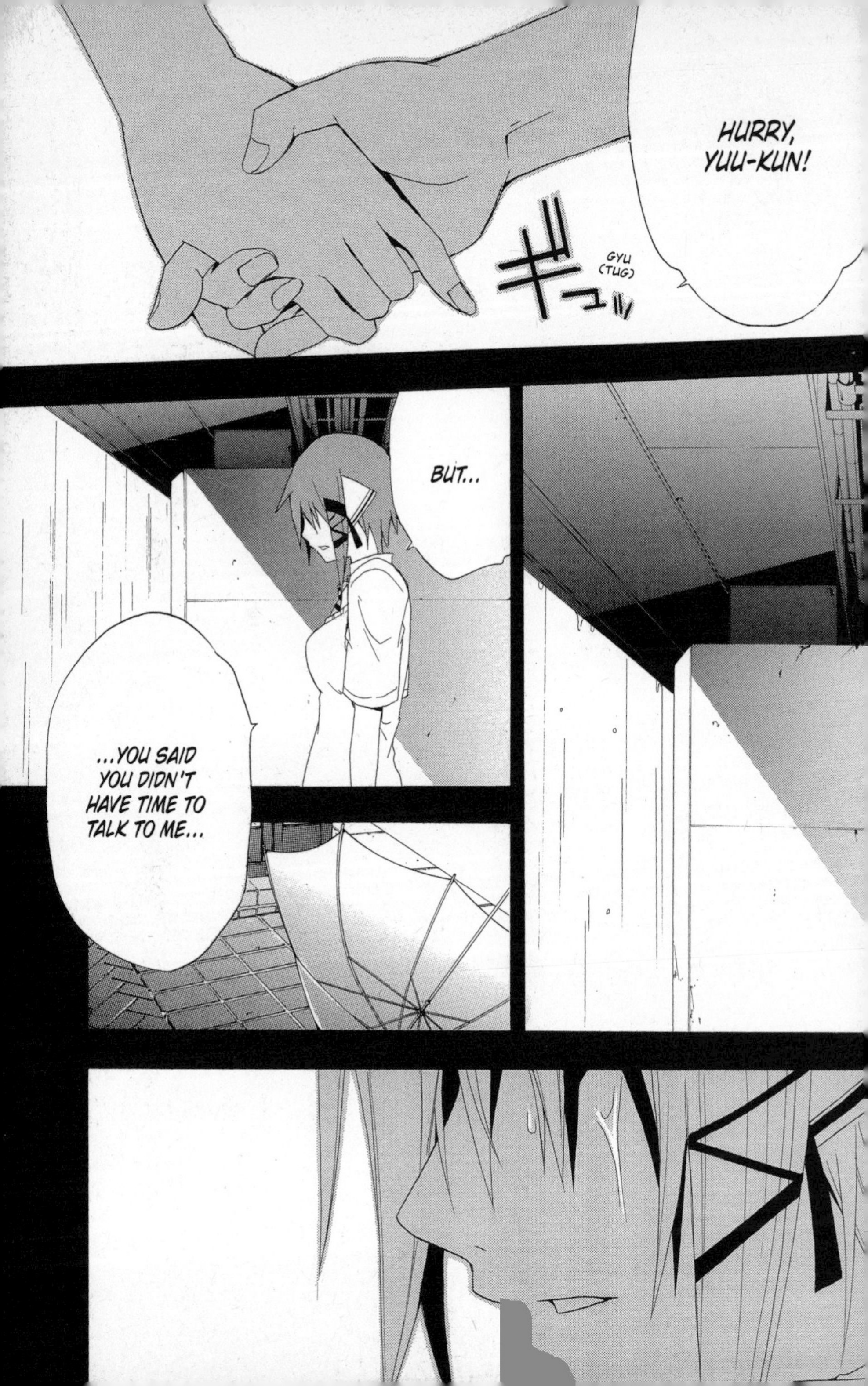
HURRY, YUU-KUN!
ギュッ
GYU (TUG)
BUT...
...YOU SAID YOU DIDN'T HAVE TIME TO TALK TO ME...

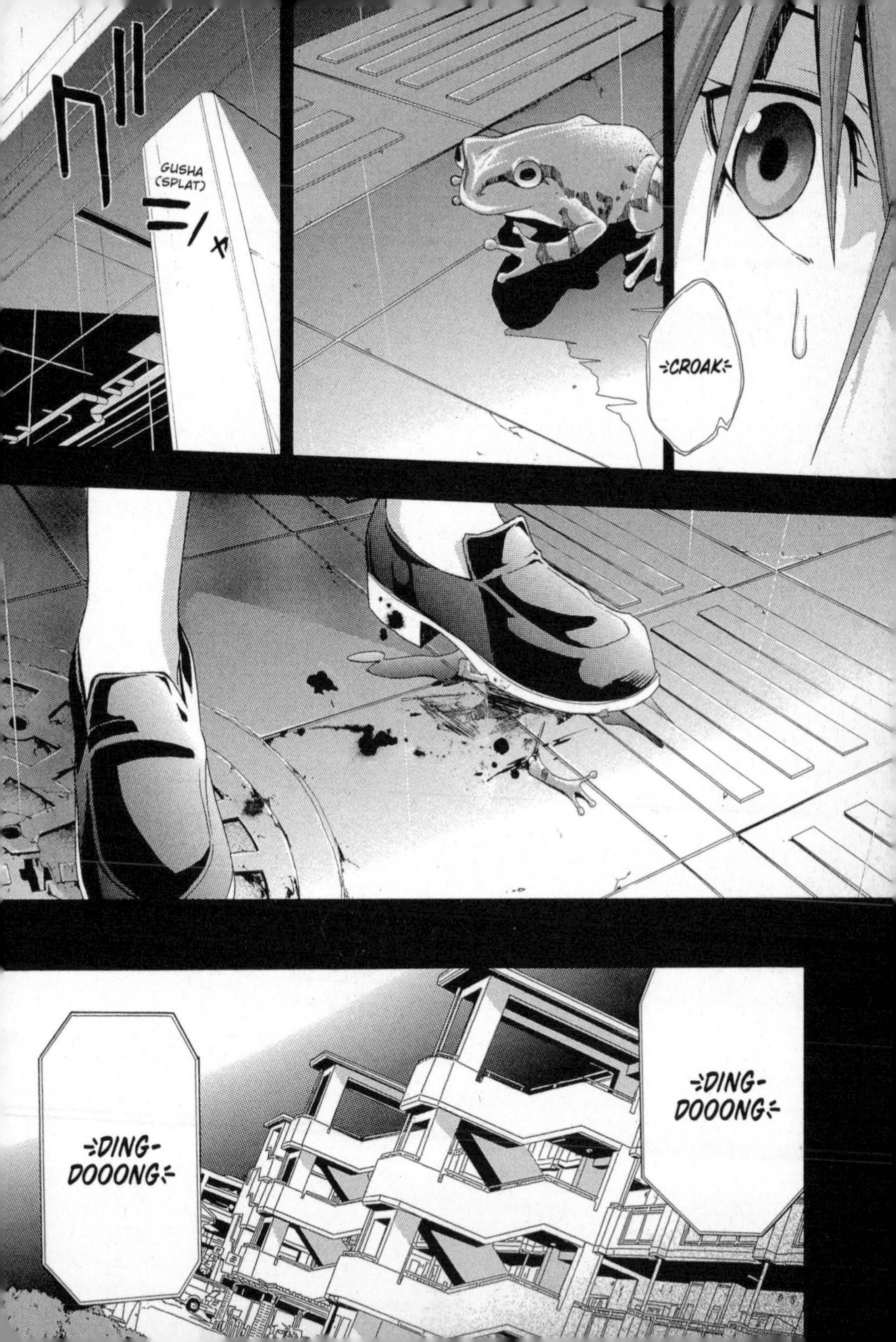
CROAK
GUSHA (SPLAT)
DING-DOOONG
DING-DOOONG

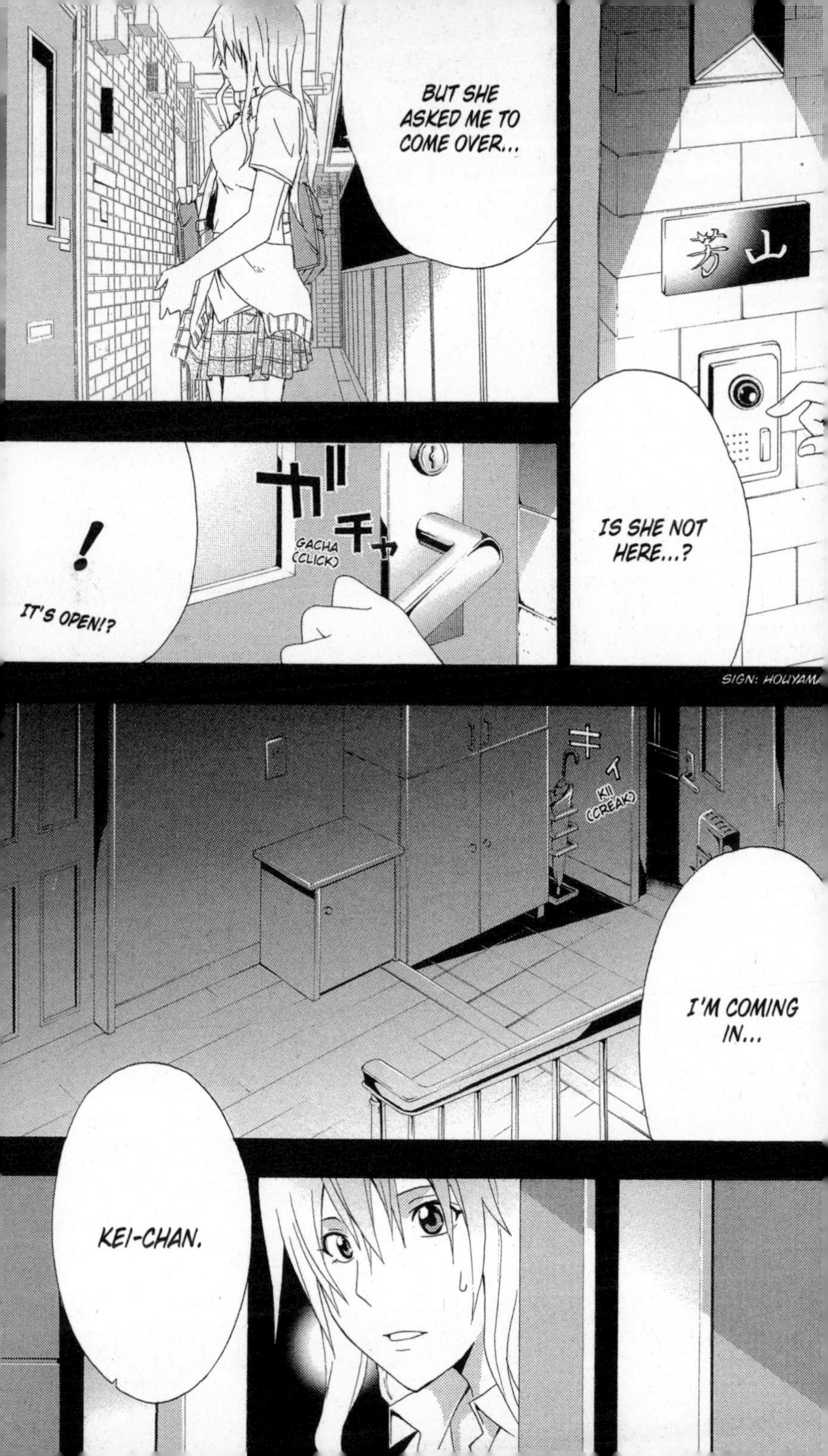
芳山
IS SHE NOT HERE...?
BUT SHE ASKED ME TO COME OVER...
!
ガチャ
GACHA (CLICK)
IT'S OPEN!?
SIGN: HOUYAMA
キィ
KII (CREAK)
I'M COMING IN...
KEI-CHAN.

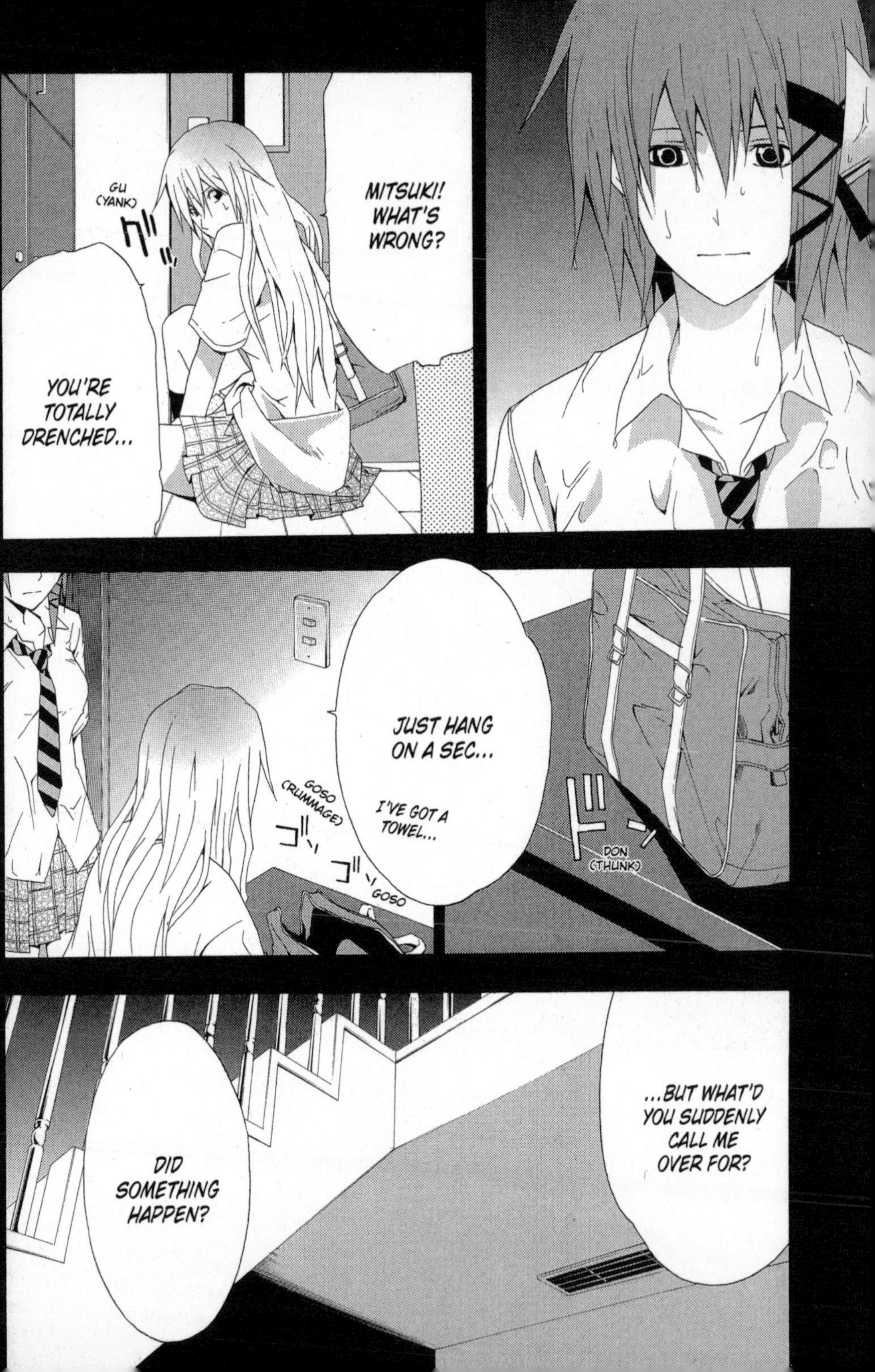
MITSUKI! WHAT'S WRONG?
GU (YANK)
YOU'RE TOTALLY DRENCHED...
DON (THUNK)
JUST HANG ON A SEC...
I'VE GOT A TOWEL...
GOSO (RUMMAGE)
GOSO
...BUT WHAT'D YOU SUDDENLY CALL ME OVER FOR?
DID SOMETHING HAPPEN?

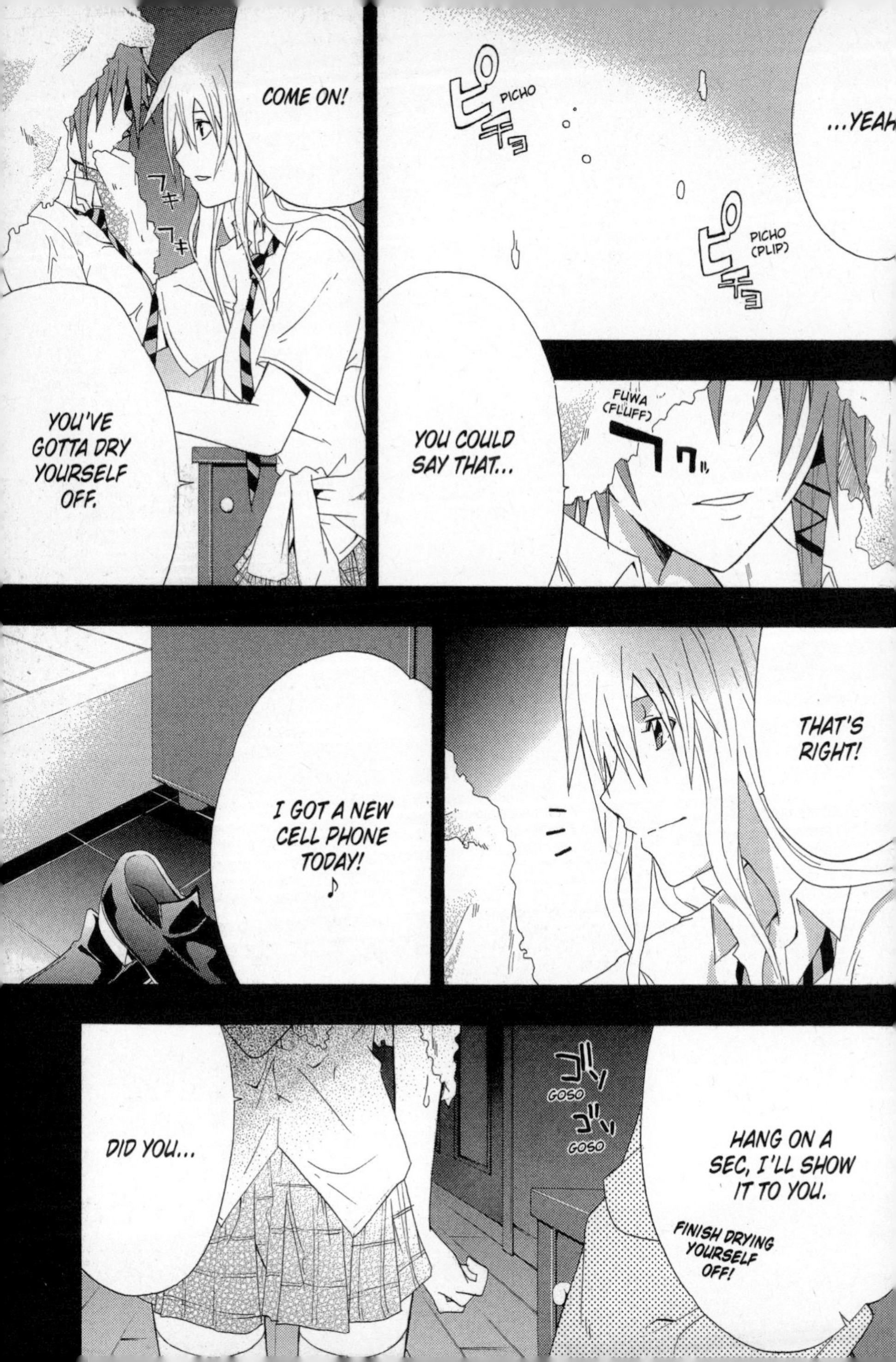
...YEAH
ピチョ
PICHO
ピチョ
PICHO (PLIP)
FUWA (FLUFF)
YOU COULD SAY THAT...
COME ON!
フキフキ
YOU'VE GOTTA DRY YOURSELF OFF.
THAT'S RIGHT!
I GOT A NEW CELL PHONE TODAY! ♪
HANG ON A SEC, I'LL SHOW IT TO YOU.
FINISH DRYING YOURSELF OFF!
ゴソ
GOSO
ゴソ
GOSO
DID YOU...

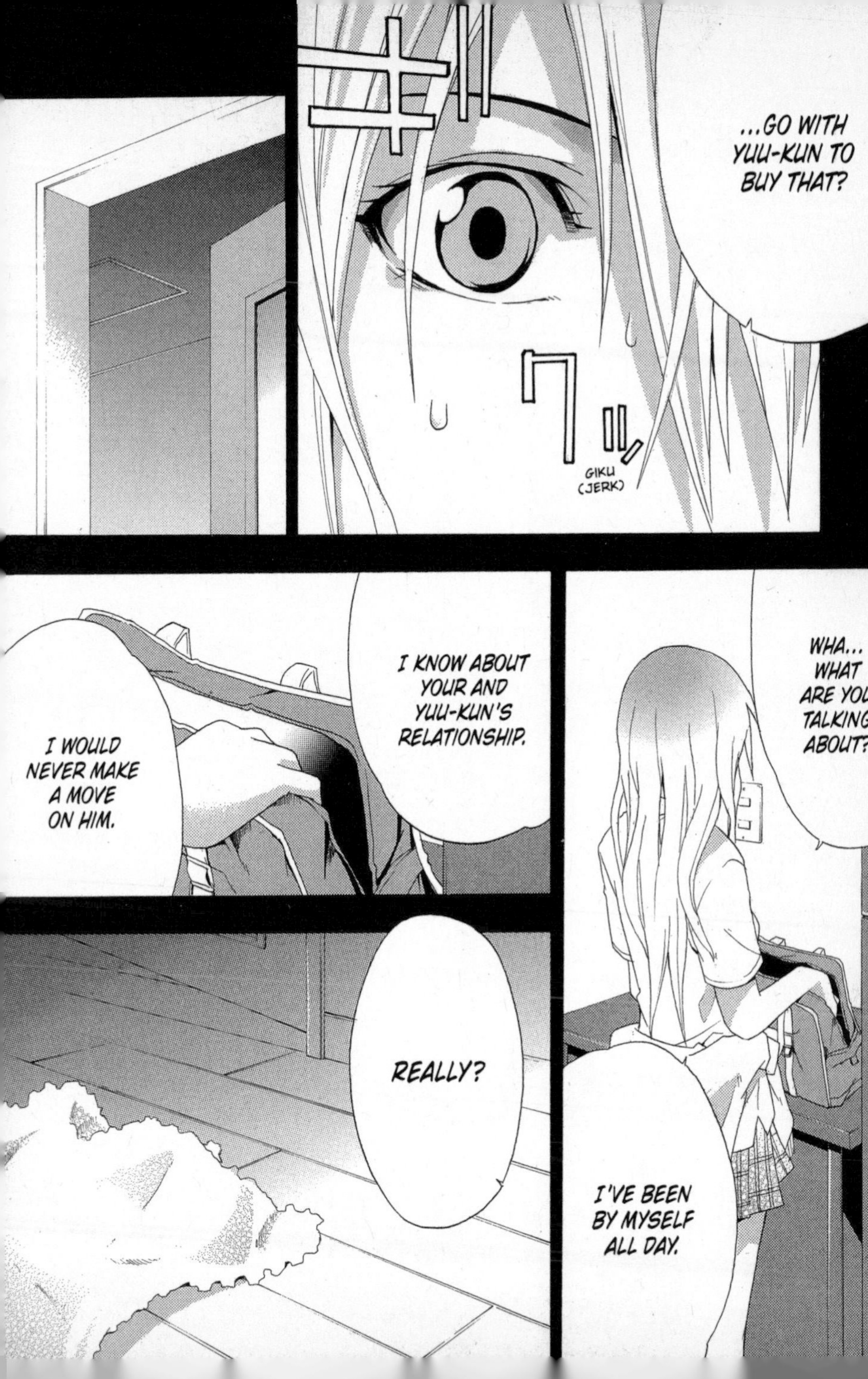
...GO WITH YUU-KUN TO BUY THAT?
GIKU (JERK)
WHA... WHAT ARE YOU TALKING ABOUT?
I'VE BEEN BY MYSELF ALL DAY.
I KNOW ABOUT YOUR AND YUU-KUN'S RELATIONSHIP.
I WOULD NEVER MAKE A MOVE ON HIM.
REALLY?

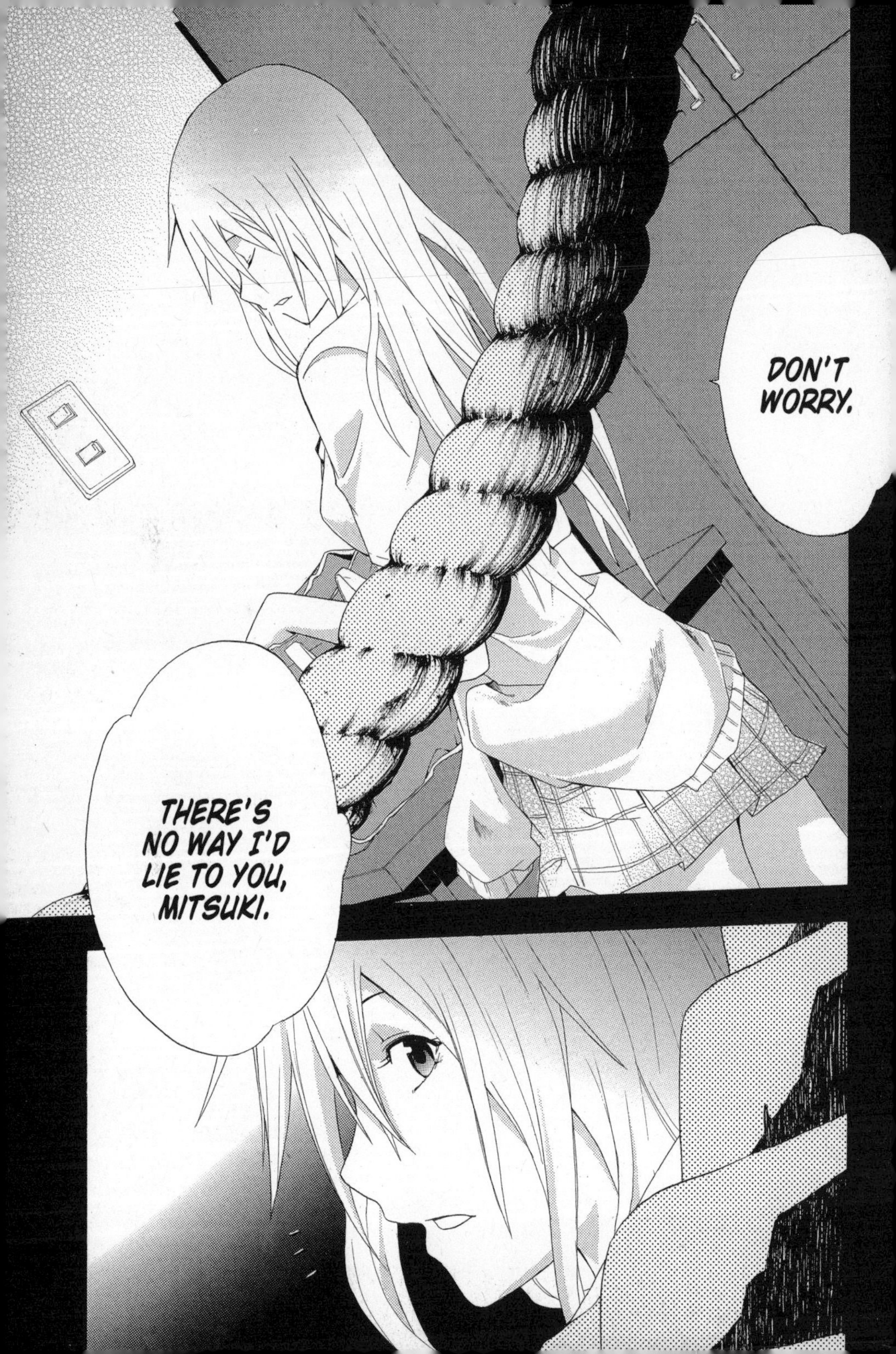
DON'T WORRY.
THERE'S NO WAY I'D LIE TO YOU, MITSUKI.

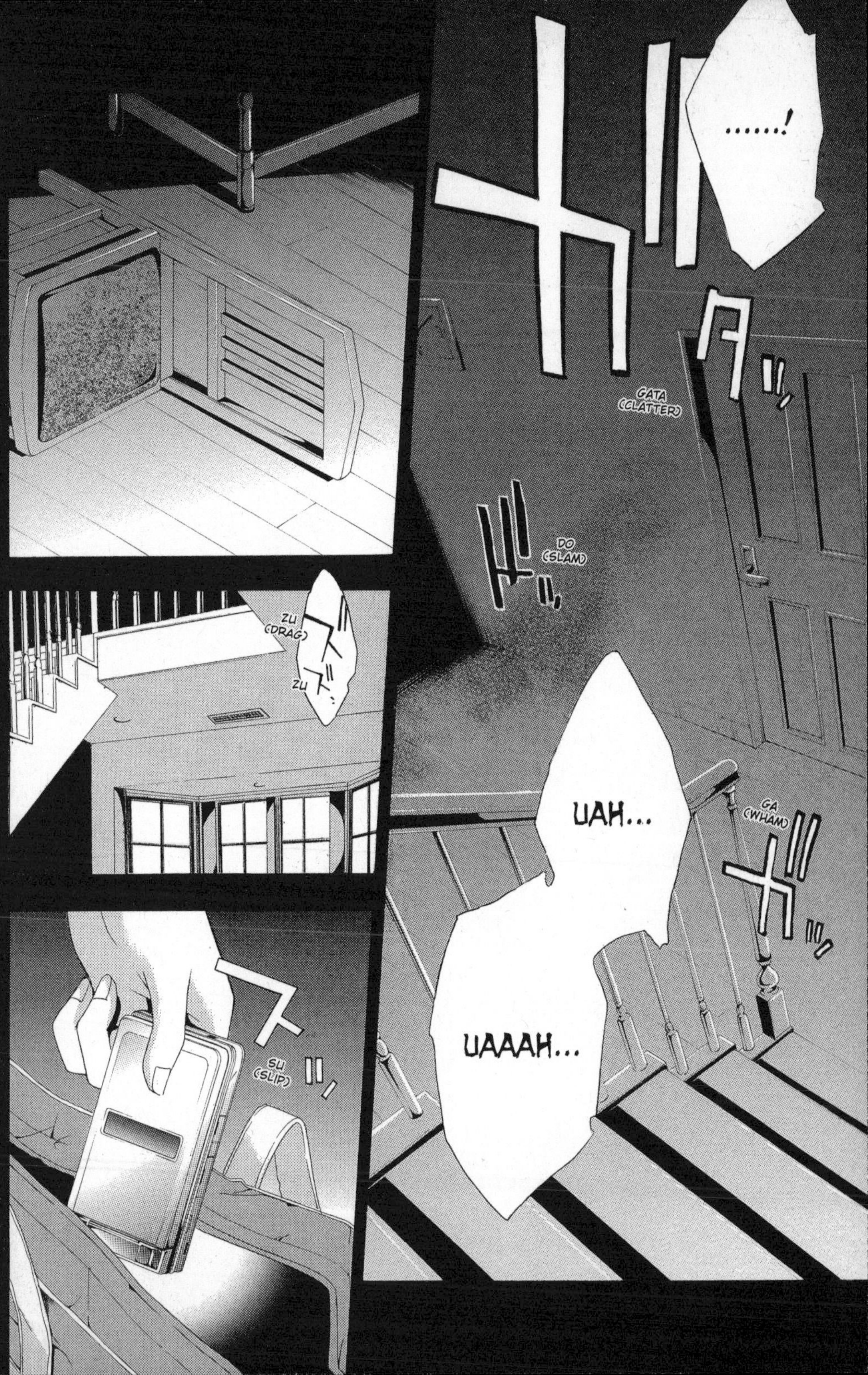
......!
GATA (CLATTER)
DO (SLAM)
UAH...
GA (WHAM)
UAAAH...
ZU (DRAG)
ZU
SU (SLIP)

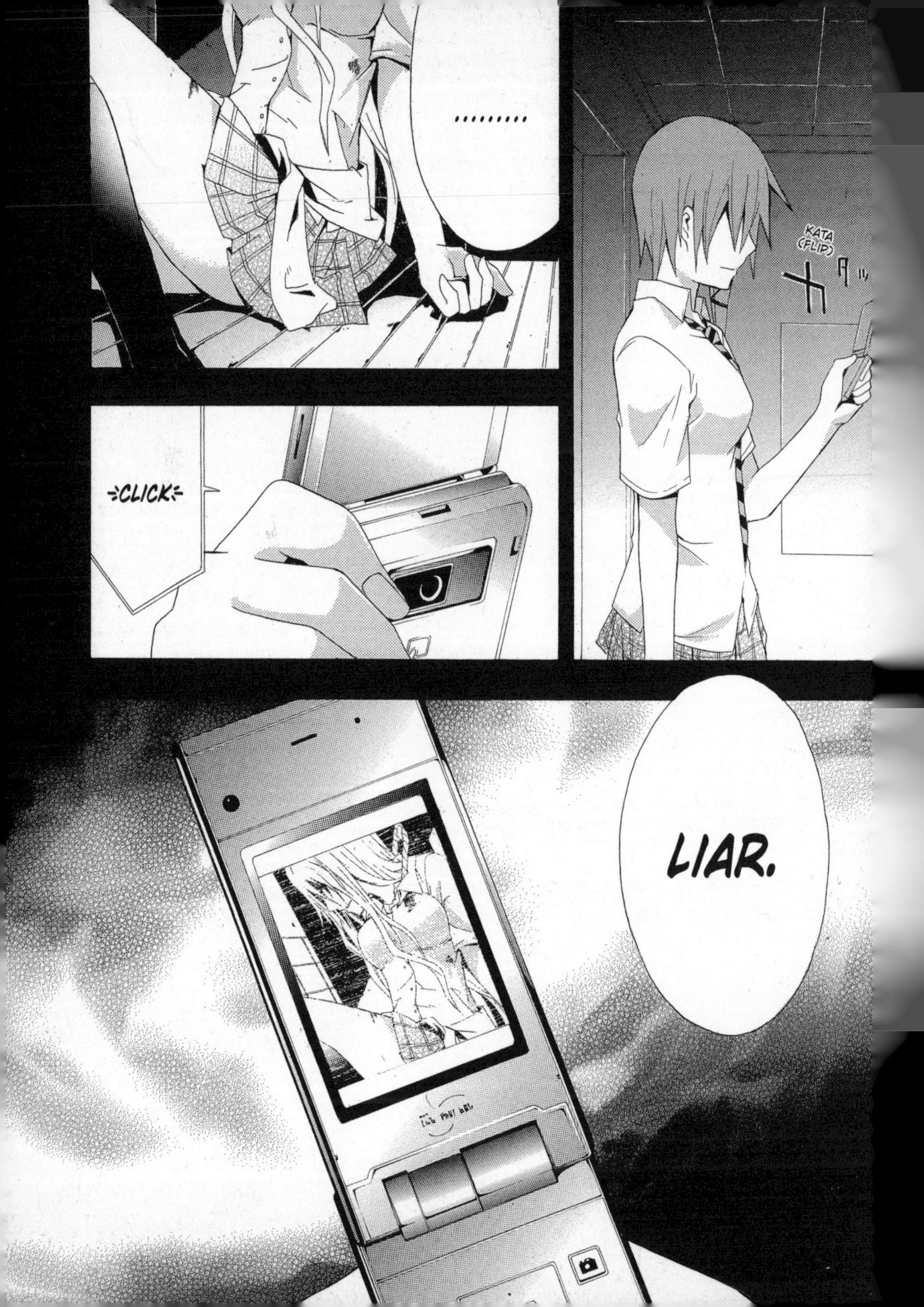
KATA (FLIP)
カタッ
....
-CLICK-
LIAR.

N...

GUSHA
(CRUMPLE)

NO
WAY...

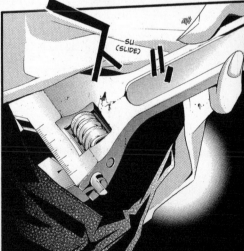

SU
(SLIDE)

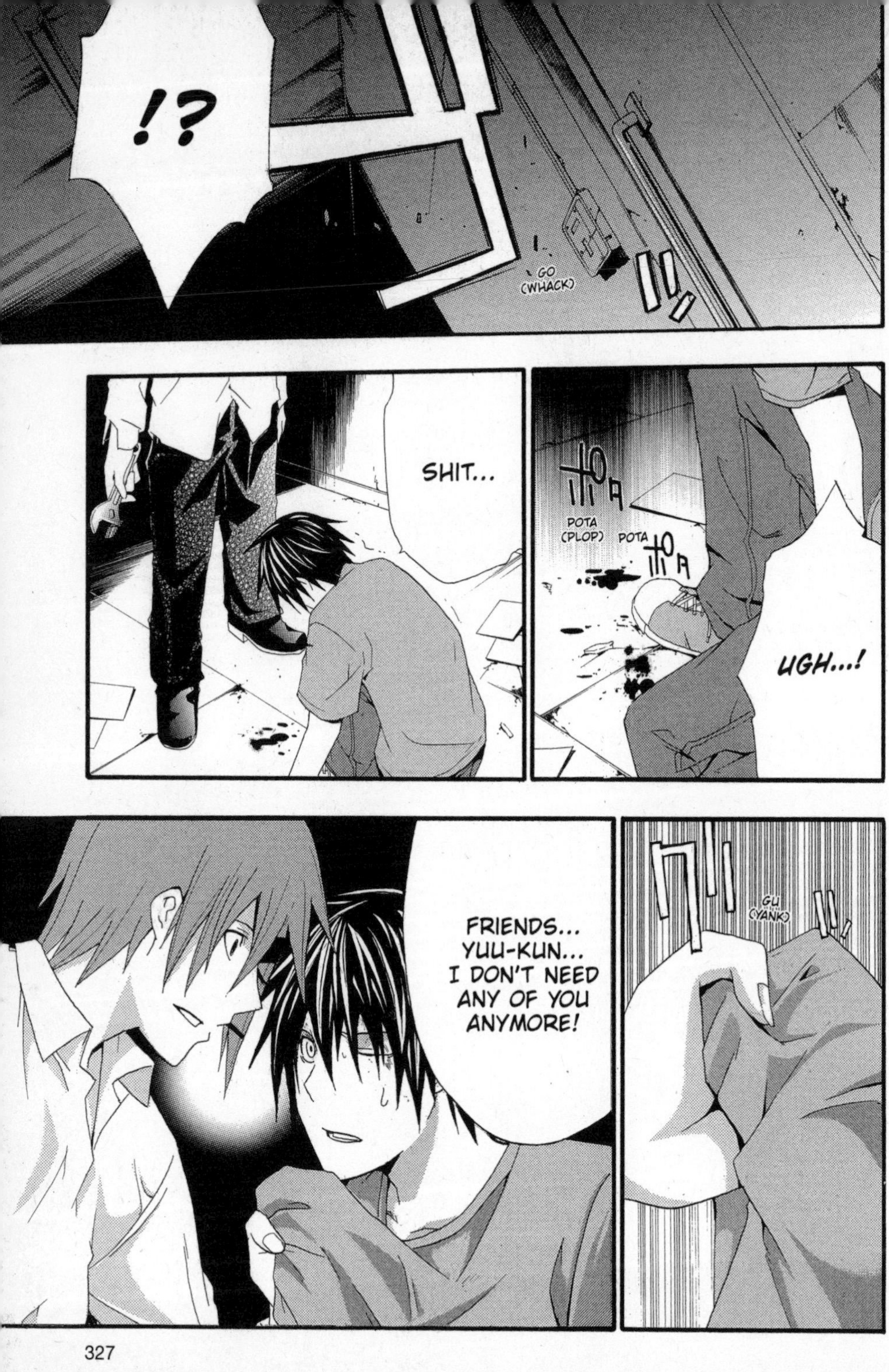
!?
GO (WHACK)
POTA (PLOP) POTA
UGH...!
SHIT...
GU (YANK)
FRIENDS... YUU-KUN... I DON'T NEED ANY OF YOU ANYMORE!

AS LONG AS I HAVE MY DAD...!

GU (GRAB)

...YOU'VE GOT IT WRONG.

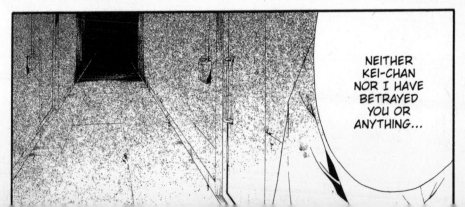

NEITHER KEI-CHAN NOR I HAVE BETRAYED YOU OR ANYTHING...

GIRI
CGRITO

IT'S TRUE THAT...

...I WAS WITH KEI-CHAN THAT DAY...

BUT...

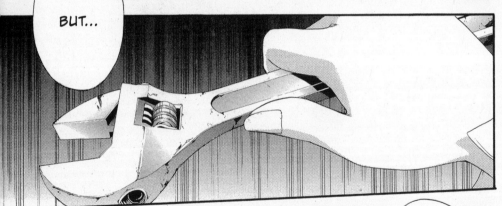

...THAT WAS...

...TO GO BUY YOUR BIRTHDAY PRESENT.

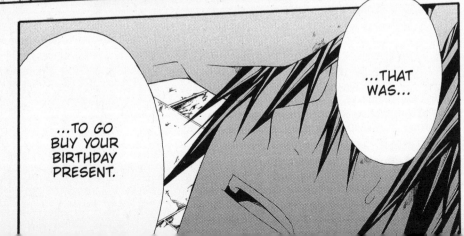

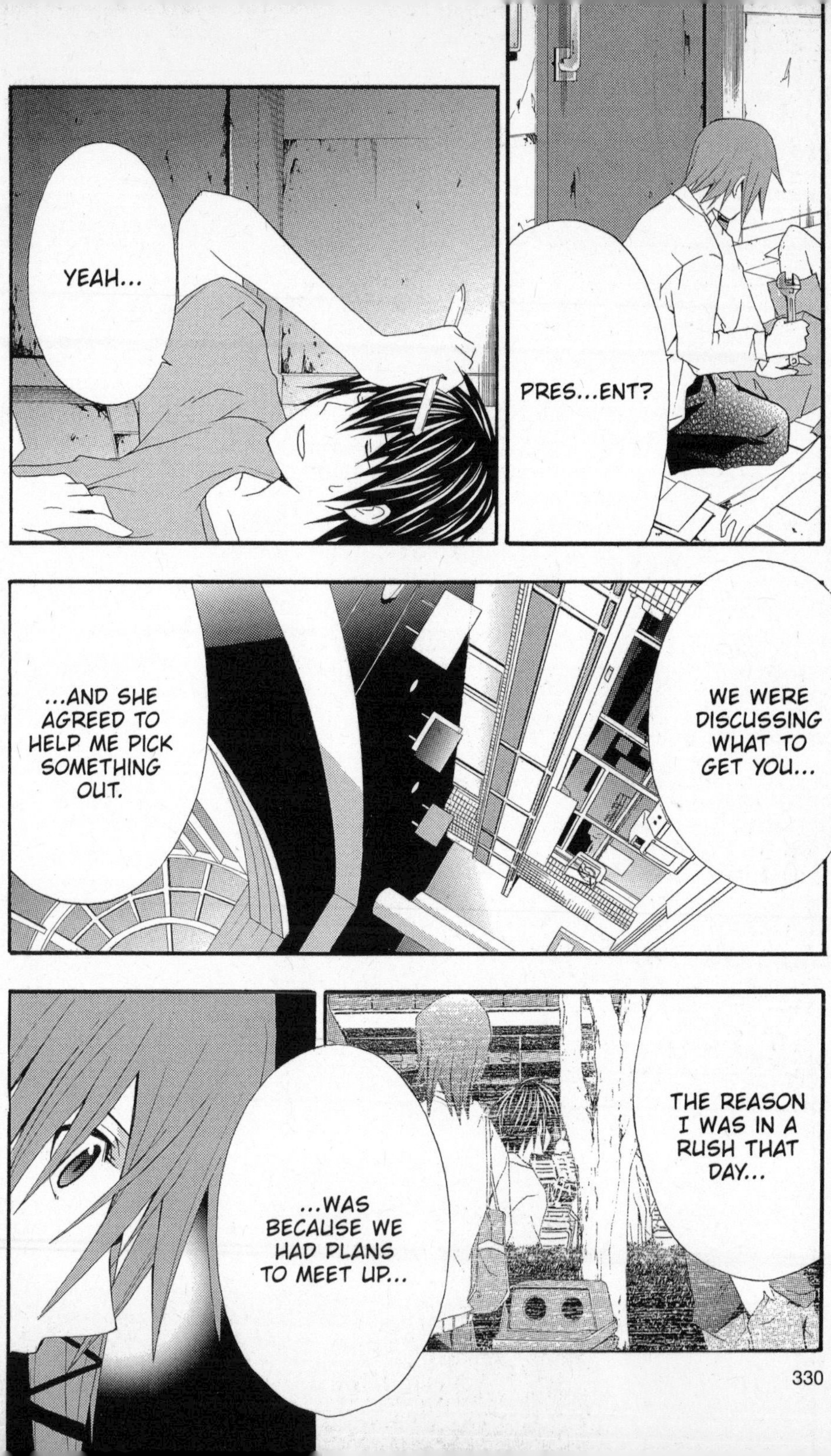
PRES...ENT?
YEAH...
WE WERE DISCUSSING WHAT TO GET YOU...
...AND SHE AGREED TO HELP ME PICK SOMETHING OUT.
THE REASON I WAS IN A RUSH THAT DAY...
...WAS BECAUSE WE HAD PLANS TO MEET UP...

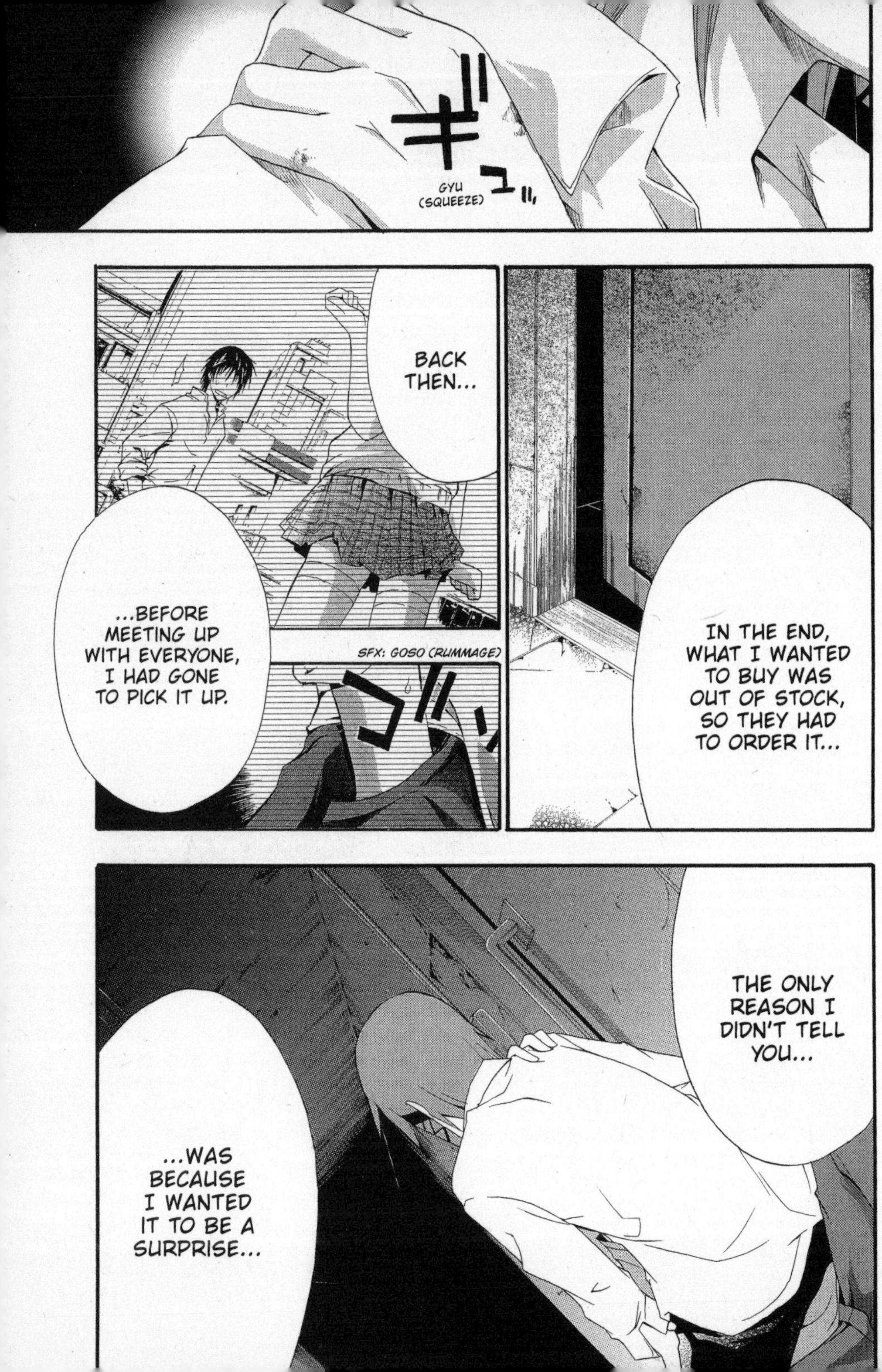
GYU (SQUEEZE)
IN THE END, WHAT I WANTED TO BUY WAS OUT OF STOCK, SO THEY HAD TO ORDER IT...
BACK THEN...
...BEFORE MEETING UP WITH EVERYONE, I HAD GONE TO PICK IT UP.
SFX: GOSO (RUMMAGE)
THE ONLY REASON I DIDN'T TELL YOU...
...WAS BECAUSE I WANTED IT TO BE A SURPRISE...

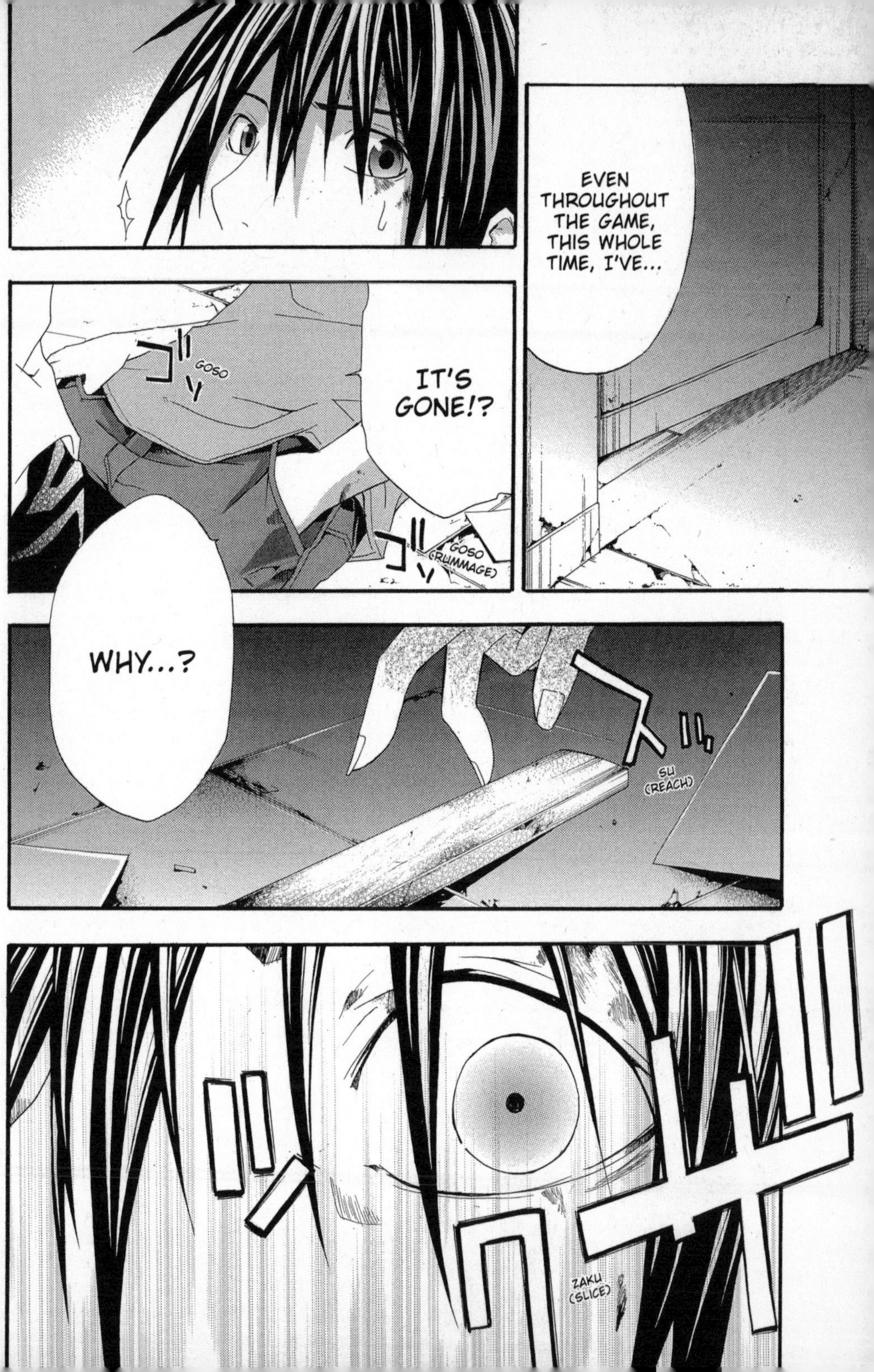
EVEN THROUGHOUT THE GAME, THIS WHOLE TIME, I'VE...
IT'S GONE!?
GOSO
GOSO (RUMMAGE)
WHY...?
SU (REACH)
ZAKU (SLICE)

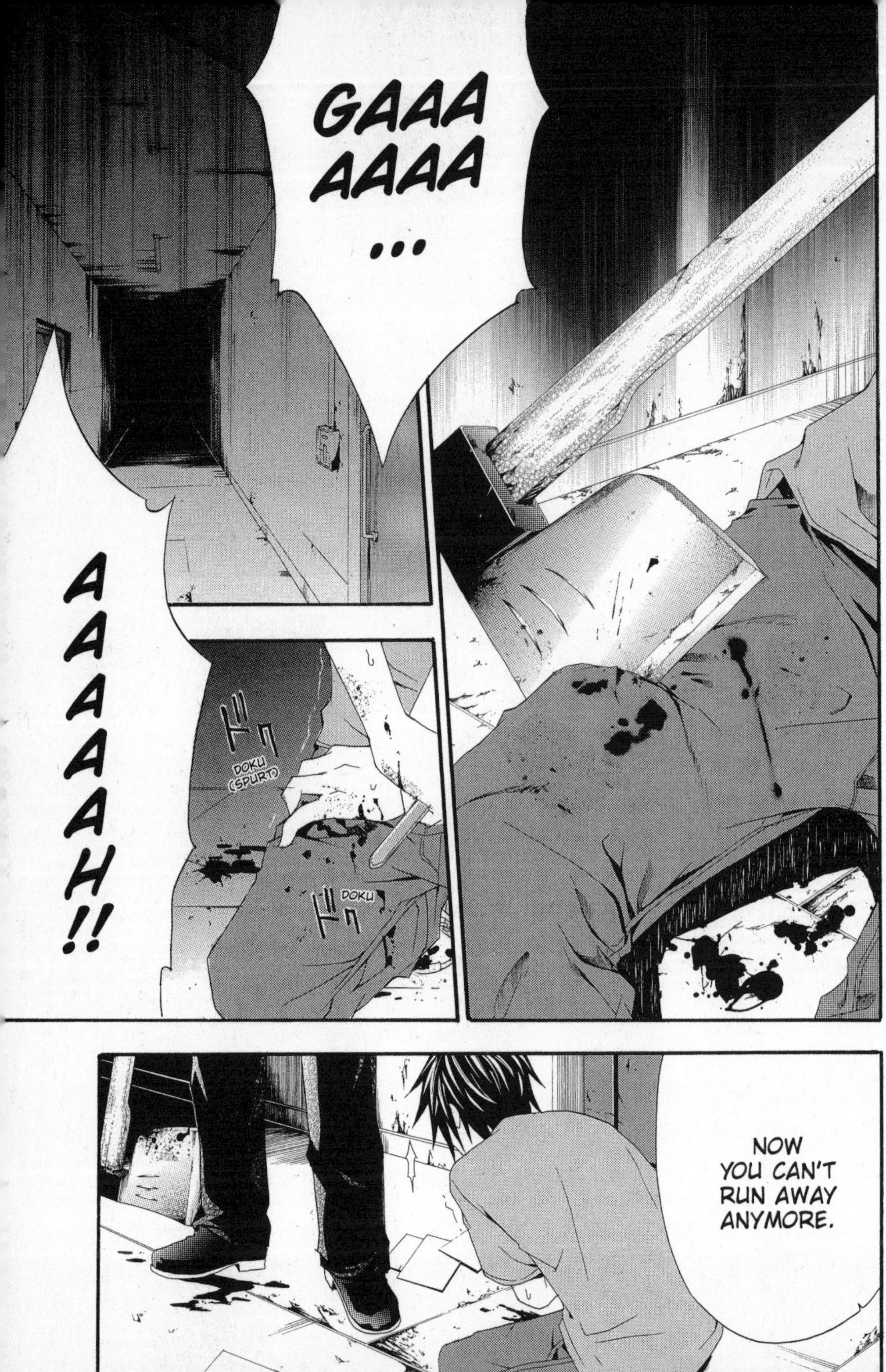
GAAA AAAA...
AAAAAAAH!!
ドク
DOKU (SPURT)
ドク
DOKU
NOW YOU CAN'T RUN AWAY ANYMORE.

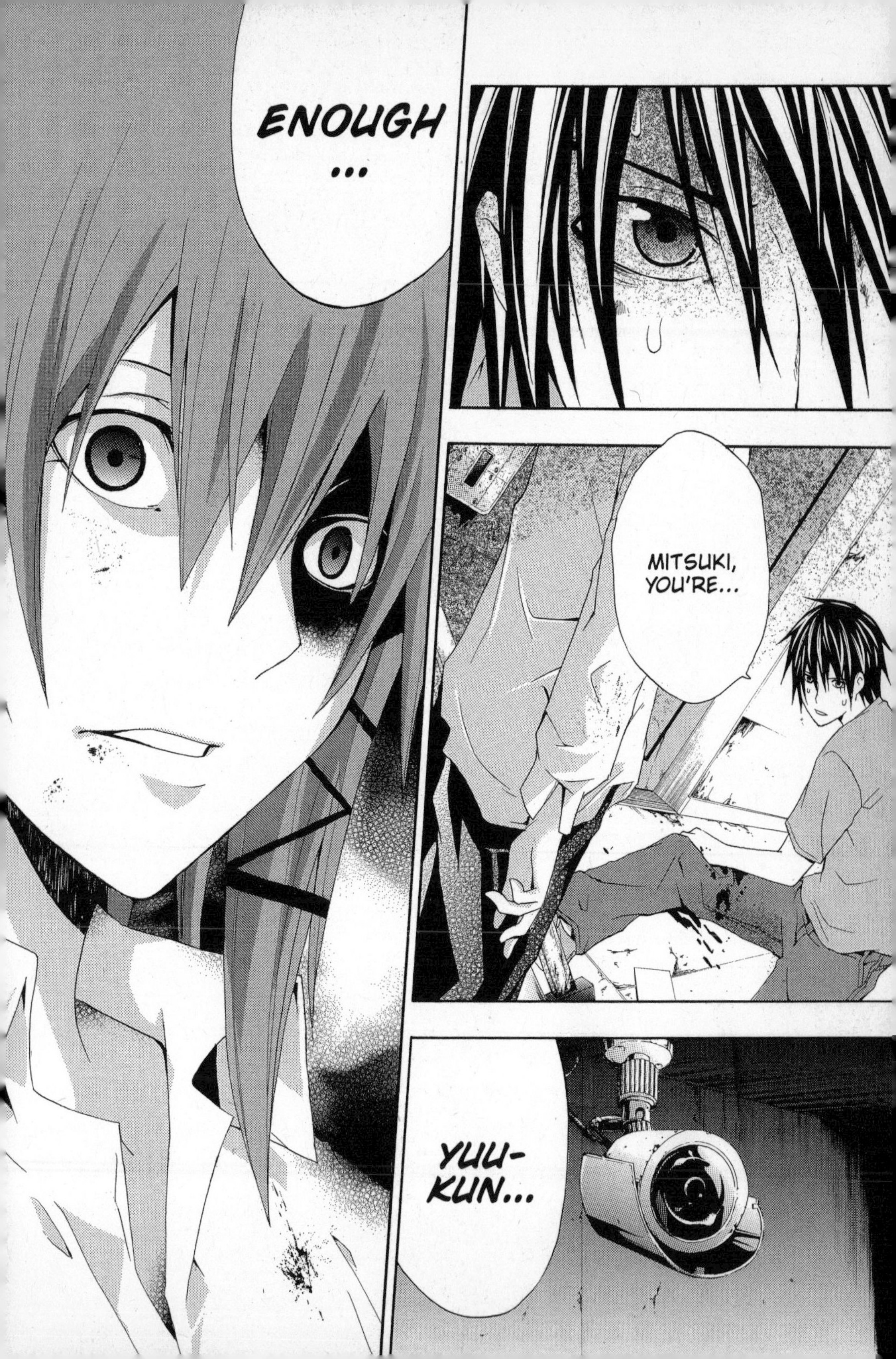
MITSUKI, YOU'RE...
YUU-KUN...
ENOUGH ...

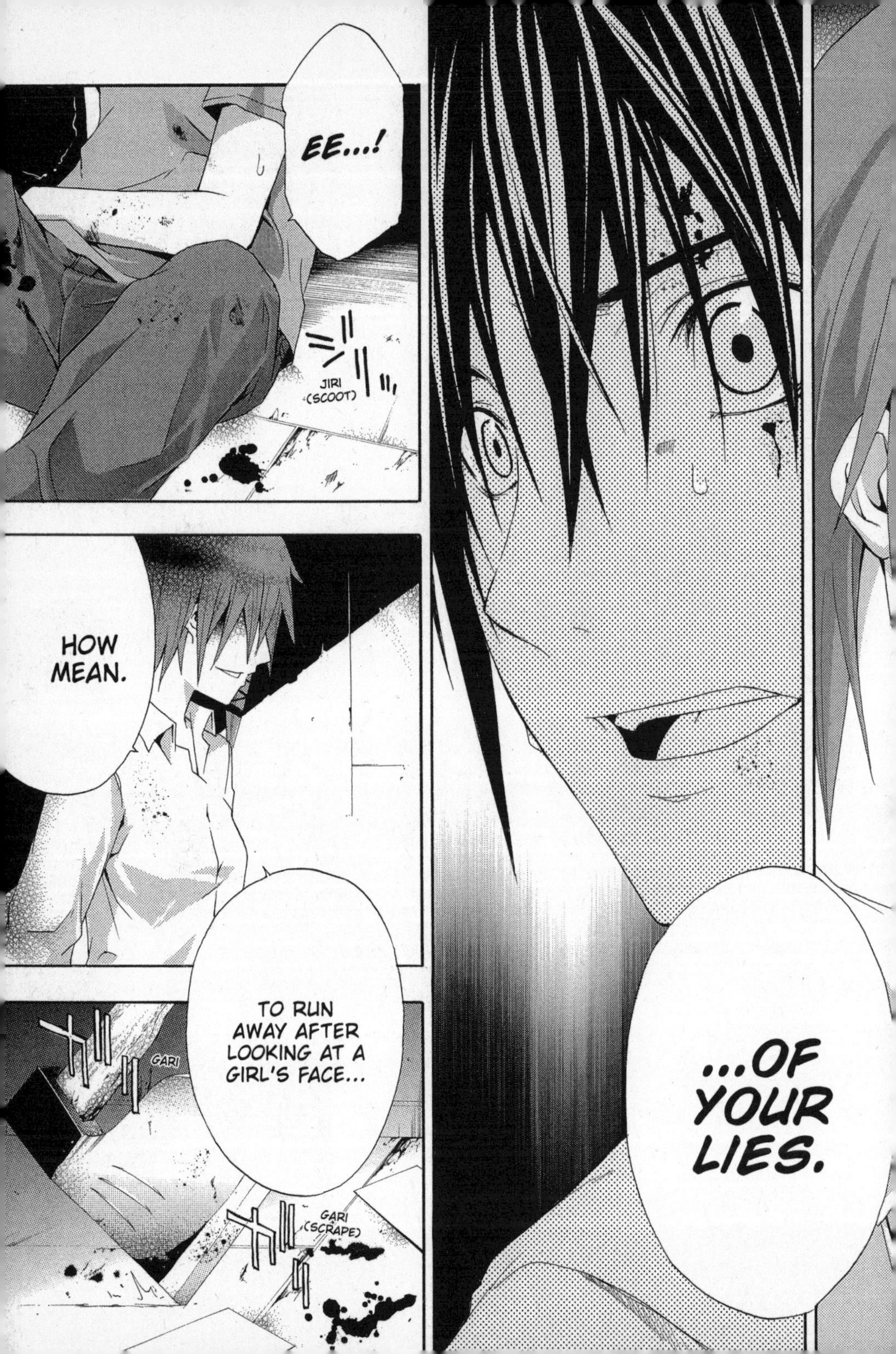
...OF YOUR LIES.
EE...!
JIRI (SCOOT)
HOW MEAN.
TO RUN AWAY AFTER LOOKING AT A GIRL'S FACE...
GARI
GARI (SCRAPE)

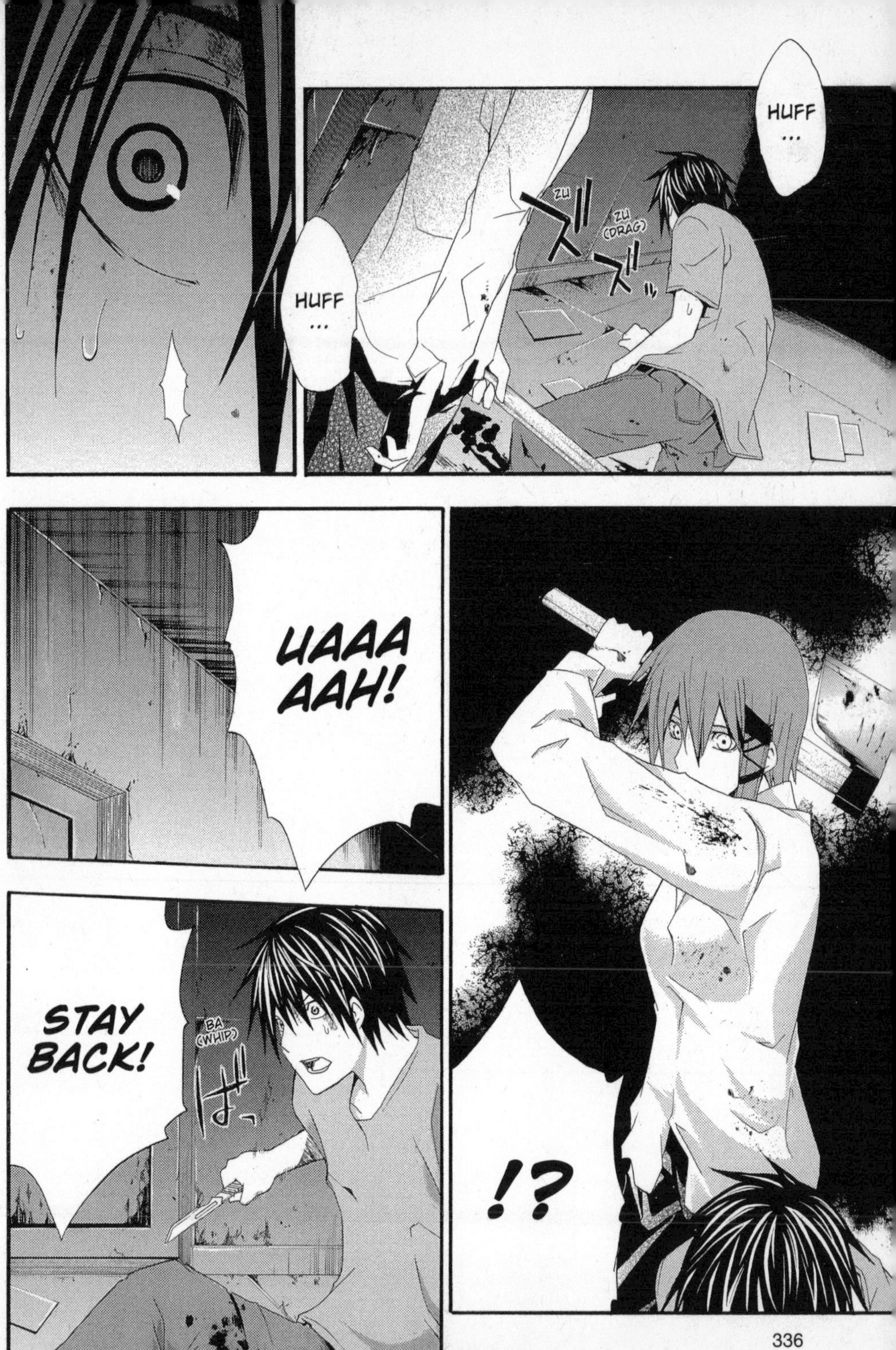
HUFF ...
ZU
ZU (DRAG)
HUFF ...
!?
UAAAA AAH!
STAY BACK!
BA (WHIP)

GA
(WHAM)

DON'T COME ANY CLOSER!!

JIKU
(STAB)

ZUKI
(THROB)

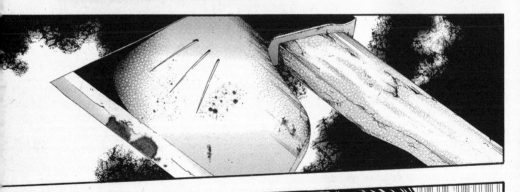

GA
(WHACK)

EEP...!

BIKU
(FLINCH)

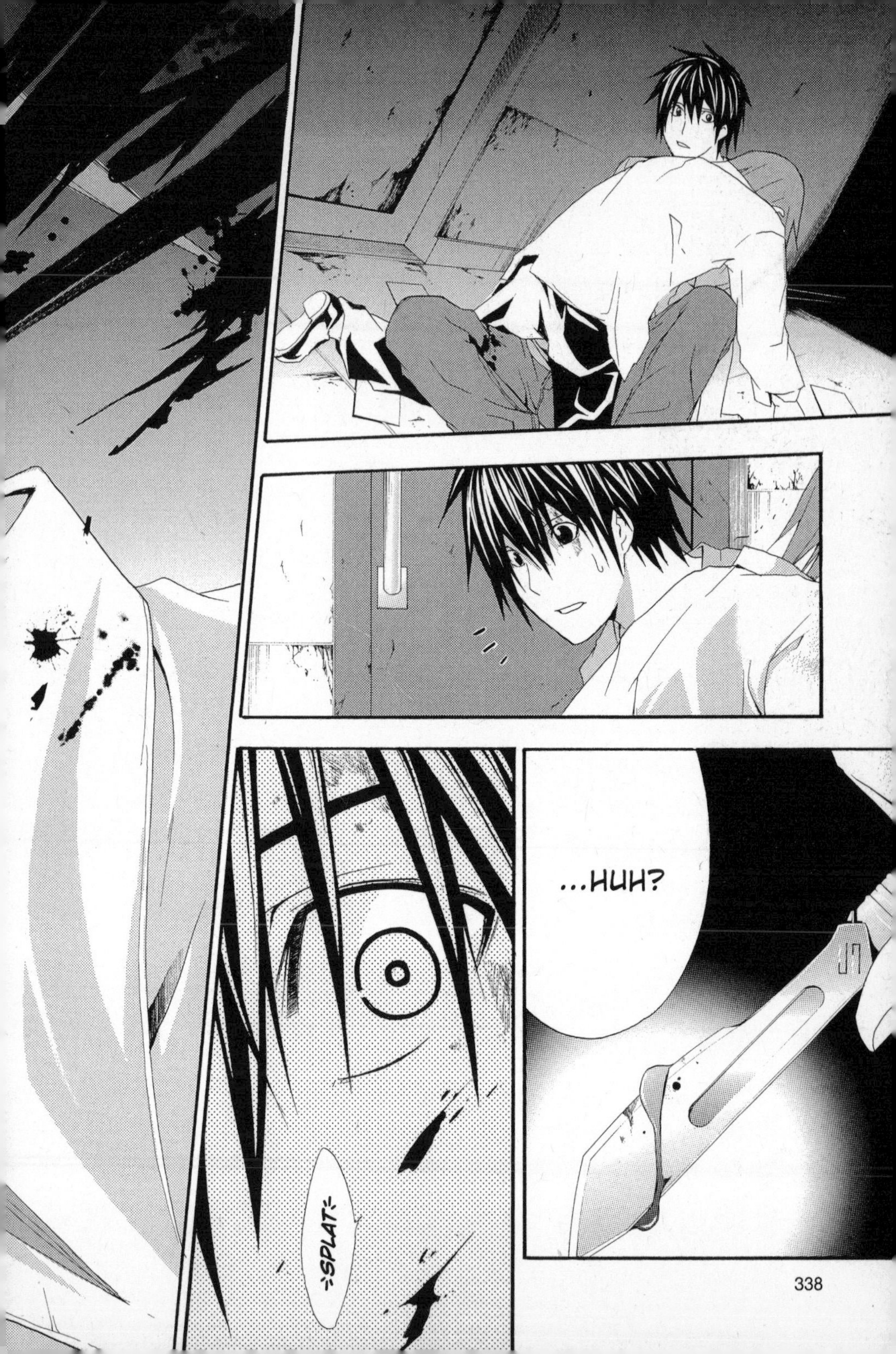
...HUH?
SPLAT

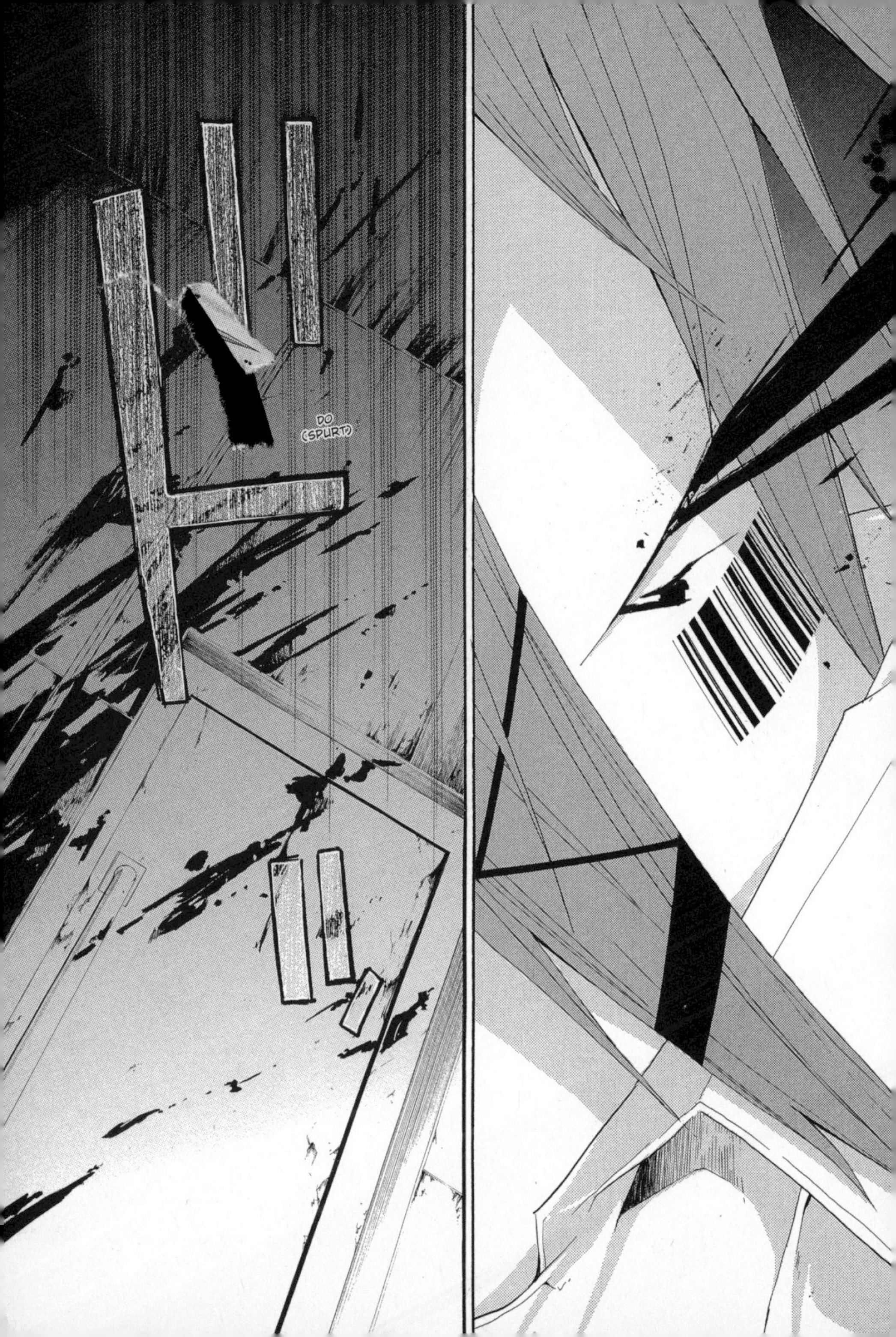
DO
(SPURT)

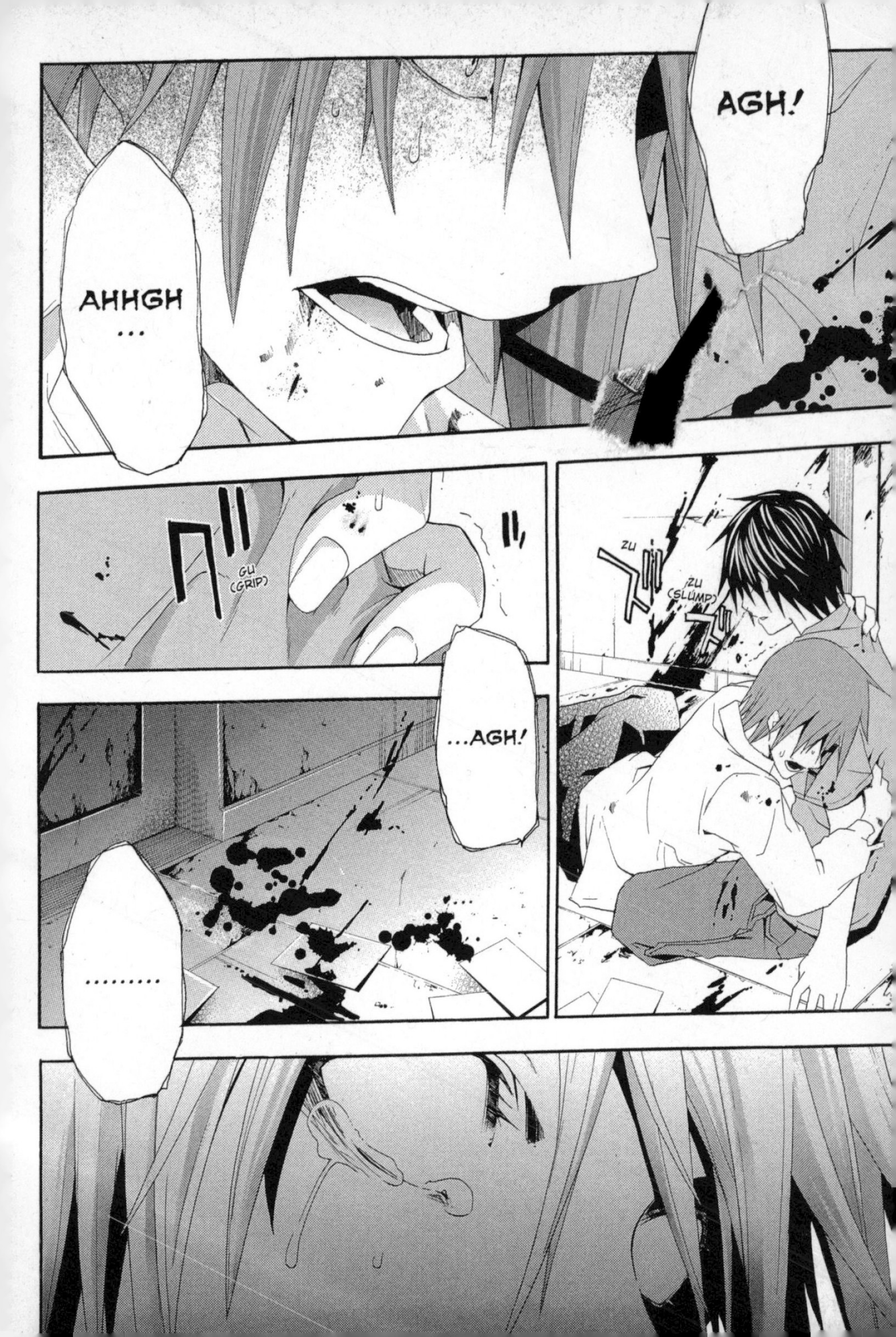
AGH!
AHHGH ...
ZU
ZU (SLUMP)
GU (GRIP)
...AGH!
....

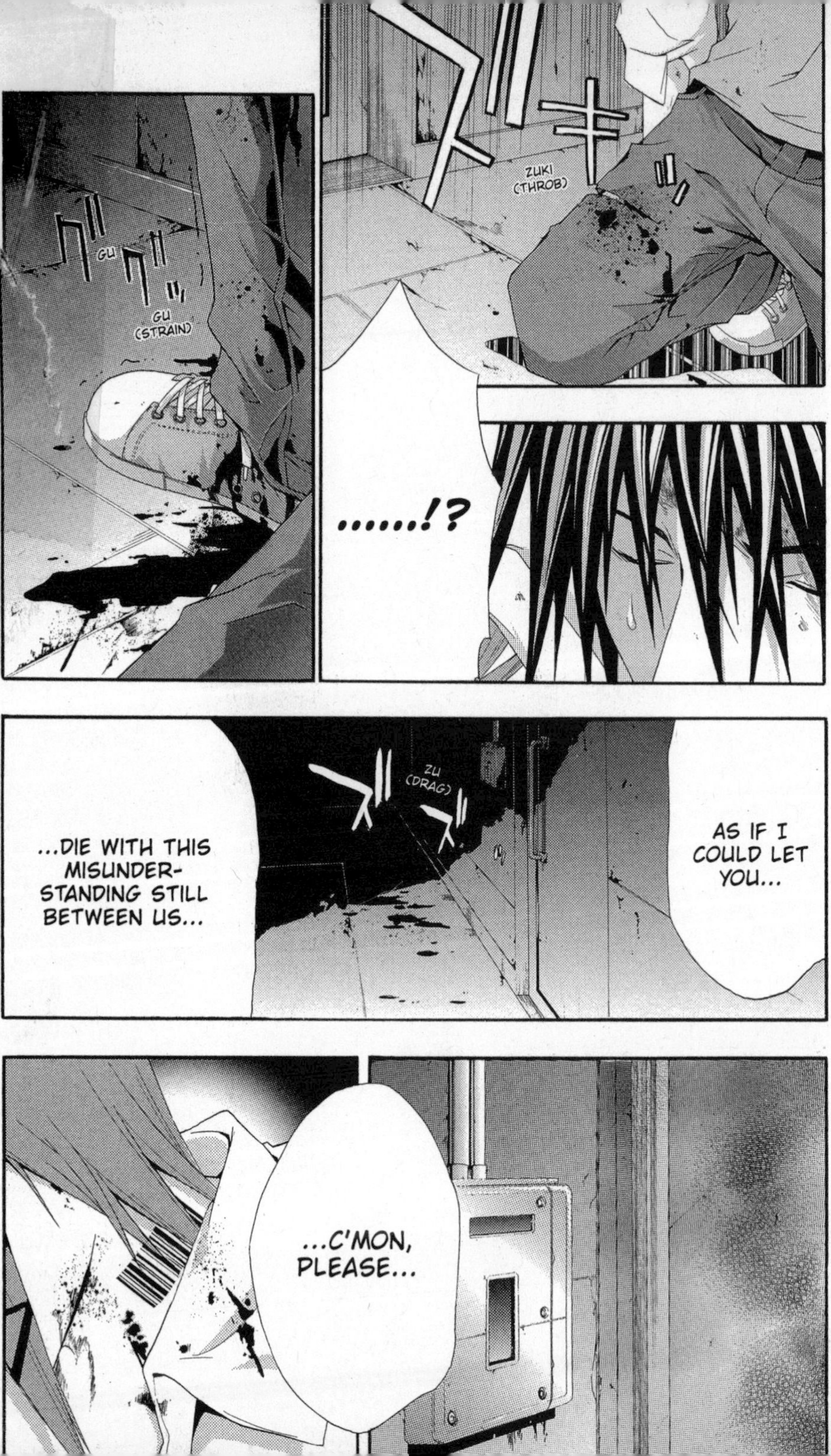
ZUKI
(THROB)
......!?
GU
GU
(STRAIN)
AS IF I COULD LET YOU...
ZU
(DRAG)
...DIE WITH THIS MISUNDER-STANDING STILL BETWEEN US...
...C'MON, PLEASE...

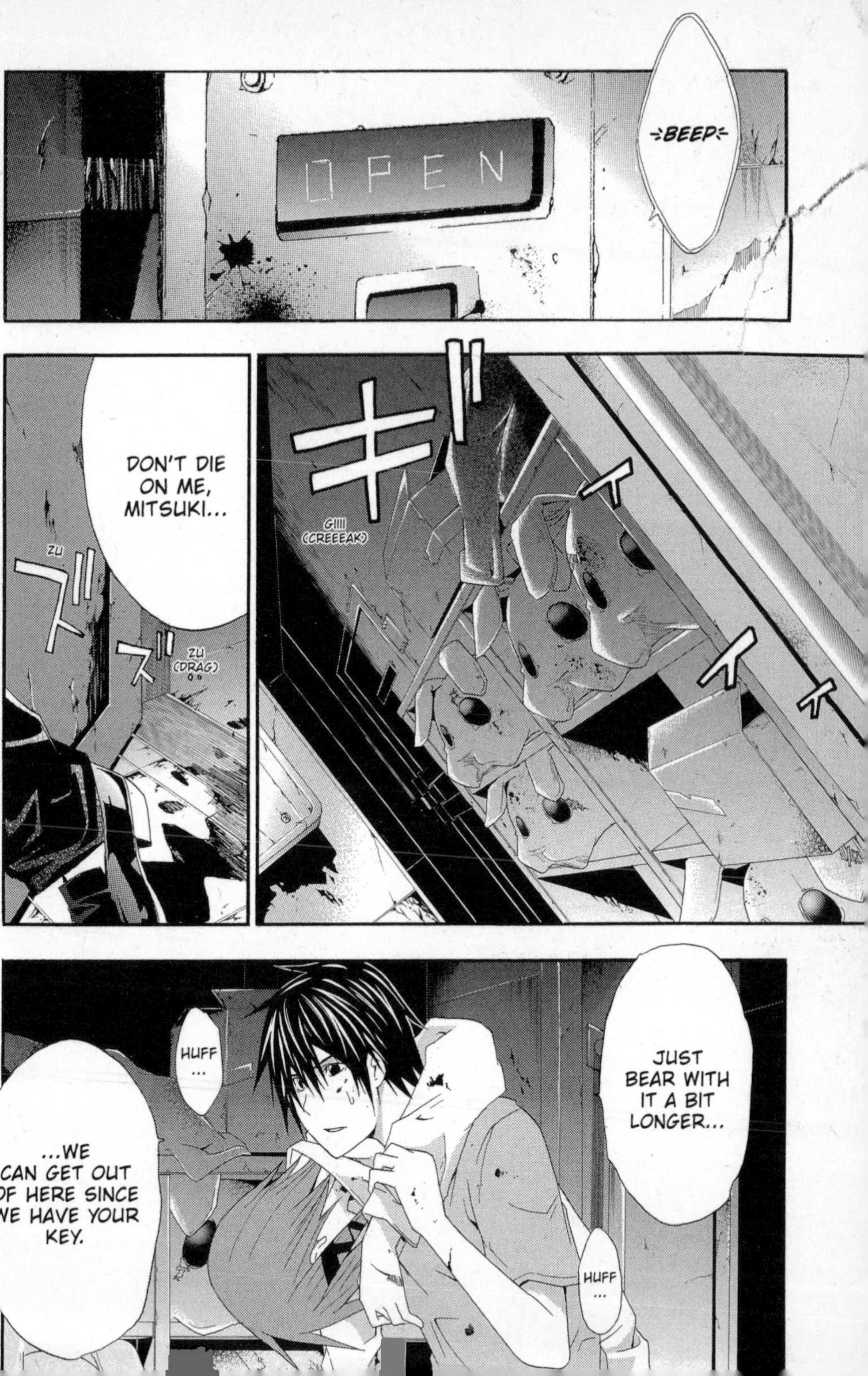
BEEP
OPEN
GIII (CREEEAK)
DON'T DIE ON ME, MITSUKI...
ZU ZU (DRAG)
JUST BEAR WITH IT A BIT LONGER...
HUFF...
HUFF...
...WE CAN GET OUT OF HERE SINCE WE HAVE YOUR KEY.

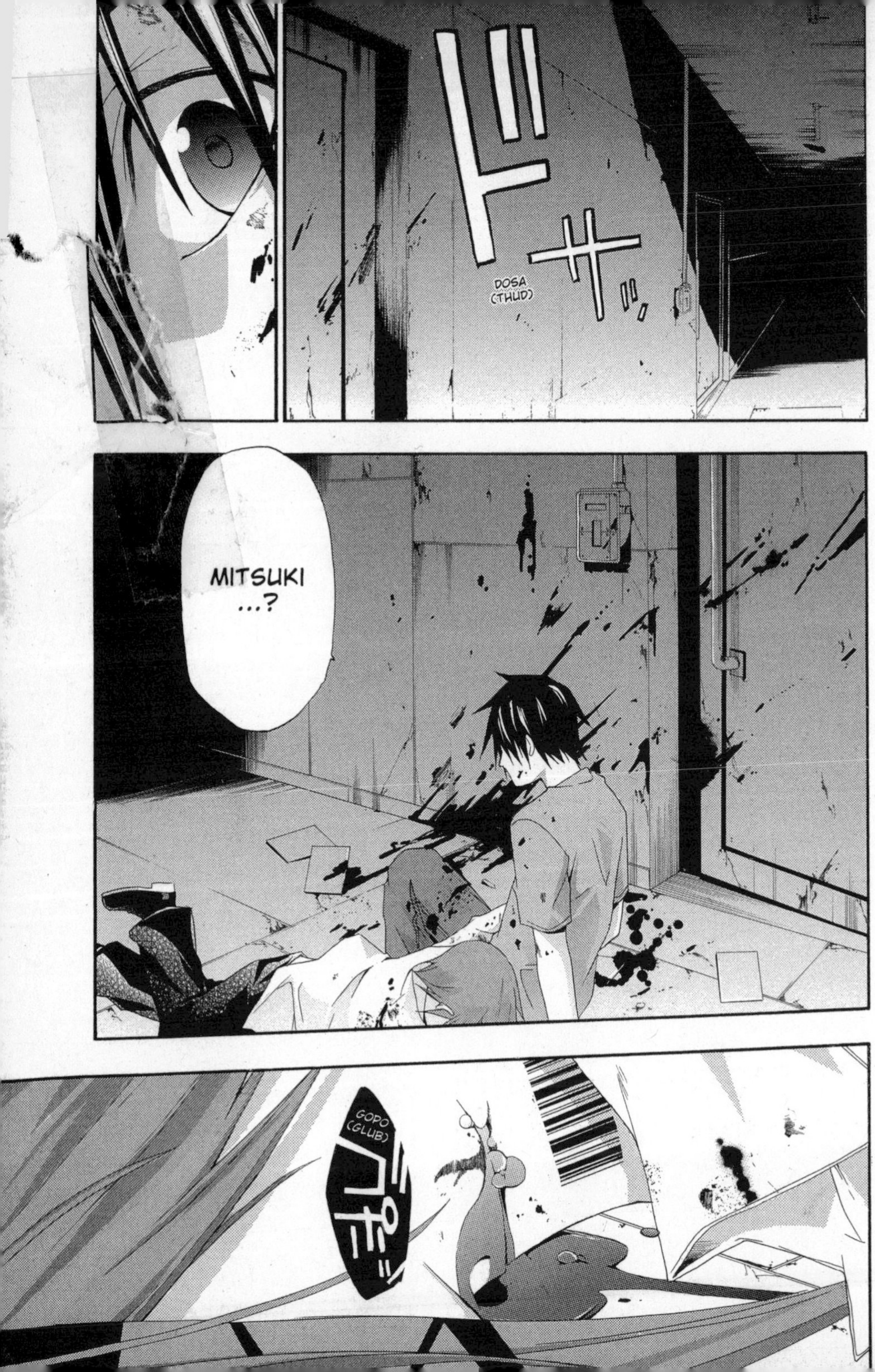
ドサッ
DOSA (THUD)
MITSUKI ...?
GOPO (GLUB)

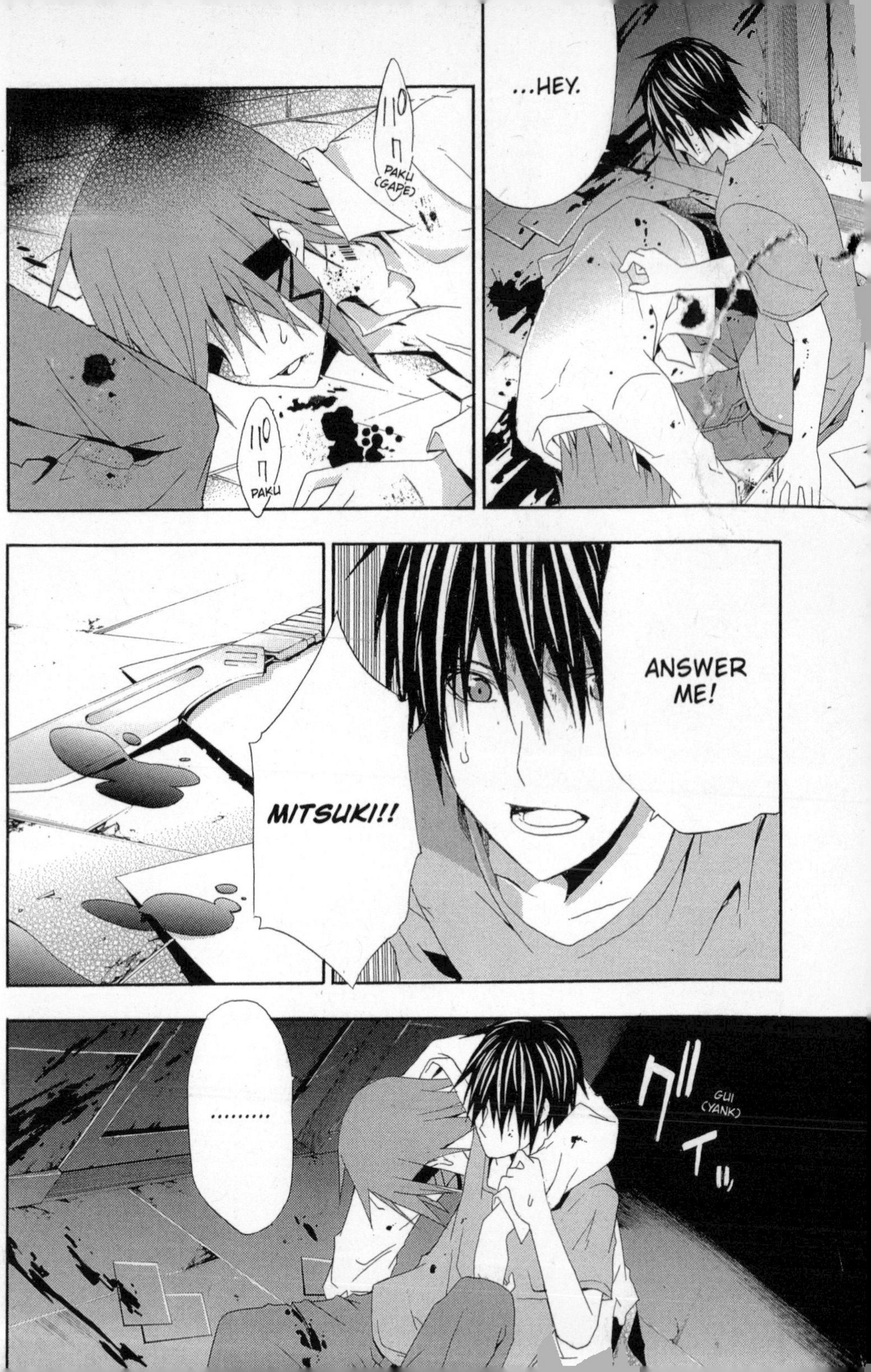
...HEY.
パク
PAKU (GAPE)
パク
PAKU
ANSWER ME!
MITSUKI!!
グイッ
GUI (YANK)
....

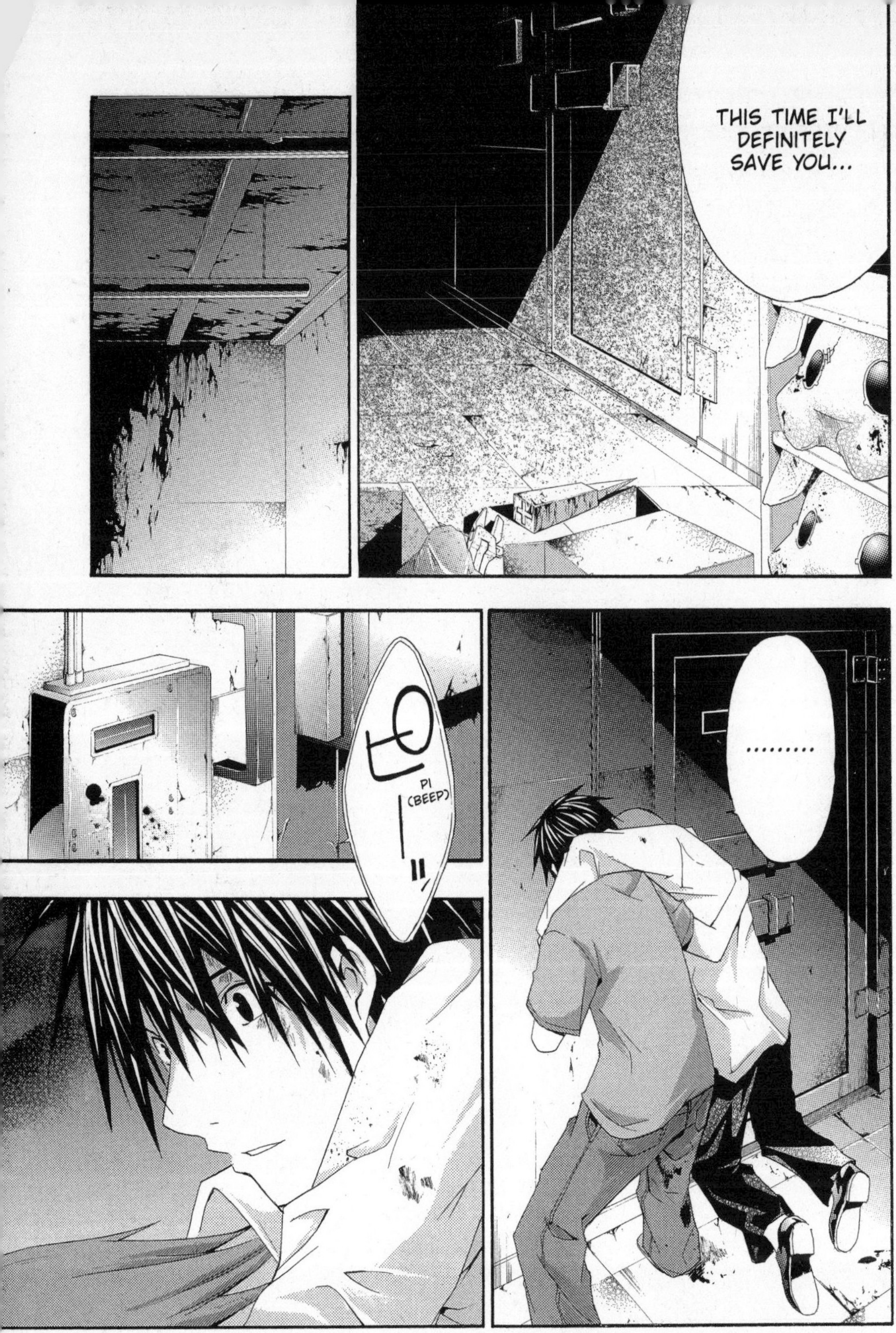
THIS TIME I'LL DEFINITELY SAVE YOU...
....
ピーッ
PI (BEEP)

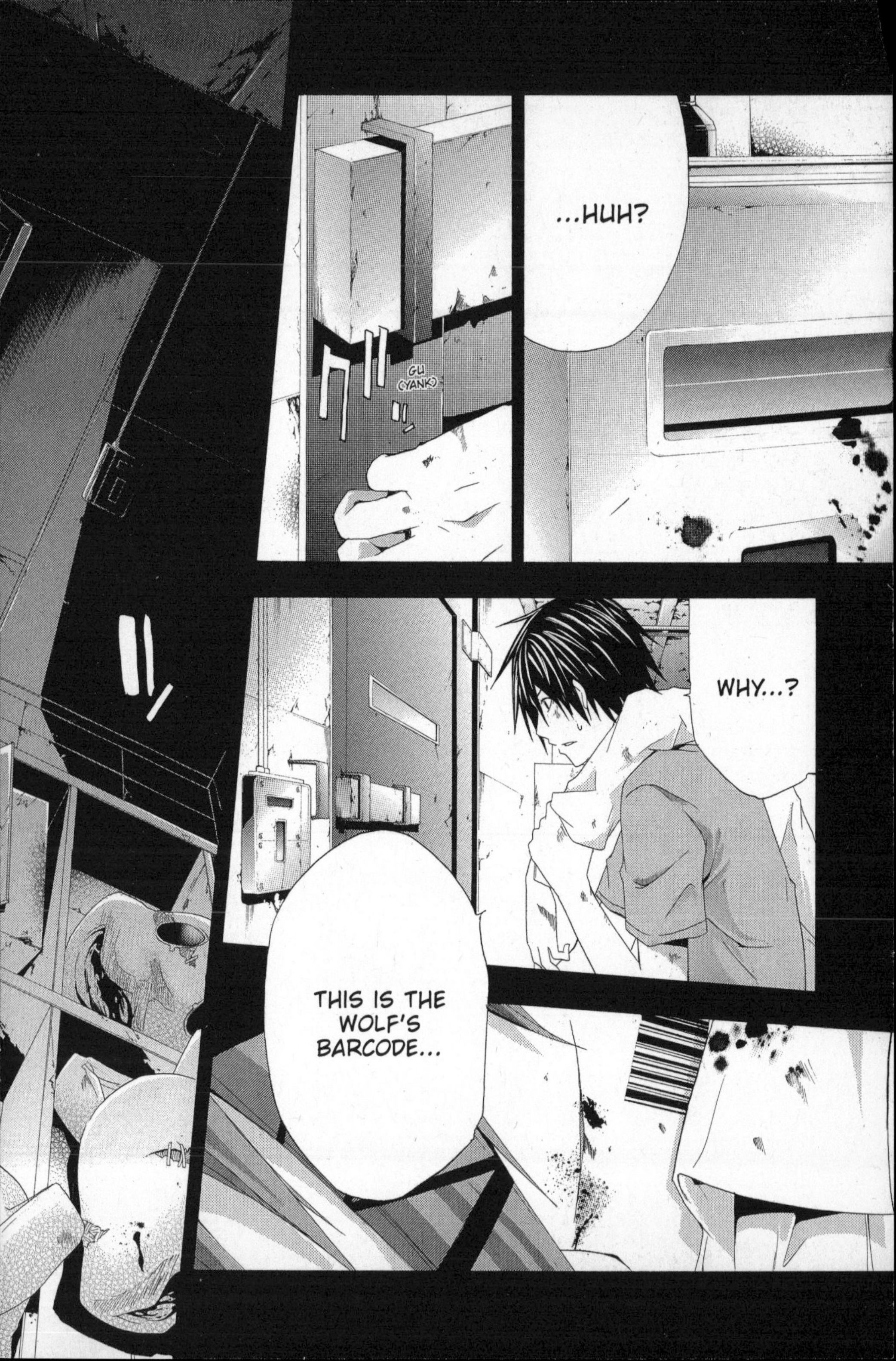
...HUH?
GU (YANK)
WHY...?
THIS IS THE WOLF'S BARCODE...

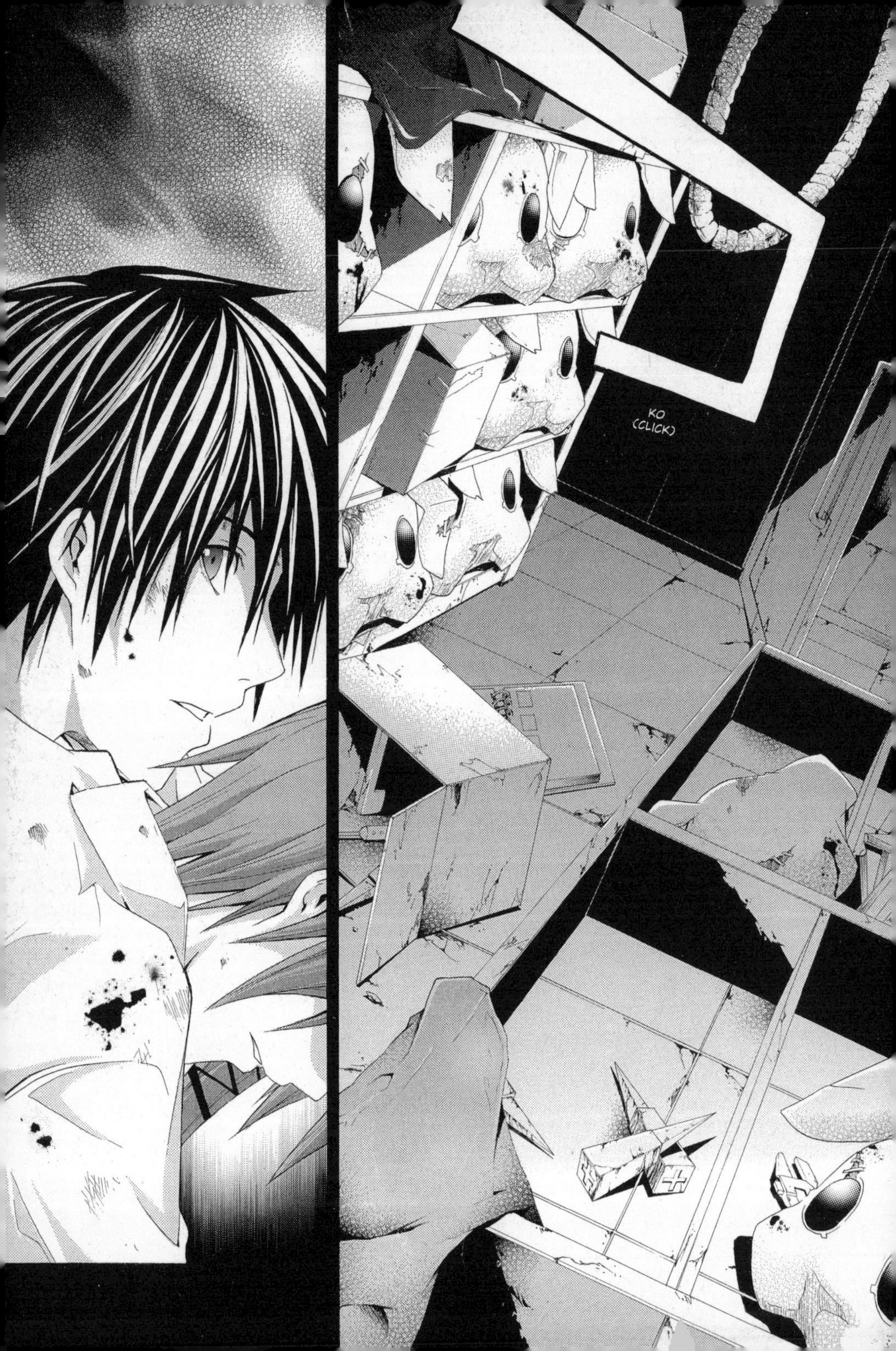
KO
(CLICK)

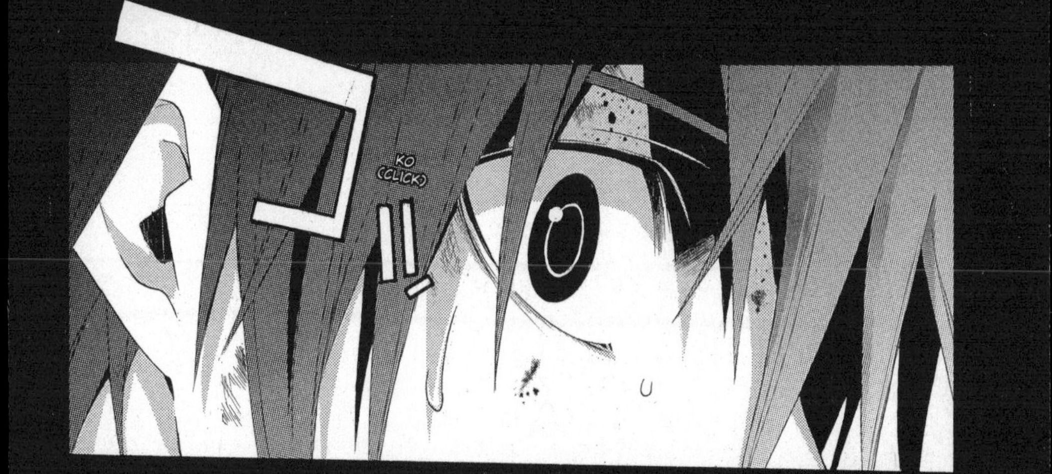
KO
(CLICK)
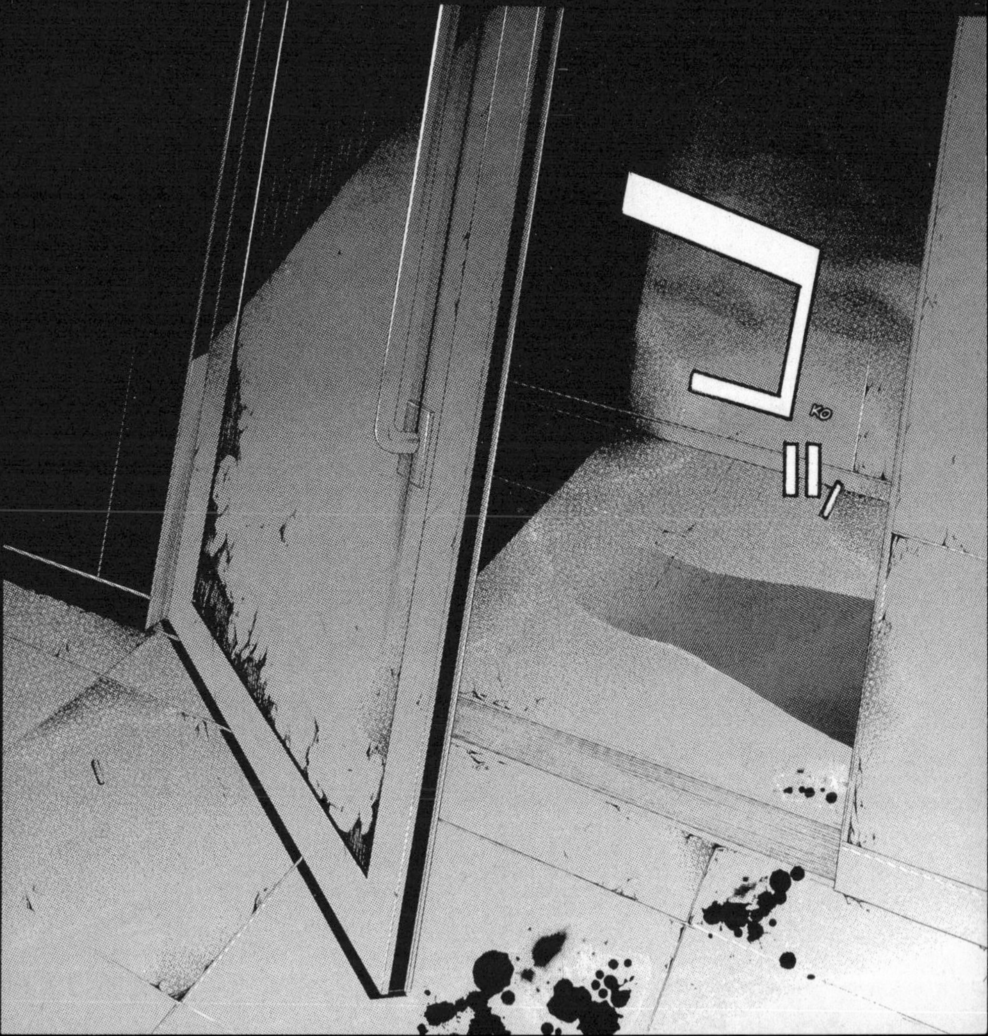
KO

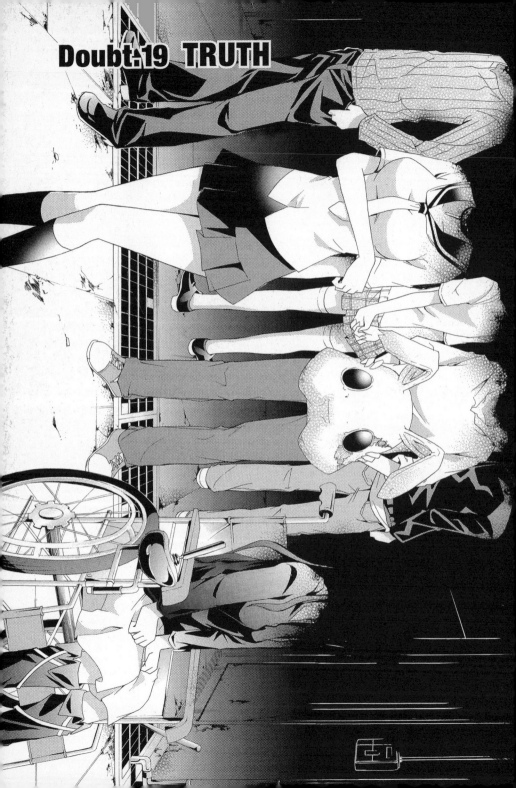

Doubt:19 TRUTH

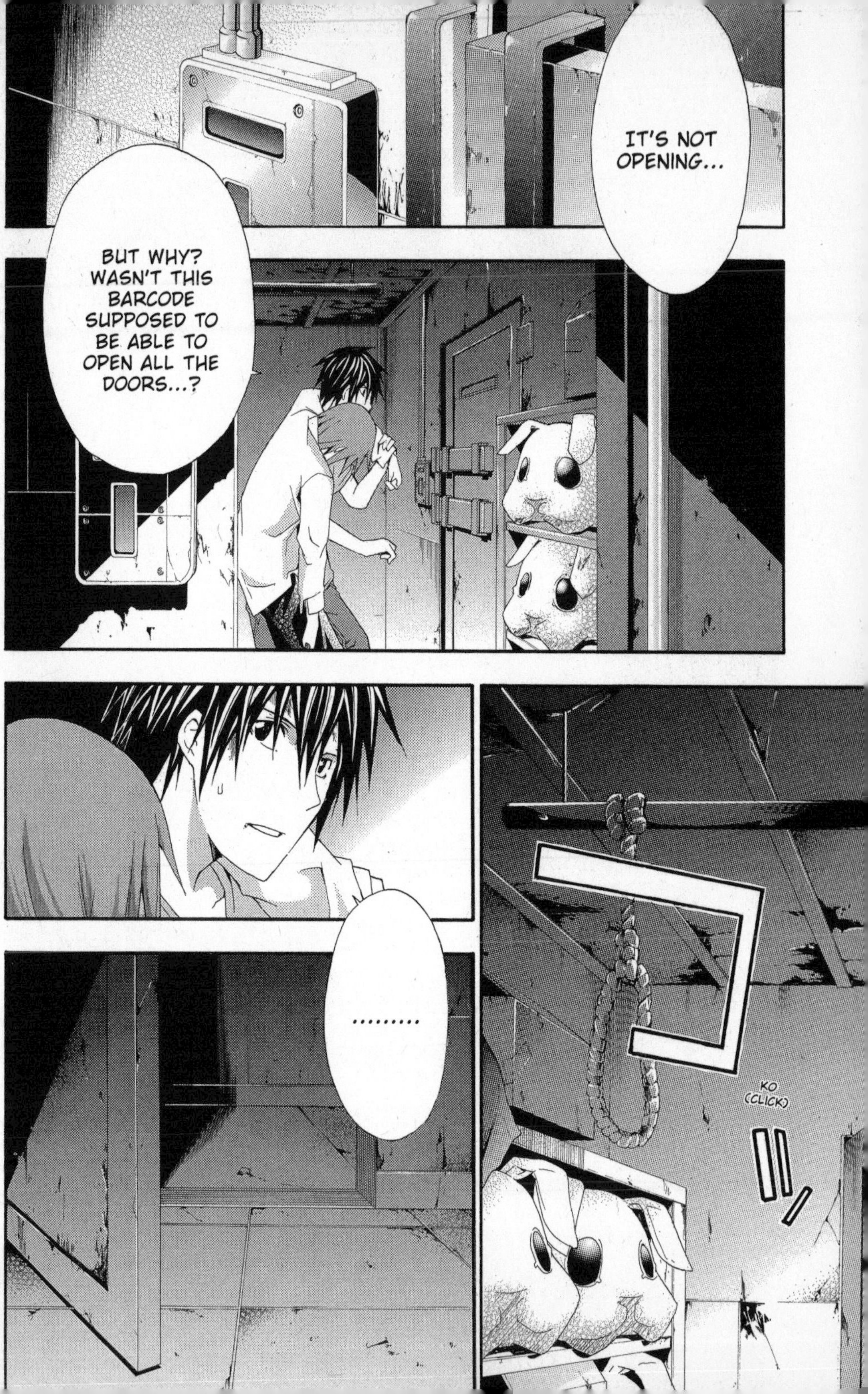
IT'S NOT OPENING...
BUT WHY? WASN'T THIS BARCODE SUPPOSED TO BE ABLE TO OPEN ALL THE DOORS...?
KO (CLICK)
....

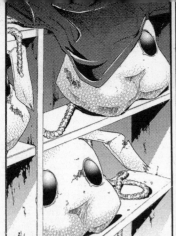

WHO'S THERE ...?

KO

....

HAJIME?

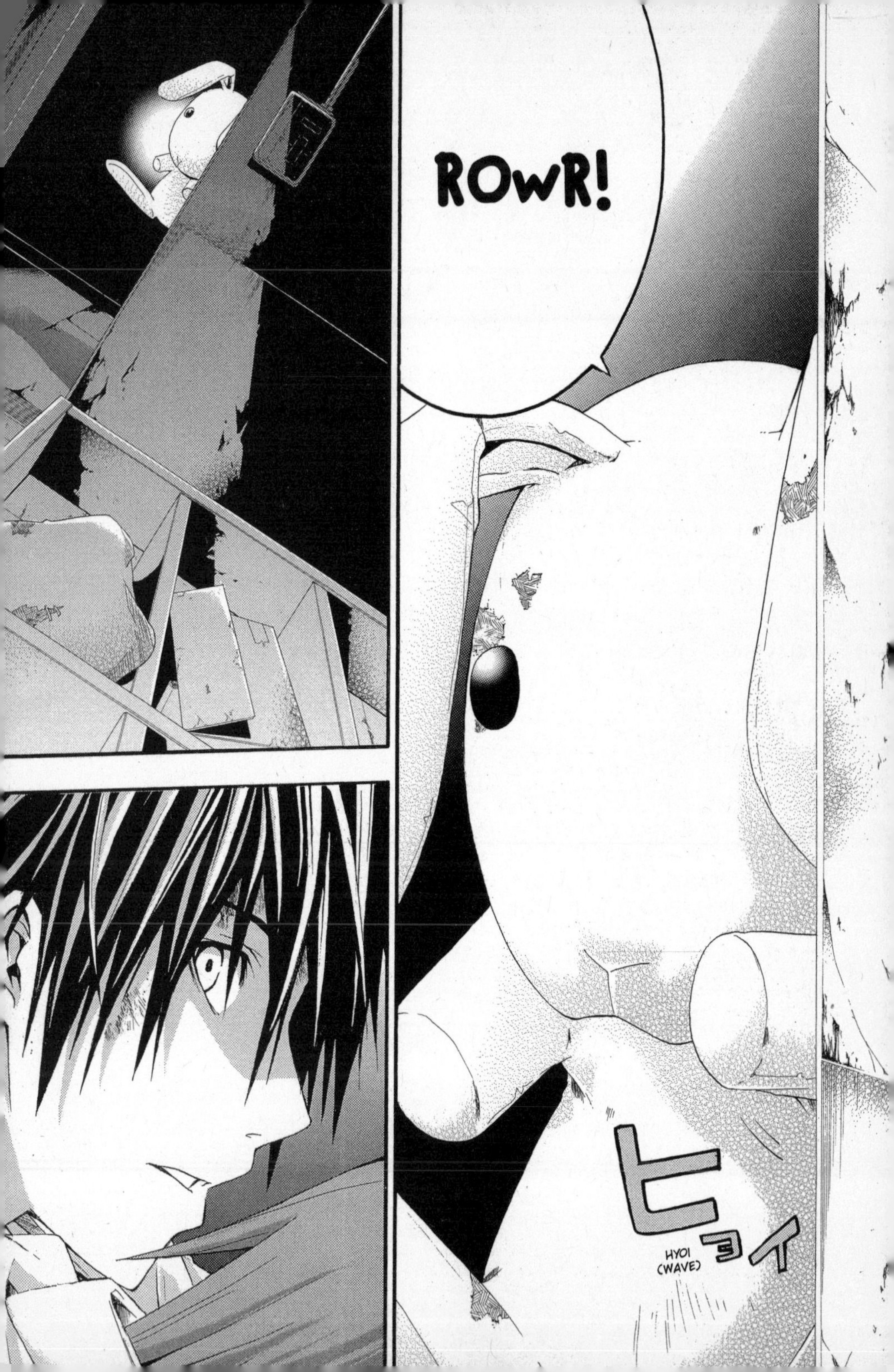
ROWR!
ヒョイ
HYOI (WAVE)

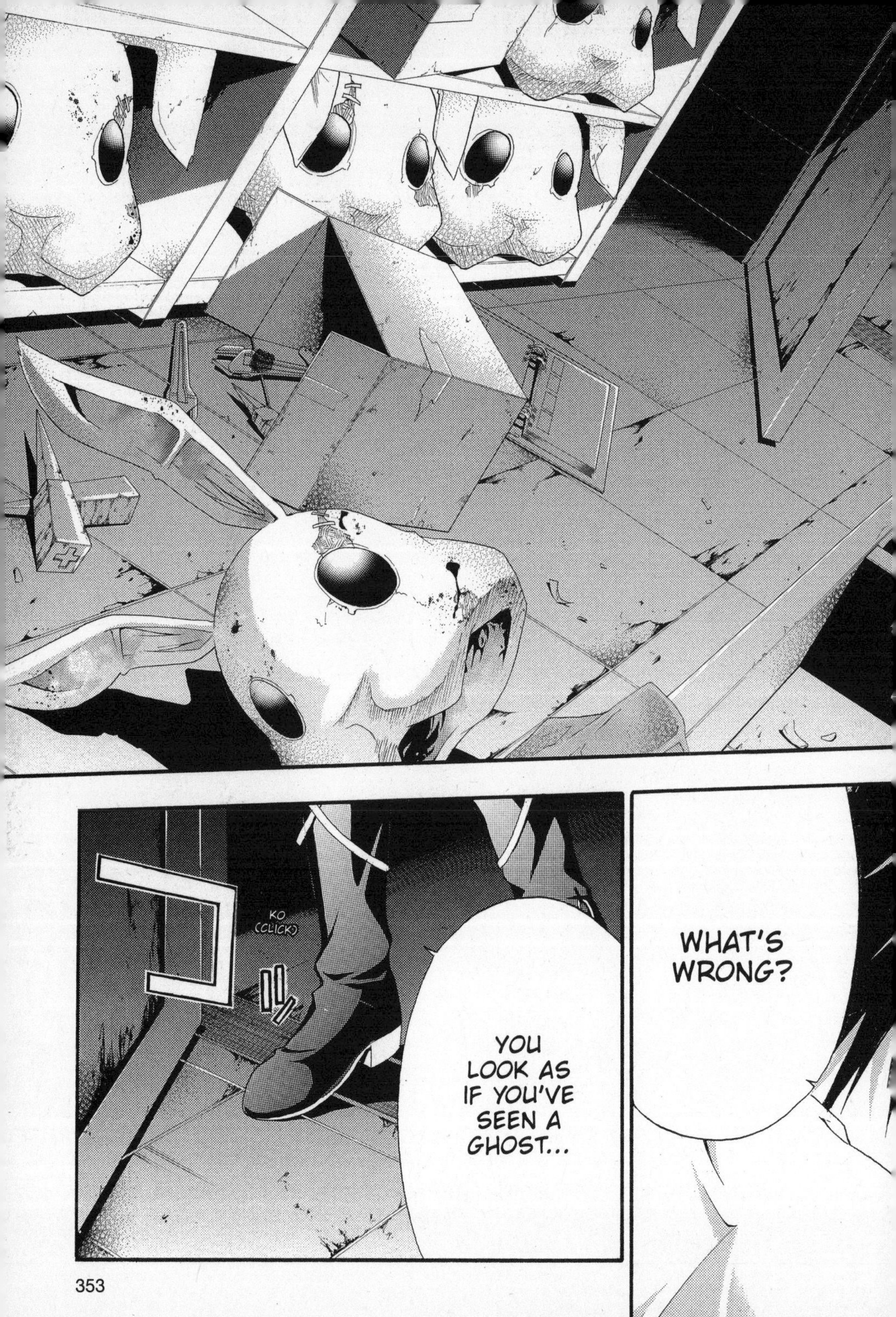
WHAT'S WRONG?
KO (CLICK)
YOU LOOK AS IF YOU'VE SEEN A GHOST...

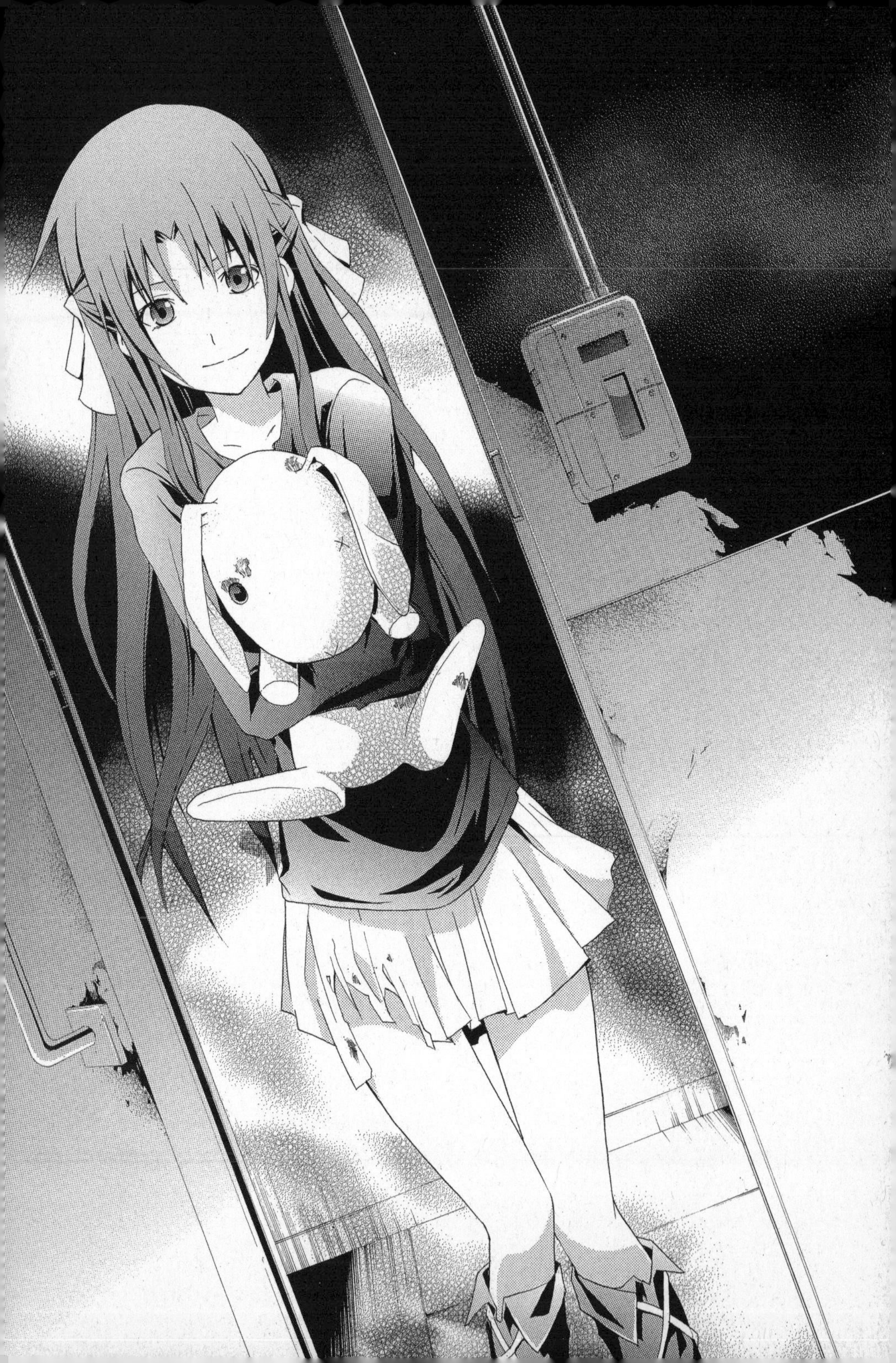

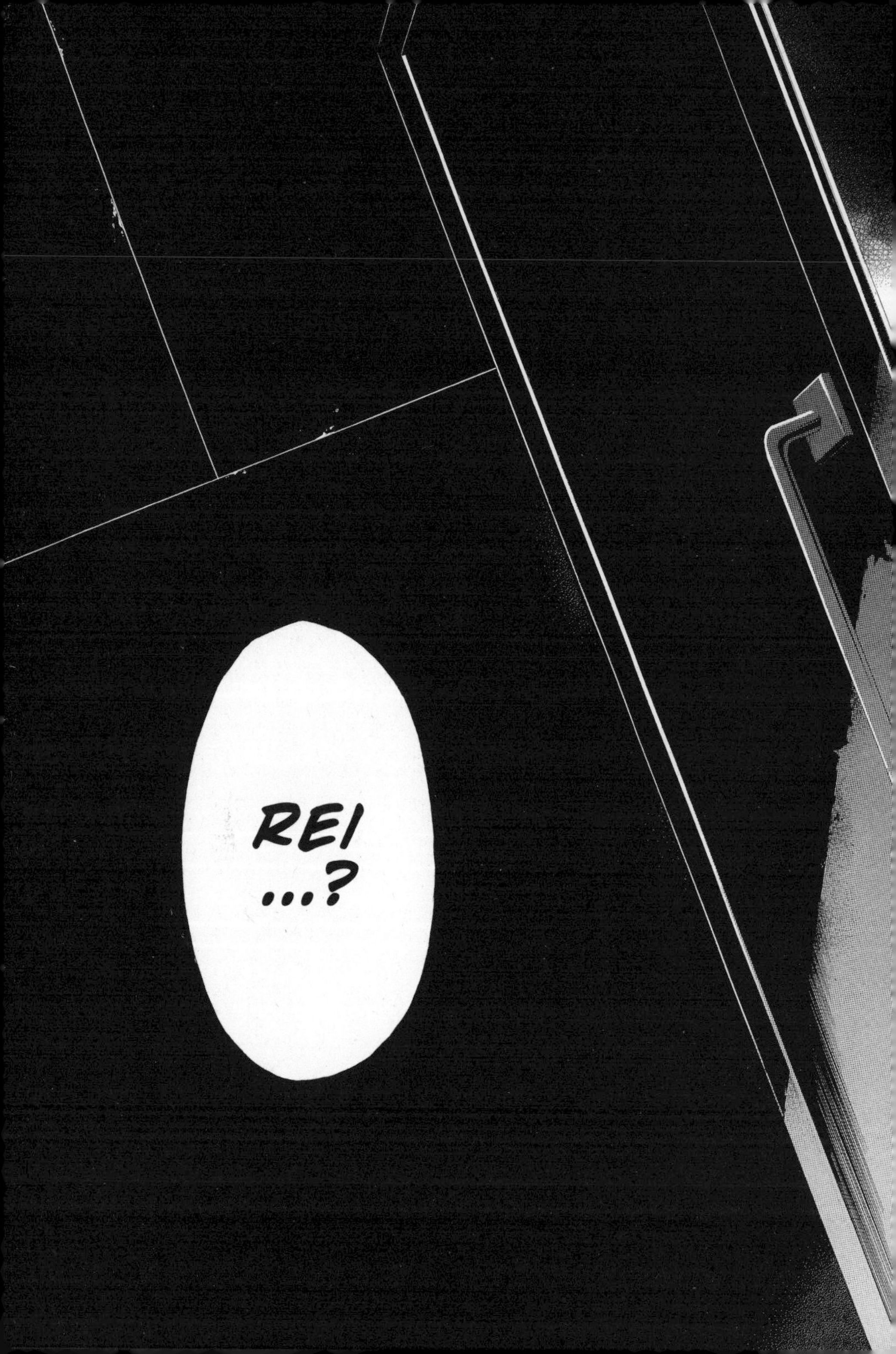
REI ...?

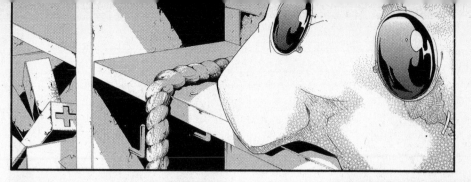

THIS HAS TO BE A LIE...

WHAT'S A LIE?

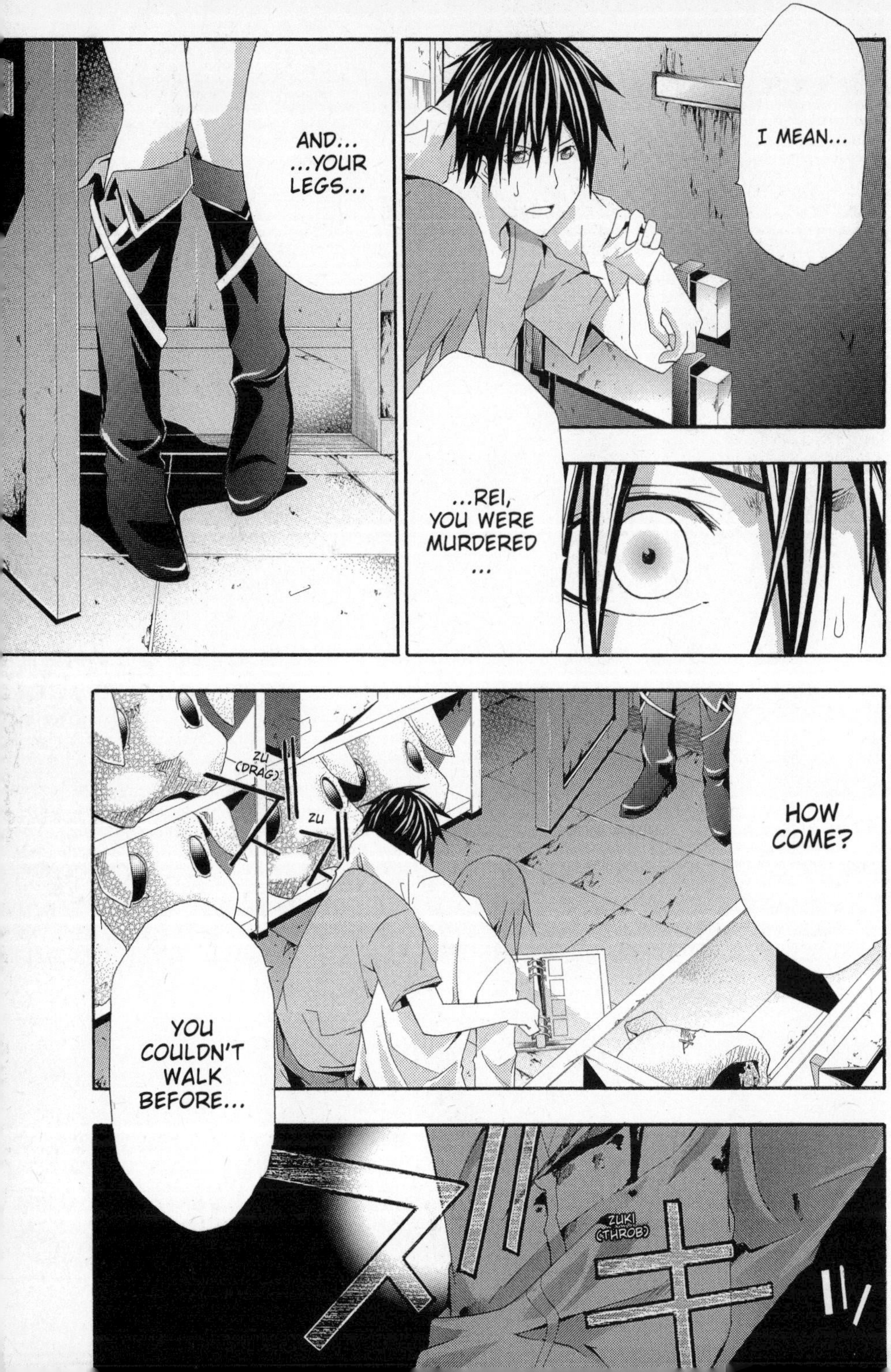
I MEAN...
...REI, YOU WERE MURDERED ...
AND... ...YOUR LEGS...
HOW COME?
ZU (DRAG)
ZU
YOU COULDN'T WALK BEFORE...
ZUKI (THROB)

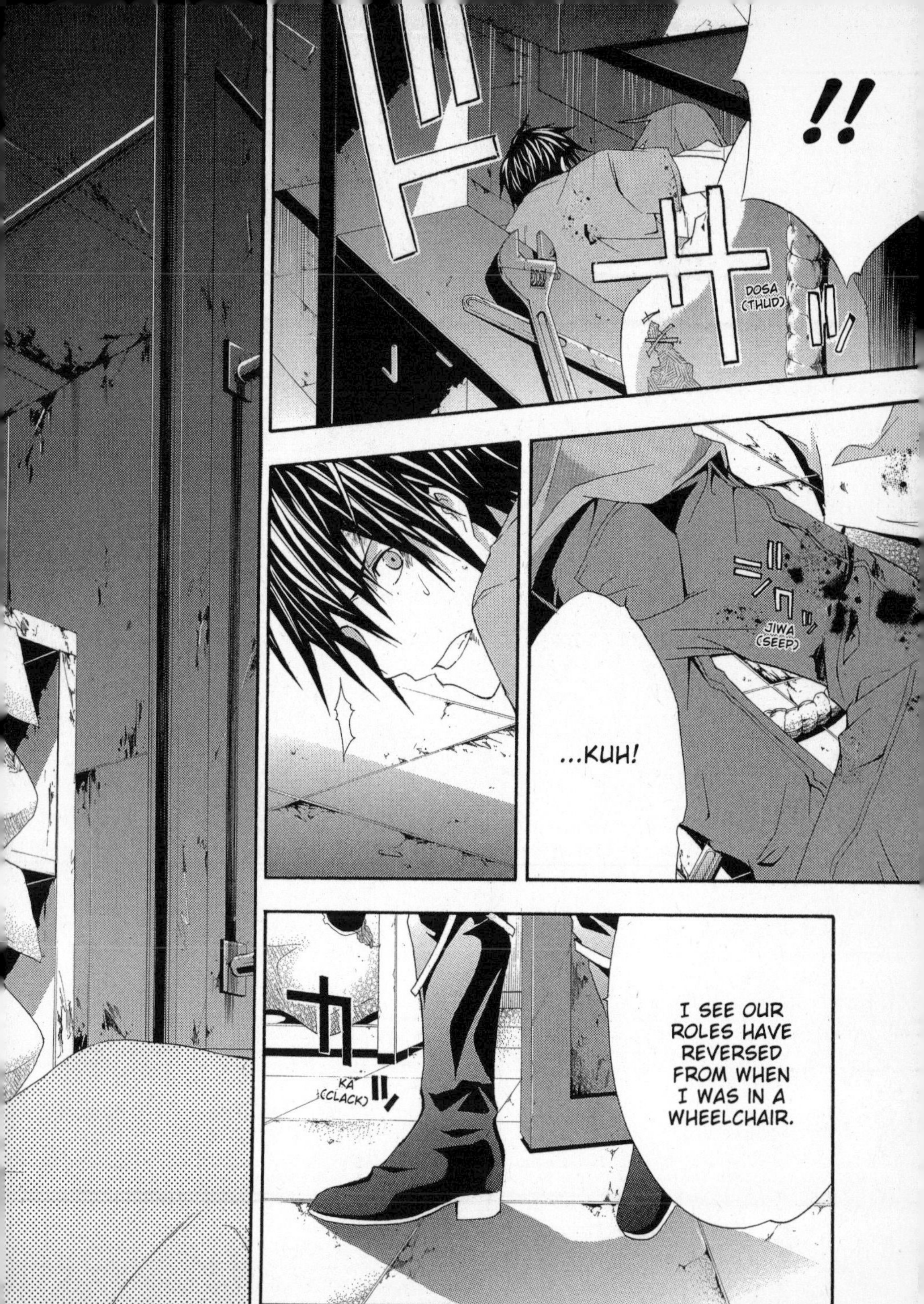
!!
DOSA (THUD)
JIWA (SEEP)
...KUH!
KA (CLACK)
I SEE OUR ROLES HAVE REVERSED FROM WHEN I WAS IN A WHEELCHAIR.

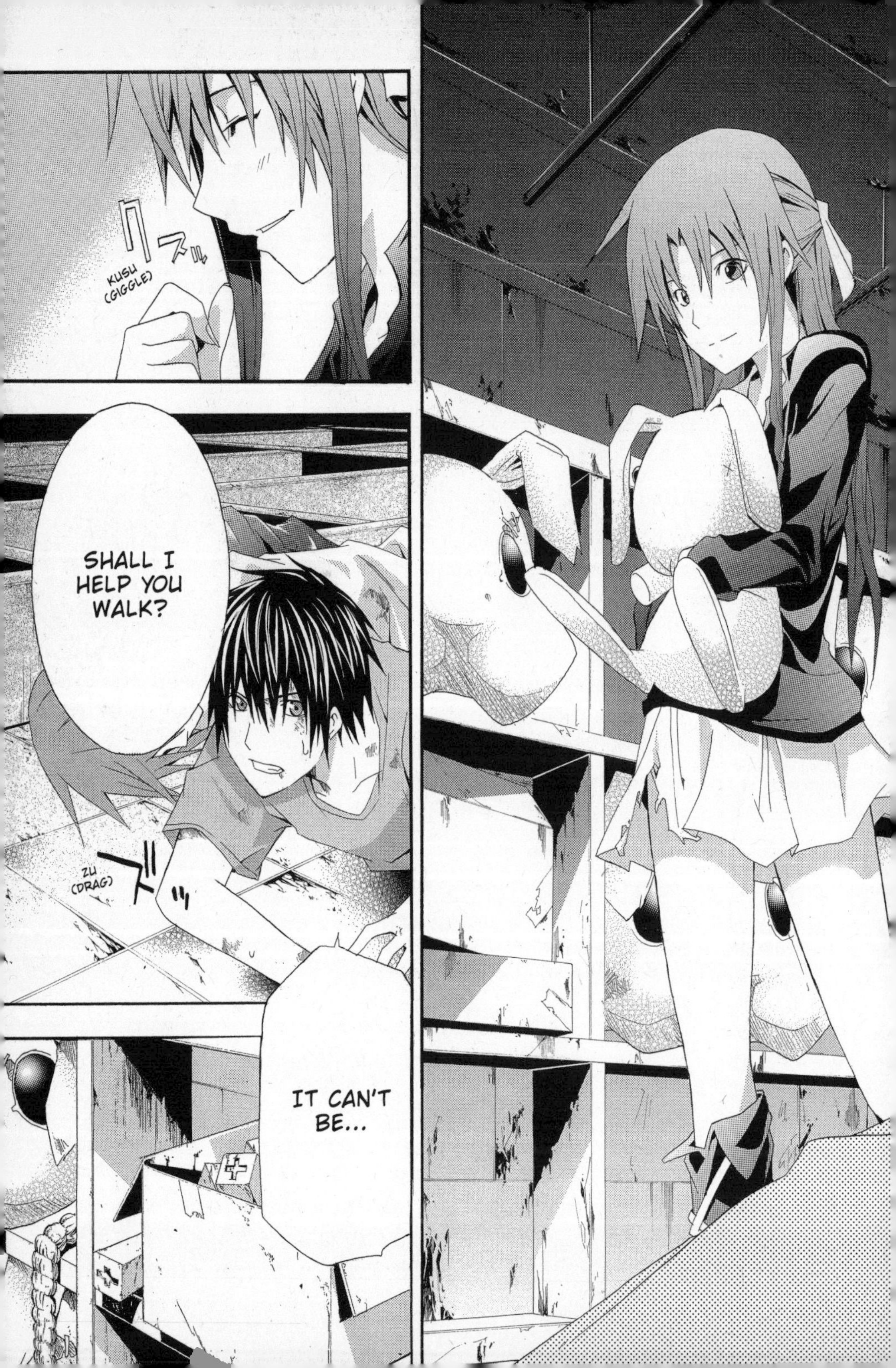

クスッ
KUSU (GIGGLE)
SHALL I HELP YOU WALK?
ズッ
ZU (DRAG)
IT CAN'T BE...

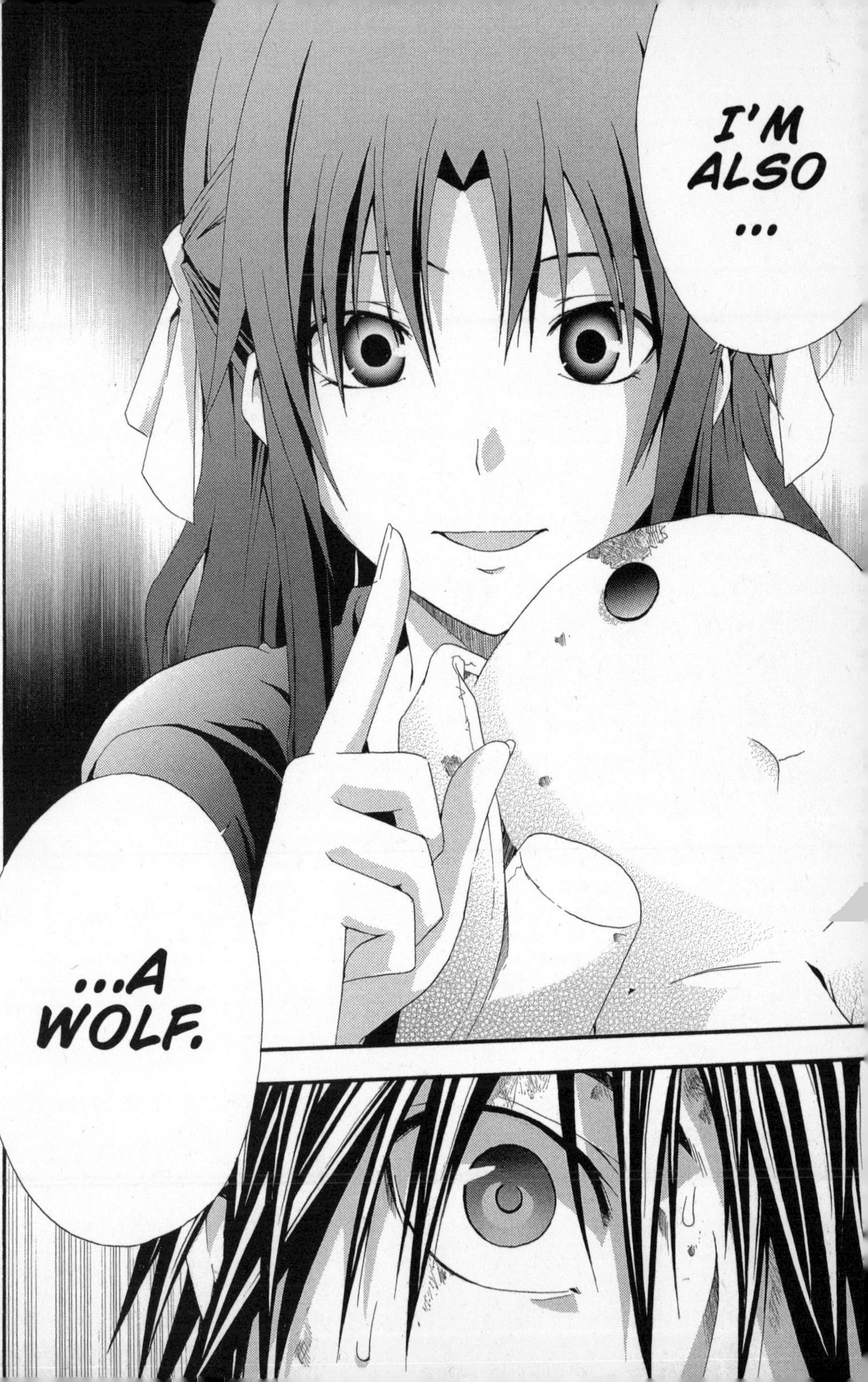
I'M ALSO ...
...A WOLF.

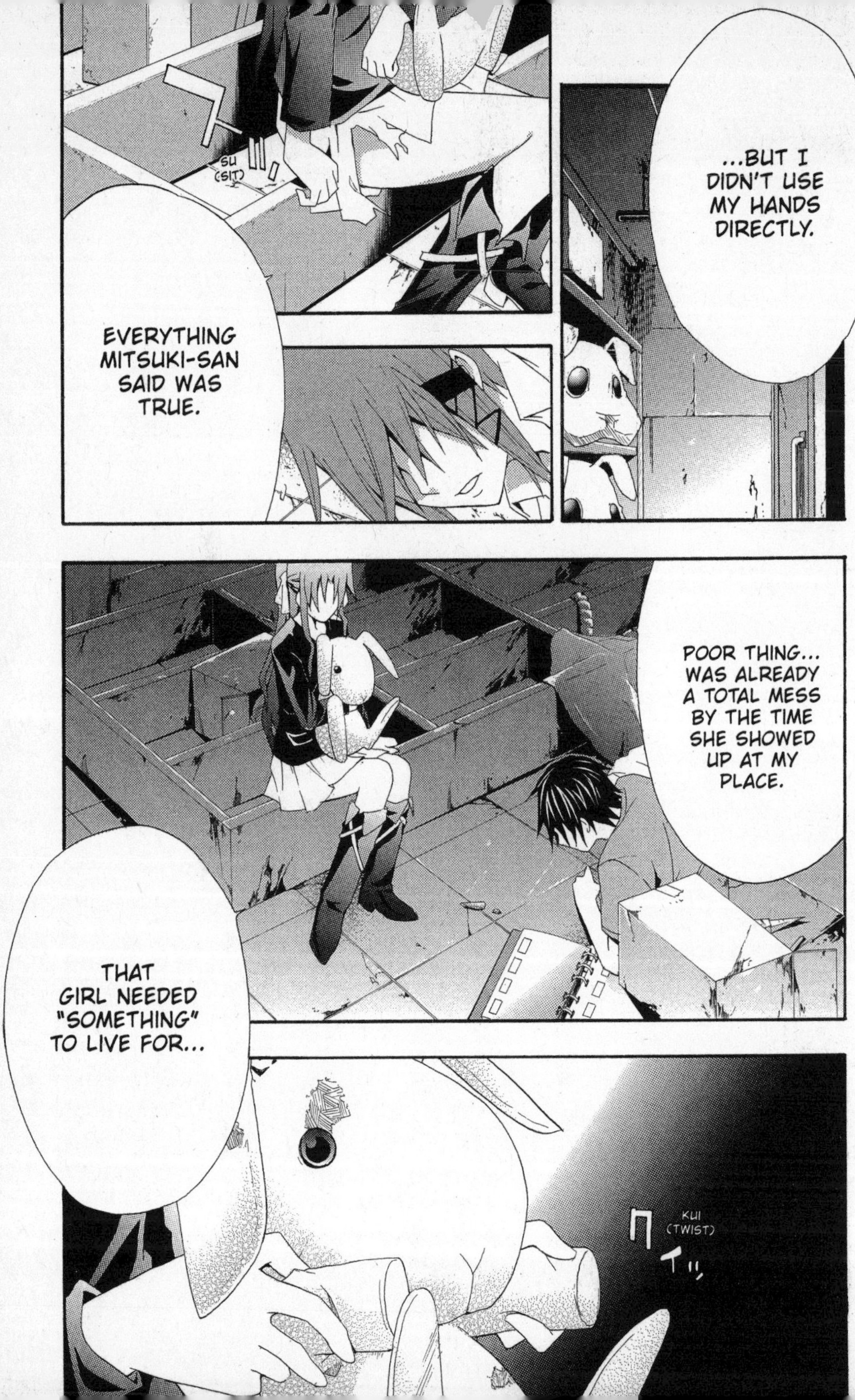
...BUT I DIDN'T USE MY HANDS DIRECTLY.
SU (SIT)
EVERYTHING MITSUKI-SAN SAID WAS TRUE.
POOR THING... WAS ALREADY A TOTAL MESS BY THE TIME SHE SHOWED UP AT MY PLACE.
THAT GIRL NEEDED "SOMETHING" TO LIVE FOR...
KUI (TWIST)

THE SENSE OF LOSS AND DESPAIR ONE FEELS...

...AFTER LOSING A LOVED ONE...

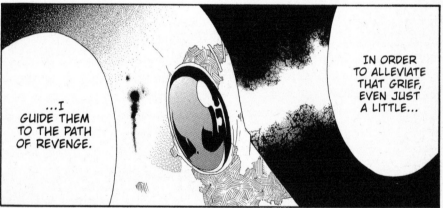

IN ORDER TO ALLEVIATE THAT GRIEF, EVEN JUST A LITTLE...

...I GUIDE THEM TO THE PATH OF REVENGE.

ALL I DO IS GIVE THEM A LITTLE PUSH...

YOU DON'T MEAN...

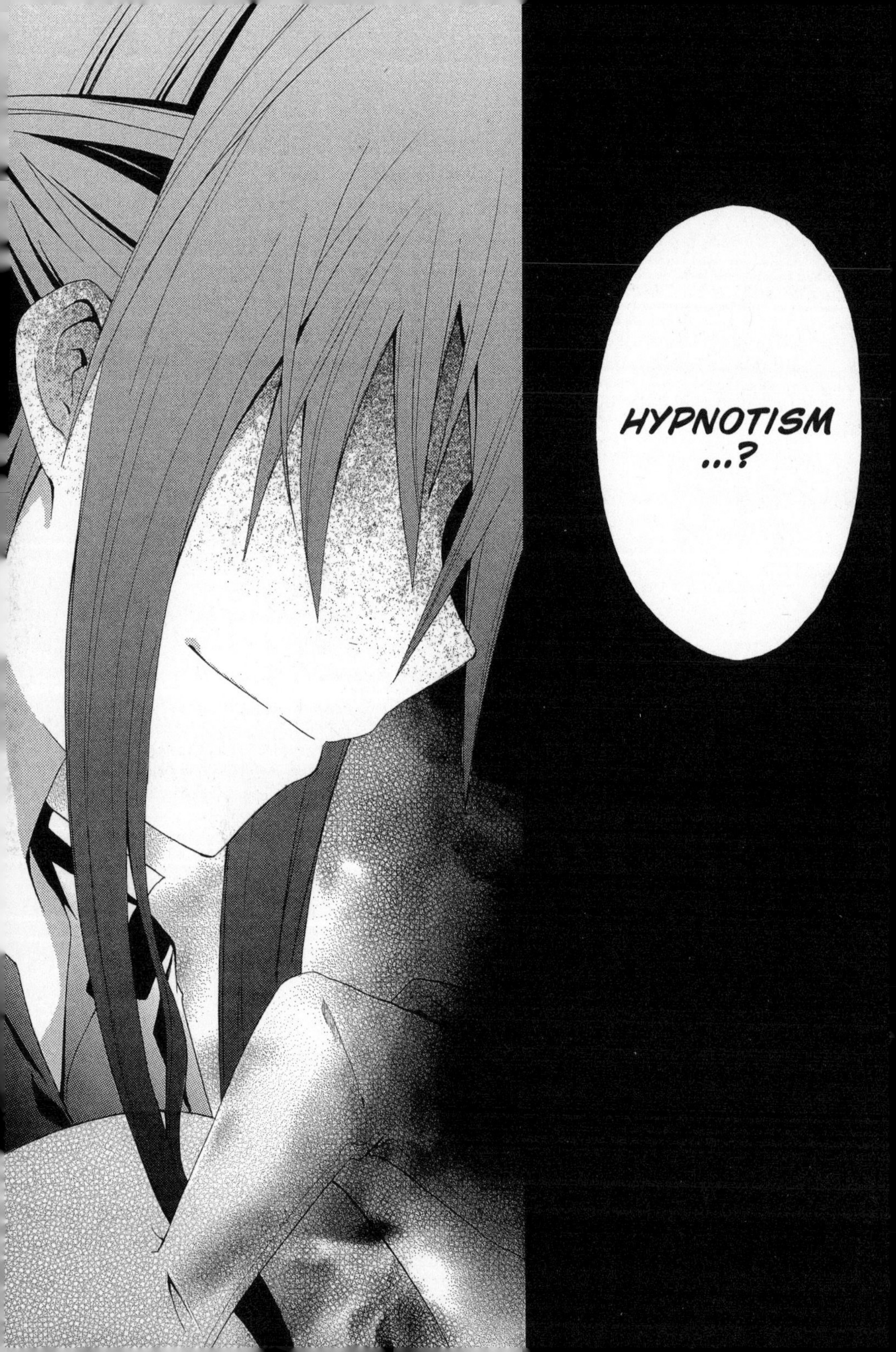
HYPNOTISM ...?

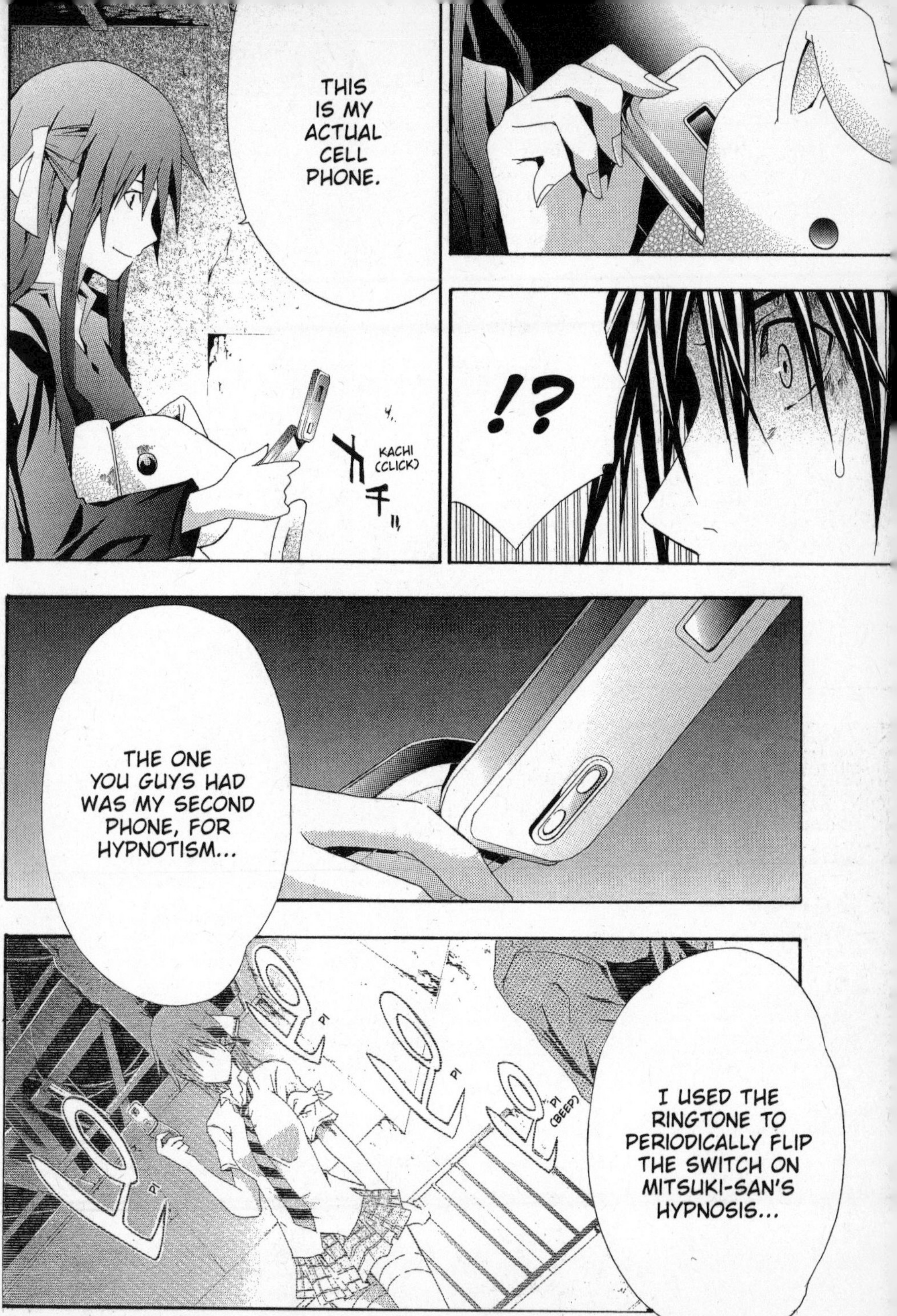
!?
THIS IS MY ACTUAL CELL PHONE.
KACHI (CLICK)
THE ONE YOU GUYS HAD WAS MY SECOND PHONE, FOR HYPNOTISM...
I USED THE RINGTONE TO PERIODICALLY FLIP THE SWITCH ON MITSUKI-SAN'S HYPNOSIS...
PI (BEEP)
PI
PI
PI

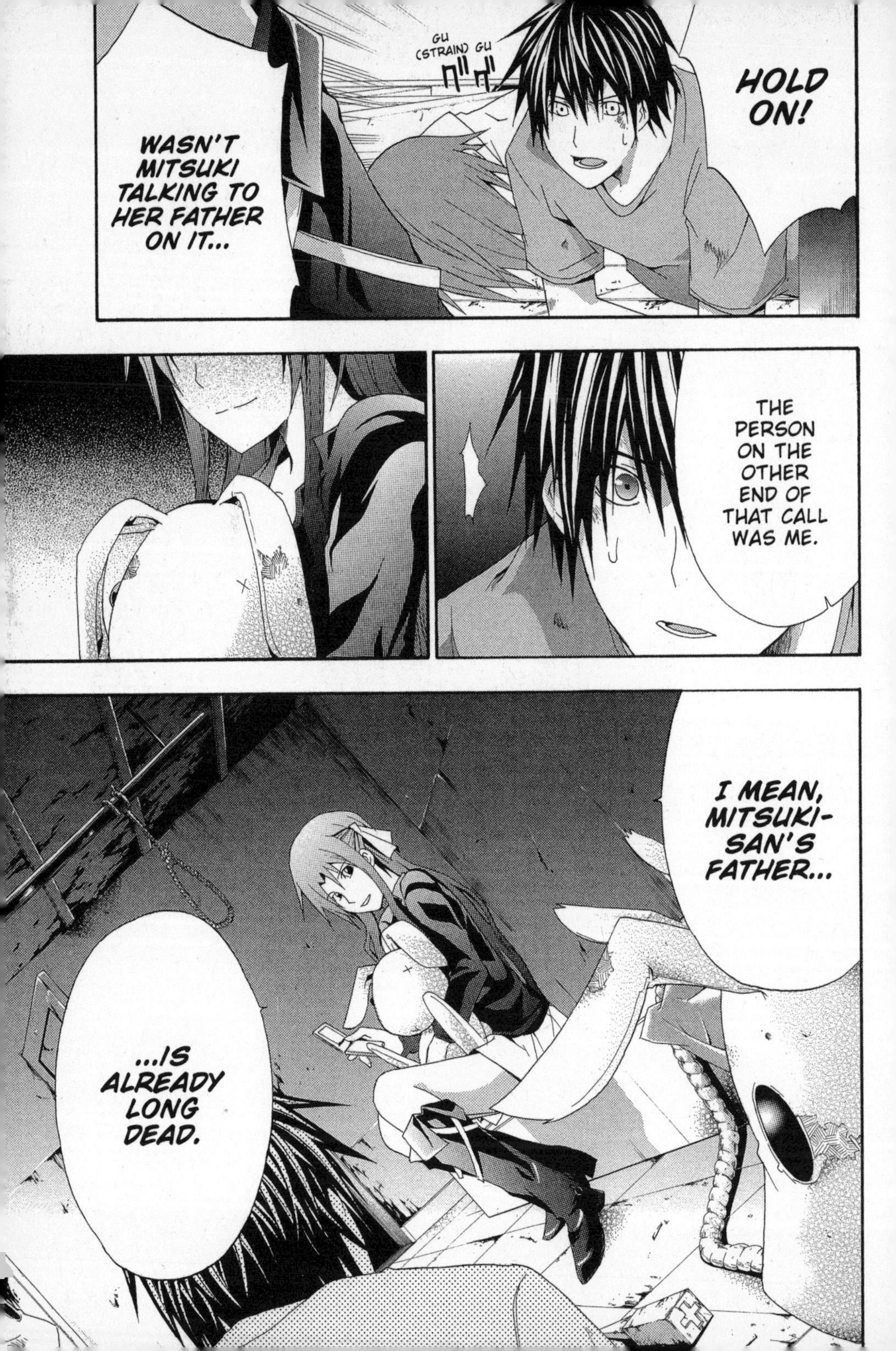
HOLD ON!
GU (STRAIN) GU
WASN'T MITSUKI TALKING TO HER FATHER ON IT...
THE PERSON ON THE OTHER END OF THAT CALL WAS ME.
I MEAN, MITSUKI-SAN'S FATHER...
...IS ALREADY LONG DEAD.

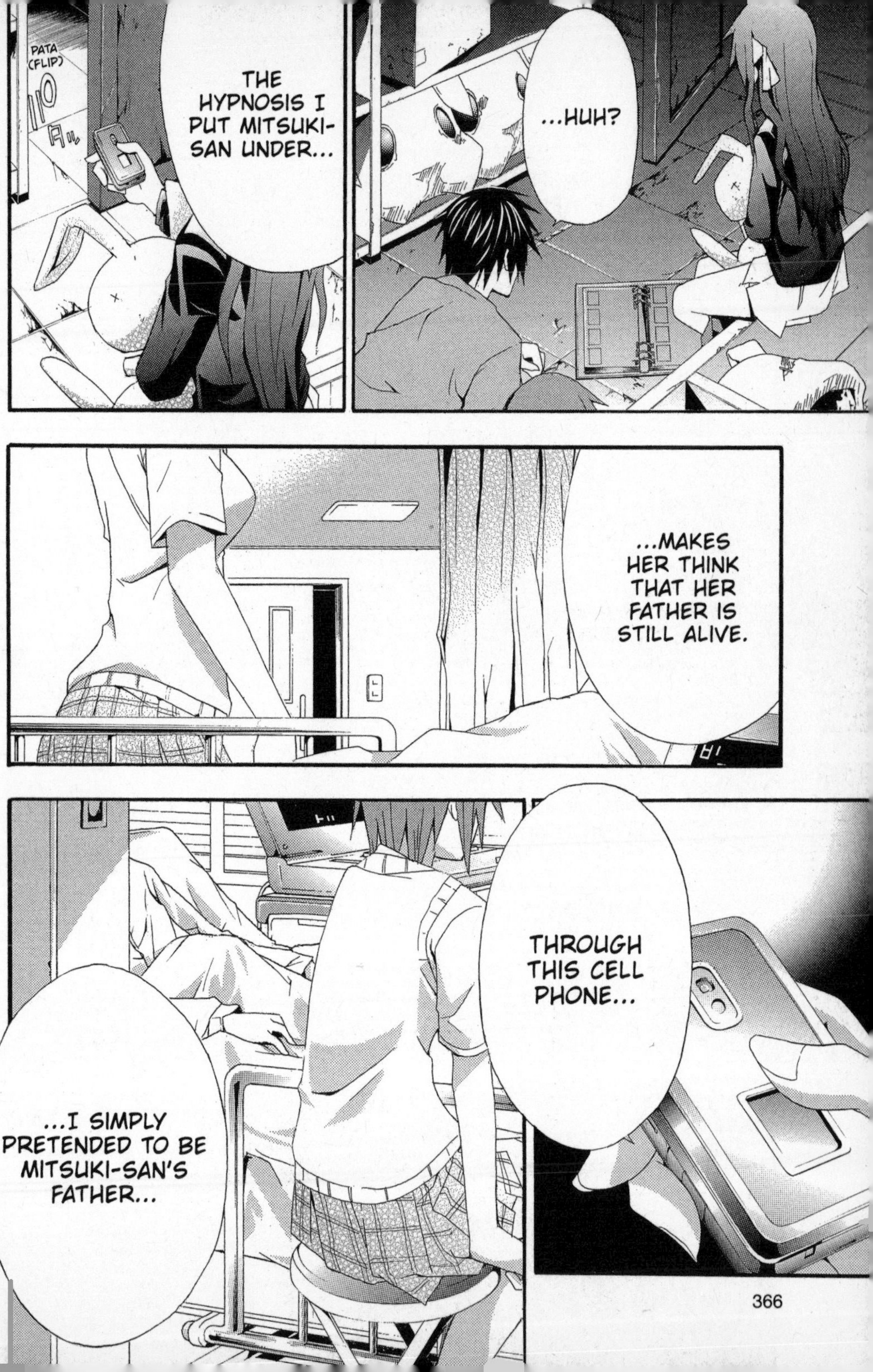
...HUH?
THE HYPNOSIS I PUT MITSUKI-SAN UNDER...
PATA (FLIP)
...MAKES HER THINK THAT HER FATHER IS STILL ALIVE.
THROUGH THIS CELL PHONE...
...I SIMPLY PRETENDED TO BE MITSUKI-SAN'S FATHER...

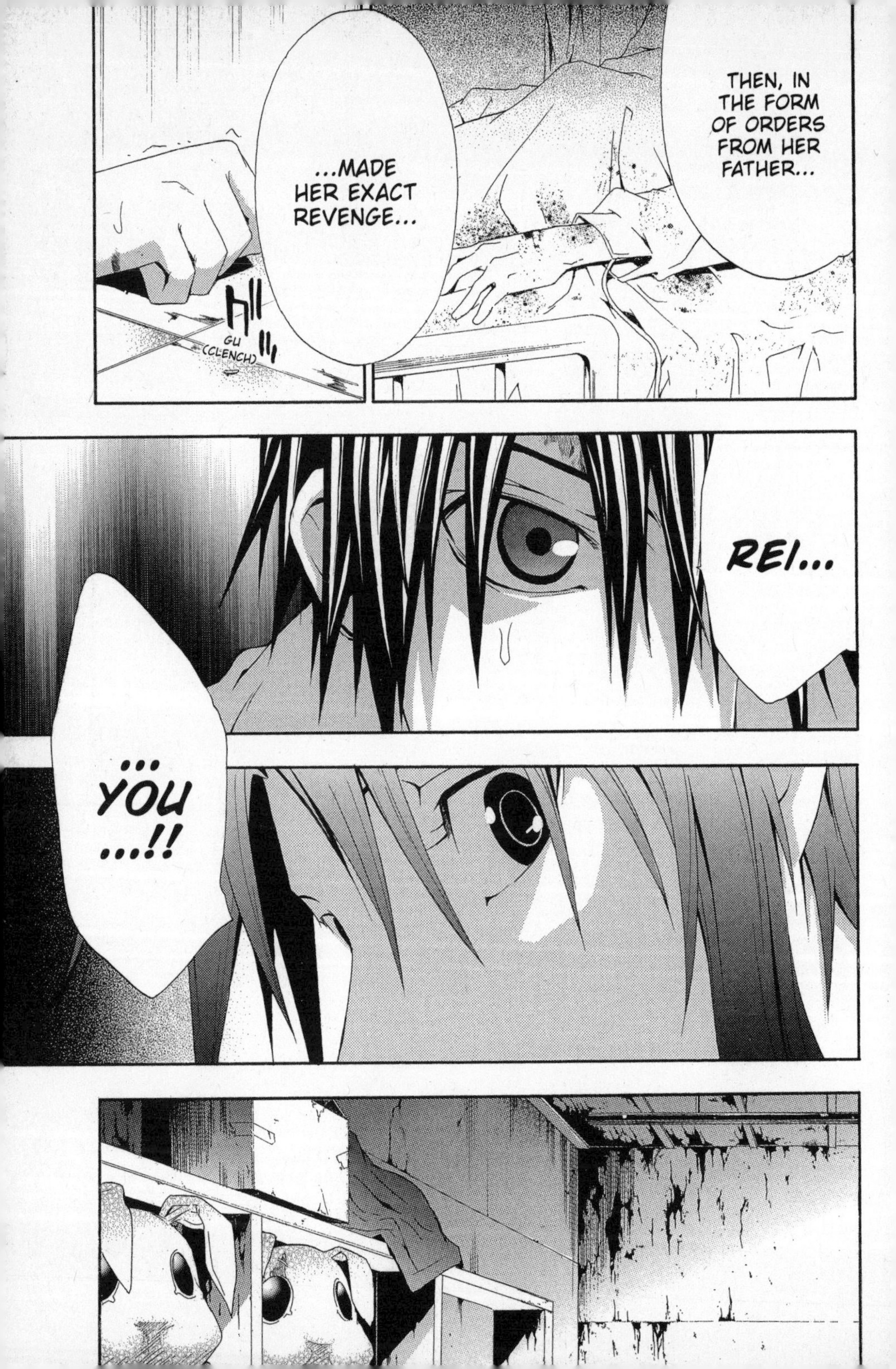
THEN, IN THE FORM OF ORDERS FROM HER FATHER...
...MADE HER EXACT REVENGE...
GU (CLENCH)
REI...
...YOU...!!

WHY WOULD YOU DO SOMETHING LIKE THIS!?

WHY ...?

"EXPOSE THE TRUTH BEHIND HYPNO-GIRL."

POFU
(FWUMP)

....

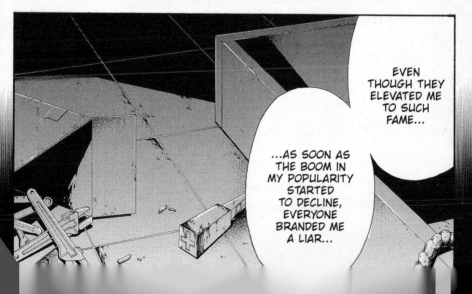

EVEN THOUGH THEY ELEVATED ME TO SUCH FAME...

...AS SOON AS THE BOOM IN MY POPULARITY STARTED TO DECLINE, EVERYONE BRANDED ME A LIAR...

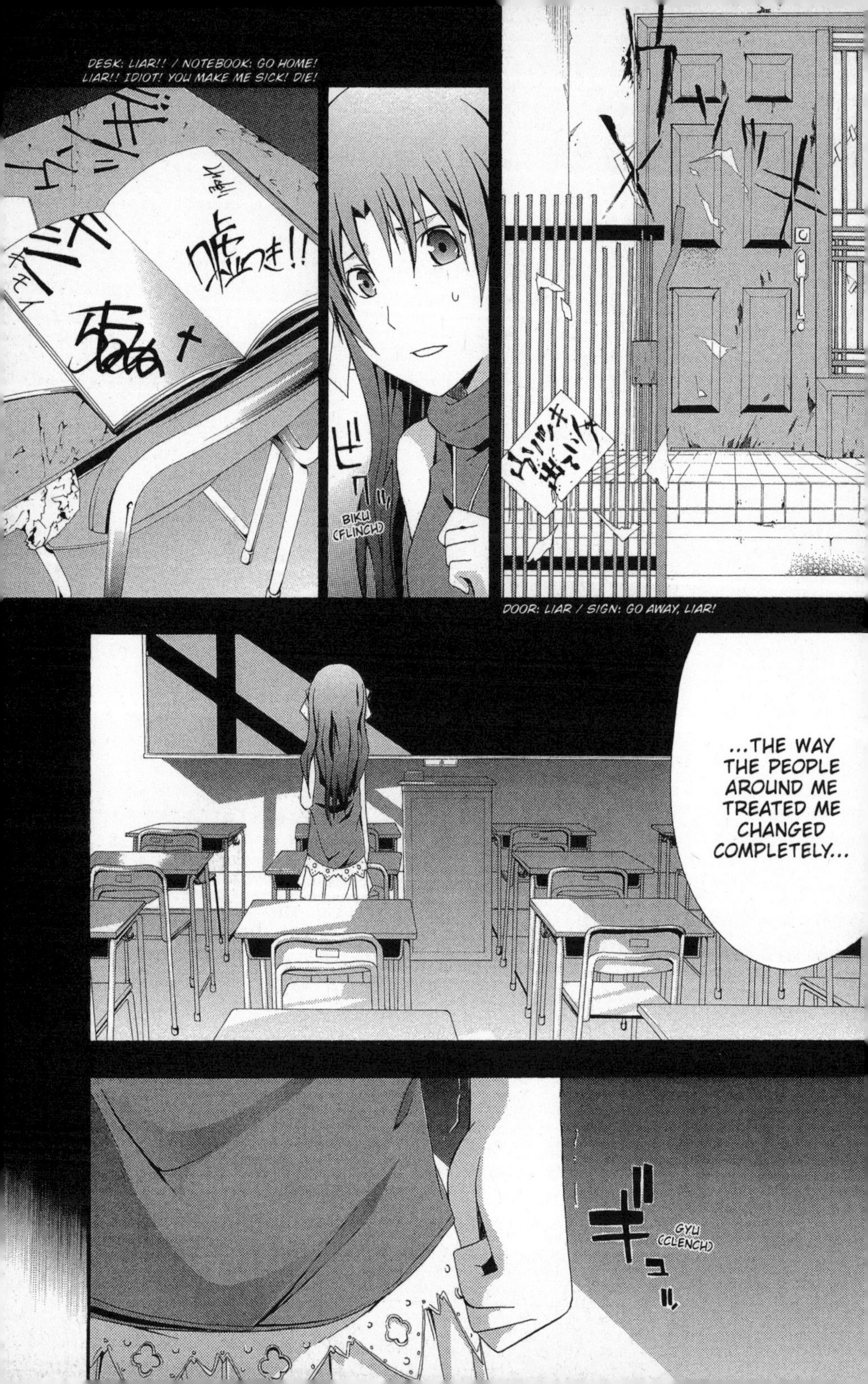
DOOR: LIAR / SIGN: GO AWAY, LIAR!
BIKU (FLINCH)
DESK: LIAR!! / NOTEBOOK: GO HOME! LIAR!! IDIOT! YOU MAKE ME SICK! DIE!
嘘つき!!
...THE WAY THE PEOPLE AROUND ME TREATED ME CHANGED COMPLETELY...
GYU (CLENCH)

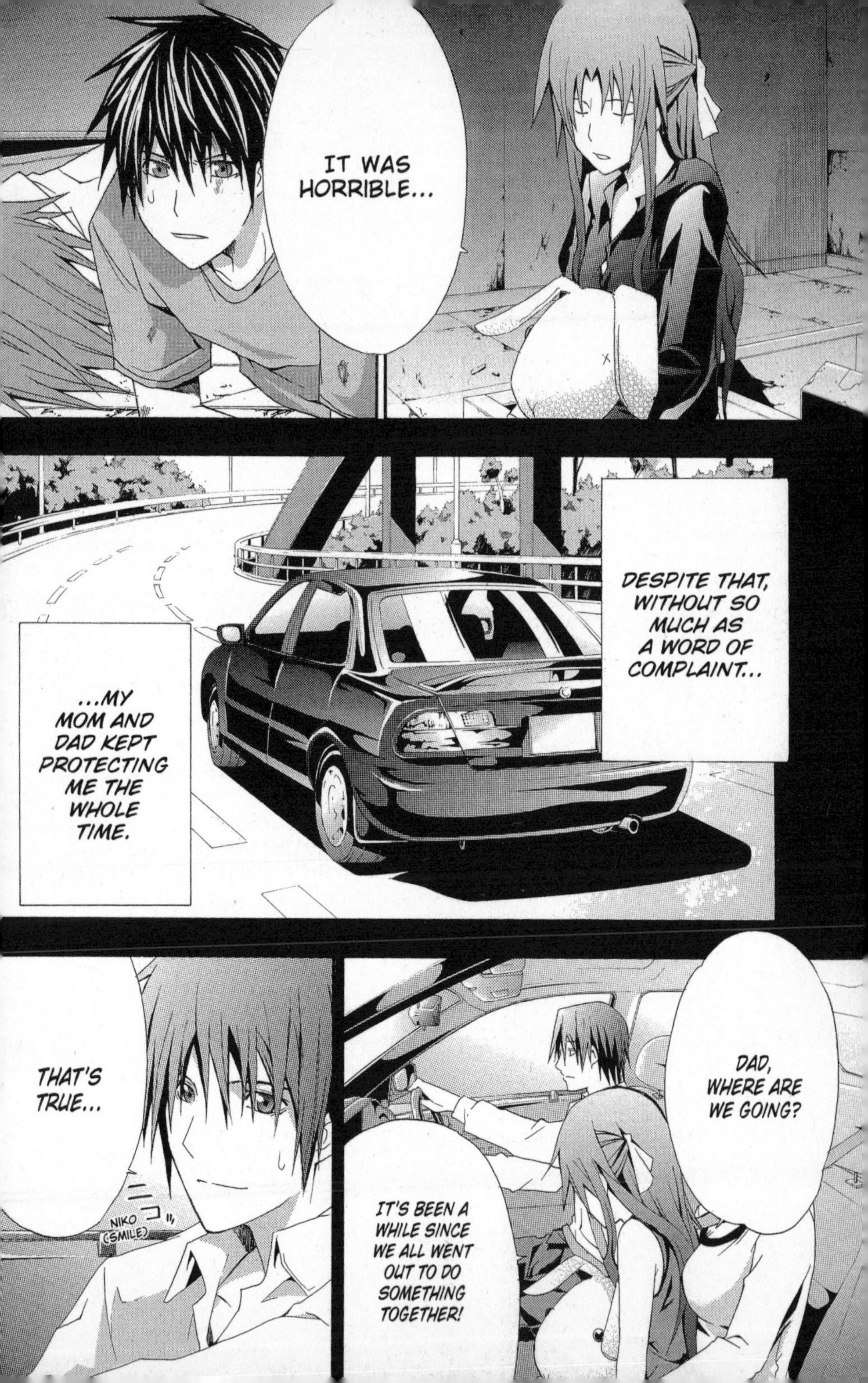
IT WAS HORRIBLE...
DESPITE THAT, WITHOUT SO MUCH AS A WORD OF COMPLAINT...
...MY MOM AND DAD KEPT PROTECTING ME THE WHOLE TIME.
DAD, WHERE ARE WE GOING?
IT'S BEEN A WHILE SINCE WE ALL WENT OUT TO DO SOMETHING TOGETHER!
THAT'S TRUE...
NIKO (SMILE)

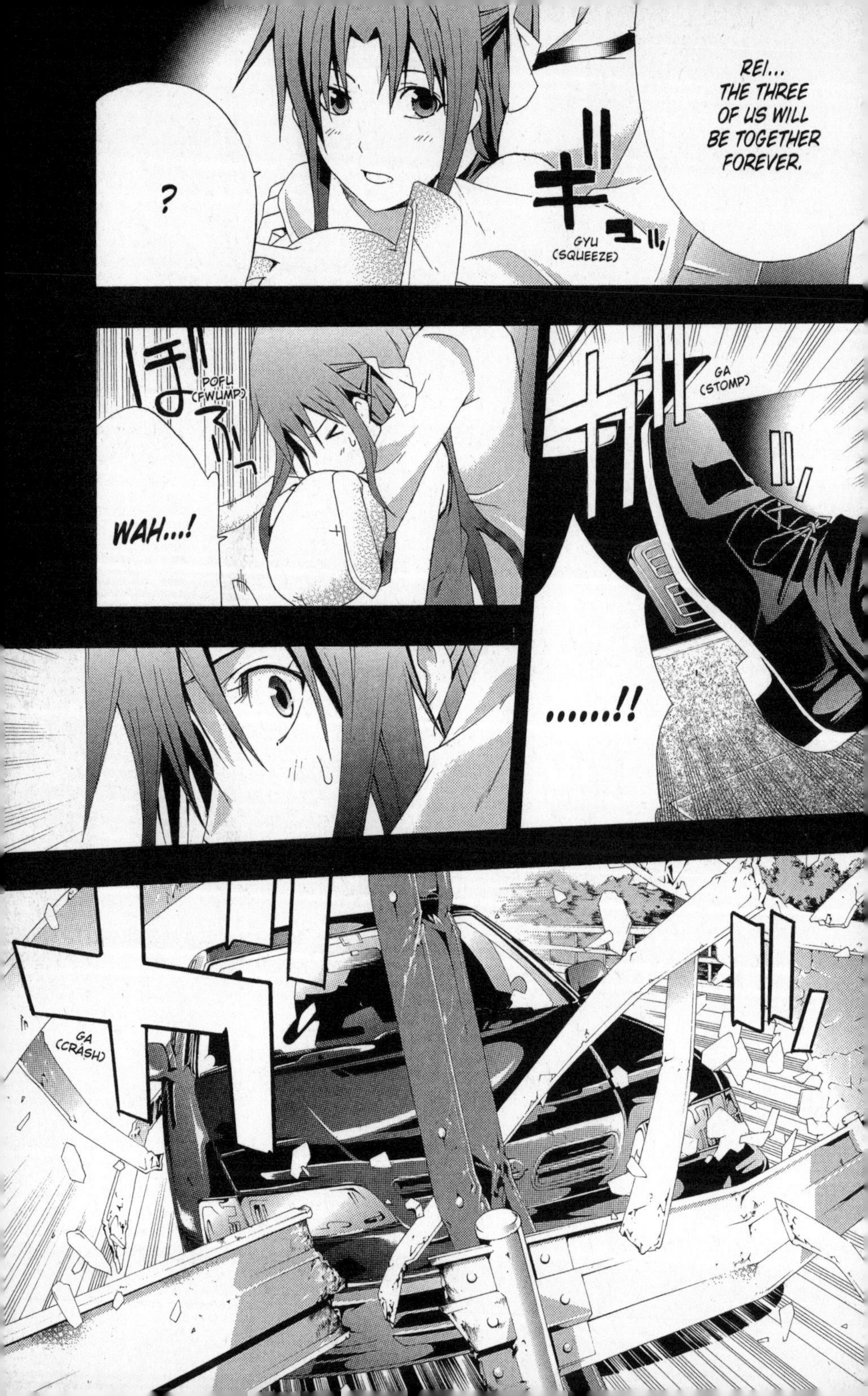
REI... THE THREE OF US WILL BE TOGETHER FOREVER.
?
GYU (SQUEEZE)
GA (STOMP)
......!!
POFU (FWUMP)
WAH...!
GA (CRASH)

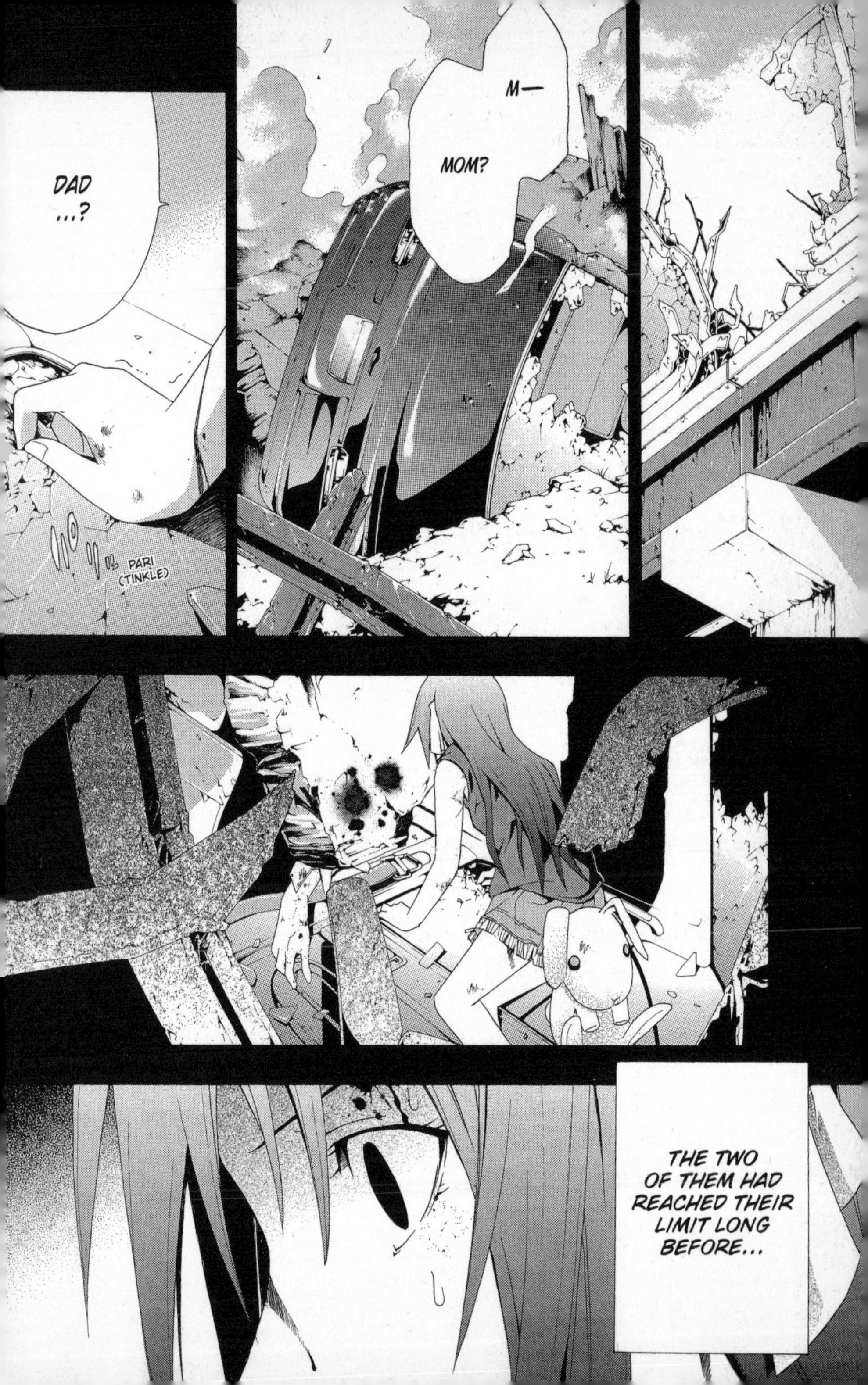
M—
MOM?
DAD ...?
PARI (TINKLE)
THE TWO OF THEM HAD REACHED THEIR LIMIT LONG BEFORE...

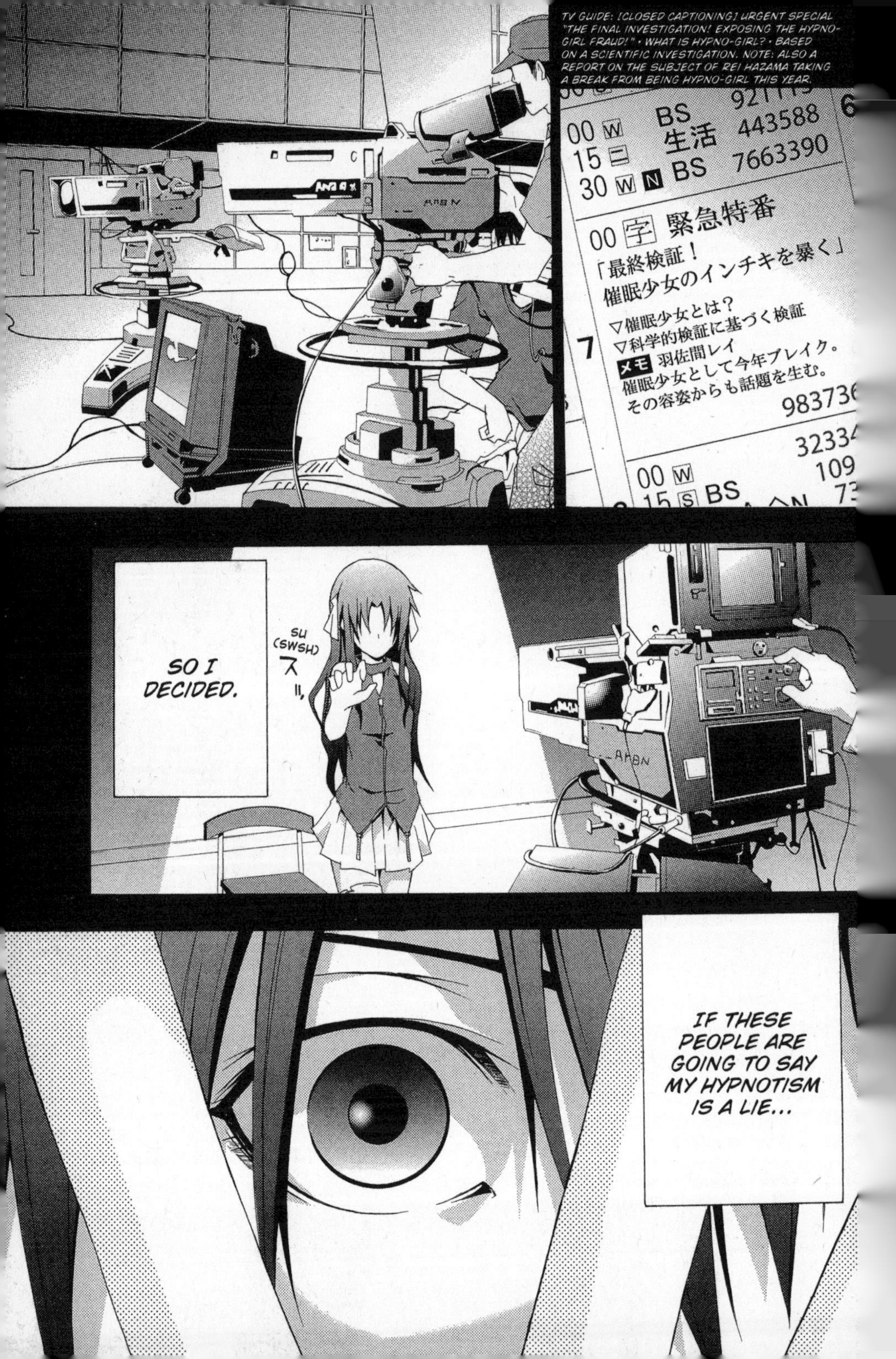
TV GUIDE: [CLOSED CAPTIONING] URGENT SPECIAL "THE FINAL INVESTIGATION! EXPOSING THE HYPNO-GIRL FRAUD!" • WHAT IS HYPNO-GIRL? • BASED ON A SCIENTIFIC INVESTIGATION. NOTE: ALSO A REPORT ON THE SUBJECT OF REI HAZAMA TAKING A BREAK FROM BEING HYPNO-GIRL THIS YEAR.
00 W BS 921115
15 二 生活 443588
30 W N BS 7663390
00 字 緊急特番
「最終検証！
催眠少女のインチキを暴く」
▽催眠少女とは？
▽科学的検証に基づく検証
メモ 羽佐間レイ
催眠少女として今年ブレイク。
その容姿からも話題を生む。
983736
SO I DECIDED.
SU (SWSH)
ス
IF THESE PEOPLE ARE GOING TO SAY MY HYPNOTISM IS A LIE...

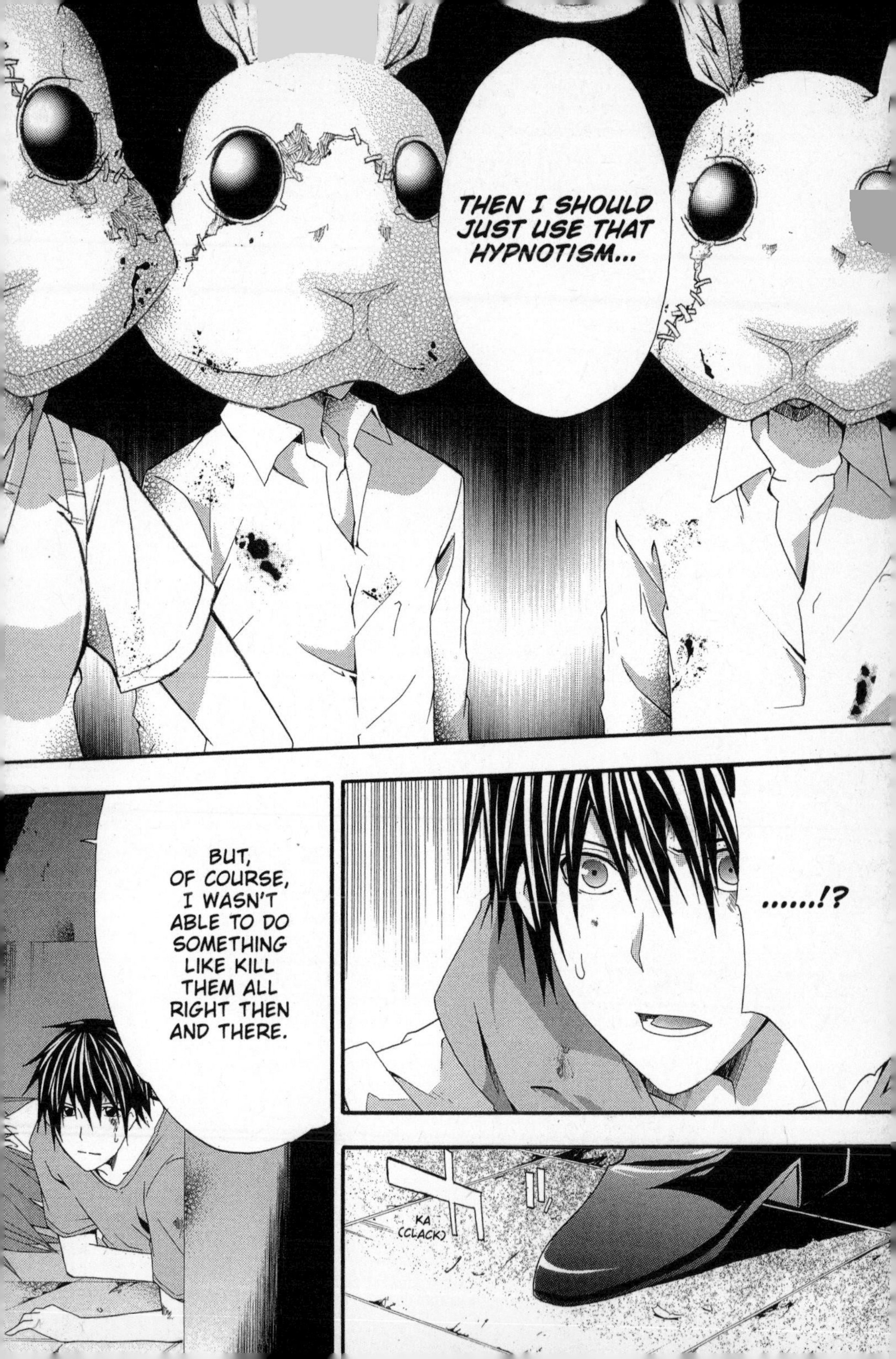
THEN I SHOULD JUST USE THAT HYPNOTISM...
......!?
KA (CLACK)
BUT, OF COURSE, I WASN'T ABLE TO DO SOMETHING LIKE KILL THEM ALL RIGHT THEN AND THERE.

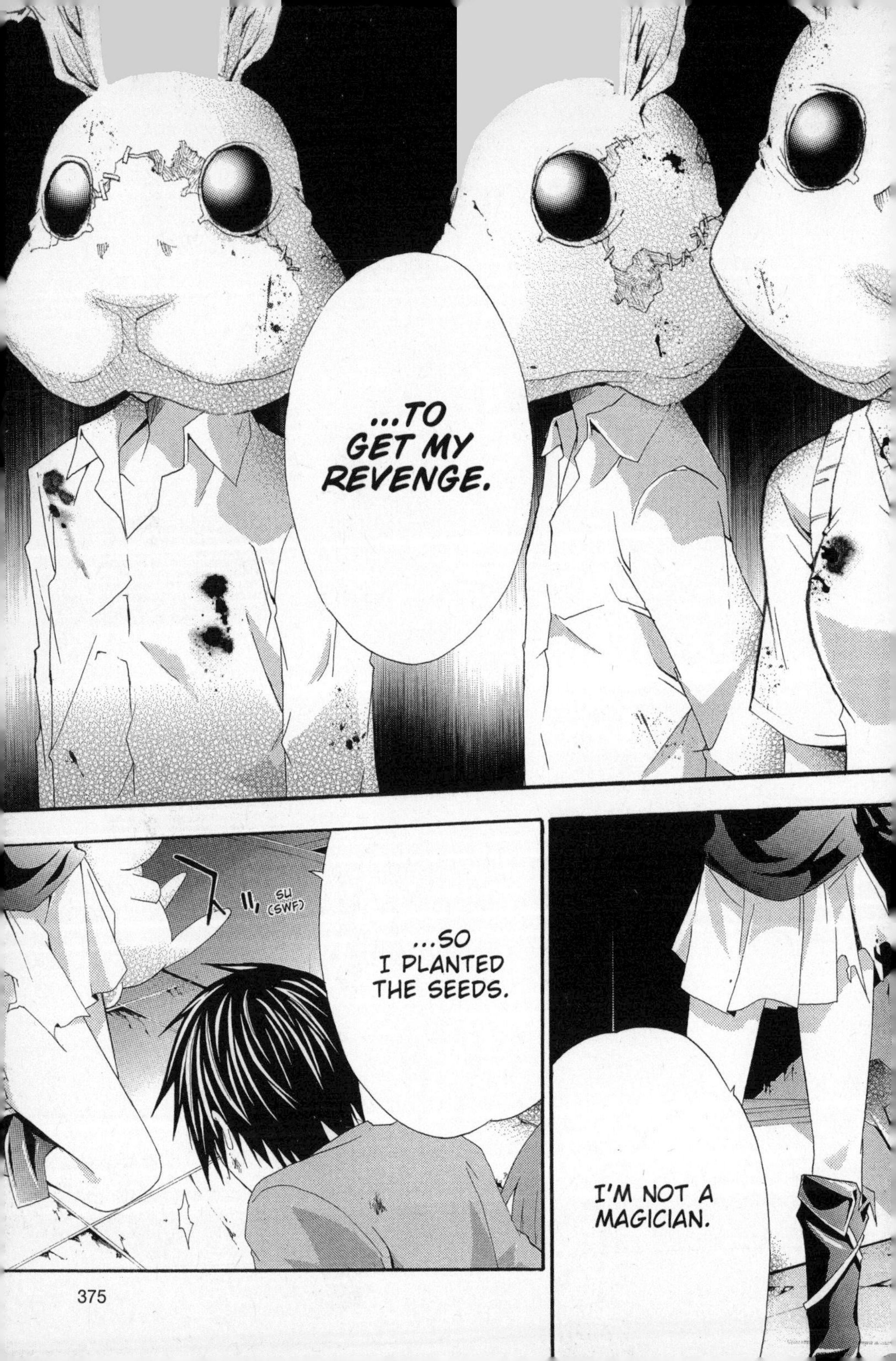
...TO GET MY REVENGE.
I'M NOT A MAGICIAN.
SU (SWF)
...SO I PLANTED THE SEEDS.

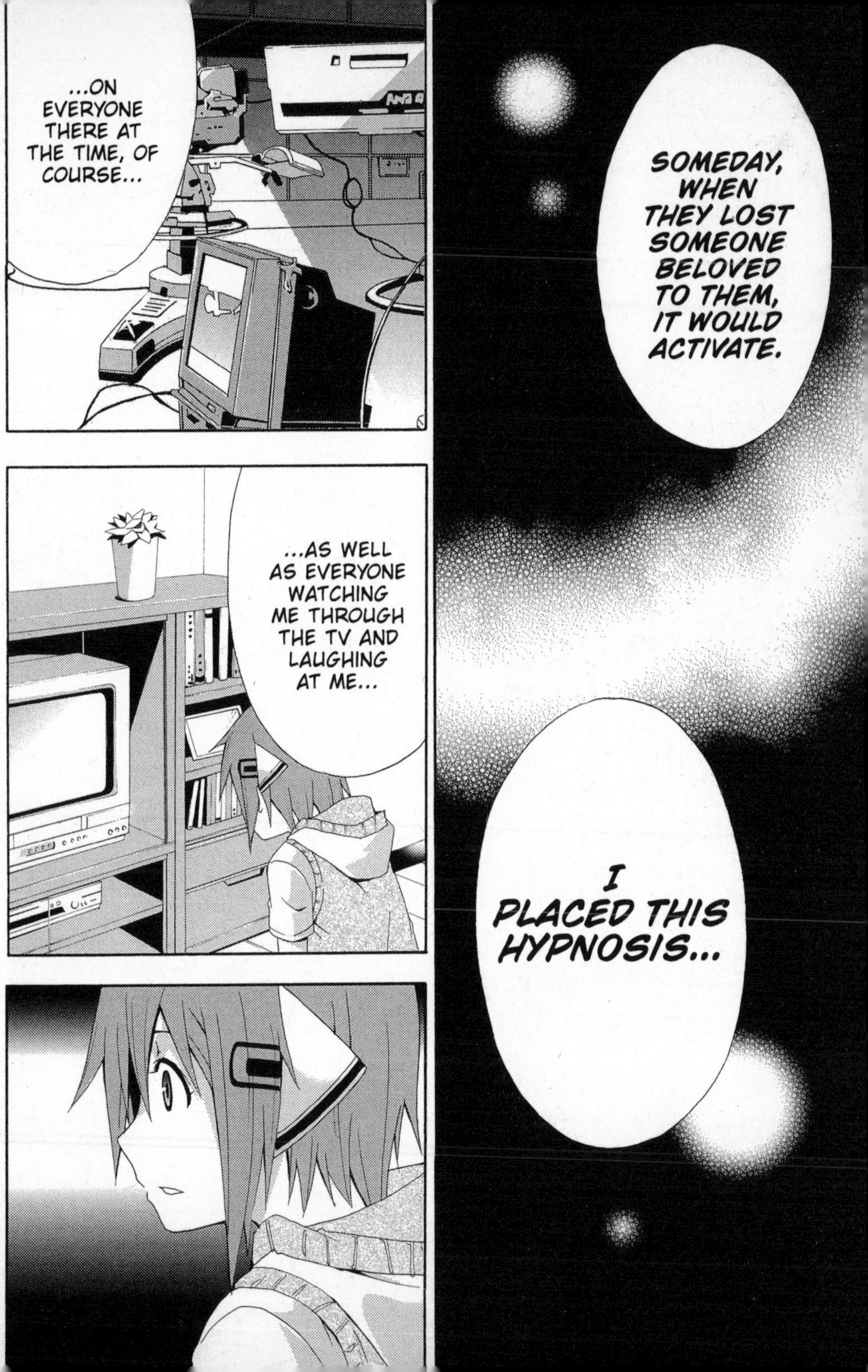
SOMEDAY, WHEN THEY LOST SOMEONE BELOVED TO THEM, IT WOULD ACTIVATE.
I PLACED THIS HYPNOSIS...
...ON EVERYONE THERE AT THE TIME, OF COURSE...
...AS WELL AS EVERYONE WATCHING ME THROUGH THE TV AND LAUGHING AT ME...

IMPOSSIBLE...!

THERE'S NO WAY YOU COULD DO SOMETHING LIKE THAT...

ズリ
SU
(SLIDE)

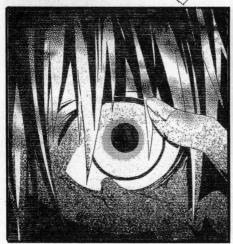

YOU WATCHED ME TOO, YUU-KUN.

....

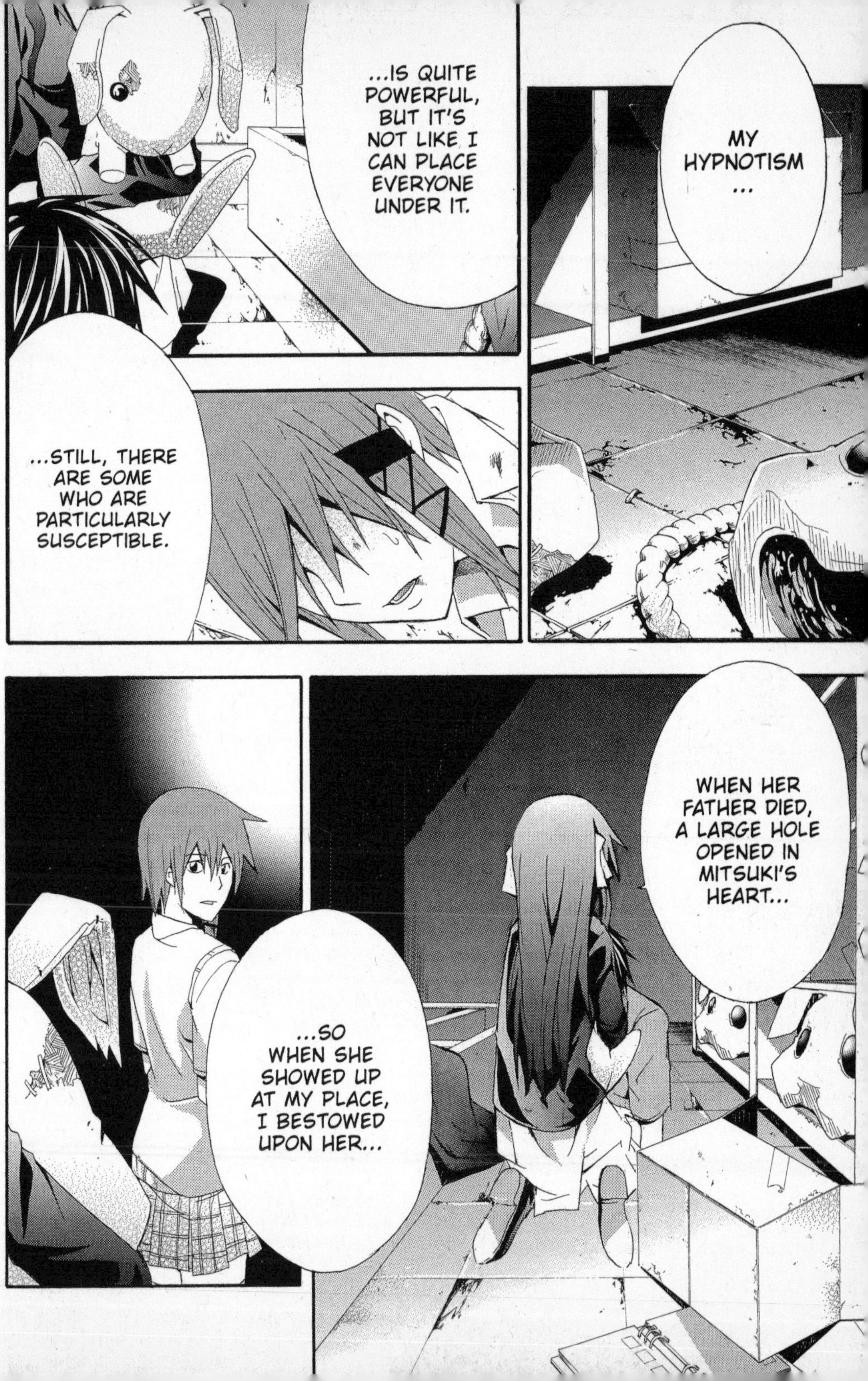
MY HYPNOTISM ...
...IS QUITE POWERFUL, BUT IT'S NOT LIKE I CAN PLACE EVERYONE UNDER IT.
...STILL, THERE ARE SOME WHO ARE PARTICULARLY SUSCEPTIBLE.
WHEN HER FATHER DIED, A LARGE HOLE OPENED IN MITSUKI'S HEART...
...SO WHEN SHE SHOWED UP AT MY PLACE, I BESTOWED UPON HER...

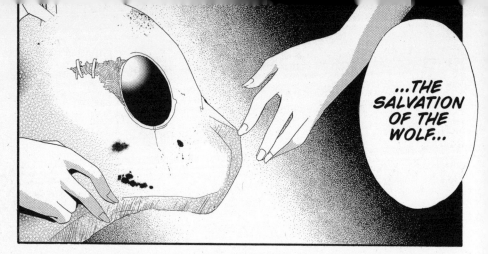

...THE SALVATION OF THE WOLF...

THAT BALD MAN WAS JUST LIKE MITSUKI-SAN.

IN THE PREVIOUS GAME, HE DOLED OUT HIS IMAGINED REVENGE...

...AND MURDERED EVERY SINGLE PARTICIPANT...

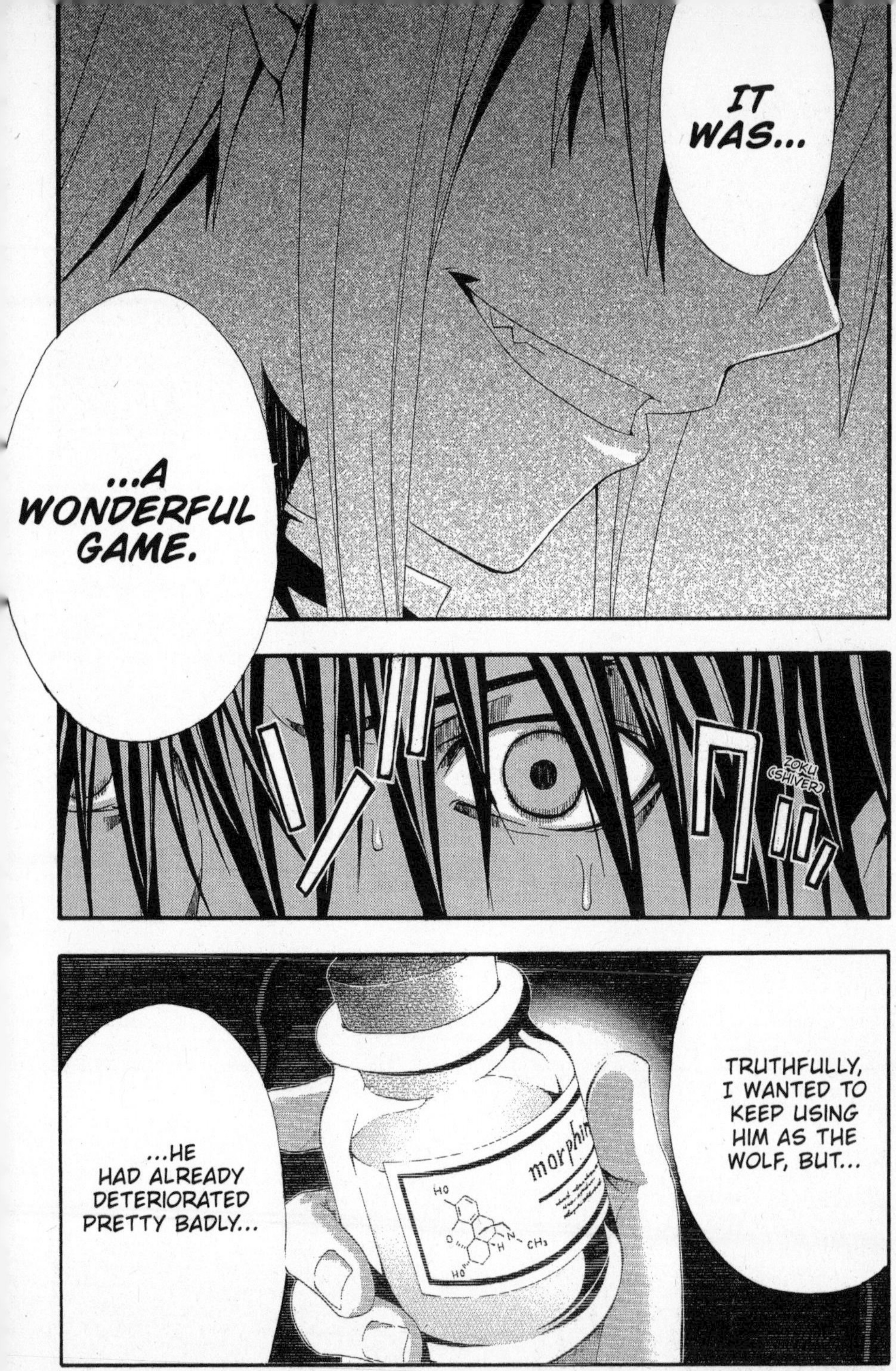
IT WAS...
...A WONDERFUL GAME.
ZOKU (SHIVER)
TRUTHFULLY, I WANTED TO KEEP USING HIM AS THE WOLF, BUT...
...HE HAD ALREADY DETERIORATED PRETTY BADLY...

I BROUGHT HIM BACK TO WORK BEHIND THE SCENES...

...DOING THINGS LIKE KNOCKING YOU OUT AND CARRYING EVERYONE HERE.

...I'D PLANNED FOR THE NEW WOLF TO TAKE HIS PLACE IN THIS GAME.

AND THEN...

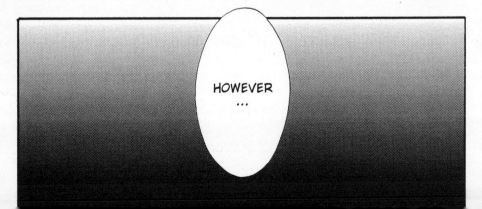

HOWEVER ...

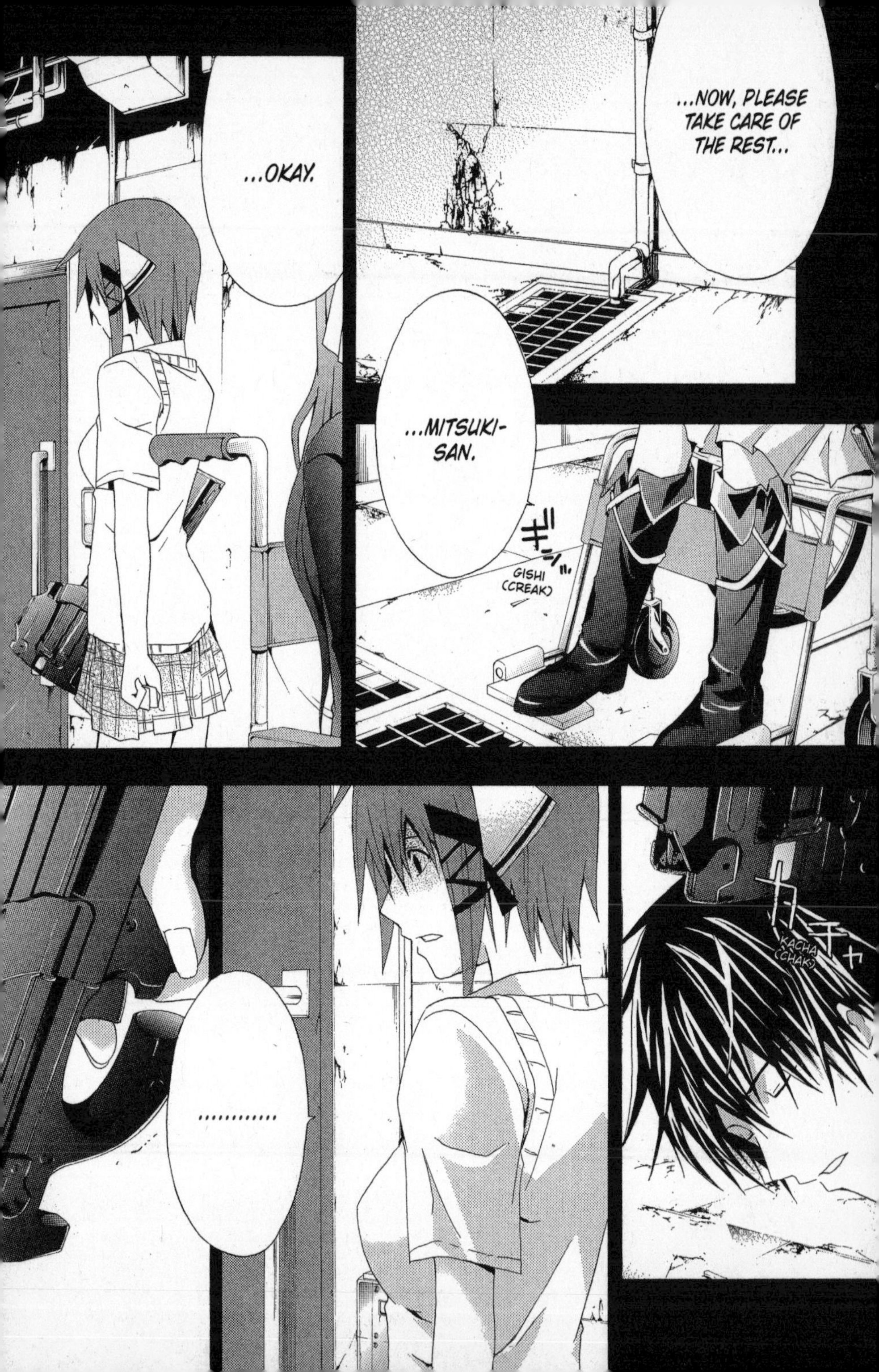
...NOW, PLEASE TAKE CARE OF THE REST...
...MITSUKI-SAN.
ギシッ
GISHI (CREAK)
...OKAY.
カチャ
KACHA (CHAK)
....

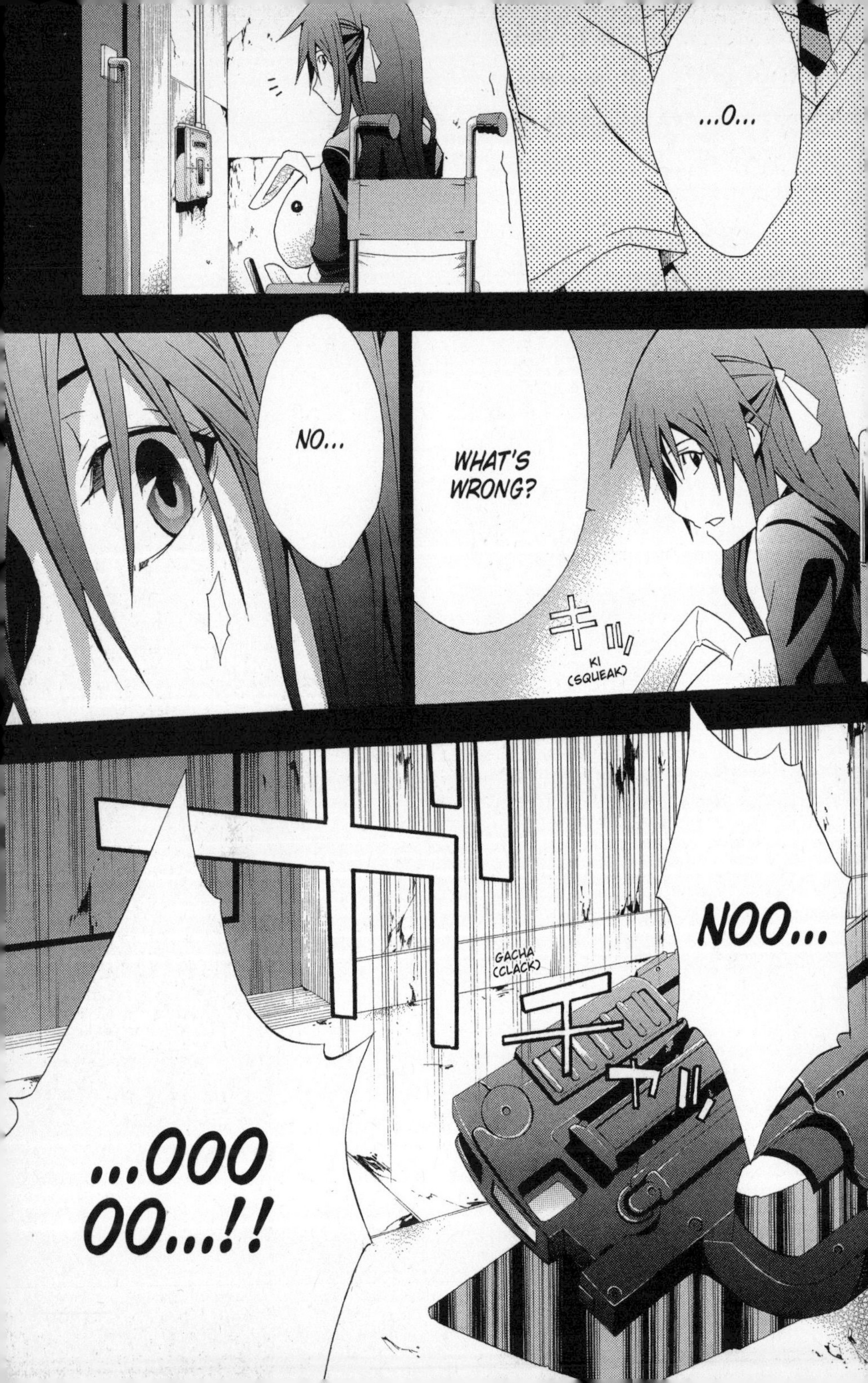

...O...
WHAT'S WRONG?
KI (SQUEAK)
NO...
NOO...
GACHA (CLACK)
...OOO OO...!!

ALL OF A SUDDEN...

...MITSUKI-SAN SNAPPED OUT OF THE HYPNOSIS I'D PLACED HER UNDER.

WHEN YOU'RE BY HER SIDE...

...THE HYPNOSIS INTERMITTENTLY DISSIPATES...

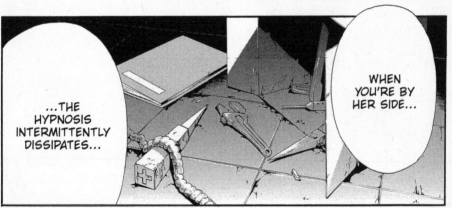

IT'S THE FIRST TIME SUCH A THING HAS HAPPENED...

SO I FIGURED IT COULDN'T BE HELPED...

...AND DECIDED NOT TO PUT A BARCODE ON YOU.

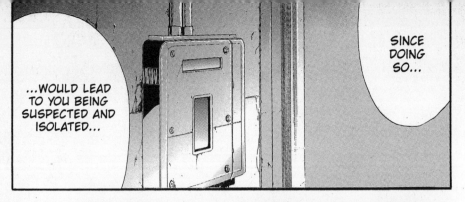

SINCE DOING SO...

...WOULD LEAD TO YOU BEING SUSPECTED AND ISOLATED...

....

GU
(GRIMACE)

SU
(SLIDE)

...WHY WOULD YOU...!!?

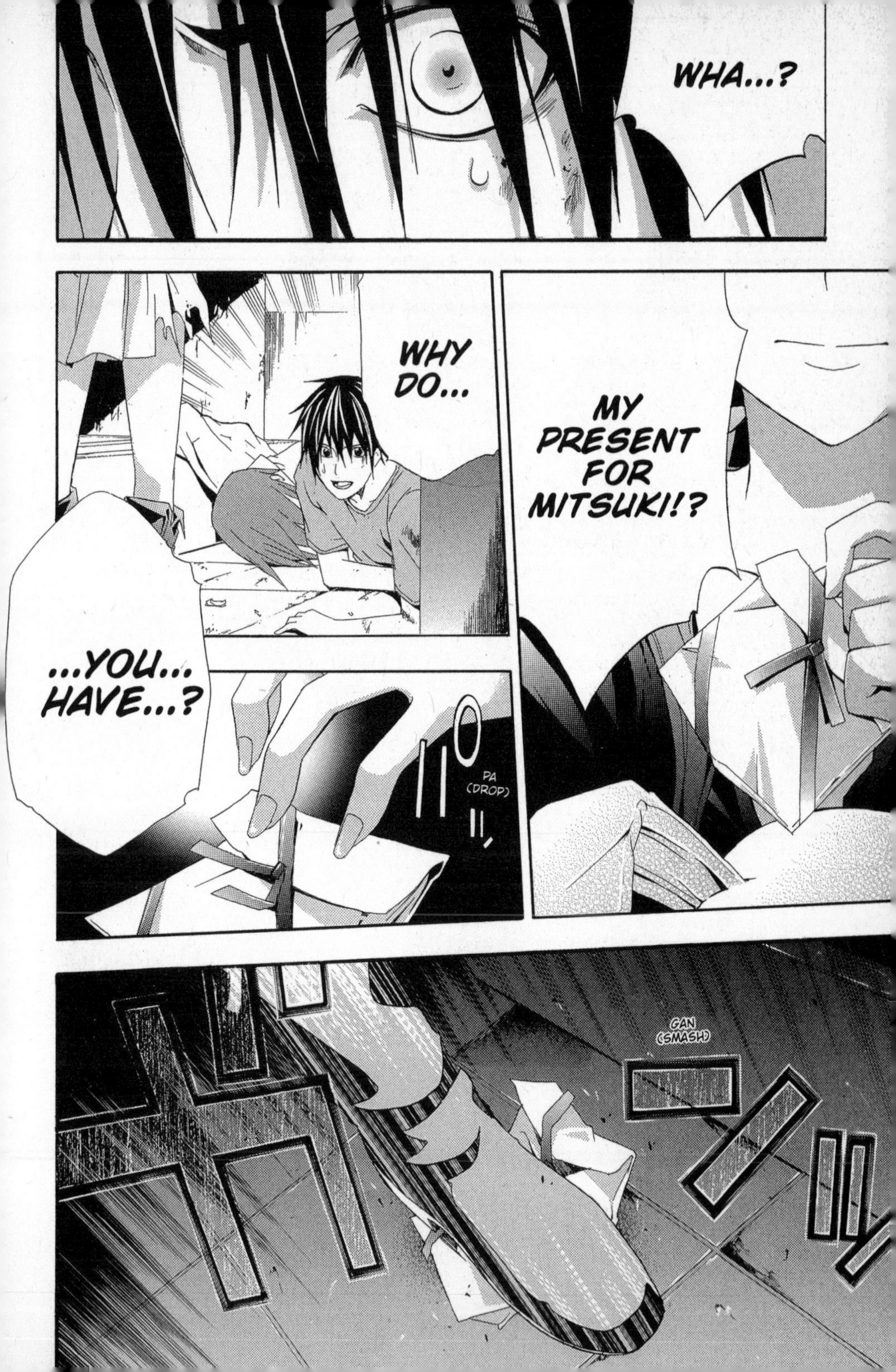
WHA...?
MY PRESENT FOR MITSUKI!?
WHY DO...
...YOU... HAVE...?
PA (DROP)
GAN (SMASH)

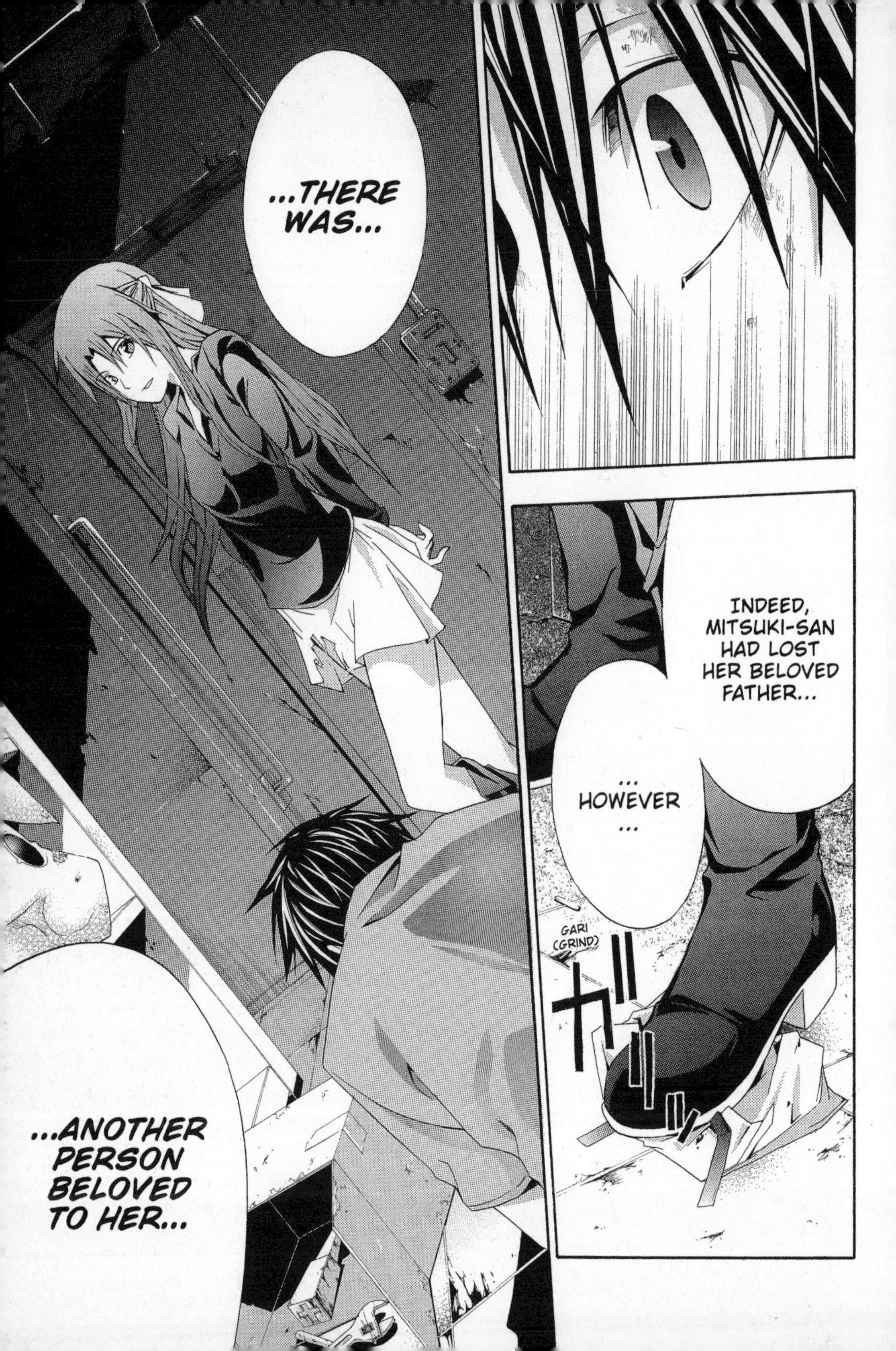
INDEED, MITSUKI-SAN HAD LOST HER BELOVED FATHER...
...HOWEVER...
GARI (GRIND)
...THERE WAS...
...ANOTHER PERSON BELOVED TO HER...

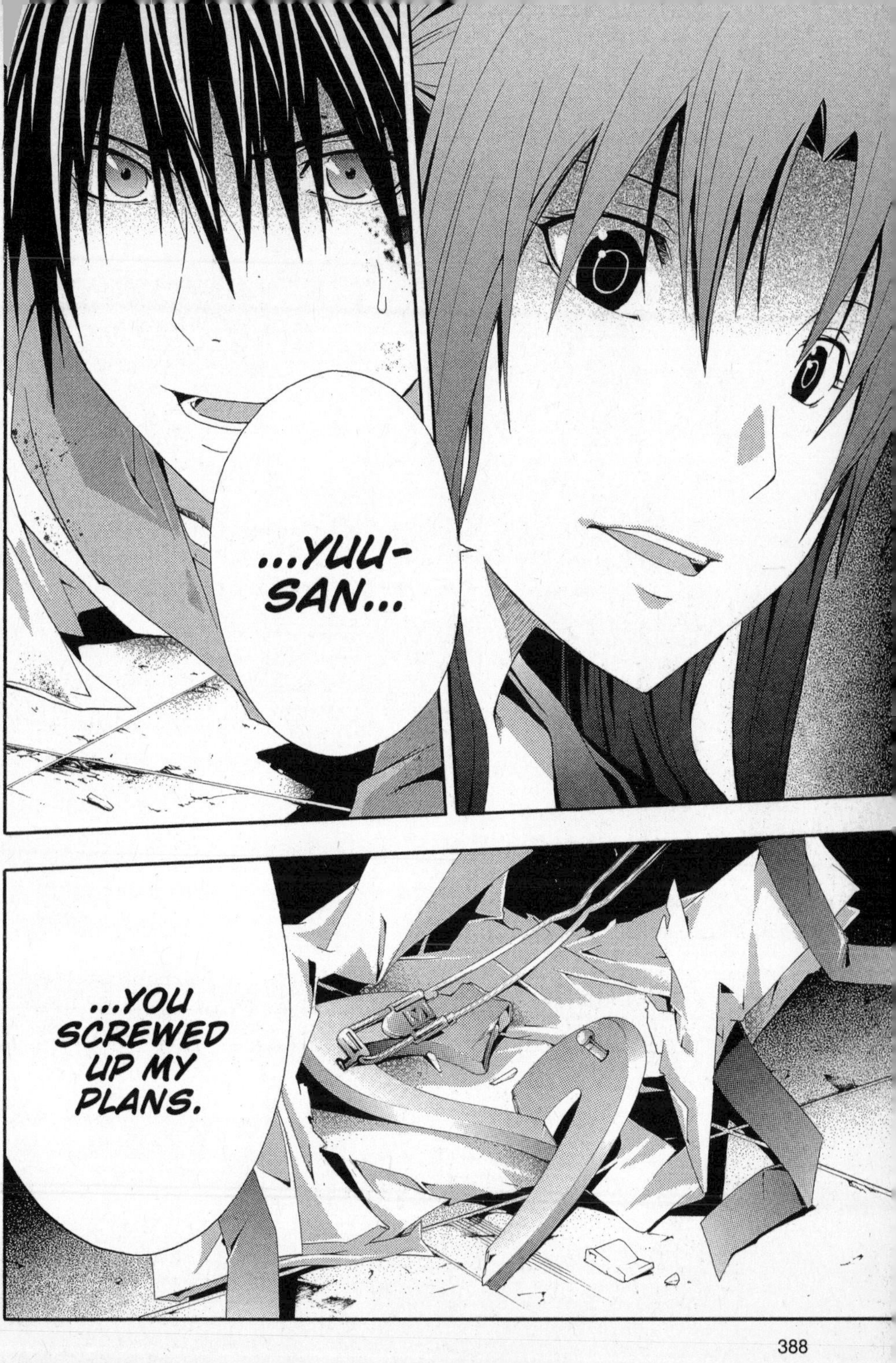
...YUU-SAN...
...YOU SCREWED UP MY PLANS.

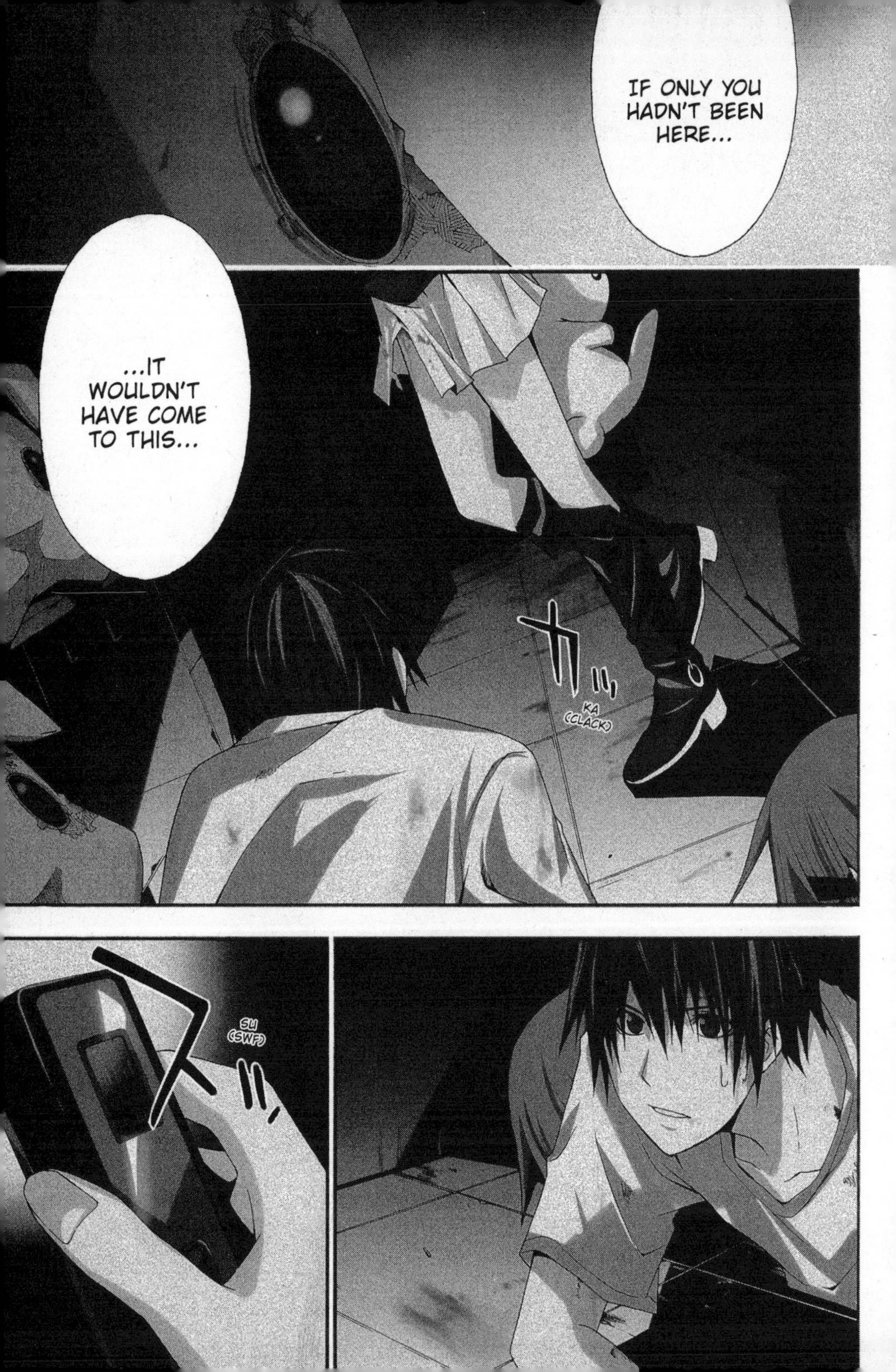
IF ONLY YOU HADN'T BEEN HERE...
...IT WOULDN'T HAVE COME TO THIS...
KA (CLACK)
SU (SWF)

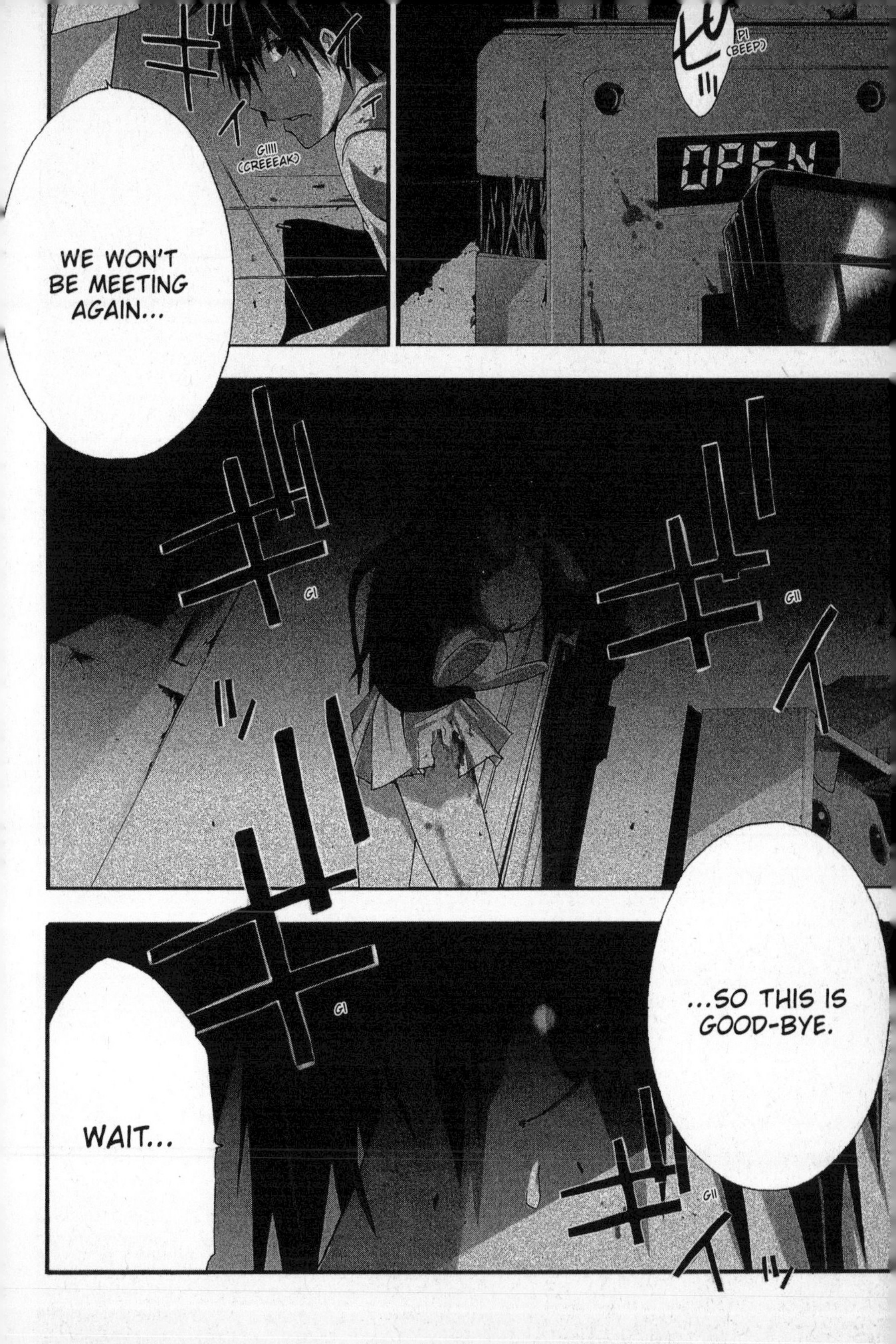
PI (BEEP)
OPEN
GIIII (CREEEAK)
WE WON'T BE MEETING AGAIN...
GII
GI
...SO THIS IS GOOD-BYE.
GII
GI
WAIT...

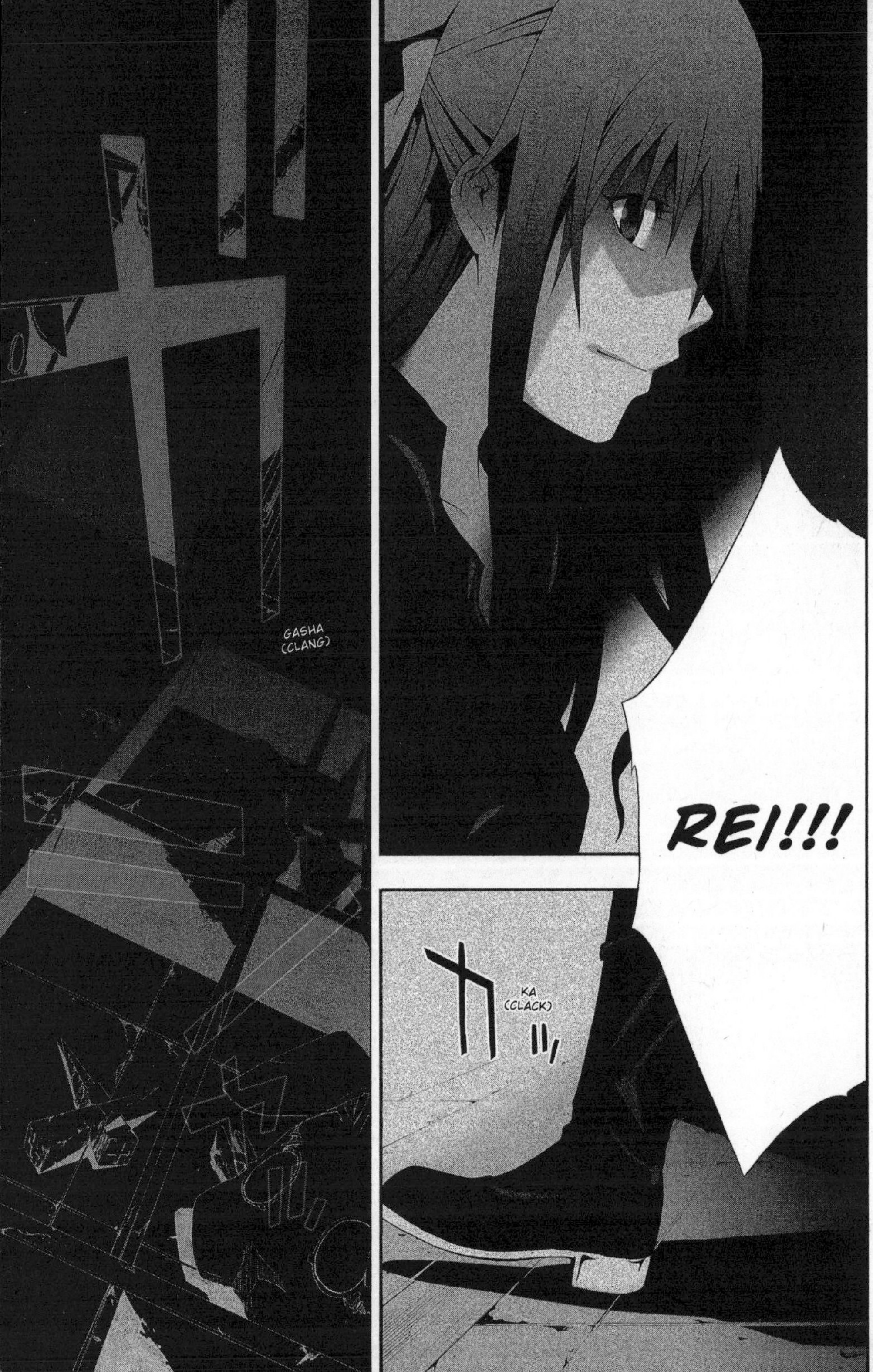
REI!!!
KA (CLACK)
GASHA (CLANG)

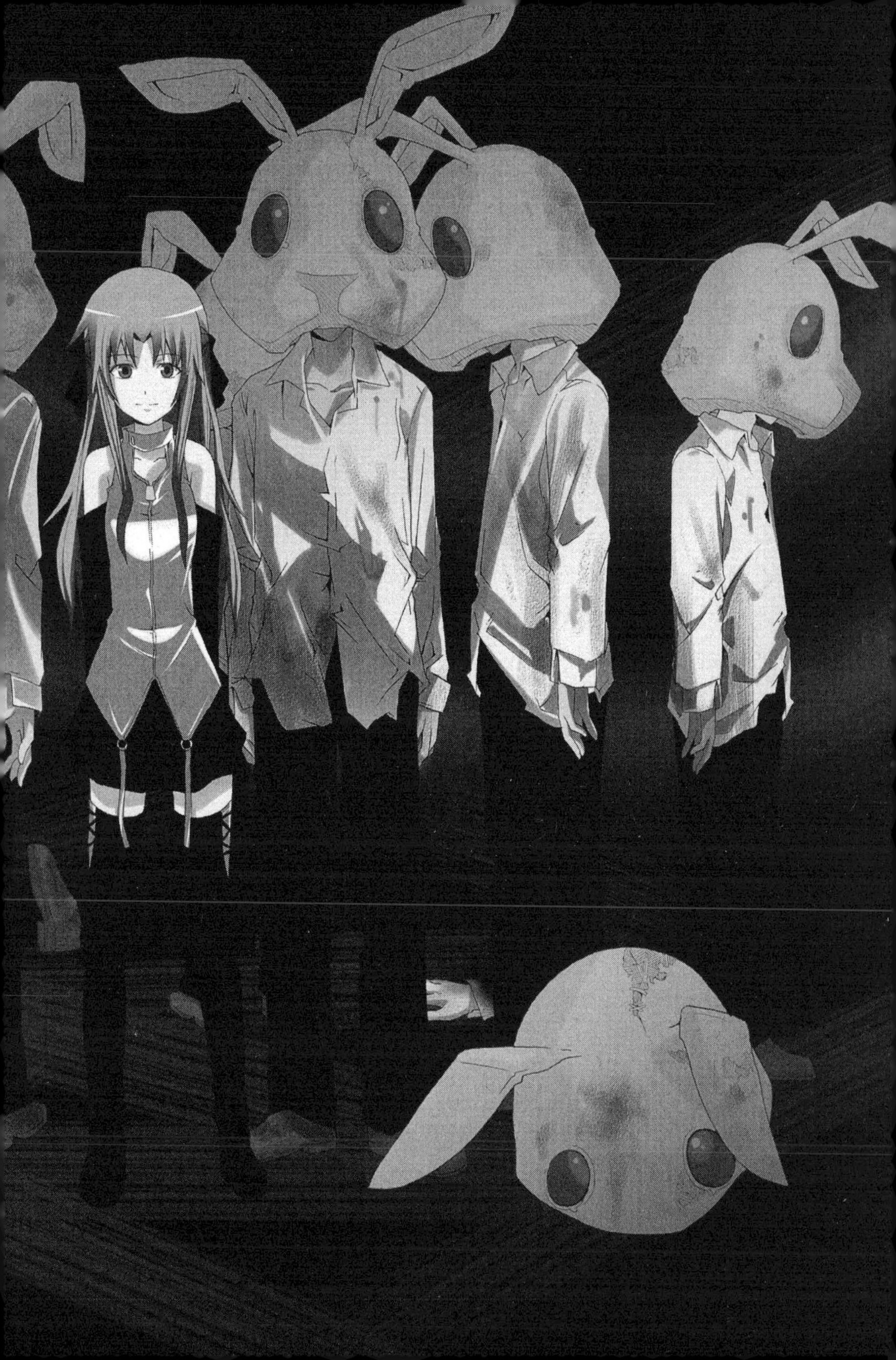

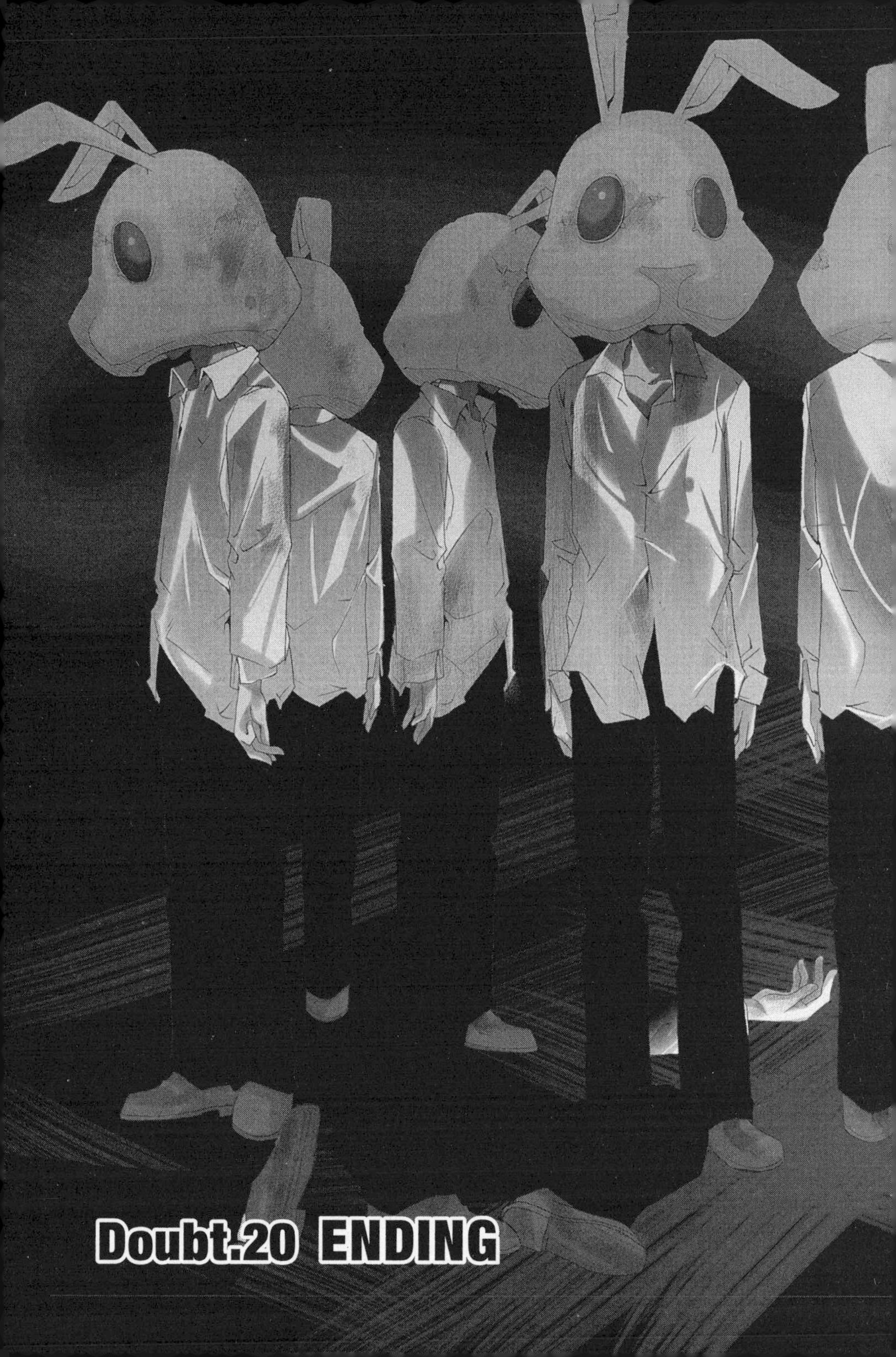

Doubt.20 ENDING

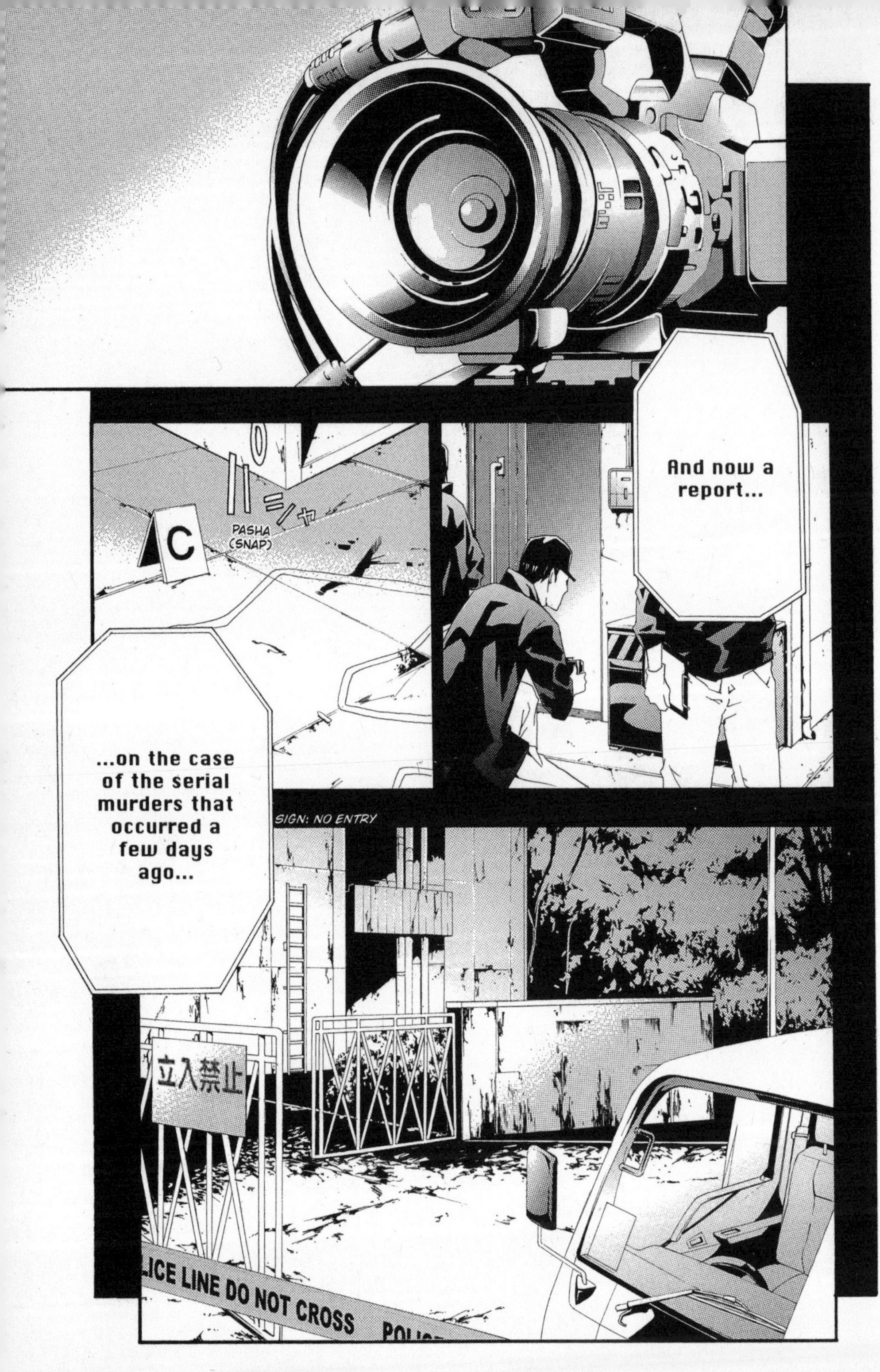
And now a report...
PASHA (SNAP)
...on the case of the serial murders that occurred a few days ago...
SIGN: NO ENTRY
立入禁止
LICE LINE DO NOT CROSS

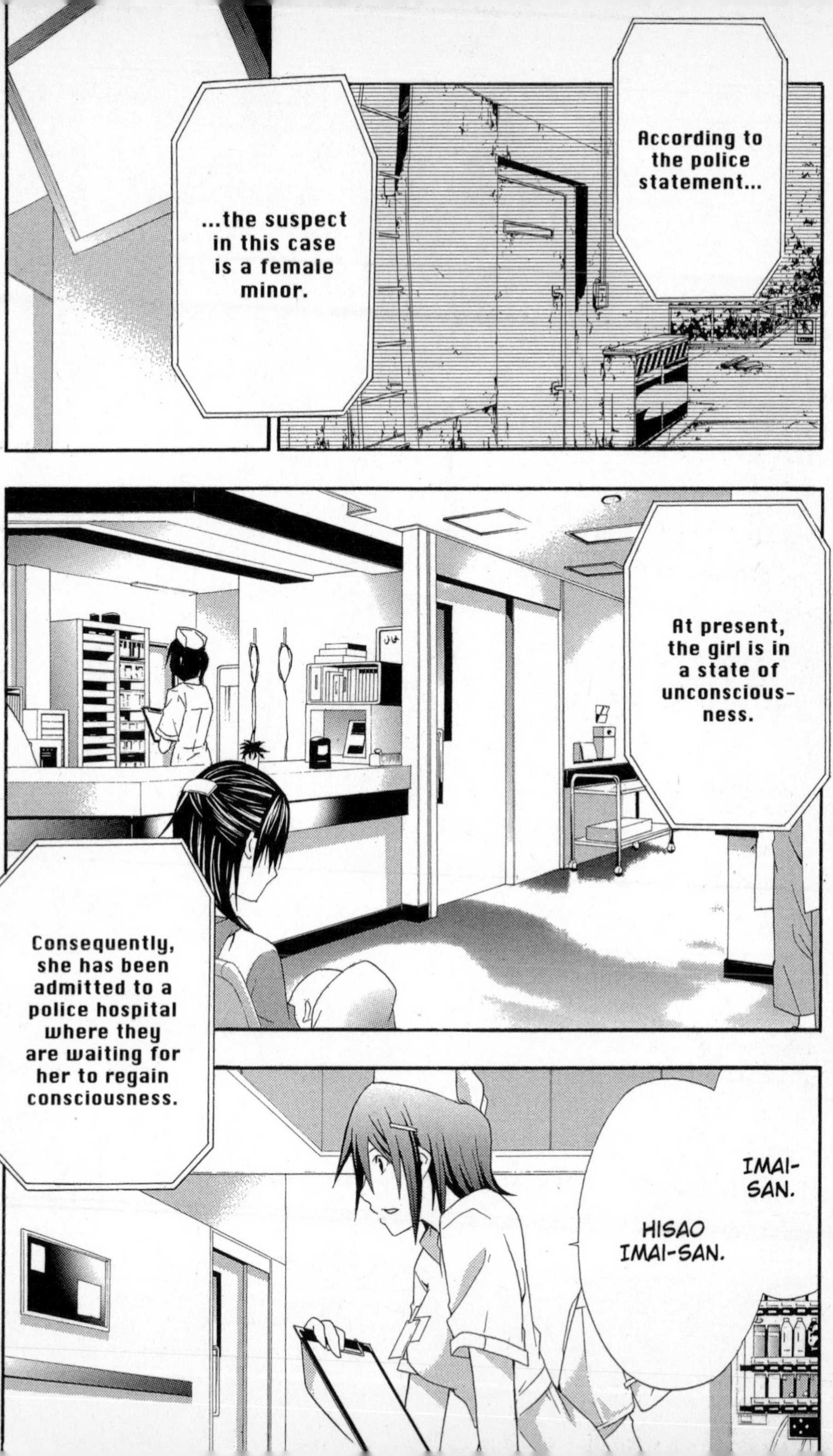
According to the police statement...
...the suspect in this case is a female minor.
At present, the girl is in a state of unconscious-ness.
Consequently, she has been admitted to a police hospital where they are waiting for her to regain consciousness.
IMAI-SAN.
HISAO IMAI-SAN.

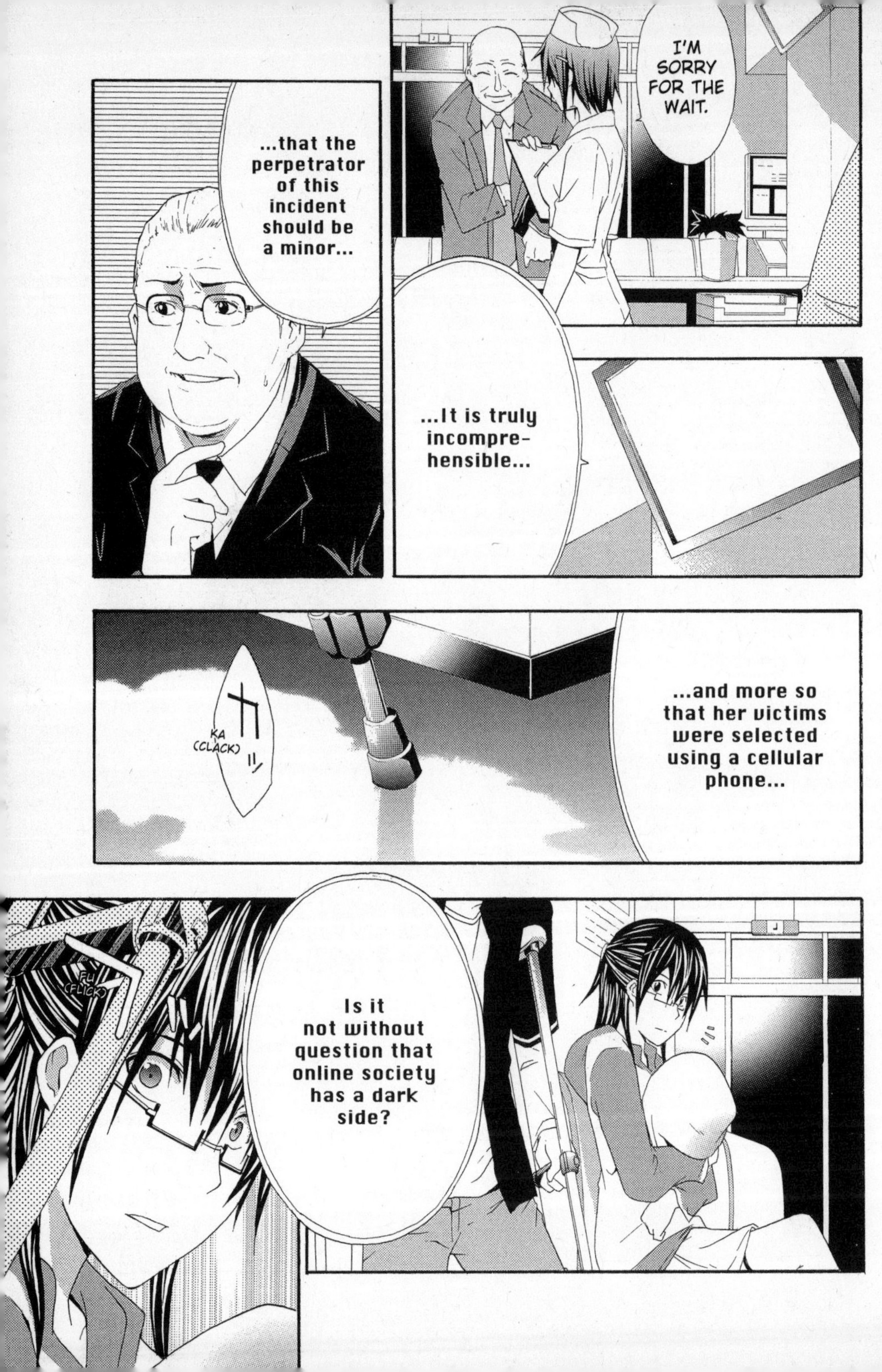
I'M SORRY FOR THE WAIT.
...It is truly incompre-hensible...
...that the perpetrator of this incident should be a minor...
...and more so that her victims were selected using a cellular phone...
KA (CLACK)
Is it not without question that online society has a dark side?
FU (FLICK)

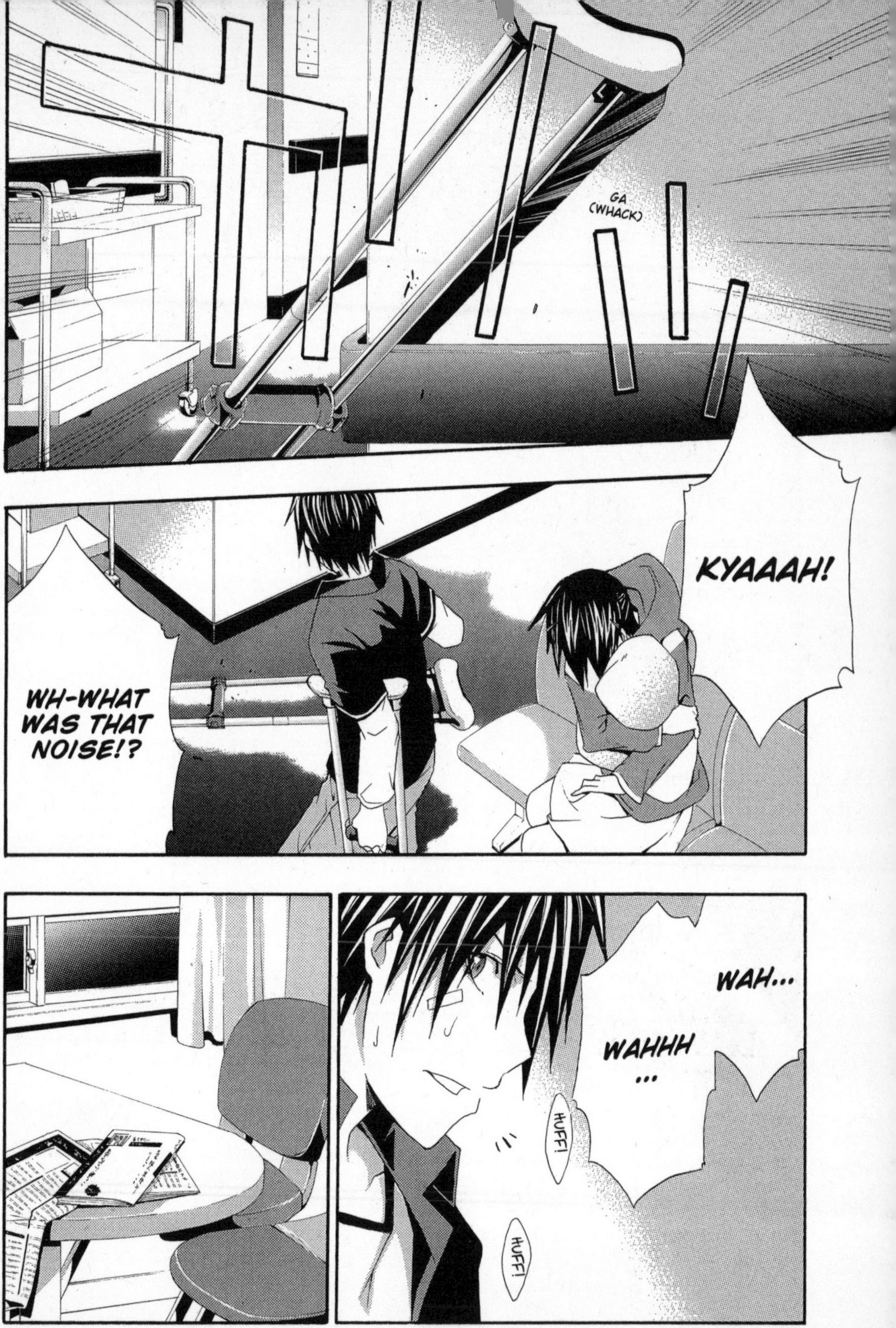
GA (WHACK)
KYAAAH!
WH-WHAT WAS THAT NOISE!?
WAH...
WAHHH ...
HUFF!
HUFF!

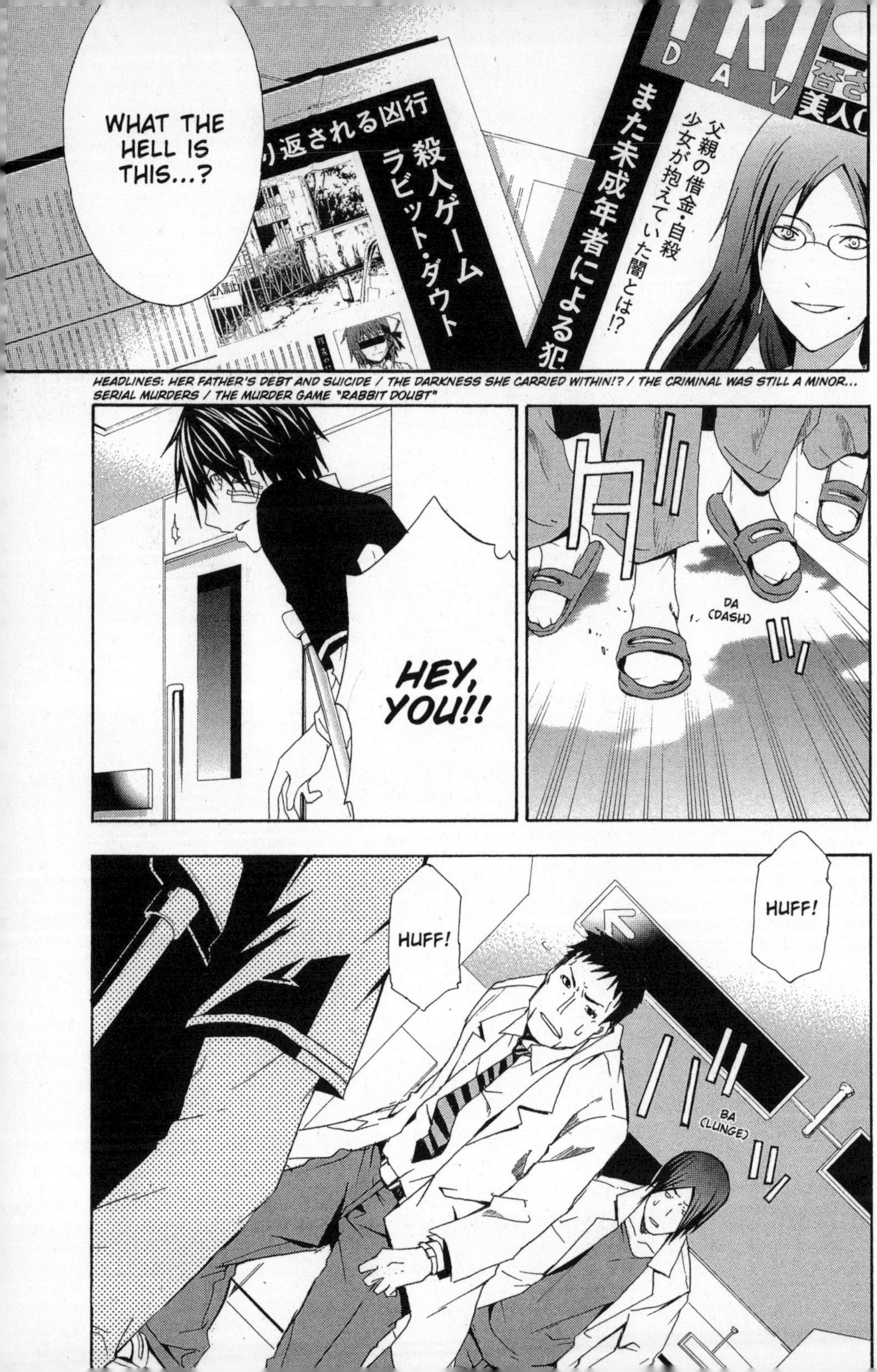

父親の借金・自殺
少女が抱えていた闇とは!?
また未成年者による犯
殺人ゲーム
ラビット・ダウト
り返される凶行
WHAT THE HELL IS THIS...?
HEADLINES: HER FATHER'S DEBT AND SUICIDE / THE DARKNESS SHE CARRIED WITHIN!? / THE CRIMINAL WAS STILL A MINOR... SERIAL MURDERS / THE MURDER GAME "RABBIT DOUBT"
DA (DASH)
HEY, YOU!!
HUFF!
HUFF!
BA (LUNGE)

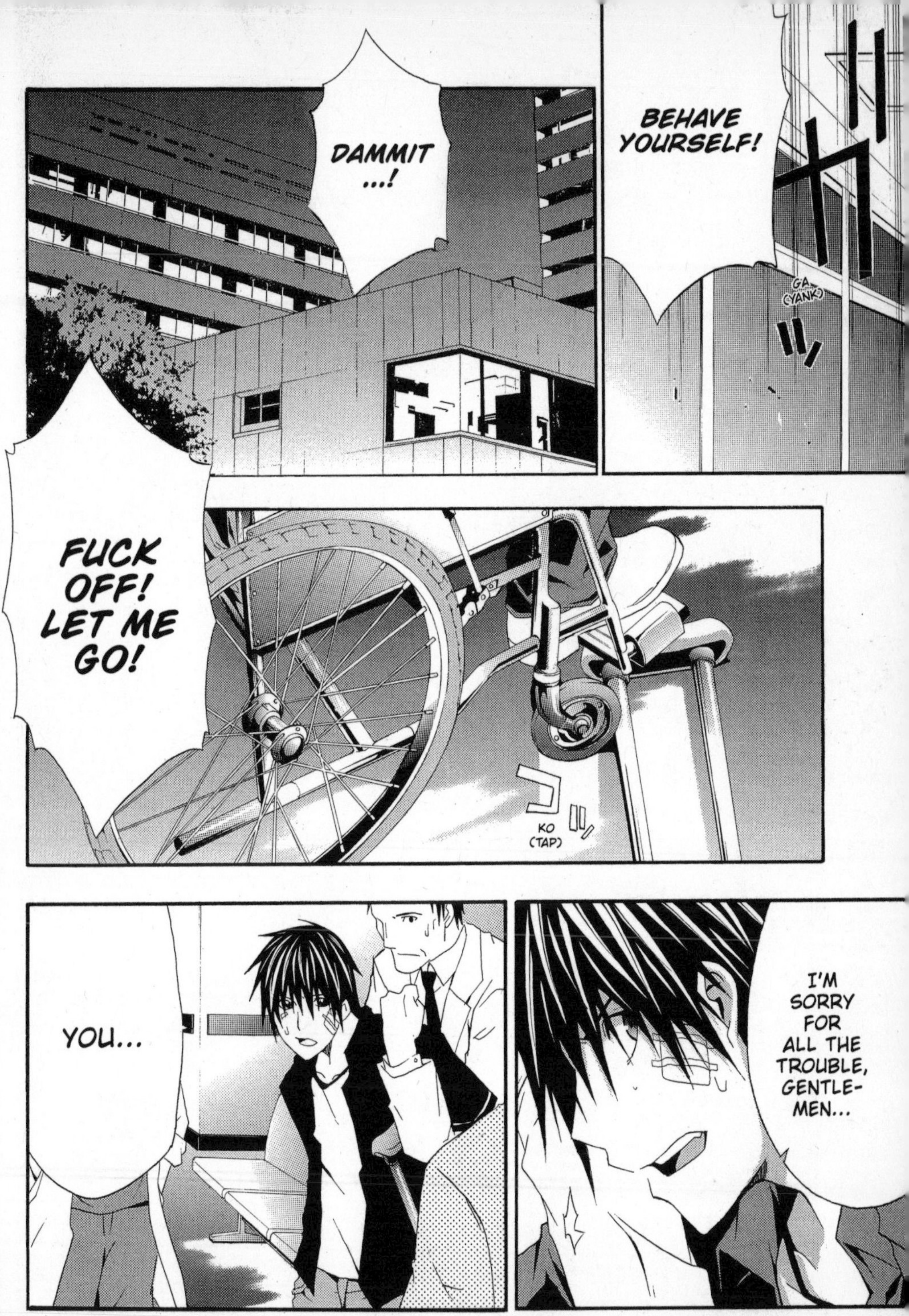
BEHAVE YOURSELF!
GA (YANK)
DAMMIT ...!
FUCK OFF! LET ME GO!
KO (TAP)
I'M SORRY FOR ALL THE TROUBLE, GENTLE-MEN...
YOU...

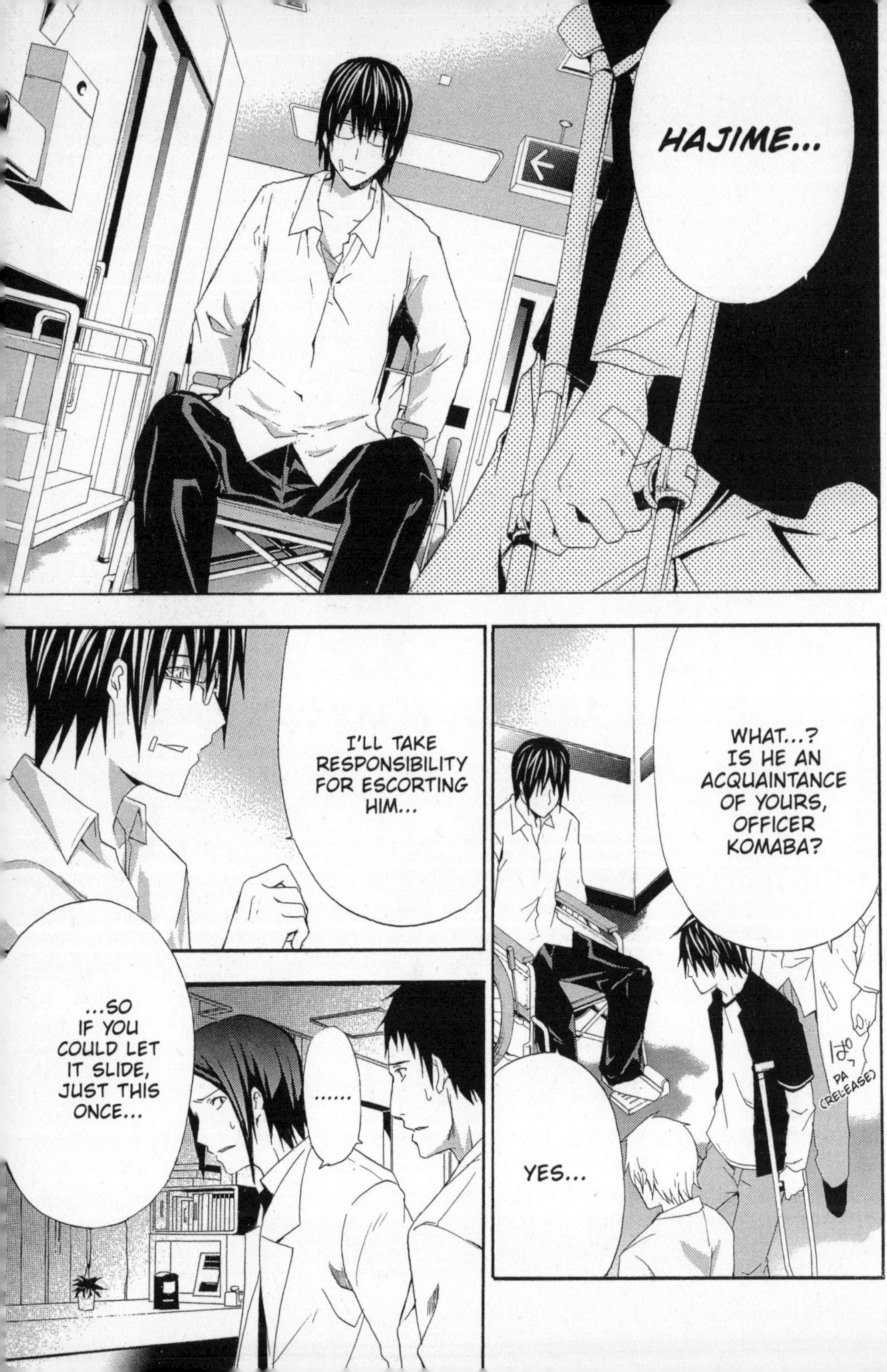
HAJIME...
WHAT...? IS HE AN ACQUAINTANCE OF YOURS, OFFICER KOMABA?
ぱっ
PA (RELEASE)
YES...
I'LL TAKE RESPONSIBILITY FOR ESCORTING HIM...
...SO IF YOU COULD LET IT SLIDE, JUST THIS ONCE...
......

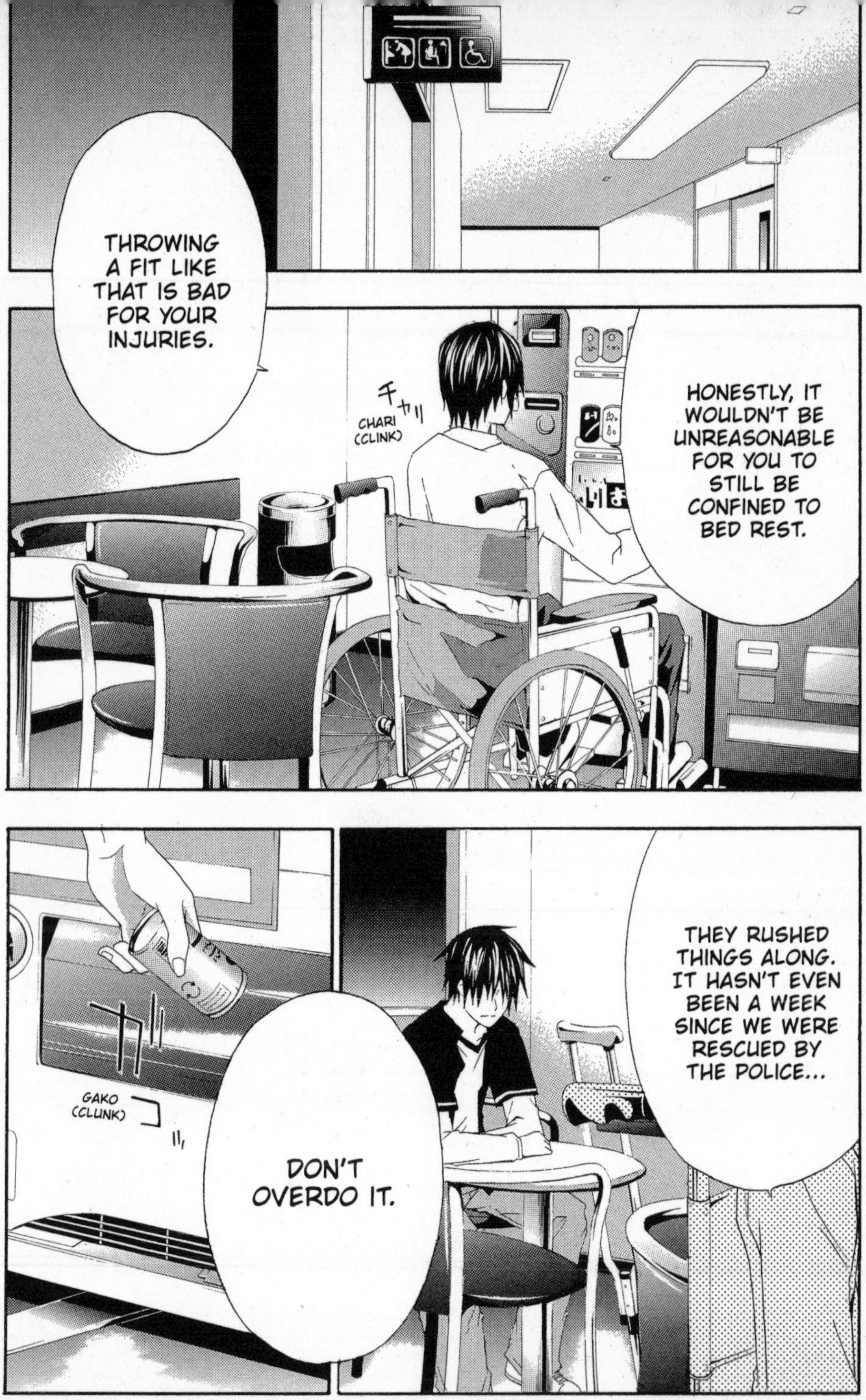
THROWING A FIT LIKE THAT IS BAD FOR YOUR INJURIES.
HONESTLY, IT WOULDN'T BE UNREASONABLE FOR YOU TO STILL BE CONFINED TO BED REST.
CHARI (CLINK)
THEY RUSHED THINGS ALONG. IT HASN'T EVEN BEEN A WEEK SINCE WE WERE RESCUED BY THE POLICE...
DON'T OVERDO IT.
GAKO (CLINK)

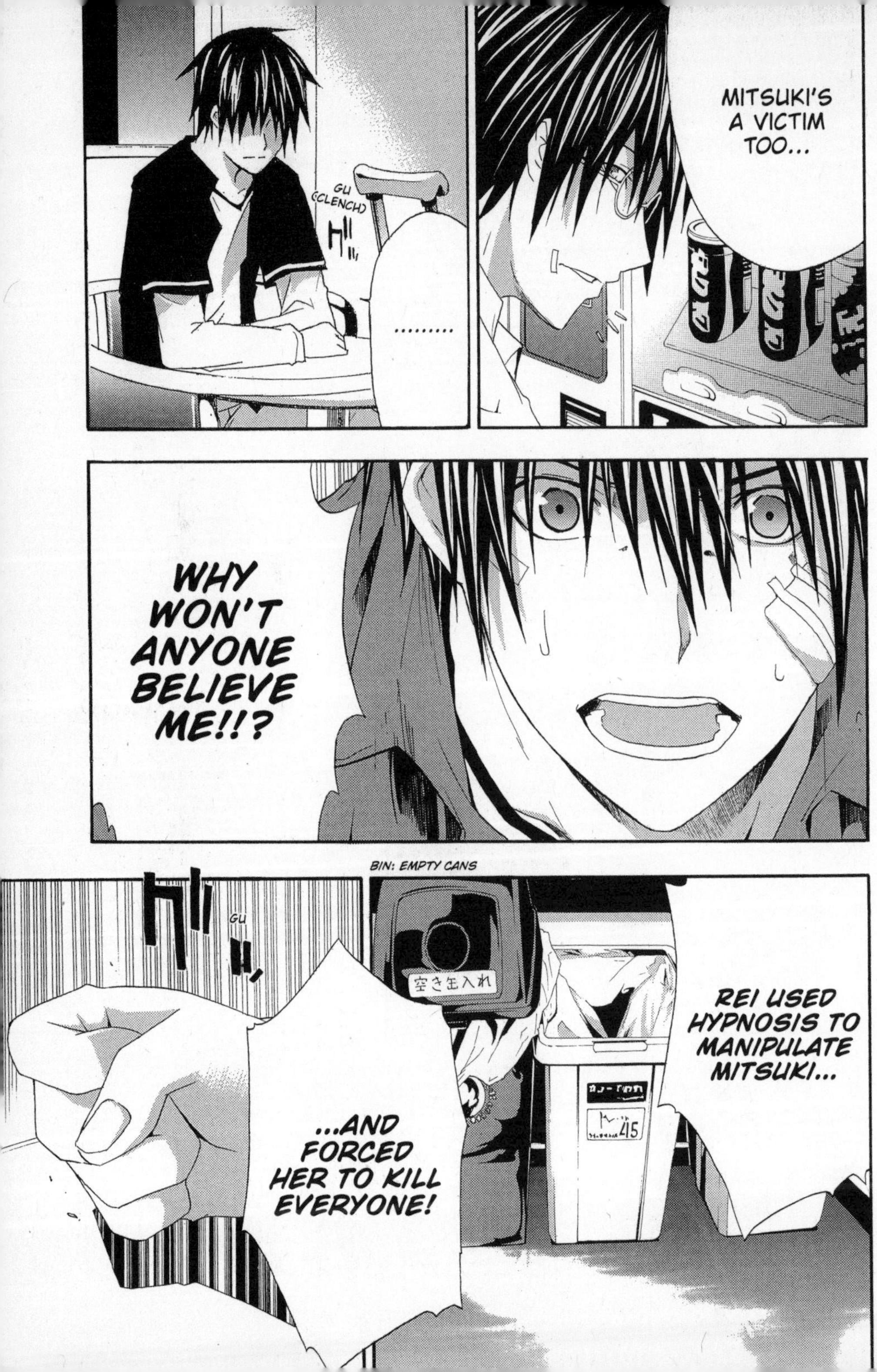
MITSUKI'S A VICTIM TOO...
GU (CLENCH)
....
WHY WON'T ANYONE BELIEVE ME!!?
BIN: EMPTY CANS
REI USED HYPNOSIS TO MANIPULATE MITSUKI...
...AND FORCED HER TO KILL EVERYONE!
空き缶入れ
GU

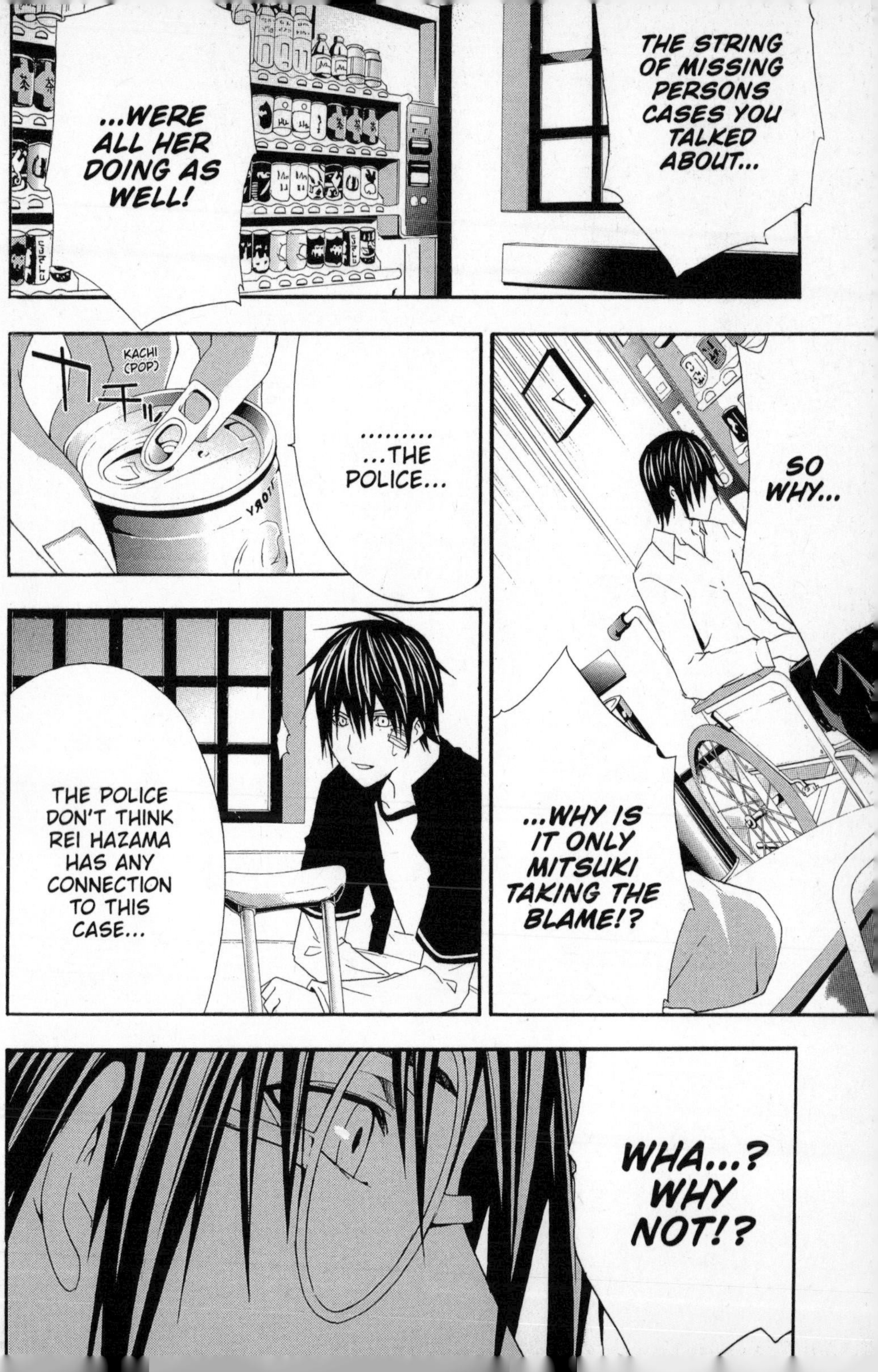
THE STRING OF MISSING PERSONS CASES YOU TALKED ABOUT...
...WERE ALL HER DOING AS WELL!
SO WHY...
...WHY IS IT ONLY MITSUKI TAKING THE BLAME!?
カチッ
KACHI (POP)
....
...THE POLICE...
THE POLICE DON'T THINK REI HAZAMA HAS ANY CONNECTION TO THIS CASE...
WHA...? WHY NOT!?

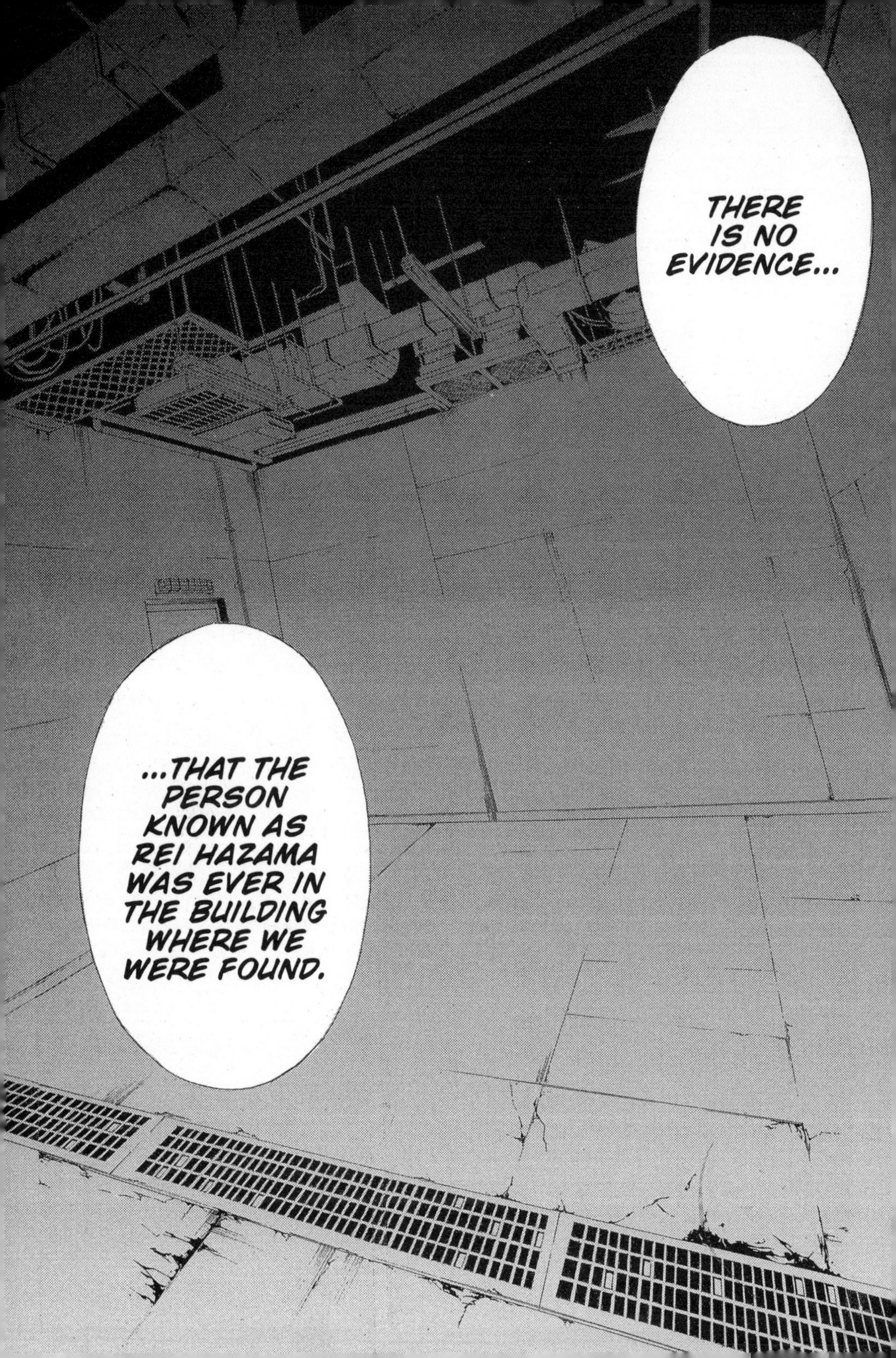
THERE IS NO EVIDENCE...
...THAT THE PERSON KNOWN AS REI HAZAMA WAS EVER IN THE BUILDING WHERE WE WERE FOUND.

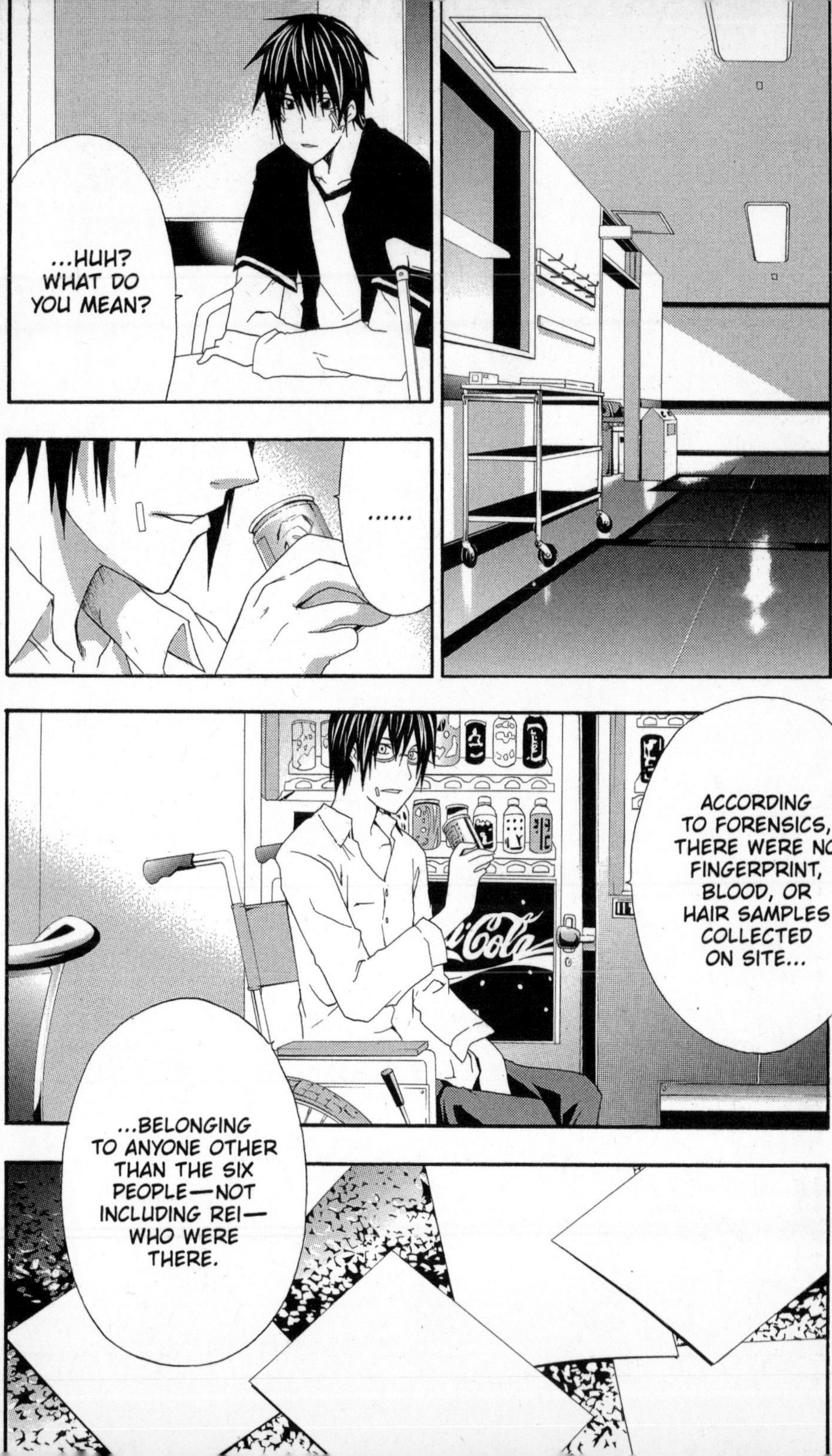
...HUH? WHAT DO YOU MEAN?
......
ACCORDING TO FORENSICS, THERE WERE NO FINGERPRINT, BLOOD, OR HAIR SAMPLES COLLECTED ON SITE...
...BELONGING TO ANYONE OTHER THAN THE SIX PEOPLE—NOT INCLUDING REI—WHO WERE THERE.

THAT CAN'T BE!

EVEN YOU SAW THAT REI WAS THERE, RIGHT!?

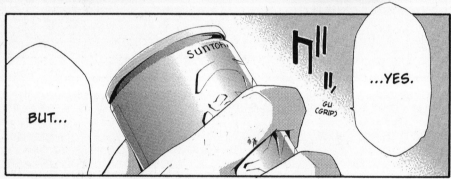

...YES.

BUT...

GU (GRIP)

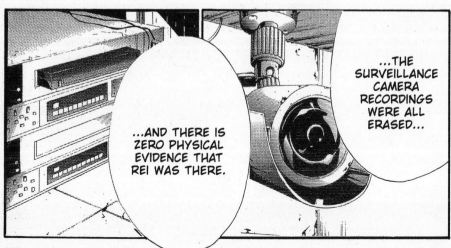

...THE SURVEILLANCE CAMERA RECORDINGS WERE ALL ERASED...

...AND THERE IS ZERO PHYSICAL EVIDENCE THAT REI WAS THERE.

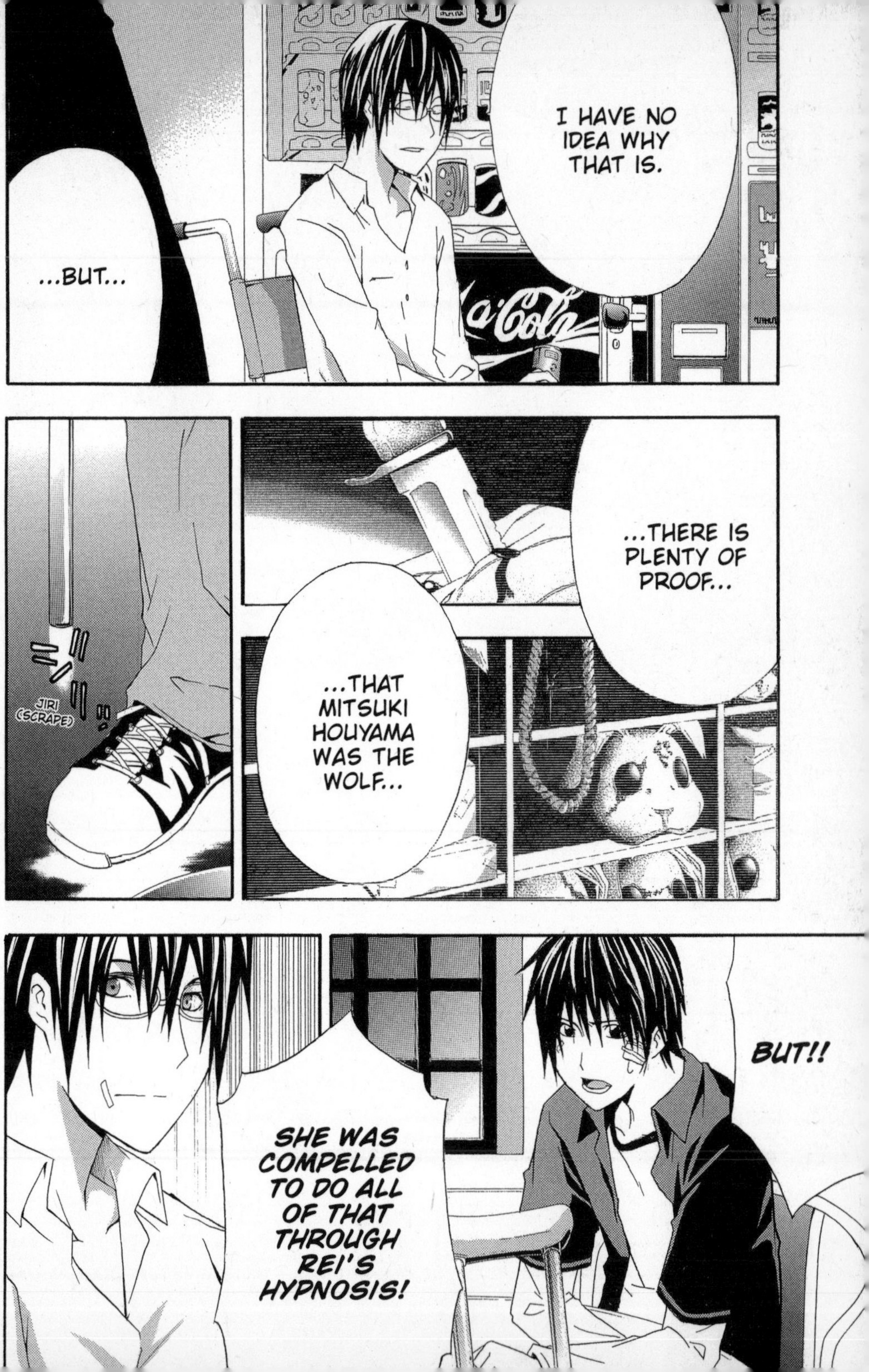
I HAVE NO IDEA WHY THAT IS.
...BUT...
...THERE IS PLENTY OF PROOF...
...THAT MITSUKI HOUYAMA WAS THE WOLF...
JIRI (SCRAPE)
BUT!!
SHE WAS COMPELLED TO DO ALL OF THAT THROUGH REI'S HYPNOSIS!

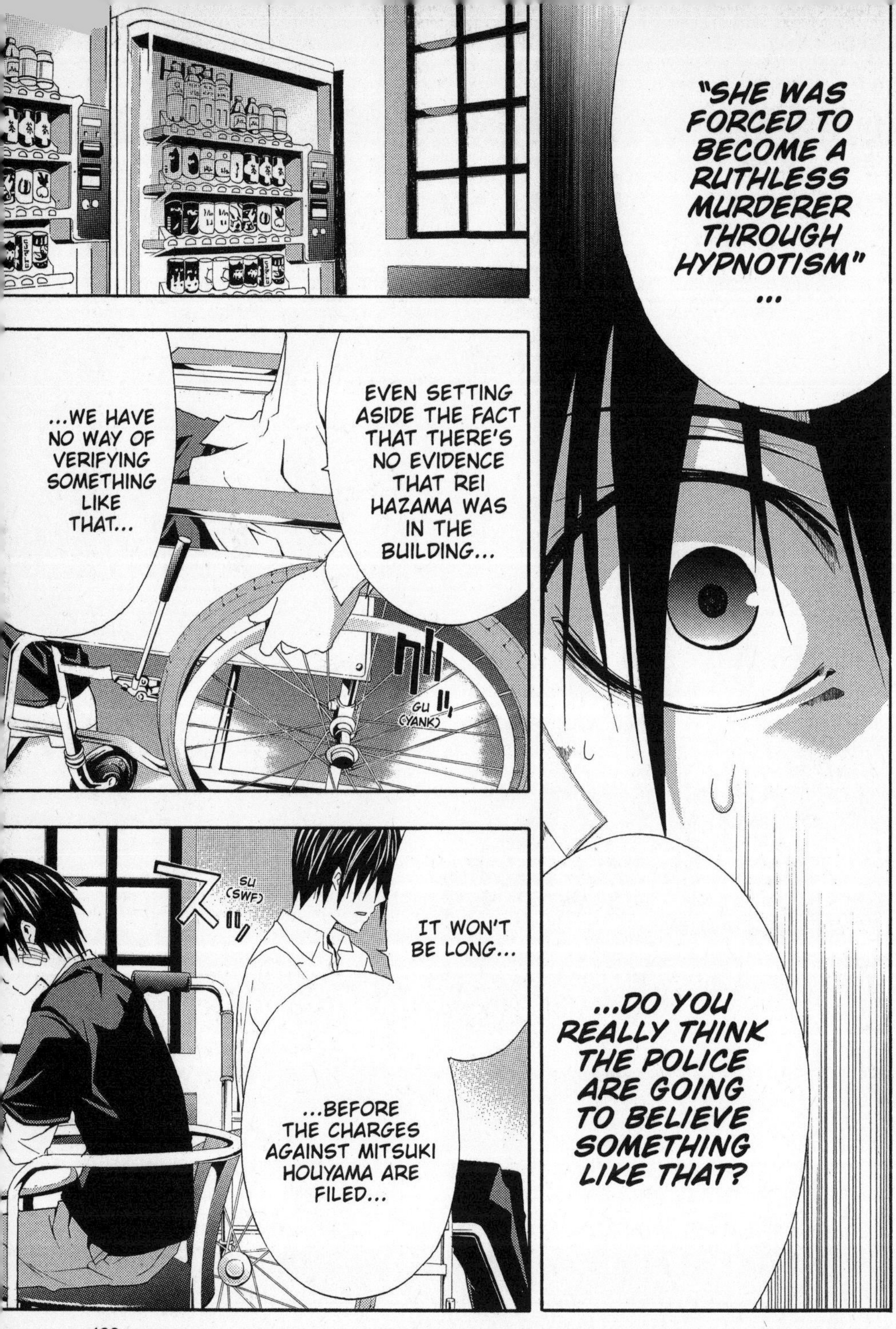
"SHE WAS FORCED TO BECOME A RUTHLESS MURDERER THROUGH HYPNOTISM" ...
...DO YOU REALLY THINK THE POLICE ARE GOING TO BELIEVE SOMETHING LIKE THAT?
EVEN SETTING ASIDE THE FACT THAT THERE'S NO EVIDENCE THAT REI HAZAMA WAS IN THE BUILDING...
...WE HAVE NO WAY OF VERIFYING SOMETHING LIKE THAT...
GU (YANK)
SU (SWF)
IT WON'T BE LONG...
...BEFORE THE CHARGES AGAINST MITSUKI HOUYAMA ARE FILED...

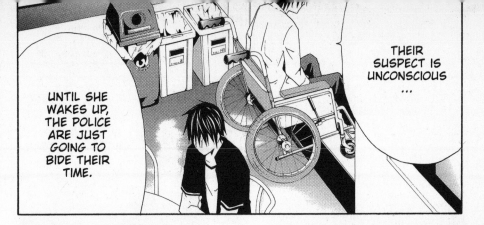

THEIR SUSPECT IS UNCONSCIOUS...

UNTIL SHE WAKES UP, THE POLICE ARE JUST GOING TO BIDE THEIR TIME.

I'LL SEE IF I CAN CONVINCE FORENSICS TO DO A REINVESTIGATION IN THE MEANTIME.

YOU SHOULD STAY BY HER SIDE.

KI (SQUEAK)

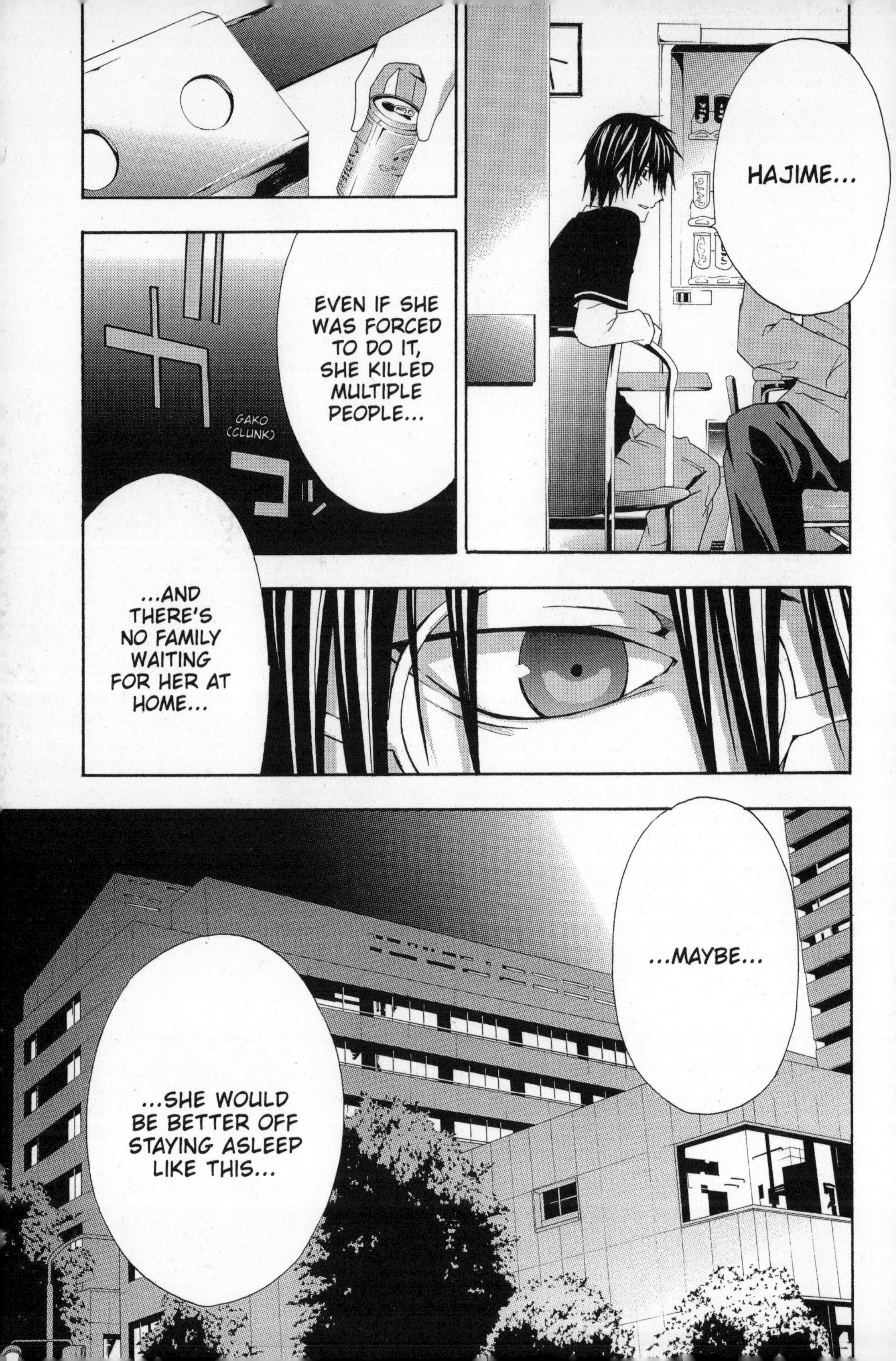
HAJIME...
EVEN IF SHE WAS FORCED TO DO IT, SHE KILLED MULTIPLE PEOPLE...
GAKO (CLUNK)
...AND THERE'S NO FAMILY WAITING FOR HER AT HOME...
...MAYBE...
...SHE WOULD BE BETTER OFF STAYING ASLEEP LIKE THIS...

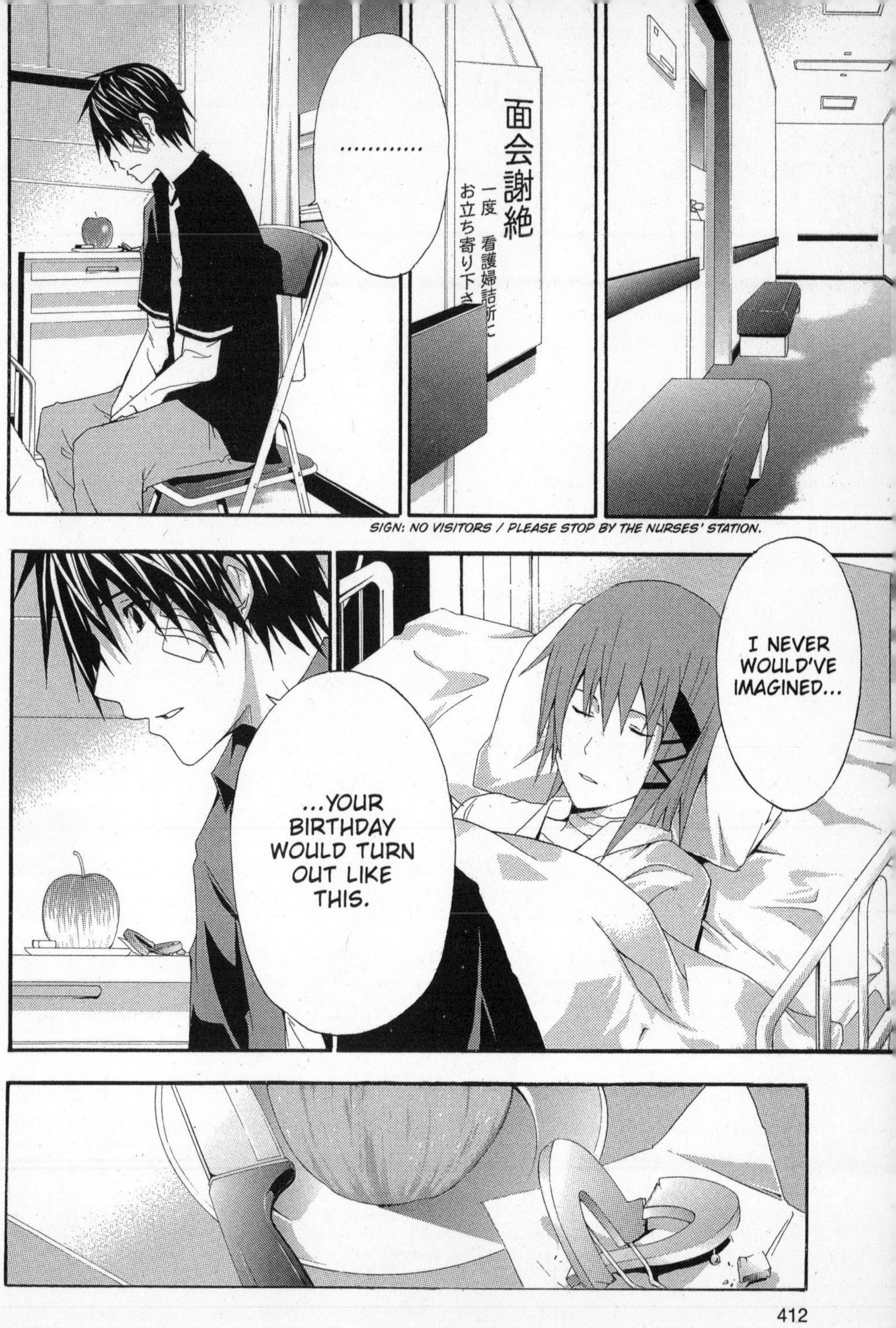
面会謝絶
一度 看護婦詰所に
お立ち寄り下さ
....
I NEVER WOULD'VE IMAGINED...
...YOUR BIRTHDAY WOULD TURN OUT LIKE THIS.

SIGN: NO VISITORS / PLEASE STOP BY THE NURSES' STATION.

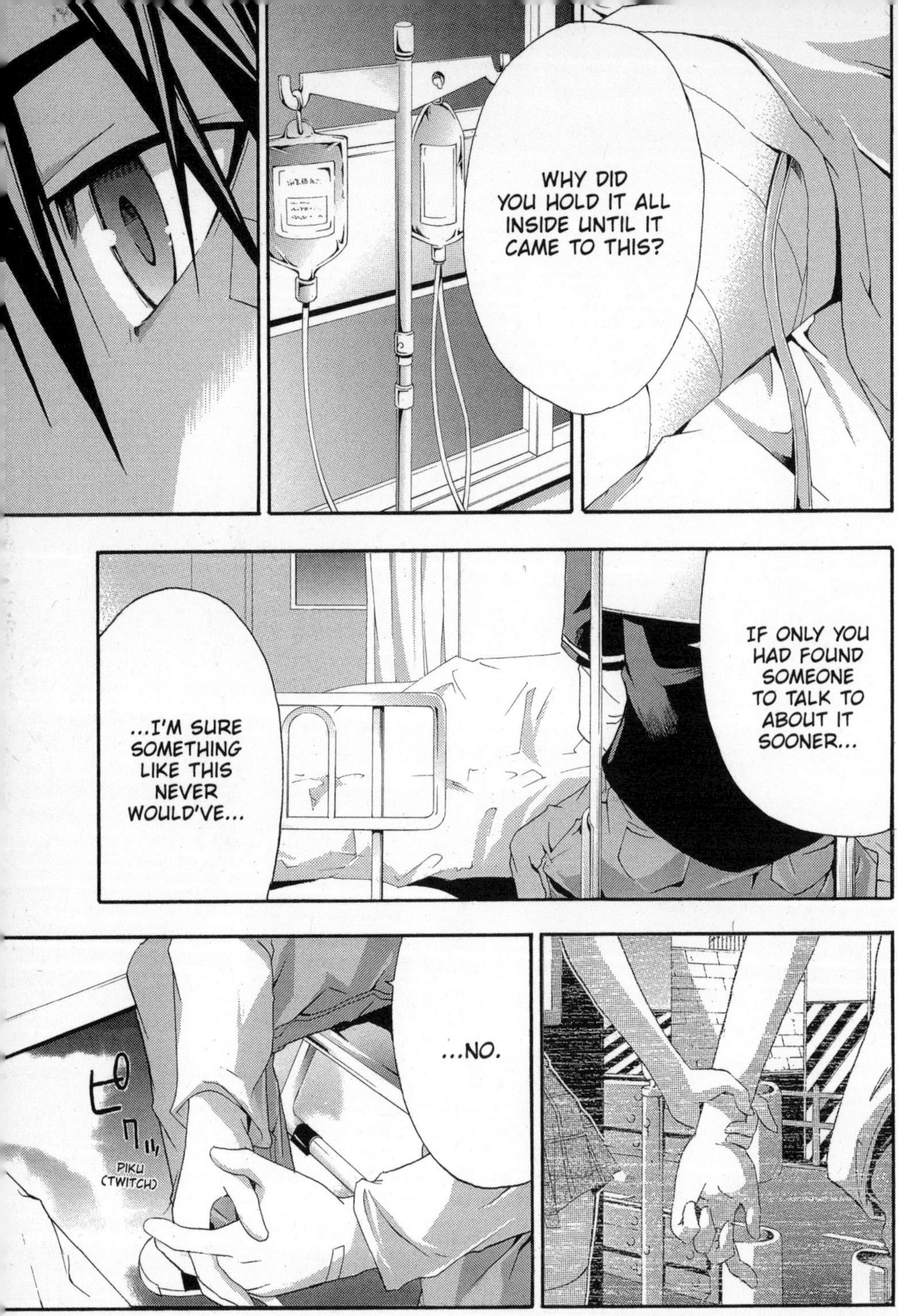
WHY DID YOU HOLD IT ALL INSIDE UNTIL IT CAME TO THIS?
IF ONLY YOU HAD FOUND SOMEONE TO TALK TO ABOUT IT SOONER...
...I'M SURE SOMETHING LIKE THIS NEVER WOULD'VE...
...NO.
ピクッ
PIKU (TWITCH)

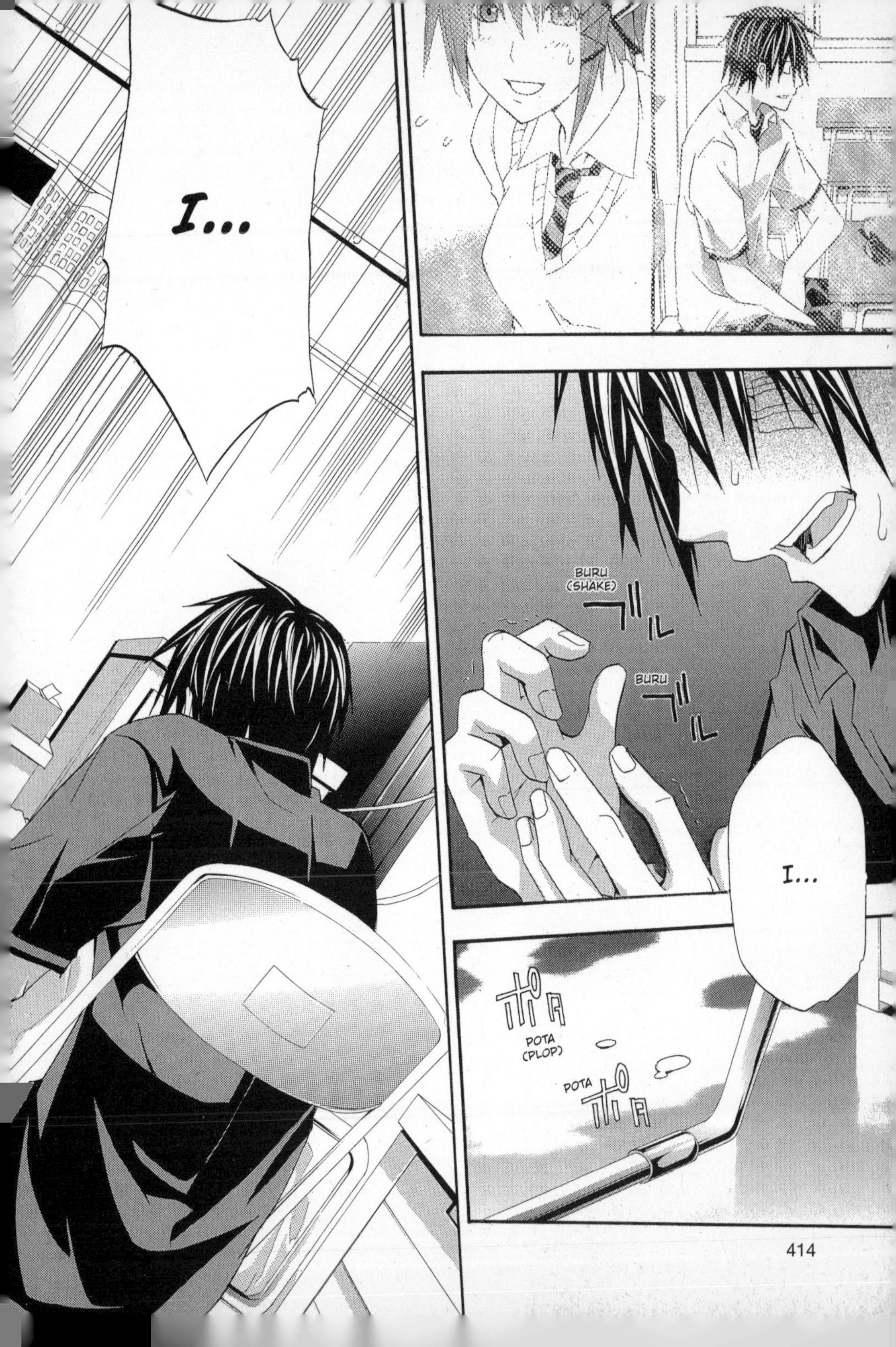
BURU (SHAKE)
ブル
BURU
ブル
I...
ポタ
POTA (PLOP)
POTA
ポタ
I...

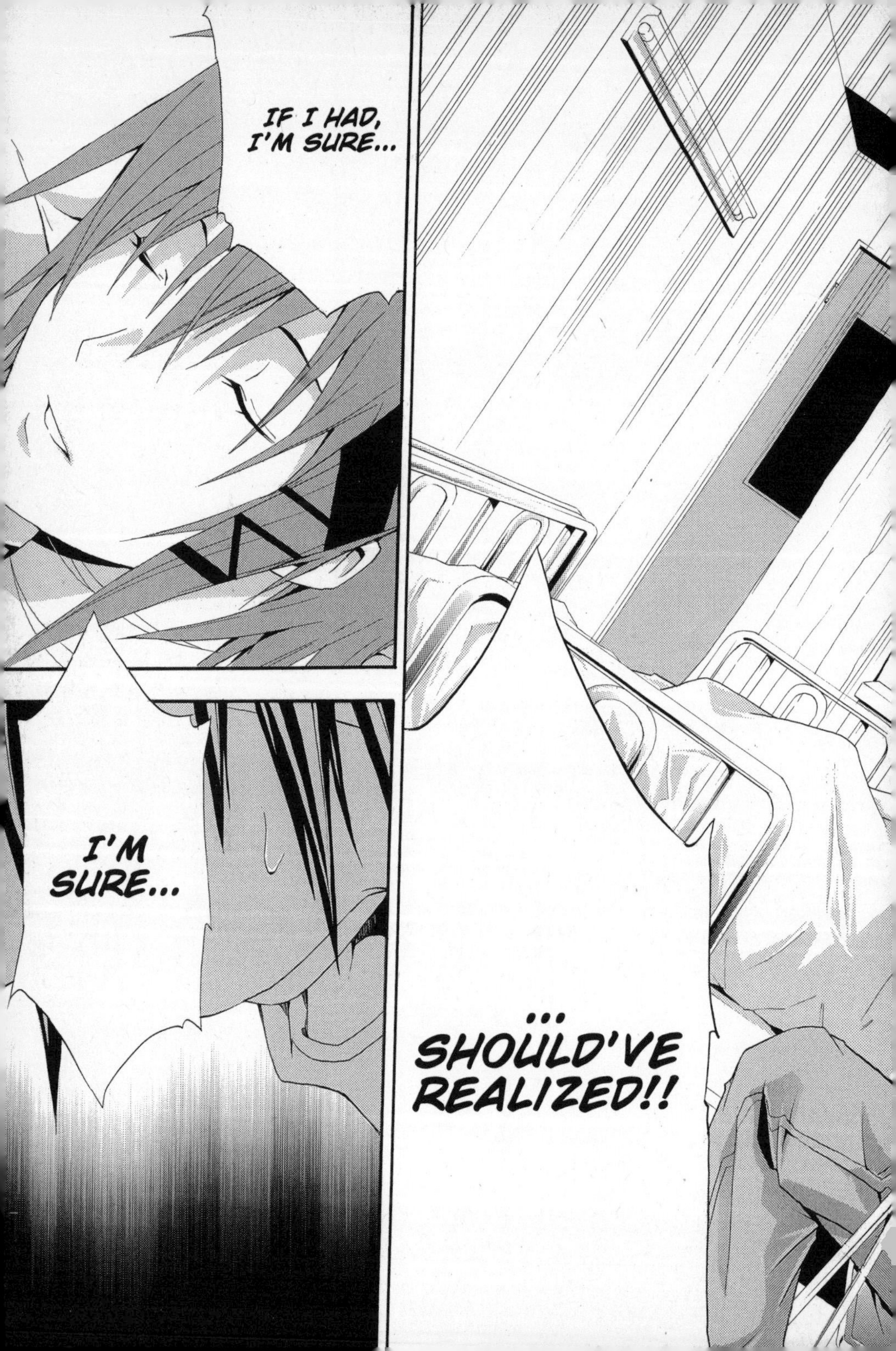
IF I HAD, I'M SURE...
I'M SURE...
...SHOULD'VE REALIZED!!

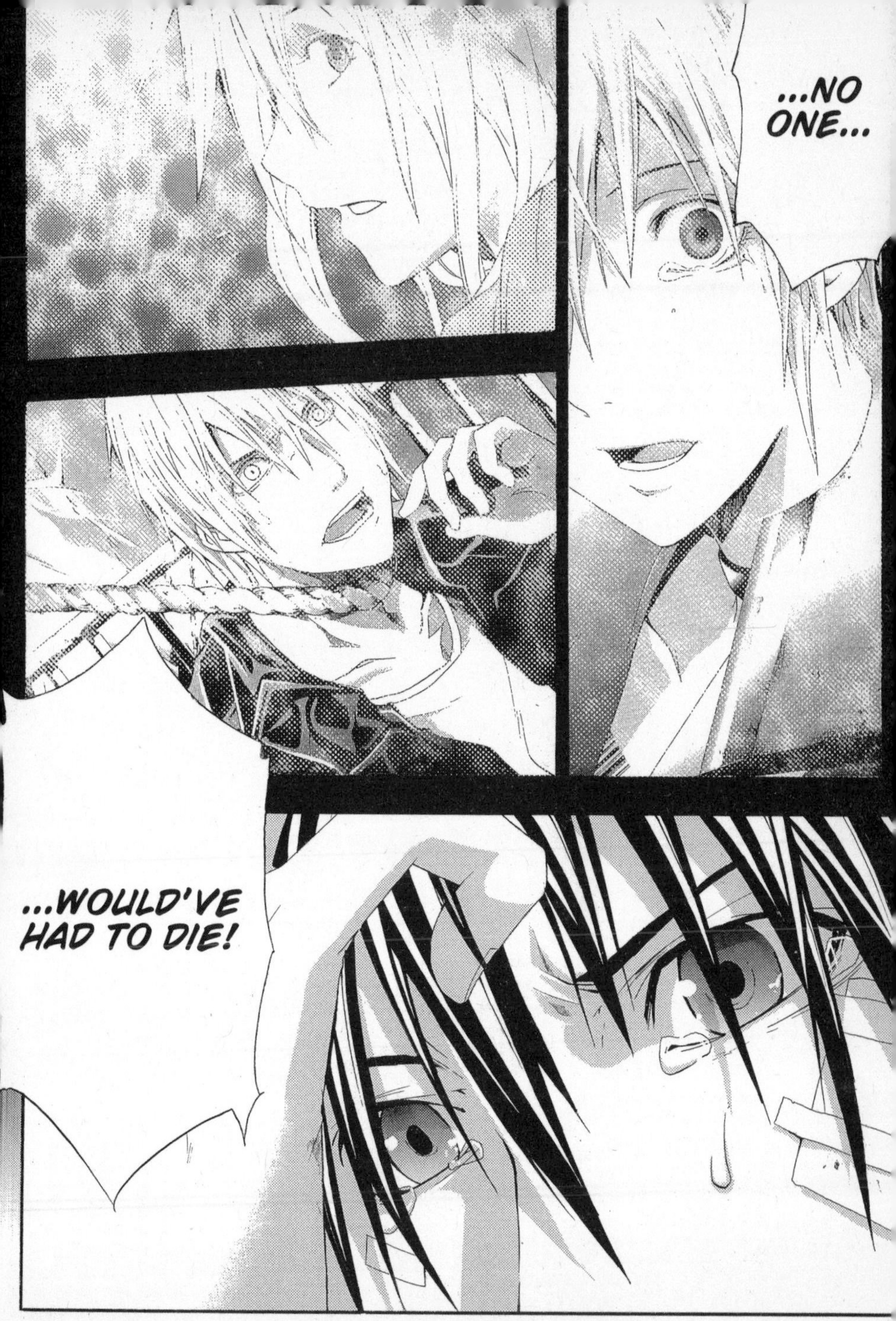
...NO ONE...
...WOULD'VE HAD TO DIE!

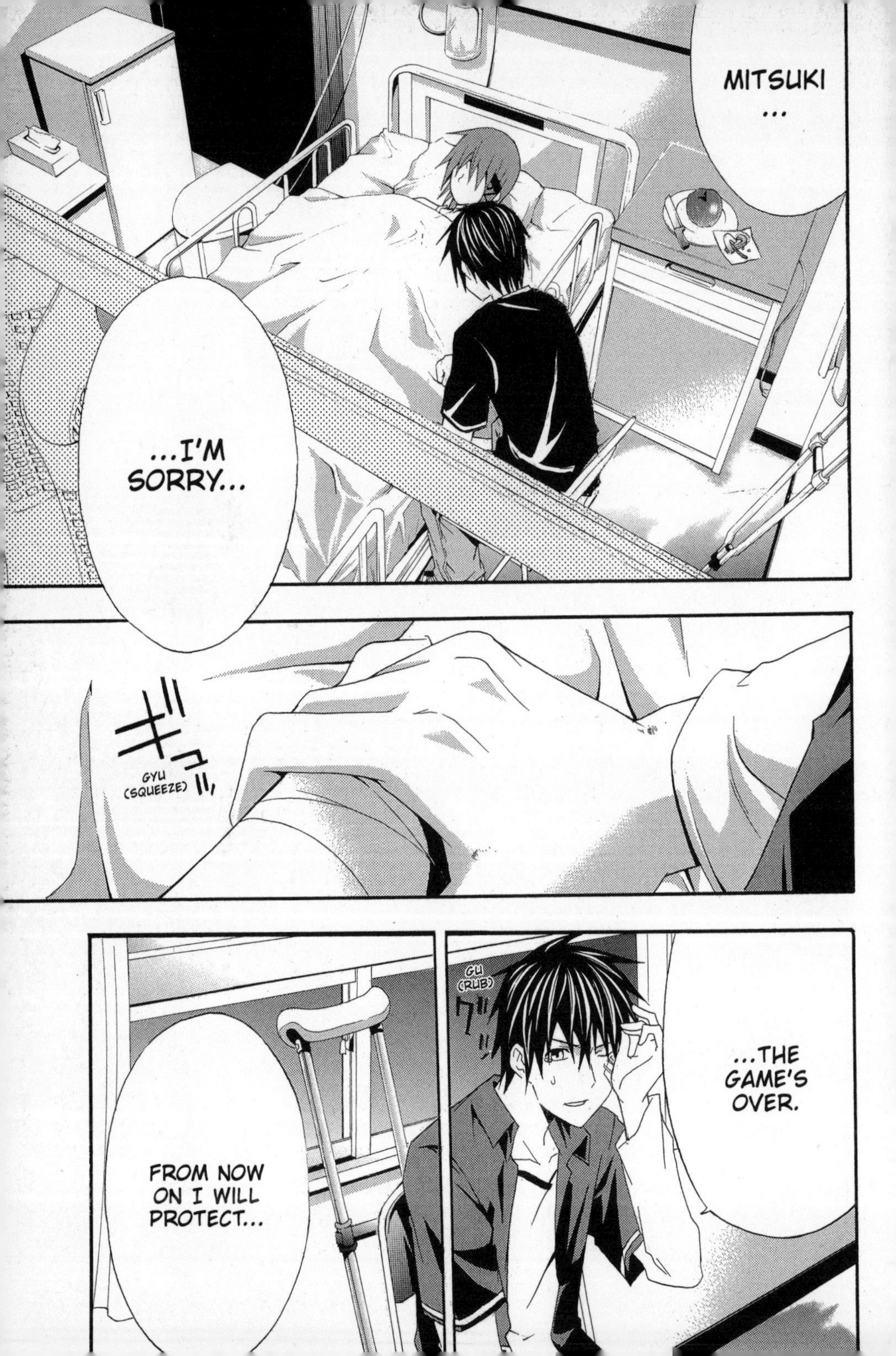
MITSUKI ...
...I'M SORRY...
ギュッ
GYU (SQUEEZE)
...THE GAME'S OVER.
グッ
GU (RUB)
FROM NOW ON I WILL PROTECT...

BEEP
BEEP
BEEP

...A CELL PHONE?

...WHAT'S THAT DOING IN HERE...?

PIKU (TWITCH)

...DID SOMEBODY DROP IT...?

SU (REACH)

BEEP
BEEP
BEEP

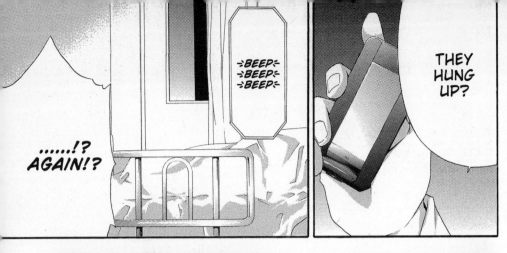

≈BEEP≈
≈BEEP≈
≈BEEP≈

......!?
AGAIN!?

THEY
HUNG
UP?

UH...
UMM...

...I JUST
FOUND THIS
PHONE,
BUT...

KA
(CLACK)

≈BEEP≈

...HELLO?

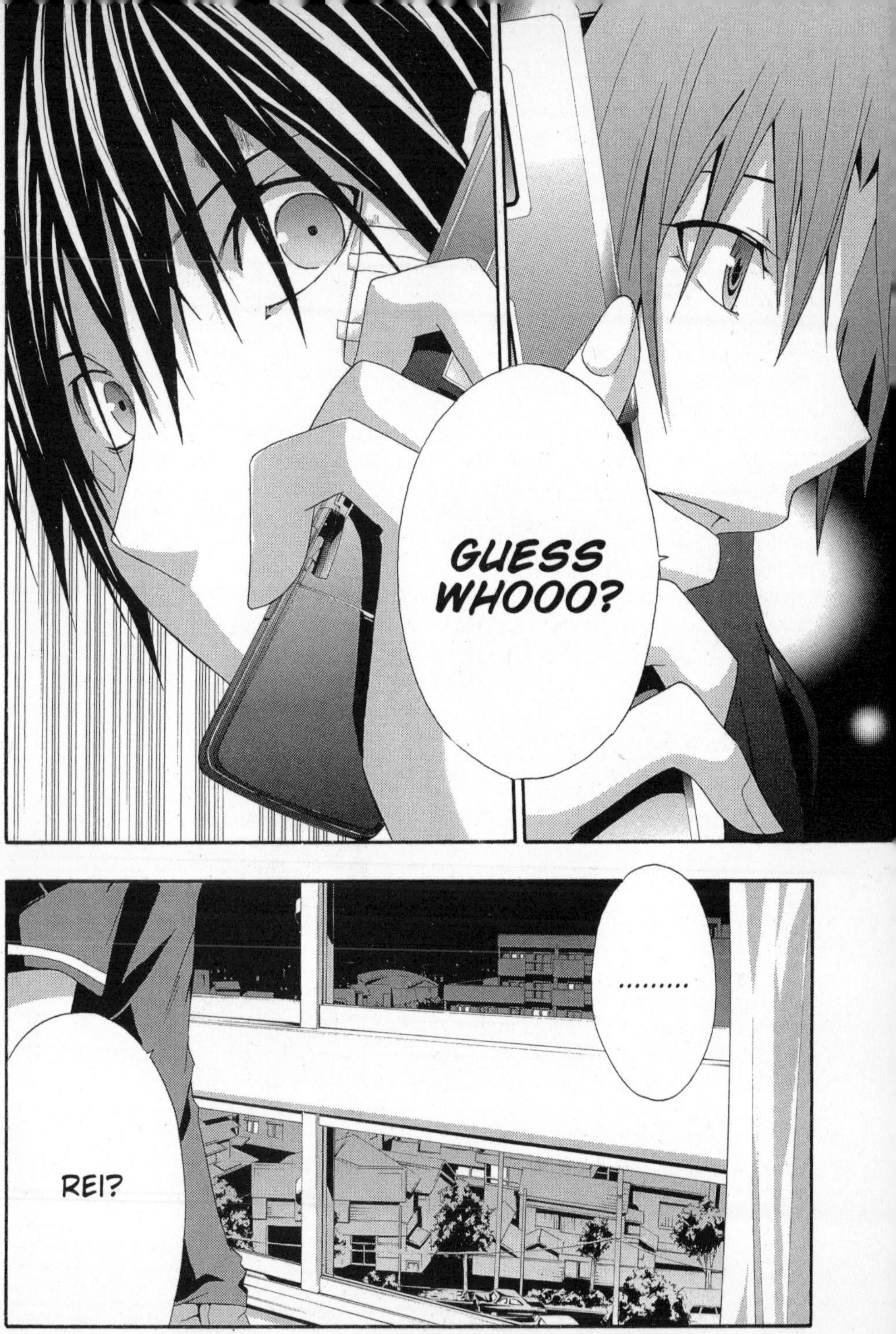
GUESS WHOOO?
....
REI?

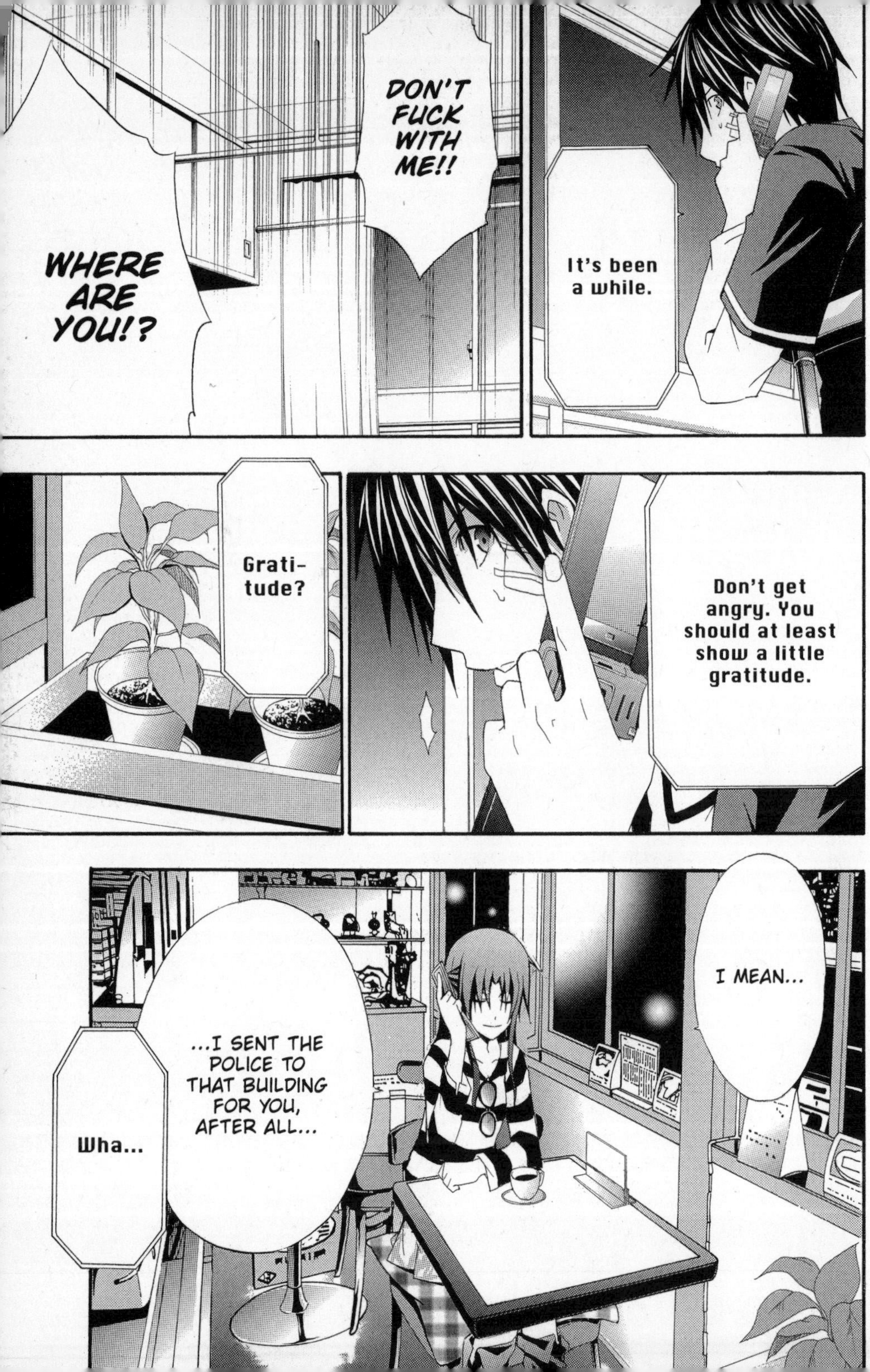
It's been a while.
DON'T FUCK WITH ME!!
WHERE ARE YOU!?
Don't get angry. You should at least show a little gratitude.
Grati-tude?
I MEAN...
...I SENT THE POLICE TO THAT BUILDING FOR YOU, AFTER ALL...
Wha...

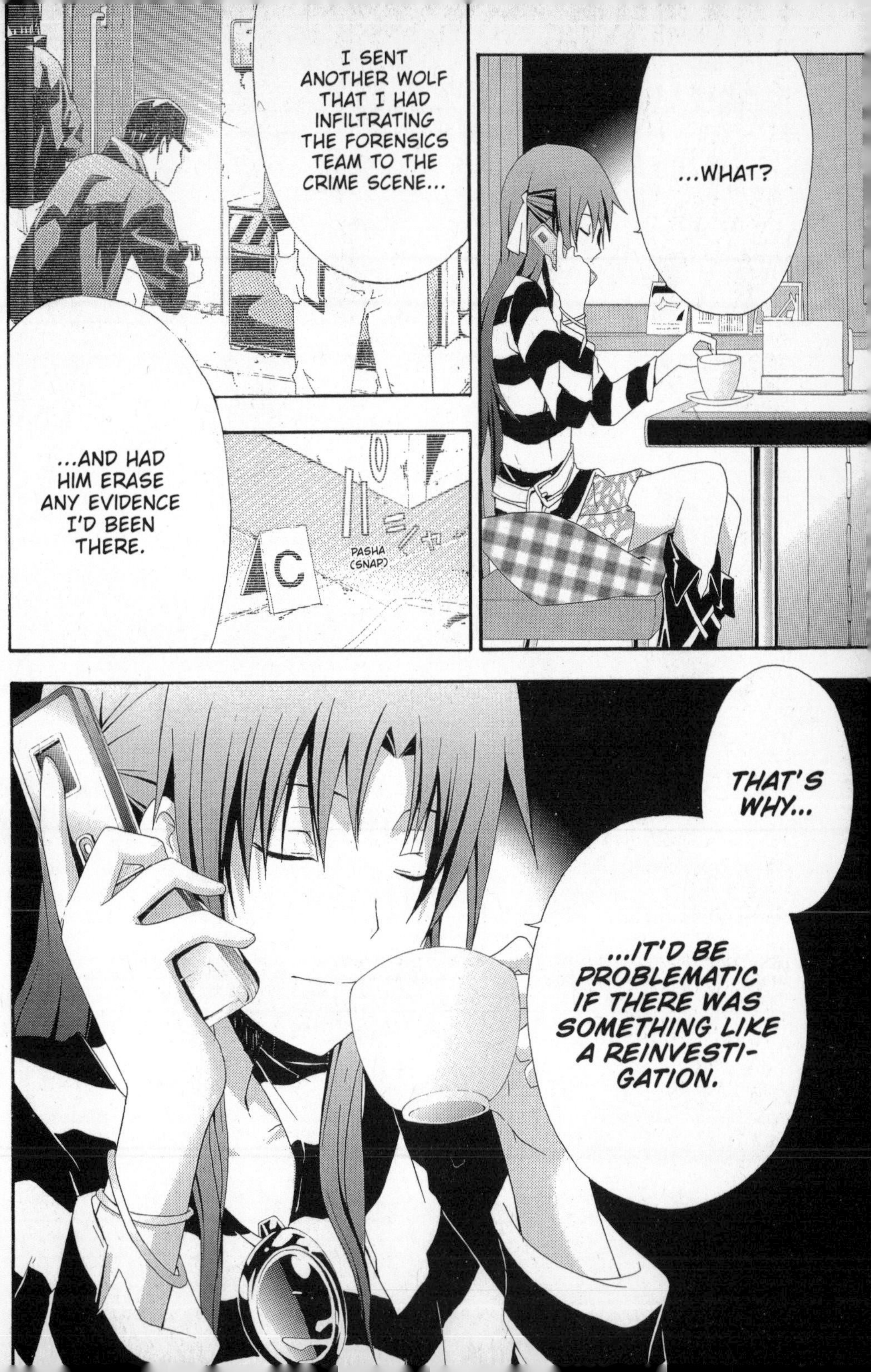
...WHAT?
I SENT ANOTHER WOLF THAT I HAD INFILTRATING THE FORENSICS TEAM TO THE CRIME SCENE...
...AND HAD HIM ERASE ANY EVIDENCE I'D BEEN THERE.
C
PASHA (SNAP)
THAT'S WHY...
...IT'D BE PROBLEMATIC IF THERE WAS SOMETHING LIKE A REINVESTI-GATION.

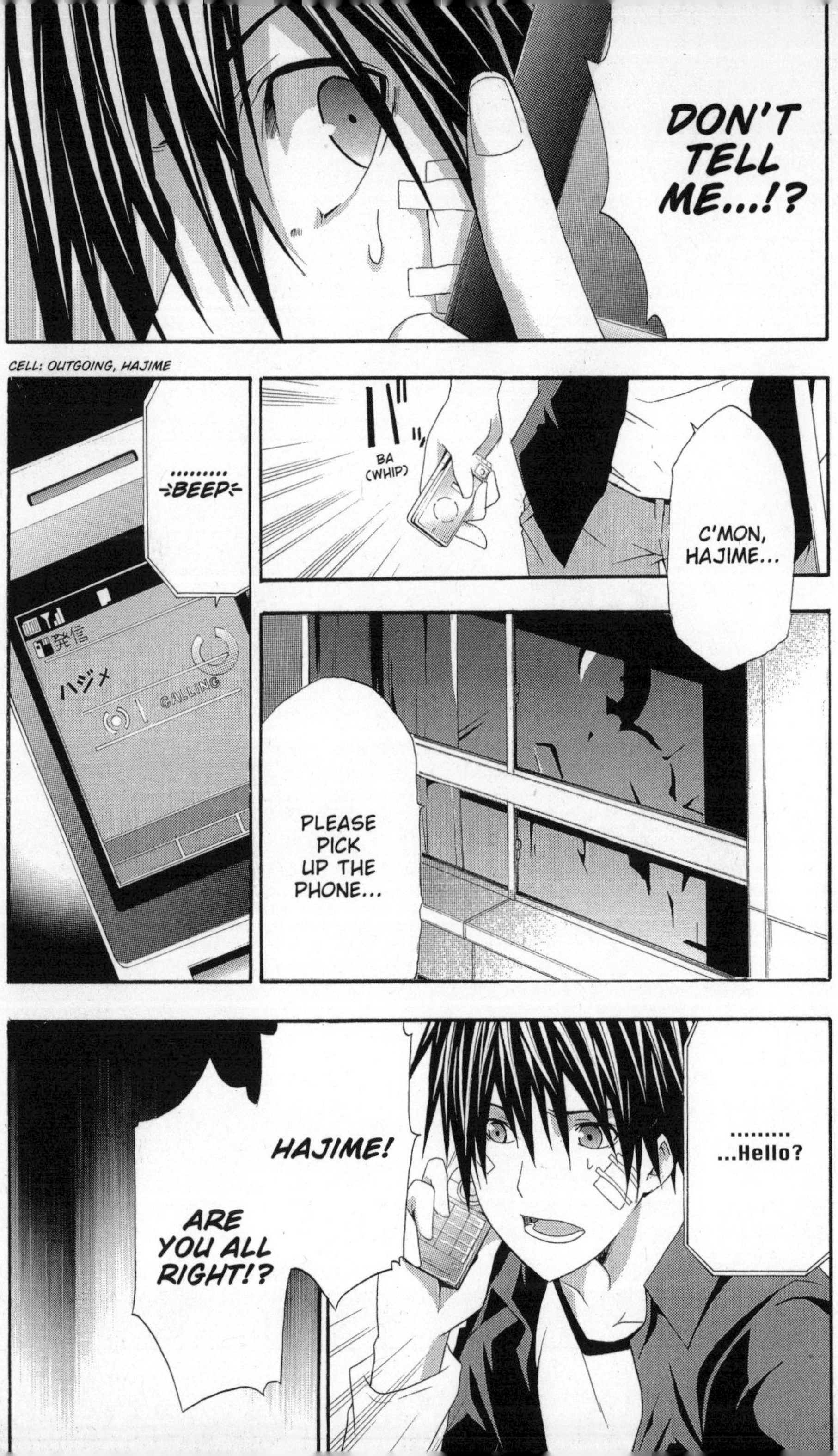
DON'T TELL ME...!?
CELL: OUTGOING, HAJIME
BA (WHIP)
C'MON, HAJIME...
PLEASE PICK UP THE PHONE...
....
BEEP
発信
ハジメ
CALLING
....
...Hello?
HAJIME!
ARE YOU ALL RIGHT!?

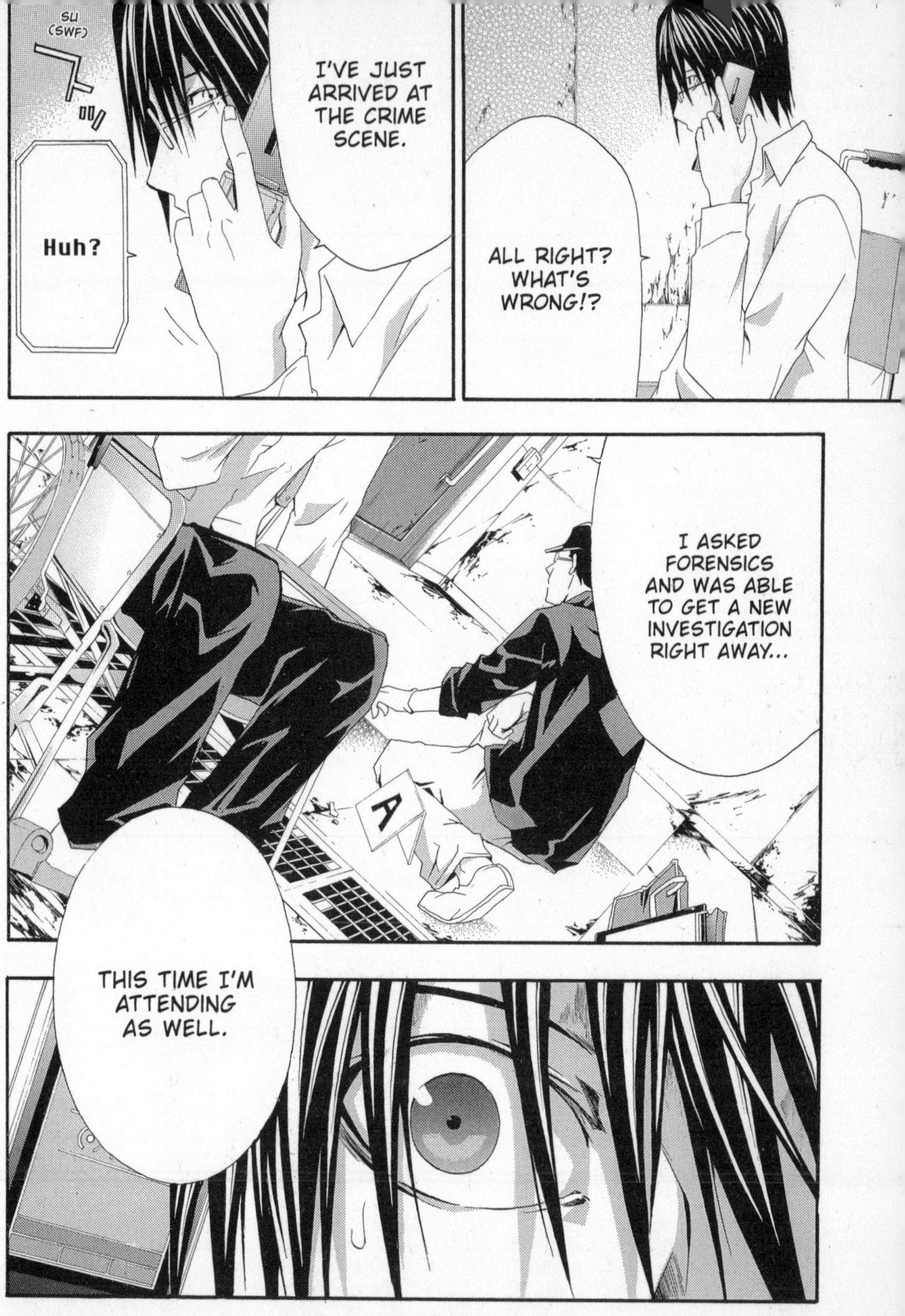
ALL RIGHT? WHAT'S WRONG!?
I'VE JUST ARRIVED AT THE CRIME SCENE.
SU (SWF)
Huh?
I ASKED FORENSICS AND WAS ABLE TO GET A NEW INVESTIGATION RIGHT AWAY...
A
THIS TIME I'M ATTENDING AS WELL.

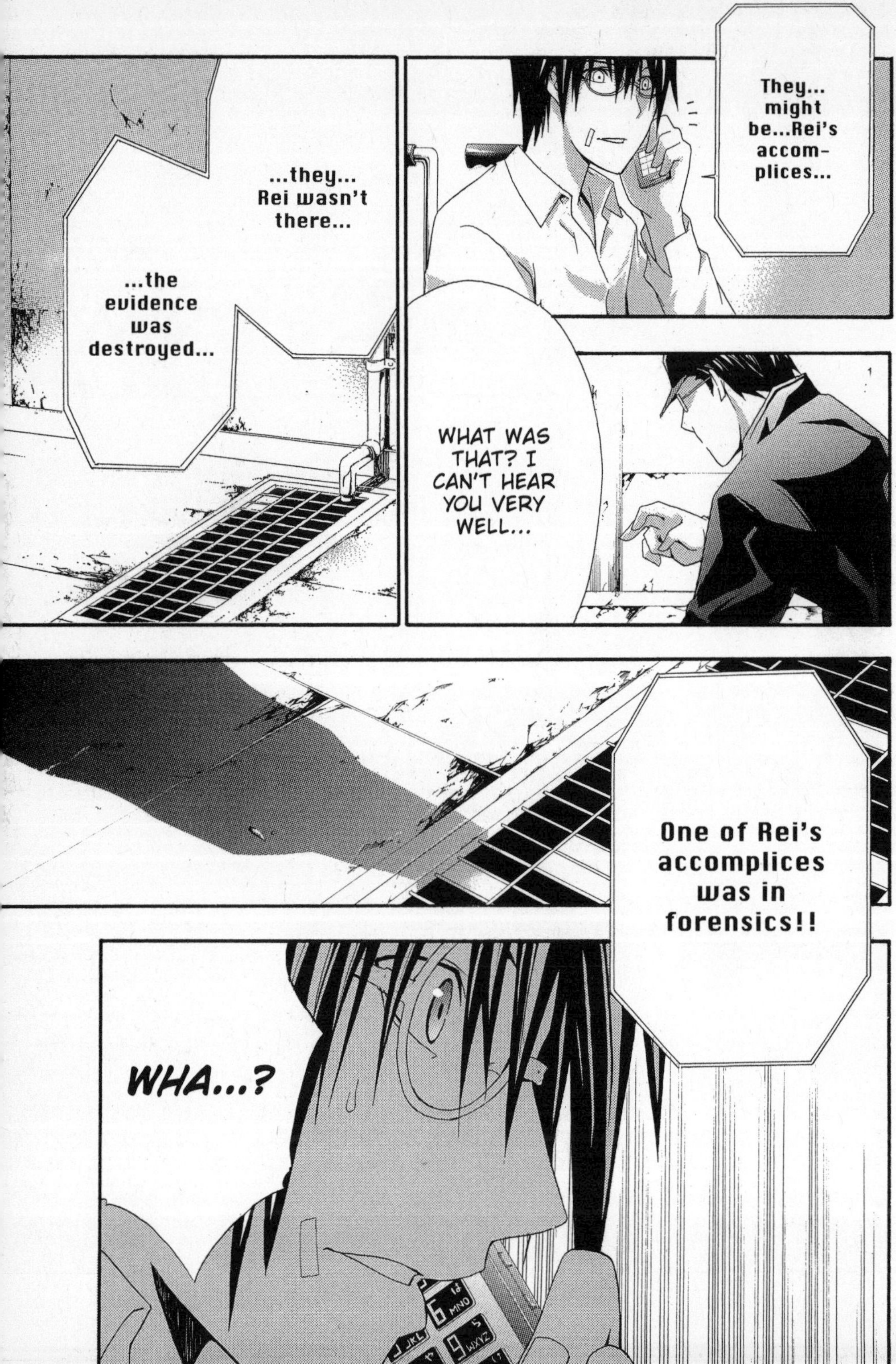
They... might be...Rei's accom-plices...
WHAT WAS THAT? I CAN'T HEAR YOU VERY WELL...
...they... Rei wasn't there...
...the evidence was destroyed...
One of Rei's accomplices was in forensics!!
WHA...?

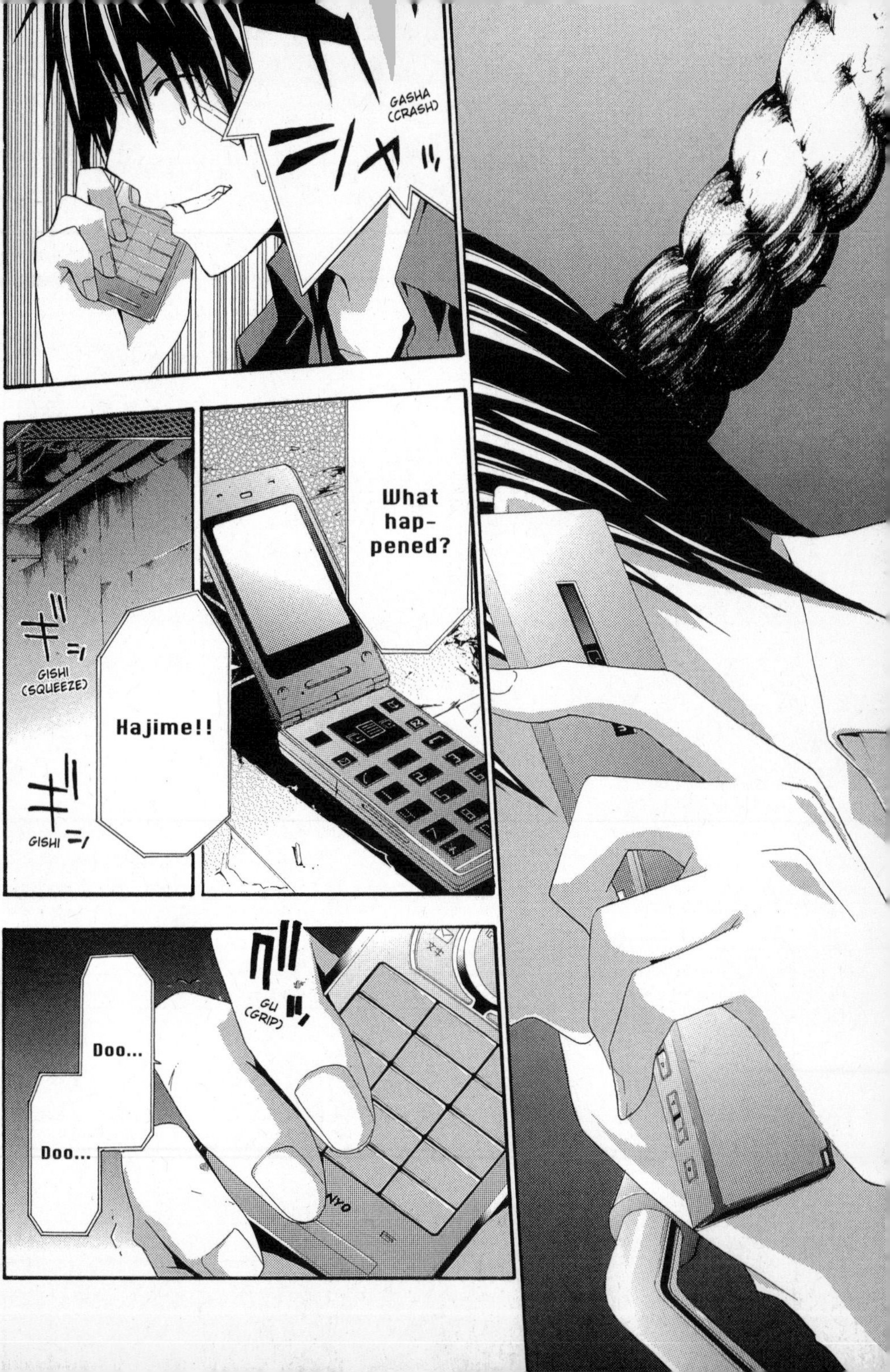
GASHA
(CRASH)
What hap-pened?
Hajime!!
GISHI
(SQUEEZE)
GISHI
GU
(GRIP)
Doo...
Doo...

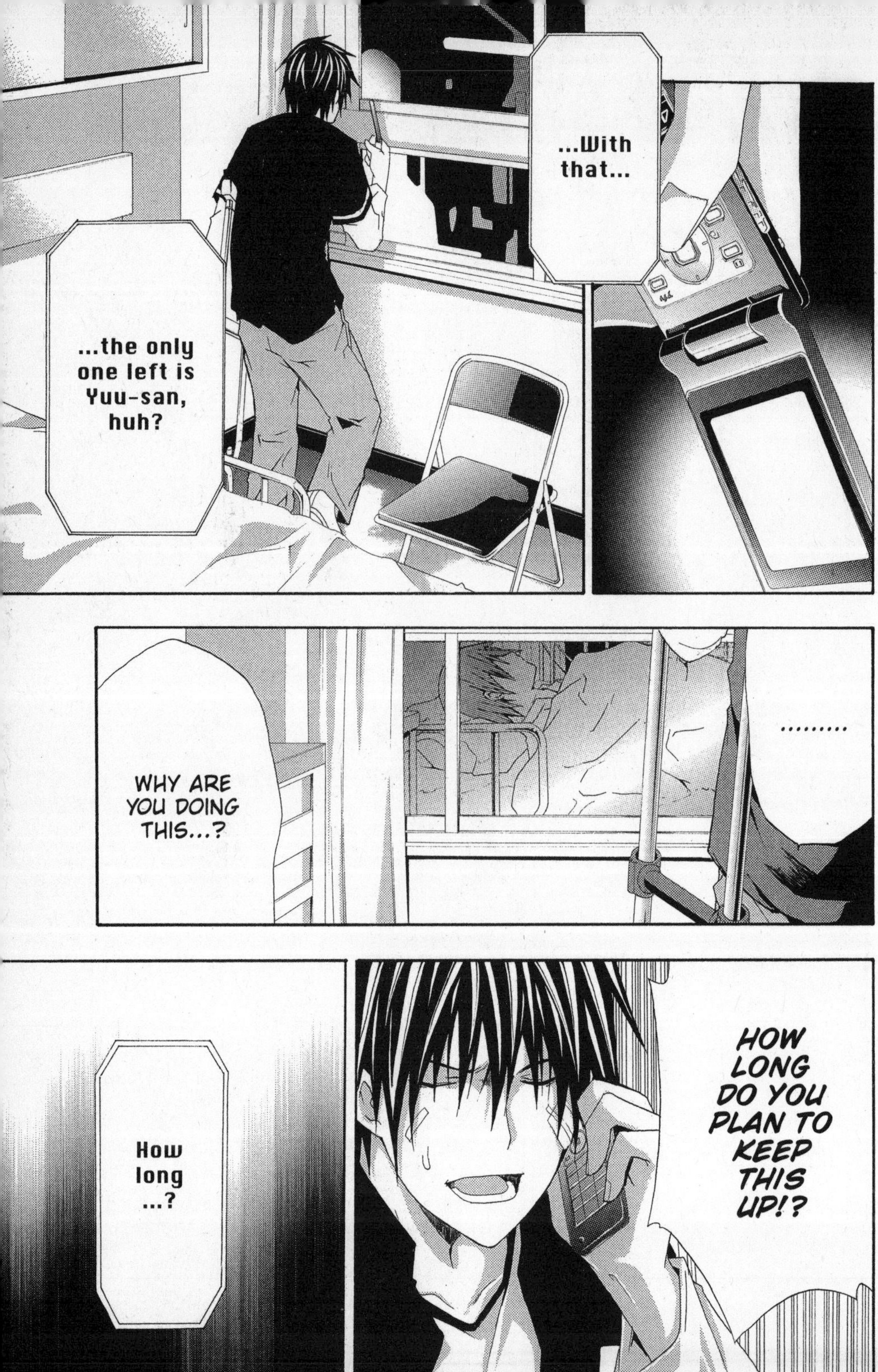
...With that...
...the only one left is Yuu-san, huh?
....
WHY ARE YOU DOING THIS...?
HOW LONG DO YOU PLAN TO KEEP THIS UP!?
How long ...?

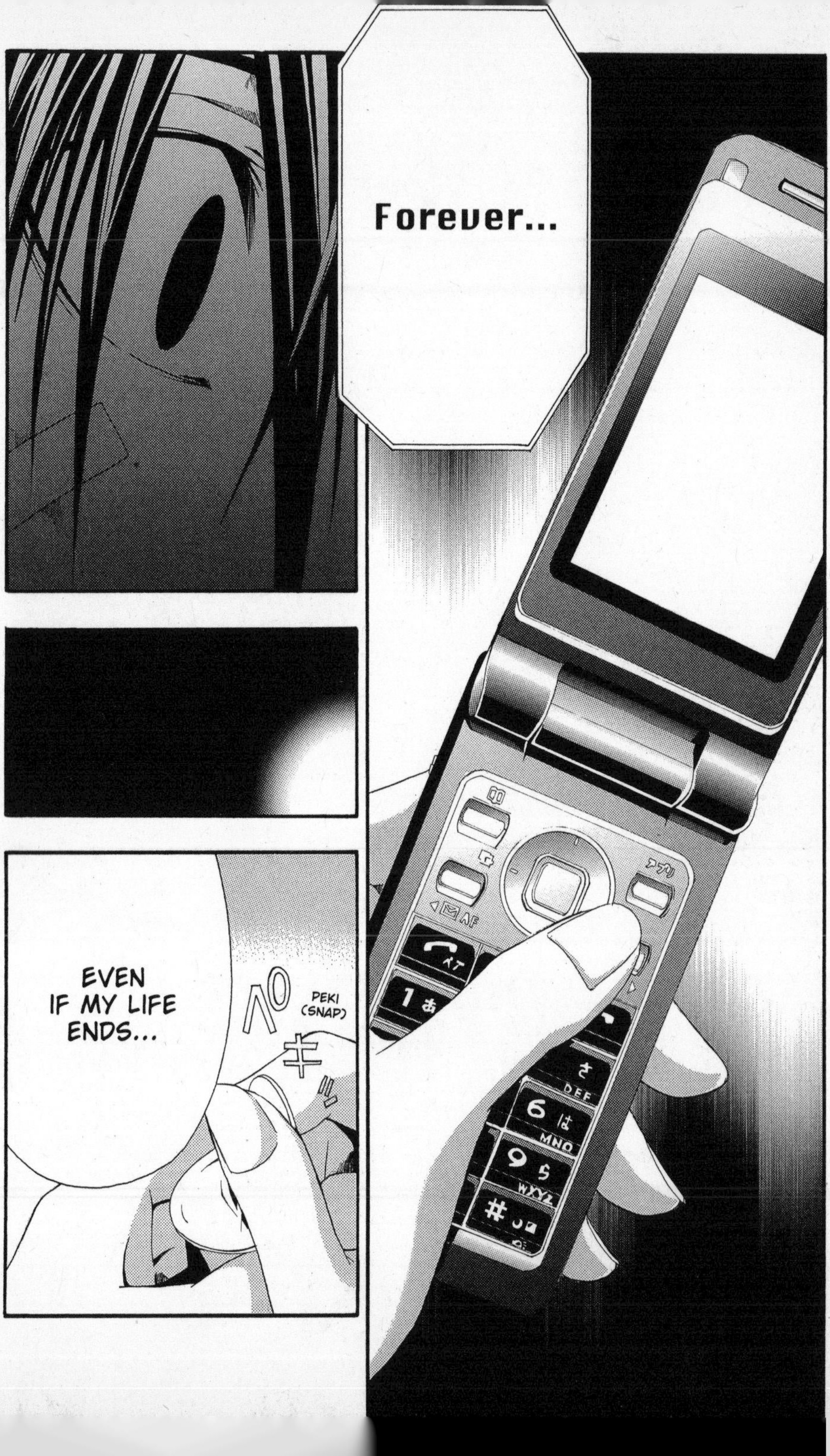
Forever...
EVEN IF MY LIFE ENDS...
PEKI (SNAP)

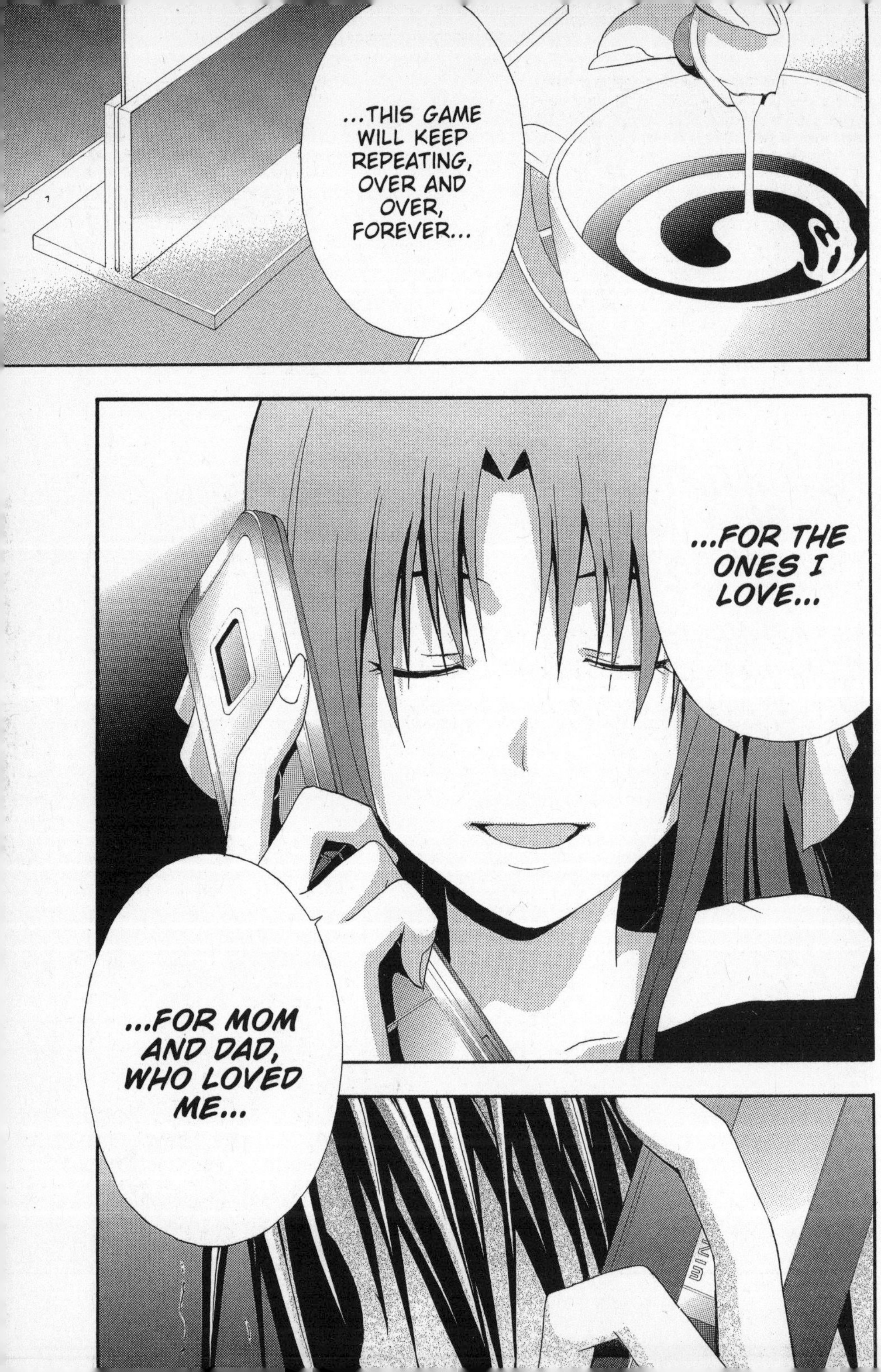
...THIS GAME WILL KEEP REPEATING, OVER AND OVER, FOREVER...
...FOR THE ONES I LOVE...
...FOR MOM AND DAD, WHO LOVED ME...

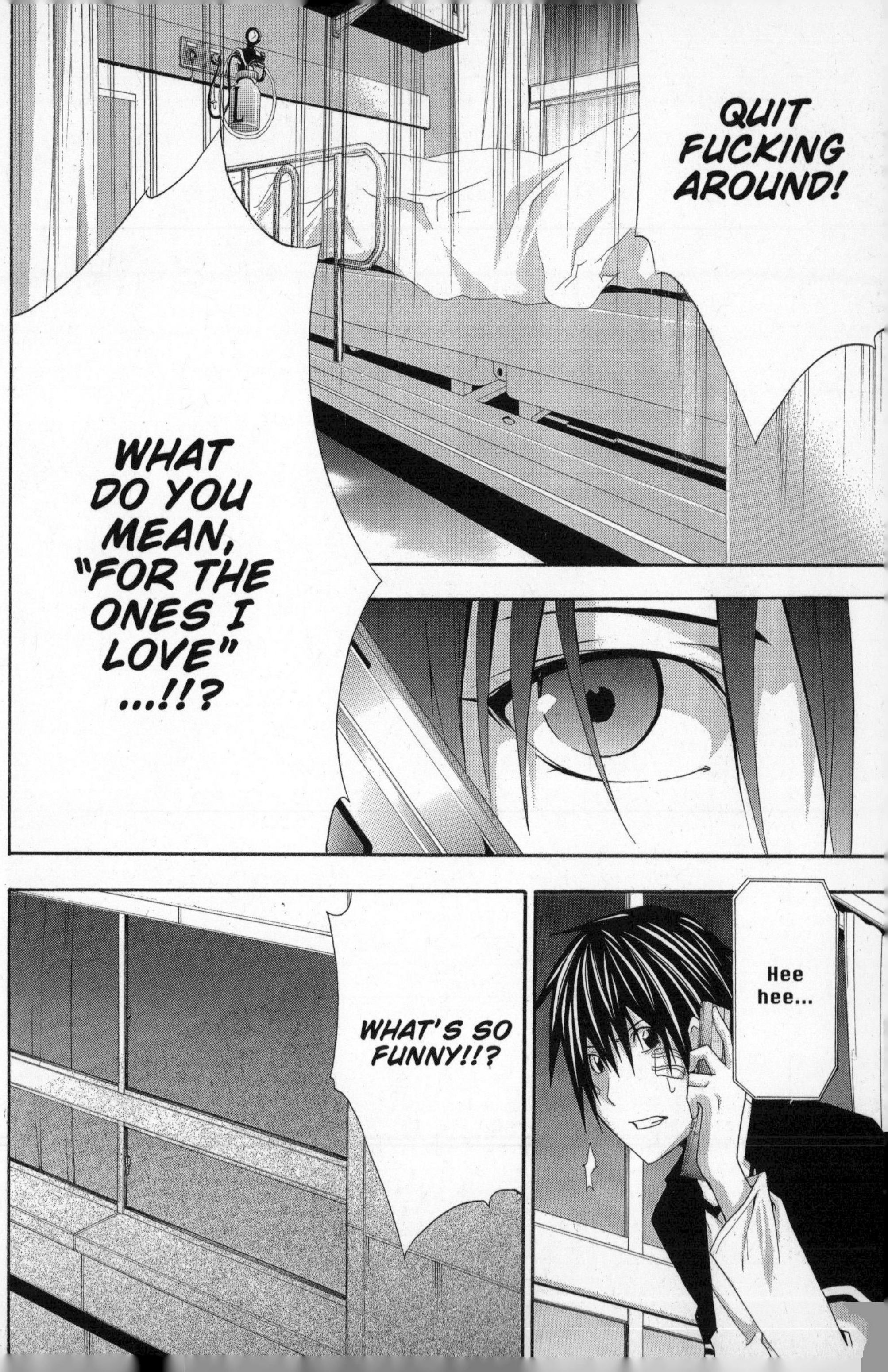
QUIT FUCKING AROUND!
WHAT DO YOU MEAN, "FOR THE ONES I LOVE"...!!?
Hee hee...
WHAT'S SO FUNNY!!?

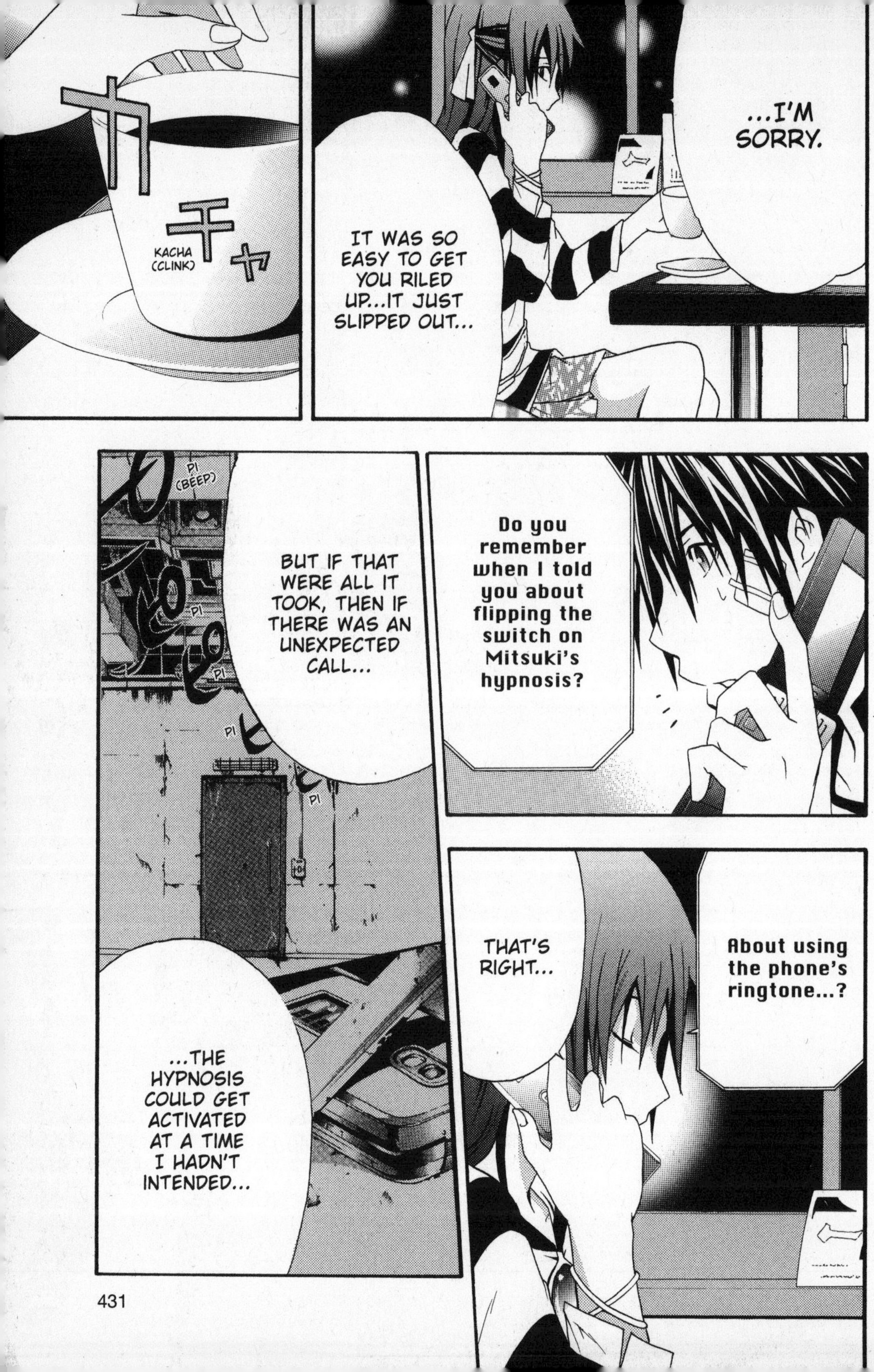
...I'M SORRY.
IT WAS SO EASY TO GET YOU RILED UP...IT JUST SLIPPED OUT...
KACHA (CLINK)
Do you remember when I told you about flipping the switch on Mitsuki's hypnosis?
About using the phone's ringtone...?
THAT'S RIGHT...
PI (BEEP)
BUT IF THAT WERE ALL IT TOOK, THEN IF THERE WAS AN UNEXPECTED CALL...
PI
PI
PI
PI
...THE HYPNOSIS COULD GET ACTIVATED AT A TIME I HADN'T INTENDED...

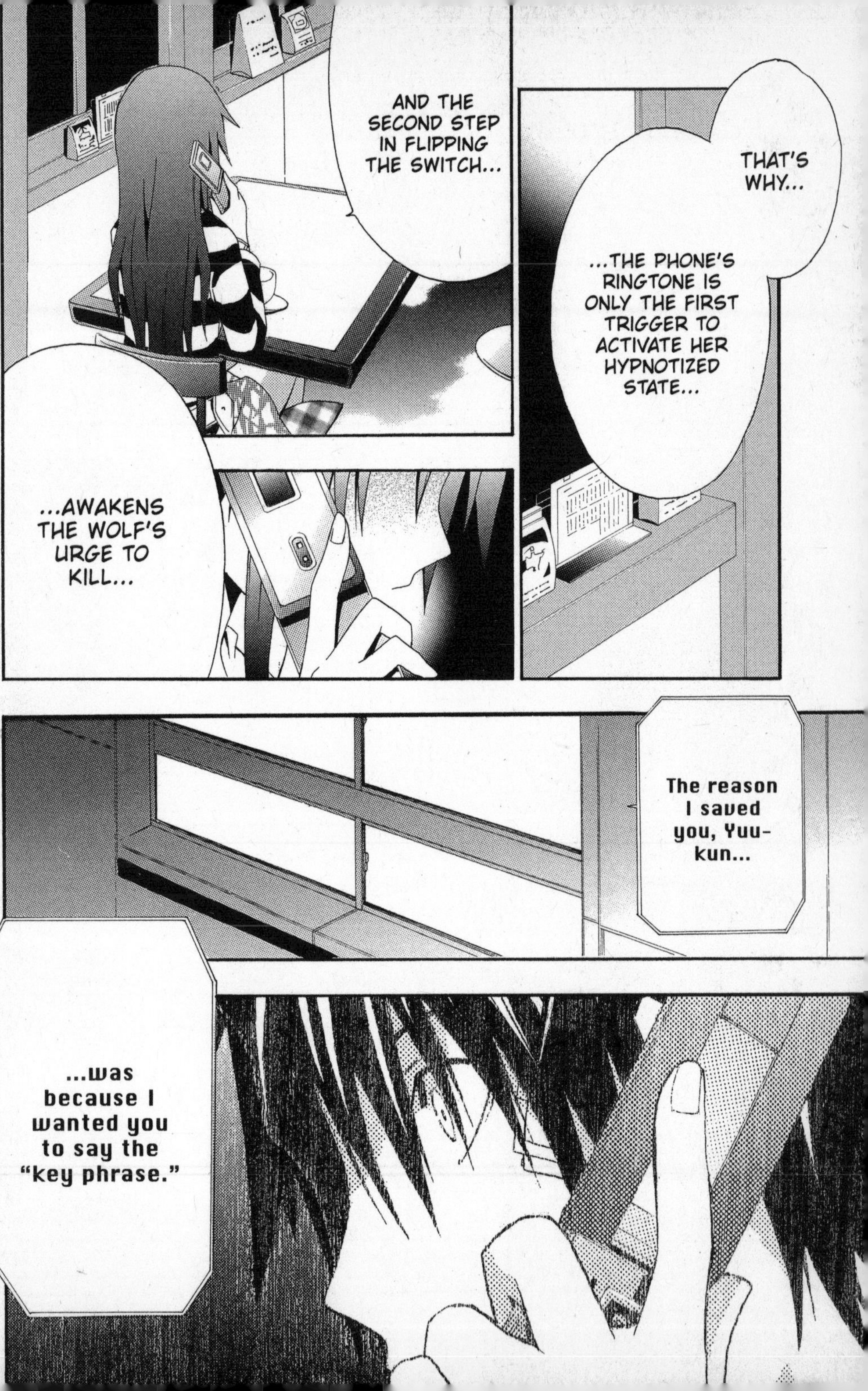
THAT'S WHY...
...THE PHONE'S RINGTONE IS ONLY THE FIRST TRIGGER TO ACTIVATE HER HYPNOTIZED STATE...
AND THE SECOND STEP IN FLIPPING THE SWITCH...
...AWAKENS THE WOLF'S URGE TO KILL...
The reason I saved you, Yuu-kun...
...was because I wanted you to say the "key phrase."

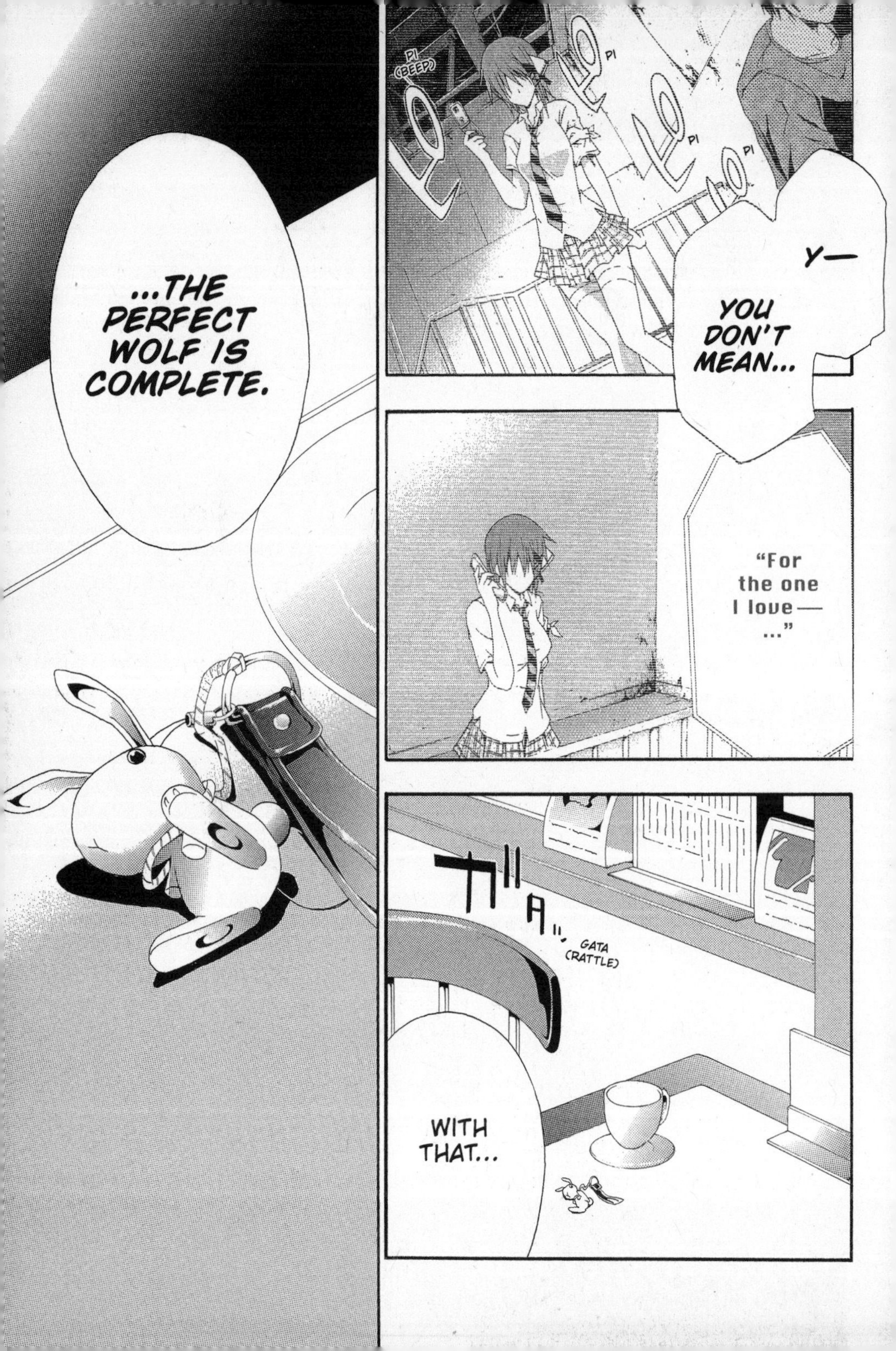
PI (BEEP)
PI
PI
PI
Y—
YOU DON'T MEAN...
"For the one I love— ..."
GATA (RATTLE)
WITH THAT...
...THE PERFECT WOLF IS COMPLETE.

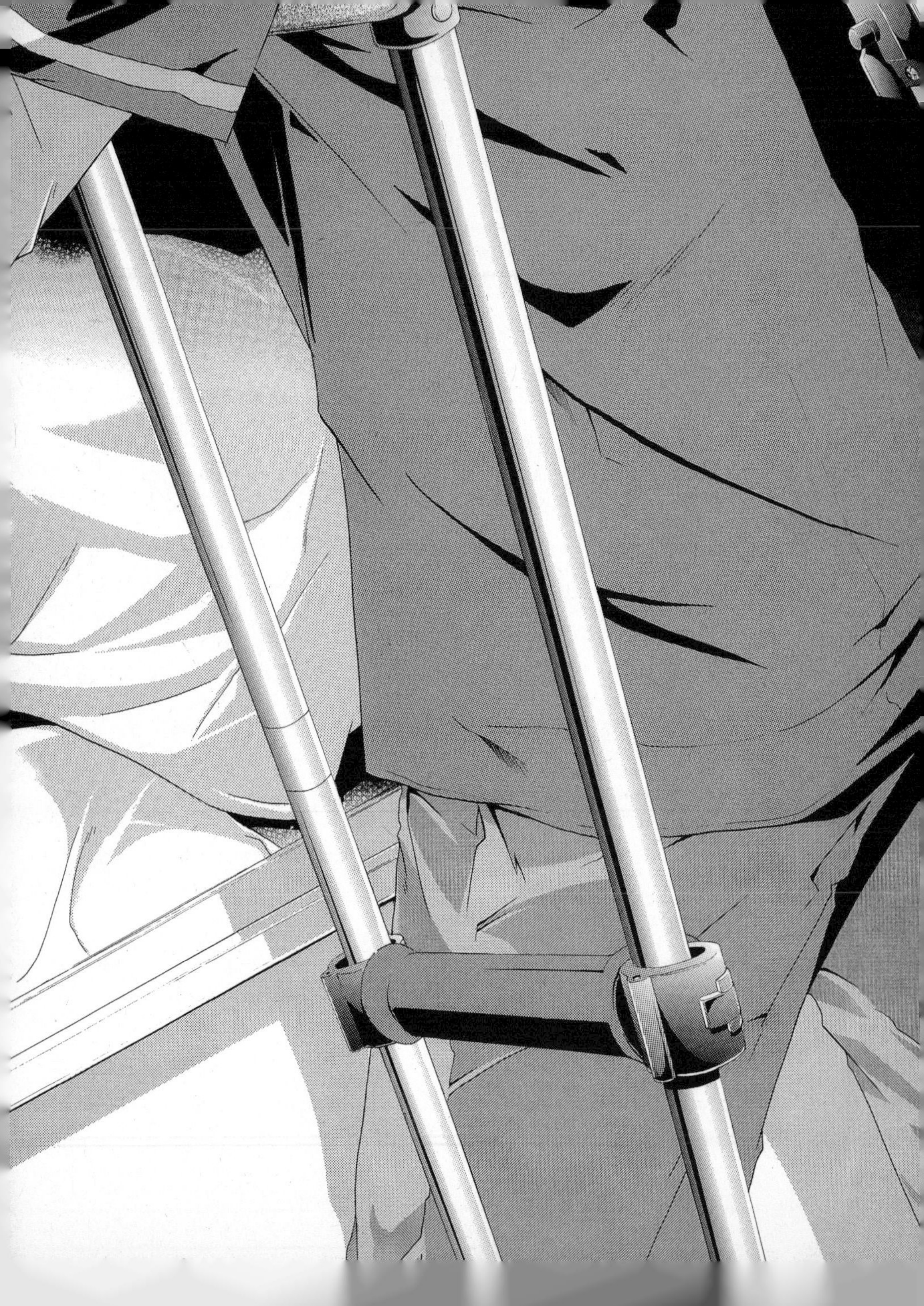

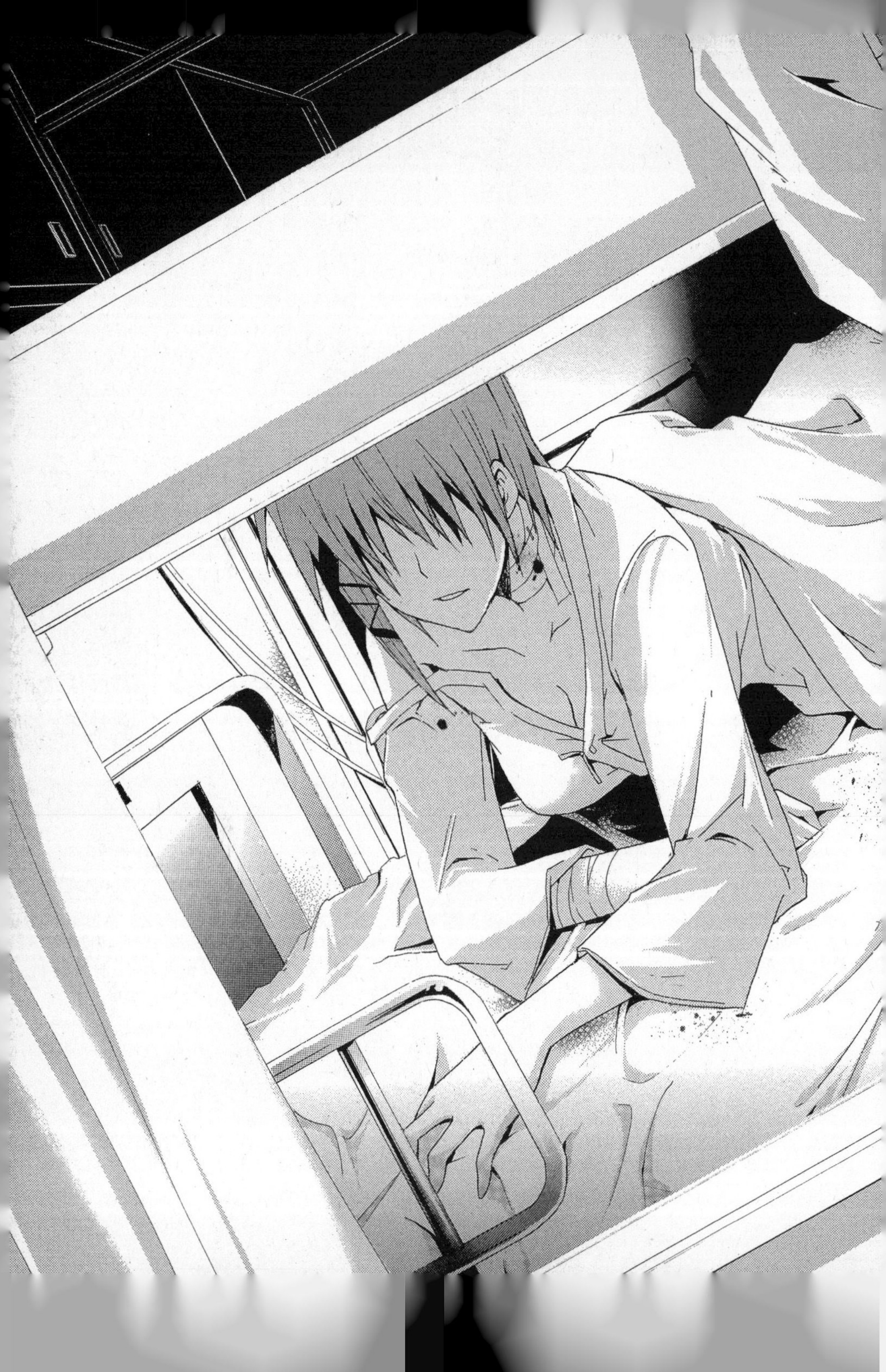

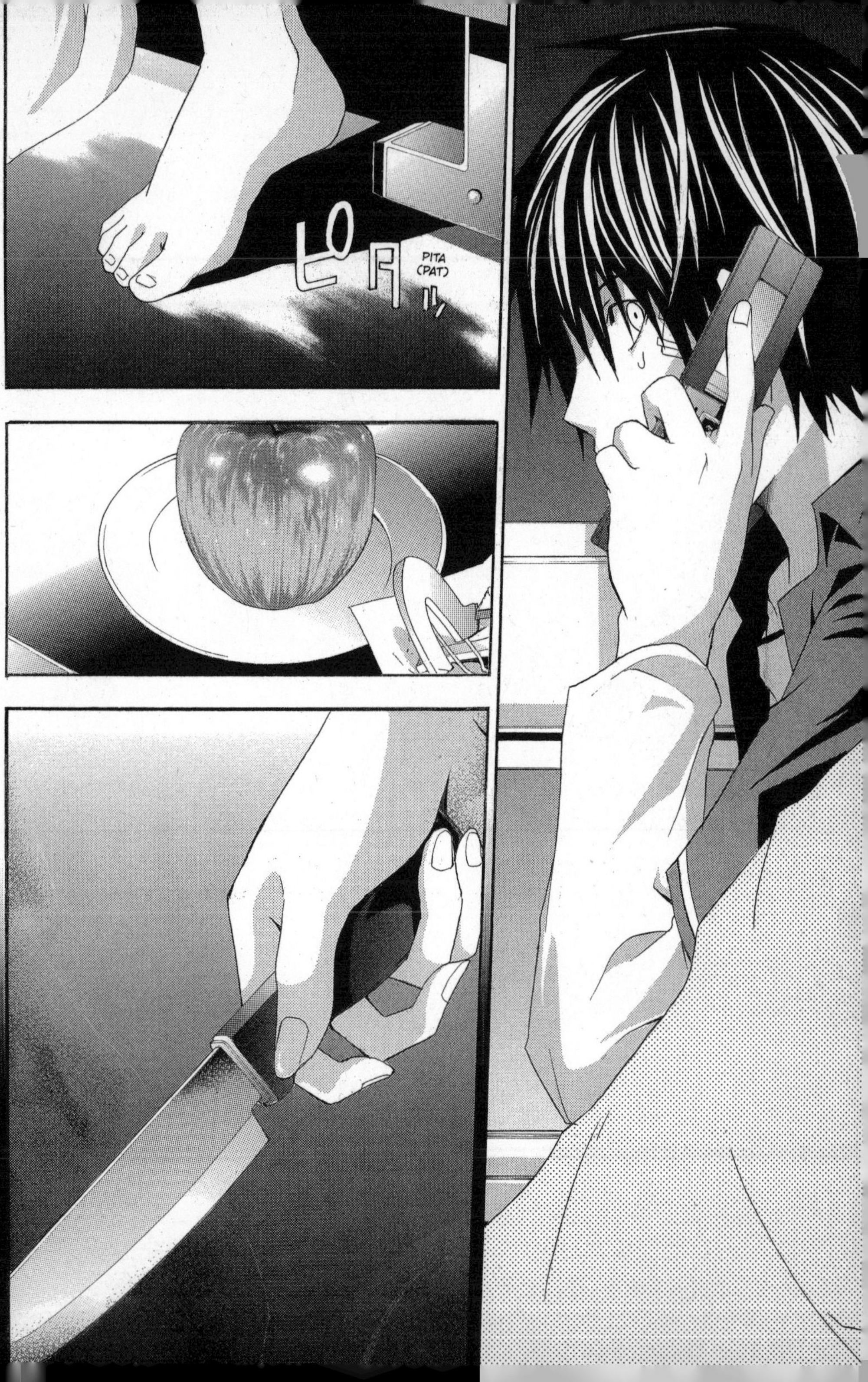
ピタッ
PITA
(PAT)

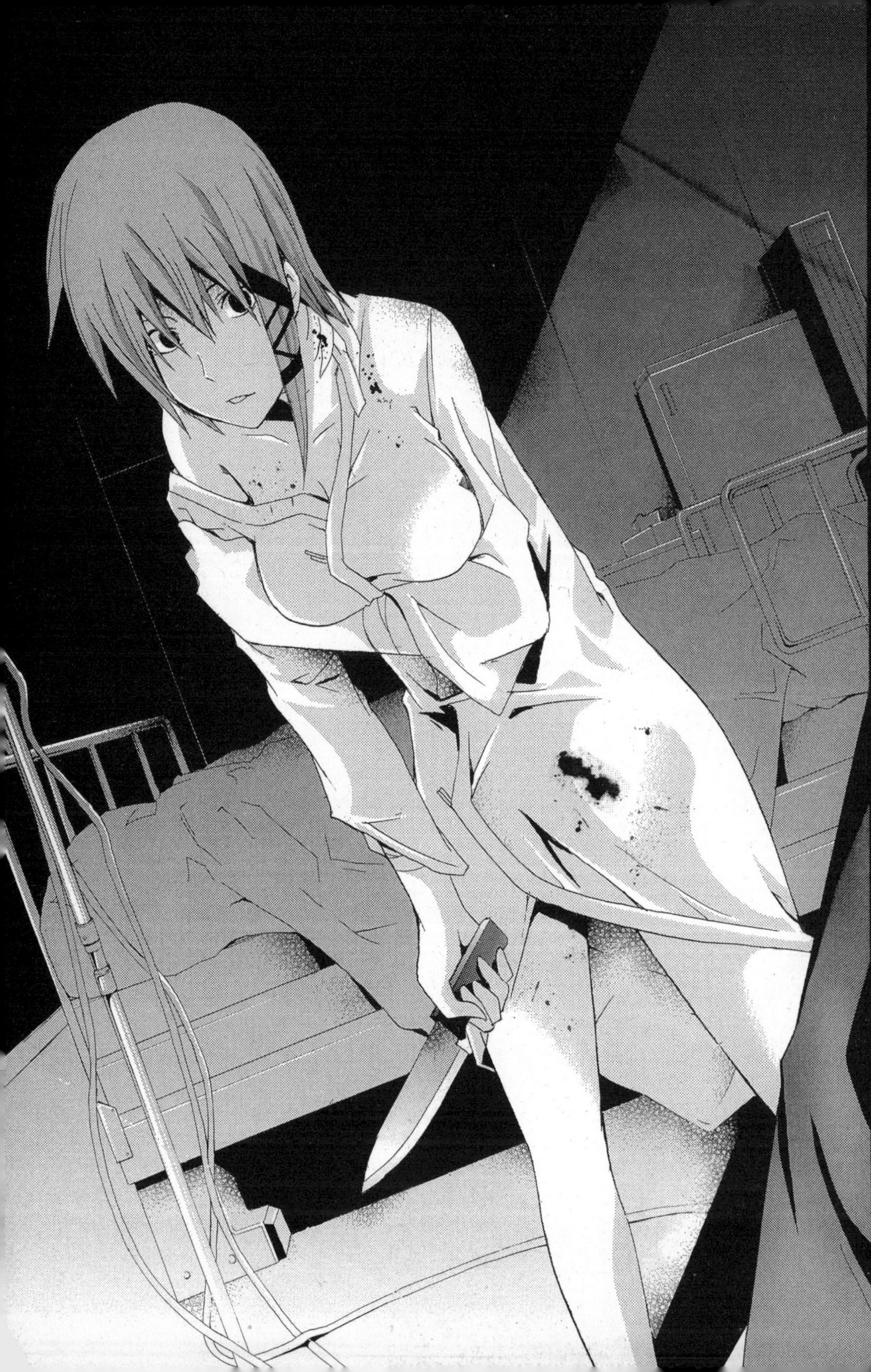

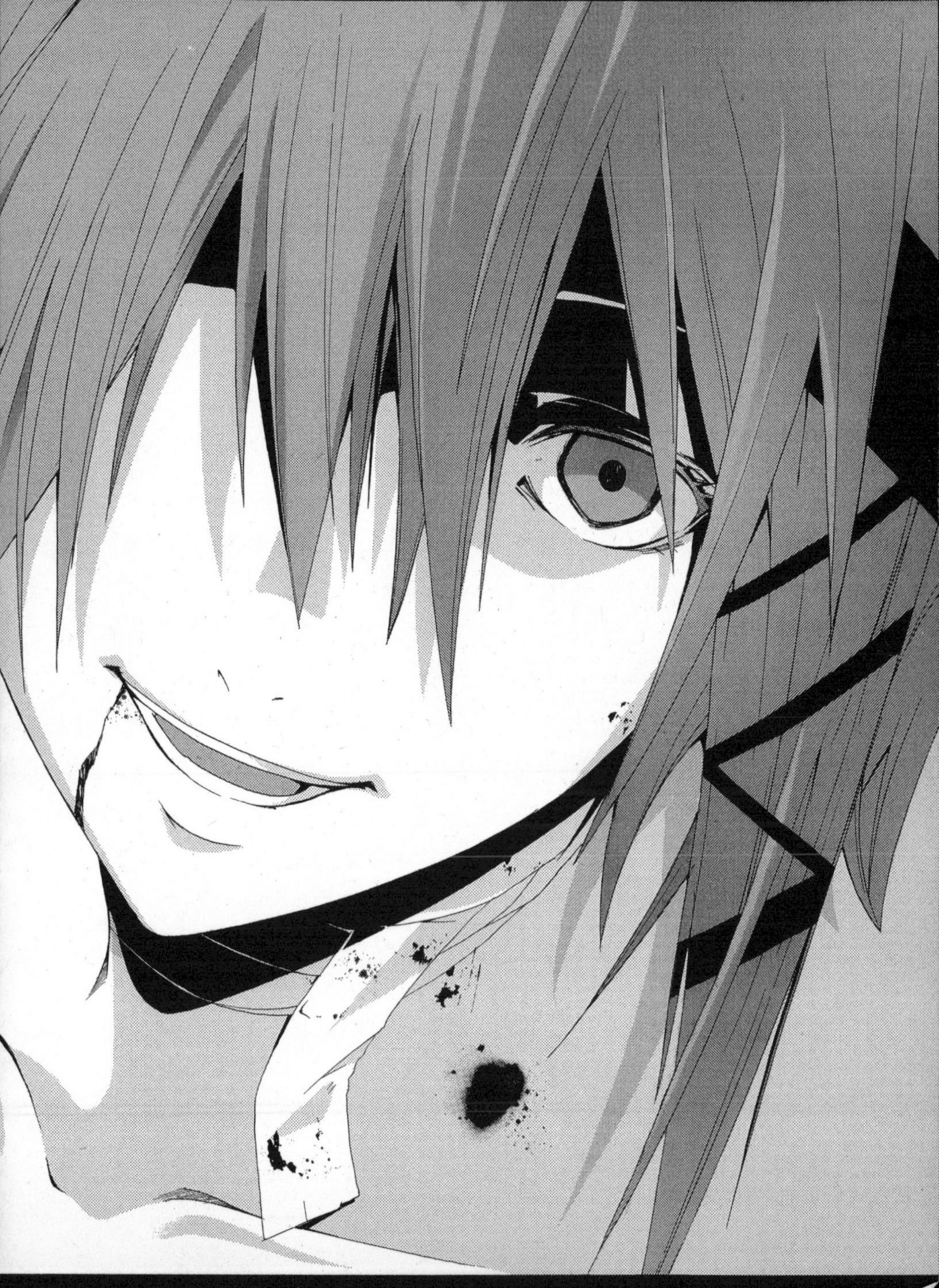

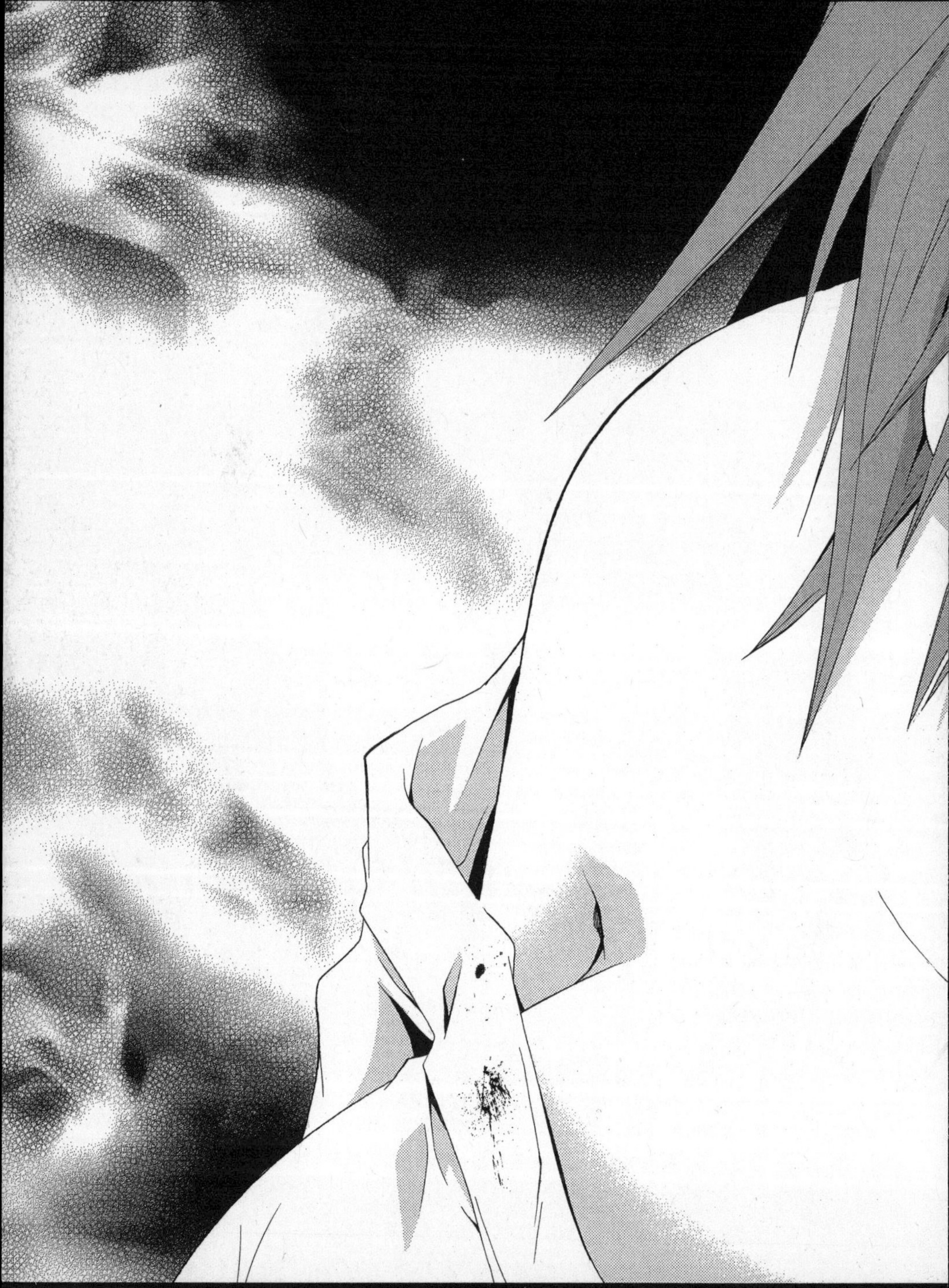

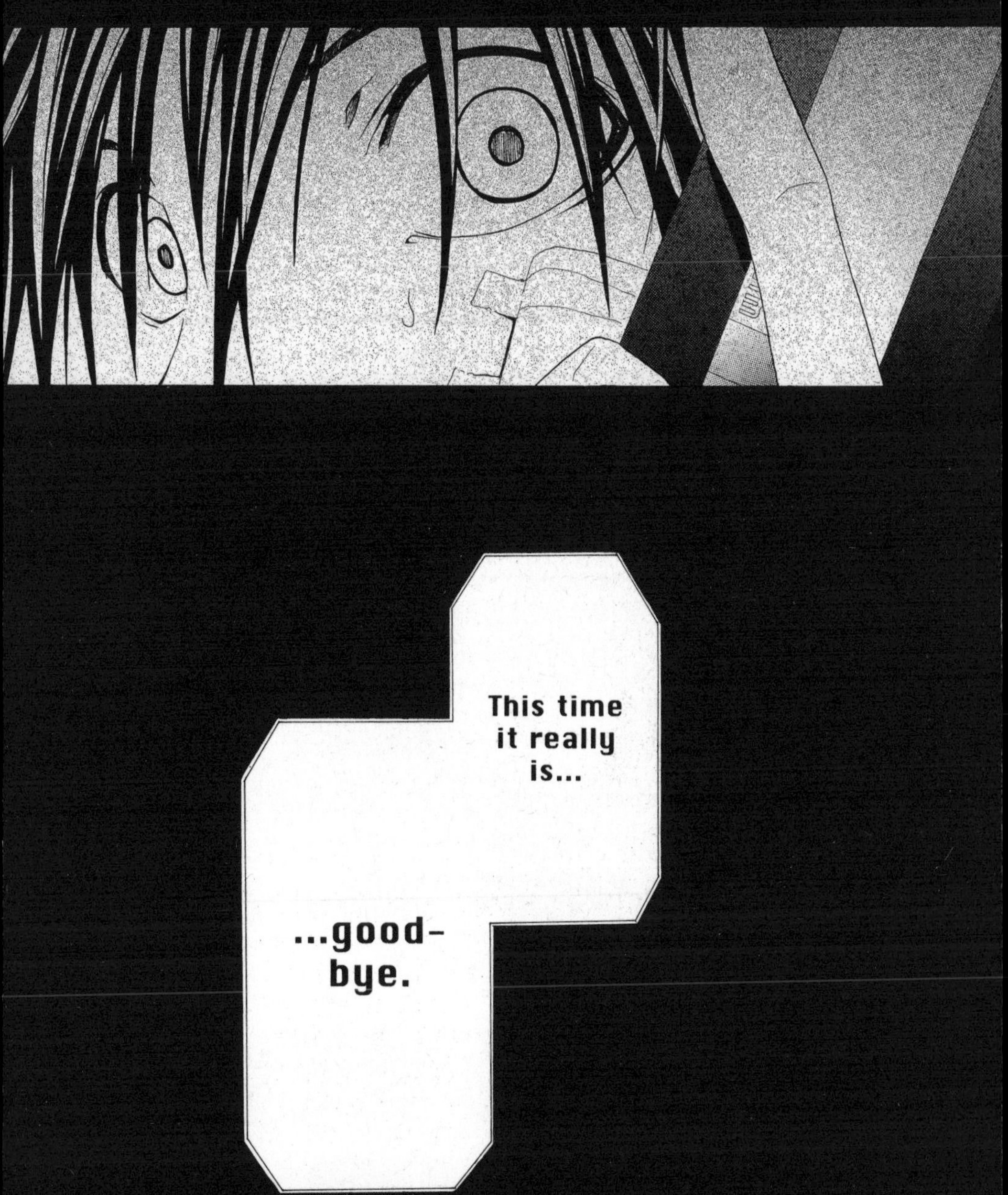
This time it really is...
...good-bye.

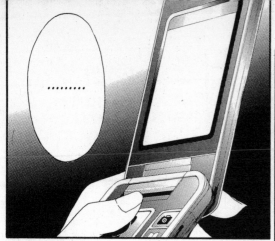

....

WOULD YOU LIKE A REFILL ON YOUR COFFEE?

...I'LL STOP FOR TODAY.

THIS GAME'S ALREADY OVER...

NIII (SMILE)

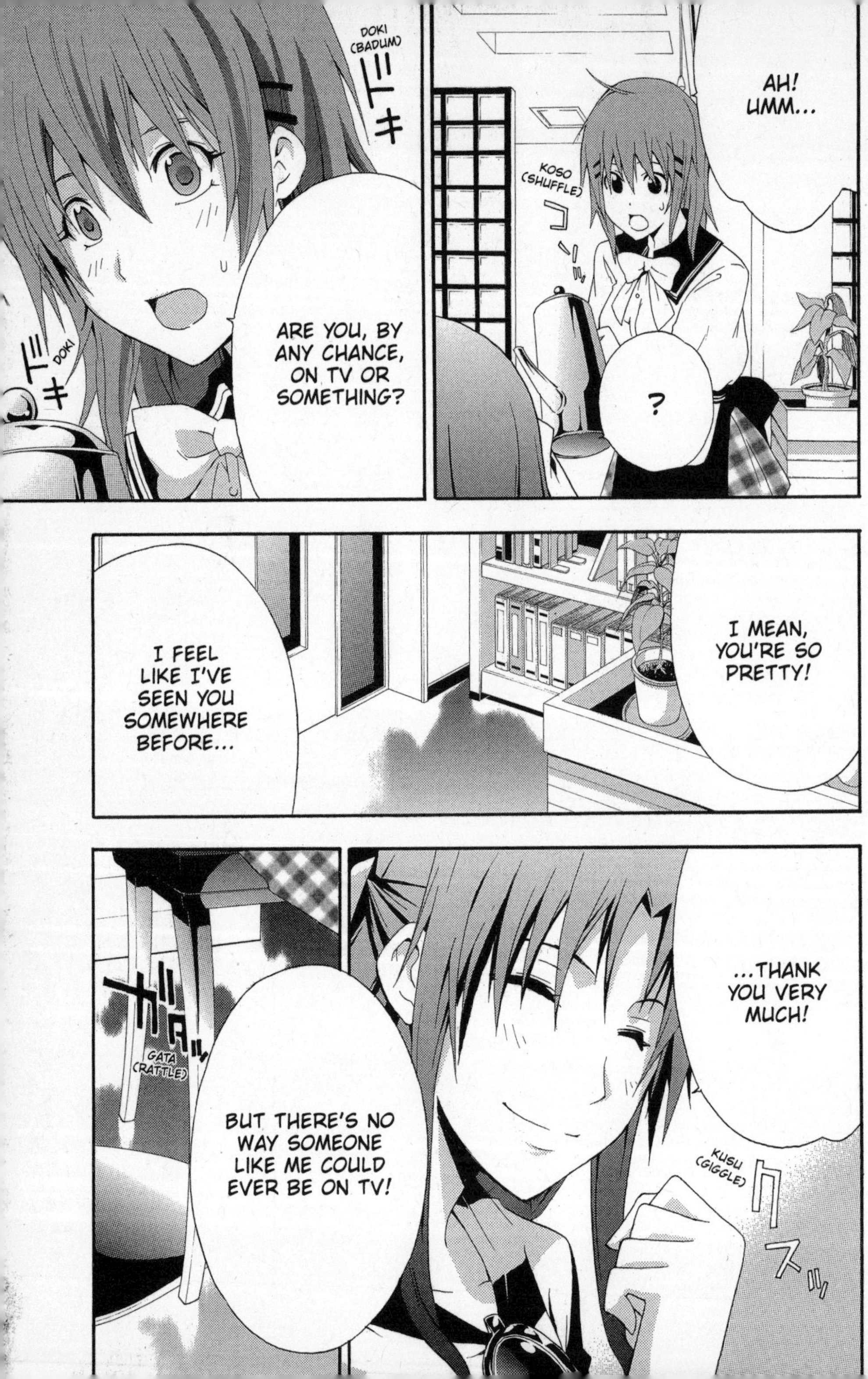
AH! UMM...
KOSO (SHUFFLE)
?
DOKI (BADUM)
ARE YOU, BY ANY CHANCE, ON TV OR SOMETHING?
DOKI
I MEAN, YOU'RE SO PRETTY!
I FEEL LIKE I'VE SEEN YOU SOMEWHERE BEFORE...
...THANK YOU VERY MUCH!
KUSU (GIGGLE)
BUT THERE'S NO WAY SOMEONE LIKE ME COULD EVER BE ON TV!
GATA (RATTLE)

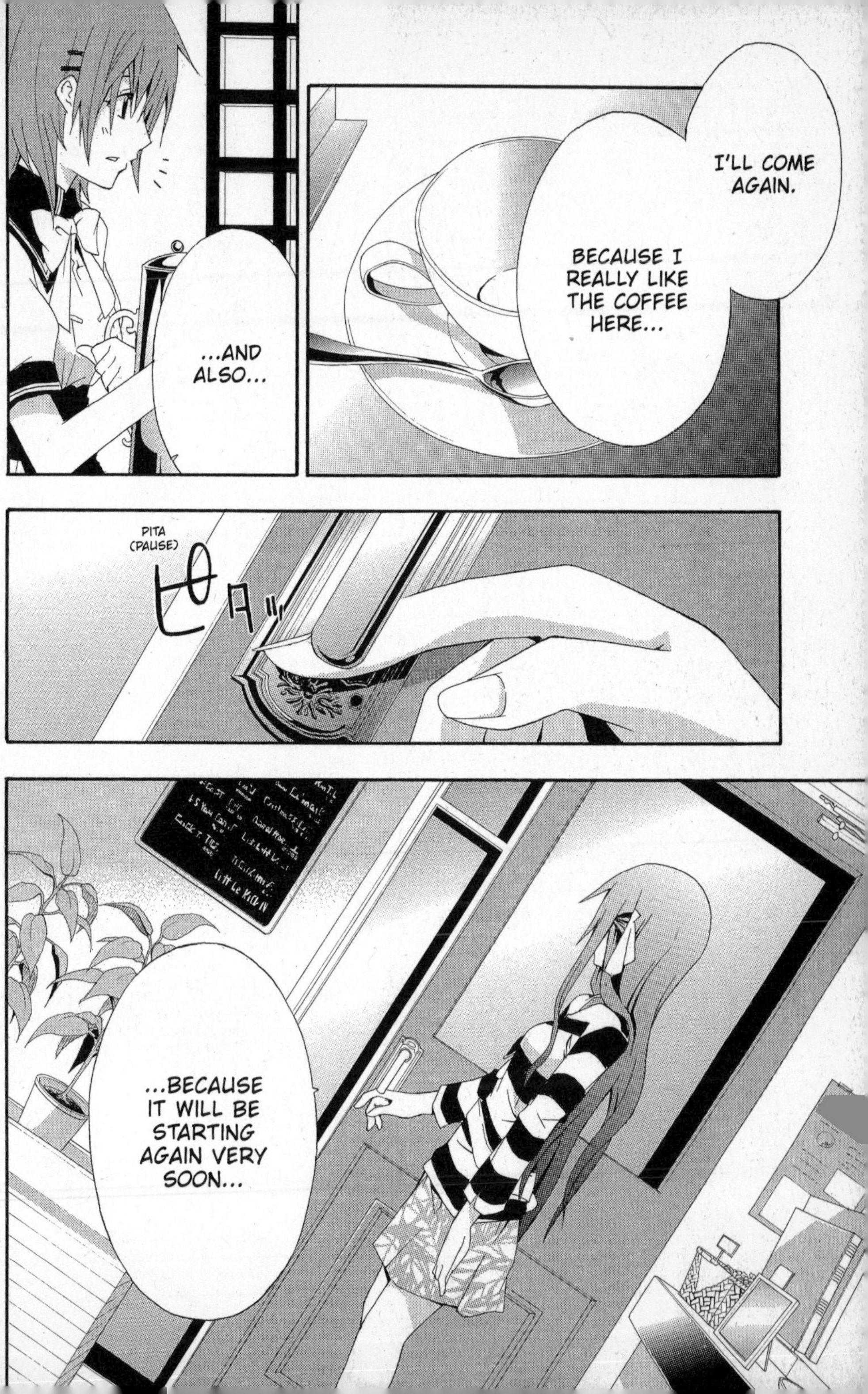
I'LL COME AGAIN.
BECAUSE I REALLY LIKE THE COFFEE HERE...
...AND ALSO...
PITA (PAUSE)
ピタッ
...BECAUSE IT WILL BE STARTING AGAIN VERY SOON...

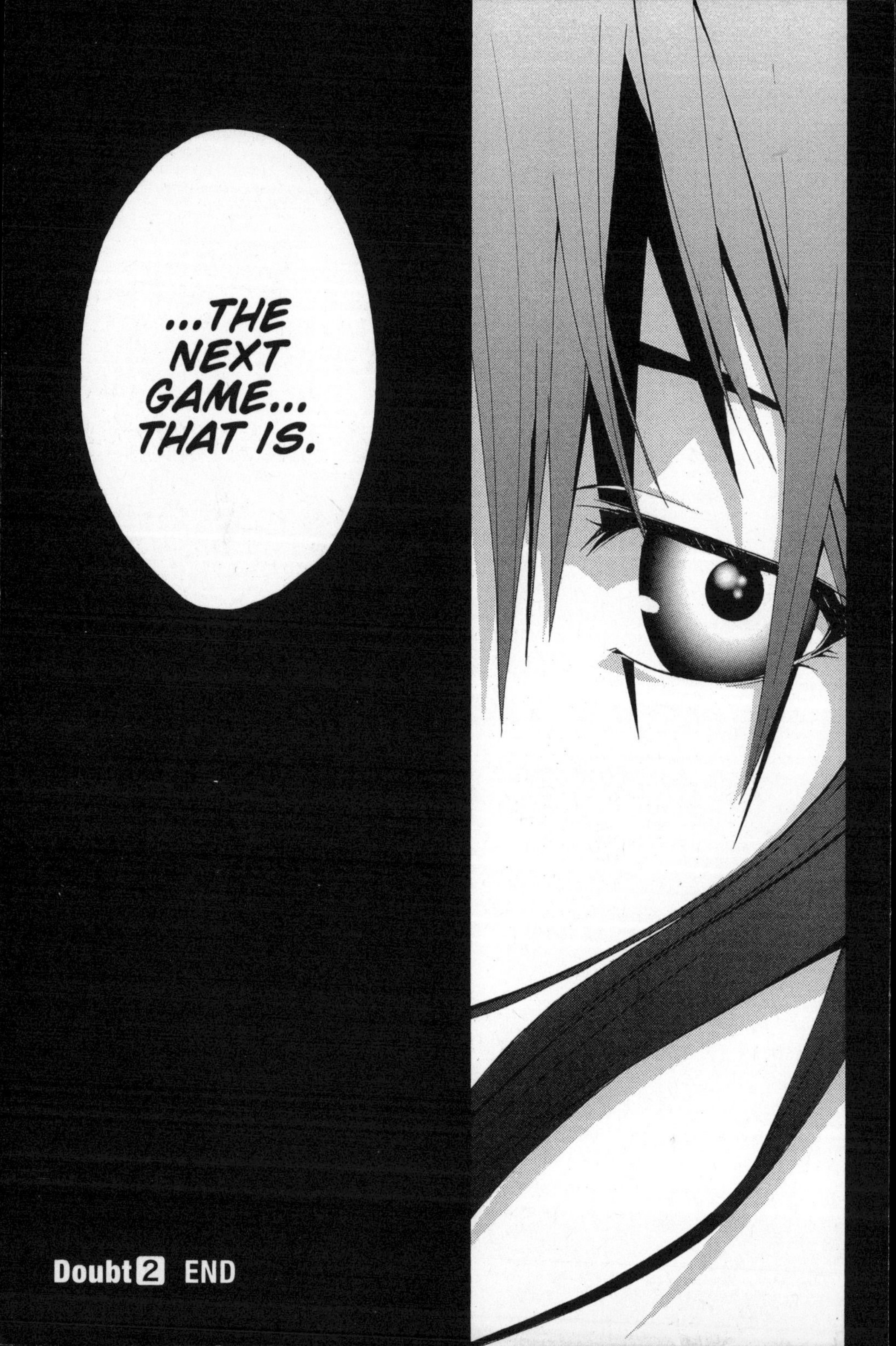
...THE NEXT GAME... THAT IS.
Doubt 2 END

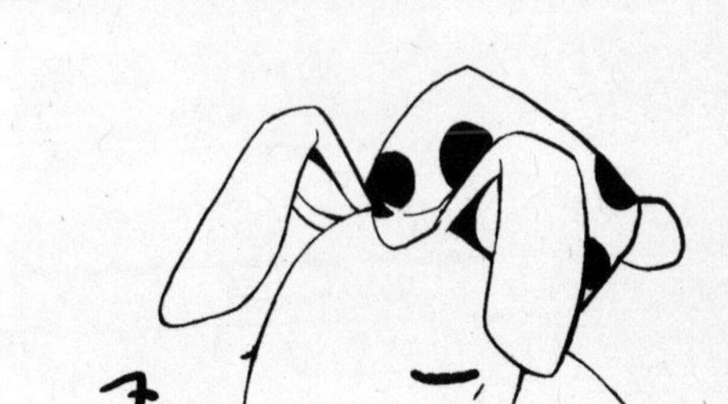
Z Z..

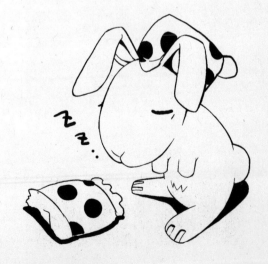

Doubt

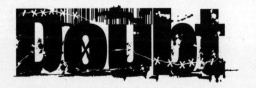

STAFF

[VOLUME 3]

[MANGA]

TONOGAI

MIZOE

KATOU

MIYASHITA

SHINOMIYA

NOMURA

OIKAWA

TAKAHASHI

[EDITOR]

NOZAKI

STAFF

[VOLUME 4]

[MANGA]

TONOGAI

MIZOE

MIYASHITA

NOMURA

OIKAWA

TAKAHASHI

[THANKS]

SHINOMIYA

[EDITOR]

NOZAKI

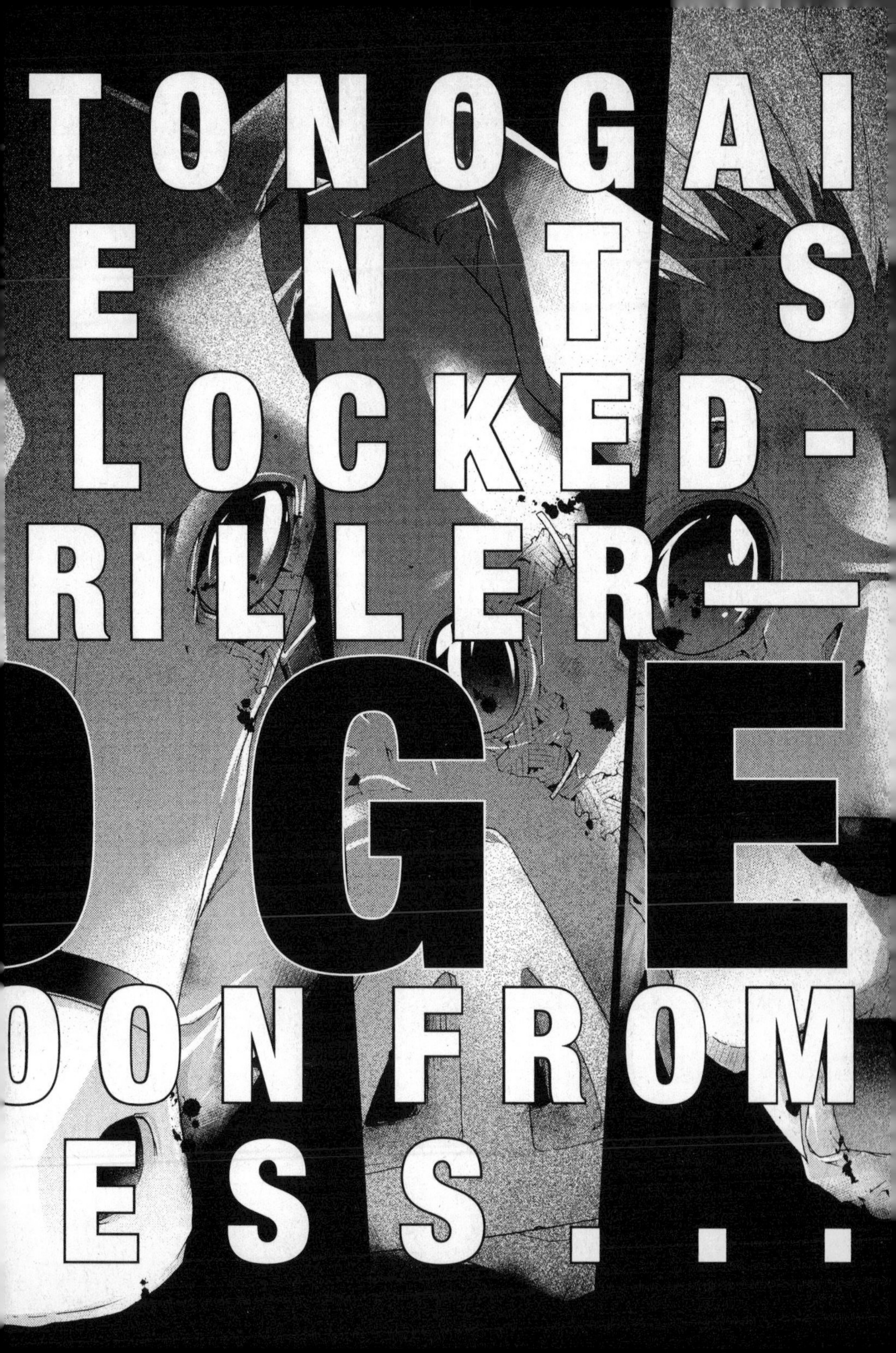

TONOGAI
ENTS
LOCKED-
RILLER—
DGE
OON FROM
ESS...

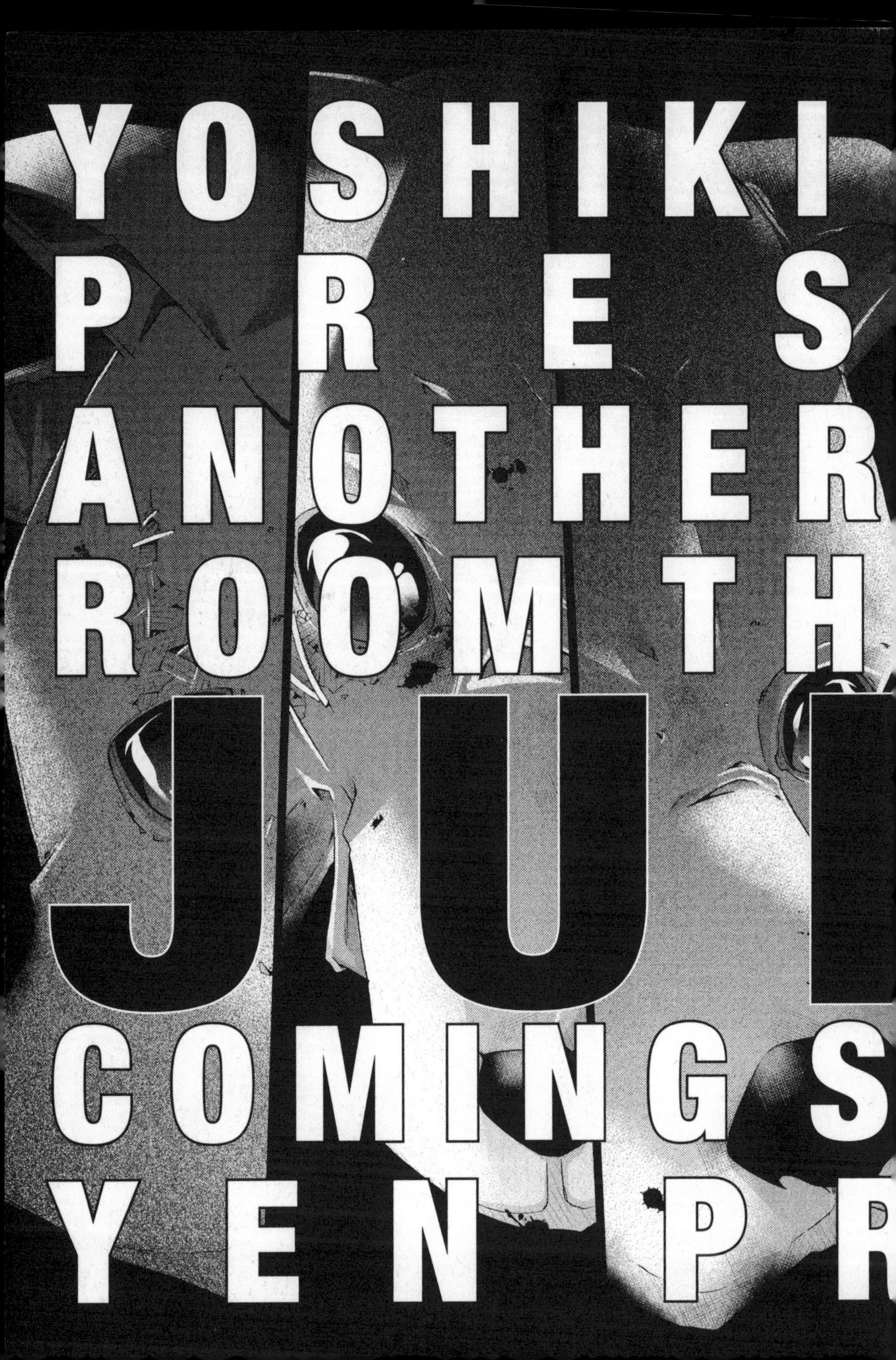
YOSHIKI
PRES
ANOTHER
ROOMTH
JU
COMINGS
YEN PR

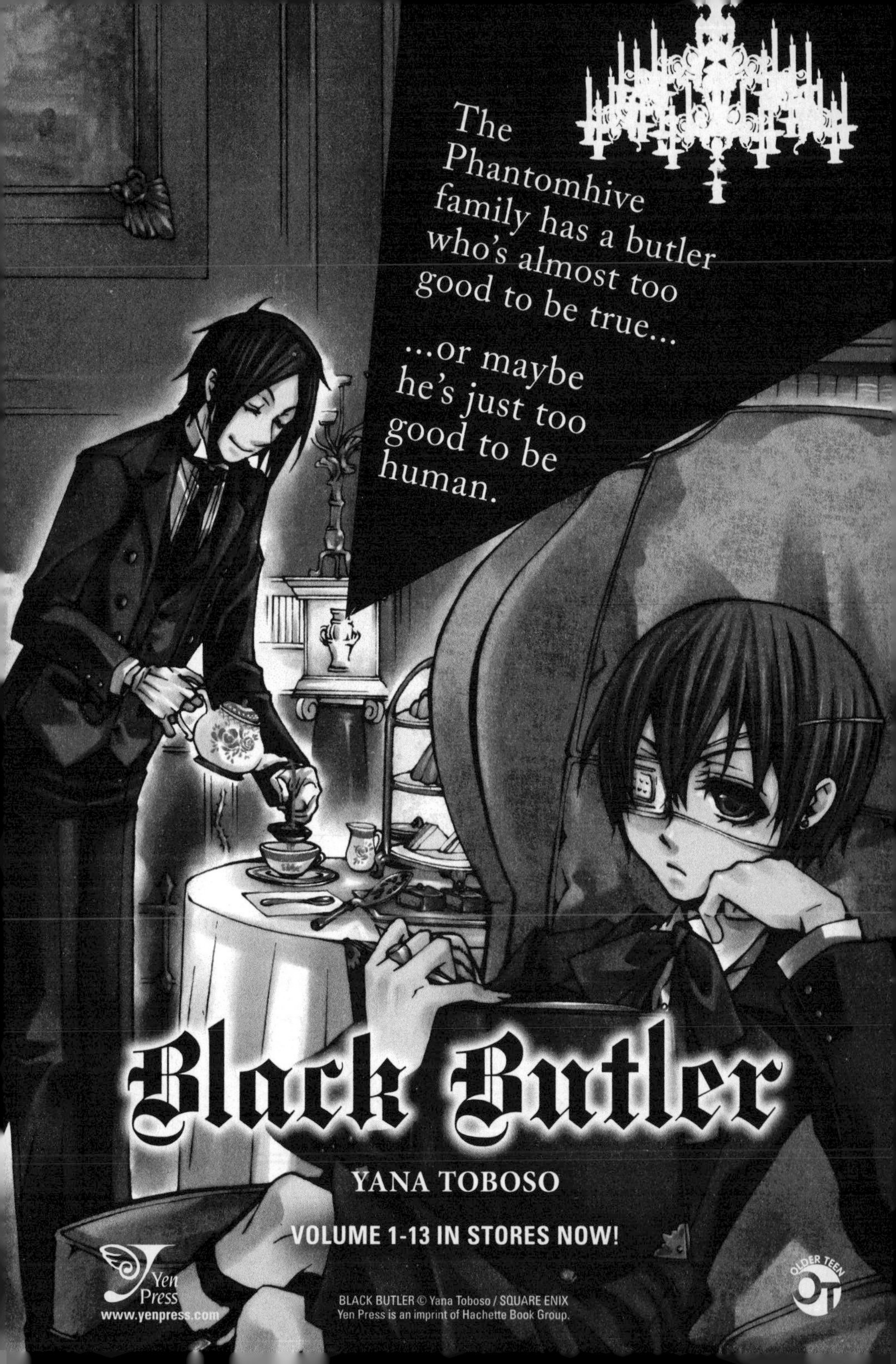
The Phantomhive family has a butler who's almost too good to be true...
...or maybe he's just too good to be human.
Black Butler
YANA TOBOSO
VOLUME 1-13 IN STORES NOW!
Yen Press
www.yenpress.com
BLACK BUTLER © Yana Toboso / SQUARE ENIX
Yen Press is an imprint of Hachette Book Group.
OLDER TEEN
OT

DOUBT ②

YOSHIKI TONOGAI

Translation and Lettering: Alexis Eckerman

DOUBT Vol. 3, 4 © 2008, 2009 Yoshiki Tonogai / SQUARE ENIX CO., LTD. All rights reserved. First published in Japan in 2008, 2009 by SQUARE ENIX CO., LTD. English translation rights arranged with SQUARE ENIX CO., LTD. and Hachette Book Group through Tuttle-Mori Agency, Inc.

Translation © 2013 by SQUARE ENIX CO., LTD.

Yen Press
Hachette Book Group
237 Park Avenue, New York, NY 10017

www.HachetteBookGroup.com
www.YenPress.com

Yen Press is an imprint of Hachette Book Group, Inc. The Yen Press name and logo are trademarks of Hachette Book Group, Inc.

First Yen Press Edition: July 2013

ISBN: 978-0-316-24531-9

10 9 8 7 6 5 4 3 2 1

BVG

Printed in the United States of America

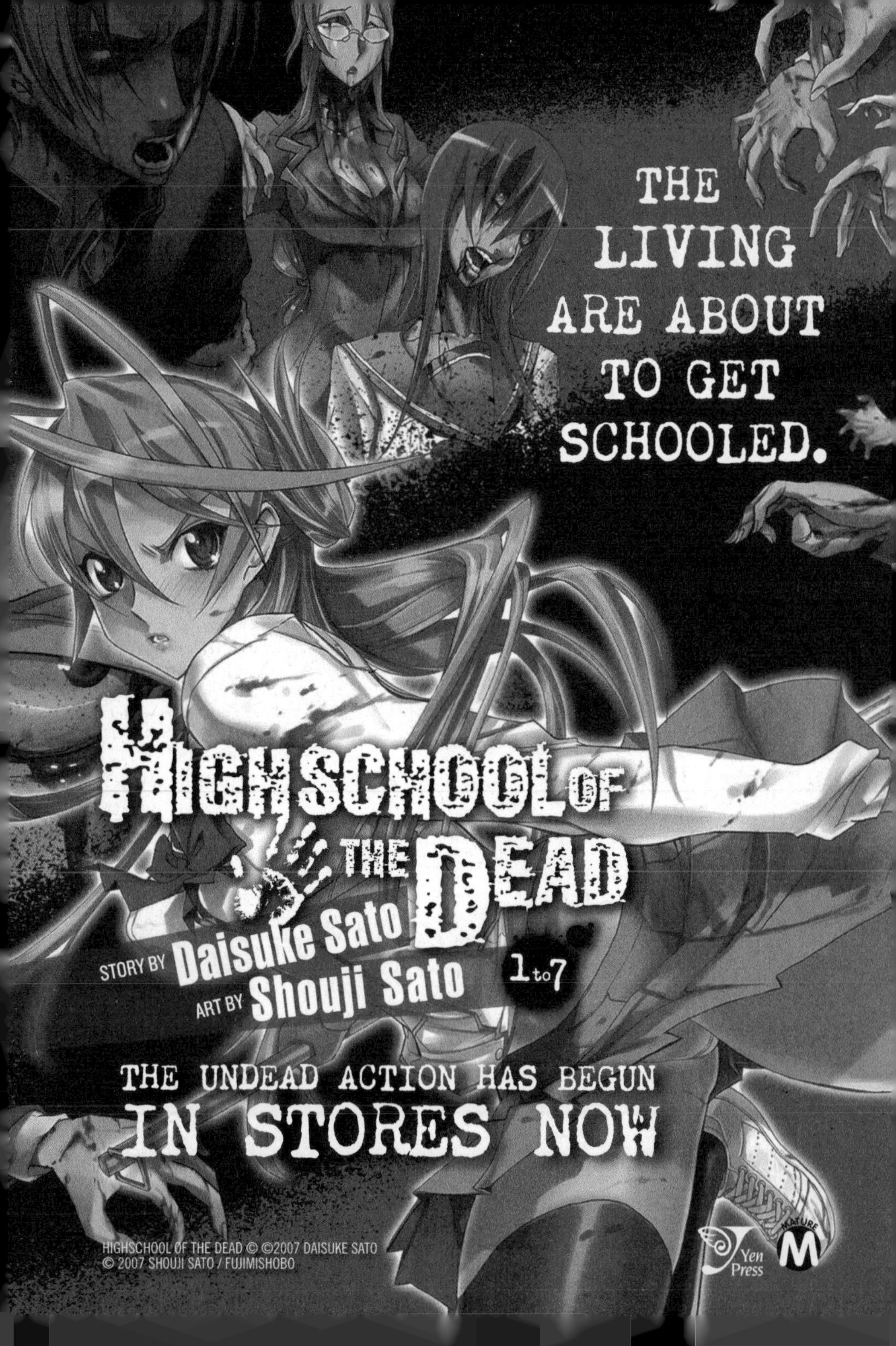
THE LIVING ARE ABOUT TO GET SCHOOLED.
HIGHSCHOOL OF THE DEAD
STORY BY Daisuke Sato
ART BY Shouji Sato
1 to 7
THE UNDEAD ACTION HAS BEGUN
IN STORES NOW
HIGHSCHOOL OF THE DEAD © ©2007 DAISUKE SATO
© 2007 SHOUJI SATO / FUJIMISHOBO
Yen Press
MATURE
M